Continued on last page of book

Code Listings

Linux System Administration

Vicki Stanfield
Roderick W. Smith

SYBEX

San Francisco Paris Düsseldorf Soest London

Associate Publishers: Neil Edde, Richard J. Staron
Contracts and Licensing Manager: Kristine O'Callaghan
Acquisitions and Developmental Editor: Maureen Adams
Editors: James A. Compton, Carol Henry, Ronn Jost
Book Production and Graphic Illustration: Publication Services
Technical Editors: Don Hergert, Joe Kirby
Book Designer: Bill Gibson
Proofreader: Publication Services
Indexer: Ted Laux
Cover Designer: Ingalls & Associates
Cover Illustrator: Ingalls & Associates

Library of Congress Card Number: 00-106435

ISBN: 0-7821-2735-5

Manufactured in the United States of America

10 9 8 7 6 5 4 3 2 1

Foreword

The Craig Hunt Linux Library is a series of highly technical books focused on specific Linux system administration tasks. Individual books provide in-depth coverage of essential computer services. The library includes books on DNS, Samba, sendmail, security, Apache, and NFS and Amd. An experienced system administrator can pick up one of these books and have all of the information necessary to master a given service. But all of these topical texts assume that the reader understands basic Linux system administration. Where do you start if you need to master the basics?

Start with *Linux System Administration,* by Vicki Stanfield and Roderick W. Smith. This book covers the fundamental skills of system administration that must be mastered before more advanced system administration tasks can be undertaken.

Daily system administration tasks are an essential part of running any Linux system. The importance of good system administration cannot be exaggerated. The most vital part of a secure, reliable computer system is a skilled system administrator. If you need help building that skill, a system administration book is a good place to start. There is nothing intuitive or obvious about the inner workings of any operating system, including Linux. A good book, like *Linux System Administration,* helps you draw on the experience of others who have already faced many of the challenges you will encounter.

Use *Linux System Administration* as the foundation volume of your own personal Linux library. Start here and build your Linux bookshelf adding books from the Craig Hunt Linux Library that address the special topics you need to master.

Craig Hunt

December 2000

Acknowledgments

The authors would like to thank everyone who supported the project, including Sybex associate publishers Neil Edde and Richard J. Staron, acquisitions and developmental editor Maureen Adams, editor James A. Compton, technical editor Don Hergert, and production liaisons Colleen Strand and Judith Hibbard. We are also grateful for the expert teamwork of Jan Fisher and the group at Publication Services: Patricia Oman, Foti Kutil, and Don Waller.

Vicki Stanfield and Rod Smith

Thanks to Craig Hunt for all his work on this series. It was nice to get to know you a little bit.

Thanks to Marty Ferguson, my good friend and ranting-instructor.

Thanks to the Linux Users of North Alabama (LUNA). You guys are all crazy, but you know a lot of stuff.

Thanks, in particular to Chris Frost, Chris Key, Chris Adams, Joe Robertson, Rod Montgomery, Mark Spencer, and all the other [Ch|K]ris and non-[Ch|K]ris members who've answered the call.

Thanks to Pat for keeping me reasonably sane throughout this arduous process.

Thanks to all those who said they'd buy this book even though they don't speak Linux. Your support is appreciated.

Vicki Stanfield

Contents at a Glance

Contents

Introduction

Linux has made its mark in the commercial world as a server operating system. Current figures from IDC give Linux a 24 percent share of the commercial server market, which is second only to the 38 percent market share held by Microsoft. Additionally, the acceptance of Linux for commercial installation is accelerating with the endorsement of companies like Dell, Compaq, and IBM, which all optionally ship Linux preinstalled on their hardware. The knowledge that a company such as IBM provides support for an operating system comforts even the most timid IT manager.

Yet remote support, even from IBM, is insufficient for most servers. Servers are simply too important. Critical corporate data is stored on servers. Desktop systems rely on servers for vital services such as e-mail and file sharing. Organizations depend on their servers, and servers depend on skilled on-site support from knowledgeable system administrators. This book focuses on providing the necessary knowledge for you to become a skilled Linux system administrator.

If you're reading this introduction, you are already a Linux system administrator or are planning to become one. Either way, you have made a good choice. Knowledge of Linux is an excellent skill for now and for the future. As the current market share of Linux server systems continues to grow, so does the demand for Linux system administrators.

Knowledge of Linux is an important "crossover" skill that can give you many more job opportunities. If you come to Linux with a Unix background, you're well on your way to mastering Linux. Linux uses the same command shells, file structure, and command-line tools as Unix does. A good book may be all you need to turn Unix skills into Linux skills, even if your Unix experience was limited to the Unix system you worked on in college.

A Windows NT/2000 administrator can use newly acquired Linux skills as a gateway to both Linux and Unix jobs, which often pay more than do comparable jobs administering Windows systems. Many organizations have mixed environments with both Unix and Windows systems. In those organizations an employee with multiple skills is highly valued.

The Benefits of Linux

Linux didn't always get the recognition it now has as a serious server operating system. It began its life as a computer enthusiast's dream—a free operating system available in source code that actually encouraged enthusiasts to create their own operating system code. It originally entered the corporate computer room through the back door. System administrators and programmers knew that Linux could be used to address corporate computing problems. They just couldn't convince management of that fact, and yet they brought Linux in anyway.

There are so many benefits to Linux it is easy to understand why system administrators were willing to take this approach. These benefits are:

Open source code   Linux is open source code. Nothing is hidden. The entire operating system is available in source code that can be read by in-house support staff or third-party support personnel. Having the source code means that support staff can really know how the system works. This knowledge gives Linux better third-party and in-house support than is possible for a proprietary operating system. With a proprietary system the inner workings of the operating system are trade secrets. Linux removes the veil of secrecy to let you know exactly how things work.

Reliability   Linux is extremely reliable. It simply does not crash. The Linux kernel is protected from misbehaving applications and the kernel itself is very stable.

Availability   Routine maintenance does not require taking the system offline. Software can be installed, configured, started, stopped, and removed without rebooting the system.

Proven tools   Although Linux has only been in widespread commercial use for a few years, the software tools that run on a Linux system are well proven. Many of the tools come from Unix, which has a 30-year history. For example, a tool like sendmail, which provides Internet e-mail service, has been in continuous production use for decades. Tools such as BIND for domain name service and Apache for Web service are the most widely used software packages of their types in the world. Linux gives you access to the best-known, best-tested software tools in existence. The reliability of Linux is matched by the proven reliability of the tools that it uses.

All of these reasons and more contributed to the increasing popularity of Linux as a server operating system. As more companies include Linux in their operating system mix or switch to Linux as their only operating system, administrators find themselves looking for a good reference on Linux as a server. This book fills that role.

Who Should Buy This Book

This book is written for the administrator responsible for the planning, installation and support of Linux servers. It was not written for the Windows user migrating to Linux with no Linux experience. There are a number of books available for the Linux beginner. This book is for the administrator who understands operating systems and hardware and has some understanding of Linux or Unix.

The Unix professional will benefit from the crossover of Unix to Linux knowledge presented by this book. If you have Linux experience, this book delves into those areas of system administration that you may not have investigated to provide you with a guide to server operations. The emphasis is on performance, reliability, and availability rather than desktop applications.

Some knowledge of Linux or Unix is assumed. If you are a system administrator migrating from another operating system, such as Windows NT/2000, you may find the philosophy of system administration the same, but the techniques are very different. Before jumping into this book, you should read an introductory text such as *Mastering Linux* by Arman Danesh (Sybex, 1999).

How This Book Is Organized

This book consists of eighteen chapters that illustrate different aspects of Linux system administration. The chapters are grouped into five parts that take you from basic administration to troubleshooting. If you're new to system administration, read Part 1 first—it covers the basics. Beyond that, you can read chapters in any order. Each chapter stands on its own. For example, if you are specifically interested in performance tuning, you could jump directly to Chapter 9. Here's a chapter-by-chapter summary.

Chapter 1: The Basics of System Administration

This chapter describes the goals of a system administrator and provides an introduction to the tools and techniques that the administrator uses to reach these goals.

Chapter 2: Installing Linux

Hardware selection is crucial when setting up a server. This chapter covers issues to consider in hardware selection and the actual installation of a Linux operating system. Some variations between different Linux distributions are covered.

Chapter 3: Linux Files and Processes

When Linux is installed and running, there are a number of important processes running on the system and key files distributed throughout the filesystems. This chapter describes the structure and layout of a Linux filesystem. It also explains the process life cycle.

Chapter 4: Tools of the Trade

This chapter covers the basic command-line tools available on Linux systems and how to use these tools to make the job of system administrator easier. Also covered are the concepts of the command-line interface, including pipes and redirection of input and output. The chapter also directs you to some additional sources of documentation on these tools.

Chapter 5: Startup and Shutdown

During the startup and shutdown of an operating system, many housekeeping activities are performed. This chapter takes a close look at the files that are used to control the events in startup and shutdown. The files used to configure the startup are also discussed.

Chapter 6: Creating and Maintaining User Accounts

Everyone with a computer on their desktop does some system administration. Managing multiple users is one of the things that separate the professional system administrator from the part-time administrator. This chapter covers the management of user accounts. The purpose and maintenance of groups is also covered.

Chapter 7: Security

Good security is good system administration. Every server must be secured. This chapter describes the security threats and the steps you must take to counter those threats. The tools used to secure your system and monitor its security are discussed.

Chapter 8: Software Administration

The installation, maintenance, and removal of software are important parts of the administrator's task. This chapter covers the details of software administration from locating and installing software to keeping the operating system updated.

Chapter 9: Performance Tuning

Selecting the right hardware and properly installing the software get you only part of the way to optimal performance. In this chapter you will learn how to tune your system to achieve maximum performance. Everything from locating the bottlenecks to tuning the filesystem and the kernel is addressed.

Chapter 10: Filesystems and Disk Management

The system administrator is responsible for managing the Linux filesystem. This chapter covers the native, foreign, and networked filesystems used by Linux. You will learn how to add new disks, replace disks, and transfer data. You'll also learn how to work with removable media.

Chapter 11: Backing Up and Restoring

Data backup and recovery are crucial elements of maintaining a reliable system. Things can and do go wrong. When important data is lost, it is the administrator's job to recover it. Backup strategies, disaster recovery techniques, and the Linux tools and media used to implement these plans are covered. Third-party tools are also covered in this chapter.

Chapter 12: Serial Communications, Terminals, and Modems

Modems, terminals, and some printers rely on serial communications. Modems can be particularly complex because they often require custom scripting. This chapter covers the various serial devices and provides the knowledge necessary to set up serial communications.

Chapter 13: Printers and the Spooling Subsystem

Printers and the print subsystem on any operating system often give administrators more than their share of problems. This chapter explains printers, the print spooling system, printer installation, and the kernel support for printers.

Chapter 14: Making Your Job Easier with Scripts

Automation of repetitive tasks makes the administrator's job much easier. Backups, report generation, and disk cleanup are just a few areas where automation of tasks can provide relief. This chapter covers shell scripts and Perl scripts. You will learn how to configure the cron utility to schedule jobs for you. Additionally, you will learn how to use awk and sed to make better and simpler scripts.

Chapter 15: TCP/IP Linux Networking

Linux networking is built upon the Internet's TCP/IP protocols. This chapter describes these protocols and explains how they are configured on a Linux system. It covers file sharing across the network, including both the NFS system used to share files with Unix computers and the Samba system used to share files with Windows computers. You'll also learn how to run network applications from inetd and xinetd.

Chapter 16: The X Window System

X is the windowing system used by Linux. X is more than a windowing system; it is also a network protocol. This chapter describes the nature of X. You'll learn how to configure an XFree86 server, including the version 4.0 server, and how to build a user desktop environment with X.

Chapter 17: Setting Up Your Mail Server

E-mail is still the most basic of all network services. Users expect it and they expect it to work. In this chapter you'll learn about the protocols that underlie the e-mail system and you'll learn how to properly configure them on a Linux server. Sendmail configuration is covered, as are techniques for blocking unwanted "spam" mail.

Chapter 18: Troubleshooting Your Linux System

Troubleshooting is one of the most important jobs of a system administrator. Many times a system administrator is judged almost solely on this skill. This chapter describes general troubleshooting techniques that can improve you skills as a troubleshooter. This chapter also covers some of the most commonly encountered problems and provides solutions to those problems.

Conventions Used in This Book

This book uses certain typographic styles in order to help you quickly identify important information, and to avoid confusion over the meaning of specific words. The conventions are listed below.

- *Italicized text* indicates technical terms that are introduced for the first time in a chapter. (Italics are also used for emphasis.)

- A `monospaced font` is used to indicate the contents of configuration files, messages displayed at a text-mode Linux shell prompt, filenames, and Internet URLs.

- *`Italicized monospaced text`* indicates a variable—information that differs from one system or command run to another, such as the name of a client computer or a process ID number.

- **`Bold monospaced text`** is information that you're to type into the computer, usually at a Linux shell prompt. This text can also be italicized to indicate that you should substitute an appropriate value for your system.

In addition to these text conventions, which can apply to individual words or entire paragraphs, a few conventions are used to highlight segments of text:

NOTE   A Note indicates information that's useful or interesting, but that's somewhat peripheral to the main discussion. A Note might be relevant to a small number of networks, for instance, or refer to an outdated feature.

TIP   A Tip provides information that can save you time or frustration, and that may not be entirely obvious. A Tip might describe how to get around a limitation, or how to use a feature to perform an unusual task.

WARNING   Warnings describe potential pitfalls or dangers. If you fail to heed a Warning, you may end up spending a lot of time recovering from a bug, or even restoring your entire system from scratch.

Sidebars

A Sidebar is like a Note, but is longer. Typically, a Note is one paragraph or less in length, but Sidebars are longer than this. The information in a Sidebar is useful, but doesn't fit into the main flow of the discussion.

Administrator's Logbook

Because the importance of logging all the configuration changes you make to a system is a major theme of this book, throughout various chapters we have included "Administrator's Logbook" sidebars illustrating the kinds of information you would record for the activity at hand.

Finally, note that Linux commands and output are often formatted for a screen display that is wider than our printed page. To indicate where we have had to "wrap" part of a longer command onto a separate line, we use the symbol ➡ at the beginning of the continued portion. For example:

```
' /etc/printcap > ${TMP1} && cat ${TMP1} > /etc/printcap
        ➡&& rm -f ${TMP1}
```

To include this statement in an initialization script (as discussed in Chapter 14), you would type it as a single line, omitting the line break and the ➡ symbol. (In other words, don't look for a ➡ key on your keyboard!)

Help Us Help You

Things change. In the world of computers, things change rapidly. Facts described in this book will become invalid over time. When they do, we need your help locating and correcting them. Additionally, a 600-page book is bound to have typographical errors. Let us know when you spot one. Send your suggested improvements, fixes, and other corrections to support@sybex.com. To contact Craig Hunt for information about upcoming books and talks on Linux, go to http://www.wrotethebook.com. Rod Smith can be reached at rodsmith@rodsbooks.com. Vicki Stanfield can be reached at vicki@thepenguin.org.

Part 1

How Things Work

Featuring:

- The role of a system administrator
- Linux tools for system administrators
- Selecting a Linux distribution
- Sample installation: Red Hat Linux
- The ext2 filesystem and file types
- Processes and the concept of multitasking
- Finding help resources and technical support
- Working with the Bash command line
- LILO and the Linux boot process
- Initialization and startup scripts
- Shutting down the system

1

The Basics of System Administration

If you ask ten system administrators what their job entails, you'll get ten different answers. Linux system administration is a job that defines itself over the time you hold it, and redefines itself over and over thereafter. In simple terms, the system administrator is the person responsible for maintaining a computer system at peak efficiency. The analysis required to maintain the system makes the job both challenging and rewarding. Users are the wildcards that make system administration much more unpredictable than simple system maintenance. Changing user needs, changing security environments, and changing applications, all conspire to change the system administrator's role over time. Despite its changing nature, certain tasks confront all system administrators on all Linux systems.

This chapter introduces some of the tasks that you will be expected to perform as a Linux system administrator, along with a collection of tools that you'll need to be familiar with to do those tasks successfully. A logbook is a critical, job-saving activity, so this chapter discusses some of the issues involved in keeping one. The section on communicating with users discusses different methods of communication and offers some hints about keeping the confidence of your users. Finally, you'll learn about the superuser privilege and related security issues.

Essentially, this chapter outlines what system administration is. In that sense it is a map to the contents of the rest of this book. When we describe a task that you'll perform as a Linux system administrator or a tool that you'll use, we will point you to the chapter where that topic is described in more depth. This book is, in a sense, a "mentor in a box," allowing you to benefit from our experiences, both positive and negative, as you begin your endeavors as a Linux system administrator.

Your Role as a System Administrator

A system administrator aims to be as transparent to the user as possible. How much the users need to contact you is a good indicator of how well you are doing your job. If you do your system administration tasks well, users will seldom need to think of you at all, except to recruit you for the company softball team or, of course, when they want additional services from the Linux system.

Your workload will vary dramatically. You'll learn to cherish the lull times when there is little external pressure, because they will enable you to work on projects to improve service and because you'll know from experience that just around the corner something will happen that requires working through the night or even several consecutive nights. If you spend the lull times evaluating your system for potential security problems or areas where performance could be improved, you'll find that there will be more low-pressure times as a result. Use the information in Chapter 7, "Security," when looking at security and in Chapter 9, "Performance Tuning," when examining how to improve your system's performance. The dynamic nature of system administration is the norm rather than the exception.

It is impossible to estimate when a critical piece of hardware might require replacement or when the operating system might crash, requiring you to come in and restart/troubleshoot it. For example, in a network one of the authors worked on, the backup scripts were set to run at night, when system usage was at its lowest, and to send e-mail to her pager upon completion of the backup process. When it didn't, she'd have to come in to find out what was wrong and get the backups going again. This, too, is part of the job. When you run into problems, Chapter 18, "Troubleshooting Your Linux System," contains many troubleshooting tips; some of these have been lifesavers and all have been useful as we progressed both as system administrators and as Linux users.

But what exactly is system administration? The term is so broad that no definition will give the whole picture. A simple definition might be "the installation and maintenance of a computer system." However, because a computer system might be anything from one computer to a networked system containing hundreds of computers, and because each employer expects something different, these few words don't define system administration in any strict sense. The real definition must include the system administrator's role as the mediator between machine and user, since you are the judge who decides whether problems are computer- or user-induced and the jury who determines what should be done about it. Certainly you must be a doctor, capable of performing healing rituals when the equipment is sick, but you must also be the counselor who breaks the news to the family when something has gone wrong. You are mother, father, baby-sitter, guru, mentor, mechanic, technician, programmer, hero, and villain to the users of your network.

Tasks of a System Administrator

A better way to define system administration might be to develop a list of tasks performed by a system administrator. This is not a comprehensive list, largely because every time we become comfortable with our job descriptions, something else is added, but it is a fairly complete list of tasks you can expect to perform:

- Configuring hardware
- Installing the operating system
- Installing application software
- Implementing system security
- Configuring the kernel
- Creating users and groups
- Updating software
- Performance tuning
- Disaster recovery
- Capacity planning

Configuring Hardware

Any hardware configuration that is required to get the system up and running is the duty of the system administrator. This includes determining which hardware will best meet the corporate goals; selecting hardware in turn requires you to consider capacity, expected capacity, cost, compatibility, resource availability, and many other things that are job-specific. The installation and configuration of that hardware also is your job. If the system does not come ready to run, you might have to assemble it from its component parts. Even if the system arrives fully assembled, you'll find that replacing components or disassembling a system that is being phased out will be your responsibility. In the Linux world, you'll be far more likely to perform hardware configuration than in the Microsoft or Unix world because Linux is a more hands-on system—or at least the general public sees it that way. Don't worry, though; if you're like us, you'll love it!

Installing the Operating System

In the Unix and Microsoft Windows world, computers often come with the operating system preinstalled, but in the Linux world the operating system is most often installed by the system administrator. Although computers are now available with the Linux operating system preinstalled, most companies prefer to avoid the additional cost and the restrictions imposed by the reseller's preconceived notions about what a Linux system is, so they have their administrators install and configure the computers. If you have multiple systems with similar configurations, you'll want to do something like a "kickstart" installation, which allows you to script the installation and let it run while you do one of the thousand other tasks you've been assigned. Sometimes you will inherit a working system, thereby missing out on the experience of installing the operating system from scratch, but eventually the system will require an upgrade or reinstallation, and that will be your responsibility. Chapter 2, "Installing Linux," demonstrates the procedure for a typical Red Hat installation and includes information on kickstart installations as well.

Installing Application Software

It is the system administrator's duty to install application programs and to make them available to the appropriate users while restricting access by those who aren't intended to use these programs. Typically this software exists on a networked machine and is available via either some type of remote login or an NFS mount. These topics will be discussed in Chapter 15, "TCP/IP Linux Networking." Protecting shared files also involves setting permissions, which we discuss in Chapter 7. You'll also be directly involved with supporting the installation of software on individual desktop computers. This includes determining what the user is allowed to install without you or your staff and providing assistance when needed. Additionally, you will probably be responsible for monitoring software licensing, since strict financial penalties often befall those who are caught abusing a software license. Fortunately, most of the software that you will use on a Linux machine will be nonproprietary, so that will lessen your load.

System Security

Perhaps the most difficult duty of a system administrator is system security. This is the area that can cause the most trouble for you. A corporate system is likely to have 24-hour Internet access, which makes it a prime target for crackers who consider it fun to break into the system and cause unexpected behavior or even crash the entire system. As you can probably imagine, the management is not likely to have much patience in this area. Maintaining system security is a manageable task, however, if you are methodical and cautious. Usually you'll be responsible for changing passwords when the existing ones have exceeded their expiration dates or when an employee has left the company. This involves developing a hard-to-guess password, or several of them, changing them on the systems, and distributing them to those who need them. The topic of passwords is covered in Chapter 7. Check the system's security even when it appears that things are fine and follow the guidelines in Chapter 7, and you'll be fine.

Configuring the Kernel

The heart of the Linux operating system is a component called a *kernel*. This component is basically an interface between the system hardware and the system application software. As system administrator, you will have to do any configuration of the kernel that is required. This includes things like restricting the size or number of files that a user can create, activating or disabling its inherent capabilities to meet the needs of the system, adding support for new hardware or filesystems, and configuring a variety of kernel-controlled parameters. We'll talk about the kernel, and how to configure it, more in Chapters 4, "Tools of the Trade," and 8, "Software Administration." Many new system administrators find this to be a daunting task, but after a few kernel compilations, you'll feel comfortable with it and wonder why it seemed so intimidating.

Creating Users and Groups

Whenever new users are added to the system, accounts must be created and configured to allow them to do their work without creating a security risk. It is often difficult for you to know what resources, for example, a new accountant really needs access to; so you'll benefit from working closely with company management to determine what's appropriate for each position. At a minimum, a mail spool must be established for each user, and you'll be responsible for configuring access to the mail spool and to an adequate mail client. Chapter 6, "Creating and Maintaining User Accounts," discusses the topic of users and groups, and Chapter 17, "Setting Up Your Mail Server," covers the configuration of a mail server.

Software Updates

Inevitably, a network and its client machines will need updates to the software they use, both system and application. In system software, these may be security fixes that lessen a cracker's opportunity to exploit a flaw in a particular software package that could have been used to get superuser access to the system. These are usually published on the manufacturer's Internet sites, and you must make it your habit to check those sites on a regular basis and apply the updates as soon as possible. On the application side, the update may be requested by end users or by management—simply to add functionality to a software package. The users will remind you of these, probably more often than you'd like. Chapter 8 discusses these and other software administration tasks in more detail.

Performance Tuning

One of the administrative tasks most noticeable to users is how well the administrator has tuned the system. Although a systems person might view efficiency in terms of memory usage, users generally makes this judgement based on how long it takes to bring up a Web browser or how long it takes to load a page. As discussed in Chapter 9, "Performance Tuning," you can often tweak the system to optimize these factors. Of course, no amount of optimization will make a system that is inadequate for its workload run well. Users also judge system administrators by how quickly they can replace or repair components that break. If the user's mouse stops functioning, the correction of this problem is the most important thing in that user's immediate future. If you do not give these problems adequate attention, you will likely find yourself a frequent scapegoat when a task doesn't get finished.

Disaster Recovery

The creation and preservation of copies of the system in different states of development is an extremely important task. After all the configuration of a system is performed, the last thing you want to do is reload the operating system and application programs from the original media. You might choose to use a disaster recovery package or just decide to be fastidious about your backups. Reconfiguring a system is frustrating at best. It is difficult to reproduce the exact configuration that you had before, and that is exactly what the users expect. You can take some of the pain out of backing up a system by selecting a backup medium that is reasonably easy to handle and by obtaining or creating the software to run the backups unattended. Added features, like a script that e-mails you when the backups have finished, also provide some peace of mind. When the system crashes and there is data that is not contained in a backup, other methods of data recovery are required. Your familiarity with these methods will help you get through troubled times with less frustration. Backups and disaster recovery are covered in Chapter 11, "Backups and Restoring."

Capacity Planning

As a Linux system administrator, you'll need to be aware of the limitations imposed by the hardware and software involved in your system. You'll need to watch the network traffic to determine when high usage creates a need for new hardware/software to be added. You'll need to watch disk space usage to determine when a system is about to outgrow its storage. You'll also want to ensure that you have sufficient printing and backup resources for the number and type of users in the system. We'll discuss each of these elements in Chapters 10, "Filesystems and Disk Management," 13, "Printers and the Spooling Subsystem," and 15 "TCP/IP Linux Networking."

"When You Have a Minute, ..."

There are so many tasks that are performed by a system administrator that it is impossible to mention them all. Our duties have included building network cables, installing a network, configuring routers, answering user questions, assembling tables upon which the system equipment will sit, and almost anything else you can think of. A system administrator who appears to have free time is fair game. Never mind that you are compiling a kernel on a remote machine while downloading accidentally deleted files from a backup. Users, managers, salespeople—they all think they have the right to interrupt you and start you off on a wholly unexpected task if you aren't obviously doing something already—and sometimes even when you are. Life for a system administrator is never boring.

Tools of the Linux Administrator

Many tools and techniques are available to make the job of system administration less maddening, and seasoned administrators usually have a suite of them that have proven useful. Some of these are commonly used Linux commands, while others are scripting tools or methods that allow you to automate your tasks. Whichever they are, the items listed below are general categories of tools that will prove invaluable to you, as a system administrator. There are a number of Internet sites that allow you to download some of these software tools and try them yourself. A site that provides access to a number of system tools specifically for Linux may be found at

```
http://home.xnet.com/~blatura/linapp1.html#sysad
```

Most Linux distributions contain some tools that the distributors have found to be both stable and useful. However you get them, you will find that they are essential to happy system administration. Here is a brief list of tools that you shouldn't be without.

Commands

There are hundreds of commands you can use to perform your administrative work. These commands may be compiled programs written in C or some other language, programs written in an interpreted language such as Python or Perl, or shell scripts that use the shell's inherent capabilities to perform some task. Whichever type the command represents, each command is executed by entering the command and any applicable parameters on the Linux command line. We'll discuss specific commands in Chapter 4.

Linuxconf

Practically every flavor of Unix has several individual tools that each performs a single administrative task, but most also have a general tool that combines many of the individual capabilities into a single interface. IBM has its smit utility; Solaris uses the admintool, and Red Hat Linux has Linuxconf. A product of the GNOME project, Linuxconf is designed to perform many administrative duties. Few tools handle so many different types of configuration tasks as the Linuxconf utility. Linuxconf is used to manage user accounts, network and Domain Name Server configuration, PPP setup, mail server and client configuration, Samba, NFS, Apache configuration, and filesystem setup. The main screen of Linuxconf is shown as Figure 1.1.

Linuxconf has a command-line mode, a character-cell mode (the same style as the installation program), an X-based mode, and a Web-based mode. We'll demonstrate Linuxconf's many uses in various chapters throughout the book.

Special-Purpose Shell Scripts

Many repetitive day-to-day functions, whether simple or complex, are accomplished by a specially designed shell script. A shell script is a list of shell commands batched together in a file so that they can be executed on demand. As Linux system administrators, we have written many, many shell scripts, and you will as well. Chapter 14, "Making Your Job Easier with Scripts," is dedicated to this topic.

System Logbook

To maintain some semblance of sanity, you need to keep your network—and your administrative activities—organized. Many system administrators, at least the ones who have learned from prior mistakes, keep a journal of the overall network configuration and the operating system and software configurations for each computer. The lack of such preparation makes an unexpected reinstall a painful experience. If you ever need to use your backup tapes to reinstall a system, time will be a critical factor, since few users understand the time involved in such a procedure. You can minimize the time required by knowing exactly what you had set up on that system. A journal of each change you made to the system is invaluable at this point. You must keep the journal just as loyally as you make your backups, because it is the combination of the two that will allow you to reinstall and reconfigure quickly and efficiently.

We recommend that you buy several blank log books to be used exclusively for journal-keeping. The hard-backed composition books used for college English classes are particularly good. These are available in most grocery stores and in any office supply store. Buy one for each computer, or in a really large network, for each class of computer. The books are cheap, and keeping one system's journal separate from another system's journal makes it much easier to keep track. Think about what separation makes sense in your system. If you can keep different categories of notes in different colors, it makes it easier to find an entry that you need to reference. For instance, red might denote major system

Figure 1.1   The Linuxconf main screen

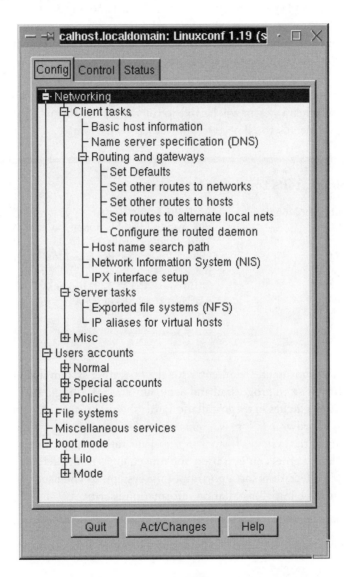

problems, blue might be used for application installation and configuration, etc. Keep all the logbooks in the same location, label them clearly, and use them without fail.

Start each journal by defining the system itself, specifically annotating each configuration detail. A system's initial entry should include the computer's identification number as assigned for tracking purposes and all the hardware information you can record. Include the CPU type and speed, the type of motherboard and any configuration you performed, how much memory, the type and size hard drive(s), the type of video card and how much video memory it contains, what other drives the system contains, what other cards the system contains and how they are configured, and identification numbers for each component, IRQ and DMA settings for any card, and any other information which might be useful when installing or upgrading later. It's a lot of work to capture this data, but when you need to assess whether a system will be able to run the newest Virtual Reality software package, these are the details you'll need to know. Here's an example.

Administrator's Logbook : Initial Entry

System: E12345678	AMD K6-3 400MHz
MB: FIC503+	VIA Apollo MVP3 Chipset 1AGP,3PCI,3ISA,2DIMM
	1MB Pipeline Burst SRAM
	2 dual-channeled PCI Bus Mastering IDE
	Baby AT
Memory:	2XCorsair PC-133 128MB sticks
Video:	AGP Matrox Marvel G400
Sound:	SB16
CD-Writer:	Sony CRX140S/C

Next you'll want to create an entry for the operating system installation, to define just how the installation progressed and detail any special configuration features. Certainly if there are any glitches in the installation, this should be noted for future reference. Tracking down a hardware failure is often a step-by-step process in which the diagnosis is made by looking at the system's history of problems rather than a single failure. Include information about kernel configuration and any changes to the default initialization process. You are, in effect, drawing a portrait of the system, so you need to catch as many details as you can. The initial installation information is critical.

Administrator's Logbook: Operating System Installation

System: E12345678

Red Hat 7.0 stock KDE workstation installation

SWAP	64MB	/dev/hda1
/boot	16MB	/dev/hda2
/	8112MB	/dev/hda3

Guest user account created.

If you add a user account, list the date, the command, the user-specific data, and anything else you'd need to replicate the action. It will take a little while to make this second nature, but when you encounter a system failure, you'll consider the journal-keeping time well spent.

Some new system administrators realize that they need a journal, but they attempt to keep one on one of the computers under their control. This is fine for a while, but if that system develops a problem, there may be no journal available for use. You might say that you'd never make that mistake. If so, congratulations, but we've heard a number of horror stories in which a computer that was used to maintain the journal was the one that failed.

Throughout the rest of this book, we will include examples of possible journal entries for the topic being discussed, in order to enforce the importance of journal-keeping and to illustrate the information that's relevant in that context.

Communicating with Users

We've alluded to the lack of understanding that users will have of your job and the time required in doing it. This is often caused by a lack of communication between system administrators and users. Sometimes, in a rush to explain a delay that was not immediately communicated to the user, a system administrator will make claims that are simply untrue. "I got called away to do something for the boss, so I was unable to setup your mail client. I'll get to it as soon as I can." Sometimes this is true, of course, but many system administrators make these claims so often that they aren't believed or taken seriously by the users they serve. This makes the job of communicating with users all the more difficult.

We have each found that once we establish ourselves as credible, users are not irritated when we have to tell them that their task has been assessed a lower priority than another. Yes, they want the job done as soon as possible, but most people have more than one responsibility and understand when you do. Earn the trust of your users by being responsible and responsive, and your job will be significantly less taxing. When there is a delay in a promised repair or configuration, a quick phone call or e-mail will usually allow you to keep the user's trust. Many system administrators think that they'll just explain the delay when they actually do the work. "Do unto others as you would have them do unto you." Truthfully, if you show respect to your users, you will have their respect as well, and your work environment will be all the better for it. Of course, most of you learned this from your mothers, but the number of system administrators who don't follow this maxim is astonishing.

There are several ways to communicate with your users. Reluctant computer users may respond better to a telephone call; the more computer-savvy may prefer e-mail. E-mail is essential whenever you need to communicate something to more than one user, but unless you use return receipts on your e-mail, you won't know if users have even checked their e-mail at all.

However you communicate, be sure to give an approximate completion time for the requested task, if only to give users some way to better estimate when they'll get their own tasks done. If your estimate is far off the mark or you are interrupted by a higher-priority task, you will find that a follow-up e-mail will decrease the users' frustration, and you won't be called or e-mailed every few minutes to find out when you'll get to their tasks.

Whichever method of communication is appropriate to your purpose, communication is a critical factor in maintaining a good working relationship with the users who rely on you.

Working on the System as Root

Root access is the power of the system administrator. There's a t-shirt that bears the message, "Bow down before me for I am root," and that isn't far from the way many system administrators view things. For a new system administrator, having access to the root password is a very cool thing. Root access means you are unstoppable. The root user, also known as the superuser, has the authority to do anything, anywhere on the entire system. This may include any computers that are networked to that machine as well. You can do very significant things, but inherent to your new power is the potential to make very significant mistakes! Root access allows you to make huge mistakes if you are careless. The general rule is "don't log in as root unless you need to." If you need to log in as root, perform the task that requires root access and immediately reassume the identity of your normal user. You can use the sudo utility, which is described shortly, to minimize the number of commands that you or your staff have to log in as root to perform.

You can also use the /etc/securetty file to restrict the set of terminals from which root can log in. This file is a list of TTY numbers, from vc/1 through vc/11 and tty1 through tty11 by default, which the login program reads when it is run. The default settings mean that root is allowed to log in from any of the virtual terminals but not remotely. Adding pseudoterminals (ttyp*n*) would allow root to log in remotely. This is not very secure and in most cases should not be done. To completely disable root login, forcing the use of su instead, /etc/securetty should be an empty file. Do not delete the /etc/securetty file, since doing so means that root can log in from anywhere. The default setup is very good and should very rarely be changed.

NOTE In Linux, *terminal* and *TTY* most commonly refer to a virtual terminal, which is simply an alternative login session. There are also physical devices called terminals, which should not be confused with workstations. These teletypewriter (TTY) devices, consisting of little more than a keyboard and monitor, were the only means of connecting to Unix mainframe and minicomputers through the 1980s and still have uses today. Chapter 12, "Serial Communications, Terminals, and Modems," shows how to configure these terminals.

Train yourself and the other users who are allowed access to the root password to be very deliberate when logged in as root and not to abuse the power it gives. A mistake you make while logged in as root could delete files that are required for the system to run properly. We once heard of a system administrator who deleted the /tmp directory, causing the whole system to become unstable. Another system administrator deleted the password file. Still another deleted the entire /home directory, taking all the users' files and functionality away until it could be dumped from a backup tape and making his boss very unhappy. In truth, most of these mistakes are recoverable if you perform regular backups, but they are embarrassing and time-consuming.

Becoming the *Root* User

How does one become the root user? This section outlines the most commonly used techniques.

su

If you logged in to the system under your own user account, you need to use the su command to assume the privileges of root. The su command allows you to initiate a new shell in which your user ID and group ID are temporarily replaced with the username you specify. It is important to note that although you seem to "become" root, you are actually only using an effective user ID and group ID. Your identity is still known to the system; your actions are still very traceable. The command to change to the superuser is:

```
$ su root
```

You will be prompted for the root password and must properly authenticate to be granted root access. Failure to do so will send a message to the root user about a failed su attempt.

If you successfully authenticate, you will retain the environment of your original user account but will be allowed to change into directories owned by root, execute binaries that would not be executable by your normal account, create files in directories that are restricted to root, and much more. Your PATH will remain as it was with your normal user, so many of the more dangerous commands will not be accessible unless you specify their full path.

su –

Adding the – parameter starts a root login shell wherein the environment of the root user is assumed as well. The command for this would be:

```
$ su - root
```

You will be prompted for the root password, and failure to authenticate will leave you as your own user and send a message of the failed su to the root user. If you authenticate successfully, however, your working directory will be changed to root's home directory. From this point on, you are effectively root, although your identity is still known.

Starting an X Session as Root

If your network uses the X Window System GUI interface (discussed in Chapter 16, "The X Window System"), you can run an entire X session as root by changing to the root user and then starting X. Everything done in that session will be performed as if you had logged in as root from the original login prompt, although again your true identity will be recorded. It is easy to forget that you have assumed superuser privileges, so this session should be handled with special care. One method of ensuring that you don't forget that you started an X session as root is to use a totally different X environment for the root user than for the other users. You might make the background of the root user's X session red or yellow to flag the session as initiated by the superuser.

Because of the potential for disaster that is associated with doing general work as the superuser, it's better to use your normal user account to log in and to initiate the X session. Once you have the X session up and running, you can then bring up a terminal and use the su command to "become" root within that terminal and perform the required tasks. As soon as you've finished, exit from the superuser identity and proceed as your normal user. This method is far less dangerous.

sudo

sudo (which stands for "superuser do") is a Linux command that system administrators commonly use to grant "superuser" or root privileges to a user or group of users temporarily so that they can perform specific operations they would not otherwise be allowed to do.

sudo logs its use, keeping track of who used it and what was done. It also sends e-mail to the superuser if someone tries to invoke sudo who does not have the necessary access to do so. Once authenticated, sudo grants the requested privilege for five minutes at a time (this default is configurable), and each command issued gets its own five minutes. The command looks like this:

```
$ sudo shutdown -r now
```

sudo first validates the user's identity by querying for a password. It then consults a file, /etc/sudoers in Red Hat Linux, to determine whether that user has permission to execute a command as the specified user or as root if no other user is specified. The /etc/sudoers file looks like this:

```
# sudoers file.

#

# This file MUST be edited with the 'visudo' command as root.

#

# See the sudoers man page for the details on how to write a sudoers
file.

#


# Host alias specification


# User alias specification


# Cmnd alias specification


# User privilege specification
root     ALL=(ALL) ALL
someuser    ALL=(ALL) ALL
```

If the user is listed in /etc/sudoers, a password prompt is issued. If the user can authenticate with the appropriate password, the referenced operation is performed and a five-minute timer will be set. During that five minutes, the authenticated user can perform sudo commands without reauthenticating.

Sudo is a critical tool. Thanks to it, you can grant certain users and administrative staff access to perform some high-level tasks without actually giving them the root password. (Of course, you'll do this only when the benefit of letting the user handle the task outweighs the potential risks. The user needs to be not only trustworthy but technically competent.) This tool is available on most standard distributions of Linux and is available for most flavors of Unix. For a more extensive description of sudo, visit its home page at http://www.courtesan.com/sudo/man/sudo.html.

In Sum

This chapter has discussed many aspects of Linux system administration, but since the entire book is about administration, it has only scratched the surface. Use this chapter as a guide to future chapters. Next we'll work through the installation process, using Red Hat Linux as a model.

2

Installing Linux

Linux system administrators often find themselves at the transition point between some other operating system and Linux. In the process, they are called on to make hardware recommendations, install Linux on servers and workstations, and set these systems up for use. These systems may be installed via a CD-ROM, from a hard disk, or even across a network (using NFS, FTP, HTTP, or some other protocol). Sometimes they are installed individually and sometimes in batch. Sometimes as an administrator you aren't transitioning but developing a plan for a Linux-based network of servers and workstations and implementing that plan. Whatever the case, the information in this chapter will help you along your way. To achieve the perfect system, you need to have both optimized operating system and application software and state-of-the-art hardware. In this chapter, we'll look at hardware performance issues that affect your selection as well as the installation and initial configuration of the very capable Linux operating system onto a server and a workstation.

Benchmarks

Although many claims are made about what hardware works most efficiently, it is very difficult to compare the performance of differently configured systems. There are many benchmarking tools available for Linux; these provide ratings that are easier to compare, but even with these you must ensure that you're comparing systems that differ only in the item being compared. This controlled comparison is not always possible but is preferable if it can be obtained. If you read benchmark results in a white paper or on a Web site, remember to consider the source for dependability and impartiality.

Here's an example. Ziff-Davis Media Inc., one of the leading information authorities for assessing technology and the Internet, in January of 1999 posted on their site a synopsis of benchmarks comparing several distributions of Linux and Windows NT running on like hardware. The Linux boxes were running Apache and Samba only and the Windows NT boxes were running Internet Information Server 4.0 with service pack 4. No unneeded services were running on any of the machines being compared. The benchmarking tool was Ziff-Davis Media Benchmarks, one of the industry standards. This test gave all of the Linux flavors tested a clear win over the Windows NT boxes. Read the results on the Ziff-Davis site at: `http://www.zdnet.com/sp/stories/infopack/0,5483,387506,00.html`.

Now consider another example. In April of 1999, a company called Mindcraft developed a set of benchmarks comparing a Microsoft NT 4 server with a Linux server wherein Windows NT came out the clear and decisive winner. Mindcraft admitted that Microsoft had funded the benchmarks but claimed that they were fair. Read the report and decide for yourself what to believe: `http://www.mindcraft.com/whitepapers/first-nts4rhlinux.html`.

To give you the whole story, Mindcraft offered to run the tests again with some Linux personnel involved this time. The results were in favor of Microsoft again, but there was a lot of room for doubt. The story is available here: `http://www.mindcraft.com/whitepapers/openbench1.html`.

This is not the only set of conflicting benchmarks between Linux and Windows—far from it. The point is that benchmarks can be developed that will support any claim. Never take benchmarks at face value unless you have carefully and methodically run them yourself. Don't immediately trust your own benchmarks. Too many system administrators download benchmarking packages, run them, and depend on the results. Evaluate the system load, configuration, and appropriateness of the hardware/software combination for the task. Ensure that the systems are as equal as you can make them, and then use the benchmarks for guidance.

Selecting Hardware

There are many factors that determine how well a computer system will perform. Certainly the hardware plays a large part. Older or less capable hardware generally slows down a system. Anyone who has upgraded from a low-end processor to a top-rated processor can tell you the significance of the upgrade. Everything seems to go faster, even though only some functions have actually sped up. Now try running poorly configured software on a state-of-the-art machine. It runs better than on lesser hardware, but it is not the best that it can be. Reconfiguring will make a great difference provided that the hardware can handle the system load. Optimized software on low-end hardware is similarly disappointing. The trick is to optimize the software on the best hardware for the intended task.

Just as a car's engine can determine how fast it will go, the hardware components in your Linux system determine how it will perform. We'll look at the minimum acceptable hardware for a Linux system and some example architectures for different types of Linux systems. We'll also discuss some issues to consider in achieving optimal performance.

Minimal Acceptable Hardware

One of the best-known facts about Linux is that it can make use of old computer parts that you have stored away somewhere. Many a high school student has salvaged an old 80386 machine and turned it into a decent print server or mail server. Originally, Linux was designed to install on an 80386 with as little as 4MB of memory, but with the rapid changes in processor speed and memory size, designing anything to work with only 4MB of memory became unnecessary. Red Hat recommends at least 16MB of memory and 500MB of hard drive space for its 7.0 release. Other distributions have slightly different recommended requirements, but these don't reflect differences in the needs of identically configured systems; rather, they reflect differing default installations and usage assumptions.

Below is some basic information about selecting performance-oriented hardware for a Linux system.

CPU Performance

One of the most important elements in determining a computer's performance is the Central Processing Unit (CPU). A new CPU seems to hit the market almost weekly. In the Intel-compatible $x86$ market, there are basically four players: Intel, Advanced Micro Devices, Inc. (AMD), VIA (which bought Cyrix in 1999), and startup Transmeta. New faces are appearing in the microprocessor technology market, but many target architectures other than the $x86$. Linux is known to run on all of those listed here:

- Intel/AMD/Cyrix 386SX/DX/SL/DLC/SLC
- Intel/AMD/Cyrix 486SX/DX/SL/SX2/DX2/DX4
- IDT WinChip
- NexGen NX586
- Cyrix 6x86, 6x86MX, and M-II
- VIA Cyrix III

- AMD K5, K6, K6-2, K6-III
- AMD K7/Athlon (including the Duron series)
- Transmeta Crusoe
- Intel Pentium and Pentium MX
- Intel Pentium Pro
- Intel Pentium II (including the Celeron series)
- Intel Pentium III

NOTE IDT and NexGen were bought out by VIA and AMD, respectively. Transmeta CPUs have yet to become popular, but they're poised to make inroads in portable devices because of their low power requirements. Many third parties resell CPUs under their own names, often with adapter boards to make the CPUs work on a wider range of motherboards than originally intended.

The current leaders of the market are the Pentium III and the AMD K7 Athlon, the latest entries from Intel and AMD. Historically, Intel has been the market leader, with AMD playing catch-up, but recent tests between these two chips show the Athlon to be faster in both game playing and video rendering. The competition between Intel and AMD, however, is ongoing, so soon Intel will certainly come out with a new CPU that outperforms the Athlon—until the next round. Although Linux also supports VIA Cyrix chips, they are not really competitive with their AMD and Intel counterparts. VIA Cyrix processors will give you no problems in Linux, but if it's performance you're looking for, look to the Athlon.

Linux also runs on a wide variety of non-*x*86 CPUs. Of particular interest, the Linux ports to the PowerPC (PPC), Alpha, and SPARC CPUs are all mature, and all these CPUs are supported by several Linux distributions. But unless you need an unusual feature of one of these CPUs (such as extraordinary floating-point power), you're probably better off going with an *x*86 CPU for Linux use, because *x*86 hardware is inexpensive and Linux is still best supported on *x*86 systems. If you've got an existing Macintosh or Alpha box, though, and want to run Linux on it, you can certainly do so.

Random Access Memory

There are two main categories of Random Access Memory (RAM): system and video. Although video RAM is important in issues of rendering speed and graphic resolution, system RAM affects the performance of all software, whether or not it is graphics-intensive. There are several types of RAM on the market today. Of course, if you have made a motherboard selection already, your RAM type will be dictated by the type supported by that motherboard. If you haven't, however, you may find yourself wading through the many subcategories of RAM available today. In early 2001, synchronous dynamic RAM (SDRAM) and Rambus dynamic RAM (RDRAM) are the most common types of system RAM. Older systems used ordinary dynamic RAM (DRAM) or variants of it.

Whenever possible, you should buy memory modules in the largest amounts that will support your configuration. For instance, if there are four slots that will accept up to 256MB modules, it would be better to buy two 256MB modules than four 128MB modules, since the former allows for system growth without forcing you to replace existing modules. You can later add two more 256MB modules for a total of 1GB instead of having to pull out the four 128MB modules and add four 256MB modules. Plan the most efficient upgrade path when you purchase computer components.

We've just outlined the bare-minimum hardware required to run Linux. As a system administrator, your job is to develop systems that are performance-oriented rather than just inexpensive, so you'll probably want more than the minimum. The next section describes system hardware requirements in terms of the tasks that a given system needs to perform.

Selecting Hardware by Intended Usage

Now that we've seen the minimum hardware required for any Linux system, we can look at three different categories of computer—a low-end workstation, a high-end graphics workstation, and a basic server—and the minimal requirements for serving those roles effectively. These are opinions based on our own experience. As Linux users often say, your mileage may vary. Use our experience as a guideline, keeping in mind that the minimum requirements may be insufficient if the system load becomes unusually high. We have tried to allow for a high system load, but at some point, a more capable CPU, more memory, and/or hard drive space might be required. Always consider the work being done and which parts of the system are being stressed the most. Look to Chapter 9 for more optimization techniques and ways to determine when the current system is overly taxed, and upgrade components as needed.

Configuration A: A Basic Workstation

The first configuration we'll look at is pretty much the minimum for any system that you will purchase. Configuration A is a workstation used primarily for word processing:

- Pentium or AMD K5 or K6 CPU
- 64MB of RAM
- CD-ROM drive
- Floppy drive

- 10GB hard drive (IDE or SCSI)
- IDE or SCSI disk controller (as appropriate)
- SVGA graphics card with at least 4MB of video RAM
- Ethernet card (10BaseT or as appropriate)
- 15-inch SVGA monitor

The hardware in this configuration is available for very little money overall. There is really no reason to buy less than this. We consider 64MB of memory to be the minimum because most systems come with this amount by default. Sometimes a system will come with only 32MB of memory, but with a little extra effort you can usually find a system with 64MB from a different vendor for close to the same cost. A system used for word processing is not very CPU-intensive. There generally are not multiple tasks waiting to be serviced, so a high-speed CPU is really unnecessary. Similarly, such a system is not generally going to require more than 64MB of memory. Documents are usually broken into small enough pieces as to be manageable on this system. The floppy drive and CD-ROM drive are simply for software update purposes and other general tasks. The 10GB hard drive is the smallest that's readily available today, and is more than adequate for a basic installation. Certainly storage space should continually be monitored to determine if and when additional space is warranted. You can use either SCSI or IDE hard drives since speed is not critical on such a system. The SVGA graphics card and monitor are the minimum since this system is not geared toward graphic applications. The network card need only be suitable to connect this system to the local network. Usually this will be 10BaseT, although 100BaseT is growing more common, and 100BaseT cards cost little more than 10BaseT cards. You may want to add more components if you have additional specific needs, such as a modem, scanner, or CD-ROM burner.

Configuration B: A High-End Graphics Workstation

Configuration B is a workstation used to develop graphics or do desktop publishing:
- Pentium II or AMD K6-2 or Athlon
- 128MB of RAM
- CD-ROM drive
- Floppy drive
- 20GB hard drive (IDE or SCSI)
- IDE or SCSI disk controller (as appropriate)
- SVGA graphics card with 16–32MB of video RAM
- Ethernet card (10BaseT or as appropriate)
- 17- or 21-inch SVGA monitor

Configuration B needs a more powerful processor since graphics production and desktop publishing will each put a slightly higher load on the processor. The memory has been increased to 128MB to allow the system to handle the large amounts of data involved in graphics or to load large documents into memory. More hard drive space is needed since graphics files are generally quite large, especially at higher resolutions. Similarly, a larger monitor is needed since the job of editing graphics and other printed matter involved in the publishing process can cause eyestrain if performed at too low a resolution.

Configuration C: A Basic Server

Configuration C is a server running basic services that the popular distributions turn on by default:

- Pentium III or AMD Athlon
- 128MB of RAM
- SCSI CD-ROM drive
- Floppy drive
- 10GB SCSI hard drive
- SVGA graphics card with 4MB of video RAM
- Ethernet card (10BaseT or as appropriate)
- 15-inch SVGA monitor

In configuration C, we have left the memory at 128MB even though a smaller amount would probably be adequate if the Web serving or mail serving load were particularly light. You can use a smaller hard drive than with the graphics workstation, since with POP3 mail that is retrieved from the server to the user's workstation will no longer be stored on the server. Your specific needs may dictate a larger hard disk, though. Restrictions to the size of incoming mail also negate the need for more storage. Certainly a system that has more than 50 users or is used in support of a Web site whose content is linked to a database would benefit from additional space. The server's hard disk is SCSI because SCSI better handles heavy disk-access loads, particularly in a multi-device configuration.

Specialized Hardware Performance Solutions

Beyond the minimal systems for specific uses described in the preceding examples, there are other items the administrator should consider in planning a high-performance system. These include support for multiple processors and disk subsystems. These items can make for a huge performance gain in specific situations and almost none in other situations.

Symmetric Multiprocessing

One way to add computing power to a computer is to add additional processors to a motherboard that supports Symmetric Multiprocessing (SMP). SMP allows you to share the processor's workload across up to 16 processors in a single computer. In practice, because of limitations of the $x86$ architecture, actual implementation has not exceeded eight processors. Still, that's enough to significantly speed up programs written to support SMP or systems that run multiple CPU-intensive programs. Only multithreaded programs will truly benefit from SMP. Multithreading, also simply referred to as threading, is the process of cloning processes to split the workload within a program into separate processes that can be routed to separate processors in an SMP system. Basically, the rule is: processes and kernel-threads are distributed among processors; user-space threads are not. If you notice that your single processor is idle much of the time because of a slow disk drive, the system probably won't benefit much from additional processing power. If your system has many simultaneously executing processes, and CPU load is very high, then you are likely to see increased system performance with SMP. Since SCSI disk drives process multiple commands without tying up the CPU, you can see significant gain when using multiple processors. The Linux make command, used to compile kernels and other software packages, has a –j parameter that allows it to take advantage of SMP and significantly speed up the process of building a kernel. The syntax is shown below:

```
make [modules|zImage|bzImages] MAKE="make -jX"
```

(X is the maximum number of processes.) The distribution of the workload is not, by definition, symmetrical since some specific functions may be assigned to a specific processor rather than spread across all processors within the system. Be that as it may, you can see extremely significant performance gains when adding up to three additional processors; beyond four processors, however, the performance gains diminish. Adding a second processor does not usually double the speed of the process compared to a single processor. It allows for portions of that process or an entirely separate process to be handled by the second processor, thereby giving a performance gain. However, if the process has not been designed to spread the workload among multiple processors, there may be no gain at all.

Linux Clusters

Clustering is the process of coordinating the workload for a given project among several independent computer systems, an alternative to the sharing of processors within one computer that we just discussed. One example of clustering is Linux Virtual Server (LVS) clustering, as supported in the Linux kernel and implemented by, among other things, Red Hat's Piranha environment. Figure 2.1 illustrates the basic idea behind an LVS cluster. Essentially, one system (there are two in Figure 2.1, so that this point of failure has a backup) interfaces between the Internet and a group of identically configured servers. Instead of running a heavy Web server off just one computer, then, LVS spreads the work across several computers. Provided the LVS router has fast enough network interfaces, the result is an improvement in speed and reliability.

LVS provides for floating server IP addresses. The LVS router has a fixed IP address for the outside world. The IP address will be assigned to either the primary LVS router or its

Figure 2.1   LVS cluster topology

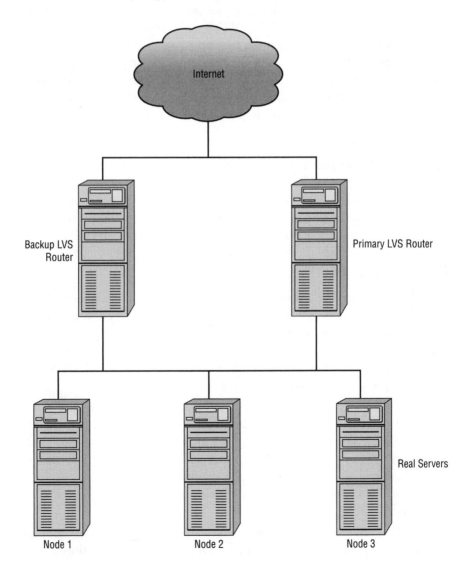

backup and will automatically be transferred if the machine to which it is assigned goes down (a process known as *failover*). In this instance, the IP address and the routing tables are synced from the downed machine by the `lvs` daemon, which handles communication between the two machines. The `pulse` daemon runs on both LVS machines to allow the secondary node to determine whether the primary node is active. The `ipvsadm` command is the command-line tool for administering the LVS machines in the cluster.

The rest of the cluster consists of real server machines to which FTP or HTTP service requests are routed via the LVS machines' second network card. The LVS router machines each run one daemon for each FTP or HTTP server running on each real server machine. This LVS router daemon will connect to the port of the real server to ensure that the system is still available to take the FTP or HTTP requests. Load balancing between the real servers may be based simply on which server's turn it is, or it can be sophisticated enough to qualify as true load balancing. For more information about this type of cluster, refer to the `http://www.linuxvirtualserver.org` Web site.

Disk Subsystems

Disk I/O is another potential bottleneck for systems that require very high performance. Disk access is measured in milliseconds, RAM in nanoseconds. The two basic techniques for making disk I/O more efficient are RAID (Redundant Arrays of Inexpensive Disks) and disk caching, both described below. The method you choose depends entirely on your specific situation. A RAID array, which requires a significant hardware investment, may or may not give you significant gain; maximizing your disk cache is almost always a good thing.

RAID Arrays   There are six different levels of RAID, all of which use multiple hard disks connected to a single computer to improve speed, reliability, or both. Levels 1–5 are primarily concerned with reliability (data redundancy) but do offer performance increases in read operations. Redundancy allows for multiple copies of the same data on different drives so that if one drive fails, the data is not lost. The different levels vary in performance as measured in read or write times:

RAID0   This level is aimed specifically at increasing performance and provides no redundancy. In RAID0, data is *striped* across multiple disks. Striping is a procedure whereby several drives appear to the computer system as a single drive. On these drives, the data is distributed into small partitions, intermixed in such a way that the virtual drive seen by the computer is composed of stripes from each drive. This allows simultaneous reads from multiple drives, which can give a significant performance boost.

RAID1   This level performs *mirroring* of data, meaning that the same data is stored on all drives. Reads tend to be faster than with a single drive since data can be read simultaneously from both drives. Read-balancing had some problems in Linux kernels, although this has been ironed out in the 2.4 kernels. If you wish to take advantage of this, you should probably consider a kernel upgrade. Writes tend to be slower since two copies of the data must be written. RAID1 may mirror data between two local drives or between drives on two different hosts.

RAID2 Not supported in Linux, RAID2 uses error correction codes to compensate for drives that do not have built-in error detection. Since most drives include error correction now, RAID2 is seldom used.

RAID3 Not supported in Linux, RAID3 stripes the data across all drives at the byte level. Parity information is stored on one of the disks in the array to protect against data loss in the event of a single disk failure.

RAID4 Similar to RAID3, except that the data is striped at the block level. Parity is maintained on one disk as in RAID3. This causes the parity disk to be the bottleneck.

RAID5 Similar to RAID4, except that parity is now split between all the disks in the array. A RAID5 array can withstand a single disk failure. Write performance is significantly slowed since a single write operation requires old data and parity to be read from each disk, the new parity to be calculated, and the new data and parity to be written to each disk in the array. However, the improvement in reading speed from striping across multiple spindles goes a long way toward offsetting the overhead of performing the write parity calculations. It is not unusual for a well-configured RAID5 software array to perform as well as or better than the individual disks would.

RAID can be implemented in hardware or software. The hardware implementations are extremely fast and extremely costly. The software implementations, on the other hand, are relatively inexpensive. As of kernel 2.2.16-22, which is standard for Red Hat 7.0, RAID0, RAID1, and RAID4/RAID5 can be configured in the kernel. There is also an option to auto-detect RAID partitions; this works by detecting any partitions created with a partition ID of 0xfd, as opposed to the usual Linux partition type code of 0x83. (You can check or change a partition type code with the Linux fdisk utility, as described in Chapter 10.)

To see what RAID support you already have installed, look at the /proc/mdstat file. If you are not running any of the RAID modules that exist in /lib/modules/2.2.16-22/block, the file will not exist or will contain the following:

```
Personalities : []
read_ahead not set
unused devices: <none>
```

If you have any RAID modules running, you'll see the RAID level(s) listed between the brackets after `Personalities`.

NOTE   Just because RAID support is *present* on your system doesn't necessarily mean that it's being *used*. It's also possible to use RAID on some disks or partitions but not on others.

Let's assume a case where you want to stripe data (RAID0) across two partitions that you marked as RAID partitions when you created them with the `fdisk` utility. We're using IDE here, but SCSI works also. Now you need to configure the `/etc/raidtab` file for your particular configuration. On the standard Red Hat 7.0 system, this file won't exist until you create it. There are several examples you can use as models; look at the `raidtab` man page for one of them. Listing 2.1 is a sample `/etc/raidtab` file, tailored to our scenario.

Listing 2.1   A Sample /etc/raidtab File

```
raiddev /dev/md0                    /* RAID device name */
        raid-level           0      /* RAID Level we use */
        nr-raid-disks        2      /* # of RAID disks */
        persistent-superblock 1     /* use the pers-sb */
        chunk-size           8      /* stripe size bytes */

        device               /dev/hda9    /* partition */
        raid-disk            0           /* index */
        device               /dev/hdb6 /* partition */
        raid-disk            1           /* index */
```

The `/etc/raidtab` file uses C-style comments—anything between /* and */ is a comment and is ignored by the system. Important elements of Listing 2.1 include:

    `raid-level`   The RAID level, as described above.

    `nr-raid-disks`   The number of disks in the RAID array.

    `chunk-size`   The number of bytes that go into each stripe.

    `device`   For each disk (up to the value specified for `nr-raid-disks`), you must specify a Linux partition device file to be used in the disk array. These partitions don't need to be in equivalent positions on the physical disks—for instance, in Listing 2.1, the array uses /dev/hda9 and /dev/hdb6.

`raid-disk`   For each RAID device, you must specify the position in the RAID array—which device is the first in the striping sequence, which is second, and so on. These values are numbered starting with 0.

Now we have our `raidtab` file set up, and we've created the partitions to be auto-detected. Auto-detection is configured into the Red Hat 7.0 kernel by default. Now use the `insmod` command to start RAID-0 as follows:

```
# insmod raid0
```

Finally, you need to run the `mkraid` command to configure your RAID-0 array and format the metadisk for use.

```
# mkraid
# mkext2 /dev/md0
```

> **WARNING**   Issuing the `mkraid` command destroys any data that might have existed on the partitions specified in the `/etc/raidtab` file. If you want to convert existing partitions to a RAID configuration, you must first back them up, then do the conversion and restore data.

Disk Caching   Disk caching uses system memory to cache disk I/O (input/output). Caching data from the disk into RAM improves performance significantly because RAM access is much faster than disk access. The disk cache stores the most recently used data from the hard drive in a memory buffer that was allocated when the system started. When a program makes a disk read request, the disk caching software intercepts the call and checks the cache buffer to see if it contains the required data. If so, the data is read from memory instead of the disk. Buying hard drives with lower access times and activating disk caching in your BIOS settings will give you significant performance gains.

The effectiveness of a cache is pretty much determined by its size. If the cache is too small, the data is often flushed before it is even reused, rendering the cache useless. A cache that is too large uses up free memory and can cause the system to swap to disk, which is also slow. Linux uses all free RAM as a buffer cache, but this cache is automatically reduced in size when additional memory is required by an application. There is no configuration required.

Types of Hardware to Avoid

Just as there are types of hardware that can make your system more efficient or easier to use, there are types that can make it less so. Some hardware devices will actually slow the system down, while others simply will be hard to support.

Proprietary Hardware

Proprietary hardware is any device for which the manufacturer supplies its own driver directly to buyers rather than making the necessary information available for operating-system developers to create the driver. This approach may pose a problem since all too often companies create drivers for Microsoft products but neglect to create drivers for other operating systems, like Linux. The Linux community is sometimes able to reverse-engineer a driver, but this takes time. More and more companies are creating Linux-compatible drivers for their products, but this is a new trend, so proprietary hardware remains a gamble. Until a few years ago, the information required to create drivers for some Diamond video cards was considered proprietary, so these cards were not recommended. Now Diamond makes this information available, and Diamond cards are supported Linux hardware.

Some types of proprietary hardware (particularly modems and printers) are commonly referred to as "Windows-only" devices, because drivers are typically only available for Windows. This designation is fluid, however; today's "Windows-only" device may have a Linux driver available tomorrow. Nonetheless, you shouldn't assume that any given device will have a Linux driver available in the future.

Some proprietary devices use stripped-down hardware that requires extra attention from the computer's CPU. This is particularly common in inexpensive internal modems (often called *WinModems* or *software modems*, although the former term is a trademark of 3Com, and so technically only applies to certain 3Com products), low-end laser printers, and so-called *AC-97* sound hardware. Linux drivers are appearing for some of these devices, but it's usually best to avoid them even when drivers are available, because they chew up CPU time that might be better spent elsewhere.

> *TIP*   If you're stuck with a software modem, check http://www.linmodems.org for information on drivers for these devices. The Linux Printing Support Database (http://www.linuxprinting.org/printer_list.cgi) hosts information on drivers for printers, including the handful of proprietary-protocol printers for which Linux support exists, but may not ship with Linux.

Hardware Compatibility

For other types of hardware, like CD-ROM drives, sound cards, and so on, Red Hat maintains a compatibility list at http://www.redhat.com/support. We have run across hardware that was not supported, but most of it was supported in subsequent versions. SuSE lists its supported hardware at http://www.suse.com/us/support/hardware/index.html. Caldera posts its hardware compatibility information at http://www.calderasystems.com/support/hardware/. Most other distributions rely on the

Linux-Hardware Compatibility HOWTO available at `http:www.//ibiblio.org/mdw/HOWTO/Hardware-HOWTO.html`.

Despite the fact that various distributions have different hardware compatibility lists, hardware compatibility actually varies very little between distributions. Most hardware support resides in the kernel, which is the same from one distribution to another (give or take some minor tweaks). Distributions may ship with slightly different kernel versions (2.2.16 versus 2.2.17, say), or one distribution may incorporate experimental drivers into its kernel whereas another may forego that uncertain benefit. If hardware works in one distribution, though, it's almost certain that you can make it work in another by obtaining an updated kernel, possibly applying some patches, and recompiling the kernel. (Chapter 8 discusses kernel compilation.) A few devices, such as video cards, printers, and scanners, require support in non-kernel applications, but similar comments apply to these devices.

Selecting a Linux Distribution

A Linux distribution is a package consisting of a selected kernel and supporting software that meets the distributor's acceptable standards for hardware support and stability. The major Linux distributions are generally considered to include Red Hat, Mandrake, Caldera, SuSE, Slackware, Debian, and Corel. Each of these is available on CD-ROM. All of these except SuSE are also available via FTP over the Internet in a form designed to be written to a CD-ROM or, in the case of Slackware, to floppies designed to initiate a network installation. (One good clearinghouse site for distribution image files is `http://www.linuxiso.org`.)

If you mention which distribution you intend to use to a Linux advocate, be ready for an explanation of why a different distribution is better. On any Linux mailing list, friendly arguments called *distro wars* frequently occur: one user mentions his distribution by name, and other members of the list feel compelled to compare that distribution with whatever they are currently using. The fact that these are e-mail lists usually prevents bloodshed.

Because Linux kernel development is separate from the development of individual distributions, there are several common elements among the different distributions. Some of the more basic common truths about Linux installations are listed below:

- All distributions need to follow the Filesystem Hierarchy Standard (FHS) or its predecessor the Linux File System Standard (FSSTND). Chapter 3 discusses the FHS in detail.

- All major distributions, with the exception of Slackware, have some sort of package-management system to help keep track of what packages have been installed and what files these packages contain. The Red Hat Package Manager (RPM) is the most common Linux package manager. It is used with Red Hat, Mandrake, SuSE, and Caldera. Debian and Corel can handle RPM packages, although these two work best with Debian packages. Slackware uses *tarballs* natively—file compilations created with the Linux tar utility. It's possible to create a tarball from an RPM or Debian package. Chapter 8 covers installation of packages in RPM, Debian, and tarball formats.

- All major Linux distributions use the Linux kernel, which has grown from Linus Torvalds' original code. A few, like Debian, intend to be kernel independent, meaning that the distribution will run with kernels other than that used in other Linux distributions. In Debian's case, the HURD project is working toward producing a kernel that can be used instead of the Linux kernel, but the HURD kernel is not available for use as yet.

The following sections discuss these distributions in sufficient depth to see the similarities, the differences in the targeted user bases, and basic features of each.

WARNING   Don't try to compare version numbers across distributions. For instance, Red Hat Linux 7.0 is not necessarily more advanced than Corel Linux 1.2.

Red Hat Linux

Red Hat Linux is currently the most popular distribution in the United States and possibly worldwide. It has a reputation for being easy to install and configure. Large improvements were made in the install process as version 6 evolved. Now in version 7.0, Red Hat's installation is very smooth. Red Hat's official Web site is located at `http://www.redhat.com`.

Installation Features

Here are some of the most important installation features of Red Hat Linux. New features are added all the time; check Red Hat's home page periodically for updated information.

Kudzu   The Red Hat distribution has made great progress in the area of hardware detection during the install process with the introduction of the Kudzu utility. This utility, included beginning in version 6.1, looks for new hardware and allows the user to configure any new hardware that Kudzu recognizes. In support of this, Kudzu maintains a file that defines the current hardware configuration. For example, Figure 2.2 shows Kudzu's display for a system that was installed without a mouse but now has a generic mouse attached.

Figure 2.2 The Kudzu utility recognizing a mouse

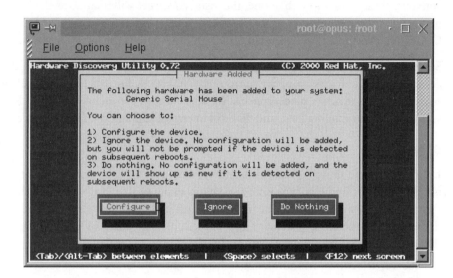

Kudzu runs automatically each time you boot the computer, or you can run it anytime thereafter. It probes for hardware and checks the current configuration to see if any hardware is new. If hardware has been added or removed, it queries the user whether to add or remove the necessary drivers now or wait until a later time. If the update is deferred, of course, Kudzu will present the same question whenever it runs. Since any attempt by Kudzu to remove serial devices like consoles would negatively impact the system, Kudzu does not check serial devices except when run from the installation.

The Kernel Versions of Red Hat Linux from 6.0 on have made more extensive use of kernel *modules* than did previous versions. Kernel modules are drivers for hardware, filesystems, and so on, which are compiled separately from the main kernel file. Under Linux, kernel modules can be loaded and unloaded at any time after the main kernel has loaded, provided that the necessary hardware exists (when unloading a module, the hardware must not be in use). As a result of the increased modularization of recent versions of Red Hat, the system better adapts itself to your computer at install time, loading more drivers you're likely to need and fewer drivers you don't need.

An example of this new kernel flexibility is the handling of Symmetric Multiprocessing (SMP) support. Red Hat has included SMP support for some time now, but in order to take advantage of it, you had to install the kernel source files, set up the appropriate configuration file, and compile the new kernel. That is, the monolithic kernel that remained on the system after an installation did not include SMP support by default. Beginning in Red Hat 6.1, however, the install program probes to determine how many processors the system contains. If there are more than one, the installed kernel will include SMP support automatically. If there is only one processor, SMP support will not be compiled into the kernel. Of course, if you add a processor later, you could recompile the kernel to add SMP support.

Since Red Hat is a commercial company, they are able to offer support to their user community. We discuss support options in Chapter 4, but for the purposes of comparison, Red Hat offers paid support, Web-based support including the archives of the various Red Hat mailing lists, and 90 days of e-mail support with the boxed distribution.

Mandrake

Linux Mandrake (`http://www.linux-mandrake.com/en/`), at version 7.2 at press time, is a derivative of Red Hat Linux, and so shares many of Red Hat's features, including the RPM package format, the Linuxconf utility (although Mandrake's interface is somewhat different), and the basic system startup procedures (discussed in Chapter 5). Mandrake distinguishes itself from its progenitor distribution in several ways:

Server selection Mandrake includes a slightly different mix of servers than does Red Hat. Most noticeably, Mandrake 7.2 uses the Postfix mail server, rather than sendmail, which comes with Red Hat.

Package optimizations Mandrake compiles most of its packages with Pentium CPU optimizations. This means that Mandrake runs slightly faster on Pentium-class CPUs (including compatible models from AMD and VIA/Cyrix), but it won't run at all on 386 or 486 CPUs.

Installation details Although the earliest Mandrake packages used a system install program that was virtually identical to Red Hat's, the latest versions differ somewhat. Most noticeably, Mandrake includes a partitioning utility that allows the user to resize existing Windows partitions.

Of the popular Linux distributions, Mandrake is the most similar to Red Hat—aside from Red Hat itself, of course. This fact makes Mandrake very compatible with binary packages built for Red Hat, and makes it easy to transition from Red Hat to Mandrake.

Caldera

Caldera System's OpenLinux is designed for corporate commercial use. It is available only for the Intel architecture. Caldera is a proven player in the Linux world and thus is likely to continue to improve its distribution over time. OpenLinux has an eServer version as well as an eDesktop version, specially tailored to those individual purposes. Caldera's Linux site is `http://www.calderasystems.com`. At press time, the current version of Caldera is 2.4.

Installation Features

OpenLinux includes LIZARD (Linux Wizard), a graphical installation program that detects your basic hardware: mouse, keyboard, video, sound card, CD-ROM, hard drives, floppy drive, PCMCIA, and Ethernet card. LIZARD then installs the Linux packages you've selected and does a basic configuration for them. We successfully installed OpenLinux on an ACER laptop that wouldn't accept a Red Hat installation without some tweaking.

On the other hand, Caldera's graphical startup screen is a little slow to appear, compared to other distributions. LIZARD does not use the data that it probes during the installation to build a kernel specific to your machine. The kernel it does leave is small but highly modularized. It does not contain SMP support, but this can be added when you build a custom kernel. Caldera requires 32MB of RAM and a minimum of 300MB to install.

SuSE Linux

SuSE (pronounced "SUE-zuh") Linux, developed originally in Germany, is the leading distribution of Linux in Europe. It is growing fast in the United States as well. SuSE is another favorite distribution of ours for its ease of use and general feel. Its English Web page is located at `http://www.suse.com`. At press time, SuSE 7.0 is the latest release of this distribution, and it's available for x86, PowerPC, and Alpha CPUs.

Installation Features

Readers of *Linux Journal* voted SuSE the easiest distribution to install in 1999, thanks largely to its smooth graphical installation tool, YaST2, which provides extensive hardware detection and configuration. YaST2 provides a basic configuration in support of networking, Internet access, sound support, and printing. SuSE is the only major distribution installable by DVD-ROM (the Professional retail package comes on DVD-ROM and CD-ROM, but the less expensive Personal retail package comes only on CD-ROM). Like most distributions, SuSE leaves the same kernel on each system to which it is installed no matter what hardware was detected during a basic installation or upgrade; this kernel contains all of the drivers for what SuSE considers common hardware.

Slackware Linux

Slackware, first released in April of 1992, is Walnut Creek Software's interpretation of the most "Unix-like" Linux distribution available. Slackware's Web site is available at `http://www.slackware.com`. The latest version of the software at press time is 7.1.

Installation Features

Many of us began with Slackware in the days when CD-ROM drives were uncommon and you had to download the whole distribution onto about 50 floppy disks, which you could then use to install to your hard drive. You can still install Slackware from downloaded floppies; it is the only major distribution that still supports a floppy installation (although it is essentially a network installation now). Most users prefer to install from a CD-ROM, an FTP site, or by NFS. Slackware provides fewer GUI tools than do most major distributions, but this is by design; the philosophy is that the user will better know the system if configuration files are set up manually rather than by a GUI setup tool. This knowledge becomes especially critical when you are administering the system remotely and because of firewall constraints can't bring up an X session. Slackware and Debian are the only major distributions whose installation programs don't provide at least a minimal X configuration. Many users prefer to postpone this task until after the initial system has been installed.

A minimal installation requires only 16MB of memory and 80MB of hard drive space.

Debian

Debian Linux is a rather unusual distribution in that it has been developed by a team of volunteers rather than a company like Red Hat or Caldera. In the more formal distributions, decisions about the installation process and which packages to include in the distribution are made by the board that runs the company, in this case Red Hat, Inc. or Caldera Systems. Debian, however, quite willingly accepts modifications from its user base. There is no single commercial backer for Debian. Given that, there is no commercial support available, but there are mailing lists and IRC chats that provide support from the user base. This apparent shortcoming is not seen as one by Debian users, who take pride in the fact that Debian is developed by hackers for hackers. Security is tighter on the default Debian system than any of the others that we've installed. Debian users tend to like having more control over its development than with other distributions. Debian's Web site is located at http://www.debian.org.

Debian contains a package called apt, which automates the downloading and installation of packages. Simply run apt-get install *program* and apt will download the program, download any packages it requires, install them in the correct order, and query you for any data it requires. User receptiveness to this concept varies widely. Many of us prefer to have a more direct involvement. It's easy enough to download the updates from the distribution's Web site and install them individually to watch the process and any errors it might generate.

Installation Features

You may install Debian from floppies, CD-ROM, a hard drive partition containing the installation files, or by NFS. A minimal Debian 2.2 installation requires at least 12MB of memory and 65MB of hard disk, although in order to install X and the most commonly used packages, you would require just under 1GB and would benefit greatly from a memory increase to at least 16MB. (If you have an unusually slim system, the older Debian 2.1 can install in just 4MB of RAM and 35MB of disk space.) The Debian installation procedure does not try to anticipate your choices about even the most basic decisions. It won't select which disks you wish to use nor which partitions on those disks will be used as the root partition or even which will be used as swap. Debian installs a minimal "base" system from its installation medium. It then reboots into this base system, which has just enough functionality to install any other packages you choose. The base system only has to support floppy drives and hard drives. From that point, you can choose which kernel modules to load during this initial phase of the installation.

Debian installs a highly modularized kernel, which means that most modules are available with the default kernel. This kernel includes SMP support, as of Debian 2.2, but it still works on single-CPU systems.

Corel

Corel Linux (`http://linux.corel.com`) is the Linux distribution from the company that sells WordPerfect. Currently at version 1.2, which also goes by the moniker "Corel Linux Second Edition," this distribution is based on Debian but includes a more user-friendly installation routine and default desktop configuration. Corel aims its distribution at people with little or no Linux or Unix experience who want to use Linux as a desktop OS. It comes with fewer packages than most Linux distributions, but they're the packages that Corel believes are most important for desktop use.

In building on the Debian base, Corel has added user-friendly GUI configuration tools similar to the Linuxconf tool used by Red Hat, Mandrake, and a few others. Unfortunately, the 1.2 release includes code that enforces its way of doing things in startup scripts. The result is that if you have a nonstandard system that requires customizations not easily handled through the GUI, you must dig into startup scripts to disable parts of the system that don't need disabling with most other distributions. One of us did a test installation of Corel Linux 1.2 on a computer that used the System Commander boot loader, for instance, only to discover that Corel Linux disabled System Commander after every boot.

On the whole, Corel Linux works best as a workstation OS, particularly when the administrator isn't perfectly familiar with the Linux or Unix way of doing things. For heavy server use, or if you want to modify the base configuration much, the original Debian is probably a better choice, as are several RPM-based distributions.

The Choice Is Yours

The difficulty of the typical Linux installation is a controversial topic. Many Microsoft advocates say that Linux is too difficult for the average person to install. Conversely, you may often hear Linux advocates state that Linux installation is simple. In our experience, neither is the exact truth. In fact, you can't really speak of Linux installation generically, because each major distribution uses a different install program. The various Linux install programs have come a long way to simplify the installation process in the past few years, and some are definitely more advanced than others. As you've seen, different distributions have different goals for the installation; some work to be user-friendly for the new Linux user, while others target a more Linux-knowledgeable audience. For this reason, a distribution is often selected by this criterion alone.

No book can cover all of the different Linux installation programs. In the following section we proceed step by step through a Red Hat installation. Despite the fact that the underlying functions of an installation are always the same, the installation details vary from distribution to distribution. Always rely on the documentation that comes with your distribution for information about installation.

Installing Red Hat Linux

Now that we've discussed some of the basics about the major Linux distributions, it's time to do a walk-through of a real install. We will use Red Hat as an example since it is the most commonly installed distribution in the United States. We will first try a basic server installation and then look at what would be different for a workstation installation.

Preparing for Installation

Before beginning an installation, you should do a few things to prepare. First, you should obtain the installation media that you will use for the installation. For this installation, we'll use a CD copy of Red Hat version 7.0.

Next you should identify the components of your computer system. Write down the manufacturer, model number, DMA channel, and interrupt (if applicable) of your video card, modem, network card, CD-ROM, hard drive(s), SCSI card, and sound card. Also note the number of cylinders and heads and total size of the hard drive(s). You may never need this information; but if you do, you won't need to shut down your system and take it apart to find it. You should keep this information near the computer after the system is installed since you might need to reference it later. Add an entry to the Administrator's Logbook detailing the installation.

Administrator's Logbook: Initial Installation

System: E12345678

Action: Installed Red Hat Linux 7.0

Installation Options: Basic server-class installation

Modifications: Added jed and joe editor packages

Hardware:

  Video: ATI Xpert 98 (Mach 64, 8MB RAM)

  Modem: External USR Sportster 56K Voice

  Network Card: Linksys LNE100TX (PNIC Tulip Clone Chipset)

  CD-ROM Drive: Pioneer DVD-113

  Hard drives: Western Digital AC26400B 6.4GB & Maxtor 91000D8 9.1GB

  SCSI Card: Generic Symbios 53c860-based host adapter

  SCSI Device: External Iomega Zip-100 drive

  Sound card: Integrated motherboard VIA 82c686a sound chipset

---

If you've purchased a Red Hat Official boxed set, it will include the image to create a boot diskette which supports a CD-ROM installation like the one we'll perform. If your computer supports booting from a CD-ROM, you can boot directly from the Red Hat CD-ROM and will not need to create a boot disk. If it does not, or if you are installing from a different medium, you might have to create your own boot disk as described later in this chapter.

Choosing a Partitioning Scheme

Disk partitioning is the division of the hard drive into logical parts that contain specific components of the operating system.

Although most people choose a more structured file system layout, Red Hat 7.0 requires only one Linux partition. Assuming its size is sufficient, this partition can contain both the root partition and all the other directories that fall beneath. An advantage of this simplistic approach is that you don't have to guess how large each filesystem will eventually grow to be. A disadvantage is that you cannot set quotas for individual directory structures and you cannot mount any of the directories under the root partition as read-only, since that requires the directory to live on its own partition. More important still is the fact that dynamic data as exists within the /home directory coexisting with the root filesystem is generally a bad idea, since corruption can cause the entire system to become unstable and possibly even unable to boot at all.

In a more structured approach, you might find that you've set aside too little space for a partition and need to find more space. There are several options for adding space:

- Back up and reinstall, enlarging the partition in question.
- Add a new drive to the system and move some of the data from the bloated partition to the new one.
- Move some of the data from the bloated partition to another existing partition.
- Create a symbolic link so that users will find the data where they expect it to be.

NOTE   Just as there are "distro wars," there are also partitioning scheme wars. Linux users have long argued about the optimum scheme, and there is no sign that they will stop. One of the premiere features of Linux, after all, is the freedom to disagree.

Red Hat has simplified the situation for new users by setting up installation classes. These classes select a partitioning scheme and software packages appropriate to the chosen use. In each case, you have the option of overriding that class' standard partitioning scheme and package selection. There are three established installation classes: the Workstation-Class, the Server-Class, and the Custom-Class. In this case, we'll be performing a Server-Class installation. The others are listed below for completeness.

Workstation-Class Installation

Use the workstation-class installation on an end-user desktop system. A system installed in this way is not intended to act as a server, but it does set up the X Window System environment.

A workstation-class installation requires at least 850MB of free disk space. If your hard drive already contains partitions of other types, like Windows, the workstation-class installation will preserve those partitions and set up the Linux Loader (LILO) to allow you to boot into either operating system. The default partitioning for this class is a 64MB swap partition, a 16MB /boot partition, and a root partition that uses the hard drive's remaining space; a partition that is set to use the remaining space in a partition is said to be *growable*. If you are unclear on what a root or a swap partition is, we'll study the actual filesystem layout in Chapter 3 and discuss swapping and additional partitioning options in Chapter 10.

Server-Class Installation

The server-class installation by default installs a prepackaged Linux-based server. Much of the required configuration is included, although certainly there are things that Red Hat couldn't guess about your system, and these you have to set up yourself. The server-class installation requires 1.7GB of free disk space. It is important to note that any previously created partitions, regardless of type, will be deleted during the server-class install. By default the disk is partitioned into a 64MB swap partition, a 256MB / partition, a growable /usr partition of at least 512MB, a growable /home partition of at least 512MB, a 256MB /var partition, and a 16MB /boot partition.

> **NOTE** The partition sizes described here are approximate. Because of the way the *x86* BIOS handles hard disks, partitions must fall on cylinder boundaries. Depending upon the disk size and how the cylinders, heads, and sectors are arranged, a cylinder can easily be 5–10MB or so in size. Therefore, Linux may not be able to create, say, a /boot partition that's exactly 16MB in size, and may instead create a 23MB /boot partition.

Custom-Class Installation

The custom-class installation is the most flexible of the three. No decisions are made for you. You must choose how the disk will be partitioned, which packages will be installed, and whether or not to use a boot loader. Choose this class of installation when you want to avoid writing over a partition that contains data that you want to keep. This also allows you to pick and choose packages.

Installing a Server

Once you've determined which partitioning scheme to use, whether your own or one provided by Red Hat, you'll need to boot the computer. In most modern computers, the motherboard's BIOS will support booting from a CD-ROM. This is the method we'll use here. Ensure that the BIOS has the correct boot sequence selected, put the CD-ROM in the drive, and reboot. On older computers, you'll need to use the boot disk that was included with the boxed set or that you made. Regardless of the method you use, a minimal Red Hat system will be loaded into RAM, and the installation will be run from this minimal system.

Other Installation Media

Although the basic procedure presented here assumes you are installing from a CD-ROM (or from a boot floppy with the CD-ROM in the CD drive), Red Hat Linux also allows you to install over a network or from a hard drive. The standard procedure uses the boot.img file from the CD-ROM. Other methods use different boot image files, which you must copy onto a floppy disk from the CD-ROM's images directory. You can install from a network server via NFS image, FTP, or HTTP using the bootnet.img file. You can also install from a CD-ROM, NFS image, FTP, HTTP, or hard drive accessed via a PCMCIA device using the pcmcia.img file. And you can install from a hard drive using the same boot.img image that you use for a local CD-ROM installation. The installation sequence is much the same, with the exception of the boot disk. You'll need to create a boot disk if you wish to install from a network server or a PCMCIA devide. To write the boot images to a floppy, you may use one of the methods listed below.

- On a Windows system, use the RAWRITE command that is located on the CD-ROM in the dosutils directory by booting into Microsoft Windows and executing RAWRITE. When asked which image to copy, specify the correct one from the images directory on that same CD-ROM. The Microsoft COPY command will not make a workable boot floppy.

- Use the following command under Linux or Unix to create a boot floppy:

  # **dd if=/*mnt/cdrom*/images/boot.img of=/dev/fd0 bs=1440k**

  The dd utility is quite a useful tool. An explanation in short is that if stands for *in file* and of stands for *out file*. You are thus writing the boot.img out to /dev/fd0 using a block size (bs) of 1440KB. Usually this may be run without specifying a block size.

- Under Linux or Unix, you can also cat the image to /dev/fd0. The command would be as follows: **cat /mnt/cdrom/images/boot.img > /dev/fd0**

Essentially, the installations are all the same once you've located the medium that contains the packages to be installed.

A few seconds after rebooting, you'll see a text-based welcome screen that offers several options for the installation process:

- Graphical mode

- Text mode
- Expert mode
- Rescue mode

Graphical installation is the default when you've booted from a CD-ROM. Text-based installation is the default if you used the boot floppy image that came in the Red Hat package. It does essentially the same things as a graphical installation, so you should be able to follow this procedure if you choose that route. You probably won't need to use expert mode unless the installation mode fails to recognize some of your hardware. It allows you to enter specific parameters for the devices that aren't detected. Choose rescue mode when you need a way to boot a basic Linux system in order to recover an installation that's gone bad (say, because you've edited the startup files in a way that prevents the system from booting).

Selecting an Installation Method

The first two screens ask you to select the language you speak and the type of keyboard you use. Assuming you started this installation using the standard boot.img as we did, the next screen you'll see Mouse Configuration, discussed in the next section. If you're using one of the other installation media, however, you'll see the Installation Method screen.

Booting the boot.img image from a floppy without the CD-ROM in the drive will take you to an Installation Method screen, offering you the options of Local CDROM or Hard Drive.

However, if you have a non-IDE CD-ROM drive, you'll be offered an additional choice between SCSI and Other. If you choose SCSI, you'll be prompted to select your SCSI Adapter from a list. Choose the adapter that most closely resembles the one in your system. If your adapter is not recognized, you may enter additional options for the driver. These options are the same that would be specified at the boot prompt to give LILO information about an unrecognized SCSI adapter. These options are discussed in Chapter 5 and Chapter 18 where LILO is detailed.

If your CD-ROM drive is neither SCSI nor IDE, you must select the Other option. CD-ROM drives in this category are usually those run from a proprietary sound card. Such drives are extremely rare in modern computers; you're only likely to find them in old 386 or 486 computers. You might have to specify options for the driver that supports such a card.

If you've forgotten to put the CD-ROM into the drive, you'll be prompted to do so.

Configure the Mouse

The install next moves on to the Mouse Configuration screen, which offers a number of style choices for PS/2, bus, and serial mice. Select the brand and style that matches your mouse. If none look right, you may select the appropriate Generic choice, and it should work. Select the correct device and port; if your system has been running Windows before, your selection should match the COM port used there. If you have a two-button mouse, you'll want to select the Emulate 3 Buttons option near the bottom of the screen. This will allow you to simulate the third button by pressing both buttons at the same time. Three buttons are useful on a Linux system because X is built around a three-button mouse. The middle button is often used to paste text selections in X applications.

Partition the Disk

The Install Options screen appears next. It requires that you choose the Install Type you've decided to use to partition your disk.

The options you'll see on the Install Options screen are divided into Install options and the Upgrade option. The Install options are the ones we discussed before: Workstation, Server System, and Custom System. These provide the partition schemes described earlier. There is only one Upgrade option. It keeps the existing partition scheme and just upgrades the software. For this example, we're using the Server System installation since, as a system administrator, you are likely to be setting up server machines. You could also set up a server using a Custom installation to take advantage of the greater flexibility in partitioning and package selection. In the end, the Server System setup is easier and quicker to run through, but is likely to produce a Linux installation that's bloated with packages you never use. A Custom System setup can produce a trimmer system, but takes more up-front time and knowledge about what individual packages do. Because the server installation will write over any existing installation, the subsequent Automatic Partitioning screen warns you that it is about to erase any existing partitions on your hard drive and offers you the alternative of creating your partitions manually with either Disk Druid or fdisk. You are also offered the option of retracing your steps and performing a customized installation. To try out the partitioning process for yourself, select the Manually Partition with Disk Druid option and press the Next button. Figure 2.3 shows the Disk Druid Partitioning screen.

If the system previously had Red Hat installed, the existing partitions will show up in the Partitions area. Otherwise, you will begin with the standard partitioning for the Server-Class Installation. Figure 2.3 shows a slightly altered version of this partitioning scheme. You can delete any existing partition by highlighting it and then selecting Delete. The partition will be removed and the Drive Summary at the bottom will show the available space.

NOTE If you have selected any of the remaining partitions as growable, the Drive Summary will still reflect that it is 99% used.

Figure 2.3   The Disk Druid Partitioning screen

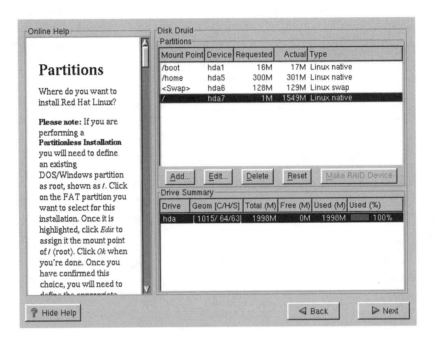

If there are existing partitions that you want to keep, highlight each partition in Disk Druid, click the Edit button, and ensure that the mount point (described shortly) and partition type are correct. Delete any partitions that you don't want, or click the Add button to add additional ones. Clicking the Add button will bring up this dialog box:

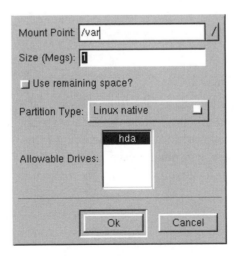

The swap partition will not have a mount point. Once you select the swap Partition Type, the Mount Point option will be grayed out. Each of the other partitions must be assigned a mount point. Some examples of mount points include /usr if this directory is to be on its own individual partition or /tmp if it is separate. Some directories must not be on a separate partition from the / directory, because files in these directories must be accessible during the boot process, before separate partitions will have been mounted. These partitions are /etc, /lib, /bin, /sbin, and /dev.

Specify the size of the partition in megabytes. The default is 1MB, which is fine if you mark the partition as growable. You'll need to change it if you want to specify a size. Also, if the system has more than one drive, you'll need to highlight the appropriate drive in the Allowable Drives field.

If you have a Windows partition, it will show up on the Partition screen as well. You'll want to assign it a mount point like /mnt/windows or /msdos. This will make it easy to access, since it will be configured to be mounted at boot time.

You could more easily have chosen the Automatically Partition and Remove Data option in the Automatic Partitioning screen and let the install process set up a typical server partition scheme as described earlier. This is certainly the easier course of action, but doesn't give you the flexibility to decide your own partition sizes or specify unusual partition layouts.

Configuring Networking

Following partition configuration, if your system has a network card, Red Hat Linux asks you to specify your network configuration, as shown in Figure 2.4. Enter the necessary information manually, or click the Configure Using DHCP button if your network uses a DHCP server to dish out IP addresses. Chapter 15 describes the TCP/IP networking options in more detail, if you need to set these options manually and don't know what to enter. (In this case, you'll need to consult with your network administrator to learn what to enter.)

Configuring the Time Zone

Following the Partition screen, you'll see the Time Zone Selection screen. There are so many time zone options as to make this a bigger task than it sounds. Select the appropriate zone for your location or the offset from Universal Coordinated Time (UTC). In either case, you must specify whether your system clock uses UTC. If you use the offset method, you must also specify whether or not Daylight Savings Time is needed.

Figure 2.4   If you enter TC/IP networking information during installation, you won't have to do so again after installation.

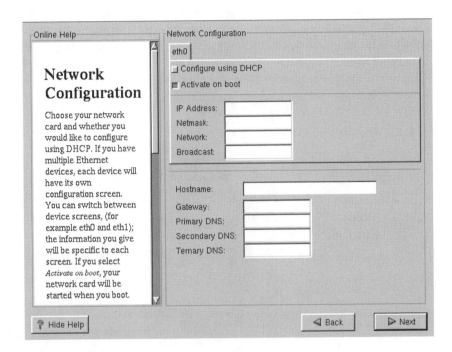

NOTE   Historically, Unix systems have set their clocks according to UTC, or the time in Greenwich, England, and have adjusted local time settings based on the computer's location in the world. *x*86 PCs, by contrast, have historically set their clocks to the local time. Linux therefore needs to understand both methods. A dedicated Linux server is generally best off with its hardware clock set to UTC, because this is less likely to result in problems for various Linux utilities derived from Unix utilities or when Daylight Savings Time changes are required. A system that dual-boots between Linux and Windows or some other OS that uses a hardware clock set to local time is better off using local time, to keep time synchronized between the OSs.

Configuring User Accounts

You'll need to set up an account to access when the system is rebooted; you'll do that in the Account Configuration dialog box shown in Figure 2.5. You are required to set up the root account. This process consists of specifying and verifying root's password. You can then either click Next to continue or add one or more normal user accounts. It's a good idea to set up at least one user account, so that you are not forced to log in as root. To do so, input the account name (user name), the password for that account, the same password again for verification, and the full name of the user. At this point, you may continue to add other users or continue to the next screen, Selecting Package Groups. You have several options for creating new users after the system has been installed. See Chapter 6 for more information about creating user accounts.

Figure 2.5   The Account Configuration screen

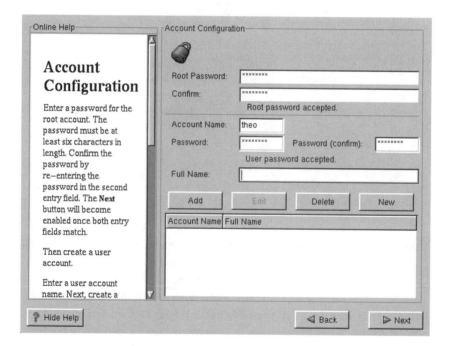

Selecting Package Groups

Finally, the moment you've waited for: the Selecting Package Groups screen allows you to select which software packages will be installed on your system, selecting them in preset server groups or individually. The only server group that is selected by default for the server class installation is the Web Server group. You can also choose to install a news server, an NFS server, or a DNS name server. The total install size is listed in the bottom-right corner of the screen above the Back and Next buttons. If you'd rather have a direct hand in package selection, click the Select Individual Packages button near the bottom of the screen. When you click the Next button, you'll be taken to the Individual Packages screen, shown in Figure 2.6.

Figure 2.6   The Individual Package Selection screen appears only if you click Select Individual Packages in the Selecting Package Groups screen.

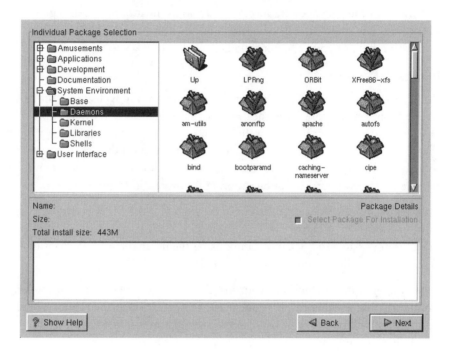

Here you can double-click on a specific package to see what it contains. Folders and individual packages represented by boxes will be displayed on the right. If you highlight a single package, information about that package appears near the bottom of the screen. This information includes the name, the size in kilobytes, and a description of the package's function. A red check mark will appear on each package selected for installation. If you're unfamiliar with what individual packages do, it's best to leave the defaults until you're more familiar with the packages. You can always install or remove packages after installing the OS proper, as described in Chapter 8. When you have completed your selections, hit the Next button.

Although the term "package" implies a self-contained unit, some packages rely on others for support, and in some cases, your selections will not include a software package that is required to support one that you have selected. This situation is called an *unresolved dependency*. The Unresolved Dependencies screen will list these. You must then either click the Install Packages To Satisfy Dependencies button to allow the installation program to include everything it needs or go back and attempt to fix these dependencies yourself. When you are finished, click Next.

Now that you've finished most of the larger interactive tasks of the installation, sit back and watch as the packages are installed. Or do as most of us do, and go get a Coke or something. The speed of your computer and the number of packages you've targeted for installation will, of course, determine how long a break you'll get.

Boot Disk Creation

You'll next see the Boot Disk Creation screen. Insert a floppy disk into the drive and click the Next button. You are given the option of skipping this step by checking the Skip Boot Disk Creation box, but it is generally a bad idea to skip this step, since a boot disk can save you if your computer refuses to boot. Problems with the root filesystem cannot be solved this way, because the boot disk does not contain a root filesystem but instead uses the one on the computer. Troubleshooting is covered in Chapter 18.

Another use for the boot disk is to boot the system if the MBR is overwritten. Some versions of Microsoft Windows will overwrite the MBR if it is installed after Linux. This makes it impossible to boot into Linux using the normal methods. Booting from a boot disk, however, allows you to reinstall LILO.

When the boot disk is finished, your installation is complete. Pop out the boot disk to avoid initiating another installation, select Exit, and watch the reboot. A great deal of information will scroll by. If you need to see it again, use the `dmesg` command once the system has booted and you've logged in to page it to the screen.

Installing a Workstation

Since the ratio of workstations to servers is typically quite high, chances are you'll be installing a lot more workstations than servers. This section describes the differences between the installation of a server, as presented in the previous section, and the workstation installation. The initial steps are the same as with a server-class installation.

Selecting Package Groups

Of course, when you get to the Selecting Package Groups screen, the server options that we saw before are not there. Instead you get to choose between a GNOME workstation, a KDE workstation, or a Games workstation. GNOME (GNU Network Object Model Environment) and KDE (K Desktop Environment) are desktop environments that enhance your X experience by providing an easy-to-use GUI "desktop," similar to those used by Windows, MacOS, or other OSs. Chapter 16 covers X, including desktop environments and X-based programs.

Despite the differences in precisely what package groups are available, workstation and server installation are similar in that you can select package groups if you click the Select Individual Packages option on the Selecting Package Groups screen. In principle, you could build nearly identical systems starting from the server and workstation installation options by modifying the individual package selections. In practice, of course, it's much faster to start with an appropriate server or workstation installation option.

Configuring Your Video Card and Monitor for X

Next you'll encounter the X Configuration screen, shown in Figure 2.7. Configuring the X Window System (Chapter 16) essentially means telling the installation program what video card and monitor you'll use with that GUI. You will be asked to select your monitor from a list. Unless you're using an unsupported video card, the Xconfigurator program

Figure 2.7   The X Configuration screen

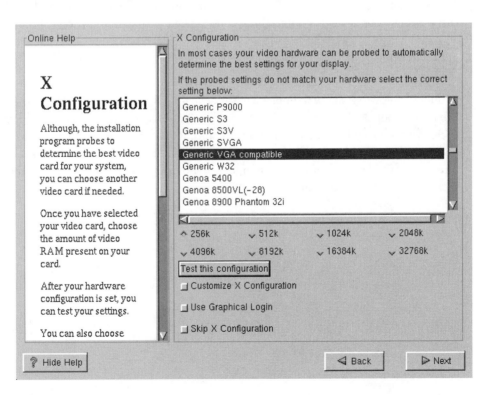

will have detected it, and the information about it will be displayed. The monitor information will be displayed also. Now you must choose what you want to accomplish in the area of X configuration. You can customize X configuration, set up the system to use a graphical login screen instead of the usual command-line one, or skip X configuration entirely. For this example, select Test This Config. If you see a box asking whether or not you can read it, click the OK button.

Tying Up Loose Ends

Next you will be greeted with the message that your Red Hat installation is complete. Remove any floppy or CD-ROM still in its drive and reboot the system. Remember that if you skipped the LILO installation, you must put your boot disk into the floppy drive. After your computer finishes powering up, you'll see the `boot:` prompt. Enter a boot label corresponding to the operating system that you wish to work in. The default boot label for your Red Hat system will be `linux`. If you specified any other boot labels during the installation, you may boot them by typing the label at the `boot:` prompt. If you press the Enter key alone, the default boot entry will be booted. If you do nothing, LILO will pause for the specified timeout period (5 seconds by default) and then will boot the default boot entry. When your system is booted, you'll be greeted with a login prompt. Enjoy.

In Sum

In this chapter we saw how to implement disk caching, RAID, and clustering using Linux. We took a look at the most popular Linux distributions and the hallmark features of each. We discussed hardware configuration and, if you were following along, you have now installed a Linux server and a Linux workstation. In the next chapter we get into the internals of the Linux operating system, discussing the history and features of the ext2 filesystem developed for Linux.

3

Linux Files and Processes

A Linux system is made up of files of various types; essentially, everything on the system is a file. These files are organized hierarchically into directories, since having all files in one large directory would be far too chaotic. As development in Linux is often done individually or in small groups, it became obvious early on that the hierarchy needed some defined structure that all developers could work within so that pieces developed by one group would fit with those developed by another. The basic characteristics of the hierarchy were defined first in the File System Standard (FSSTND), which was the consensus resulting from a lengthy discussion on a specially created Linux mailing list. The Filesystem Hierarchy Standard (FHS), a subsequent version of the FSSTND, was intended to standardize file systems between Linux and Unix for compatibility between different software packages, distributions, and networked systems.

This chapter discusses the history of these two standards and what they brought to Linux. It explains the file concept, including file types and file naming. It looks at the filesystem hierarchy as it has evolved and describes what an inode-based filesystem is. The chapter also discusses the components that together form Linux. Finally, you'll learn about the processes that perform the actual work on a Linux system, how to track them, and how to administer them. As a system administrator, you must know the filesystem that you are working on and its restrictions and limitations in order to allocate system space efficiently and avoid pitfalls. Just as with city ordinances, you can sometimes get by without knowing them intimately, but you might find that your lack of knowledge gets you into trouble.

The Filesystem Hierarchy Standard

The history of the Filesystem Hierarchy Standard encapsulates the open-source development of Linux as a whole. Even if you're not a history buff (or an open source "true believer"), understanding the issues that the developer community set out to solve in defining the standard can help you better understand the system you're working with today.

Linus Torvalds intended that the Linux operating system compensate for the problems he encountered when trying to use the Minix operating system. In its very early days, Linux was developed in tandem with the Minix operating system, allowing Linus to share disks between the Minix and Linux sides. At that point, the Linux filesystem was in fact the Minix filesystem. Soon thereafter, a Virtual Filesystem (VFS) layer was developed to handle the file-oriented system calls and pass the I/O functions to the physical filesystem code, allowing Linux to support multiple filesystems. Developed for use as an instructional tool, the Minix filesystem supported only 14-character file names and limited its filesystem support to those smaller than 64 megabytes. In April 1992, after the integration of the VFS into the kernel, a new filesystem, the Extended File System or extfs, was implemented and added to Linux version 0.96c.

Although extfs was significantly more usable than the Minix filesystem, it still lacked some features that Linus wanted. Additionally, its practice of tracking free blocks and inodes via a linked list did not allow for optimum performance, because, as the filesystem was used, the list became unsorted and the filesystem became fragmented. Released in alpha version in January of 1993, the Second Extended File System (ext2fs) grew out of the desire to fix the problems of extfs and to ensure a focus on excellent performance, robustness, and flexibility to allow users to use new features without having to reformat their filesystems. Ext2fs supports filenames as long as 255 characters and filesystems as big as 4GB. Linux is still using this file system, although as described in Chapter 10, several more advanced alternatives are starting to become viable as replacements for ext2fs.

Although ext2fs solved many technical problems, procedural problems remained; administrators did not always agree on *how to use* the filesystem. That is, administrators and distribution maintainers didn't always put the same files in the same locations, leading to confusion. In August 1993, a programmer named Olaf Kirsh posted a message to one of the most important Linux discussion groups, discussing the possibility of designing a common standard for filesystem layout. It turned out that many Linux users had something to say about this topic, and soon a new mailing list was created specifically to house the discussion. The goal was to form a consensus about creating a standard filesystem hierarchy that would support the needs of the Linux file and directory structure.

> **NOTE** The word *filesystem* has two meanings. The first refers to the low-level layout of data on the disk, as defined by filesystems like the Minix filesystem, extfs, and ext2fs. The second meaning refers to the placement of files and directories within the directory structure on the disk. Which meaning is intended should be clear from context.

A few of the problems that the Linux community sought to solve were:

- The need to define which binaries belonged in /bin and which belonged in /usr/bin
- The disorder caused by having both binaries and configuration files in /etc
- The need to separate site-wide configuration files from local configuration files to facilitate the sharing of these files where appropriate
- The need to move changeable files out of /usr so that partition could be mounted as read-only

The consensus for solving these and other problems was formalized into a filesystem hierarchy standard specific to the Linux operating system, called FSSTND. The first official version of the FSSTND was released in February 1994, and two subsequent revisions were released over the next year. The FSSTND defined a standard filesystem structure for Linux systems, mapped where specific types of files and directories belong and clarified what was intended to be contained in specific system files. Linux FSSTND 1.2 is the final version of this standard. The major limitation of this standard was simply that it applied only to Linux and thus could not be used on networks with "mixed" operating systems. It didn't take long before the Linux specificity drove a push toward a new, more open standard.

An effort to create a filesystem hierarchy standard that would serve Unix operating systems in addition to Linux began in 1995. Many BSD supporters participated in this effort. The goal was to change the focus of the FSSTND, to generalize it so that it applied across the board to any Unix-like system. The name of the standard was changed to Filesystem Hierarchy Standard (FHS) to emphasize that it was a new standard.

The FHS may be applied to any filesystem layout that:

- Conforms to a hierarchical structure
- Handles file data consistently
- Includes data-protection mechanisms

The FHS begins by defining shareable data and unshareable data. Shareable data can be used by more than one host without alteration. Unshareable data is exclusive to one host and would require tailoring for use by another host. For example, it might be beneficial to share a text document across hosts, but sharing a configuration file that is tailored to the specific hardware on the host machine would not be beneficial.

FHS ensures that shareable files are not interspersed with unshareable files, so that a partition containing shareable data may be shared with another host without making an unshareable file available to that host. In the old Unix standard, shareable files and unshareable files existed together on the same partition. The /usr partition is a good example. It contained unshareable data until the /var system was created. Now, unshareable /usr files are stored in /var and linked into the /usr directory tree, leaving /usr perfectly shareable.

FHS further distinguished between static files and dynamic files. Static files are files that require superuser permission to change. Program files are a perfect example. Dynamic files are those that may be changed without the superuser's involvement, either by some process that runs automatically on schedule or manually by a user without root privileges. Examples include user data and log files.

The ext2 Filesystem

In order to understand what can be done with files, directories, and filesystems in the directory structure sense, it's helpful to understand some of the data structures that underlie a filesystem in the low-level partition data structure sense. Because ext2fs is the most common Linux filesystem, this section describes ext2fs and its data structures. Other Linux native filesystems use similar structures, although some of the details differ. Non-Linux filesystems often differ in more details, but many of the basic principles still apply. (For a discussion of various Linux and non-Linux filesystems, see Chapter 10.)

The Physical Structure

The ext2 filesystem is composed of block groups, which may or may not be sequential on the physical disk. Figure 3.1 shows the physical structure of an ext2 filesystem.

Each block group contains filesystem control data: a superblock and filesystem descriptors. It also contains filesystem data: a block bitmap, an inode bitmap, an inode table, and data blocks. Inodes are explained in the next section. Normally about 5 percent of these blocks are set aside to allow the superuser room to recover a filesystem that has reached its maximum number of user processes and become unusable by ordinary users.

Figure 3.1   Each block group is largely independent of the others, which can aid recovery in the event of data corruption.

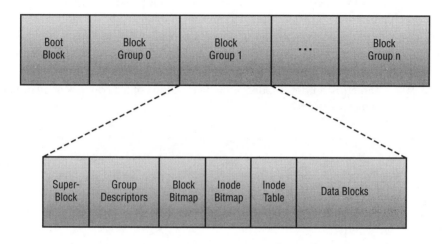

> **TIP**   Ext2fs allows you to choose the logical block size when you create the filesystem, commonly 1024, 2048, or 4096 bytes. Larger block sizes can speed up I/O since fewer disk head seeks are needed when more data is read during each seek. Large blocks do, however, waste more disk space since the last block is almost never full. Larger block sizes therefore leave a larger amount of unused space than do smaller block sizes.

Inodes

All of the important information about a file, except for its name and location, is stored in a data structure called an *inode*. The inode stores:

- Locking information
- The access mode
- The file type
- The number of links to the file
- The owner's user and group IDs
- The size of the file in bytes
- Access and modification times
- The inode's time of last modification
- The addresses of the file's blocks on disk

Each file is assigned a unique inode when it is created. The name of the file is stored separately in a directory-name cache entry. The inode number of each entry in the directory-name cache can be used to obtain the corresponding inode cache entry, which contains the specific information about the file represented by that inode. Figure 3.2 illustrates this structure. In this way, a command to obtain a directory listing is fast since it doesn't have to concern itself with the actual data in a file but only that contained in the inode.

Figure 3.2   Directory entries, inodes, and the locations of files on disk need not all come in the same order.

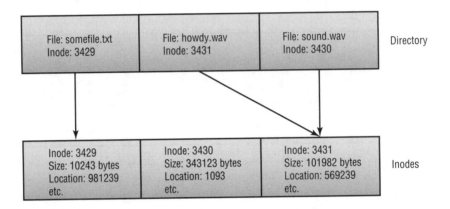

When a file is opened, it locks its entry into the inode cache to indicate that it is in use. Inactive files are kept in memory, with an inactive inode that may still contain data pages from its previously associated file if the inode has not yet been reclaimed by the filesystem. When an inactive inode is reused, its data pages are flushed to make room for the inode's new data.

Directory Layout

The Linux directory layout is largely determined by the FHS requirement to group similar data and not blur the boundaries between the groups. The top-level directories are intended to contain specific groups of data. Likewise, the subdirectories within each top-level directory contain data that meets the constraints for the top-level directory as well as some further constraint. As a result, each top-level directory is defined in terms of what it contains. Although there are still variations among the different Unix-like systems, the top-level directories in a Red Hat system provide a model that can be used to describe any Linux system.

/   (mandatory) The root filesystem is the base of the directory hierarchy. Although the root user's home directory on most Linux distributions is /root, if /root doesn't exist, / is used instead. The / filesystem is intended to remain uncluttered, so as a rule, you should avoid creating new directories or files there.

WARNING   Although / and /root are both pronounced "root," they're very different directories. The former is the base of the Linux filesystem, and the latter is the home directory for the superuser.

/bin   (mandatory) The /bin directory contains binaries that are required in single-user mode regardless of their assigned execution privilege. This directory is not intended to have subdirectories. Commands intended to be run primarily by individual users should be placed in /usr/bin instead.

/boot   (mandatory) The /boot directory contains all the files needed to boot the system except configuration files and the map installer. This directory stores data which are used before the kernel begins the system initialization as defined by /etc/inittab. (See Chapter 5 for a discussion of the system startup process.) The Linux kernel may be stored in /boot or in /, but kernels stored in /boot should be given filenames that include the complete version as well, such as /boot/vmlinuz-2.2.14-5.0, since more than one kernel image is likely to be stored there.

/dev   (mandatory) The /dev directory contains block and character device files as well as sockets and named pipes. As you'll see later in this chapter, it is the directory where all of your devices hang out.

/etc   (mandatory) The /etc directory, usually pronounced "et-see," contains configuration files for the host. Over the past few years, directories have been added under /etc to better organize configuration files. For example, there has long been an /etc/X11 directory, which contains the X configuration files. Recent additions include /etc/ppp and /etc/httpd. This directory structure makes finding a file in /etc a little easier.

/home   (optional) The /home directory contains the individual users' home directories. Some system administrators prefer not to use the /home directory concept but instead place user directories in a /var/users directory or even a /usr/users directory. Sometimes the /home directory is actually a symbolic link to /usr/home or some other directory within the /usr hierarchy; this is probably a bad idea since the /usr directory is intended to be mountable as read-only and home directories typically contain dynamic data. Most Linux system administrators simply leave the user's home directories in /home.

/lib   (mandatory) The /lib directory contains shared libraries needed at system bootup or to run top-level commands (located in the /bin directory). Libraries in support of the commands in /usr are stored in /usr/lib.

/mnt   (optional) The /mnt directory contains temporary mount points for storage devices like hard drives or floppy drives specific to the host. Each mount point is actually a directory that will contain the device's filesystem once it is mounted. In the case of a mounted CD-ROM containing an /etc directory and file1 and file2 in its root, the files would be available as /mnt/cdrom/etc/, /mnt/cdrom/file1, and /mnt/cdrom/file2. By the standard, this directory must contain mount points for the CD-ROM and the floppy drive at a minimum, but each Linux distribution determines which mount points to include and usually includes many more than this. Some distributions place mount points for CD-ROM and floppy drives in the / directory, rather than in /mnt.

/opt   (optional) The /opt directory is intended to contain all of the data required to support software packages added to the original system. The /opt directory is a feature borrowed from the AT&T SysV Unix filesystem hierarchy.

/proc   (optional) The /proc directory contains a virtual filesystem—that is, one that doesn't correspond to a physical disk device. This filesystem contains process and kernel information specific to the kernel that is currently running. The information stored in /proc is very useful when you are trying to track down problems with your system. /proc contains a listing of interrupts, devices, I/O ports, and a lot more. It also contains a directory for each process currently running; the directory name is the process number. This directory includes such things as the command line that initiated the process and other environmental information pertaining to the process. The last section of this chapter provides a detailed look at processes and their role in the Linux filesystem.

/root   (optional) The /root directory contains configuration files for the root user's account. This directory was created to prevent cluttering up the / directory with the root user's configuration files. Most distributions are set up so that if there is no /root directory, the root user's account defaults to /.

/sbin   (mandatory) The /sbin directory originally contained only static binaries but now contains binaries that are administrative in nature and are restricted to superuser use only. These binaries may also be used by the system during the boot process. Binaries that do not require execution prior to the mounting of the /usr partition are stored in /usr/sbin or, if host-specific, in /usr/local/sbin.

/tmp   (mandatory) The /tmp directory is used whenever a program needs to write a file that will be removed when the program is terminated. The /tmp directory is typically flushed at reboot or at some interval defined by the administrator. If /var is on its own partition, /tmp is often a link to /var/tmp; this frees up space on the root partition. The Red Hat distribution uses the tmpwatch command to automatically clean out any file in /tmp or /var/tmp that has not been accessed in 10 days (240 hours). tmpwatch is run from a script in the /etc/cron.daily directory. See Chapter 14 for more information on the cron daemon and scripting. The time period may be adjusted as appropriate for your system. The actual command is:

```
/usr/sbin/tmpwatch 240 /tmp /var/tmp
```

/usr~MS(mandatory) the /usr directory stores shareable read-only data. Because of this, /usr, if made a separate partition, can be mounted as read-only. To facilitate this, /usr should contain only static data, using links to changeable data in the /var directory to preserve this characteristic.

/var (mandatory) The /var directory contains variable data files like logs, lock files, and process-specific data files. The existence of a /var directory makes it possible to mount /usr as read-only since files written during system operations are stored in /var instead of in /usr. Since /var contains the system log, /var/log/ messages, any problem that sends frequent error messages could fill the /var directory. For this reason, /var is often created on a separate partition from the rest of / to avoid filling up the / partition and not being able to log in. It is important to note that not all directories under /var are shareable; /var/log is an example of one that is not.

Of course, anyone with superuser privileges can create directories in the / directory. This is generally to be avoided because the top-level directories were created largely to prevent cluttering up the / directory. For more information on the underlying directory structure, reference the FSSTND, which may be found at http://www.pathname.com/fhs/.

File Characteristics

To the average user, a *file* is a sequence of information bytes, stored together and named as a collective entity. A file can be an executable program, a document, a database, a shell script, or any other collection of bytes that has meaning. In fact, virtually everything in Linux is seen by the system as a file, including the directories and devices.

Filenames in Linux can range up to 255 characters and may or may not be terminated with an extension. Filenames are case sensitive, like nearly everything else in Linux. This means that the names File.txt, FILE.txt, file.txt, and FiLe.txt would all refer to different files. The case sensitivity of filenames, combined with their variable length, gives you great flexibility. Not only are there more names available to you, but you can use specific capitalization patterns to indicate certain types of files. For instance, you might start directory names with a capital letter.

> ***NOTE***   In DOS, file names are always eight characters, followed by a period, followed by a three-character extension. The VFAT filesystem used by Windows 9*x* and ME adds long filenames, but keeps the short filenames as well. You can see the short filenames by starting a DOS shell and using the DIR command.

Determining a Linux File's Type

Knowing a file's type tells you a great deal about the file itself. For example, each different graphic file type has a different internal format; most include a header containing specific information about that graphic's size and other attributes. If you write a translator to read in a graphic of a given type and output that same graphic in a different file format, you need to know the file's format so you can parse the file properly. Since Linux files aren't required to have a file extension, you sometimes have to determine a file's type using another method. File types may be determined in a number of ways. Certainly the file extension, if present, does the work for you, but when it doesn't, you can use commands like ls and file to determine the type.

The *file* Command

The file command was created to allow a user to determine a file's type and is the best tool for this purpose. The format for the file command is:

file [*options*] [-f *namefile*] [-m *magicfiles*] *file*

Whereas the ls command doesn't differentiate between the various "normal" file types (as discussed in the next section), the file command does. The file command is supported by a file named magic (/usr/share/magic by default on a Red Hat system) which contains information on all the file types that the file command knows about. The –f option reads in a file which contains names of files whose type is to be determined. You can specify a different magic file with the -m option on the command line. The file command will use this magic file to determine, to the best of its "knowledge," what type of file you've specified. The file command's output will usually include one of the following key words: *text*, *executable*, or *data*. Below are two examples of the data produced by the file command.

Listing 3.1   The Output of the file Command Varies with the Type of File It Examines.

```
$ file ssh-1.2.27.tar.gz
ssh-1.2.27.tar.gz: gzip compressed data, deflated, original filename,
       ➥last modified: Wed May 12 06:20:20 1999, os Unix


$ file test_table.c
test_table.c: C program text
```

You'll notice that the first file was identified as compressed data created on a Unix system, and modified Wed May 12 06:20:20 1999. If the file is a text file, the `file` command tries to determine its computer language as in the second example, where some code written in the C language was correctly identified.

The *ls* Command

The `ls` command is one of the most often used Linux commands. `ls` provides information about a file, including its type. The name `ls` means *listing* because the command lists all of the files in a directory. The syntax for `ls` is simple:

```
ls [options] [file or directory name]
```

The `ls` command without arguments produces output like that in Listing 3.2.

Listing 3.2   The Output of the `ls` Command Entered without Arguments

```
$  ls
sshd   sshd.old    sshd1    sshd1.old    visudo
```

If no arguments are specified, you simply get a listing of file names, which by default does not include any file names that begin with a dot. You can use arguments to further define what the listing will include. The -1 option (which stands for "long listing") allows you to examine the permission string, the owner, the file size, the date it was last modified, and the filename as in Listing 3.3.

Listing 3.3   The Output of the `ls -1` Command

```
$  ls -1
lrwxrwxrwx    1 root   root         5    May    3 18:24   sshd->sshd1
lrwxrwxrwx    1 root   root         5    May    3 18:20   sshd.old->sshd1
--rwxr-x-x    1 root   root    649246    May    3 18:24   sshd1
-rwx--x--x    1 root   root    649246    May    3 18:20   sshd1.old
---x--x--x    1 root   root     56712    Sep    2 11:00   visudo
```

You'll remember that directories, symbolic links, devices, and text files are all files under Linux. The first character in the permission string located in column 1 of the `ls -1` output indicates the file type. It only differentiates between regular files (-), directories (d), links (1), character special files (c), block special files (b), pipes (p), and sockets (s). These file types are discussed further in the "File Types Defined" section later in this chapter.

TIP Although the sample output in Listing 3.3 shows each of the file types that we've mentioned, the character special files and block special files do not typically appear in the same directory with other files. They are primarily found in the /dev directory and are included in this example for illustration purposes.

The ls command has several other arguments. These are the most commonly used:

-a Lists the files whose names begin with a period (.) in addition to the normal ls output. There's nothing special about these files, except that they're normally not shown in ls output and other directory listings; the leading period is simply Linux's way of hiding files, similar to the hidden bit on DOS or Windows computers.

--color[=*WHEN*] Indicates whether or not to use colors to distinguish file types. *WHEN* may be never, always, or auto.

-d or --directory Lists the directory names instead of their contents.

-G or --no-group Does not display group information.

-i or --inode Prints index number of each file.

-n or --numeric-uid-gid Lists numeric UIDs and GIDs instead of names.

-R or --recursive Lists subdirectories recursively.

-s or --size Prints the size of each file in blocks.

-S Sorts by file size.

-t Sorts by modification time.

File Types Defined

Although the file command generally recognizes text, executable, and data as distinct file types, and extensions can help identify the application that produced a file, it is helpful to think in terms of the strict file types used by the ls command. Table 3.1 lists the file types that ls recognizes. The Symbol column shows the symbol that appears at the beginning of the permission string set for a file of that type. We'll talk more about permission strings in Chapter 7. The last column contains an example of the specified type of file.

Table 3.1   File Types Recognized by ls

Type	Symbol	Example
Normal file	none	chapter1.doc, myprogram.c
Directory	d	/usr

Table 3.1   File Types Recognized by ls *(continued)*

Type	Symbol	Example
Links	l	/dev/mouse
Named pipe	p	/dev/initctl
Socket	s	/dev/printer
Block device file	b	/dev/fd0
Character device file	c	/dev/console

Normal Files

Normal files include binaries, text files, shell scripts, image files, and generally any file that does not fall under one of the other categories. Most of the files on your system fall into this category. The word *normal* is applied as a catchall to differentiate these files from the other, more specialized file types discussed below.

A binary file is an executable file, in binary format; that is, a program that has been converted to machine language so that it might be executed. Scripts are executable also. We'll discuss this more thoroughly in Chapter 14. Image files, compressed archive files, and various other files also contain binary data, but they aren't executable. These files are sometimes referred to as binary files but sometimes not, depending upon context. Text files contain minimally formatted or unformatted text. Some applications, such as word processors, may produce text with some binary data. These files could be considered either text or binary (in the non-executable sense), depending upon the details of the format and the exact criteria used in classifying the files. Executable files in Linux do not typically carry an extension. The program ls that we referenced above is in fact an executable file. The permissions for a binary file usually give the owner permission to execute the file and may give others permission to do so as well.

Directories

Directories are logical containers for files; they allow you to organize your files into a hierarchy instead of storing all of them in the root directory. A directory may contain other directories as well as individual files. A directory can be identified in ls -l output by the d prefixed to its permission string.

In Linux, directories are created with the mkdir command, browsed with the ls command, and removed with the rmdir command. We've discussed the ls command earlier in the chapter. The mkdir command will create a directory if the supporting directory structure already exists and the specified directory within this structure does not. The mkdir command syntax is very simple:

    mkdir [*options*] [*path*] *directory_name*

The mkdir command has only three possible parameters:

   -m, --mode=*MODE*   Sets the permission mode for the new directory (as in chmod).

   -p, --parents   Prevents generation of an error if the directory exists.

   --verbose   Prints a message for each created directory.

The rmdir command removes the specified directory if it is empty. If the directory is not empty, an error is generated. The syntax for the rmdir command is similar to the mkdir command.

    rmdir [*options*] [*path*] *directory_name*

The rmdir command has the following arguments:

   --ignore-fail-on-non-empty   By default, a directory must be empty before it can be removed; this option tells Linux to ignore that rule.

   -p, --parents   Removes any parent directories that become empty after the specified directory is removed.

   --verbose   Gives diagnostic data upon each successful removal of the directory.

The benefits of grouping related files into a hierarchical structure should be thoroughly familiar to every system administrator (in fact, to every user). First, by grouping the data in a rational fashion, you avoid the need to wade through every file on your system to find the one you want. Thus you might have an Images directory, a Sound directory, etc.

Another benefit of separating your files into directories is that they are easier to back up. If you place all variable files in a separate directory structure from the static files, you can then back up just the files that might have changed since the previous backup, without having to continuously back up all the files that never change. You might want to create a Document directory to contain all of the documents created using StarOffice or some other word processing software. This makes it easy for you to back up everything on your system once a week and to back up these document files daily. We'll talk more about backup strategies in Chapter 11.

Links

A *link* is a way of allowing several filenames access to the same file. Links come in two varieties: hard links and symbolic links, often called soft links. Hard links are simply files with different names that have separate directory entries, each pointing to the same inode.

Referencing Figure 3.2 from the earlier discussion of inodes, howdy.wav and sound.wav are hard links to the same file, because they share the same inode.

Since an inode is device-specific, both files in a hard-linked pair must be contained on the same disk partition. Deleting the link will not remove the original file and vice versa. If a file was linked to another file and then either file is deleted, recreating a new file with the same name as the old one will not reestablish the link between the two files, since the new file will have a different inode. Hard links cannot be used to link two directories, because the standard commands for removing directories won't remove the link.

Hard links are created with the ln command. The syntax for this command is as follows:

    ln [*options*] *target* [*link_name*]

    ln [*options*] *targets directory_name*

The link command shown below creates a hard link to the /usr/local/netscape/netscape-navigator file; this link is called netscape and is located in the /usr/local/bin directory.

    # **ln /usr/local/netscape/netscape-navigator /usr/local/bin/netscape**

The link is only created if the file and directory permissions allow the user to do so. If the last argument is a link name, a link with that name will be created. If the last argument is an existing directory's name, links named for each specified target will be created in that directory.

A symbolic link is basically a pointer to another file. In the case of symbolic links, the linked file is assigned a completely different inode. To create a symbolic link to illustrate this, we again use the ln command, but we add the –s option. For example,

    ln –s /home/user/example_file /tmp/example

Now, by using the –i option to the ls command, we can see that the two inode numbers are different.

    $ **ls -i example_file /tmp/example**

    176449 /tmp/example   719925 example_file

Most operations performed on a symbolic link are actually performed on its target file. If an editing command uses a symbolic link as its argument, the edit will actually take place in the file referenced by the symbolic link. Some commands, like rm (remove), act on the link itself, leaving the target file intact. The permission string on a symbolic link is not used. It will always be rwxrwxrwx. The actual permissions are determined by the referenced file's permission string.

In contrast to hard links, a symbolic link can be used to link directories. If you move or delete the linked-to file, the symbolic link will be left "dangling," pointing at nothing, unlike a hard link in which the file contents would still exist and be accessible from the link. If you delete a symbolic link, re-creating a new file of the link's name won't automatically restore the link; you must use the ln command again to re-create the link.

Pipes

A named pipe, also called a FIFO (first in, first out), is a special file type that allows independent processes to communicate with each other. The first process opens a specified file—the pipe—for writing. The other opens the same file for reading. The processes communicate via that file. All communication between the process and the pipe is unidirectional. Each time the file is opened, whether for reading or writing, the open function blocks other processes from opening the same pipe for the same activity. That is, if the pipe is opened for read-only, the open function will not return, thereby blocking any requests to open that same pipe for read-only; attempts to open the pipe for writing will cause the open for read-only to terminate. If, on the other hand, the pipe is opened for writing, all attempts to open the same pipe for writing will be blocked, but the first attempt to open it for reading will be allowed. The rules for blocking are as follows:

- If you open the pipe for both reading and writing, then the open function will not perform blocking.

- If you open the pipe for reading, the open function will not return until another process opens the FIFO for writing, unless O_NONBLOCK is specified, in which case the open succeeds.

- If you open for writing, the open function will not return until another process opens the FIFO for reading, unless O_NONBLOCK is specified, in which case the open fails.

For example, suppose you want to display a daily fortune as your .signature file. You could use the name of that file as a pipe from a fortune-generating program. Now every time any program tries to read from your .signature file, the reading program will pause for your program to supply a fortune as your .signature.

The specifics for reading and writing using named pipes require programming functions which are beyond the scope of this book. The creation of a named pipe, however, is very much part of a system administrator's job. There are two ways to create a named pipe: using the mkfifo command or using the mknod command if mkfifo isn't available. These two commands each create a named pipe called test_fifo:

```
$ mkfifo test_fifo
$ mknod test_fifo p
```

The ls command may be used to verify that the FIFO was created:

```
$ ls -l test_fifo
prw-rw-r--   1 user     user          0 Jan 29 14:50 test_fifo
```

Sockets

Sockets are virtual connections between two processes. Unlike named pipes, sockets may be unidirectional or bidirectional. The standard input-output library contains a socket library function, called `socket()`, which creates a communication endpoint and returns a file descriptor containing its local host's network address and the port number to which the second process may attach in order to communicate with the first. If you have ever used an Internet address in the format `http://12.34.56.78:10`, you were connecting to a specific socket.

Devices

Linux recognizes two kinds of devices, differing in the way they exchange data with the CPU. The first type is the random-access *block* device, such as SCSI, floppy, or IDE disk drives. A block device file is a buffered file. Data is added to the buffer until some predetermined event occurs, typically a full buffer. At this point the buffer is flushed to the device, and the data-collection process begins again. Your hard drives are prime examples of block devices. If data were saved to a hard drive character by character, it would be exceedingly slow.

The second type of device is the character device, such as a tape drive, modem, or serial mouse. Character device files are used for unbuffered reads and writes. This means that the data is sent out as soon as it is received. The character device `/dev/console` is a great example. Of course, you don't want your system buffering the keystrokes before sending them to the console. You want to see them as they are being typed.

Devices of either type are represented in the filesystem as *device files* and are stored in the `/dev` directory, which also includes sockets and pipes. The `/dev/printer` device is one such socket. When you read or write a device file, the data comes from or goes to the device represented by that file. For instance, if you used the `cat` command and directed the output to `/dev/printer`, the output that would have been written to the screen will instead be piped to the printer represented by `/dev/printer`.

Processes

The filesystem that we have examined is only one of the internals of Linux. This filesystem by itself is static. The activity on a Linux system is represented as processes, which open and manipulate files within the filesystem.

Each program that is run by a computer's Central Processing Unit (CPU) is called a *process*. A command may include many processes. There are several processes running at any one time on a Linux system. As a system administrator, you will be directly responsible for ensuring that the necessary system processes are run and the schedule by which they are run. You are further responsible for managing the system so that the higher-priority processes get the CPU's attention first. Last, you must ensure that the memory space is adequate to house all the processes that must be run. To do these things, you need to know the fundamental details about what a process is and how it works.

The Concept of Multitasking

The most precious resource in the system is the CPU. There is usually only one CPU, so its usage must be optimized. Linux is a multiprocessing operating system, which means that one of its goals is to dish out CPU time among various processes. If there are more processes than CPUs, the rest of the processes must wait for the CPU to become available. Multiprocessing is conceptually simple; processes execute until some situation forces them to stop. Typically this is because a system resource that is needed is unavailable. In a multiprocessing system, several processes are kept in memory at the same time so that when one process is forced to stop, the CPU can be used by another process instead of sitting idle. The CPU is shared among multiple processes (tasks); hence the name *multitasking*.

Types of Processes

There are three basic types of processes: interactive processes, batch processes, and daemon processes. The kernel manages these processes and assigns each a unique process ID (PID) in ascending order until the highest defined process number is reached; at this point it starts at the first unused number again. The only process ever assigned a PID of 1 is the init process, which has a parent PID of 0 to distinguish it from the other processes. We'll talk more about this important process in a moment.

Processes are owned in much the same way that files are owned; the user ID of the user who starts the process is assigned as the real user ID of the process. Likewise, the group ID of the user is assigned as the real group ID of the process. But it is not the real user ID and group ID that determine the process's access rights and who can start and stop it. Instead, entities called the effective UID and GID are used. If the executable has its permission set suid, then the process will be run as if the owner of that file had executed it and will allow access for anyone in the group it was assigned. The assumed UID and GID are referred to as the effective UID and GID. If the executable has not been set suid, the real UID and GID are also the effective UID and GID.

> **WARNING** It's somewhat common to use a set suid binary to allow ordinary users to perform tasks that would otherwise require superuser privileges. The mount command, for example, has its suid bit set and is owned by root, so ordinary users can mount partitions under certain circumstances. This practice is potentially dangerous, however, because a bug in an suid root program can give local users superuser access to the system. Programs that are routinely installed in this way are therefore subjected to extraordinary security scrutiny. You should not use this feature willy-nilly, because it can easily produce a security breach.

Interactive Processes

Some processes are run interactively by users in a terminal session. If you log into a Linux system and run a mail reader, the mail reader process is an interactive process. While you are interacting with the mail reader, it is running in the foreground, actively attached to the terminal process. A process running in the foreground has full control of the terminal until that process is terminated or interrupted. A background process is suspended, returning terminal control to the parent of the suspended process. The background process may be able to continue its work in the background—if the continuation does not require interaction with the terminal. Interactive process control, or *job control* as it is commonly called, allows a process to be moved between the foreground to the background, restarted in the background if applicable, or restarted in the foreground.

Let's assume that you are running a backup process in the foreground using the tar command, tar zcf /dev/st0 /. You have observed the output and determined that the backup is properly running. You might want to do something else on that terminal, necessitating that you move the tar process to the background. Type Ctrl+Z. You will see a message on your terminal to indicate that the process has been stopped:

```
[1]+    Stopped         tar zcf /dev/st0  /
```

The process will be stopped, waiting in the background. But what if you aren't sure that the process is actually running? Use the jobs utility to list the background processes.

```
$ jobs
[1]+    Stopped         tar zcf /dev/st0  /
```

As you see, the stopped process is just out there waiting for you. To allow the backup process to continue in the background, type **bg** at the command line. Running the jobs program again will yield:

```
[1]+    Running         tar zcf /dev/st0  /
```

At this point, you may let it run on in the background until it terminates when the backup has completed, or you may use the fg command to bring the process to the foreground again.

If you want to start a process in the background, simply append an ampersand to the command. The tar command would then look like this:

```
$ tar zcf /dev/st0  /  &
```

You will then be given a process ID, which looks like this:

```
[2]  4036
```

You can then bring the process to the foreground using the fg command as we did before or let it run its course in the background.

Technically, interactive processes in X work the same as they do in text mode; however, most GUI environments include default methods of launching programs that are effectively the same as appending an ampersand on a command line. Running an X program in the background doesn't make the X program inaccessible, though; it still opens a window and displays its output. Your experience is therefore one in which programs appear to run side-by-side, and you use mouse clicks, or perhaps merely mouse *movements*, to bring one process or another to the foreground. All the visible programs are active and running, even if they are not doing much when you're not interacting with them directly. If you launch an X program from an xterm or other terminal window, however, the xterm will become unresponsive unless you include the ampersand in the command. If you use Ctrl+Z to regain control of the xterm, the X program you launched from the xterm becomes unresponsive unless you then type bg to allow both processes to run. It's easy to become confused and think that an X program has crashed, when in fact it's just been stopped after having been launched from an xterm.

Batch Processes

Batch processes are submitted from a queue and have no association with a terminal at all. Batch processes are great for performing recurring processes at some time when the system usage is low. To accomplish this on a Linux system, use the batch and at commands. The at command is really pretty simple to use. Let's assume that you want to run the tar command that we just used in the interactive process example at 2:00 in the morning tomorrow. You would use the at command as shown below:

```
# at 2:00
at> tar -zcf /dev/st0 /
```

After entering this command, you must press Ctrl+D. The system responds with a warning that the command will be run using /bin/sh, since some shell scripts are written only for a specific shell, and then gives a recap of what command will be run and when:

```
warning: commands will be executed using /bin/sh
job 1 at 2000-09-01  02:00
```

To schedule something to happen on a specific date, use at like this:

```
# at 23:55 12/31/00
at> tar -zcf /dev/st0 /
```

Again, use Ctrl+D to terminate input to at. Now check your work with the atq command, which lists all processes that you've scheduled with the at command. The output resembles the following:

```
1       2000-09-01  02:00  a
2       2000-12-31  23:55  a
```

Now let's assume that you decide it's too risky to run your backup with only 5 minutes left in the millenium and decide to cancel that job. Use atrm like this:

```
# atrm 2
```

Now check your work with the atq command:

```
# atq
1    2000-09-01  02:00  a
```

If you want to restrict the usage of the at command, you can do so using the /etc/at.deny and /etc/at.allow files. On a Red Hat system, the default installation creates an empty /etc/at.deny and no /etc/at.allow. This means that any user can use the at facility. If you wish to deny at privileges to the user steve, simply add him to the /etc/at.deny file. If you wish to only allow root to use at, create an /etc/at.allow file with only the word root in it. If the /etc/at.allow file exists, only the users listed therein will be allowed to use at. If there is no /etc/at.allow file, any user not listed in the /etc/at.deny file can use at.

If you need to run a CPU-intensive process in the background when the system load is low, use the batch command. The batch command will try to run the command immediately, but it will only be allowed to run when the system load is less than 0.8. You can manually check the system load by looking at the /proc/loadavg file. Assuming that you want to run our trusty backup when the system usage is low, use the batch command as follows:

```
# batch
at> tar -zcf /dev/st0 /
```

Once again, use Ctrl+D to terminate input. Now when the system load drops below 0.8, the backup will start.

Daemons

Daemons are server processes. These processes run continuously in the background until the service they represent is called. For instance, httpd (the Apache Hypertext Transfer Protocol daemon) is a standalone Web server service. It is typically started at boot time but spends most of its time monitoring the port assigned to Apache, looking for work. When data comes in on port 80 (Apache's default port), httpd picks up the traffic and starts processing it as appropriate. When the job is done, it returns to a listening mode.

A special daemon exists to monitor ports for other daemons, which have been assigned to it. This daemon, traditionally called inetd, but replaced by xinetd in Red Hat 7.0, is referred to as a TCP/IP *super server*. It is started at bootup, and listens to the ports assigned the processes that are listed in the /etc/inetd.conf file (or /etc/xinetd.conf, for xinetd). Chapter 15 discusses daemons and super servers in more detail.

Parent Processes and Their Children

When a process needs to perform several functions in order to complete its task, it cannot exit until all of the functions are finished. This means that if a system needs to do several database queries to complete a task, it might not update the screen until all of the queries have been completed. In order to prevent such an obvious lag, the *parent* process can initiate *child* processes to complete the subtasks in a more expedient manner by performing as many of them as possible simultaneously. The creation of child processes is called *forking*. Each child process is assigned a new PID, but also retains its parent's ID as the PPID. This helps you track which process called which child process. The child process is a duplicate of the parent process, inheriting nearly all of its parent's environment with the exception of its PID. The child then uses the exec command to replace itself in memory with the binary code of a program that can perform the requested function. When the replacement program finishes its task, it exits.

Listing 3.4 shows an excerpt from the table of processes as output by the ps -ajx command.

Listing 3.4 Sample ps Output

PPID	PID	PGID	SID	TTY	TPGID	STAT	UID	TIME	COMMAND
0	1	0	0	?	-1	S	0	0:09	init [3]
1	2	1	1	?	-1	SW	0	0:21	[kflushd]
1	3	1	1	?	-1	SW	0	0:17	[kupdate]
1	4	1	1	?	-1	SW	0	0:00	[kpiod]
1	5	1	1	?	-1	SW	0	0:16	[kswapd]
1	6	6	6	?	-1	SW<	0	0:00	[portmap]
1	381	381	381	?	-1	SW	0	0:00	[apmd]
1	434	434	434	?	-1	S	0	0:00	syslogd -m 0
1	445	445	445	?	-1	S	0	0:00	klogd
1	477	477	477	?	-1	S	0	0:00	crond
1	493	493	493	?	-1	S	0	0:00	inetd
1	764	764	764	tty1	835	SW	0	0:00	[login]
1	766	766	766	tty3	766	SW	0	0:00	[mingetty]
1	767	767	767	tty4	767	SW	0	0:00	[mingetty]
1	768	768	768	tty5	768	SW	0	0:00	[mingetty]
1	769	769	769	tty6	769	SW	0	0:00	[mingetty]
764	788	788	764	tty1	835	SW	500	0:00	[bash]
788	810	810	764	tty1	835	SW	0	0:00	[su]
810	811	811	764	tty1	835	SW	0	0:00	[bash]
811	835	835	764	tty1	835	SW	0	0:00	[vi]

You can see that this display contains a great deal of useful information. Looking at the PID and PPID fields, you can follow the parent/child lineage. For example, the init process started several processes: kflushd, kupdate, kpiod, kswapd, portmap, apmd, syslogd, klogd, crond, inetd, login, and several mingetty processes. We know this by looking at the PPID field, since process 1 is the init process. If you look at the login process numbered 764 and then at the bash process numbered 788, you can detect that the bash process is forked off the login process. Since bash is the login shell, which is started upon login, this makes sense. The su process that is process 810 is being run under that bash shell, since the PPID is the PID of the bash process.

Looking at the parent group ID (PGID), we can see that kflushd, kupdate, kpiod, and kswapd all belong to the bin group.

The TTY field tells where the process is running. The files started up as part of the initialization process typically have a ? in this field since they are not tty-specific. The processes specific to a tty list that tty number (or, in the case of a remote login, a pts number).

TIP A tty is a login session connected to the standard output pipe; that is, it is local to the CPU. Linux has six terminals (ttys) defined by default. A pts entry indicates a login by telnet or xterm. pts/0 is the first such login.

The TIME column shows the total amount of system (CPU) time used by the process so far; this is not equivalent to the amount of clock time since the process started, because we are on a multitasking system.

The process status codes (STAT) can be interpreted using the following information as taken directly from the ps man page:

```
D uninterruptible sleep (usually IO)

R runnable (on run queue)

S sleeping

T traced or stopped

Z a defunct ("zombie") process

W has no resident pages

< high-priority process

N low-priority task

L has pages locked into memory(for real-time and custom IO)
```

We've hardly scratched the surface of the ps command, but we will revisit it when we discuss managing processes a little later in this chapter. First we will examine the initialization process used by Linux. Some of the details vary from distribution to distribution; this discussion uses the Red Hat process as a model, pointing out differences in other distributions where appropriate.

The *init* Process

The most important process in a Linux system is init. The first process started on a Linux system, it is assigned the PID 1. The init process is owned by the root user and has a PPID of 0.

The last thing the kernel does when it boots is to start the init process. The init process controls the rest of the boot process by checking and mounting the filesystems, starting the necessary daemons, and doing whatever else it has been configured to do. Chapter 5 shows how to configure the init process.

When a parent process dies before all of its child processes have died, the remaining child processes are said to be *orphan* processes. These processes are required to have a parent process, so the init process adopts the orphan processes until they, too, are completed or killed.

Listing 3.5 illustrates what happens when a user logs in to your system. Earlier in the chapter we saw the output from the ps -ajx command. This time we use the -aux parameter set, which displays the user who owns the process, the process ID, the percentage of the CPU that this process is consuming, the amount of memory that this process is consuming, and the time the process started.

Listing 3.5 Output from the ps -aux Command

```
root   4270   0.0   0.8   2212   1120   pts/2   S   20:58   0:00   login - user
user   4271   0.1   0.8   1760   1032   pts/2   S   20:58   0:00   -bash
user   4301   0.1   0.6   1708    848   pts/2   S   21:00   0:00   vi todo
```

You can see in Listing 3.5 that a login process with a PID of 4270 was started for the user user; logins are always owned by root. Since it has a pts number, it is a remote login. This login process forked off a child process with a PID of 4271. This child process is the bash shell that was initiated by the login process when the user logged in.

Since user logged in remotely, a pts was assigned instead of a tty number. In old versions of Red Hat, remote ttys are referred to as ttyp0, ttyp1, etc. In Red Hat 6.0 and later, remote ttys are referred to as pts/0, pts/1, etc. The init process runs as long as the system is active. Nothing else can run without the parent init process. We'll discuss the init process in detail in Chapter 5 when we discuss system startup and shutdown. During a system shutdown, init performs the reverse of its bootup procedure. It kills all other running processes, unmounts all filesystems, and stops the processor, along with anything else it has been configured to do.

Managing Processes

Part of your responsibility as system administrator is to manage the system's processes to prevent a runaway process (one that has started consuming system resources far beyond what it should) from causing your system to crash. You need to understand how to obtain information about the processes that are running. We have looked at a couple of examples of the ps command to illustrate earlier points. Now we'll look at ps more formally. The ps (process status) command is the most often used method of obtaining data about current processes. The ps command called without arguments will display all of the processes running from that specific login including their PIDs, tty information, CPU time, and the command that started the process. The ps command becomes more useful if you add some arguments, as you can see in Listing 3.6.

Listing 3.6 Output from the ps −e Command

```
PID  TTY    TIME      CMD
  1  ?      00:00:09  init
  2  ?      00:00:22  kflushd
  3  ?      00:00:17  kupdate
  4  ?      00:00:00  kpiod
  5  ?      00:00:20  kswapd
  6  ?      00:00:00  mdrecoveryd
296  ?      00:00:00  ppp-watch
365  ?      00:00:00  portmap
3653 tty2   00:00:00  vmware
3654 tty2   00:00:05  vmware
3655 tty2   00:00:01  vmware
3864 tty2   00:00:41  ld-linux.so.2
3887 tty2   00:00:00  netscape-commun
3946 ttyS1  00:00:00  pppd
4024 tty2   00:00:01  kvt
4025 pts/1  00:00:00  bash
4269 ?      00:00:00  in.rlogind
4270 pts/2  00:00:00  login
4271 pts/2  00:00:00  bash
4301 pts/2  00:00:00  vi
4317 pts/0  00:00:00  man
4318 pts/0  00:00:00  sh
4319 pts/0  00:00:00  sh
4322 pts/0  00:00:00  groff
4323 pts/0  00:00:00  less
4326 pts/0  00:00:00  grotty
4328 pts/1  00:00:00  ps
```

You can see that the output from ps -e gives you the basic information about all the running processes. The output includes the PID, the tty, the time, and the command itself. This is quite sufficient when you are trying to obtain the PID of a process to kill it or restart it.

The output from ps -au, as shown in Listing 3.7, displays information in a user-oriented format (u) that includes all processes on this terminal, including those of other users.

Listing 3.7   Output from the ps -au Command

```
USER   PID  %CPU %MEM VSZ  RSS TTY   STAT START   TIME COMMAND
user   4025 0.0  0.7  1760 988 pts/1  S   18:17   0:00 bash
user   4331 0.0  0.6  2532 884 pts/1  R   21:32   0:00 ps au
```

System administrators more often use a version of the ps command that gives this information for all the processes on this terminal as well as all daemon processes, such as the ps -aef command illustrated in Listing 3.8.

Listing 3.8   Output from the ps -aef Command

```
UID      PID  PPID C STIME TTY      TIME CMD
root     1    0    0 Sep28 ?        00:00:09 init [3]
root     2    1    0 Sep28 ?        00:00:22 [kflushd]
root     3    1    0 Sep28 ?        00:00:17 [kupdate]
root     4    1    0 Sep28 ?        00:00:00 [kpiod]
root     5    1    0 Sep28 ?        00:00:20 [kswapd]
root     6    1    0 Sep28 ?        00:00:00 [mdrecoveryd]
bin      365  1    0 Sep28 ?        00:00:00 portmap
root     381  1    0 Sep28 ?        00:00:00 [apmd]
root     434  1    0 Sep28 ?        00:00:00 syslogd -m 0
root     445  1    0 Sep28 ?        00:00:00 klogd
daemon   461  1    0 Sep28 ?        00:00:00 /usr/sbin/atd
root     477  1    0 Sep28 ?        00:00:00 crond
root     493  1    0 Sep28 ?        00:00:00 inetd
root     509  1    0 Sep28 ?        00:00:00 [lpd]
```

How Things Work

PART 1

This form of the command is very useful when you are looking for information on a specific daemon. Simply pipe the command into a `grep` command to see whether the daemon in question is running. This is especially useful in a script where the other output would confuse the situation. For this reason, it is one of the versions of the `ps` command that is most commonly used by system administrators. The man page for the ps command lists the many options available to tailor the output to what you need.

The command `top` uses the `/proc` filesystem to display all active processes along with the percentage of CPU power and percentage of memory that each one is using. You can also do this with a `ps` command, but `top` is better in that it is a continuous listing which is updated in real-time in order by CPU usage and is configurable. The most CPU-intensive programs are listed first, as shown in Figure 3.3. This is extremely helpful when your system is running slowly, and you want to find out which process is dominating the CPU. In the case of Figure 3.3, one process (`setiathome`) is consuming 97.8% of the CPU time. This might or might not be a sign of trouble, depending upon whether that process *should* be consuming a lot of CPU time. The `top` command also lists specifics such as uptime, the number of users, the number of processes and their status, and how real memory and swap space are being used.

Figure 3.3   Sample output of top command

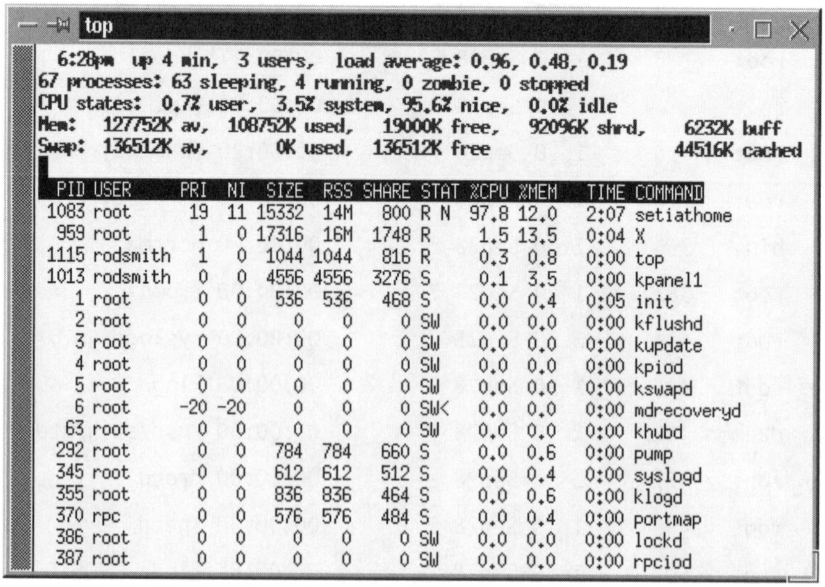

```
— -◁| top                                                    · □ ✕
   6:28pm  up 4 min,  3 users,  load average: 0.96, 0.48, 0.19
67 processes: 63 sleeping, 4 running, 0 zombie, 0 stopped
CPU states:  0.7% user,  3.5% system,  95.6% nice,  0.0% idle
Mem:   127752K av,  108752K used,   19000K free,   92096K shrd,    6232K buff
Swap:  136512K av,       0K used,  136512K free                   44516K cached

  PID USER      PRI  NI  SIZE  RSS SHARE STAT %CPU %MEM   TIME COMMAND
 1083 root       19  11 15332  14M   800 R N  97.8 12.0   2:07 setiathome
  959 root        1   0 17316  16M  1748 R     1.5 13.5   0:04 X
 1115 rodsmith    1   0  1044 1044   816 R     0.3  0.8   0:00 top
 1013 rodsmith    0   0  4556 4556  3276 S     0.1  3.5   0:00 kpanel1
    1 root        0   0   536  536   468 S     0.0  0.4   0:05 init
    2 root        0   0     0    0     0 SW    0.0  0.0   0:00 kflushd
    3 root        0   0     0    0     0 SW    0.0  0.0   0:00 kupdate
    4 root        0   0     0    0     0 SW    0.0  0.0   0:00 kpiod
    5 root        0   0     0    0     0 SW    0.0  0.0   0:00 kswapd
    6 root      -20 -20     0    0     0 SWK   0.0  0.0   0:00 mdrecoveryd
   63 root        0   0     0    0     0 SW    0.0  0.0   0:00 khubd
  292 root        0   0   784  784   660 S     0.0  0.6   0:00 pump
  345 root        0   0   612  612   512 S     0.0  0.4   0:00 syslogd
  355 root        0   0   836  836   464 S     0.0  0.6   0:00 klogd
  370 rpc         0   0   576  576   484 S     0.0  0.4   0:00 portmap
  386 root        0   0     0    0     0 SW    0.0  0.0   0:00 lockd
  387 root        0   0     0    0     0 SW    0.0  0.0   0:00 rpciod
```

Terminating/Restarting with the *kill* Command

You know how to see what processes are dominating your CPU and slowing down your system, but what do you do about it? To terminate a process on a Linux system (and in most other Unix-like systems), you use the `kill` command. Issued with only a process ID as an argument, the `kill` command will send a signal to the process telling it to terminate. Some processes are able to catch the signal and cannot be killed so easily—the "John Wayne" processes, which simply ignore the `kill` signal. For these you must use a -9 argument, making the command look like this:

```
$ kill -9 234
```

The -9 cannot be caught, so the process whose ID is specified will terminate. It's generally a good idea to try issuing the `kill` command *without* the -9 argument first, because some programs close themselves more cleanly this way, without leaving behind temporary files and so on.

If you need to restart a daemon, because it is hung up or because you've made a configuration file change, you can do this by entering the `kill` command with a -1 argument before the process ID, as in the example below.

```
# kill -1 234
```

Do not combine this with the -9 argument. Using

```
# kill -HUP 234
```

will do the same thing. You may notice when you speak to other system administrators that HUP is sometimes used as a verb, basically meaning restart.

NOTE Linux supports a command called nohup, which launches a program in such a way that it ignores the HUP kill signal. This allows you to run a program so that it survives a logout, which can be handy if you want to run a program that will be running for a very long time, but you don't want to tie up a terminal or xterm window with that program. To use this utility, just place it before an ordinary command, as in **nohup number-cruncher**.

Terminating/Restarting Processes Using Scripts

In Red Hat Linux (as in many commercial versions of Unix), each daemon has a single script that allows you to kill it, check its status, or restart it. The handling of these scripts is based on run levels. Run levels are more thoroughly discussed in Chapter 5. For now you only need to know that the system has several modes it can boot into. The selection of the run level allows only certain processes to be started by the `init` process. On Red

Hat systems, these scripts exist in /etc/rc.d/init.d, one for each daemon that is to be started or shut down by the system either at bootup or run level change. Under the /etc/rc.d/ directory, there is a subdirectory for each possible run level, which contains symbolic links to the scripts that should be run for that level. Most scripts contain the capability to start, stop, status-check, and restart their specific daemons.

To kill the sendmail daemon, for instance, you use the stop option:

> **# /etc/rc.d/init.d/sendmail stop**

If the daemon is stopped, you'll see the message:

> Shutting down sendmail: [OK]

The [OK] will be replaced by [FAILED] if the daemon was not shut down as shown below. This might happen if the daemon that you are trying to kill is not currently running.

> Shutting down sendmail: [FAILED]

If you wish to start a daemon that is not currently running, substitute the word start for stop:

> **# /etc/rc.d/init.d/sendmail start**

The system will then attempt to start up the sendmail daemon. A message confirming the successful startup will be displayed.

> Starting sendmail: [OK]

If you just want to know whether a daemon is running, instead of searching through a ps listing, you may use the script in /etc/rc.d/init.d which governs that daemon, specifying the status option, as in:

> **$ /etc/rc.d/rc.local/sendmail status**
>
> sendmail (pid 4437) is running...

Last, you may restart a daemon that is currently running—or as some would say, you can "HUP" the daemon. To do this for sendmail, you would use

> **# /etc/rc.d/init.d/sendmail restart**

You will then see the message

> Shutting down sendmail: [OK]

if the shutdown succeeded, or

> Shutting down sendmail: [FAILED]

if the shutdown was unsuccessful. Following the shutdown line, you will see

```
Starting sendmail: [OK]
```

if the sendmail daemon started or

```
Starting sendmail: [FAILED]
```

if it did not. A failure during the shutdown phase will not automatically prevent the daemon from restarting, although a problem with that daemon might cause both the shutdown and the startup to fail.

```
Shutting down sendmail: [FAILED]
```

```
Starting sendmail: [FAILED]
```

In Sum

We've looked at the ext2 filesystem: how it developed and how it is laid out. We've also looked at processes and process management using such commands as ps, fg, bg, and top. You got a first look at the init process and saw why it is so important. We'll look in more detail at the init scripts in Chapter 5 when we map out the entire startup process.

In Chapter 4, we'll discuss the different elements you'll need to perform system administration tasks. Our discussion will include command-line tools, commands, and resources to help you work through the problems you encounter.

4

Tools of the Trade

Just as mechanics must be able to use their tools skillfully to keep your vehicle in working condition, so also must a Linux system administrator be able to use the tools of the trade to maintain a workable Linux system. In either case, what looks to the layman to be magical is in fact the implementation of some skill learned via previous experience. Success comes from knowing what has to be done, having the resources to do it, and implementing what you know. Remember that every task is a tool you might need later. In view of this, system administrators must learn the basic elements of the job to the point where they are second nature. Only then can these elements be used as building blocks to accomplish tasks that are more challenging.

In this chapter, we'll identify several such building blocks. We'll discuss information tools like man pages, info pages, and Web-based Linux support services before looking at some command-line tools that will be useful in your Linux systems administration experience. We'll give you some basic commands to store in your Linux toolbox, explain how you can make commands work together to solve bigger tasks with piping and redirection, talk about the different ways of locating specific files on your system, and discuss the use of quoting, the history list, and Bash shell commands.

Locating Help Resources

One of the most important elements in establishing yourself as a system administrator is demonstrating that you know where to find an answer you don't know off-hand. Some really sharp system administrators will advise you never to admit that you don't know something. We wholeheartedly disagree with this approach. Yes, some people become angry when the answer isn't one that you can give without verifying the information, but it should never change your policy of being honest. More often than not, people are relieved to hear an honest reply as long as you come back with the answer in a reasonable time. When asked something that you don't readily know, always give the same basic answer: "*I haven't seen that one in a while, but I know where to get the information you need. I'll be back with you as soon as I get it.*"

If you can't recall the answer, take the honest approach and forget about the knowledge-able strut. The knowledgeable strut puts you in a position of having to be (or at least appear to be) omniscient, and none of us are that. We also have found that people who pretend to know all the answers tend to come off as arrogant, and some clients love to prove an arrogant system administrator wrong. You are less of a target if you are honest about your abilities—as long as one of those abilities is the ability to find an answer.

To find answers when you need them, look at the numerous information resources that are available if you know where to find them. One of the features we like most about Linux is the availability of resources. On a Microsoft Windows machine, you can't just bring up a page of useful information on a command. There are documents and online help features in Windows, but those tools generally don't answer questions unless they fit into a specific mold, or they get almost to the point where they're helpful and then stop. They don't offer enough information to piece together the answers that exist between the lines. In Linux and other Unix-like operating systems, the information is most often there if you know what you're looking for.

Man Pages

Man (short for "manual") *pages* are online documents that describe the format and functioning of commands and files as well as some other tools available on your Linux system. Man pages are not meant to be comprehensive but rather to give general information about usage. Man pages aren't meant to take the place of the source documentation, but instead to highlight how to use the referenced resource. Unless the system was installed without them, man pages are readily available from the command line. Simply type **man man** to get the man page on how to use man pages. The basic format of the command is:

```
man [options] [section] topic
```

There is a configuration file for the man command located at /etc/man.config. This file allows you to configure the environment variables that the man command uses if you don't wish to specify them on the command line. The options include the path that should be searched for man pages, the order in which the manual sections should be searched, and whether to store the man pages in a compressed format.

Man pages are grouped into sections or categories as outlined in Table 4.1. A given command can have man pages in different categories if appropriate; for example, the umount command has a page in section 2 for the programmer's system call and a page in section 8 for its use as a system administration tool. Some packages, like Tcl, separate their pages into a different section rather than including them in the categories listed.

Table 4.1   Online Manual Sections Specified in the man Command

Section	Category
1	User commands that may be started by anyone
2	System calls (kernel functions)
3	Library functions
4	Devices
5	File format descriptions
6	Games
7	Miscellaneous
8	System administration tools that only root can execute
9	More kernel routine documentation
n	New documentation that may be recategorized
o	Old documentation that may go away soon
l	Documentation referring to this specific system

If you don't remember the name of the command you want to know about, man has an option that will look for a keyword in the Whatis database, a set of files containing short descriptions of system commands. In this way, if you know that the purpose of the command you want is to add a user, you can specify:

```
$ man -k user
```

The output, an excerpt of which is listed below, will be a list of man page topics that contain the word *user* in the description, along with the section each page is in and a simple description of the topic.

access (2)   Check user's permissions for a file

chage (1)   Change user password expiry information

useradd (8)   Create a new user or update default new user
              information

userdel (8)   Delete a user account and related files

You can see from this that the command you want is useradd; running man on that command produces the display shown in Listing 4.1.

Listing 4.1 The Man Page Display for useradd

```
USERADD(8)                                                  USERADD(8)


NAME
       useradd  -  Create  a  new user or update default new user
       information


SYNOPSIS
       useradd [-c comment] [-d home_dir]
               [-e expire_date] [-f inactive_time]
               [-g initial_group] [-G group[,...]]
               [-m [-k skeleton_dir] | -M] [-p passwd]
               [-s shell] [-u uid [ -o]] [-n] [-r] login


       useradd -D [-g default_group] [-b default_home]
               [-f default_inactive] [-e default_expire_date]
               [-s default_shell]


DESCRIPTION
   Creating New Users
```

When invoked without the -D option, the useradd command creates a new user account using the values specified on the command line and the default values from the system. The new user account will be entered into the system files as needed, the home directory will be created, and initial files copied, depending on the command line options. The version provided with Red Hat Linux will create a group for each user added to the system, unless -n option is given. The options which apply to the useradd command are

[OPTIONS omitted]

NOTES

The system administrator is responsible for placing the default user files in the /etc/skel directory.
This version of useradd was modified by Red Hat to suit Red Hat user/group convention.

CAVEATS

You may not add a user to an NIS group. This must be performed on the NIS server.

FILES

/etc/passwd - user account information
/etc/shadow - secure user account information
/etc/group - group information
/etc/default/useradd - default information
/etc/skel - directory containing default files

```
SEE ALSO
        chfn(1),  chsh(1),  crypt(3),  groupadd(8),   groupdel(8),
        groupmod(8),  passwd(1),  userdel(8),  usermod(8)


AUTHOR
        Julianne Frances Haugh (jfh@bga.com)



                                                                      1

(END)
```

The useradd display is typical of a man page for a command. After the command's name, you see a synopsis of the formal syntax, a description of its use, its possible arguments (omitted here for space reasons), any caveats or restrictions on its use, any references to related commands, and the author's name and e-mail address. Non-command man pages include similar sets of data as appropriate.

Man pages, by default, use the less -is command to write the information to a file that you can view. The less command is simply a filter that pages through a file, displaying each page on your screen. (We'll talk more about it in a few pages.) Similar programs are cat and more, which you may have used before. You may change the man command's default viewer by adding the -P option followed by the name of the viewer program you wish to use. Or you can configure this change in /etc/man.conf.

If the man pages aren't installed, and there is room on the system, install them. To do this, use the rpm command as described in Chapter 8. You'll find invaluable information in these pages. Many times, we have needed to use some rarely used capability of a Linux command and found the format for that command in the man page. An added benefit in Linux is that the man pages are available in a number of languages—just in case you'd like to get an explanation of the ls command in Indonesian.

Info Pages

Although man pages have been the standard source of information about Unix commands for many years, the GNU Project has more recently introduced the concept of *info pages*, and the Linux community is moving toward replacing man pages with info pages. Man pages for many commands are no longer being updated and instead direct you to the corresponding info page for information.

From our point of view as users, info pages are very similar to man pages. They are grouped into the same categories as man pages. The critical difference that drives the info page movement is the advantage of using the Texinfo format.

Texinfo is a documentation system that uses a single file to create both online display and printed output. That is, only one file must be maintained in support of printed documentation and the info page. This is a tremendous time-saver for the program's developer who, under the man page system, had to create both a user's manual for printing and a man page for on-screen viewing.

A Texinfo file is a plain ASCII text file that also contains @-*commands* (commands preceded by an @), which tell the typesetting and formatting programs how the text is intended to be formatted. A Texinfo file may be edited with the editor of your choice, but the GNU Emacs editor has a special Texinfo mode that provides special Texinfo-related features. You can read Info files using the standalone Info program or the Info reader built into the Emacs editor. There is not a great deal of difference in the material whichever way you do it, but info pages look awkward to those of us who have gotten used to the old way. The command to list the info page for the useradd command is:

info useradd

The output looks like Listing 4.2.

Listing 4.2   The Info Page Display for useradd

```
File: *manpages*,  Node: useradd,  Up: (dir)




USERADD(8)                                                        USERADD(8)


NAME

       useradd  -  Create  a  new user or update default new user
       information
```

```
SYNOPSIS

        useradd [-c comment] [-d home_dir]

                [-e expire_date] [-f inactive_time]

                [-g initial_group] [-G group[,...]]

                [-m [-k skeleton_dir] | -M] [-p passwd]

                [-s shell] [-u uid [ -o]] [-n] [-r] login


        useradd -D [-g default_group] [-b default_home]

                [-f default_inactive] [-e default_expire_date]

                [-s default_shell]


DESCRIPTION

-----Info: (*manpages*)useradd, 184 lines --Top---------------------
-----------

Welcome to Info version 3.12h. "C-h" for help, "m" for menu item.
```

As you can see, the Info page presents essentially the same information as the old man page
format. For now, system administrators will benefit from getting to know them both.

Technical Support

Linux has a reputation as a do-it-yourself operating system, and for this reason many
would-be corporate users have not taken it seriously. Mailing lists and online Frequently
Asked Questions lists have long been available, but this informal support didn't really
gain Linux anything in the business market. Companies that would otherwise have used
Linux shied away, thinking that their customer base would hesitate to buy something
with such informal support. Fortunately, there are some enlightened corporate executives
who agree with us that getting technical support from a user community is actually better
than from a commercial vendor, for a couple of reasons. First, you get the benefit of many
of your peers' experience. Also, with commercial software you are dealing with "planned
obsolescence," and the answer for many questions turns out to be "you need to buy an
upgrade to do that." Whichever type of corporate environment you are working in,
you're likely to encounter both points of view.

In response to Linux's reputation as an unsupported operating system, several third-party
companies have begun offering fee-based technical support plans for businesses and indi-

viduals. This has been an area of substantial development in the last year or two. Companies can now point to these new support sources when pitching the use of Linux to their clients. Here's a look at the most important online support sources, both commercial and from the user community.

Configuration Support

Users of early Red Hat found the support offered by the company to be disappointingly limited to installation issues and often unresponsive. Red Hat's Web site contained a database of previously answered questions, but problems with the search engine often rendered this database unsearchable.

After the release of version 5.1 greatly increased their sales volume, Red Hat began revamping its support program. They improved their installation support and reworked their online database. Web-based support was offered as well as support through e-mail and telephone. As of Red Hat 7.0, this support is offered with the Standard Edition, the Deluxe Edition, and the Professional Edition of Red Hat. Each of these levels offers 90 days of Web or e-mail installation support. Support contracts for post-installation problems and per-incident support are available as well.

Most third-party companies that offer Linux support have searchable databases on their Web sites, which they encourage you to use as the first level of support. Many of these same companies also offer more formalized support in the form of 24/7 e-mail support, telephone support, and Web-based support, each intended to have a very quick turn-around time. You may need to exchange several e-mails with the support personnel before the matter is resolved, but this can all take place in a matter of hours. Support Web sites often have Web-based forms to gather all the necessary data and then channel it to a support engineer who responds via e-mail or telephone. Call-in telephone support is not usually intended to be the primary channel for support.

Some third-party support sites, such as Enterprise Linux Support at `http://e.linux-support.net/`, offer fee-based telephone and Web-based support at hourly or daily rates, depending on how long it takes to solve the particular problem. Web-based support is generally significantly cheaper than telephone support. This same company offers support by volunteer engineers under the name Free Linux Support at `http://support.marko.net/`. The success of the engineers is monitored, and the best engineers are offered paid positions with Enterprise Linux Support.

Other third-party support sites as well as companies like Red Hat (`http://www.redhat.com/apps/support/`) and Caldera (`http://www.caldera.com/support/`), offer pay-by-the-incident support, where the charge is a given rate per problem regardless of how much—or how little—time the problem takes to solve. The charge per incident is widely variable. Distributors generally offer installation support free for a given time after the purchase of a boxed distribution.

Also available are traditional support contracts, which offer to support any problem within a given period for a set amount of money. These contracts specify what the telephone support hours are and what the expected response time is.

Tailored Linux Development

In 1998, LinuxCare (`http://www.linuxcare.com`) began to offer distribution-neutral support programs to businesses as well as individuals. LinuxCare's primary business is to develop customized Linux software for business customers. They provide assistance in the areas of Linux kernel extension, system optimization, device driver development, and application porting. They also offer consulting services in the areas of Linux security, network management, and project management in general.

A number of small, Web-based companies, such as Linux Corporate Consulting (`http://www.corplinux.com`) and Linux Consulting (`http://www.linux-consulting.com/`), offer fee-based support services in the form of customized Linux server and client machines, Linux system administration tools and scripts, specialized Linux software, and Linux maintenance. The number of consultant firms is growing rapidly. A simple search of the Internet can find a consultant who will develop whatever Linux-related software you need.

General Web Support

Nearly every distribution has at least one mailing list available to users of the distribution or others who have distribution-specific questions. Messages are addressed to the appropriate list, and the list handler mails them to the other members of that list as appropriate. It is a very effective way to obtain support information. You simply e-mail your question to the list; others read your post and e-mail their responses to the list. Sometimes the list handler creates a digest version of the list, meaning that instead of receiving each e-mail individually, you receive a composite post when the waiting message queue reaches a given capacity.

Red Hat uses lists named `redhat-announce-list`, `redhat-watch-list`, and `redhat-list`. The announce list, as the name implies, announces events that affect the Red Hat community. The `watch` list alerts its members to security issues, and the `redhat` list is for general issues. `redhat-list` is available in digest format. Information on joining these lists is available at `http://www.redhat.com/mailing-lists`.

The Debian distribution has too many lists to mention by name, but you can find information about them and how to subscribe at `http://www.debian.org/MailingLists/subscribe`.

Corel Linux has several newsgroups: General, Hardware Compatibility, Installation, Networking, Printing, Setup/Config, German, and Other Languages. To find out about these newsgroups, check the information at `http://linux.corel.com/support/online.htm`.

Slackware has two basic lists: `slackware-announce` and `slackware-security`. Each is available in digest format as well. More information may be found at `http://www.slackware.com/lists`.

SuSE Linux also has several mailing lists, including `suse-announce-e` for announcements, `suse-linux-e` for general discussions, `suse-security`, and `suse-security-announce`. Other lists are specific to Motif, Oracle, IMAP, Applixware, and other topics. More information on these lists is available at `http://www.suse.com/support/mailinglists/index.html`.

A number of sites archive the various Linux-related lists. Very useful is Deja.com's Usenet discussion service, located at `http://www.deja.com/usenet`. What you'll find there is a search engine that will respond to your query with a list of related posts from the various lists that are archived there. Select the one that most closely resembles what you're interested in, and you'll see the text from that post. It's especially useful to enter error messages as the query, possibly followed by the word Linux. This works quite well for those errors that don't seem to be documented anywhere else.

For example, you might enter the following in the search window:

```
"Boot partition too big" Linux
```

This generates about 200 hits; several of these detail the problem. (In case you're curious, the answer is that the `/boot` partition must be contained within the first 1023 cylinders of the hard drive.)

Command-Line Tools

Linux provides a number of command-line tools to support you in your system administration duties. This section first looks at the command-line techniques that help you use commands more effectively, like pipes, redirection, wildcards, and tildes. As you'll see, all of these features are provided by the shell, which for Red Hat Linux is the Bash shell. The remainder of the chapter then summarizes the basic command-line programs—

commands—that you use every day. All of these pieces fit together to help you accomplish the day-to-day tasks of a Linux administrator.

Bash Command-Line Functionality

The shell assigned to a particular user serves as the command interpreter for that user's session. Commands are read from standard input and interpreted in a certain way by the shell; the same commands might be interpreted differently by a different shell. The default shell in Linux is the Bourne Again Shell, or Bash. The Bash shell includes features from the Bourne shell, the Korn shell, and the C shell. Bash reads its configuration from the .bash_profile and .bashrc files, which are discussed further in Chapter 5 in the context of user-specific startup scripts.

Bash, like other Unix shells, has certain special characteristics, which we will discuss here. These include its usage of environment variables, piping and redirection, wildcards, the tilde, and the history list.

Environment Variables

Environment variables are strings, set by the Bash shell or some other program, that make data available to other programs. These strings are called "environment" variables because they are globally accessible and are therefore part of the environment. The following variables are set in the /etc/profile file under Red Hat Linux:

```
PATH
PS1
USER
LOGNAME
MAIL
HOSTNAME
HISTSIZE
HISTFILESIZE
INPUTRC
CALENDAR_DIR
```

The PATH variable is redefined on several levels, since different users need to have access to different files and directories. Setting an environment variable in a Bash shell has two steps: setting the value and then exporting it. Sometimes you will see this as two separate commands:

```
HISTSIZE=1000
export HISTSIZE
```

It may be more efficient to do only one step as follows:

```
export HISTSIZE=1000
```

To display the current value of an environment variable, use the echo command:

```
echo $HISTSIZE
```

You can access these variables from within a C program using the getenv function.

Piping and Redirection

Piping and redirection are such powerful tools that it's frustrating to find yourself on a system that either doesn't handle pipes or handles them badly. Most Unix-like operating systems handle both pipes and redirection similarly.

Piping   When you execute a command in Linux, it has three streams opened for it. The first is for input and is called Standard In (stdin). The next is for output and is called Standard Out (stdout). The last is the error stream and is called Standard Error (stderr). Piping is the practice of passing the first program's stdout into the stdin of another program. You do this by listing the first command followed by a pipe (|) and then the command where the first command's output is being sent. For example, if your task is to back up certain files on your system, you can funnel the file listing that is output from a find command into stdin of the cpio command, prompting cpio to store only the listed files on your tape:

```
# find /home/user | cpio -ocvB /dev/st0
```

The output of the find command would look something like this:

```
/home/user
/home/user/.Xdefaults
/home/user/.bash_logout
/home/user/.bash_profile
/home/user/.bashrc
/home/user/calendar
```

When this output is piped into the cpio command, each of these files is added to the archive and written to the tape drive specified as /dev/st0 (the first SCSI tape drive).

If you want to exclude all sound files with the extension .au, you could pipe the find command through a grep command and then into the cpio command. The command would then look something like this:

```
# find  /home/user | grep -v *.au | cpio -ocvB /dev/st0
```

In this case, the file list output by the find command would be filtered to exclude all of the files that end in the extension .au, and only the remaining files would be added to the archive.

Redirection   *Redirection* is the practice of changing where the stream comes from or points to. One common use is to route the system log to a vacant console and update it as messages are added. If you wanted the output of the command to go to the console device designated by /dev/tty9 rather than to stdout, you would enter this:

```
# tail -f /var/log/messages > /dev/tty9
```

When you execute this command, the output of the tail command will be redirected to console 9, causing the system log (/var/log/messages) to be displayed there and, since the -f argument is present, appending new output as it is written to the system log.

Sometimes you want to take input from somewhere other than stdin. This is also redirection, and you can use the same principle illustrated above. Let's say that a file contains a list of names to be sorted in a particular order. By changing the stdin for the sort command, we can make it take the names from the file, reorder them, and write them to stdout. The command would look like this:

```
# sort < namelist
```

The sort command must come first or the shell will look for a program named namelist and give you an error.

You can use the two redirection operators in the same command sequence when you need to take stdin from one file and send stdout to another. The result is the same as if you had used the cp command. With redirection it would look like this:

```
# cat < namelist >newlist
```

One of the most common uses of redirection is to send both stdout and stderr to a file in order to save the data for examination. This is a very useful tool for tracking down a problem. This can be done for any two I/O streams and not just stdout and stderr. Using stdout and stderr, the command would look like this:

```
# backup > backup.log 2>&1
```

Redirection as above causes backup.log to write over any file previously known as backup.log. If you want to append the output from a command to backup.log instead of writing over it, you'd use the >> symbol. This is especially good for log keeping. The command would look like this:

```
# backup >> backup.log
```

Wildcards

Bash, like most other Unix shells, allows the use of special characters called *wildcards* to reference more than one file at a time. DOS and Windows, of course, also offer wildcards, but the difference is that in Linux, these special characters are expanded by the Bash shell and not by the program itself. That is, if you launch a program that has special characters in its argument string, the program does not need to know how to handle them; they are translated by the Bash shell before being passed to the application. Instead of the wildcard characters, for instance, the program would receive a space-delimited list of all files matching the wildcard construct. The user may restrict this capability if the wildcard characters are intended to be interpreted by the program rather than the shell. There are three wildcard characters frequently used in Linux, each interpreted differently by the Bash shell: the asterisk, the question mark, and the bracket pair.

The asterisk is often called the "splat"; the string b*.bmp might be pronounced as "b-splat-dot-bmp." Its purpose is to replace a string of any number of characters in sequence. Thus b*.bmp is replaced with any file whose name begins with *b* and has the .bmp extension. The files blue.bmp, barney.bmp, bermuda.bmp, and before_you_go_away.bmp would all match.

The string *.* matches all files that contain a period; be certain that you really mean to act on all files in the directory when you use this string. The string .* matches any dot file.

Many a user has deleted important files by specifying an incorrect wildcard string as an argument to the rm command. The "joke" that is often played is trying to get the new guy to run rm -rf * from the root directory. This is a forced removal of all files and directories. It's ugly if you have no backup.

The question mark represents any one character. The string file_? would match all of the following: file_1, file_2, file_A, or file_b. The string file.??? would match any file named file that has a three-character extension.

The bracket pair is used to define a list or range of characters to be matched. The string file[0-9] would match file0, file1...file9. The string [a-zA-Z] would match any single alphabetical character. The string [a-zA-Z0-9] would match any alpha or numeric character.

Quoting

As you've seen, shell commands assign special meanings to ordinary alphanumeric characters, so when these characters are used within strings literally, there needs to be some way to prevent the shell from interpreting the quoted string as a command. In the Bash shell, quoting is the basic technique for this. There are three quoting mechanisms: the escape character, single quotes, and double quotes:

- The backslash (\ ) is the Bash escape character. It causes the next character to be taken literally.

- Single quotes preserve the literal value of each character within the quotes. A single quote may not occur between single quotes, since the enclosed quote would be interpreted as the closing single quote.

- Double quotes protect the literal value of all characters contained within, except for the dollar sign ($), the tick mark (`), the double quote ("), and the backslash (\). If your quoted string contains an environment variable that is to be expanded, double quotes would prevent this. Single quotes would allow the expansion.

The Tilde

The tilde can save you several keystrokes every day. If a pathname/file combination begins with a tilde, everything preceding the first / is treated as a possible login name. In the case of ~user/some_files, the ~user would be replaced by the home directory of user. In most cases, this would be expanded to /home/user/some_files. If the resulting login name is a null string, as in ~/myfiles, the tilde is replaced by the username of the user who executed the command.

If the tilde is followed by a plus sign, the ~+ is replaced by the present working directory. If the plus sign is replaced by a dash, the previous working directory is used instead.

Command and Pathname Expansion

One of the most convenient features of the Bash shell is *command-line completion*. Using this feature, you can type in the first few letters of a command until your string becomes unique, and hit the Tab key to force the Bash shell to complete the command name for you. Here's an example. If you enter the letters **lp** and press Tab, nothing will happen since several commands begin with the letters *lp*. If you hit the Tab key again, Bash will list all of the commands in your PATH that meet that description.

You can then simply enter the lptest command, if that's what you're looking for. If you'd prefer, however, you may type only enough letters to uniquely match that command—in this case, **lpt** and then hit the Tab key. This time, the lptest command will be completed for you.

This works equally well for filenames. If you go to your home directory and type **ls m** and hit the Tab key, nothing will happen—unless you have only one file or subdirectory beginning with the letter *m*. Pressing Tab again, however, will yield a list of all files or subdirectories within your home directory that begin with *m*. You can then type in the complete file or directory name or enough letters to make it unique followed by the Tab key.

The History List

The history list allows you to retrieve previously entered commands for reuse instead of having to remember and retype them. This is useful when the command is lengthy or frequently used. The `.bash_history` file is a list of commands like those shown in Listing 4.3.

Listing 4.3   The `.bash_history` File

```
man lsattr

lsattr

lsattr |more

man find

man ls

pine myfriend@hometown.com

clear

pine

clear

exit

pine

su

pine otherfriend@nothome.com

clear

exit

pine myfriend@hometown.com

su

startx

exit
```

To create the history list, the shell stores all of the commands that were executed during a session in a file called by default `.bash_history`. (You can rename this file by setting the environment variable HISTFILE to the new name, and you can determine how many commands will be retained by setting the HISTSIZE environment variable.)

The easiest way to retrieve a command from the history list is by using the arrow keys, especially if the command was recently entered. The up arrow retrieves the previous command from the history list, and the down arrow retrieves the next command. You may traverse the entire history list this way if you wish, but if HISTSIZE is large, this can become tedious.

An alternate way to search the history list is to enter on the command line an exclamation point followed by the first few letters (until it is unique) in the command you wish to retrieve. The most recent iteration of the command is then retrieved and executed. Entering **!pine** at the command line would retrieve the last pine command in the .bash_ history file, pine myfriend@hometown.com. If you knew that you had recently used the pine command to write to otherfriend, you could type **!pine o** at the prompt and the pine otherfriend@nothome.com command would be retrieved.

Basic Commands

Although there are exceptions, basic Linux commands generally take one of the following forms:

```
command [-option] target

command [-option] source destination
```

Linux command names, like filenames, are case-sensitive. Although most commands are completely lowercase, some options are uppercase. The man pages discussed above are invaluable in your use of unfamiliar commands. Even someone who has been administering a system for 20 years can learn something about the functionality of the basic commands. New options are being added all the time, as are entirely new commands.

The Linux commands presented below are some of the most commonly used. These definitions are not intended to be comprehensive but to give you a general idea of their use. Although we show the general syntax of each command listed, this is not a formal command reference, defining every option of each command. For a complete reference, see the appropriate man page. Later chapters discuss many of these commands in more detail, in the context of their administrative uses.

User Account Commands

The commands in this section allow you to work with user accounts. They include the commands to create a user, to delete a user, and to perform various other common user functions. More information on user-specific tasks is available in Chapter 6.

adduser

There is actually no adduser command under Red Hat Linux; to accommodate users who have used this command in other Unix varieties; it is symbolically linked to the useradd command, explained below.

finger

```
finger [options] [username][@host]
```

The finger command is used to display information about the system's users. Since this command can be used remotely by giving the target user's name as user@hostname, it is usually disabled as a security measure.

groups

```
groups [username]
```

The groups command prints a list of groups to which the specified user belongs. If no user is specified, the groups are given for the user who issued the command.

newgrp

```
newgrp [group]
```

The newgrp command is used to change the user's group identity. The specified group must exist in the /etc/groups file, and if the group has been assigned a password, the user is first prompted for that password. Once the password is accepted, the user retains the current user name but is given the privileges belonging to the specified group.

last

```
last [-num] [options] [ -f file ] [name] [tty]
```

The last command searches the /var/log/wtmp file and lists all the users who've logged in since the file was created. The *num* option may be used to specify how many logins back from the last login to include. The -f option allows you to specify a different file to search instead of the wtmp file. The *name* and *tty* options will filter the output by user and/or tty.

mesg

```
mesg [y|n]
```

The mesg command controls write access to a workstation. If write access is allowed, other users may use the write command to send messages to the terminal. An argument of y turns on access, and n turns off access. If no argument is provided, the current setting will be displayed.

passwd

```
passwd [options] [username]
```

The passwd command is used to change the password of the user executing the command. If you are the superuser, you can specify a different *username* in order to change that user's password instead. Password security is discussed in Chapter 7.

pwd

```
pwd
```

The pwd (print name of working directory) command is used to list the path of your current directory. If you need the full path for a script and don't want to type it all in, you can issue the pwd command, cut the output, and paste it into the editor being used to create the script.

repquota

```
repquota [options] filesystem
```

The repquota command prints the current number of files and amount of disk space in kilobytes used by each user.

su

```
su [options] [-] [user] [args]
```

The su command runs a shell with the effective user ID and group ID of user. This is typically used to become the root user for a task requiring that level of privilege, but it is much safer if the system is set up for the use of sudo.

sudo

```
sudo [options]
```

The sudo command is used to allow users to execute commands on their workstations that are normally reserved for the superuser. It is discussed more thoroughly in Chapter 3.

useradd

```
useradd [options] login_name
```

The useradd command creates a new user on a Red Hat Linux system. Different options allow you to specify things like the password, the shell, and the user identification number. When invoked with the -D option, the information is used to update the default new user information.

userdel

```
userdel [-r] login_name
```

The `userdel` command deletes the system account files for a user and removes the user's entry from /etc/passwd. Unless the -r option is given, the `userdel` command leaves that user's home directory and all the user's files in place.

usermod

```
usermod [options] login_name
```

The `usermod` command modifies the specified user's account information. The options allow you to change several settings, including the home directory, login name, password, and shell.

File-Handling Commands

This section contains commands geared toward file creation and management. Most of these are the basic commands you are likely to use almost daily.

cat

```
cat [options] filename(s)
```

The `cat` command dumps a file to `stdout`. Often `stdout` is then redirected into another command via a pipe or to a different file. It is often used to concatenate two or more files, thereby creating a new file. The command to do this is

```
cat file1 file2 file3 >newfile
```

chmod

```
chmod [options] mode(s) filename(s)
chmod [options] octal_mode(s) filename(s)
```

The `chmod` command is used to change the access mode of files. Only the owner of the file or the superuser may alter its access. There are two methods for expressing the mode you wish to assign. The first is the symbolic method, wherein you specify letters representing the mode. This requires that you specify the following information.

Who is affected:

u	User who owns the file
g	Group (only users in file's group)
o	Other users
a	All(default)

What operation:

+	Add permission
-	Remove permission
=	Set permission, overwriting old permissions

What kind of permission:

r	Read
w	Write
x	Execute
s	User or group ID is temporarily replaced with that of the file
t	Set sticky bit: keep executable in memory after exit

For example, ug+x would add execute privileges for the user and members of the group, and o+rw would allow other users not in the specified group to read and write the file.

Some administrators prefer the octal method, which uses a sequence of three numbers to represent the permissions for the user, group, and others. The new permissions completely override the previous assignment. Three digits are computed, representing the user, group, and others, respectively. To compute them, you add up the integers corresponding to the permissions you wish to grant at each level. The result is a three-digit number in which the first number represents the User permissions, the second the Group permissions, and the third the Other permissions. The values assigned to each permission are as follows:

1	Execute
2	Write
4	Read

Thus, read and write permissions would assign a 6 (2+4). Read, write, and execute would assign a 7 (1+2+4). Using this method, 755 would grant the user read, write, and execute privileges, and both group members and all others would have read and execute.

chown

```
chown [options] newowner filename(s)
chown [options] newowner.newgroup filename(s)
```

The chown command changes the owner of the specified file or files to the owner listed as an argument. This command can also be used to change both the owner and the group settings on the specified file. To do this, append a period followed by the new group to the owner name.

chgrp

```
chgrp [options] newgroup filename
```

The chgrp command is used to change only the group setting for the file. You must own the file or be the superuser to use this command. The new group may be specified by group name or ID.

cp

```
cp [options] source destination
```

```
cp [options] source directory
```

The cp (copy) command is used to copy the source file to destination. If the source and destination are both filenames, the duplicate will be placed in the current directory. They can also be full paths, meaning that either the source file or the destination file might not be in the current directory. Alternately, the second argument may be a directory, in which case source will be copied into the new directory, retaining its old name. You may specify the –r option to recursively copy the source directory and its files and subdirectories to destination, duplicating the tree structure in the new location.

dd

```
dd [options] if=infile of=outfile [bs=blocksize]
```

The dd command makes a copy of the input file specified as if=infile using the given blocksize if included to standard output or to the output file specified as of=outfile. This command may be used to write data to a raw device. This command is often used to write a bootable image to a floppy disk:

```
# dd if=boot.img of=/dev/fd0
```

diff

```
diff [options] file1 file2
```

The diff (difference) command displays the lines that differ between the two files listed as arguments. This is useful when you need to see the exact changes made to a file. For example, if a program source file won't compile after several additions have been made, and you'd like to back out of the changes one at a time, you would diff the current version against the last compiled version.

file

```
file [options] [-f namefile] [-m magicfiles] file
```

This command determines the file type of the named file using the information in the default magic file or the one passed as a parameter. The file command was discussed in Chapter 3.

find

```
find [path] [expression]
```

The find command is discussed in detail later in this chapter.

grep

```
grep [options] string targetfile(s)
```

The grep (get regular-expression pattern) command searches for a specified string in the target file or the stdin stream if no filenames are given. grep is used quite often in a piped command to filter data before passing it on or in scripts. A list of characters enclosed in ([]) brackets as the string argument matches any of the characters in the list. For example, the string [Hh]ello matches either *Hello* or *hello*. The string [A-Za-z] matches any letter in either lowercase or capital form. The string [0-9] represents any one-digit number. The carat ^ indicates the beginning of a line, and the dollar sign $ indicates the end of a line. Thus the use of the string ^[A-Z] would match any line that began with a capital letter. Options include –i to ignore differences in case between the string and the input file line, -l to print the names of files containing matches, -r to attempt to match the string within all subdirectories as well, and –v to return all nonmatching lines.

head

```
head [options] filename(s)
```

The head command prints by default the first ten lines of the specified file(s). The optional -n argument allows you to define how many lines, starting with line 1, will be printed.

ispell

```
ispell filename
```

The ispell program checks the spelling of all words in the named file and prompts the user to accept the present spelling, replace it with a suggested spelling, add it to the dictionary, look up a specified string in the dictionary, change capital letters to lowercase, or quit the program. To learn about other more sophisticated uses see the man page.

less

```
less [options] filename
```

The less command starts up a file viewer that allows up and down movement within the file being viewed. The less command doesn't require the entire file to be read in before starting, so it tends to start up faster than commands that do. This command is very frequently used on the command line as well as from within another program.

ln

```
ln [options] target linkname
ln [options] target(s) directory
```

The `ln` (link) command creates a link, named *linkname*, to *target*. If a directory is specified in place of a link name, the link will be created in that directory and named the same as the target. This concept was discussed in Chapter 3.

more

```
more filename
```

The `more` command starts a very primitive but often used file viewer. It outputs a page of data to the screen (or `stdout`) and scrolls to a new page when the user hits the spacebar. The `more` command is often the last part of a pipe command, allowing the user to page through the output.

mv

```
mv file1 file2
```

The `mv` (move) command moves the file from the location specified by `file1` to that specified as `file2`. In Linux, this command is also used to rename a file.

rm

```
rm [options] filename(s)
```

The `rm` command removes or unlinks the given file or files. This may take effect recursively if the -r option is given or interactively if the -i option is given. By default, Red Hat Linux aliases `rm` to `rm -i` in an attempt to protect the user from accidentally removing files, by forcing acknowledgement before actually unlinking the file(s).

tail

```
tail [options] filename(s)
```

The `tail` command prints by default the last 10 lines of the specified files. The optional -n argument allows you to define how many lines starting backward from the last line will be printed.

Process-Oriented Commands

The commands in this section are used to control processes and are all pretty common. We looked at processes in Chapter 3.

ps

> ps [*options*]

The ps (print status) command gives the status of the current processes. The process list may be filtered or the output format may be changed by specifying related options.

pstree

> pstree [*options*] [*pid|user*]

The pstree command displays a tree of processes with the root at the specified PID or at init if no PID is specified.

halt

> halt [*options*]

The halt command annotates the /var/log/wtmp file that the system is being rebooted and then halts it. If halt is called when the system is not in run level 0 or 6 (the run levels that cause the system to reboot), the much gentler shutdown command will be issued instead. Any users who are logged in will be notified that the system is going down, and no additional users will be allowed to log in. All processes are notified as well, giving them time to exit gracefully. Run levels are discussed in more detail in Chapter 5.

shutdown

> shutdown [-t *sec*] [*options*] *time* [*warning-message*]

The shutdown command brings down the system in a safe way. The shutdown command issues a warning to the users and to the currently running processes so that they can clean up before the system goes down. The shutdown command then sends a run level change request to the init process. If the shutdown is intended to halt the system (option –h), the requested run level is 0. If the system is to be rebooted (option –r), the run level is 6. If the shutdown is intended to put the machine in single-user mode (neither option –r nor –h), the run level is 1.

reboot

> reboot [*options*]

The reboot command is identical to the halt command described above, except that the system is returned to the default run level upon completion of the shutdown.

init

```
init [run level]
```

The init command initiates a change to the specified run level. The /etc/inittab then calls the /etc/rc.d/rc script, passing it the specified run level. The rc script causes the appropriate processes to be started for that run level. For example, to go to run level 3, the rc script runs the scripts pointed to by the symbolic links contained in the /etc/rc.d/rc3.d directory. The /etc/rc.d directory only exists in systems with SysV=style initialization scripts. The rc#.d directories are directly under /etc in Linux distributions that use the BSD=style initialization scripts. SuSE Linux does it a little differently still, putting the scripts that on a SysV system would be in /etc/rc.d/init.d directly in the /etc/rc.d directory. The init process was described in some detail in Chapter 3, and we'll talk about it again in Chapter 5.

kill

```
kill [-s signal] [-p] [-a] PID
kill -l [signal]
```

The kill program sends the given signal to the process whose PID is listed. By default this is the SIGTERM signal, which requests that the process terminate. Sometimes the process ignores the SIGTERM signal and has to be given a different variation of the kill command, kill -9 PID. Either the number or the signal name may be used. The number is preceded only by the hyphen, as in the kill -9 example; the signal name, however must be preceded by -s:

kill -s SIGKILL PID

The kill program with the -p option does not send a signal but only outputs the PID of the process that would receive the signal if sent. To generate a list of signals, use the kill -l format, the output of which is shown below:

1) SIGHUP	2) SIGINT	3) SIGQUIT	4) SIGILL
5) SIGTRAP	6) SIGIOT	7) SIGBUS	8) SIGFPE
9) SIGKILL	10) SIGUSR1	11) SIGSEGV	12) SIGUSR2
13) SIGPIPE	14) SIGALRM	15) SIGTERM	17) SIGCHLD
18) SIGCONT	19) SIGSTOP	20) SIGTSTP	21) SIGTTIN
22) SIGTTOU	23) SIGURG	24) SIGXCPU	25) SIGXFSZ
26) SIGVTALRM	27) SIGPROF	28) SIGWINCH	29) SIGIO
30) SIGPWR			

killall

```
killall [options] [-s signal] process_name
```

The killall command kills processes by name rather than PID as kill does. It is a much newer command than the kill command, so many of us forget about it. It is a more intuitive version, though, and saves you the trouble of determining the PID.

top

```
top [options]
```

The top command yields a continuous real-time listing of active processes, listing the most CPU-intensive first and also including memory usage and runtime information. This is very useful if your system suddenly seems to be running slowly, and you're trying to track the cause. Simply run the top command.

nice

```
nice [options] [command [arguments]]
```

The nice command runs the included command at an adjusted scheduling priority. It allows you to be "nice" to other users by making a really resource-intensive job run at a lower priority. The priority range is between 20 and –20. A priority of 0 is average; 20 holds the process until nothing else is placing demands on the system; and –20 indicates the maximum priority. If no command is specified, nice prints the current scheduling priority.

When you issue a command, you can precede it with the word nice to cause it to assume a lower priority. For example, this command starts a backup process, setting its nice value to 19 so that it won't dominate other processes. (Note that you must precede a priority by a dash, so a positive nice value looks like a negative value, and a negative value would use two dashes.)

```
# nice -19 backup
```

renice

```
renice priority [[-p] PID] [[-g] group] [[-u] user]
```

The renice command changes the priority of the running processes specified by PID, process group name, or user name to the given priority. The priority range is between 20 and –20. A priority of 0 is average, 20 holds the process until nothing else is placing demands on the system, and –20 indicates the utmost urgency. Users may only renice their own processes, but the superuser can renice any user's processes.

Since the `renice` command is used for processes that are already running, use the `top` command to determine which of them are dominating the system's resources. To do so, simply type **top** at the command prompt. The `top` output as shown below includes a %CPU column and a %MEM column which indicate what percentage of each of these resources the process is using. (We have omitted the SIZE, RSS, SHARE, STAT, and LIB columns to make the data easier to interpret.)

```
PID  USER PRI  NI     %CPU       %MEM       TIME  COMMAND

3652 user  19   0     29.6       34.1     614:16  backup

1452 root   1   0      1.9       11.1      14:30  X
```

You can see that the backup process is taking more than its fair share of the system's resources. If you want to give it a lower priority, 19, simply issue the `renice` command like this:

```
# renice -p 3652
```

Filesystem Commands

In Chapter 3, we looked at how the Linux ext2 filesystem developed and learned some general characteristics of this filesystem. The commands in this section allow you to do things like check, fix, and mount a filesystem. We revisit this important topic in Chapter 10.

df

```
df [options] filesystem
```

The `df` (disk filesystem usage) command reports the number of free disk blocks and inodes on the specified device, mount point, directory, or remote resource. This information, if checked periodically, can let you know when you are about to outgrow a filesystem. Likewise, it can show when you have a runaway process generating errors in the `/var/log/messages` file, thereby filling up the `/var` partition (or / if `/var` is not a separate partition). Looking at the sample `df` output shown in Listing 4.4, you can see the number of blocks used and available and the percentage of the filesystem that is currently being used.

Listing 4.4   Sample df Output

```
Filesystem         1k-blocks     Used Available Use% Mounted on
/dev/hdb1           2016016    467476   1446128  24% /
/dev/hdb6           7558368   4987292   2187128  70% /usr
/dev/hda8           6048320   2393976   3347104  42% /home
```

fdisk

```
fdisk [options] device
fdisk [-s] partition
```

The fdisk (fixed disk) command allows you to view and change partition table information for the given device. Use the second form shown above to get the size of the specified partition. If you use the first form, the session will become interactive, and a menu of commands will be available to you. This command is useful when you want to reinstall or add a new disk to the system.

Another useful option is –1, which allows you to list the partitions on a specified device as shown in Listing 4.5.

Listing 4.5   Sample Output of the fdisk –1 Command

```
# fdisk -1 /dev/hda
```

```
Disk /dev/hda: 255 heads, 63 sectors, 2491 cylinders
Units = cylinders of 16065 * 512 bytes
```

Device Boot		Start	End	Blocks	Id	System
/dev/hda1	*	1	255	2048256	83	Linux
/dev/hda2		256	2491	17960670	5	Extended
/dev/hda5		256	893	5124703+	83	Linux
/dev/hda6		894	1021	1028128+	83	Linux
/dev/hda7		1022	1054	265041	82	Linux swap
/dev/hda8		1055	1819	6144831	83	Linux

fsck

```
fsck [options] [-t fstype] filesystem
```

The fsck (filesystem check) command is used to check and repair a filesystem. This command is run at bootup by the rc.sysinit process with the -a option, which tells it to check each filesystem listed in /etc/fstab unless the sixth field for that filesystem in the /etc/fstab is zero. If it detects a problem, it will report that there was an "unexpected inconsistency." You will have the option of entering the root password to do maintenance or dropping to single-user mode, where you can run fsck manually and fix the problem. When you run it manually, `fsck` will evaluate the problem and fix it (although some data will most likely be lost), and make the system bootable again.

tune2fs

```
tune2fs [options] device
```

The `tune2fs` command is used to fine-tune the characteristics of a filesystem. You can change the number of times the filesystem may be remounted before a filesystem check is forced, the maximum time that can elapse before it must be checked, the error behavior of the filesystem, and so on. Attempting to adjust parameters on a filesystem that is mounted as read/write will damage the filesystem! More on the usage of `tune2fs` is found in Chapter 9.

mkdir

```
mkdir [options] director(ies)
```

The `mkdir` (make directory) command creates one or more directories with the names specified. If a fully qualified path is given, the directories will be created there; otherwise, they will be created in the current directory. We discussed the `mkdir` command in Chapter 3. Here is an example of how it would be used to create a directory under user's home directory:

```
mkdir /home/user/new_dir
```

mke2fs

```
mke2fs [options] device [blocks-count]
```

The `mke2fs` command is used to create a Linux filesystem on the specified device. The `blocks-count` argument sets the number of blocks on the device, although it may be omitted to allow `mke2fs` to set the file system size.

mount

```
mount [options] [mountpoint] [device_node] [-t filesystem_type]
```

The `mount` command attaches the filesystem referenced as `device_node` to the mount point specified as `mountpoint`. If the filesystem is listed in the `/etc/fstab` file, either the mountpoint or the `device_node` may be supplied alone. If the filesystem type is different than specified in `/etc/fstab` or if the filesystem is not listed there, a filesystem type must be specified (although it is sometimes recognized automatically). The following example mounts the CD-ROM located at /dev/hdc on the mount point /mnt/cdrom.

```
# mount /dev/hdc /mnt/cdrom -t ext2
```

umount

> umount [*options*] *device|mount_point* [-t *vfstype*]

The umount command detaches the listed filesystem or the filesystem mounted on the specified mount point from the Linux tree. The filesystem cannot be unmounted when it contains open files, has a user currently located somewhere in its directory tree, or contains a swap file that is in use.

showmount

> showmount [*options*] [*host*]

The showmount command queries the mount daemon on a remote machine about the status of its NFS server. If no options are specified, the showmount command returns a list of all clients who are mounting from that host.

ulimit

> ulimit [*options*] [*limit*]

The ulimit command can be used to determine resource limits for a shell and the processes started by it. The arguments to ulimit include -a to report all current limits, -c for maximum core size, -f for maximum file size, -n for the number of open files, and -u for the number of processes available per user. The ulimit may also be used to adjust these limits by specifying the correct argument followed by the new numeric value. Preceding the options with an H sets hard limits, which cannot be increased once set. A soft limit, preceded with an S, can be increased until it reaches the hard limit. If neither H nor S is given, a soft limit is assumed.

To determine what the hard limit is on the maximum core size, use the ulimit command as listed below. The return value shows that on a Red Hat system, there is no hard limit to the size of a core file.

```
# ulimit -Hc
unlimited
```

To set the maximum core size to 1024, issue the following command:

```
# ulimit -c 1024
```

Now check your work by issuing the ulimit -c command without a value. The result should be the value you specified.

mkswap

```
mkswap [options] device [size]
```

The mkswap command creates a swap area on the specified device or file. A swap area is used to hold pages written out from memory, making it possible to read them back into memory more quickly. In Linux, a swap space twice the size of the amount of memory in the system is usually sufficient. Most often, the device that contains the swap space is a disk partition, but a file created with a dd command can also be used, like this:

```
# dd if=/dev/zero of=/dev/swapfile bs=1024 count=65536
```

The copy command will not work to create a swap file. When the device or file is created, the swapon command must be used to activate the swap area.

A swap partition is typically created when the Linux system is first installed. Refer to Chapter 2 for more information on how to create swap space as a separate partition.

swapoff

```
swapoff [-a]
```

```
swapoff specialfile(s)
```

The swapoff command disables swapping on the specified devices or files. If swapoff is called with an -a option, all swap entries in /etc/fstab will be disabled.

swapon

```
swapon [-v] [-p priority] specialfile(s)
```

```
swapon [-a]
```

The swapon command enables swapping on the specified devices or files or on all devices listed in /etc/fstab if the -a option is given. This is usually done by the rc script when the run level is changed.

sync

```
sync [options]
```

The sync command flushes the filesystem buffers, thereby forcing any data waiting there to be written to the disk. This command is necessary when you mount another filesystem and make changes to it to ensure that everything that was to be written to the mounted filesystem actually was.

fuser

    fuser [options] filesystem

The fuser (file user) command determines which user is using a file from a given filesystem or is currently in a directory belonging to the given filesystem. This is important if you try to unmount a filesystem and are told that it is busy. The –m option is necessary if the filesystem is mounted. Using the -u option gives both process and corresponding user information for the filesystem. The c after several process IDs in the following example indicates that those processes are running from the current directory.

    # fuser -mu /home
    /home: 1456(user) 4271c(user) 4301 4301c(user)
                    4456c(user) 5729(user)

Network Commands

The commands in this section work with network connections and are used frequently. These commands allow you to determine whether a network interface is operational and to check its efficiency. Chapter 15 deals with TCP/IP connections and Chapter 7 deals with the security issues related to such a connection.

ifconfig

    ifconfig [interface]

    ifconfig interface [address_family_type] [options] address

The ifconfig command displays the status of currently active network interfaces. If an interface is listed as the only argument, ifconfig will return the status of that interface. The ifconfig command may also be used to configure network interfaces, although it is seldom used that way except in configuration scripts. Listing 4.6 shows the output from this command.

Listing 4.6   Sample Output from the ifconfig Command

    eth0   Link encap:Ethernet HWaddr 00:40:05:A0:52:33
            inet addr:192.168.1.1 Bcast:192.168.1.255
            ➥Mask:255.255.255.0
            UP BROADCAST RUNNING MULTICAST MTU:1500 Metric:1
            RX packets:5861 errors:1 dropped:0 overruns:0 frame:1
            TX packets:5051 errors:0 dropped:0 overruns:0 carrier:0
            collisions:1 txqueuelen:100
            Interrupt:9 Base address:0xf600

```
lo        Link encap:Local Loopback
          inet addr:127.0.0.1  Mask:255.0.0.0
          UP LOOPBACK RUNNING  MTU:3924  Metric:1
          RX packets:4404 errors:0 dropped:0 overruns:0 frame:0
          TX packets:4404 errors:0 dropped:0 overruns:0 carrier:0
          collisions:0 txqueuelen:0


ppp0      Link encap:Point-to-Point Protocol
          inet addr:216.126.175.225  P-t-P:216.126.175.2
          ↙Mask:255.255.255.255
          UP POINTOPOINT RUNNING NOARP MULTICAST  MTU:1500  Metric:1
          RX packets:2191 errors:0 dropped:0 overruns:0 frame:0
          TX packets:2125 errors:0 dropped:0 overruns:0 carrier:0
          collisions:0 txqueuelen:10
```

netstat

```
netstat [options]
```

The netstat command displays network connections, routing tables, interface statistics, masquerade connections, netlink messages, and multicast memberships. The –n option forces the output to use numeric IP addresses rather than hostnames.

ping

```
ping [options] host
```

The ping command is used to test network connections. It sends a signal to the indicated host, waits to receive a reply packet, and reports the receipt or lack of response. The ping command is primarily used for troubleshooting network connections. Examples are given in Chapter 18.

route

```
route
route [options] add [-net|-host] target [options]
route [options] del [-net|-host] target [options]
```

The route command is used to display and manipulate the IP routing table. It is primarily used to set up static routes to hosts or networks already configured by the ifconfig command.

ftp

    ftp [*options*] *host*

The ftp command starts the interface to the Internet's File Transfer Protocol, allowing users to transfer files to and from a remote site. It is typically run interactively, although this can be turned off with the -i option.

telnet

    telnet [*options*] [*host|port*]

The telnet command uses the Telnet protocol to communicate with the specified host or in command mode if no host is given. In command mode, telnet takes commands like OPEN (to open a host site), CLOSE (to close a host site), QUIT (exits the telnet session completely), STATUS, and a few others.

traceroute

    traceroute [*options*] *destination_host*

The traceroute command allows you to determine how long a packet takes to make each hop along the way to the destination host. This is very helpful information when a transmission to that host is significantly delayed or not received at all. Each intermediate host is listed with the time (in milliseconds) that the hop took. Listing 4.7 shows sample output.

Listing 4.7   Sample Output from the traceroute Command

```
traceroute to 216.15.152.66 (216.15.152.66), 30 hops max, 38 byte
    ↵packets
  1  lvhun1.popsite.net (216.126.175.4)  107.606 ms  98.544 ms
     ↵99.231 ms
  2  bhm1-core1.popsite.net (216.126.175.1)  106.141 ms
     ↵109.084 ms  109.090 ms
  3  atl-core1-s1-3.popsite.net (216.126.168.221)  116.211 ms
     ↵108.875 ms  109.361 ms
```

```
 4   h4-0.atlanta1-cr4.bbnplanet.net (4.0.138.245)  176.592 ms
        ↙238.687 ms   209.170 ms
 5   p1-1.atlanta1-nbr1.bbnplanet.net (4.0.5.206)  113.971 ms
        ↙108.913 ms   119.981 ms
 6   p11-0-0.atlanta1-br1.bbnplanet.net (4.0.5.121)  119.803 ms
        ↙114.610 ms   114.952 ms
 7   4.0.2.142 (4.0.2.142)  120.051 ms   2099.758 ms   2069.831 ms
 8   104.ATM3-0.XR1.ATL1.ALTER.NET (146.188.232.58)  169.836 ms
        ↙159.737 ms   159.888 ms
 9   195.at-2-0-0.TR1.ATL5.ALTER.NET (152.63.81.26)  169.878 ms
        ↙159.800 ms   159.851 ms
10   129.at-6-0-0.TR1.STL3.ALTER.NET (152.63.0.190)  169.855 ms
        ↙169.727 ms   229.888 ms
11   289.ATM7-0.XR1.STL1.ALTER.NET (152.63.89.157)  2049.869 ms
        ↙169.716 ms   169.912 ms
12   193.ATM11-0-0.GW1.STL1.ALTER.NET (146.188.224.65)  179.874 ms
        ↙169.756 ms   169.876 ms
13   cybercon-gw.customer.alter.net (157.130.124.126)  149.941 ms
        ↙149.748 ms   149.872 ms
14   server.dialupnet.com (216.15.152.66)  159.815 ms   159.665 ms
        ↙4049.903 ms
```

Printer Management Commands

The commands in this section deal with the printers on your network and how they schedule print jobs. Chapter 13 gives more detail on managing printers.

lpc

```
lpc [command [argument]]
```

The lpc (line printer change) command allows you to control printing jobs that have been sent to a printer on your network. You can disable or enable a printer or printer queue, thereby preventing or allowing additional jobs to be sent to that printer. You can prioritize the waiting print jobs. You can also check the status of a printer or printer queue or printer daemon. All of these are tasks you will be asked to do on a fairly regular basis as a system administrator. Chapter 13 explains the specifics of this command.

lpq

        lpq [-1] [-Pprinter] [job #] [user]

The lpq (line printer queue) command looks at the print spool for the specified printer (or the default printer) and reports the status of the specified job or all jobs for the specified user if no job number is specified. This command is discussed more thoroughly in Chapter 13.

lpr

        lpr [-Pprinter] [-#num] [-C class] [-J job] [-T title] [-U user]

        [-i [numcols]] [-w pagewidth] [filetype_options] [name]

The lpr (line printer) command spools named files for printing when resources become available. Among its options, you can specify the printer device with -P, the number of copies to print, and the page width. This command is discussed in Chapter 13.

lprm

        lprm [-Pprinter] [-] [job #] [user]

The lprm (line printer remove) command is used to remove print jobs from the queue of the specified or default printer. If a job number is specified, only that job will be removed. If a user name is specified by the superuser, all jobs for that user will be removed. If only a dash is given, all jobs owned by the user who issued the command will be removed. If the superuser gives this command with the – (minus sign) option, the printer spool will be emptied.

Other Useful Commands

A few commonly used commands don't fit into any of the other categories.

date

        date [options] [+FORMAT]

        date [options] [MMDDhhmm[[CC]YY][.ss]]

The date command prints or sets the system's date and time. If no option is specified, the current date and time will be printed to stdout in this format:

        [DAY MON DD hh:mm:ss TIMEZONE YYYY]

You may change the format by adding + and a format string to the command. The format string can take any form you like as long as you use a defined set of symbols, which you can find in the man page.

Here are a couple of examples:

```
# date +%m/%d/%y
9/1/00
```

When you specify date information as an argument in the form:

```
[MMDDhhmm[[CC]YY][.ss]
```

the system's date will be changed to the given date and time:

```
# date 0901182600.00
Fri  Sep   1  18:26:00   CDT  2000
```

hdparm

```
hdparm [options] device
```

The hdparm (hard disk parameters) command retrieves or sets specified parameters of the specified hard drive. This command was primarily developed for use with IDE hard drives, but some parameters apply to SCSI drives, too.

dmesg

```
dmesg [-c] [-n message_level] [-s buffersize]
```

The dmesg (display messages) command displays the messages that scroll across the screen during bootup. Assume that Sam User was working on one of your Linux systems today and began complaining that the system's sound card didn't work anymore. You know that a friend of yours is far better at troubleshooting sound problems, and she owes you a favor. Run the dmesg command, redirecting the output to a file. Mail the resulting file to your friend and race her to the answer.

free

```
free [options]
```

The free command is used to show how memory is being used on the system, allowing you to determine whether adding memory would be advantageous. It displays the amount of free and used physical and swap memory. In Linux, memory is used very efficiently;

any memory not being used by a process is used for buffering to allow the system to react more quickly. As a result, the output from the `free` command might be confusing. Listing 4.8 shows an example.

Listing 4.8   Output of the free Command

```
                total     used     free    shared   buffers   cached
Mem:           127808   124668     3140    105668      3264    65716

-/+ buffers/cache:       55688    72120

Swap:          265032    20504   244528
```

You see in the `free` output that there is a total of 127,808KB (128MB) of memory but that only 3140KB is listed as free. Some of the memory usage is normal but much of it is due to the Linux use of chip memory for buffers and cache. The `-/+ buffers/cache` line shows the memory used and free (respectively), not counting disk cache—in other words, it reflects memory used by the kernel, programs, and data, but not memory used by buffers and disk cache. The best indicator of whether you need more memory is the swap usage displayed. In this example, the system is using only 20,504KB of 265,032KB of the available swap space. Since so little swapping is being done, it is clear that this system has sufficient memory—at least for the current level of operations.

umask

```
umask [-S] [mode]
```

The `umask` command sets the permission mode assigned to a file created by the initiating user. The mode is interpreted as octal if it begins with a number and symbolic if it begins with a letter. To print the current umask as octal, simply call `umask` with no arguments. The `umask` command may be run with only a –S argument if you want the output in symbolic mode.

uname

```
uname [options]
```

The uname command prints out system information including the hardware type, the hostname, the operating system's name, release, and version number, and the processor type.

uptime

```
uptime
```

The uptime command tells how long the system has been running since its last reboot. It lists the current time, how long the system has been up, how many users are logged in, and system load averages.

In Sum

Now that we've discussed some of the basic tools that you'll use, you're ready to look at how the system works. Experiment with the tools in this chapter; familiarity with them will make your system administration duties much easier. We'll look at the boot process and the initialization process that follows in Chapter 5. Knowing the intricacies of this process well greatly helps your troubleshooting ability.

5

Startup and Shutdown

The process of starting up Linux is multifaceted. So much happens during a system boot that it is easy to lose touch with what procedures actually take place. Much of the wizardry of system administration is simply familiarity with a process such as booting. Knowing this process well makes it fairly easy to configure the system, to fix it when it breaks, and to explain it to your users. To understand the Linux startup, we'll walk through it from start to finish in this chapter. Linux startup and shutdown are further complicated by the fact that there are two different standards for how they are done: the BSD-style startup method and the System V-style method. Understanding the differences between the two is important since some Linux distributions—Debian and Slackware for example—use BSD-style system initialization scripts, while other distributions, such as Red Hat and Caldera, use System V-style startup scripts.

In this chapter we talk about the Linux Loader (LILO)—what it is and how it works. We look at different boot methods, including booting into single-user mode and booting from a floppy. We examine the Linux startup scripts in some detail, and the related user startup files that run when a user logs in to the system. Finally we discuss the log files that help you to troubleshoot when a system won't start up normally.

The system performs a similar sequence of tasks after you command it to shut down. There are many active processes that must be shut down and devices and filesystems that must be unmounted to avoid causing damage to your system. This process also occurs in stages. We'll also walk through this process to gain a full understanding of how shutdown works and what it does. The shutdown scripts and log files are discussed in order to make the whole process clear.

The Linux Boot Process

When you start up a Linux system, a series of events occur after you power up and before you receive a login prompt. This sequence is referred to as the boot process. Although this sequence can vary based on configuration, the basic steps of the boot process can be summed up as follows:

1. The Basic Input/Output System (BIOS) starts and checks for hardware devices. Stored in the computer's ROM (Read-Only Memory), the BIOS is a program described as firmware because it is built into the hardware memory. The computer will automatically run when the power is applied to the computer. The purpose of the BIOS is to find the hardware devices that will be needed by the boot process, to load and initiate the boot program stored in the Master Boot Record (MBR), and then to pass off control to that boot program. In the case of Linux, the BIOS performs its checks and then looks to the MBR, which contains the first-stage boot loader, such as LILO. After finding LILO, the BIOS initiates LILO.

NOTE   Sometimes, however, the MBR contains another boot loader, which in turn finds LILO on the first sector of a Linux partition.

---

2. The BIOS hands over control to the first-stage boot loader, LILO, which then reads in the partition table and looks for the second-stage boot loader on the partition listed in the /etc/lilo.conf file.

3. LILO runs the second-stage boot loader (/boot/boot.b). The second-stage boot loader finds the kernel image and runs it.

4. The kernel image contains a small, uncompressed program that decompresses the compressed portion of the kernel and runs it. The kernel scans for system information, including the CPU type and speed. Its drivers scan for other hardware and configure what they find. The kernel then mounts the root filesystem in read-only mode since the filesystem has to be checked with fsck.

5. The kernel starts the init process by running /sbin/init.

6. As outlined in the later section "Initialization and Startup Scripts," the init process starts up getty programs for the virtual consoles and serial terminals and initiates other processes as configured and monitors them until shutdown.

This general boot process can be affected by various factors even within the same distribution. For instance, the steps above assume the system has only one bootable kernel image. That's probably the case when you first install, but you might also have a bootable sector installed with another operating system, like Windows, or a different distribution of Linux. Later, if you install a different version of the kernel and compile it, you'll have to configure LILO to see it. As you'll see later in the chapter, there are a number of parameters that you can specify at the LILO boot prompt, but first let's take a closer look at the Master Boot Record.

The Master Boot Record

The Master Boot Record (MBR) plays a crucial role in the bootup process. Located on the first disk drive, in the first sector of the first cylinder of track 0 and head 0 (this whole track is generally reserved for boot programs), it is a special area on your hard drive that is automatically loaded by your computer's BIOS. Since the BIOS is loaded on an electronically erasable programmable read-only memory (EEPROM) chip, which is generally not reprogrammed at the user/administrator level, the MBR is the earliest point at which a configured Linux Loader can take control of the boot process. Figure 5.1 shows a hard drive with its MBR and five Linux partitions. Three of these (/dev/hda1 through /dev/hda3) are *primary partitions* that are pointed to directly, and two (/dev/hda5 and /dev/hda6) are *logical partitions* that reside within an *extended partition* (/dev/hda4). This baroque arrangement is the result of early limitations on the number of partitions in the PC's partition table and is further discussed in Chapter 10. Linux uses the Second Extended Filesystem (ext2fs), which is also detailed in Chapter 10. Basically, the filesystem is the structure imposed on each partition for the purpose of organizing files. It is the underlying frame to which the data is added.

As you can see in Figure 5.1, the MBR contains program code (LILO), a 64-byte partition table identifying four primary partitions, and a 2-byte magic number used to determine whether or not the sector is really a boot sector. Since a sector is 512 bytes long and since LILO must share this space, LILO is limited in size to 446 bytes. In order to accommodate this restriction, the boot loader has been split into two phases. The first phase uses LILO in the MBR to locate the second-stage boot loader, which is almost always located in /boot/boot.b on the drive that contains the root Linux filesystem or the /boot partition if it is separate from the root partition. This second-stage boot loader then gets copied into the MBR over the first-stage boot loader to continue the boot process.

Figure 5.1 A hard drive's partition layout

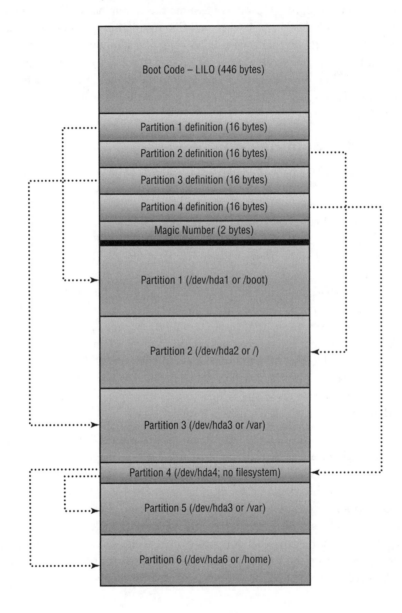

LILO: Definition and Configuration

You've seen that the first step in the boot process is the execution of the boot loader—typically LILO. Unless another boot loader is being used in conjunction with LILO, LILO is the first non-BIOS step in the boot process.

How Things Work

PART 1

> **NOTE**   LILO isn't the only boot loader in existence. Alternatives include System Commander, NTLDR, and the Grand Unified Bootloader (GRUB). System Commander is a boot management utility that allows you to choose from up to 100 operating systems at boot time. Information is available at http://www.v-com.com. NTLDR is the boot manager for Windows NT. More information about NTLDR is available at http://www.microsoft.com/TechNet/win2000/win2ksrv/reskit/sopch15.asp. GRUB is an alternative to LILO that ships with some distributions, such as Mandrake. Whichever you choose, this boot loader will reside in the MBR where LILO normally lives. Most boot loaders must launch LILO to complete the Linux boot process. In such situations, LILO resides in the first sector of the Linux boot partition. In this scenario, LILO is known as the secondary boot loader. GRUB, however, can boot Linux directly, without invoking LILO. For our purposes, we'll assume that LILO is loaded in the MBR.

LILO is very versatile and allows you to boot multiple kernel images as well as the boot sector of any other bootable partition on the system. This bootable partition might point to a Windows 95 or 98 partition, a Windows NT partition, or any of a number of other operating systems, allowing you to boot any one of them. You must make LILO aware of the images and any other operating systems that it is expected to boot. To do that, you'll add information about each kernel image or operating system into the /etc/lilo.conf file, including a label by which to refer to each image. Then you'll run the LILO program as described later in this section. LILO loads the selected kernel image and the corresponding initrd image—if there is one—into memory and relinquishes control to that kernel.

initrd Images

Linux includes support for RAM disks, which are disk filesystems loaded from a floppy or hard disk but stored in RAM during use. RAM disks can be useful during system installation or maintenance, because they obviate the need for physical disk access. An initial RAM disk (initrd) image is a kernel-specific image that allows some setup functions to occur before the root filesystem is mounted. An initial RAM disk causes the system startup to occur in two stages: the kernel comes up first with a minimal set of drivers, and then the RAM disk image loads additional modules as needed. This allows the boot process to take advantage of devices that require modules that would not normally be available until the boot process is completed. This is especially important if you wish to load a Linux system that is on a RAID array, since support for any RAID other than RAID-0 is modular and not found in the default kernel. Until recently, initrd was used during an installation from a PCMCIA or SCSI hard drive or CD-ROM. Now, however, the Red Hat installation program allows you to find your SCSI or PCMCIA-driven hard drives and CD-ROMs. If you need to create an initrd image, use /sbin/mkinitrd. This command has the following format:

mkinitrd *image-name kernel-version*

So for the 2.2.16-22 kernel (the *kernel-version* number must match the /lib/ modules/ directory name), the command would look like this:

 # /sbin/mkinitrd initrd.2.2.16-22.img 2.2.16-22

Then just add the initrd line into that kernel's stanza in your /etc/lilo.conf file, as described shortly, and you're set.

LILO is configured using the /etc/lilo.conf file. The basics of LILO are very simple, but its power lies in the many options that can be passed if needed. The lilo.conf file in Listing 5.1 demonstrates many of these options. The sample file in Listing 5.1 is suitable for a computer that boots two different Linux distributions (installed on /dev/hdb1 and /dev/hdc1), both of which use the same kernel. The computer has an Adaptec 152*x* SCSI adapter and a SoundBlaster sound card, both of which require certain kernel options (set via the append line) to work correctly. The following sections describe the lilo.conf file's details.

Listing 5.1 A Sample `lilo.conf` File

```
#Global Section
boot=/dev/hda
map=/boot/map
install=/boot/boot.b
compact
prompt
timeout=50
message=/boot/message
linear
default=linux
append="aha152x=0x140,12,7,0,0 sb=240,5,1,5,300"

#Per-Image Section
image=/boot/vmlinuz-2.2.16-22-1
    label=linux
    read-only
    root=/dev/hdb1

image=/boot/vmlinuz-2.2.16-22-1
    label=debian
    read-only
    root=/dev/hdc1
    initrd=/boot/initrd-2.2.16-22-1.img

image=/boot/vmlinuz-2.2.16-22
        label=orig
        read-only
        root=/dev/hdb1
```

```
other=/dev/hda1
    label=msdos
```

The Global Section

The first section of the /etc/lilo.conf file applies globally to any kernels that are to be booted from LILO. The first line in the global section shows that LILO is to be installed in the MBR on the first disk, /dev/hda. If LILO were to be the secondary boot loader, this reference would be to the Linux boot partition, writing LILO there.

The system map in use is /boot/map. This file is a symbolic link to the system map for a kernel that you have created. It is basically made up of debugging information for that kernel. Even Linux system administrators don't usually use this file unless they are doing kernel development work.

The next line identifies the boot loader code proper. Typically this is /boot/boot.b. This file contains both the code that will reside in LILO's space in the boot sector and the extra code LILO relies upon to complete the boot process.

Adding the compact parameter allows LILO to read the hard drive more quickly by transferring several sectors at once instead of doing single-sector reads. It works on most modern systems but might cause an older system to hang. If so, remove the line.

LILO's default behavior is to wait 4 seconds for you to press the Shift key and boot the default kernel if you do not. The prompt instruction tells LILO to instead prompt the user for which image to boot. This is what causes the lilo: prompt that you have probably seen.

The timeout parameter in the next line sets the time (in tenths of a second) to wait for keyboard input. After this period, the default kernel is automatically booted. If you enter the timeout parameter without a numeric value, the timeout period is infinite. During the timeout period, pressing Tab displays a listing of available images.

The next line identifies a file containing a message to display before the boot prompt. The message file is limited to 65,535 bytes. Changing or removing the message file requires you to rebuild the map file.

If the linear parameter is included, it forces the generation of linear sector addresses instead of the sector/head/cylinder addresses that are used by default. This is necessary if you've configured your BIOS to use any drives in Linear Block Addressing (LBA) mode.

The default parameter sets the default kernel image to be booted if no other image label has been given. If no default parameter exists, LILO treats the first kernel specified as the default.

The append line is particularly important. Any parameters that the kernel needs in order to boot correctly can be appended. Typically this line is used to specify parameters for hardware that isn't automatically detected, as in this example. The append line in Listing 5.1 includes the information for an Adaptec 1520B SCSI interface card and a Sound-Blaster sound card. Notice that there is no comma between the two append strings, since each one includes commas. Likewise, there are no spaces in each individual append string since the list of strings is space-delimited. The format for these items varies depending upon the item type. Information about hard drives is commonly appended and is specified as follows:

```
append="hd=cccc,hhhh,ssss"

linear
```

where *cccc* indicates the number of cylinders that the drive has, *hhhh* indicates the number of heads, and *ssss* indicates the number of sectors. To include information on two different drives, use two representations as follows:

```
append="hd=cccc,hhhh,ssss hd=CCCC,HHHH,SSSS"

linear
```

When run on some motherboards, Linux doesn't correctly detect memory above 64MB, or sometimes even 16MB. If you have more memory than this, you can use the free command to see if Linux has detected it. If it hasn't, you may use an append line to let LILO know about the additional memory. You can also use this option to test how the system would run with less memory, by indicating less memory than you actually have. The amount of memory can be specified in kilobytes (with a suffix of k) or in megabytes (using a suffix of M). To specify an amount of memory, use the following append line:

```
append="mem=128M"
```

If you happen to be running a Linux system with two Ethernet cards, you might have to append a line that contains the information for the two cards as in this example:

```
ether=9,f600,eth0 ether=10,6800,eth1
```

The Per-Image Section

Each section that defines a bootable kernel or non-Linux partition is known as a *stanza*. The stanzas that follow the global section in Listing 5.1 define three specific Linux kernel images and a bootable Windows partition. For each one, the image= line specifies the image or partition location. The label= line identifies the name that will be used at the LILO prompt. If read-only is included in the stanza, the root filesystem will be mounted as read-only originally (when it is subject to a filesystem check); it is remounted read-write later in the boot process. The root= line tells where the root directory for the specified kernel is located. Finally, if there is need for an initrd image, its location is specified on a line that begins initrd=.

Now let's look at the specific stanzas to understand the differences. The first stanza, with the label linux, boots a kernel image located at /boot/vmlinuz-2.2.16-22-1, initially as read-only. The root partition to use is located at /dev/hdb1, the boot sector of the first partition of disk 2.

Now, looking at the second stanza, labeled debian, we see that it uses the same kernel image, also booted as read-only, but it uses a different root directory and includes an initrd image. The difference in the root partition is because this stanza boots a different Linux installation—specifically, a Debian Linux setup instead of the Red Hat distribution booted with the linux stanza. The root files for the Debian distribution are located on the first partition of the third IDE disk, /dev/hdc1. Since we are using the same kernel in both places, we use an initrd image to change the modular information as appropriate for the Debian distribution.

The third stanza is for the original kernel as installed with Red Hat 7.0. It is a good idea to keep this image, since a simple mistake when compiling a new image can generate a kernel panic, forcing you to use rescue mode if you can't boot the original kernel. (As discussed later in the chapter, a kernel panic can occur when the system can't find or can't execute the kernel image referenced by the LILO label or location it has been given.) The setup for this booting scenario is basically the same as the linux stanza, since the Red Hat 7.0 installation is the same.

The fourth stanza points to a Windows 98 installation. This stanza is simpler than the previous three. It doesn't need to contain anything beyond an other= line, to specify the path to that operating system's boot sector, and a label line, which specifies the name to be input at the LILO prompt to start up that operating system. The information needed to boot Windows is contained in the boot sector of /dev/hda1 because it is a secondary boot loader, run by the primary Linux Loader.

Running the LILO Program

After lilo.conf is configured as you want it, you must use the lilo program to install it to the Master Boot Record. This is typically done with the following command:

```
# /sbin/lilo
```

There are many options you can use on the command line here for unique situations, but they aren't frequently needed. The one option that gets a lot of use is –r, which is used when you are in rescue mode or some other situation where the drive containing the lilo.conf file is mounted and not part of the active system. The –r option tells the system to chroot to the specified directory and run the command from there. For instance, let's say that you are booted into rescue mode and have mounted /dev/hda1 as /mnt/tmp. You have repaired the incorrect lilo.conf, which is actually located at /mnt/tmp/etc/lilo.conf at present. If you try to run /sbin/lilo, the system will look for /etc/lilo.conf instead. You use the following command to tell it to pretend that /mnt/tmp is the / directory, thereby forcing LILO to read /mnt/tmp/etc/lilo.conf as if it were /etc/lilo.conf. The command looks like this:

```
# /sbin/lilo -r /mnt/tmp
```

Another option that you might need is –u. This removes LILO from the MBR. The command looks like this:

```
# /sbin/lilo -u
```

There are so many options available with LILO that it is impractical to list them all in a general book like this one. The BootPrompt-HOWTO provides an exhaustive list and is available on-line at http://www.linuxrx.com/HOWTO/sunsite-sources/BootPrompt-HOWTO.html.

Now let's look at different ways to boot your system.

Creating a Boot Floppy

What do you do to recover from disk or system failure like a lost boot sector or a disk head crash, when the kernel you've created won't boot the system and you've forgotten to create a LILO stanza for your working kernel, or when you've copied a new kernel over an old one and forgotten to rerun LILO? One method is to boot from a floppy. A boot floppy is a basic requirement for every computer, whether workstation or server. This section shows how to create one.

There are two types of floppy boot disk installation. One uses LILO, while the other boots directly from the kernel on the disk without the benefit of LILO. If you need to pass parameters to the kernel during the boot, use a LILO floppy.

Creating a LILO Boot Floppy

Let's assume that you don't want to write LILO to the MBR but instead want to boot from a floppy disk. You need to change the boot line of the /etc/lilo.conf file to tell it to write the LILO image to /dev/fd0 or whatever designation represents your floppy drive. Running /sbin/lilo after that change will create a LILO boot floppy that contains the information normally written to the MBR.

Most distributions give you an easier method, an executable called mkbootdisk, usually located in /sbin. Any boot disk you create using /sbin/mkbootdisk will contain a kernel image, an initrd.img file, a /boot directory containing the second-stage boot loader and a system map, a /dev directory containing the floppy device and the root filesystem device, and an /etc directory containing lilo.conf. When you boot from this disk, you will get a LILO prompt and a chance to enter any extra information that LILO might need. The command looks like this:

```
# /sbin/mkbootdisk 2.2.16-22
```

Creating a Boot Floppy without LILO

Alternately, you can copy the kernel to a floppy using the dd command, which produces a boot disk that is independent of LILO. If your kernel is vmlinuz-2.2.16-22, do the following:

```
# dd if=/boot/vmlinuz-2.2.16-22 of=/dev/fd0
```

Then tell the kernel on the floppy what your root partition is, using the rdev command. The rdev command can be used to set the image root device, as in our next example, or less commonly, the swap device, RAM disk size, or video mode. If no setting information is included, the current values are displayed. The command to set the root partition to the first partition on the second IDE disk is as follows (this example assumes that your root partition is located in the first partition of the second drive):

```
# rdev /dev/fd0 /dev/hdb1
```

With or without LILO, the floppy boots much the same way as the system did before. The difference is that the boot program uses the boot sector on the floppy instead of the MBR on the first disk drive. Also, if you are using the floppy without LILO, and if your BIOS is set to try booting from the floppy disk, your system will boot the kernel contained in the disk without offering a LILO prompt.

Using LOADLIN

LOADLIN (Load Linux) is a DOS executable that can initiate a Linux system boot. This program comes with most Linux distributions. Red Hat 7.0 places it in the dosutils directory of the first installation CD-ROM. Copy the LOADLIN.EXE file to a DOS partition or DOS boot floppy. (You might want to create a C:\LOADLIN directory.) You'll also need to copy a Linux kernel image file, probably located in /boot on your Linux system, to the DOS partition or floppy. From this point, you can boot Linux (which we will assume is located on the first partition on the second IDE drive) as follows:

```
C> LOADLIN C:\vmlinuz root=/dev/hdb1 ro
```

To boot using a RAM disk image, use this form of the command:

> C> **LOADLIN C:\vmlinuz root=/dev/ram rw initrd=C:\rootdsk.gz**

To boot from a root floppy in drive A, use this command:

> C> **LOADLIN C:\image root=/dev/fd0 rw ramdisk=1440**

LOADLIN is sometimes used if your Linux system won't boot because of a LILO configuration problem and you need to get back into the system to fix the LILO boot information; it's also useful if you are forced to restore from a backup and don't have a running system from which to start the restore. This can also be done with a Linux boot floppy as we've already described, so it really comes down to personal preference.

TIP   LOADLIN can be particularly handy if you have a piece of hardware that requires initialization in DOS before it can be used in Linux. For example, some sound cards must be initialized into a special SoundBlaster compatibility mode before they can be used in Linux, and the programs to do this only run under DOS. You can create a DOS partition that runs the sound card initialization program from CONFIG.SYS or AUTOEXEC.BAT and then launches LOADLIN. The result is a Linux boot with the hardware in a condition that Linux can accept.

WARNING   Although LOADLIN works from the DOS compatibility mode of Windows 95 and 98, that mode has been effectively removed from Windows Me. Therefore, LOADLIN does not work from a full Windows Me boot, although it does work from a Windows Me emergency floppy.

Single-User Mode

Single-user mode is a maintenance mode in which a root shell is started and no other users may log in. The prompt will change to a pound sign (#) to indicate that this is a root shell. This mode may be initiated using the command init 1 or by adding the word single or the number 1 after the image label at the LILO prompt. If you are on the system doing work and decide you need to go into single-user mode, type init 1. If you have rebooted because of a kernel panic or the like, simply add a 1 after your image label when the LILO prompt comes up, as in:

> LILO: **linux single**

or

> LILO: **linux 1**

If your system is booted into single-user mode, the initialization tasks relating to the multiuser environment are skipped, and if the init program is used to switch to single-user mode, all daemon processes are stopped. The init process next starts a Bourne shell as the root user on /dev/console. The root filesystem is mounted, and other filesystems are available to be checked or mounted. No daemons are run automatically, and some resources may not be available because their home filesystem is not mounted.

If, for instance, /usr is on a separate partition (that is, if it's a separate filesystem), any commands in /usr/bin, /usr/sbin, or /usr/X11R6/bin won't be available unless you mount the /usr partition manually. Typing exit at the prompt will log you out of the single-user shell, while Ctrl+D will boot the system into its normal multiuser mode.

You might also reach a system-initiated single-user mode if there is a problem in the boot process. In this case, you are dropped to a root shell, where you have **root** access and can make the changes necessary to make the system bootable. This most often occurs when the fsck process run during the boot fails and the system needs you to check and repair the filesystem manually.

One use for single-user mode is to change the **root** password when it is unknown, for example when an employee leaves the company without providing the password. There is no way to retrieve the old password, but single-user mode gives you **root** access so you can use the passwd command to enter a new **root** password. When you reboot into multiuser mode, the new password will allow you **root** access as before.

This illustrates the security threat posed by allowing unrestricted access to the system console and the danger of single-user mode. Obviously, you don't want just anyone to be able to boot your system and change the **root** password. To secure single-user mode, you can make LILO require a password. Simply add a password=*password* line in the global options section of your lilo.conf, replacing *password* with your password. Alternatively, you may add a password parameter in each individual stanza to protect certain boot setups differently. In the example lilo.conf file that we used, you might choose to password-protect the Debian setup but not the Red Hat setup. Typically, the option is global.

For the best security, you should password-protect the BIOS and set it to *not* boot from a floppy. These two actions configure the computer to be unbootable from a floppy disk unless the user has the BIOS password. If you don't take these steps, an intruder with physical access to the computer could simply insert a Linux boot floppy and modify the system on disk. Given more time, though, an intruder with physical access could remove the hard disk or use recovery jumpers on the motherboard to bypass these precautions. Short of encrypting all data on your disk, there's nothing you can do to prevent tampering if an intruder can open the computer's case.

Initialization and Startup Scripts

Earlier in the chapter, we identified initialization as the final stage of the startup process. The initialization process varies a bit between distributions. These differences range from the locations and names of the scripts to what is actually run by default. We'll start by looking at the process, discussing differences as we come across them. The initialization process begins when the kernel starts the init program. This program parses the /etc/inittab file to determine the specifics of what programs to run and what run level to leave the system in when it is finished. We'll look at an example from Red Hat (which uses the System V-style script) and another from Debian (which uses the BSD model). Slackware and SuSE's methods are very similar to that seen in the Debian model. Slackware comes with an empty rc.local by default.

The Red Hat Model

All distributions customize their initialization scripts somewhat, but most inittab files are very similar. Listing 5.2 shows an example inittab file from a Red Hat 7.0 system.

Listing 5.2   A Sample inittab File

```
#
# inittab      This file describes how the INIT process should set
#              up the system in a certain run-level.
#
# Author:      Miquel van Smoorenburg,
#              <miquels@drinkel.nl.mugnet.org>
#              Modified for RHS Linux by Marc Ewing and Donnie
#              Barnes
#


# Default runlevel. The runlevels used by RHS are:
#   0 - halt (Do NOT set initdefault to this)
#   1 - Single-user mode
#   2 - Multiuser, without NFS (The same as 3, if you do not have
#       networking)
#   3 - Full multiuser mode
```

```
#    4 - unused
#    5 - X11
#    6 - reboot (Do NOT set initdefault to this)
#
id:3:initdefault:

# System initialization.
si::sysinit:/etc/rc.d/rc.sysinit

l0:0:wait:/etc/rc.d/rc 0
l1:1:wait:/etc/rc.d/rc 1
l2:2:wait:/etc/rc.d/rc 2
l3:3:wait:/etc/rc.d/rc 3
l4:4:wait:/etc/rc.d/rc 4
l5:5:wait:/etc/rc.d/rc 5
l6:6:wait:/etc/rc.d/rc 6

# Things to run in every runlevel.
ud::once:/sbin/update

# Trap CTRL-ALT-DELETE
ca::ctrlaltdel:/sbin/shutdown -t3 -r now

# When our UPS tells us power has failed, assume we have a few
# minutes of power left. Schedule shutdown for 2 minutes from now.
# This does, of course, assume you have powerd installed and your
# UPS connected and working correctly.
pf::powerfail:/sbin/shutdown -f -h +2 "Power Failure; System
    ➥Shutting Down"
# If power was restored before the shutdown kicked in, cancel it.
```

```
pr:12345:powerokwait:/sbin/shutdown -c "Power Restored;
   ➥Shutdown Cancelled"


# Run gettys in standard runlevels
1:2345:respawn:/sbin/mingetty tty1
2:2345:respawn:/sbin/mingetty tty2
3:2345:respawn:/sbin/mingetty tty3
4:2345:respawn:/sbin/mingetty tty4
5:2345:respawn:/sbin/mingetty tty5
6:2345:respawn:/sbin/mingetty tty6


# Run xdm in runlevel 5
# xdm is now a separate service
x:5:respawn:/etc/X11/prefdm -nodaemon
```

The file begins with a block of comments, including a summary of the run levels used in Red Hat; let's take a moment to look at the six run levels and their uses:

0   Used to halt the system. To do this, the system performs an `init 0` command and the system is halted. As the comment says, you should *not* set `initdefault` to this.

1   Puts the system into single-user mode.

2   Puts the system into a multiuser mode but does not support networking.

3   Puts the system into the standard full multiuser mode but does not automatically start X.

4   Unused

5   X11; puts the system into standard multiuser mode with a graphical (X-based) login.

6   Signals the system to reboot itself. Again, do *not* set `initdefault` to this.

NOTE The meaning of run levels between 2 and 5 is somewhat arbitrary. Although most distributions use the conventions outlined here, not all do. For example, SuSE uses run level 2 as a full multiuser mode with networking, and starts X with run level 3 rather than 5.

In the first uncommented line, the `init` program is told what run level to use after a reboot. The line looks like this:

```
id:3:initdefault:
```

The first part of this line, `id`, simply represents the word `initdefault`. The number 3 indicates that the system should start in run level 3 by default. For a system that uses the X Window System graphical environment (discussed in Chapter 16), you would instead use this command:

```
id:5:initdefault:
```

Keep in mind that specifying an initial run level of 5 will cause an inability to log in if X has a problem that prevents it from starting. Typically, you'll see one of two things happen: Either the screen will repeatedly clear as the system tries to start X, fails, tries again, and so on; or the system will try to start X once, fail, and drop back to run level 3.

Following the run level line, the next uncommented line in Red Hat's `inittab` file tells the `init` program which script to start:

```
si::sysinit:/etc/rc.d/rc.sysinit
```

Here we've chosen to run the `rc.sysinit` script, which we'll look at in detail in a moment. Since the second colon-delimited field, the run level field, is empty, this script will be run only at boot time. The rest of the line, `/etc/rc.d/rc.sysinit`, is the exact command to run.

After the `rc.sysinit` file exits, the `inittab` starts the `/etc/rc.d/rc` script with the appropriate run level as an argument. The `rc` script then executes all of the scripts pointed to by the symbolic links contained in the directory for that run level. If the run level is 3, for example, the scripts pointed to by the links in `/etc/rc.d/rc3.d` are run. Listing 5.3 shows this directory for a default Red Hat 7.0 installation.

Listing 5.3 The `/etc/rc.d/rc3.d` File Contains Links to the Scripts for Run Level 3.

K01pppoe	K84ypserv	S25netfs	S80sendmail
K10ntpd	S05kudzu	S35identd	S85gpm
K20nfs	S08ipchains	S40atd	S85httpd
K20rstatd	S10network	S45pcmcia	S90crond
K20rusersd	S12syslog	S50xinetd	S90xfs
K20rwalld	S13portmap	S55sshd	S95anacron
K20rwhod	S14nfslock	S56rawdevices	S97rhnsd
K34yppasswdd	S16apmd	S60lpd	S99linuxconf
K35smb	S18autofs	S75keytable	S99local
K45arpwatch	S20random	S80isdn	

You'll notice that each file begins with an S or a K. The system first runs the scripts whose names start with K to kill their associated processes, if running. Next, the system runs the scripts whose names start with S to start the associated processes. Changing a K name to start with S (such as renaming K20nfs to S20nfs) makes Linux start the process rather than kill it when entering the run level, and changing an S name to K causes Linux to kill the process when entering the run level. This is how Linux controls what processes to start in a given run level.

After the run level 3 processes are killed or started, the /sbin/update command in the inittab file is run. This command flushes the kernel buffers and writes their data to the hard drive. This is basic housekeeping to improve kernel performance.

The next line sets the Ctrl+Alt+Delete key combination to indicate a reboot of the system. The –t option indicates that the init process is to wait 3 seconds before telling its dependent processes to restart themselves. The shutdown occurs as if you had initiated the following shutdown command:

```
# /sbin/shutdown –t3 –r now
```

The pf line of the inittab file then sets the system up to run a different kind of shutdown if an attached uninterrupted power supply (UPS) indicates that power has failed. This shutdown is scheduled to occur 2 minutes after this notification. The following pr line, however, indicates that the shutdown is to be cancelled if the init process receives a notification that the power was restored before the shutdown was initiated.

The next six uncommented lines, with identifiers 1–6, run getty programs for the virtual terminals. These getty programs are essential since they initialize the ttys, provide the login and retrieve the user-input data, and then start a login process for the user. Without these lines, no users could log into the system.

The last line, with the identifier of x, is set by the 5 in the second colon-delimited field to run the X Display Manager (XDM) process for run level 5 only. An XDM allows you to log into run level 5 directly. Red Hat 7.0 uses prefdm as its XDM program, but the program used varies from one distribution to another.

If /etc/inittab contained any additional lines that specified no run level (meaning to run at boot time only) or run level 3, they would be run. You can add any such lines yourself, if you have something that you need to start only in a certain run level. Usually the Red Hat default inittab is fine as it comes.

After running /etc/inittab, the system turns its attention to the rc.sysinit script, which performs many functions. These include:

- Setting the path and the hostname, and checking whether networking is activated
- Mounting the /proc filesystem

- Setting the kernel parameters
- Setting the system clock
- Loading keymaps and fonts
- Starting swapping
- Initializing the USB controller (if present) along with its attached devices
- Checking the root filesystem, if required
- Setting up PPP
- Remounting the root filesystem as read-write
- Loading modules as appropriate

You don't typically add to this file, since the rc.local file was included for that purpose; however, this file's task is critically important.

Finally, the /etc/rc.d/rc.local file is run. This is the file where you make your local changes to the startup process. This file runs after all of the other initialization files and can therefore be used to override any settings made during the earlier initialization steps. By default, this file creates the login banners /etc/issue and /etc/issue.net. These files are used to set the display that will precede the login prompt when a user logs in locally (/etc/issue) or remotely (/etc/issue.net). By default, the /etc/issue file contains something like this:

```
Red Hat Linux release 7.0 (Guinness)
Kernel 2.2.16-22 on an i586
```

Many system administrators think this is too much information to give to someone who may be trying to crack your system. It might be better to change the /etc/issue banner to something more generic like "Welcome to localdomain" or to give your users any information you believe they need before entering your system. If you change the /etc/issue file directly, it will be overwritten when the /etc/rc.d/rc.local file is run again. You must change this in /etc/rc.d/rc.local to make the change permanent. Since this file is one big if clause, any commands that you wish to add should be added before the last fi.

The Debian Model

Debian's inittab file is only slightly different from Red Hat's version. Listing 5.4 shows the Debian inittab.

Listing 5.4   Debian's inittab File

```
# /etc/inittab: init(8) configuration.
# $Id: inittab,v 1.8 1998/05/10 10:37:50 miquels Exp $


# The default runlevel.
id:2:initdefault:


# Boot-time system configuration/initialization script.
# This is run first except when booting in emergency (-b) mode.
si::sysinit:/etc/init.d/rcS


# What to do in single-user mode.
~~:S:wait:/sbin/sulogin


# /etc/init.d executes the S and K scripts upon change
# of runlevel.
#
# Runlevel 0 is halt.
# Runlevel 1 is single-user.
# Runlevels 2-5 are multi-user.
# Runlevel 6 is reboot.


l0:0:wait:/etc/init.d/rc 0
l1:1:wait:/etc/init.d/rc 1
l2:2:wait:/etc/init.d/rc 2
l3:3:wait:/etc/init.d/rc 3
l4:4:wait:/etc/init.d/rc 4
l5:5:wait:/etc/init.d/rc 5
l6:6:wait:/etc/init.d/rc 6
# Normally not reached, but fallthrough in case of emergency.
```

```
z6:6:respawn:/sbin/sulogin


# What to do when CTRL-ALT-DEL is pressed.
ca:12345:ctrlaltdel:/sbin/shutdown -t1 -a -r now


# Action on special keypress (ALT-UpArrow).
kb::kbrequest:/bin/echo "Keyboard Request--edit /etc/inittab to
    ➥let this work."


# What to do when the power fails/returns.
pf::powerwait:/etc/init.d/powerfail start
pn::powerfailnow:/etc/init.d/powerfail now
po::powerokwait:/etc/init.d/powerfail stop


# /sbin/getty invocations for the runlevels.
#
# The "id" field MUST be the same as the last
# characters of the device (after "tty").
#
# Format:
#   <id>:<runlevels>:<action>:<process>
1:2345:respawn:/sbin/getty 38400 tty1
2:23:respawn:/sbin/getty 38400 tty2
3:23:respawn:/sbin/getty 38400 tty3
4:23:respawn:/sbin/getty 38400 tty4
5:23:respawn:/sbin/getty 38400 tty5
6:23:respawn:/sbin/getty 38400 tty6


# Example how to put a getty on a serial line (for a terminal)
#
```

```
#T0:23:respawn:/sbin/getty -L ttyS0 9600 vt100
#T1:23:respawn:/sbin/getty -L ttyS1 9600 vt100


# Example how to put a getty on a modem line.
#
#T3:23:respawn:/sbin/mgetty -x0 -s 57600 ttyS3
```

Under Debian, the first uncommented line in inittab sets the default run level to level 2. You'll remember that this level is a multiuser mode that doesn't include networking.

The next line in inittab instructs the init process to run the /etc/init.d/rcS file, which we'll look at next. Like its Red Hat counterpart, it executes the S and K scripts for the specified run level. It sets up Ctrl+Alt+Del slightly differently than the Red Hat model, and adds an Alt+Up-Arrow shortcut to define a keyboard request function. The rcS script then sets up UPS power functions similar to Red Hat's, adding a function for immediate shutdown. The getty programs are set up, although Debian only has the first tty respawning a getty when the system is at run level 5. The last part of Debian's inittab gives examples of how to run getty programs on a serial line and a modem line.

Listing 5.5 shows the Debian rcS file mentioned earlier.

Listing 5.5   The Debian rcS File

```
#! /bin/sh
#
# rcS      Call all S??* scripts in /etc/rcS.d in
#          numerical/alphabetical order.
#
# Version: @(#)/etc/init.d/rcS  2.76  19-Apr-1999
miquels@cistron.nl
#


PATH=/sbin:/bin:/usr/sbin:/usr/bin
runlevel=S
prevlevel=N
umask 022
export PATH runlevel prevlevel
```

```
#
#  See if system needs to be set up. This is ONLY meant to
#  be used for the initial setup after a fresh installation!
#
if [ -x /sbin/unconfigured.sh ]
then
  /sbin/unconfigured.sh
fi


#
#    Source defaults.
#
. /etc/default/rcS
export VERBOSE


#
#  Trap CTRL-C &c only in this shell so we can interrupt
#  subprocesses.
#
trap ":" INT QUIT TSTP


#
#    Call all parts in order.
#
for i in /etc/rcS.d/S??*
do
    # Ignore dangling symlinks for now.
    [ ! -f "$i" ] && continue

    case "$i" in
```

```
        *.sh)

            # Source shell script for speed.

            (

                trap - INT QUIT TSTP

                set start

                . $i

            )

            ;;

        *)

            # No sh extension, so fork subprocess.

            $i start

            ;;

    esac

done


#

#    For compatibility, run the files in /etc/rc.boot too.

#

[ -d /etc/rc.boot ] && run-parts /etc/rc.boot


#

#    Finish setup if needed. The comment above about

#    /sbin/unconfigured.sh applies here as well!

#

if [ -x /sbin/setup.sh ]

then

   /sbin/setup.sh

fi
```

The rcS file sets up some environmental variables, including the PATH variable. It then runs a special configuration shell script if the system is running for the first time after installation. The rcS script then runs other scripts, which do things like enable virtual memory, mount filesystems, clean up certain log directories, initialize Plug-and-Play devices, load kernel modules, configure PCMCIA devices, set up serial ports, and run System V `init` scripts. The `rcS` script will call certain scripts in `/etc/rc.d` before it relinquishes control. These include:

`rc.local`   Similar to the Red Hat `rc.local`, it serves the same purpose.

`rc.modules`   Loads kernel modules: network card, PPP support, and other modules. If this script finds `rc.netdevice`, it will call that script as well.

`rc.pcmcia`   Probes for any PCMCIA devices that exist on the system and configures them. This is most useful for laptop users, who probably have a PCMCIA modem or network card.

`rc.serial`   Configures the serial ports by running the appropriate `setserial` commands.

`rc.sysvinit`   Looks for System V `init` scripts for the desired run level (symbolic links in /etc/rc.d/) and runs them. Similar to the Red Hat version, this `rc.sysvinit` script runs the scripts pointed to by the symbolic links in the appropriate subdirectory. In the case of run level 3, all links in /etc/rc3.d/ will be run.

Again, once this work is finished, the `init` program initiates a Bash shell, which reads in the user configuration files as described in "User Initialization Files" below, displays a login prompt, and then waits for some process that needs its attention.

Modifying the Startup Procedure

As a general rule, you should not have unused services running on your computers; you should turn off any services that are automatically initiated at boot time but are not used. Conversely, any services that you want to have started automatically but are not turned on at boot time by default should be configured to start in the appropriate run levels. For example, PCMCIA runs by default in a standard Red Hat 7.0 installation; but most desktop computers do not use PCMCIA, so it should be disabled. Similarly, any of the *r* command services (`rsh`, `rlogin`, `rexec`, and so on) for remote users should be disabled if they are not being used. These commands are commonly targeted by outsiders looking for security vulnerabilities to exploit. Leaving such services running provides a port that expects input, and this port could potentially be used to access the system. To disable the service, thereby closing the port, modify the set of services that are automatically started at bootup; to do this, use the `ntsysv` utility, which is part of the standard Red Hat 7.0 distribution. This console-based utility configures the current run level by default but may be passed a `-level` option to configure another level. Figure 5.2 illustrates the `ntsysv` utility. The `ntsysv` utility is used at system installation but may also be run from the command line. You may select or deselect the listed services by selecting or deselecting the box in front of the service name; in this case, PCMCIA is disabled for the current run level.

Figure 5.2   Use the ntsysv utility to control which services are automatically started at bootup.

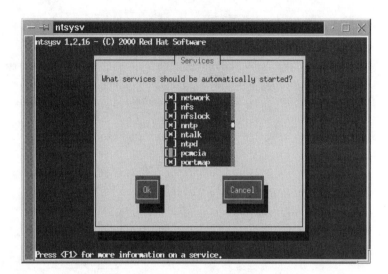

Another tool for adding, deleting, or reordering services in run levels 2–5 is the tksysv utility, which is available as part of the Red Hat distribution. This utility is X-based and is quite good. It presents a display of each of the services that are started and stopped at the various run levels and allows you to delete or add as needed. The principles of its use are basically the same as for ntsysv. Figure 5.3 shows the tksysv utility.

The KDE environment has its own graphical manager for SysV scripts, ksysv. It is also quite nice and features drag-and-drop capabilities. This utility is also included with the Red Hat distribution. Since it is a KDE tool, it is X-based. In resolutions higher than 640×480, you need to display it at full size since the smaller default size obscures the process names. (The program does, however, provide help when you mouse over a process name.) Figure 5.4 illustrates the ksysv utility.

Still another option is the command-line chkconfig utility, which gets bonus points for being easy to use and independent of X. If you pass it a --list switch, it will display a list of all SysV scripts and whether each is turned on or off at each run level. Listing 5.6 shows the output. The --add and --del switches allow you to alter the processes in each run level.

Figure 5.3   The tksysv utility

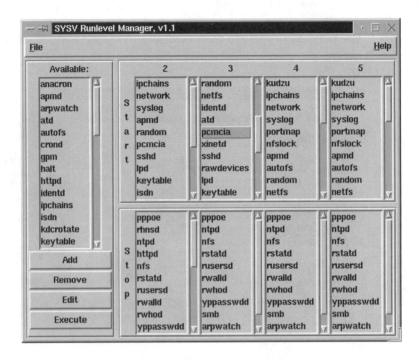

Figure 5.4   The ksysv utility

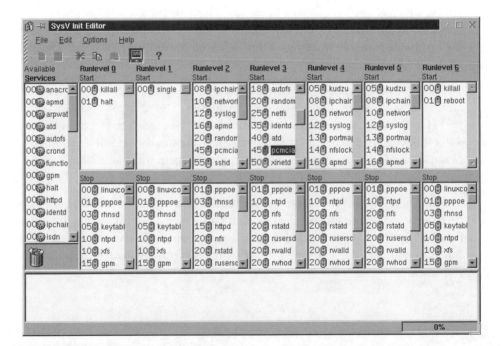

Listing 5.6   Sample chkconfig Output

```
syslog        0:off   1:off   2:on    3:on    4:on    5:on    6:off
crond         0:off   1:off   2:on    3:on    4:on    5:on    6:off
netfs         0:off   1:off   2:off   3:on    4:on    5:on    6:off
network       0:off   1:off   2:on    3:on    4:on    5:on    6:off
random        0:off   1:off   2:on    3:on    4:on    5:on    6:off
rawdevices    0:off   1:off   2:off   3:on    4:on    5:on    6:off
xfs           0:off   1:off   2:on    3:on    4:on    5:on    6:off
xinetd        0:off   1:off   2:off   3:on    4:on    5:on    6:off
reconfig      0:off   1:off   2:off   3:on    4:on    5:on    6:off
anacron       0:off   1:off   2:on    3:on    4:on    5:on    6:off
httpd         0:off   1:off   2:off   3:on    4:on    5:on    6:off
apmd          0:off   1:off   2:on    3:on    4:on    5:on    6:off
atd           0:off   1:off   2:off   3:on    4:on    5:on    6:off
named         0:off   1:off   2:off   3:off   4:off   5:off   6:off
keytable      0:off   1:off   2:on    3:on    4:on    5:on    6:off
gpm           0:off   1:off   2:on    3:on    4:on    5:on    6:off
ipchains      0:off   1:off   2:on    3:on    4:on    5:on    6:off
pcmcia        0:off   1:off   2:on    3:off   4:off   5:off   6:off
kdcrotate     0:off   1:off   2:off   3:off   4:off   5:off   6:off
kudzu         0:off   1:off   2:off   3:on    4:on    5:on    6:off
linuxconf     0:off   1:off   2:on    3:on    4:on    5:on    6:off
lpd           0:off   1:off   2:on    3:on    4:on    5:on    6:off
nfs           0:off   1:off   2:off   3:on    4:on    5:on    6:off
nfslock       0:off   1:off   2:off   3:on    4:on    5:on    6:off
sshd          0:off   1:off   2:on    3:on    4:on    5:on    6:off
identd        0:off   1:off   2:off   3:on    4:on    5:on    6:off
portmap       0:off   1:off   2:off   3:on    4:on    5:on    6:off
pppoe         0:off   1:off   2:off   3:off   4:off   5:off   6:off
rstatd        0:off   1:off   2:off   3:off   4:off   5:off   6:off
```

How Things Work

PART 1

rusersd	0:off	1:off	2:off	3:off	4:off	5:off	6:off
rwalld	0:off	1:off	2:off	3:off	4:off	5:off	6:off
rwhod	0:off	1:off	2:off	3:off	4:off	5:off	6:off
smb	0:off	1:off	2:off	3:off	4:off	5:off	6:off
sendmail	0:off	1:off	2:on	3:on	4:on	5:on	6:off
rhnsd	0:off	1:off	2:off	3:off	4:off	5:off	6:off
ypbind	0:off	1:off	2:off	3:off	4:off	5:off	6:off
yppasswdd	0:off	1:off	2:off	3:off	4:off	5:off	6:off
ypserv	0:off	1:off	2:off	3:off	4:off	5:off	6:off
autofs	0:off	1:off	2:off	3:on	4:on	5:on	6:off
dhcpd	0:off	1:off	2:off	3:off	4:off	5:off	6:off
mysqld	0:off	1:off	2:off	3:off	4:off	5:off	6:off
nscd	0:off	1:off	2:off	3:off	4:off	5:off	6:off
ntpd	0:off	1:off	2:off	3:off	4:off	5:off	6:off
squid	0:off	1:off	2:off	3:off	4:off	5:off	6:off
vmware	0:off	1:off	2:off	3:on	4:off	5:off	6:off

```
xinetd based services:
        amandaidx:      off
        amidxtape:      off
        finger: on
        linuxconf-web:  off
        rexec:  off
        rlogin: on
        rsh:    off
        swat:   off
        telnet: on
        tftp:   off
        wu-ftpd:        on
        talk:   on
        ntalk:  off
```

```
pop-3:   on
auth:    on
chargen:          off
chargen-udp:      off
daytime:          off
daytime-udp:      off
echo:             off
echo-udp:         off
time:             off
time-udp:         off
```

You can also use Linuxconf to configure services to be run. Use the Control Panel ➢ Control Service Activity option on the Control tab. You'll see a list of services. Click one, and you'll be able to set the run levels in which the service is active, as shown in Figure 5.5. Linuxconf offers many additional capabilities, so it is well worth the time spent learning how it works.

Tracking Startup Problems

If your system won't start up, the cause could be any of a number of things. One common problem is that something is wrong with the LILO installation. Troubleshooting LILO startup problems is tricky for newcomers to Linux because the error messages are cryptic. They do have clear meanings, however, which Table 5.1 demystifies.

LI Only

The most common of the LILO errors is the LI message, which means that the second-stage boot loader has loaded but could not be started. Sometimes this is the result of a disagreement between the BIOS and LILO about the disk parameters. If the number of cylinders, heads, and sectors are not agreed upon, you will see this error. Using the hard drive append line that was described in the lilo.conf section, specify the correct parameters for the drive. If the drive is in BIOS LBA mode, use the linear option in the /etc/lilo.conf.

At other times this is the result of a BIOS limitation, which prevents the /boot partition from booting if it is not contained within the first 1024 cylinders of the disk. As of LILO version 21.4.2, this limitation has been overcome on systems where the BIOS supports EDD BIOS extensions.

Figure 5.5   Linuxconf's run level selection tab for a service

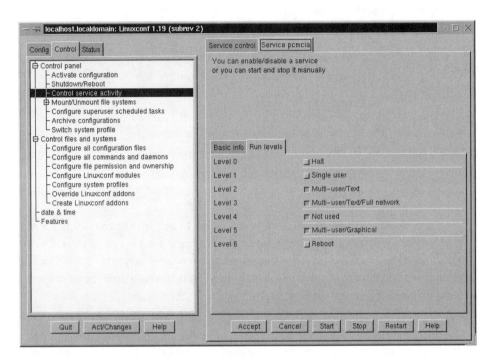

Table 5.1   Errors Indicated by the LILO Prompt

LILO Display	Meaning
Nothing	LILO hasn't been loaded.
L	First-stage boot loader is loaded and started.
LI	Second-stage boot loader is loaded.
LIL	Second-stage boot loader is started.
LIL?	Second-stage boot loader loaded at incorrect address.
LIL-	The descriptor table is corrupted.
LILO	LILO loaded correctly.

The first thing to try is to boot another kernel image or from a boot disk and then rerun LILO. If that doesn't fix the problem, boot from a boot disk, mount the filesystem that contains the root filesystem (and /etc as well), and try changing the linear option in /etc/lilo.conf. Don't forget to type lilo again to re-install the boot loader!

If your version of LILO is earlier than 21.4.2 and if your boot disk is larger than 8GB, try upgrading LILO. (Red Hat 7.0 ships with LILO 21.4.4, so it's capable of handling large hard disks from the start.) If your BIOS is very old (older than 1995 or so), you may need to upgrade it or re-partition your disk so that a small /boot partition falls below the 1024-cylinder limit (about 8GB). 10–20MB should be large enough for this partition.

If all else fails, it's conceivable that GRUB will do a better job than LILO. Check http://www.gnu.org/software/grub/ for more information on this tool.

Kernel Panics

Another possible problem is a kernel panic. These events are really not frequent occurrences if you aren't doing a lot of bleeding-edge kernel testing and don't make a lot of typos in important files like /etc/lilo.conf and /etc/fstab. Many Linux system administrators have never experienced even one kernel panic. A kernel panic is often quite frustrating for new system administrators, since it can be the result of several different problems—including both hardware and software problems. One key thing to remember is that kernel panics may be caused by problems with arguments passed to LILO, but if the LILO phase was successful and the problem is not hardware, the culprit is probably something that was run from /etc/rc.d/rc.sysinit. Look through this file and see if you can determine what it was. Another possible cause is an error in the /etc/fstab file that prevents the root filesystem from being mounted.

Now that we have the system initialized, let's look at what happens when a user logs in. You will need to know this process well so that you can troubleshoot user login problems.

User Initialization Files

A different type of initialization happens when a user logs in. This is not a system-wide initialization like the boot process. It is another sequence for user-specific initialization. But just as with the system initialization files on each desktop, the system administrator is responsible for the user initialization files.

When a user logs in, the system user configuration files are run first. These files are scripts and are sourced in instead of being executed. A file is sourced via the "dot" command. To source the .login file, for example, use the following command:

```
. /home/someuser/.login
```

> **NOTE** *Sourcing* a file executes each command as if it were typed in at the command prompt rather than as a separate program. The sourced file's environment becomes part of the shell in which it is run. A file does not have to be executable to be sourced.

The first to be sourced is /etc/profile. This file is intended to contain system-wide environmental variable definitions and programs to be started by all users when they log in; for example, it can include a calendar program that lists company events and other useful information. It also sources in any files that exist in the /etc/profile.d directory. This directory exists because it is easier for an RPM to add a script file there than to add lines to /etc/profile.

When the /etc/profile script is finished, the system looks in the user's home directory for a .bash_profile, a .bash_login, or a .profile in that order. The first of these that it finds is sourced in. Usually this is the .bash_profile file. The first thing this file does is to source in .bashrc if it exists in the user's home directory. After that it sets some environmental variables. The .bashrc file contains user-specific aliases and functions. The .bashrc file in turn sources the /etc/bashrc file, which contains system-wide functions and aliases, including the prompt that the users of the system will see.

When the user logs out of the Bash shell, the .bash_logout file will be sourced. It should contain any commands necessary to clean up after the user. This may include deleting any files in a temporary directory owned by that user.

Startup Log Files

Sometimes it is helpful to see what the system did when booting up. The most common way to do this is to view the /var/log/dmesg file, which is a record of the kernel ring buffer. This file gives basically the same information that scrolls quickly down the screen at bootup. You may view this file with an editor like vi or Emacs if you have root privileges or by running the /bin/dmesg binary, which anyone on a system can execute:

```
# /bin/dmesg
```

There is also useful information in /var/log/boot.log. This file logs successful and unsuccessful starts and stops of the /etc/rc.d/init.d scripts. If the start or stop is unsuccessful, this log may indicate why.

Another useful log file is /var/log/messages. This file contains information written by klogd, the logger for kernel messages. The syslogd daemon, which logs system messages from processes that do not belong to the kernel, also writes to /var/log/messages.

How Things Work

PART 1

Administrators should examine this file on a regular basis so that problems not immediately obvious to a user do not go unnoticed.

System logs like /var/log/dmesg and /var/log/messages are rotated on a regular basis by the logrotate script. This script is configured by the /etc/logrotate.conf file. This file allows you to specify how to rotate the files, whether to store them in a compressed format, when to remove a file from /var/log, and whether to mail the log to someone.

Finally, since /proc is a virtual filesystem that contains information pertaining to the kernel currently being run, it provides a lot of helpful information. Following are some of the more helpful files and directories in /proc:

File	Contents
/proc/interrupts	IRQ information
/proc/cpuinfo	CPU information
/proc/dma	DMA information
/proc/ioports	I/O information
/proc/meminfo	Available, free, swap, and cached memory information
/proc/loadavg	System load average
/proc/uptime	Time since last reboot
/proc/version	Information about kernel version
/proc/scsi	Information about SCSI devices
/proc/ide	Information about IDE devices
/proc/net	Network information
/proc/sys	Kernel configuration parameters

Shutdown

Red Hat Linux uses the BSD-style shutdown command. This command's syntax is:

    shutdown [*options*] *time* [*message*]

When the system has been signaled to shut down, all logged-in users are notified that the system is going down using either the standard message or the one specified as a parameter to the shutdown command. All processes are then sent a SIGTERM signal to tell them that the computer is going down. This gives these processes time to shut down cleanly. The shutdown command then signals the init process to change the run level to 0 (halt) if the option -h was provided or 6 (reboot) if the -r option was used instead.

The /etc/rc.d/rc script is run with an argument of 0 or 6 as appropriate. This changes the run level and runs the scripts pointed to by the symbolic links in /etc/rc.d/rc0.d or /etc/rc.d/rc6.d as determined by the argument passed to the /etc/rc.d/rc script. If a user hits Ctrl+Alt+Del to initiate a shutdown, the shutdown command will check for an /etc/shutdown.allow file. If this file exists, it is read in and used to determine whether the user who initiated the shutdown has permission to shut down the system. The /etc/shutdown.allow file contains pairs of hostnames and usernames. If the hostname of the system attempting to shutdown is listed, and the username next to it is a user who is currently logged on, the shutdown will proceed.

Most modern Linux distributions also provide a shutdown option on the XDM login screen. This allows inexperienced users to shut down after logging out, in a manner reminiscent of Windows NT or 2000.

Warning Users

The shutdown command sends the users on the system a message telling them that the system is being shut down, whether it is a reboot or a halt, and when the shutdown will occur. You may add a message of your own to tell why, when the system will be brought back up, or any other information which you'd like your users to know. As the shutdown time approaches, the message will be repeated. The frequency of the message increases as the shutdown time gets nearer.

It is best not to make the shutdown period so short that users cannot finish with their applications and exit the system. Of course, there will be times when the shutdown must occur right away; this can't be helped, but adding a message telling the users when they can expect access to the system again may help soften the blow.

Shutdown Log Files

Some of the same log files used with the startup process are also used for logging shutdown. Any problems with the kernel that occur during shutdown will be annotated in /var/log/messages. The /var/log/boot.log will report any problems relating to the processes run by the init program from /etc/rc.d/init.d. The distinction between these files is not clear-cut, however, and messages about the same problem tend to show up in both. If, for instance, the eth0 device wasn't detected, you'd see something like the following in /var/log/boot.log:

```
May 21 13:03:46 somedomain ifup: Delaying eth0 initialization.
May 21 13:03:46 somedomain network: Bringing up device eth0 failed
```

While this won't tell you everything you need to solve the problem, it will point you in the right direction. The messages in `/var/log/messages` tend to be more helpful. The message about the same problem from `/var/log/messages` looks like this:

```
May 21 12:03:46 somedomain modprobe: modprobe: Can't locate module
➥eth0

May 21 12:03:46 somedomain ifup: Delaying eth0 initialization.

May 21 12:03:46 somedomain network: Bringing up device eth0 failed
```

These more helpful messages tell you that the problem occurs when attempting to load the modules, usually meaning that this module or one of its dependencies can't be found.

In Sum

Starting a Linux system involves the interaction of a wide range of software, from the computer's BIOS to the Linux startup scripts. Critical components that you can configure include the installation of a boot loader (LILO, GRUB, and LOADLIN are common for Linux) and the specification of what services should be run. Most Linux systems use scripts in the `/etc/rc.d` directory tree to control these services, and these configurations can be edited manually or by using tools such as `ntsysv` or `tksysv`. Shutting a system down is also a process that involves running specialized system scripts. At all steps along the way, information is logged to assorted files, which you can consult when troubleshooting your system.

In the next chapter we'll look at adding users and what that involves. Adding and managing users and groups is, after all, a major part of a system administrator's job.

Part 2

Managing Users and Software

Featuring:

- Creating and maintaining user accounts
- Creating and working with groups
- Common types of attacks on network security
- Authorization and authentication techniques
- Firewalls and other security techniques
- Installing binary packages
- Compiling source code
- Compiling the kernel
- Keeping your operating system updated

6

Creating and Maintaining User Accounts

Managing and maintaining user accounts is the first step toward maintaining system security. Without individual user accounts, we would all be working in a single large common directory, in a state of chaos. Managing user and group accounts allows us to partition and control the access of users with respect to one another.

Managing users and groups is a large part of your job as a system administrator. Setting up user accounts allows you to provide your users with access while still retaining the ability to track what your users do as well as the ability to limit their access as appropriate. It is one of the most visible jobs you'll have. Learning to do it efficiently will save you hours in the long run, and the confidence you'll exude from knowing it well will put you in good standing with your users.

Linux uses two or three files to maintain user and group information. The /etc/passwd file stores information about user accounts, and /etc/group stores information about groups. Most systems also use a file called /etc/shadow to maintain passwords. Later in the chapter you'll see examples of these files. You'll also see that all the basic administrative tasks of adding, removing, and modifying user and group accounts can be done in any of three ways: by manually editing the account's entry in /etc/passwd or /etc/group, by using Linux command-line utilities that pass the relevant information to those files, or by using a GUI tool like Linuxconf to enter the same information.

User Accounts

Different types of users have different needs and may be assigned different types of accounts. Selecting the right type of account will ensure that the user has the needed access without allowing access beyond his or her scope. Common account types include:

- TCP/IP network access accounts (PPP and SLIP) to link users to the server (and perhaps beyond) via TCP/IP networking protocols
- UUCP network accounts, which allow for networking using older protocols
- Normal login accounts (also called *shell accounts*)
- Mail accounts (POP, virtual POP, or IMAP) for mail retrieval

The two special account types you'll encounter most frequently are Point-to-Point Protocol (PPP) and Post Office Protocol (POP) accounts. Both of these account types obviate the need for a user's home directory to exist. Both POP and PPP users never directly log in to a user shell on the system, so such users have no need for a home directory. Using Linuxconf, POP users' login shells are set to /bin/false. This way, even if the user attempted to log in at a console or through a protocol such as Telnet, the session would immediately terminate with an error exit code of -1–in other words, the login attempt would fail, even if the user presented a correct password.

The POP user's Mail User Agent (MUA) authenticates with the mailer system itself. The PPP user does need a login shell of sorts, though. The login shell is effectively the PPP daemon itself, and authentication is performed when the connection is created. Under Red Hat 7.0, Linuxconf creates a home directory for the PPP user at /home/loginname where loginname is the user's login. The PPP user's login shell is set to /usr/lib/linuxconf/lib/ppplogin.

The */etc/passwd* File

Information about each user is contained in the /etc/passwd file. As a system administrator, it is critical that you clearly understand this important file. In the excerpt shown in Listing 6.1, you'll notice that root is listed first. The root user is always assigned the user ID (UID) 0 and group ID (GID) 0. Other special users and accounts associated with services and daemons are listed after root and always have UID and GID values below 500. Last, regular and special accounts for individual users are listed.

Listing 6.1   An Example of an /etc/passwd File

```
root:x:0:0:root:/root:/bin/bash
bin:x:1:1:bin:/bin:
daemon:x:2:2:daemon:/sbin:
adm:x:3:4:adm:/var/adm:
lp:x:4:7:lp:/var/spool/lpd:
sync:x:5:0:sync:/sbin:/bin/sync
shutdown:x:6:0:shutdown:/sbin:/sbin/shutdown
halt:x:7:0:halt:/sbin:/sbin/halt
mail:x:8:12:mail:/var/spool/mail:
news:x:9:13:news:/var/spool/news:
uucp:x:10:14:uucp:/var/spool/uucp:
operator:x:11:0:operator:/root:
games:x:12:100:games:/usr/games:
gopher:x:13:30:gopher:/usr/lib/gopher-data:
ftp:x:14:50:FTP User:/home/ftp:
nobody:x:99:99:Nobody:/:
xfs:x:43:43:X Font Server:/etc/X11/fs:/bin/false
named:x:25:25:Named:/var/named:/bin/false
marty:x:500:500:Not Feldman:/home/marty:/bin/bash
ernie:x:501:501:Earnest too:/home/ernie:/bin/csh
betty:x:502:502:Ready Betty:/home/betty:/bin/pop
donald:x:503:503:Unka Donald:/home/donald:/bin/bash
```

Looking at the last entry, Donald's record, you can see the following colon-delimited fields:

Username   Donald's username is not capitalized. Typically, initial capitalization is not used in order to avoid upper/lower case confusion. There is no default value for the username field.

Encrypted Password   Technically, this field holds the password for users; however, this particular Linux system is using *shadow passwords*, which are held in /etc/shadow.

Therefore the /etc/password file contains an x in the second field to indicate to login that the actual password is held elsewhere.

User ID Throughout the system, any file owned or created by Donald will have this number associated with it. It is actually this UID that will be associated with Donald's files, and the human-friendly donald is what is displayed to us, for example by the ls command. Also, every process executing on the system will be associated with a UID. Typically it's the UID of the user who starts up the process.

Default GID This is Donald's login group. All files are owned by both a user and a group. When Donald creates a new file, it will by default receive his GID value, which will also be associated with the file. It is no coincidence that Donald has a GID equal to his UID, as do all of the other users listed in the password file in Listing 6.1. This is by design under Red Hat Linux, an approach called *user private groups*. We will explore this approach later. Other Linux distributions, for example SuSE, use the traditional approach where all users are default members of one large collective group, typically named users. One of your jobs as a system administrator is to decide whether to use your distribution's default group assignment scheme or use another one.

User Description This field holds descriptive information about the user (Unka Donald in this example). In some organizations, it contains phone numbers, mail stops, or some other contact information. Its contents are included with the finger utility's report.

User's Home Directory When the user is authenticated, the login program uses this field to define the user's $HOME variable. By default, in all Linux distributions, the user's home directory will be assumed to be /home/username. If the user's home directory can't be accessed, the user will be defaulted to the root (/) directory. "Landing" in the root directory when you log in is always an indication that something is awry.

User's Login Shell When the user is authenticated, the login program also sets the users $SHELL variable to this field. By default, in all Linux distributions, a new user's login shell will be /bin/bash, the Bourne Again Shell. If no shell is specified, it defaults to the Bourne shell, /bin/sh. Special user accounts sometimes require that the user's login shell be set to something other than a shell path. For a POP user or a Virtual POP user, you don't need to assign a shell at all, since they don't ever actually log on to the system. Instead, use /bin/false to prevent the user from getting a login shell if access is attempted while preserving his or her ability to retrieve mail.

Listing 6.1 reveals over a dozen system accounts (with UIDs of less than 500) in addition to the user accounts (with UIDs of 500 or above). Some of these accounts, such as root, bin, daemon, and halt, are more-or-less required on any Linux system. Others, such as `mail`, `news`, `games`, `gopher`, and `ftp`, are associated with specific servers or program collections. Your Linux system can get by without these accounts, but if you install certain programs, they may not work correctly, because they'll assume that these accounts are present. Other accounts, such as `nobody`, fall in between these two cases; they may be used by several different packages but aren't strictly required for basic functionality.

Some programs add users to `/etc/passwd` during installation. The qmail mail server, for example, adds several entries for its own use. If you install such a program but then remove its users, the program may fail to operate correctly, or at all. You should, however, remove any such accounts if you remove the software that required them.

> **TIP** It's a good idea to back up the `/etc/passwd` file (as well as the `/etc/shadow` file, which stores passwords, and `/etc/group`, which stores group information) soon after system installation, as well as after adding or deleting users. This can make it easier to recover the system if you ever need to reinstall. It can also help you track down system breakins, because crackers often create their own accounts. These often have a UID of 0, giving them root privileges even if they use another username on the account. Crackers also sometimes add passwords (revealed in `/etc/shadow` on most systems) and login shells to normal system accounts, such as `ftp`.

Shadowed Passwords

When a user picks or is assigned a password, it is encoded with a randomly generated value referred to as the *salt*. Using the salt, any password can be stored in 4096 different ways. The salt value is stored with the encrypted password. When a user logs in and supplies a password, the salt is first retrieved from the stored encrypted password. The supplied password is then encoded with the salt value and compared with the stored password. If there is a match, the user is authenticated.

Because it is used to obtain user and group names from the system-held UIDs and GIDs, the `/etc/passwd` file must be readable by anyone on the system, and this makes it vulnerable to attack. Anyone can pull out a user's encrypted password string and compare it against a generated list of dictionary words that have been encrypted using the same algorithm used to encode the password. A cracker trying to break the password generates the list by encrypting simple dictionary words using all 4096 salt values. If the password string matches one in the list, the person running the test has that user's password. In order to combat this security risk, the concept of *shadowing* was adopted.

Shadowing solves the problem by relocating the passwords to another file (/etc/shadow). Only root can read and write to the /etc/shadow file. After shadowing, donald's line in the /etc/passwd file would look like this:

```
donald:x:503:503:Unka Donald:/home/donald:/bin/bash
```

The password is replaced with an x, which indicates that it is shadowed. A line in /etc/shadow contains the encrypted version of Donald's password as well as some other information:

```
donald:HcX5zb8cpoxmY:11088:0:99999:7:0::
```

NOTE By default, Red Hat Linux 7.0 uses shadow passwords. Listing 6.1 shown earlier reflects this fact; all its password entries are x.

The fields in the /etc/shadow file are as follows:

Username This is Donald's login name, which matches the one we saw in the /etc/passwd file.

Encrypted Password This is where the actual encrypted password is stored on a system using password shadowing.

Last Password Change This number represents the number of days since January 1, 1970 that the last password change took place.

Days Until Change Allowed This number represents the number of days until a password change will be allowed. This is typically set to 0, allowing the user to change the password as often as desired.

Days Before Change Required This number represents the number of days before the user will be forced to change the password. If password changes are not forced, this field is set to 99999.

Days Warning Before Password Expires This field is used to set the number of days prior to password expiration you want the user to be notified. Typically the user is notified a week in advance, so this field is set to 7.

Days Between Expiration and Deactivation This number represents the number of days that an account may be expired before the account is disabled. If inactivation is not intended to be automatic, the field is set to −1 or left empty.

Account Expires This field shows the date the account will be disabled, represented as the number of days since January 1, 1970. This is particularly useful for students with set graduation dates and temporary employees. If this type of automatic deactivation is not to be used, the field is set to −1 or left empty.

Special Flag This field is reserved for future use. It typically remains empty.

Shadow passwords were first used in SCO Xenix, but the Shadow Suite was freely distributable. Red Hat Linux doesn't use the Shadow Suite, but instead uses the PAM modules to perform the same function. The utilities involved in maintaining shadowed passwords include the following:

pwconv   Uses the values of PASS_MIN_DAYS, PASS_MAX_DAYS, and PASS_WARN_AGE from /etc/login.defs to add new entries to the /etc/shadow file and removes any entries in /etc/shadow that don't have corresponding entries in /etc/passwd.

pwunconv   Checks the /etc/passwd file against the /etc/shadow file, updating the /etc/passwd entries with corresponding /etc/shadow entries by putting the /etc/shadow password field into the corresponding line in /etc/passwd. The /etc/shadow file is removed upon completion. Some password aging information is lost. This effectively disables shadow passwords. You're only likely to need to do this if you must use some outdated utility that insists on seeing passwords in /etc/passwd, or if you want to manipulate accounts as one file, as when migrating users from another system.

grpconv   Performs the same function as the pwconv utility but on groups from the /etc/group file instead.

grpunconv   Performs the same function as the pwunconv utility but on groups instead.

Administrator's Logbook: Password Conversion

Date: 01/20/2001

System: E12345678

Action: Used pwunconv to convert from shadowed to nonshadowed passwords in order to integrate usernames from System E12248271, which uses nonshadowed passwords

Date: 01/22/2001

System: E12345678

Action: Used pwconv to re-enable shadowed passwords after successful integration of accounts from System E12248271.

Adding New Users

To add a new user to the system, you must have **root** access, and you must follow a series of general steps. The required steps are:

1. Create a record for the user in /etc/passwd.

2. Set the user's password.

3. Specify a login shell for the user.

There are also two optional steps. These help to configure a useful environment, but not all account types require these steps. They are:

4. Create a home directory for the user.

5. Populate the user's home directory with various useful files. (This step isn't described further because it's very system-specific. You might want to add a README file, for instance, for the benefit of new users.)

You can perform these as single discrete steps, but you can ease your administrative burden by automating the process using either user-creation scripts, which have existed for years, or graphical user interfaces, which have appeared more recently.

Adding a User from the Linuxconf GUI

For the simplest default accounts, many administrators find it best to work from the command line, specifying switches to the **useradd** and **passwd** commands, as described in the next section. To create accounts that include some nondefault elements, however, you may prefer to work with a GUI, such as Linuxconf. In particular, creating any of the special accounts mentioned earlier in this chapter from within Linuxconf takes care of the peculiarities of that account's specific authentication sequence. For that reason, creating these accounts is most easily done with the Linuxconf tool. The format of the GUI itself provides excellent cues for the optional fields.

In order to create a user account using Linuxconf under a Red Hat Linux system, simply invoke the utility from a root shell in either the X Window System or a text console by typing **linuxconf**. If you invoke Linuxconf when you're running X, the program produces an X-based display. You can run it without X, however, in which case the program produces a text-mode display.

Once the Linuxconf screen comes up, you'll need to select Users Accounts ➢ Normal ➢ User Accounts from the menu. Doing so will expand the window and bring up a list of users on the right side of the Linuxconf window, as shown in Figure 6.1. To add a user, click the Add button. You'll then be presented with the User Account Creation screen shown in Figure 6.2.

Figure 6.1   The Linuxconf User Accounts module lets you edit existing accounts or add new ones.

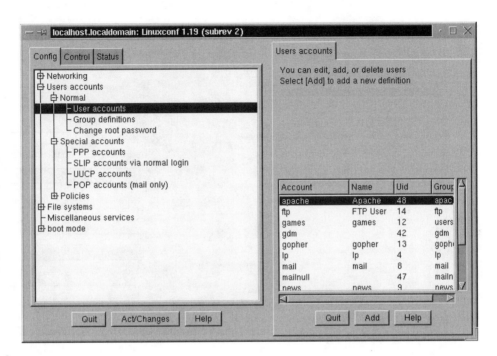

The only information you truly *must* enter to add a user is the username, entered via the Login Name field. It's also useful to enter something in the Full Name field, however. Once you've done this, click Accept to create an account—Linuxconf asks you to enter a password (twice, to be sure you type it correctly) and then creates the necessary entries in /etc/passwd and /etc/shadow. If necessary, you can enter a nonstandard home directory or group, or specify a particular user ID for the user. If you leave these fields blank, Linuxconf will assign default values. As simple as it is to add a new user, you may be tempted to utilize many of the options presented on the interface, but for the most part the system defaults are adequate.

As shown in Figure 6.2, there are three major categories of information you can add:

Base Info   Basic information provided in /etc/passwd and /etc/group.

Params   Policy enforcement for password aging—the account's expiration date, number of days between enforced password changes, and so on.

Privileges   Special permission management, such as whether the user may use Linuxconf, shut down the computer, and so on.

Figure 6.2 The User Account Creation screen has three tabs for entry of assorted information.

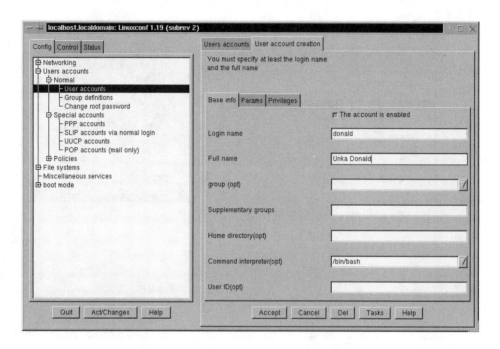

If you want to change any of these characteristics, do so *before* you click Accept to create the account. Alternatively, you can alter an account's settings after it's been created by clicking the account name in the User Accounts module (Figure 6.1). This brings up the User Information module, which provides the same options as the User Account Creation module (Figure 6.2).

Adding Users from the Command Line

Adding a user from the command line also requires the five steps listed earlier. You can use the useradd command to accomplish all of the steps except assigning a password. The useradd command accepts the information needed for the individual fields in the /etc/ passwd file as arguments, as follows:

```
useradd [-D] [-g default_group] [-b default_home] [-s default_shell]
```

The useradd command creates a new user account using the values given on the command line (supplying default values for any items not specified). useradd enters data into the appropriate system files. It then creates the user's home directory at /home/username by default or at the location specified by the –b option. The useradd command copies sample configuration files from /etc/skel. In Red Hat Linux, a group with the same name as the user is created, and the user is added to that group. (Other distributions may handle groups differently, as explained further in the "The Function of Groups" section later in this chapter, which also describes Red Hat's approach in more detail.)

Next you'll want to give the user a password, using the passwd command:

```
# passwd donald
New UNIX password:
Retype new UNIX password:
```

The configuration files contained in /etc/skel are intended to be set up for the typical user in that system. The files in this directory include .Xdefaults, .bash_logout, .bash_profile, .bashrc, .kderc, .kde/, and Desktop/. You may add any files that will routinely be contained in your users' home directories.

Default values for certain user characteristics may be set in the /etc/login.defs file. The mail directory, which typically is set to /var/spool/mail/*username*, is set via the MAIL_DIR variable in that file. Password aging information is also stored in the login.defs file. The minimum and maximum UID and GID values are stored there for automatic selection by the useradd command.

Migrating Users from Other Unix Systems

Since most Unix variations use the same format for their /etc/passwd files, it is possible to migrate users directly from a Unix platform to Linux. If the Unix system is using shadowed passwords, you must first run the command to "unshadow"— pwunconv. The pwunconv utility requires no arguments. Copy the appropriate user lines from the passwd file of the other machine into the /etc/passwd file on Linux and run /sbin/pwconv to reapply shadowing.

Modifying User Accounts

Most system administrators make changes to user accounts by editing the appropriate files. It is often easier to use a text editor to edit the passwd file to change a simple configuration detail like the user's shell than to bring up a GUI utility or use usermod at the command line. We'll show you all three, and you can decide which you prefer.

Manually Modifying User Accounts

The most direct way to modify a user's account information is to edit the corresponding entry in /etc/passwd. For example, suppose you wish to change our hypothetical user Donald's shell to the C shell. Use your favorite editor to open the /etc/passwd file. Donald's line looks like this:

```
donald:x:503:503:Unka Donald:/home/donald:/bin/bash
```

Simply change the /bin/bash to /bin/csh, and save the file. The next time Donald logs in, he will be using the C shell. Of course, other information, including the user's name string, Unka Donald, may be changed as well. You can change the home directory, but you must create the new directory and move any files from the old directory to make it usable. Do not change the UID or GID unless you really know what you're doing. If you change these fields inadvertently, Donald will lose access to his files, since the system sees the owner and group designation numerically and uses the /etc/passwd file to convert them for output in human readable format to the user.

In principle, it's also possible to edit the contents of /etc/shadow in a similar manner. In practice, though, most of its contents come in a form that's less easily handled by humans. The password is encrypted, so you can't change it by hand unless you're simply copying a password from another system (which is potentially risky). The time information is entered in units of days since 1970, which is awkward to compute. All in all, it's best to leave /etc/shadow alone.

Modifying User Accounts with Linuxconf

To modify any user's account, take the following steps:

1. Start Linuxconf by selecting it from a drop-down menu or typing **linuxconf** at a shell prompt.

2. Open Config ➤ Users Accounts ➤ Normal ➤ User Accounts.

3. Select the account that you'd like to change. You will then be presented with the User information screen, which is essentially identical to Figure 6.2, with any existing values filled in.

4. Change the appropriate fields, and select Accept to accept the modified user information.

5. Click Quit from the User Accounts screen, which follows.

6. Click Act/Changes from the main Linuxconf screen.

7. Click Activate the Changes from the Status of the System screen.

8. Click Quit from the main Linuxconf screen.

Modifying User Accounts with *usermod*

To use the usermod utility to alter a field in a user's password record from the command line, use the following command:

```
usermod [-c comment] [-d home_dir [-m]] [-e expire_date]
     ➥[-f inactive_time] [-g initial_group] [-G group[,…]]
     ➥[-l login_name] [-p passwd]
     ➥[-s shell] [-u uid] [-o] [-L|-U] login
```

The important `usermod` options and their meanings are:

-c *comment*   The string that will replace the current comment.

-d *home_dir* [-m]   New home directory. If –m is specified, move the contents of the old home directory to the new home directory, which is created if it doesn't already exist.

-e *expire_date*   The date, in YYYY-MM-DD format, on which the user account will be disabled.

-f *inactive_time*   The number of days after password expiration until the account is permanently disabled. Use –1 to turn off the automatic disabling feature and 0 to disable the account immediately upon password expiration.

-g *initial_group*   The user's new initial login group. The group must exist.

-G *group*   Other groups to which the user should belong. The list is comma-delimited, with no white space. The groups listed must already exist. If the user is currently a member of a group that isn't listed, he or she will be removed from that group.

-l *login_name*   The name of the user will be changed to this login name. This will cause the files owned by this user to show the new login name as owner since the UID will be matched to the entry in the /etc/passwd file. You probably want to change the home directory to use this new *login_name* as well. You may not change the *login_name* of a user who is currently logged in.

-p *password*   The user's new password as encrypted by the `crypt` command. If you pass plain text, it will appear in /etc/passwd as plain text. If you then run `pwconv`, the /etc/shadow file will contain the plain text password. If the user attempts to log in using the same text string, access will be denied, because the system will attempt to decrypt the text string taken from /etc/shadow before it matches it to the input password string. To change a password, you normally use the `passwd` command, not `usermod`.

-s *shell*   This is the shell that the user will be assigned at login. Entering a blank for this option causes the system to select the default shell, which in Linux is Bash.

-u *uid*   The numeric value of the user's ID. This value must be unique unless you also specify the –o option. System accounts will normally be assigned a UID between 0 and 99. User accounts on most systems begin with 500, leaving 100–499 for other uses. When the UID is updated using `usermod`, any files owned by the user and existing in the user's home directory will be updated to the new UID so that the /etc/passwd file will assign the correct owner to these files. Files outside the user's home directory will retain the old UID number, meaning that an `ls -l` of these files will show the numeric version of the old UID or a different user's name if a new user has been assigned the old UID.

Managing Users and Software

PART 2

-L   Places an exclamation mark in front of the user's password in the /etc/passwd file, which disables the user's ability to log in.

-U   Removes the exclamation mark from the user's entry in the /etc/passwd file, re-enabling the user's password.

login   The user's login name.

Disabling User Accounts

If you need to deactivate an account but believe that the account will be needed again in the future, you'll want to disable it instead of deleting it. A deleted account and a disabled account look exactly the same to a user attempting to log in using that account, but a disabled account does not remove the user's home directory or any files owned by that user.

Manual Disabling

The simplest way to disable an account is to make sure that the user's password has expired. To do this, you can modify the user's entry in /etc/shadow. As discussed earlier, dates in this file are represented as the number of days since January 1, 1970. The third field in an entry is the date the password was last modified, and the eighth field is the date the account will expire. So you first want to change the user's password; the third field in the entry will then reflect today's date. Subtract one from that number, insert the new number immediately before the last colon, and save the file.

```
donald:HcX5zb8cpoxmY:11088:0:99999:7:0::
```

Subtracting 1 from 11088 yields 11087, so you'd change the entry to this:

```
donald:HcX5zb8cpoxmY:11088:0:99999:7:0:11087:
```

Disabling an Account with Linuxconf

To disable a user's account, follow these steps:

1. Start Linuxconf as previously described.
2. Open Config ➤ Users Accounts ➤ Normal ➤ User Accounts.
3. Select the account that you'd like to disable. You'll then be presented with the User Information screen, which resembles Figure 6.2.
4. Uncheck the Account Is Enabled box.
5. Click Accept to accept the modified user information.
6. Click Quit on the User Accounts screen that follows.
7. Click Act/Changes from the main Linuxconf screen.
8. Click Activate the Changes from the Status of the System screen.
9. Click Quit from the main Linuxconf screen.

Disabling an Account with *chage*

There is no useradd/usermod equivalent that allows you to disable a user's account, but you can use the chage (change aging) command to update the user's password expiration date to yesterday. chage allows you to input this as the number of days since January 1, 1970, or in the YYYY-MM-DD format as follows:

```
# chage -E 2000-8-12 someuser
```

If the date is passed, the account will be disabled but can be enabled later using the same method. When the user attempts to log in, he or she will see the following message:

```
Your account has expired; please contact your system administrator
```

Deleting User Accounts

If you are sure that you will not need a user's account again, you can delete it. Deleting an account basically reverses the steps you took to create it. Those steps were:

1. Create a record for the user in /etc/passwd.
2. Set the user's password.
3. Specify a login shell for the user.
4. Create a home directory for the user.
5. Populate the user's home directory with various useful files.

The order in which you reverse these steps is unimportant, however. Of course, you'll need to delete the files you've created in the user's home directory as well as the user's home directory itself. You'll also need to search the system for any other files owned by this user and either remove them or reset their ownership. You must also remove the user's /etc/passwd entry. This may all be done by hand or via tools as before.

Manually Deleting an Account

First you'll want to remove the user's /etc/passwd entry. When pwconv is run again, the /etc/shadow entry for that user will be automatically removed as well. Next, remove the home directory and all of the files contained therein using an rm command like the following:

```
# rm -r /home/donald
```

The rm command will remove the /home/donald directory and all the files and subdirectories it contains. If you're confident enough and would rather not be prompted, you can add the –f option to the above command (making it **rm -rf /home/donald**), which instructs Linux not to prompt you about removing files. This is very dangerous, so you might want to just endure the prompts.

> ***TIP*** It's a good idea to back up a deleted user's account. You can do this by archiving the files using the `tar` backup utility (described in Chapter 11) and storing the files on floppy disk, high-capacity removable disks like Iomega Zip disks, CD-R discs, or tape. Keeping a deleted user's files on hand in this way can be handy if you discover you've deleted the wrong account or if you need to recover a particular file from the ex-user's account for some reason.

Next you need to search the computer for other files owned by the deleted user and determine what to do with these files. Use the `find` command for this as follows:

```
# find / -gid 503 -uid 503
```

Assuming Donald's user ID was 503 and his original group ID had never been changed, this command would generate a list of files by full path that were owned by Donald or had his group ID. You'll then need to look through the file list and determine what to do with each file. If you decide to keep a file but change its ownership, you can use the chown command, as follows:

```
# chown betty.users /opt/somefile
```

The above command changes the ownership of `/opt/somefile` to `betty`, and changes group ownership to the `users` group. You can omit the period and group name if you don't want to change it, or add an `-R` parameter before the username to recursively change every file within a directory. For instance, the following command changes the ownership of the `/home/samba/sharedfiles` directory and all its files and subdirectories to `betty`, but doesn't change the group associated with the files:

```
# chown -R betty /home/samba/sharedfiles
```

Deleting an Account with Linuxconf

You can also delete a user using the Linuxconf utility. To do so, follow these steps:

1. Start Linuxconf as previously described.
2. Navigate to Config ➢ User Accounts ➢ Normal ➢ User Accounts.
3. Select the account that you'd like to delete. You will then be presented with the User Information screen, which is similar to Figure 6.2, with any existing values filled in.
4. Click the Del button to delete the user listed and remove all of the user's files from the user's home directory.
5. Activate the changes as before.

You will still need to locate files owned by this user in other folders and delete or reassign them.

Deleting an Account with *userdel*

The `userdel` utility will remove a user's entry in the `/etc/passwd` file and optionally remove that user's home directory and all the files and subdirectories it contains. Any files owned by that user outside the home directory will remain on the system and will appear as owned by the user's ID when displayed via an `ls -l` command. The `userdel` command to delete our hypothetical Donald's `passwd` entry and home directory looks like this:

```
# userdel -r donald
```

You may also choose to delete Donald's `/etc/passwd` entry but leave all the files in his home directory by omitting the –r.

You may choose to use the `find` command shown earlier to locate all files owned by Donald or in his group.

Groups

You saw earlier in the chapter that each user has a default group identity, called a login group, which is assumed upon logging in to the system. Once authenticated by `/bin/login`, the user assumes the group identity specified in the `/etc/passwd` file. In Red Hat Linux, a user's default group ID is the same as the user ID; in some other Linux distributions, all users are by default put in a single group, typically called `users`. Linux administrators can create new groups, associating users for specific purposes such as projects that require certain users to have access to the same set of files. The next sections show how to add and remove groups, and how users can become members of different groups.

The Function of Groups

Groups are an integral part of Linux security. As described in Chapter 3, every file has an associated permissions string. This string specifies the presence or absence of read, write, and execute permission to each of three classes of users: the file's owner, the file's group, and all users on the system (often called *world* permissions). By controlling the group setting for files and by assigning users to particular groups, you can enhance the internal security of your Linux system. For instance, if your system is being used by two different sets of employees, each of which is working on one project, you can create two groups, one for each set of employees. By denying world access to users' files, you can prevent employees in one group from reading files created by members of the other group. If a few users belong to both groups, you can make those users members of both groups, so they can read both groups' files.

Because every Linux installation is unique, it's impossible for a Linux distribution to come with a default group setup that's appropriate for all environments. The packagers of Red Hat can't know what groups you'll need, any more than they can know what users you'll need. Nonetheless, the account creation tools make certain default assumptions about how you might group your accounts. Different distributions do things in different ways.

In Red Hat Linux, every time a new user is added, a group with the same user ID and numeric ID as that user is created. Say the user is `donald` again. A user group called `donald` would be created, and the user `donald` would be added to that *user private group*. The umask (see Chapter 4) is set to 002, which means that any file created by `donald` will have read-write permission for him (the owner) and for the `donald` group and read-only for world. This works well since we know that `donald` has membership in the group by default. Since Donald is the only member of his user private group, only he and the super-user can access files with the group set to `donald`. Anyone can be added to the `donald` group and will then have group access to any files that Donald creates with this umask.

Other distributions don't always work this way. Some create a single group (generally called `users`), and place all users in this group. Thus, both the `donald` and `betty` accounts by default belong to the `users` group. Typically, the umask is 022, so users can read each other's files, but cannot write to them. This is a *shared-group* approach.

On small workstations, both these approaches tend to work well, because workstations tend to have just one or two users, and the implications of group membership have small consequences. At worst, you may need to add one or two users to each other's groups in the user private group approach, or create a couple of new groups and change default group membership in the shared group approach. On larger systems, though, you're likely to need to create a more complex configuration. In an academic environment, for instance, you may need to create groups for different courses; and in a work environment, you may need to create groups for different working groups. The tools to do this parallel the tools used to create user accounts in many respects.

The */etc/group* File

Information about each group is contained in the /etc/group file. Just as with /etc/passwd, it is critical that any system administrator clearly understand this important file. Its structure is fairly simple. Listing 6.2 shows an excerpt from a typical /etc/group file.

Listing 6.2   A Portion of the /etc/group File

```
root:x:0:root
bin:x:1:root,bin,daemon
daemon:x:2:root,bin,daemon
```

```
<... other entries ...>
slocate:x:21:
project2038:x:1000:ernie,betty
marty:x:500:
ernie:x:501:
betty:x:502:
donald:x:503:
```

Each entry declares a group name, password, and numeric group ID, called the GID. Table 6.2 lists the default groups that Linux creates automatically upon installation.

Table 6.2   Default Linux Groups

Group	GID	Members	Description
root	9	root	Superuser group
bin	1	root,bin,daemon	Running programs
daemon	2	root,bin,daemon	Running programs
sys	3	root,bin,dam	System group
adm	4	root,adm,daemon	Administrative group
tty	5		Access to terminals
disk	6	root	Access to disk device files
lp	7	daemon, lp	Printing group
mem	8		Kernel memory access
kmem	9		Kernel memory access
wheel	10	root	Users with near-root privileges
mail	12	mail	Used by mail utilities
news	13	news	Used by Usenet news utilities

Managing Users
and Software

PART 2

Table 6.2   Default Linux Groups *(continued)*

Group	GID	Members	Description
uucp	14	uucp	Used for UUCP networking
man	15		Used for man page access
games	20		Group for storing game high scores
gopher	30		Used by the Gopher utility
dip	40		Dialup IP group (PPP, SLIP)
ftp	50		Group for FTP daemon
nobody	99		Low-security group
users	100		Default user group on many systems
floppy	19		Group for access to low-level floppy disk devices

Adding New Groups

Just as users can be added manually, with a command-line utility, or using Linuxconf, groups can also be created in any of these ways. The different methods are explained below so that you can choose the method you prefer. (Once you've created a new group, you presumably want to add users to that group. This process is described shortly, in "Changing Group Membership.")

Manually Adding a Group

Because the structure of the /etc/group file is fairly simple, administrators typically add groups by directly editing the file. To create a group with an initial set of group members, simply add the usernames of the users to the comma-delimited list at the end of the entry. For instance:

```
cs101::101:donald,betty,ernie
```

To check your work, the id command reports all of the groups a user has membership in. The output for the root user looks like this:

```
uid=0(root) gid=0(root)
groups=0(root),1(bin),2(daemon),3(sys),4(adm),6(disk),10(wheel)
```

> **NOTE** It's not normally necessary to add root to groups you create. root is a very special account, which can read and write any file or directory on the computer, so it doesn't need membership in ordinary user groups. root belongs to several system groups as a matter of convenience for handling those groups.

The groups command may be used instead to give the same basic information:

```
root bin daemon sys adm disk wheel
```

Adding a Group with *groupadd*

To add a new group, use the groupadd command, which uses the parameters passed on the command line to create a new group, relying on system defaults for any parameters you don't specify. The new group will be added to the system files as needed. The syntax for the groupadd command is as follows:

```
groupadd [-g GID [-o]] [-r] [-f] group
```

The meanings of the various groupadd parameters are as follows:

-g *GID*   The numeric value of the group's ID. The GID must be unique unless the –o option is given. The value must not be a negative number. The default is to select the smallest remaining ID that is greater than 500 and greater than the ID of any other group. System accounts use the values between 0 and 499.

-r   Designates that the added group will be a system group. The group will be assigned the first available GID under 499 unless the –g option specifies a GID to be used instead.

-f   If a group of the specified name already exists, forces the groupadd command to leave that group as it exists on the system and continue without returning an error message. (Ordinarily, groupadd would complain about the attempt to reuse a group name.) Also this option changes the way that –g behaves in Red Hat, so that if –g is given without –o, the group will be added as if neither –g nor –o were specified.

group   The name of the new group being created.

Managing Users and Software

PART 2

Adding a Group with Linuxconf

You can also use the Linuxconf utility to add new groups. To do so, follow these steps:

1. Select Config ➢ User Accounts ➢ Normal ➢ Group Definitions from the Linuxconf main menu. The result is the User Groups Linuxconf module shown in Figure 6.3.

Figure 6.3   The Linuxconf User Groups module allows you to add, remove, or modify groups in a manner similar to changing user accounts.

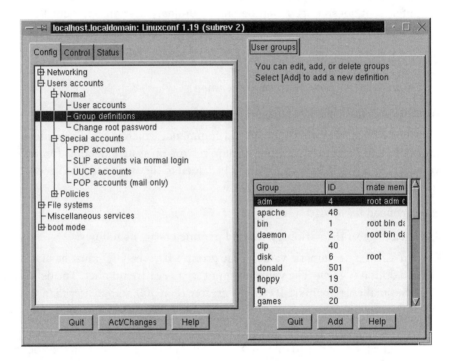

2. Click the Add button to add a new group. You will then be presented with a User Groups screen as shown in Figure 6.4.

3. Specify the group's name and any alternate members.

4. Click Accept.

5. Activate the changes as before.

Changing Group Membership

All actions performed by a user are performed under a specific user ID and group ID. Therefore, although a user may belong to more than one group (by adding the username

Figure 6.4   You can specify user group information using the Group Specification screen.

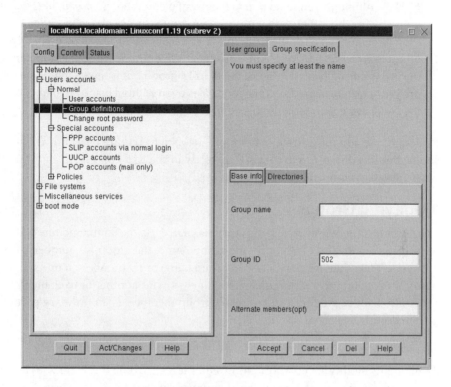

to multiple groups' /etc/group entries, as described earlier), a user may only *act* as a member of one group at a time. Ordinarily, this is not terribly important, but it can be in some cases. For instance, a user might need to create files that carry a certain group membership, so that other members of the appropriate group can read those files. Every user has a primary group affiliation, specified in the user's /etc/passwd file entry. Upon logging in, the user acts as a member of that group. The newgrp command provides a means for users to temporarily change the group associated with their actions. (The command sg is frequently a synonym for newgrp.) To use newgrp, type the command, a hyphen (which causes the system to reinitialize the user's environmental variables), and the new group name. For instance, to become a member of the project1 group, type:

```
$ newgrp - project1
```

If the user donald has used newgrp to join the group project1, when he creates a new file, such as a project document, it will show up in a long listing (ls -l) with group ownership by the new group:

```
-rw-r--r--    1 donald    project1       10332 Aug 20 16:07 proj_doc
```

> **NOTE** Although you need to use the newgrp command to *create* files with group ownership other than your primary group (or use chown or chgrp to change ownership after the fact), this isn't necessary to *read* files owned by a group to which you belong, but which isn't your primary group. For instance, if Donald is normally a member of the donald group but is also a member of the project1 group, he can read project1 files even without using newgrp, provided the files have group read permissions.

By design, the administrator can configure newgrp to require authentication for group access, but this doesn't seem to work correctly in the Red Hat distribution, so we advise you to avoid assigning passwords to groups.

Modifying Groups

The modification of groups may be done manually, via the command line groupmod tool, or via Linuxconf. You can modify the group name, the group ID number, and group members. You might need to change a group name or ID number on one system to bring two or more computers' configurations in line with one another or to change your scheme for group layouts. Adding and removing group members is an ordinary part of system administration.

Manually Modifying a Group

To manually modify group information, edit the /etc/group file. Here you can change the group name, GID, and the members. If you wish to change other information, it is much easier to use the useradd or the Linuxconf utility.

As an example, consider the following group definition:

```
project1:x:503:donald,betty
```

Suppose you want to give the group a more descriptive name and add a new user, emily. You could change the definition as follows:

```
moonshot:x:503:donald,betty,emily
```

Thereafter, the group ID will appear in program listings and the like as moonshot, not project1. (Even existing files will be changed.) When changing to this group, group members will need to specify moonshot as the group name, and the user emily will be able to use the group's resources.

> **WARNING**   Changing the GID, like changing the UID of a user, will "orphan" files owned by the group. The recovery process is the same as described earlier for altering existing files' UIDs. Unless you have a compelling reason to do so, it's best not to change the GID of an existing group.

Modifying Group Information with *groupmod*

The characteristics of a group may be modified with the groupmod command. All appropriate system files are updated. The syntax for groupmod is similar to that of groupadd:

```
groupmod  [-g GID [-o]] [-n group_name] group
```

-g *GID*   The numeric value of the group's ID. This value must be unique unless the –o parameter is specified. As with the groupadd command, group IDs must be non-negative and should not fall between 0 and 99 unless the group is a system group.

-n *group-name*   The new name of the group.

group   The old name of the group.

Linuxconf

The Linuxconf utility may be used to modify a group. Simply navigate to the Group Definitions option as before. When presented with the group list, highlight the one you wish to modify. You will then be presented with the same Group Specification screen as shown in Figure 6.4, with the existing values filled in. Make changes as needed, and then click the Accept button. Activate the changes as before.

Deleting Groups

Groups may also be deleted using the same three methods as in other account management tasks: manually editing the /etc/group file, using the command line (the groupdel command), or using Linuxconf.

Deleting a Group with *groupdel*

You can delete groups using the groupdel command; this command deletes any entries that refer to the named group:

```
groupdel group
```

The groupdel command does not, however, search for files with that GID. That must be done separately with the find command, as follows:

```
# find / -gid GID
```

Deleting a Group with Linuxconf

The Linuxconf utility can also be used to delete a group. Simply select the Group Definitions option as before. When presented with the group list, highlight the one you wish to delete. You will then be presented with the same Group Specification screen as shown in Figure 6.4, with the existing values filled in. Click the Del button, and activate the changes as before.

Manually Removing a Group

Although you can remove a group simply by editing the /etc/group file to delete the line that corresponds to the group you wish to remove, that's not as efficient as the other methods. If you remove the group's entry in /etc/group, you should probably remove the corresponding entry in the /etc/gshadow file (in which shadowed group passwords are stored, if you have elected to use group passwords). If you do not use passwords for your groups, this file will not be automatically updated.

In Sum

As a multiuser OS, Linux relies upon user accounts and groups to maintain security and keep the system usable to all its users. Over the years, manual methods, text-based tools, and GUI tools have been developed to manage these accounts and groups. However you do it, though, it's important that you understand how Linux handles its accounts and groups—the relationship between usernames and UIDs or group names and GIDs; where passwords are stored; and how users are assigned to groups. Understanding these topics will allow you to effectively manage your user base, whether it's just one or two people or thousands. These subjects are also critically important for understanding Linux system security, which is the topic of the next chapter.

7

Security

Monitor any Linux mailing list for a week or two, and you will see posts from someone whose system has been broken into or taken down by an unauthorized entry. You can tell from the tone of the messages that this is a frustrating experience. As a result, seasoned system administrators are always on the watch for holes in their security plan. They know that, as system administrators, they must constantly look for ways to improve security because there are always people outside looking to crack their security; if the system's security stays as it is for too long, different cracking techniques can be tried until one eventually succeeds. If your security motif changes over time, would-be intruders will need to spend most of their time trying to get back to the point they last reached, and the system will remain secure.

With all of the news stories of crackers being indicted, most people know that breaking into a computer system is illegal. Still there are many people who access the Internet with this goal in mind. Some are malicious, and others are just curious. What most of the world calls "hackers" can be divided into three categories: crackers, hackers, and script-kiddies.

Crackers are highly skilled computer users who intentionally break security on computer systems in order to cause damage and demonstrate superior ability. (The term was coined around 1985 by hackers to make a distinction between themselves and the destructive crackers.) A cracker is malicious, breaking into a system solely to cause damage and show superior ability. Crackers tend to steal information, use your identity to distribute spam, deny you access to your own system, and generally wreak havoc on your system. For many crackers, it is a game; others recognize that they can gain financially from their theft. To crackers, destruction is of no consequence. Their intrusion may not be obvious because they plan to be back or to use the system to relay mail, thereby disguising their identities. Crackers are the reason you need to check your system's logs on a daily basis and to watch for the telltale signs we'll discuss later in this chapter.

A *hacker* is a particularly skilled programmer who loves to hack around on computers. This person enjoys looking to learn new things and generally gets a rush out of even the smallest computer discovery. There are a great many of us out there. A hacker may fall into the cracker category, but not all hackers are crackers. In fact, the crackers probably make up a very small percentage. Most hackers do not crack systems—not because they can't, but because they are not malicious. Hackers don't break into systems to cause damage, but they may break in to learn how it is done or to test security for a colleague or client. We know some hackers who have broken into systems to learn how to protect them from intrusion. After breaking in, they leave the system undamaged and pass on information about the security flaw or create a patch to fix it.

There are numerous sites on the Internet that detail how to exploit known security flaws and provide scripts designed to do just that. *Script-kiddie* is the term commonly used to describe those who do not possess the skills required to break into a system on their own but instead download a script to perform the task. Often these break-ins are characterized by minor damage, since script-kiddies don't usually know the system well enough to know what would cause damage. They do try to make themselves known to the target system's administrator by leaving a calling card in the form of a file with a name that will be noticed or by changing the banner printed above the login (`/etc/issue`) to something offensive. Script-kiddies generally strive to make their intrusion known since they have no real skills to do further damage at a later date.

Types of Attacks

There are so many types of security attacks that it is impossible to list all the variations. We explain some of the most common here, with the emphasis on clarifying how the attack is made and what vulnerability it attempts to exploit. It is important to say that there is no such thing as absolute security from these attacks. Even if there were, some enterprising young cracker would find something else to exploit. This is true not only of Linux but of every operating system out there: all Unix versions, all Microsoft Windows versions, VMS, and any other operating system you can think of.

The goal is to maintain the highest possible level of security on your system by keeping up with new attacks as they hit. Watch your distribution's home site for updates that fix security exploits, and install them immediately. Each major distribution of Linux has a security-announce list where users and staff post news of new security exploits and other security-related news. Be sure to subscribe to the appropriate security list to stay ahead of would-be intruders.

Trojan Horse

You probably remember the story of the Trojan horse from Homer's *Iliad*. The Greeks sent a giant wooden horse as a present to end their ten-year war with Troy. When it was within the gates of Troy, Greek soldiers emerged from inside and defeated the unsuspecting Trojans.

In security, then, a Trojan horse is a program or a script that is hidden inside an authorized program. This code, when executed, causes an undesirable effect. Many of these are aimed at Microsoft machines, targeting their mailers. For example, you may remember the "Love Bug" Trojan horse from May of 2000. It appeared to be an e-mailed love letter but, when opened, it would cause problems, such as sending itself to everybody on your e-mail address book, erasing your files, and downloading another Trojan horse program that would steal your passwords. This particular Trojan horse affected only Microsoft Windows machines, but while Trojan horses are rare on Linux machines, they are not unheard of. In January of 1999, a Trojan horse was found in the `util-linux-2.9g.tar.gz` on some Web sites. This type of attack is difficult to protect against. As a result, Red Hat and many other distributions have begun adding checksums or Pretty Good Privacy (PGP) signatures to the packages they make available for download. Make use of these verification techniques if they are available to you.

Pretty Good Privacy (PGP)

Pretty Good Privacy is a software package that provides both asymmetric data encryption, which is usually used for e-mail, and secret keys and symmetric encryption for other files. PGP is generally used to ensure that the e-mail you receive is as its author intended. Mail sent through the Internet can easily be intercepted, changed, or created as if it were from someone else entirely. With PGP, you can digitally sign your e-mail, generating a mathematical value based on your e-mail's content as encrypted using your private key. If the recipient of e-mail has your public key, the PGP software makes the same calculation, thereby determining that the message has not been altered. Since only you have the private key that encrypted the hash value that was successfully decrypted with your public key, only you could have digitally signed the e-mail. Packages made available for download may be signed the same way.

The difficulty comes with obtaining the public key in such a way as to be sure that the person who claims the key actually is the one who generated it. The most secure way is to meet face to face with the person, exchanging identification and public keys at the same time. Retrieving a signed software package from a Web site is not as secure.

Typically you obtain the developer's key from a Web site or possibly via e-mail. Still, this is a step in the right direction. For more information on PGP, see its international home page at http://www.pgpi.org/.

Checksum

A checksum is another type of file signature that is usually used for validation when files are transferred by means that are considered unreliable, for instance from disk to tape. It is valuable as a security check as well. The checksum is computed from the binary bytes of the file, creating a "fingerprint" of sorts. When the file is transferred, a new checksum is computed and compared with the saved fingerprint. This method is not foolproof. A knowledgeable cracker will simply pad the file to obtain the appropriate checksum value. Like other methods, however, it is better than nothing. For more information about creating a checksum, see the chksum man or info page.

Back Door

A *back door* is code added to a program to allow unauthorized access to the host system. Take, for example, a program that has been altered to e-mail information about the person running the program to some mail account whenever the program is run. Very few users look at the size of binary files to see whether the program has been changed. Fewer still check beyond that if the sizes match. Even worse is that some programmers-for-hire include back doors in the programs they write as a matter of course. Once there is any negative interaction between the programmer and the client, the programmer exploits the back door and gets revenge. In this case, the only way to find the offensive code is to wade through the source code. Typically, if the code works, it isn't looked at until it requires some updating, so the programmer has plenty of time to play spy.

There is little if any defense against a back door if it is inserted by someone doing software development for your company. If you believe that a coder has inserted a back door in a product, you can have another programmer look at the code, but beyond that, you have to depend on your normal security watches to catch his or her entry onto the system. With a system that uses a package manager like the Red Hat Package Manager (RPM) or Debian's Package Management System, you can run a command to verify that a package as a whole has not been changed and output codes indicating any changes to individual files. Using this information, you can determine whether files on your system have been changed and how.

Trusted Host

One of the most talked-about vulnerabilities in Linux involves the *trusted host* files. Trusted host files allow users to log in without a password, because their logins and host machine names are included in the appropriate files: /etc/hosts.equiv and .rhosts in the user's home directory. The commands that rely on these files are referred to as the *r-commands* and include rlogin, rsh, rcp, and rexec. Most Linux system administrators simply disable these commands and replace them with Secure Shell (SSH).

SSH is a client/server package that encrypts all outgoing data from either direction, thus creating an encrypted tunnel. The client side sends a request to the server (sshd), and the server sends back a public host key and a public server key. The client attempts to verify the public host key by locating it in either /etc/ssh_known_hosts or the .ssh/known_hosts file in the user's home directory on the client. If the client is able to verify the public host key, it generates a 256-bit random number, encrypts it with the two keys from the server, and sends it to the server. This generated number is then used by both the server and the client to derive the session key, which is used to encrypt any further communication between the two during this session. If the process fails to generate a session key, access by the client is denied. This is a somewhat simplified description, but it illustrates the basic process. For more information, start with the SSH-FAQ at http://www.tigerlair.com/ssh/faq/ssh-faq.html.

Red Hat Linux 7.0 includes a free version of SSH that was developed by the OpenBSD Project. Called OpenSSH, the package includes the following: the ssh program, to be used in place of Telnet and rlogin; scp, to be used in place of rcp and ftp; and the server-side sshd program and its supporting utilities.

Buffer Overflow

A buffer overflow occurs when a program written to read data is not properly restricted to the intended area of memory. This is similar to when your cellular phone picks up someone else's conversation. You don't really know whose conversation you are hearing, but you might hear something that the speaker didn't intend to reveal to anyone outside the target audience. A buffer overflow causes a program to read data that was not intended for it. It is quite difficult for even skilled programmers to take advantage of this, but there are programs available on the Internet that were written explicitly for this purpose. Typically, programs prone to overflow buffers are reported on the main security lists for your distribution.

Scanning or Sniffing

Network *scanning* involves the probing of an IP address or some of its ports to determine which services are available on that system. Sniffing is the process by which data packets are intercepted as they are sent over the network. Specifically, crackers look for passwords and the like. There are packages available that help you to detect whether your system is being attacked in this way and even to fool the sniffer. Some of these packages are detailed in the "Intrusion Detecting Packages" section later in this chapter.

Spoofing

Spoofing is the process of masquerading as a known user. This can be in the form of e-mail that appears to the receiving system to have come from a known user or data packets that look like they came from a trusted machine. The details of how this is accomplished are beyond the scope of this book, but there is a way to minimize or possibly even stop it completely.

The Linux kernel can be configured to perform Source Address Verification. If your system has the file /proc/sys/net/ipv4/conf/all/rp_filter, you only need to add a little code, shown in Listing 7.1, to one of the startup scripts at some point before any network interfaces are configured. What this script does is turn on rp-filtering for each individual interface listed in the /proc/sys/net/ipv4/conf directory.

Listing 7.1   rp_filter Code

```
# Turn on spoof protection for all  interfaces.
if [ -e /proc/sys/net/ipv4/conf/all/rp_filter ]; then
  echo -n "Setting up IP spoof protection..."
  for interface in /proc/sys/net/ipv4/conf/*/rp_filter; do
    echo 1 > $interface
    done
  echo "done."
else
  echo "THERE WERE PROBLEMS. You will be dropped to a shell to"
  echo "troubleshoot. You may use CONTROL-D to exit the shell and"
  echo " continue system startup."
  echo
  # Start a single user shell on the console
  /sbin/sulogin $CONSOLE
fi
```

Denial of Service

In a denial-of-service attack, the attacker tries to make some resource too busy to answer legitimate requests for services. In recent years, several large companies, including Amazon.com, Yahoo!, and CNN.com, have had service interruptions due to denial-of-service attacks.

Here's an example. Bad Guy and his buddy have two computers on the Internet. Each uses scanning techniques to find computers on the Internet that they can spoof through. Each finds several vulnerable computers they can crack. At a given time, Bad Guy and his friend cause all the compromised computers to ping the target site, thereby increasing the load and hiding his and his buddy's identities. The target site can't handle all of the false traffic and its regular load too, so everything grinds to a halt. This is especially effective with the HTTP daemon, which attempts to confirm the address of any system that makes a request upon it. The HTTP daemon thus waits until its request to the spoofed IP times out before being "convinced" that it is a bad address. In this case, Bad Guy and his friend send so many data packets with spoofed IP addresses that the server is too busy trying to confirm IP addresses to be able to do any Web servicing.

Detecting and preventing Denial of Service attacks is difficult since the attacks come from several sources at once. To minimize the effects of the attacks, thoroughly screen incoming network packets and deny packets using firewall or routing software. This might not completely prevent delays in service, but it will reduce the load that the attack creates on your system.

Accurate logging at the Web or mail server can assist law enforcement in catching the cracker; however, this is complicated in many cases by the fact that crackers rarely launch this type of attack from their own machines. Instead, the cracker launches the attack via other compromised machines on the Internet, thereby implicating only the owners of the exploited machines.

Password Cracking

Password cracking is the acquisition by whatever means of a valid user password. This is a real threat to any system but particularly to systems whose administrators don't teach their users the importance of selecting a hard-to-guess password or don't force users to change their passwords fairly often. We'll discuss the actual authentication process in the upcoming "Securing the Authentication Process" section.

For now let's talk about how to select a secure password. Passwords should not be standard dictionary words like *misery* or *supersecret*. Passwords should have a mixture of numbers, letters, and symbols like #@$%&. Use capital letters and lowercase letters. A good password might be *R#t34%Ka*. Linux uses a tool called `cracklib` to evaluate the security of a password. Regular users cannot change their passwords to anything based on a word in the `cracklib` dictionary, although the superuser may do so. This restriction is accomplished by using Pluggable Authentication Modules, which we'll discuss in a later section.

Social Attacks

Social attacks are performed by an insider. This person might simply walk up behind a user who is logging in and watch to see the password as it is keyed in. In another form of social attack, an individual pretends to be a system administrator and obtains information—such as a user's password—that provides unauthorized access. These types of attacks are best dealt with by making your users security-conscious. Teach them to be alert for such situations, and make sure to introduce new members of your system administration staff to as many users as possible.

Physical Attacks

If an intruder gains physical access to your system, he may try to hack it, interfere with or intercept network traffic, or even physically destroy it. Linux in particular has one physical security vulnerability that you need to avoid. Anyone with a boot disk can boot the average system into single-user mode and have root access to it! Obviously this is not something you want to have happen. The vulnerability is with respect to the Linux Boot Loader (LILO), which we discussed in Chapter 5. You must change the default configuration to safeguard the system.

The first step is to assign a password that must be typed in when the system is rebooted. Without the password, the machine doesn't initialize, so no breach is possible. To do this add the `restricted` and `password` lines to `/etc/lilo.conf` as indicated in Listing 7.2.

Listing 7.2   Securing the `lilo.conf` File

```
boot=/dev/hda
map=/boot/map
install=/boot/boot.b
prompt
message=/boot/message
linear
default=linux
append="aha152x=0x140,12,7,0,0"
restricted
password=#94hd*1@
```

```
image=/boot/vmlinuz-2.2.16-22
        label=linux
        read-only
        root=/dev/hda1
```

The `password` line is self-explanatory. The `restricted` line is required if the `password` line is used. Remember to include the `prompt` line so that the system doesn't just automatically boot without asking for input. Since a `timeout` value would allow the system to boot if the user didn't enter something in the given amount of time, that option has been removed. Note, however, that while omitting the `timeout` option makes your system more secure, it also removes the ability to boot the machine unattended. You don't want a `delay` option either for a similar reason; `delay` tells the machine to boot the default selection if no user input is detected for the specified amount of time.

Now you need to secure this file to prevent an intruder from viewing the password, which is in clear text. First use the `chmod` command to set the file so that only the root user has read/write privileges.

```
# chmod 600 /etc/lilo.conf
```

Next use the `chattr` command to change the file attributes so that the immutable bit is set on the file. This prevents the file from being modified, linked to, removed, or renamed except by the superuser.

```
# chattr +i /etc/lilo.conf
```

Finally, you'll need to ensure that the machine's BIOS is set to prevent booting by floppy or CD-ROM, since there are bootable images that would allow the intruder to circumvent the LILO hurdle. Finally, password-protect your BIOS settings. Now you are secure against someone sitting down and rebooting the system unless they know the password to either the BIOS or LILO. An intruder who can open the computer's case can still steal the hard disk or reset the BIOS to gain entry to the computer, though. The best protection against this is to keep the computer in a physically secure area.

Types of Security

Security is tricky business—especially since several crackers can gang up on a computer system or network. Typically a site will have only a few people trying to set up security to block them. Of course, a computer's security needs are relative to the importance of the data it contains. Home computers that are used primarily for learning, data processing, and sending e-mail need much less security than do bank systems, which are heavily targeted by crackers. Your systems will probably fall somewhere in between. While a home user might not want the intrusive measures higher security requires, a data communications firm would probably be willing to jump through those hoops. Security requires a lot of extra effort by users as well as the system administrator, so determining just how much security you need is important. The job of securing your system, called risk assessment, has two parts: assessing vulnerability and assessing threat.

Assessing vulnerability means assessing the loss that the company would suffer if your security were breached. Ask yourself where your systems are vulnerable. Which information might be profitable to a thief? Which information might generate a profit if taken by disgruntled employees? Is the mission-critical data available to naive users who might inadvertently damage or delete it? Is the mission-critical data available to all employees or only to those who need it? How much would down time spent fixing a hacked system cost the company in man-hours, lost profit, etc.? These are the questions to ask before developing the security plan.

Assessing threat means assessing how many people out there are really going to attempt to break in. Remember that just because you're paranoid doesn't mean that no one is out to get you, or in this case, the data you're protecting. Be too cautious. If you are on the Internet, the threat of a cracker on the hunt is a real issue. Also ask yourself whether you have competitors or other groups who might seek to damage your company's reputation by stealing data or taking the system down. Try to determine the threat. Of course, you must never completely discount any of the above possibilities, but the answers to these questions can help you to focus your efforts where the threat is greatest.

Once the security system is in place, an auditing plan should be written to ensure that the security that you've set up remains effective. It is better to use a formal auditing checklist than to "shoot from the hip" since repetitive tasks like security evaluation are all too easy to rush through. A checklist forces you to be thorough. We'll discuss how to audit your security later in this chapter.

Although no system is ever completely safe from intrusion, there are ways to minimize the possibility of a break-in or other security breach. For this discussion, we'll divide security into the areas that are under the system administrator's direct control:

- User-based security basically answers two questions: "Is this user who he or she claims to be?" and "What resources should be available to this user at this time?" Linux uses Pluggable Authentication Modules (PAM) to secure the system from intrusion by unauthorized users.

- Port security in designed to protect network ports from unauthorized hosts and networks. This type of security is handled largely by the kernel but is also affected by IP firewall administration, commonly referred to as *IP chains*. Port security is important since any open port is an invitation to a cracker. Port security also helps to control outgoing information from the users on your systems.

- You must also restrict network access to system resources and services based on the requesting host. Quite often you know that the users on www.gooddomain.com should have access to a given resource while users on www.baddomain.com should not. This is the job of host-based security. Under Linux, host-based security is handled in any of several ways, including TCP Wrappers, xinetd, and individual daemon security options.

- You should restrict physical access to your systems to prevent tampering. Also use the lilo.conf securing measures that we mentioned in the "Physical Attacks" section.

- A last type of security is the assignment of permissions to exclude certain users from having access to specific files or devices. This is the most commonly discussed method of securing your system and the best understood. Unfortunately, by itself it is insufficient to defend your system adequately.

Securing the Authentication Process

The authentication process is a mystery to most of your users. Generally users don't worry about how they are authenticated as long as they gain access to their files. They type their login and password combinations and wait while the magic happens. If they are authenticated, they are content; if the authentication fails, they call you for help. As a system administrator, you need to know how this process works.

First, Linux uses two different systems for authenticating user passwords: DES (the Data Encryption Standard) and MD5 (message digest algorithm, version 5). The DES algorithm can deal with MD5 passwords, but the MD5 algorithm can't understand DES passwords. DES passwords are encoded using the Federal Data Encryption Standard algorithm. MD5 uses the RSA Data Security, Inc. MD5 message digest algorithm. By default on most Linux systems, MD5 is used now. Passwords encrypted with the MD5 hash are longer than those encrypted with the DES hash and also begin with the characters 1. A shorter password that does not begin with a $ is typically a DES password.

Hashing Passwords

On a Linux system the passwords, which are often referred to as encrypted, are actually encoded or hashed. This means that they are encoded in such a way that they generally cannot be decrypted. Figure 7.1 illustrates the process.

Figure 7.1   How Linux passwords are hashed

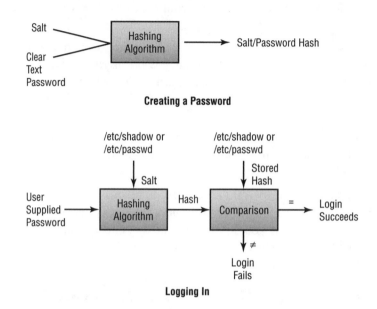

When users change their passwords, the variable-length password that they enter and a two-character salt that the system generates are run through a modified DES algorithm or MD5 algorithm to generate a hash. Although the hash is often referred to as an encrypted password, it actually is encoded instead. As described in Chapter 6, the salt is a sort of monkey wrench that changes the hash in any one of 4096 ways. Under Linux, the DES result is a 13-character one-way hash, a string of characters that is almost impossible to regenerate into its clear text form. The first two characters represent the salt, and the remaining 11 represent the hashed password. For MD5, the password is 32 characters long and begins with 1.

Linux systems do not "decrypt" the stored passwords at all during authentication. Instead, the password that a user supplies to a DES system at login and the two-character salt hash taken from the /etc/passwd file are run through the same DES algorithm, generating a one-way hash. In the case of MD5 passwords, the first two characters will be $1 and the characters between the second and third $ represent the salt, while the rest is the hashed password. As with the DES passwords, the salt is removed and passed with the login password into the appropriate algorithm. The result is compared to the hash stored in /etc/passwd. If they are the same, it is assumed the proper password was supplied. In old-school Unix, the user was considered to be authenticated if this encrypted password was identical to the second field of the user's entry in the /etc/passwd file. The potential for intruders masquerading as authenticated users was simply ignored. An /etc/passwd file has the following format:

username:*passwd*:*UID*:*GID*:*full_name*:*directory*:*shell*

An example of a password file that uses the DES algorithm is shown as Listing 7.3. A sample password file that uses the MD5 algorithm is illustrated in Listing 7.4.

Listing 7.3 Example DES /etc/passwd File

```
root:AB2dfzgfkgjfl:0:0:root,,,:/root:/bin/bash
bin:9pskwjeioxjar:1:1:bin:/bin:
daemon:f7lsdjenjfkejdl:2:2:daemon:/sbin:
adm:DIBU7epiSd4xs:3:4:adm:/var/adm:
lp:5fg63fhD3d5gh:4:7:lp:/var/spool/lpd:
sync:dsjLkwRi4d1rt:5:0:sync:/sbin:/bin/sync
shutdown:5fg63fhD3d,M.z:9406:6:0:shutdown:/sbin:/sbin/shutdown
halt:10gw4c34GeKSJ:7:0:halt:/sbin:/sbin/halt
user:G2sdqwpk75jzx:500:500:Unknown User:/home/user:/bin/bash
```

Listing 7.4 Example MD5 /etc/passwd File

```
root:$1$7t6j9J2k$2jOqc7RxD3E86Dx7.bYfI.:0:0:root,,,:/root:/bin/bash
bin:$1$45NwV/np$8DwIrkbNaFc/oeKREY/eC/:1:1:bin:/bin:
daemon:$1$Om3cvkqJ$K8ZfrewZPdv3gcX7OSYaN.:2:2:daemon:/sbin:
adm:$1$s.614WUD$79JSpeUvOmN1/IKof8mn51:3:4:adm:/var/adm:
lp:$1$K9QSOPt7$R1OOcFpwLJ3t5MKvOffH1/:4:7:lp:/var/spool/lp:
sync:$1$zjkRCMgA$TLiDMTFeTU9Io8QkylstZ1:5:0:sync:/sbin:/bin/sync
shutdown:$1$LPWwN8S2$xiNnTCB..cNhgUfMaOn980:9406:6:0:shutdown:/sbin:/
    ➥sbin/shutdown
halt:$1$I9ffuBg2$4BgcZGnqK78pbhohoAfvIO:7:0:halt:/sbin:/sbin/halt
user:$1$S8td6y.8$IYPK1ILLM8TNTUNZ7pVBk/:500:500:Unknown User:
    ➥/home/user:/bin/bash
```

The /etc/passwd file on a Linux system must be world readable for the other user information that is stored in this file to be available to the programs that need it.

Managing Users
and Software

PART 2

Unfortunately, this makes the hashes available as well. While you cannot decrypt a hash, it is possible to compare a list of generated hashes with the ones stored in /etc/ passwd to find a match, which can be exploited. Crackers simply encode a dictionary of words and common passwords using all possible 4096 salt values. They then compare the hashed passwords in your /etc/passwd file with those in their list. Once they have found a match, they have the password for an account on your system. This is referred to as a *dictionary attack* and is one of the most common methods for gaining unauthorized access to a system. The attack is significantly easier if intruders can obtain a copy of your /etc/passwd file since they then only have to encode their dictionaries with the salts that exist in the /etc/passwd file. To reduce this vulnerability, Linux adopted the practice of shadowing the passwords.

Shadow Passwords

Shadowing removes the hash strings from the /etc/passwd file and places them in /etc/ shadow, which is not world readable. Only the superuser has read and write permissions for the /etc/shadow file. This hinders the dictionary attack by making the hashes unavailable to anyone except the superuser. Additionally, the Shadow Suite gives you the ability to perform certain functions based on a password's age. It allows you to require that users change their passwords at given intervals, to restrict users from changing their passwords for given intervals, render the account inactive after a given interval, or expire the account after a given interval. This information for a specific user may be retrieved or changed via the chage (change password aging information) command. The chage command with the −l option prints the relevant data for the given user.

```
# chage -l user
Minimum:               0
Maximum                99999
Warning:               7
Inactive               -1
Last Change:           Jun 06, 2000
Password Expires:      Never
Password Inactive:     Never
Account Expires:       Dec 31, 2000
```

You can change this information interactively by not including any parameters between the command and username. This gives you a prompt for each individual item to be changed. Here is the first prompt you'll see:

```
# chage someuser
```

```
Changing the aging information for someuser
Enter the new value, or press return for the default
```

```
Minimum Password Age [0]:
```
If you'd rather change each item individually, use the following syntax:

```
chage [-m mindays] [-M maxdays] [-d lastday] [-I inactive]
    ➥[-E expiredate] [-W warndays] username
```

To change the number of days warning that someuser will get before a password change is forced, use the following command:

```
# chage -W 10 someuser
```

By default, shadow passwords are enabled at installation. You can use the authconfig command to go between shadowed and unshadowed mode after installation. authconfig is a text-based utility that allows you to enable or disable shadow passwords and MD5.

If you use authconfig to disable shadow passwords, any entries in the /etc/shadow file that do not have corresponding /etc/passwd entries will be removed and the corresponding entries will transfer their password hashes to the /etc/passwd file. Keep in mind that the password aging information stored in /etc/shadow will be lost in this transaction.

If you enable shadow passwords using authconfig, it will transfer the hashes from the /etc/passwd file to the /etc/shadow file, replacing each hash in /etc/passwd with an X. This can be accomplished outside of authconfig by the pwconv command, which converts to shadow passwords by moving the hashes from /etc/passwd file to /etc/shadow. Use pwunconv to go the other direction.

For any additional information, read the Shadow-Password-HOWTO available at http://howto.tucows.com/otherhowto/Shadow-Password-HOWTO.

Pluggable Authentication Modules (PAM)

At first, most privileges were granted based on password authentication or membership in a specific group. That was not a bad beginning. It soon became obvious, however, that it was insufficient to assume that a user's identity is known simply because the login password is correct and rely on that authentication as the sole means of determining what access should be granted. New programs began including their own authentication methods instead of assuming that the login authentication was sufficient. Each of these required the login, FTP, and other programs to be rewritten to support the new method.

Now authentication is more flexible and is handled under Linux by Pluggable Authentication Modules (PAM). The different major distributions began including PAM in the following versions:

Red Hat Linux 5.0

Debian Linux 2.1

Caldera Linux 1.3

SuSE Linux 6.2

PAM is a flexible set of library modules that allow a system administrator to configure each individual application with its own authentication mechanism—a defined subset of the available library modules. Although some operating systems look for their PAM loadable object files in /usr/lib/security, Red Hat chose to follow the Linux Filesystem Standard by locating them in /lib/security. A listing of this directory would include a number of files called pam_access.so, pam_console.so, pam_cracklib.so, and so on. These files are the shared libraries that support the various capabilities of PAM.

Any program that uses PAM modules instead of some internal security method is called a PAM client. PAM uses four modules to authenticate users, manage user accounts, manage passwords, and manage actual login sessions. The authentication module is responsible for both verifying the user's credentials and giving the OK to proceed. The account management module provides the capability to determine if the current user's account is valid. This module checks for password or account expiration and verifies that the login meets any access hour restrictions. The password module provides functionality to change a user's authentication token or password. A session management module provides functionality to set up and terminate login sessions. These modules are referenced in the configuration file, which we'll look at below.

In order to work with PAM, applications are developed to be independent of any particular authentication scheme. This means that the program is no longer concerned with which authentication scheme it will use. Instead, it will have "authentication modules" attached to it at runtime in order to work. The Linux administrator can change the authentication scheme for a PAM-aware application at any time, without rewriting the application code, by editing a PAM configuration file, which may be application-specific or used system-wide. The modules referenced within the configuration file implement the authentication scheme; so to change schemes, you edit the file to include different modules. If no existing modules meet your security needs, you may write new modules and include them instead.

For example, suppose there is an application that requires user authentication prior to performing some service for the user. In the old days, the application would have to request and read in a password and then validate that password or to use some other authentication scheme that was built into the application. Now, instead of using its own integrated authentication scheme, the PAM-aware application uses PAM to do the authentication portion.

To accomplish this, the application calls PAM, naming a configuration file, which usually shares the name of the application. If PAM has been configured to apply the same authentication scheme to all applications, the scheme is determined by the /etc/pam.conf file. If each application is free to have its own scheme, PAM looks in the /etc/pam.d directory for a configuration file with the specified name. For example, the login program that is commonly used in Linux has a configuration file named /etc/pam.d/login.

The modules are pass-fail. By default, a failed authentication process proceeds past the failed module to prevent the user from knowing where the failure occurred and using this information to break the authentication. You can change this behavior by changing required to requisite in the configuration file; if any requisite module returns failure, PAM fails immediately without calling any other modules.

The /etc/pam.conf file contains a listing of services, each paired with a service module. When a service is requested, its associated module is invoked. Each entry has the following format:

service_name module_type control_flag module_path [options]

Each module referenced in the module_path for that service is then processed in the order in which it appears in the configuration file. The control_flag determines the persistence and importance of the modules and may be set to one of the following values: requisite, required, optional, or sufficient. If all requisite and required modules succeed, then a successful status is returned, and any errors in optional or sufficient modules are ignored. If any requisite or required modules fail, the error value from the first one that failed is returned. If no service modules are designated as requisite or required, at least one optional or sufficient module must succeed before a successful status is returned. If all fail, the error value from the first failed service module is returned. If two or more lines have the same service_name and module_type pair, that service is said to be *stacked*. This allows you to perform incremental checks with different parameters and set these checks to different levels of importance.

If any entry in /etc/pam.conf is incorrect, or if a module cannot be opened, all PAM services will fail, and users will not be permitted access to the system. Likewise if the system is missing the appropriate file in /etc/pam.d, or if the /etc/pam.conf file has been deleted, no one will be able to log into the system since login is the first of the applications that rely on PAM. To fix this, the system administrator must use single-user mode to correct the errant file or to reinstall PAM completely.

If your system is set up to use different authentication schemes for each application, each will have its own configuration file located in /etc/pam.d. The general syntax of an /etc/pam.d configuration file is as follows:

> *module_type control_flag module_path* [*arguments*]

On Red Hat 7.0, the /etc/pam.d/login configuration file looks like Listing 7.5.

Listing 7.5   The /etc/pam.d/login Configuration File for Red Hat

```
#%PAM-1.0
auth        required      /lib/security/pam_securetty.so
auth        required      /lib/security/pam_stack.so service=system-
                          ➥auth
auth        required      /lib/security/pam_nologin.so
account     required      /lib/security/pam_stack.so service=system-
                          ➥auth
password    required      /lib/security/pam_stack.so service=system-
                          ➥auth


session     required      /lib/security/pam_stack.so service=system-
auth
session     optional      /lib/security/pam_console.so
```

In this example, the first library referenced for the auth service is pam_securetty.so. This library is used to prevent the root user from logging in over the network. If a user is attempting to authenticate as root, the module determines which terminal the attempt is coming from and then checks the /etc/securetty configuration file to see if that terminal is listed. The /etc/securetty file, by default, lists only those terminals that are physically connected to that machine. This is a required module, so a failure here fails the entire authentication scheme for this application.

The next library in the auth sequence is actually a stack of library checks, a reference to the system-auth file in the /etc/pam.d directory. This is new in Red Hat 7.0. Before this, each library had its own line in the login file. So the pam_stack.so line actually runs the functions in the auth section of the system-auth file shown in Listing 7.6.

Listing 7.6   The system-auth File

```
#%PAM-1.0

# This file is auto-generated.

# User changes will be destroyed the next time authconfig is run.
auth        sufficient      /lib/security/pam_unix.so likeauth nullok
                            ➥md5 shadow

auth        required        /lib/security/pam_deny.so

account     sufficient      /lib/security/pam_unix.so

account     required        /lib/security/pam_deny.so

password    required        /lib/security/pam_cracklib.so retry=3

password    sufficient      /lib/security/pam_unix.so nullok
                            ➥use_authtok md5 shadow

password    required        /lib/security/pam_deny.so

session     required        /lib/security/pam_limits.so

session     required        /lib/security/pam_unix.so
```

As a result, the next module that the auth service uses is pam_unix.so, the main authentication module. The parameters are likeauth, nullok, md5, and shadow. The likeauth argument makes the module return the same value when called as a credential-setting module and an authentication module. By default, it will reject a NULL password, but the nullok parameter overrides this. We prefer to remove the nullok parameter to prevent the system from accepting NULL passwords. The shadow parameter forces the system to check whether the information in the shadow suite requires that the login be denied, for example if the account had expired. Passing this module is also required.

The libraries for PAM are located in /lib/security/. If you are having problems with the login process, it would be wise to check the /etc/pam.d/login file to determine which PAM libraries are needed and make sure they exist in the /lib/security directory. Further, you should take some time to understand the commonly used PAM files. The better you know them, the better you'll be able to troubleshoot problems.

The beauty of PAM is in its configurability. PAM's modular design makes it easy to use and easy to change. Any application that is developed to be PAM-aware makes user's lives easier by not requiring them to learn separate passwords for each application.

To learn more about implementing PAM in Linux, see *The System Administrator's Guide*, at http://www.us.kernel.org/pub/linux/libs/pam/Linux-PAM-html.

File Permissions

We talked about file permissions in Chapter 3 and Chapter 6, but this topic is worth revisiting in the context of security. As you remember from our discussion of the chmod command in Chapter 4, each file is assigned a permission string. This string determines the type of access granted to the file's owner, to members of the file's group, and to others in the outside world. The types of access that can be granted are read (r), write (w), and execute (x). Here is a sample permission string:

```
-rwxr-xr-x   1   owner   group   240   May 1 11:00   file
```

Under Linux, each file is assigned an owner and a group. In this example, the owner is called owner, and the group is called group. Ownership is completely separate from group membership, which is to say that the file's owner does not have to belong to the file's group. Permission strings specify permission in the following order: owner, group, and others. Looking at the permission string, we see that the owner of file has read, write, and execute permissions for it. Members of the group group have read and execute permissions. All others have read and execute permission as well.

Under Red Hat Linux, when a user is created, a group of the same name is created with only the named user as a member. Red Hat calls these user private groups. Chapter 6 describes this practice.

To set appropriate access levels for a file or directory, you need to consider the use(s) that will be made of it. For example, if you plan to execute the ls command on a directory, you need to assign that directory read permission. Obviously, a file that is to be viewed requires read access. Likewise, a file that is to be changed requires write access. A file that is to be run as an executable will, of course, need executable permission. When the file is a directory, however, these requirements might not be so obvious. Generally, any directory that you want to search or whose contents you want to list will need read access. Any directory whose contents are to be changed requires write access. If you wish to change your present directory to the target directory, the directory will have to allow you execute privileges. Table 7.1 lists some commands and the required file/directory permissions.

Table 7.1 Permission Requirements for Common Commands

Command	File Permission	Directory Permission
ls /home/user	None required	Read
ls -l /home/user	None required	Read and Execute
cd /home/user	None required	Execute
rm /home/user/file	None required	Execute and Write
cat /home/user/file	Read	Execute
binary	Execute	Execute
script	Read and Execute	Execute
rm -r /home/user/ testdir	N/A	Read, Write, and Execute
binary > file	Write	Execute

You can see that if you want someone to be able to perform an ls command in a specific directory, you must set up the permissions string so that either that user or their group has read permission in that directory. If you want a user to be able to view a file, it must have read permission set for the user or the user's group and the directory must allow access permissions on either the user or group level as well. The same principle should be applied to other situations where you are attempting to give access to only a select group. In this case, create a group with a name like project1. (See Chapter 6 for instructions on how to do this.) Make each individual who should have access a member of the group project1. (Again, see Chapter 6.) Now set the permissions on the directory where the files to be accessed are going to be stored to something like drwxrwx---, thereby allowing the owner of the directory and the members of the group project1 read, write, and execute permissions. Each file that is created in this directory must also allow members of project1 permission to read, write, and execute.

File permissions are an important security measure, but you really don't want would-be intruders to get that far. Some measures must be taken to prevent any unauthorized person from getting onto the system at all.

Managing Users and Software

PART 2

Protecting Against Network Intrusion

One of the biggest tasks with regard to security is to protect the network against intrusion. Anytime you have a network, especially one that's connected to the Internet, there is potential for intrusion. A number of things can be done to minimize the danger, but no method is foolproof. Usually several methods are used in combination to maximize the chance of catching or stopping an intruder. Among these are firewalls, TCP Wrappers, and post-break-in analysis to enhance prevention (learning from your mistakes).

Firewalls

The purpose of a firewall is twofold. Firewalls keep would-be intruders out and keep local system users in. If a company wants to protect proprietary information, it can block access to the system from any IP address not within the company. This is usually more desirable than taking the machine off the Internet entirely, since it allows remote users within the company to retain access. If that same company wanted to prevent its users from having access to certain outside Web sites, it could set up a firewall, which would restrict certain IP addresses from being able to send packets through the firewall to the specified sites on the Internet. The packet itself has two parts: header and data. The header contains the IP address of the sender, the intended recipient, the packet size, and other relevant information. As a result, the firewall need not waste time on the data portion of the packet but instead inspects the header to determine what to do with the packet.

The first firewalls were simply nonrouting computers with two network cards, one connected to the Internet and the other to the local area network. If you needed Internet access, you logged on to the firewall server and performed functions from there, exporting the display to your local machine. Anything that you ran on the firewall machine had access to both networks. That type of firewall implementation is seldom used today, at least in this simple form; this configuration requires everyone who is to have Internet access to have an account on the firewall. You definitely don't want to do this if you are not sure that all users who gain such access are trustworthy.

Instead, two implementations are commonly considered when it is determined that a firewall is needed. The first is a true firewall, called a filtering firewall or a packet-filtering firewall. The filtering firewall handles packets at the network level before they get to the application layer. The second method actually uses a proxy server but is often referred to as a firewall. A proxy is basically a machine that makes network connections for the user instead of the user having a direct connection. Quite often the two methods are used in tandem.

The Packet-Filtering Firewall

A packet-filtering firewall is basically a router; its job is to examine data packets and forward them appropriately. Figure 7.2 shows one firewall configuration.

Figure 7.2   A simple firewall configuration

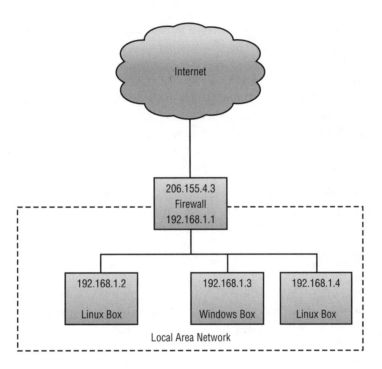

As you can see, the firewall interfaces with both the Internet and the local area network and has two IP addresses as a result. Any of the machines on the LAN can send data packets to the firewall destined for some site outside. Conversely, data packets can come over the network to the firewall intended for a local user. Either way, the firewall determines whether the packet is to be permitted to proceed.

The firewall uses specific header information from the data packet to determine whether the packet should be allowed to pass through; this information includes the packet type, the source address and port number, the destination address and port number, the protocol, and any flags or options to TCP or IP. Data packets must follow certain "rules" to gain passage through the firewall. In Linux, you configure these rules using the IP Chains package, which we'll examine next.

Your firewall can be as restrictive or open as you wish. Perhaps you simply want to prevent people outside your firewall from being able to Telnet into your system. You may do this by having the firewall reject incoming packets that are required to set up such connections. In an alternate scenario, you might want to filter packets from inside your local area network to prevent anyone from reaching a given IP address. How restrictive your firewall is depends on the rules you set in IP Chains.

The functionality for a packet filtering firewall is built into the Linux kernel, although you must recompile with certain network kernel options turned on. This is outlined in the Firewall-HOWTO, maintained by Mark Grennan. Basically, in selecting options you need to include routing, defragmentation, IP masquerading, and multicast routing (if you intend to do multicasting). Older kernels in the 1.*x.x* era used a package called `ipfwadm`, which is no longer supported. Kernels since 2.2.13 use IP Chains instead; we'll talk about that in the IP Chains section below, and you can supplement your knowledge by going to `http://www.rustcorp.com/linux/ipchains/`. The 2.4 kernels use a new firewall utility, known as `iptables`.

Read the Firewall and Proxy Server HOWTO if you are building a firewall! It will probably be helpful to read the Linux Networking HOWTO and the Linux `IPCHAINS` HOWTO as well. Most HOWTOs can be found on Red Hat's site at:

`http://www.redhat.com/mirrors/LDP/HOWTO/`

A filtering firewall does not require a high-end power computer. If you have an old 486DX66 or better with at least 16MB of memory, 300–500MB of hard drive space, and network connections, you will do fine. The work of filtering packets doesn't heavily tax a system.

IP Chains

The IP Chains package makes managing the kernel's inherent firewall capabilities much easier. An IP *chain* is a set of rules to be considered when a data packet is attempting to pass through the firewall. The default IP Chains configuration includes three permanent chains: input, output, and forward. The input chain governs incoming packets, the forward chain manages packets destined for another host, and outgoing packets are subjected to the rules of the output chain. You may add and edit other chains as needed. The IP chains process is fairly simple and is illustrated in Figure 7.3.

Figure 7.3   The IP Chains process

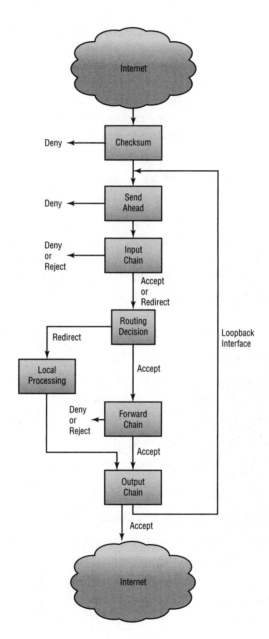

The packet enters the system and is checked by checksum to see if it is corrupted. If it is, it is denied; otherwise it is passed on to the sanity check, which checks to see whether the packet is properly formatted. If it isn't, it is denied. If the packet passes this test, it is sent on to the input chain. The packet may be accepted and sent to the forward chain, denied and dropped without an error being generated, rejected and returned to the sender with an error, or sent into a user-defined chain for further processing. If sent on to the forward chain, the packet is checked against that chain's ruleset and denied, rejected, or sent on to the output chain. If the input chain determines that the packet is intended for a local process, the packet is sent through that process to the output chain, which checks the packet against its ruleset and denies it, rejects it, or sends it to its destination on the Internet.

In an alternate scenario, the loopback interface used for debugging, a packet that is sent from a local process and destined for a local process passes through the output chain right into the input chain.

Rules and Rulesets An IP Chains rule can specify the packet source with the -s option, the protocol with the -p option, the destination with the -d option, the chain to which packets are to be sent if the rule matches with the –j (jump) option, and the port. There are two types of rules: those that affect an entire chain and those that affect the rules within a chain.

These options affect an entire chain:

-N	Create a new chain.
-X	Delete an empty chain.
-P	Change the policy for a built-in chain.
-L	List the rules in a chain.
-F	Flush the rules out of a chain.
-Z	Zero the packet and byte counters on all rules within a chain.

These options affect rules within a chain:

-A	Append a new rule to a chain.
-I	Insert a new rule at some position within a chain.
-R	Replace a rule at some position within a chain.
-D	Delete a rule at some position within a chain if passed a numeric value or delete the first rule that matches if passed a rule to match.

Now let's look at a few sample rules. This rule denies all packets from 192.168.0.11:

```
ipchains -A input -s 192.168.0.11  -j DENY
```

This rule denies all packets that are not from 192.168.0.11:

```
ipchains -A input -s !192.168.0.11 -j DENY
```

This displays a list of the rules for all chains:

```
ipchains -L input
```

Both of the following rules delete the seventh chain, the first by matching the rule number and the second by matching the rule itself:

```
ipchains -D input 7
ipchains -D input -s 192.168.1.11 -j DENY
```

Finally, this rule flushes the input chain:

```
ipchains  input -F
```

Now perhaps we want to deny FTP to the outside world but allow it on our internal network. We do this by adding a rule to the input chain that rejects FTP requests that come in on eth0 but accepts those coming in on eth1. To do this, we must run two separate ipchains commands:

```
ipchains -A input -p tcp -i eth0 --dport ftp -j REJECT
ipchains -A input -p tcp -i eth1 --dport ftp -j ACCEPT
```

Once your ipchains file is properly set up, you will need to make it run at each bootup. Red Hat Linux offers the ipchains-save and ipchains-restore binaries for this purpose. Run ipchains-save redirecting its output to /etc/ipchains.conf in order to save your rules to the ipchains.conf file:

```
ipchains-save > /etc/ipchains.conf
```

Next add the ipchains-restore command to /etc/rc.d/rc.local so that it will run automatically at bootup. You could just as easily add the ipchains commands that we stored in /etc/ipchains.conf to /etc/rc.d/rc.local, but if you expect to make a lot of changes to the ipchains configuration, the first method is more versatile.

Listing 7.7 contains an example ipchains file. This file is set up to do IP masquerading for the 192.168.1 internal network.

Managing Users
and Software

PART 2

Listing 7.7 A Sample ipchains File

```
#!/bin/bash
/bin/echo -n "Setting up IP Chains: ipchains"
/bin/echo "."


#
#         New ipchains commands for somedomain.com
#
# Define some variables
# Any system anywhere
export ANY="0.0.0.0/0"
# The Internet connection
export INET="-W eth0"
# The local network port
export LETH="-V 192.168.1.1 -W eth1"
# The local network
export LNET="192.168.1.1/255.255.255.0"
# The firewall (this system on the local network)
export FWALL="192.168.1.1/32"
# The firewall's Internet address (if known or determinable)
export INET_IP="225.126.21.1"
# Some ipfwadm flags for the TCP protocol
export OpenNewConn="-y"
export ConnEstablished="-k"


# Flush Old Rules
#/sbin/ipchains input -F
#/sbin/ipchains output -F
```

```
# Load masquerade support modules
/sbin/modprobe ip_masq_ftp
/sbin/modprobe ip_masq_irc
/sbin/modprobe ip_masq_raudio


# Create forwarding chain and set reject as default
#/sbin/ipchains -N forward
#/sbin/ipchains -A forward -j reject -S #LNET -d $LNET
#/sbin/ipchains -A forward -j reject -S #LNET -d 10.0.0.0/8
#/sbin/ipchains -A forward -j reject -S #LNET -d 172.16.0.0/12
#/sbin/ipchains -A forward -j reject -S #LNET -d 192.168.0.0/16


# Masquerade these ip's w/ default as all
/sbin/ipchains -A forward -j MASQ -s 192.168.1.1/32 -d $ANY
/sbin/ipchains -A forward -j MASQ -s 192.168.1.2/32 -d $ANY
/sbin/ipchains -A forward -j MASQ -s 192.168.1.3/32 -d $ANY
/sbin/ipchains -A forward -j MASQ -s 192.168.1.4/32 -d $ANY
/sbin/ipchains -A forward -j MASQ -s 192.168.1.5/32 -d $ANY
/sbin/ipchains -A forward -j MASQ -s 192.168.1.6/32 -d $ANY
/sbin/ipchains -A forward -j MASQ -s 192.168.200.206/32 -d $ANY


# Sets telnet and ftp to be instant, and ftp-data to have fast
# throughput
#/sbin/ipchains -A output -p tcp -d 0.0.0.0/0 telnet -t 0x01 0x10
#/sbin/ipchains -A output -p tcp -d 0.0.0.0/0 ftp -t 0x01 0x10
#/sbin/ipchains -A output -p tcp -s 0.0.0.0/0 ftp-data -t 0x01 0x08
```

```
# Create ppp-out rule set
#/sbin/ipchains -N ppp-out
#/sbin/ipchains -A output -i ppp0 -j ppp-out
# Minimum delay for Web trafic & telnet
#/sbin/ipchains -A ppp-out -p TCP -d 0.0.0.0 80 -t 0x00 0x10
#/sbin/ipchains -A ppp-out -p TCP -d 0.0.0.0 telnet -t 0x00 0x10


# Low priority for ftp data, nntp, pop-3
#/sbin/ipchains -A ppp-out -p TCP -d 0.0.0.0/0 ftp-data -t 0x00 0x02
#/sbin/ipchains -A ppp-out -p TCP -d 0.0.0.0/0 nntp -t 0x00 0x02
#/sbin/ipchains -A ppp-out -p TCP -d 0.0.0.0/0 pop-3 -t 0x00 0x02


# Default policy: allow all traffic unless explicitly blocked
#/sbin/ipchains -N input
#/sbin/ipchains -A input -P accept
#/sbin/ipchains -N ouput
#/sbin/ipchains -A output -P accept


# Tell the kernel to allow ip forwarding
/bin/echo "1" > /proc/sys/net/ipv4/ip_forward
```

Administrator's Logbook: IP Chains

System: E12345678

Added the following rule to prevent message traffic from 192.168.1.23 from being passed on:

ipchains -A input -s 192.168.1.23 -j DENY

Added the following rules to deny ftp requests coming in from the outside world (eth0) but accept internal network (eth1) FTP requests:

Administrator's Logbook: IP Chains *(continued)*

ipchains –A input –p tcp -i eth0 --dport ftp –j REJECT

ipchains -A input -p tcp -i eth1 --dport ftp -j ACCEPT

The Proxy Server

While a packet-filtering firewall handles filtering at the Network level, a proxy server works at the Application level. The filtering firewall knows nothing of which application sent the packet—only the IP address of the machine that sent it and the destination IP— but the proxy server receives data directly from an application that is set up to talk to that specific proxy on that particular port. For example, Netscape may be configured to send all requests to a proxy server that will get the requested page and return it to the Netscape application. The proxy server may also maintain a cache of the last pages visited and check each page against that cache before going onto the Internet to retrieve the requested page.

The proxy server can reside on your firewall machine (the topology looks the same as in Figure 7.2 shown earlier), on a different machine inside the firewall (as in Figure 7.4), or connected to the Internet and the local area network without the benefit of a firewall. Having a proxy server with no firewall only controls what the users on the local area network can access; it does nothing for the incoming packet traffic. It is usually preferable to have as little outside the firewall as possible, so putting the proxy server on a different machine that is protected by the firewall is a good idea.

The proxy server intercepts any Web requests coming from clients within the firewall and checks them against an access control list, which details the sites for which access must be denied. If the requested Web page is not on this list, the request is processed normally, going either directly out on the Web or through a firewall for further processing. If the request successfully passes through the ipchains filtering on the firewall, the retrieved Web page is sent back to the requestor. If the requested Web page is on the control list, the requesting machine receives a message indicating that the URL is not accessible or not valid. Many big companies set up a proxy server to allow their users Internet access and also allow themselves to monitor the traffic.

A proxy server is much more resource-intensive than a filtering firewall, since it creates a new process for each user who connects to it. If you have a lot of traffic, you'll need at least a Pentium II with 64MB of memory, two network cards, and a 2GB or larger hard drive. This should handle around 50 concurrent users.

Figure 7.4 A combined proxy/firewall implementation

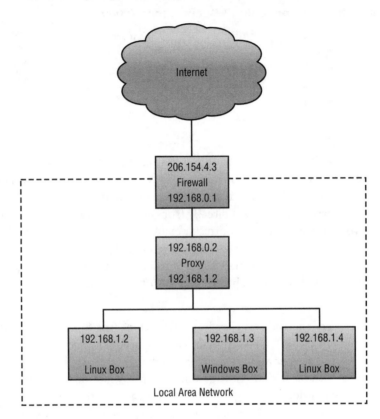

inetd

The Internet Services Daemon (inetd) can function as another step in the security process. Inetd watches all ports assigned to it and starts up the service associated with any port that has activity. This relieves each process of the need to have a daemon running to check these ports, thereby reducing the number of open ports a cracker can attempt to get through. This also prevents the system from being bogged down by several services running daemons to check their individual ports.

Use the /etc/inetd.conf file to notify the inetd daemon of the ports it is responsible for. This file contains the following information for each service being handled by inetd:

- The service name
- The socket type (stream for TCP and dgram for UDP)
- A transport protocol, which is listed in /etc/protocols

- A wait or nowait value for a dgram socket
- The user ID of the process owner
- The full path name of the service executable
- Any parameters that the service executable requires

Listing 7.8 illustrates some sample lines from /etc/inetd.conf.

Listing 7.8   Example /etc/inetd.conf File

```
# inetd.conf  This file describes the services that will be
# available through the INETD TCP/IP super server.  To reconfigure
# the running INETD process, edit this file, and then send the
# INETD process a SIGHUP signal
#
# Version:      @(#)/etc/inetd.conf    3.10    05/27/93
#
# Authors:     Original taken from BSD Unix 4.3/TAHOE.
#              Fred N. van Kempen, #
# <waltje@uwalt.nl.mugnet.org>
#
# Modified for Debian Linux by Ian A. Murdock
# <imurdock@shell.portal.com>
#
# Modified for RHS Linux by Marc Ewing <marc@redhat.com>
#
# The format of each entry is as follows:
#
#<service_name> <socket_type> <protocol> <flags> <user>
#<server_path> <args>
#
# Echo, discard, daytime, and chargen are used primarily
# for testing.
```

```
# To reread this file after changes, just use 'killall -HUP inetd'
#
#echo       stream  tcp      nowait  root      internal
#echo       dgram   udp      wait    root      internal
#discard    stream  tcp      nowait  root      internal
#discard    dgram   udp      wait    root      internal
#daytime    stream  tcp      nowait  root      internal
#daytime    dgram   udp      wait    root      internal
#chargen    stream  tcp      nowait  root      internal
#chargen    dgram   udp      wait    root      internal
#time       stream  tcp      nowait  root      internal
#time       dgram   udp      wait    root      internal
#
# These are standard services.
#
ftp       stream  tcp      nowait  root      /usr/sbin/tcpd  in.ftpd -l -a
telnet    stream  tcp      nowait  root      /usr/sbin/tcpd  in.telnetd
#
# Shell, login, exec, comsat and talk are BSD protocols.
#
shell     stream  tcp  nowait  root      /usr/sbin/tcpd  in.rshd
login     stream  tcp  nowait  root      /usr/sbin/tcpd  in.rlogind
#exec     stream  tcp  nowait  root      /usr/sbin/tcpd  in.rexecd
#comsat   dgram   udp  wait    root      /usr/sbin/tcpd  in.comsat
talk      dgram   udp  wait    nobody.tty  /usr/sbin/tcpd  in.talkd
ntalk     dgram   udp  wait    nobody.tty  /usr/sbin/tcpd  in.ntalkd
#dtalk    stream  tcp  wait    nobody.tty  /usr/sbin/tcpd  in.dtalkd
#
# Pop and imap mail services et al
#
```

```
#pop-2   stream  tcp     nowait  root    /usr/sbin/tcpd ipop2d
pop-3   stream  tcp     nowait  root    /usr/sbin/tcpd ipop3d
#imap    stream  tcp     nowait  root    /usr/sbin/tcpd imapd
#
# The Internet UUCP service.
#
#uucp stream  tcp  nowait  uucp  /usr/sbin/tcpd
# /usr/lib/uucp/uucico  -l
#
# Tftp service is provided primarily for booting.  Most sites
# run this only on machines acting as "boot servers." Do not
# uncomment this unless you *need* it.
#
#tftp   dgram   udp     wait    root    /usr/sbin/tcpd  in.tftpd
#bootps dgram   udp     wait    root    /usr/sbin/tcpd  bootpd
#
# Finger, systat and netstat give out user information which may be
# valuable to potential "system crackers." Many sites choose to
# disable some or all of these services to improve security.
#
#finger stream  tcp  nowait  nobody /usr/sbin/tcpd  in.fingerd
#cfinger stream tcp  nowait  root    /usr/sbin/tcpd  in.cfingerd
#systat stream  tcp  nowait  guest  /usr/sbin/tcpd  /bin/ps -auwwx
#netstat stream tcp  nowait  guest  /usr/sbin/tcpd
# /bin/netstat    -f inet
#
# Authentication
#
auth  stream  tcp  wait  root  /usr/sbin/in.identd in.identd -e -o
#
# End of inetd.conf
```

```
linuxconf stream tcp wait root /bin/linuxconf linuxconf --http
swat     stream  tcp     nowait.400       root /usr/sbin/swat swat
```

```
linuxconf stream tcp wait root /bin/linuxconf linuxconf --http
```

The first uncommented line shows us that the in.ftpd daemon is under the control of inetd. To find out what port it expects input on, look at the /etc/services file. This file has at least one line for each service, listing its name, port, and any alias that it uses.

The FTP daemon has the following /etc/services entry:

```
ftp            21/tcp
```

This tells us that the FTP daemon runs on port 21.

Many services have two entries to account for the TCP and UCP protocols. The lines below indicate that the http daemon passes traffic on port 80.

```
www    80/tcp    http    #WorldWideWeb HTTP
www    80/udp            #HyperText Transfer Protocol
```

It is a good idea to turn off any service that you don't intend to use; each service is a door that could potentially be opened. Add a pound sign (#) to the start of each line in /etc/inetd.conf corresponding to the service you wish to disable.

chkconfig

In addition to services controlled through inetd or similar super servers, many servers run directly, linking up to ports without using a super server. You can usually shut these down by adjusting their startup scripts, as described in Chapter 5.

TCP Wrappers

TCP Wrappers is a host-based security layer that applies to daemons started by the inetd daemon. You might have noticed in the /etc/inetd.conf excerpt above that the command being run was /usr/sbin/tcpd. The tcpd executable is a wrapper program that checks the /etc/hosts.allow and /etc/hosts.deny files to determine whether or not the specified service should be run. When tcpd is started by inetd, it reads the /etc/hosts.allow file and then /etc/hosts.deny. It grants or denies access based on the rules in these two files.

Red Hat Linux 7.0 and Mandrake Linux 7.2 have both switched to xinetd as a replacement for both inetd and TCP Wrappers. xinetd is discussed later in this chapter and in Chapter 15.

The `/etc/hosts.allow` file is a configuration file for the `tcpd` program. This file contains rules that describe which hosts are allowed to access which services on the local host. The format is as follows:

```
service_list: host_list: [optional_command]
```

The service list is a comma-delimited list of service names to which this rule should be applied. The `ftpd`, `telnetd` and `httpd` services are examples. The keyword ALL or ALL EXCEPT may be used as well. For instance, the following entry would allow all users to use all the local services except FTP:

```
ALL EXCEPT in.ftpd: ALL
```

The host list is a comma-delimited list of host names. The host name may be represented as an IP address, a specific host name, or a host name that uses wildcard characters to make the match. If the host name begins with a period, all hosts that share the string following that character will match this rule. For example, the line below would match any attempt to Telnet in from a computer on the `somedomain.com` network.

```
in.telnetd:.somedomain.com
```

If a numeric IP is used, it may be a full IP address for a specific machine or may consist of only the first three period-delimited numbers, causing any IP that starts with those three numbers to be matched. The host list may contain these keywords: ALL, LOCAL, PARANOID, and EXCEPT. The ALL keyword would cause all hosts to match. The LOCAL keyword causes any local login to match. The PARANOID keyword means that any host whose name is being spoofed will match. The EXCEPT keyword is most often used in conjunction with ALL as in this example:

```
ALL EXCEPT hostname
```

This would match every host except the one that is listed. Another variation on this theme allows for the rule to include an expression in the form

```
12.34.56.0/255.255.254.0
```

This will be interpreted as a net/mask pair and will be matched if the net portion is equal to the bitwise AND of the address and the mask portion. Thus it would allow any address between 12.34.56.0 and 12.34.57.255 access to the system.

The optional `command` argument identifies a command to be run every time the rule is matched. For example, this might be used to send e-mail to the superuser when a certain host uses the Telnet service. There are a number of expansions that may be used; they are covered in the hosts.allow man page. Table 7.2 shows example entries from /etc/ hosts.allow and what they mean.

Table 7.2   Sample /etc/hosts.allow Entries

Line	Meaning
in.ftpd:ALL EXCEPT 123.45.67.	FTP service is allowed to all except those on the 123.45.67.* domain.
ALL:ALL	All services are allowed to all hosts.
ALL: 123.45.67.89	All services are allowed to the 123.45.67.89 host.
ipop3d:LOCAL	The POP3 service is allowed to all local accounts.
in.talkd:host.somedomain.com, host2.somedomain.com	The Talk service is allowed to both host and host2 in somedomain.com.
in.telnetd:.somedomain.com	The Telnet service is allowed to any host on the somedomain.com domain.

The /etc/hosts.deny file uses the same format as /etc/hosts.allow but serves the opposite purpose. Lines in this file determine which hosts will be denied access to the specified service. The /etc/hosts.allow and /etc/hosts.deny files work in conjunction. If the /etc/hosts.allow file listed the rule ALL:ALL, allowing open access to all services, but the /etc/hosts.deny file included lines that prohibited some hosts from using some services, /etc/hosts.deny would override the open access for only the hosts and services specified. The deny file is the dominant file. An open system would include the ALL:ALL entry in the /etc/hosts.allow file and nothing in the /etc/hosts.deny file, granting access to everyone and denying it to no one. A completely closed system would have nothing in /etc/hosts.allow and ALL:ALL in /etc/hosts.deny, thereby denying access to everyone.

The TCP Wrappers package includes two tools you can use to check your TCP security. There is tcpdchk, which examines the /etc/inetd.conf, /etc/hosts.allow, and /etc/ hosts.deny files for blatant errors. To display a list of all access rules, use the following command:

```
# tcpdchk -v
```

The command will return a list of accesses explicitly permitted or denied, including the daemon to which the access pertains, the client to whom the access pertains, and the actual access determination. Here is an example:

```
>>> Rule /etc/hosts.allow line 18:
daemons:  in.telnetd
clients:  .ntrnet.net
access:   granted
```

The other tool is the `tcpdmatch` utility, which allows you to test for a specific daemon and client. The command looks like this:

```
# tcpdmatch in.telnetd www.macroshaft.com
```

The command will return the following if access is granted:

```
client:  hostname www.macroshaft.com
client:  address  117.4.137.45
server:  process  in.telnetd
access:  granted
```

If the host is denied access, the response will look like this:

```
client:   hostname www.macroshaft.com
client:   address  117.4.137.45
server:   process  in.telnetd
matched:  /etc/hosts.deny line 10
access:   denied
```

The TCP Wrappers package provides decent protection for your system once a user has gained access. Still, denial of service is not enough by itself.

xinetd

As of Red Hat 7.0, `inetd` is no longer installed by default. Instead, the more secure extended Internet Service Daemon (`xinetd`) is used. Other distributions are switching to `xinetd` as well. Both `xinetd` and `inetd` can be run concurrently on a system. In fact, the author of the `xinetd` code suggests that an admin running an RPC service do so from `inetd`. You can use your `inetd.conf` file to create a `xinetd.conf` file for the non-RPC services.

On a Red Hat 7.0 system, /usr/sbin/inetdconvert is a Python script that converts your inetd.conf file to several files in a new /etc/xinetd.d directory. The command to use this tool to convert all services that haven't already been converted is:

```
# inetdconvert --convertremaining
```

A Perl script to convert the inetd.conf script into an xinetd.conf file is included with some other versions of the xinetd package, located in the same directory as the binary. This script will be in /usr/sbin if it exists on your system and may be run using the following command, assuming that the executable is in /usr/sbin:

```
# /usr/sbin/xconv.pl < /etc/inetd.conf > /tmp/xinetd.conf
```

The transition creates several files within the /etc/xinetd.d directory. These files contain the configuration options for each service managed by xinetd, so you'll need to edit these files to configure xinetd to handle these services in the way you'd like. By way of example, Listing 7.9 shows the /etc/xinetd.d/telnet file, which configures the Telnet service.

Listing 7.9   The /etc/xinetd.d/telnet File Configures the Telnet Service and Is Typical of the xinetd Files for Individual Services.

```
# default: on
# description: The telnet server serves telnet sessions; it uses \
#        unencrypted username/password pairs for authentication.
service telnet
{
        flags           = REUSE   NAMEINARGS
        socket_type     = stream
        wait            = no
        user            = root
        server          = /usr/sbin/in.telnetd
        log_on_failure  += USERID
}
```

The entry from inetd.conf to handle the Telnet service actually contains most of the same information:

```
telnet  stream  tcp     nowait  root    /usr/sbin/tcpd  in.telnetd
```

What is different is the `flags` field. With this field, you can force some specific configuration modes, including security monitoring via TCP Wrappers. The REUSE flag is set by default to allow binding of the service's socket to the Internet address even if there are programs that use it. This might be the case if a previous instance of `xinetd` has started some servers that are still running on this socket. The second flag, NAMEINARGS, is not set in Red Hat 7.0 by default but is necessary if the `xinetd` system is to use TCP Wrappers.

Detecting Intrusion

Intruders usually, if not always, leave signs of intrusion. For some, being noticed is the game. Those who don't want to be noticed need to stay on the system just long enough to adequately mask the intrusion but still get off the system before someone notices that they are on. Crackers can alter the log files in such a way as to make it almost impossible for someone to notice that they have been on the system, but this takes a great deal of time. Many crackers simply delete the log files that would identify them or cut out the portions that detail their activities. This leaves time gaps in the logs, leaving a huge footprint. Still, you will usually only know that someone has been there and not know who it was.

Sometimes intrusion is fairly easy to detect. Although crackers tend to try to disguise their intrusion, there are always tell-tale signs. On a Red Hat Linux system, the `/var/log/secure` file is very helpful. This file logs all attempts to access services on the system along with information about whether the attempt was successful or unsuccessful. Looking at this log, you can sometimes determine that someone is trying to break in, because there are several failed attempts to access the system by a single IP or hostname. Failed login attempts, by Telnet, FTP, or some other service, are easy to spot in the logs:

```
Jun 20 11:33:01 mydomain in.telnetd[1822]: refused connect
        ➥from 121.137.226.29
Jun 23 01:23:22 mydomain in.ftpd[19650: refused connect from
        ➥209.151.118.23
```

You can then use an `nslookup` on the IP to gain any information you can about where the attempted logins are being instigated. Then add this IP to your `/etc/hosts.deny` file to make things a little rougher. Most often, however, the IP is no longer valid, because the cracker was attempting to access your system through a dial-up account. If the IP does resolve, don't immediately assume that the would-be intruder actually has an account within that system; many times, crackers will break into a system and use that system to try to access another system. Sometimes this continues until the chain is quite long. In this case, the IP would belong to another of the cracker's victims and not the cracker. Sometimes the cracker will delete the portions of the `/var/log/secure` and `/var/log/messages` files that show the attempted breach, or the relevant logs may be deleted entirely. These signs are all too often overlooked. System administrators must watch for blank spots in the logs or missing logs as well as strange patterns in these same files.

In order to keep up with the evolving set of threats and vulnerabilities, system administrators must take intrusion detection very seriously. As an old vulnerability is fixed, another one may be introduced. The intruder may be a total stranger or the boss' son. It takes a concerted effort to stay ahead. Intrusion detecting tools are one way to even the odds.

Applications for Detecting Intrusion

Intrusion detecting is a repetitive chore. It is difficult to keep up, since the break-in can happen at any time—day or night. For this reason, it is better by far to run some intrusion-detecting applications that will watch the system for you and notify you of suspicious activity or changes to files. Several such applications are available. Here are just a few.

Tripwire

Tripwire 2.2.1 for Linux produces a baseline of your files and checks existing files against this baseline when requested to do so. You'll want to keep the baseline on a floppy or other removable media to prevent an intruder from deleting or modifying it. Of course, you'll want to update the baseline file periodically or when a lot of changes have been made to your files. The version for Linux is available for free. Although it is not open-source, Tripwire planned to release an open-source version some time in the fall of 2000. To download Tripwire 2.2.1 for Linux or read about it, go to `http://www.tripwiresecurity.com/products/linux.cfm?`.

Scanlogd

Scanlogd detects port scans and writes one line per scan through the syslog mechanism. Since Denial of Service attacks typically send multiple packets to different ports to cause the system to be too overwhelmed to handle legitimate requests, if any outside IP address sends several packets to different ports on the same machine in a short time, scanlogd logs it. You can download it or read more about it on `http://www.openwall.com/scanlogd`.

Deception Tool Kit

The Deception Tool Kit (DTK) is a very clever application that allows you to spy back at the intruders who are spying on you. It fakes certain services, making it appear as if the system has multiple vulnerabilities, and then captures information about any attempt to exploit them. For instance, if the cracker tries to get the /etc/passwd file, DTK will send a fake one. The cracker then wastes time trying to crack the passwords before realizing that it does not contain valid passwords for the system. As a preventive measure, traffic on port 365 indicates that the target machine is running DTK, thereby serving as a flag to the inquiring cracker and forcing reconsideration about whether or not to pursue the attack on your system. Read more about it at `http://www.all.net/dtk/`.

Logcheck

Logcheck is part of the Abacus Project being conducted by Psionic Software (`http://www.psionic.com/abacus/`). It examines the logfiles for possible security problems or violations. It then generates a list of what it considers to be suspicious and e-mails that list to the system administrator. It is free for use at any site. Download it at `http://www.psionic.com/abacus/logcheck/`.

This list of intrusion-detecting applications is not comprehensive. It is generally a good idea to search the Internet for security sites that recommend applications of this type, since new ones are made available quite often. Running one or more of these or other applications empowers you in your attempts to prevent would-be intruders from cracking your system.

Managing Users and Software

PART 2

In Sum

Security is such a big topic that there is always more to be said. We have included the specific tools that we use or have had recommended to us. You should search the Internet and talk to other system administrators to find the specific products that meet the needs of your situation. Test everything. Be very thorough and always watch your distribution's homepage for security advisories and updated packages.

Now we go on to the topic of software administration. You'll get to know this topic quite well in your career as a Linux system administrator. Chapter 8 will get you started.

8

Software Administration

Most Linux distributions ship with a wide variety of software packages, many of which you can select during system installation and use immediately after installation. On occasion, however, you'll find that you need to install and use additional programs, or upgrade packages you've already installed. Depending on which Linux distribution you're using, you may have a choice of several different *package formats,* which are methods of distributing software in a single file, often including information about which other programs a new one requires. Most Linux programs rely upon the glibc package, for instance, and packages can specify this dependency.

In addition to the choice of package format, software can be distributed in either *binary* or *source code* form. The former is ready-to-run software. The latter consists of the original program code files, which must be *compiled* into the binary form needed by Linux. Source code packages are more portable than binary packages—you can use the same source package on both *x*86 and PowerPC computers, for example. You can also modify source code if you know how to program in whatever language the package uses. You must decide which format you want to use for any given program.

Updating existing packages can be as important as adding new ones. Updates may fix bugs and security flaws, or simply add features that new programs require. One particularly important update is that of the *kernel,* the core of the Linux system. (Technically speaking, Linux *is* the kernel; almost everything else in a Linux distribution works on other OSs, at least once recompiled.) Although kernels can be updated via package management, the usual way to update is by recompiling the kernel. This task can be intimidating to new Linux administrators, but it's very important that you understand how to do it, because kernel recompilation provides many benefits and may be the only way to accomplish certain tasks in Linux.

Installing Binary Packages

Software installation procedures vary substantially from one Linux distribution to another. Most distributions today use Red Hat Package Manager (RPM) files or Debian packages, but Slackware uses *tarballs*—files created by the tar program, which contain none of the sophisticated dependency information supported by RPM and Debian packages. A few others, such as Stampede Linux, use their own proprietary formats. As a general rule, if you get a binary package, get one that uses the package format favored by your distribution. If necessary, you can often convert from one format to another with the alien program, or you can install a tarball. (All Linux distributions can read tarballs.) It's always cleanest to start with the correct package format.

Installing an RPM

Most modern Linux distributions use the RPM format, although Debian packages are becoming more popular. Fortunately, installing RPMs is a simple process.

WARNING Upgrading an RPM package sometimes wipes out the package's configuration files. Back up these files (which may be located in a wide variety of locations but are usually somewhere in /etc) *before* upgrading a working program.

Basic *rpm* Options

Use the rpm program to install or upgrade a package at the shell prompt. This program has the following syntax:

```
rpm [operation][options] [package-files|package-names]
```

Table 8.1 summarizes the most common rpm operations, and Table 8.2 summarizes the most important options. Be aware, however, that rpm is a very complex tool, so this chapter can only scratch the surface of its capabilities. In fact, an entire book (Ed Bailey's *Maximum RPM*, Red Hat Press, 1997) is devoted to this utility. The rpm man pages contain information on operations and options more obscure than those listed in Tables 8.1 and

8.2. Many of rpm's less-used features are devoted to the creation of RPM packages by software developers.

Table 8.1   Common rpm Operations

rpm Operation	Description
-i	Installs a package; the system must *not* contain a package of the same name.
-U	Installs a new package or upgrades an existing one.
-F or --freshen	Upgrades a package only if an earlier version already exists.
-q	Queries a package: Finds if a package is installed, what files it contains, and so on.
-V or -y or --verify	Verifies a package: Checks that its files are present and unchanged since installation.
-e	Uninstalls a package.
-b	Builds a binary package, given source code and configuration files.
--rebuild	Builds a binary package, given a source RPM file.
--rebuilddb	Rebuilds the RPM database, to fix errors.

Table 8.2   Common rpm Options

rpm Option	Used with Operations	Description
--root *dir*	Any	Modifies the Linux system having a root directory located at *dir*. This option can be used to maintain one Linux installation discrete from another one, say during OS installation or emergency maintenance.

Table 8.2 Common rpm Options *(continued)*

rpm Option	Used with Operations	Description
--force	-i, -U, -F	Forces installation of a package even when it means overwriting existing files or packages.
-h or --hash	-i, -U, -F	Displays a series of pound signs (#) to indicate the progress of the operation.
-v	-i, -U, -F	Used in conjunction with the -h option to produce a uniform number of hash marks for each package.
--nodeps	-i, -U, -F, -e	Performs no dependency checks. Installs or removes the package even if it relies on a package or file that's not present, or is required by a package that's not being uninstalled.
--test	-i, -U, -F	Check for dependencies, conflicts, and other problems without actually installing the package.
--prefix *path*	-i, -U, -F	Sets the installation directory to *path* (works only for some packages).
-a or --all	-q, -V	Queries or verifies all packages.
-f *file* or --file *file*	-q, -V	Queries or verifies the package that owns *file*.
-p *package-file*	-q	Queries the uninstalled RPM *package-file*.
-i	-q	Displays package information, including the package maintainer, a short description, and so on.
-R or --requires	-q	Displays the packages and files upon which this one depends.
-l or --list	-q	Displays the files contained in the package.

rpm is an extremely useful tool because it maintains a database of information on installed packages. This database includes information on the packages (including package names and version numbers), the files associated with those packages, checksums for each file, and files and packages upon which every package depends. The database allows an RPM-based distribution to detect incompatibilities or missing features required by specific new packages. This helps you avoid damaging your system should you attempt to install a package containing files that conflict with another package. You avoid the frustration of finding that a new program relies upon libraries you don't have installed. Warned up front about such problems, you can correct them most easily.

Using Text-Based Tools

To use rpm, you combine one operation with one or more options. In most cases, you include one or more package names or package filenames, as well. (A *package filename* is a complete filename, but a *package name* is a shortened version. For instance, a package filename might be samba-2.0.7-21ssl.i386.rpm, while the matching package name is samba.) You can either issue the rpm command once for each package, or list multiple packages, separated by spaces, on the command line.

When installing or upgrading a package, the -U operation is generally the most useful because it allows you to install the package without manually uninstalling the old one. This one-step operation is particularly helpful when packages contain many dependencies, because rpm detects these and can perform the operation should the new package fulfill the dependencies provided by the old one.

To use rpm to install or upgrade a package, issue a command similar to the following:

```
# rpm -Uvh samba-2.0.7-21ssl.i386.rpm
```

You could also use **rpm -ivh** in place of **rpm -Uvh** if you don't already have a samba package installed.

WARNING It's possible to distribute the same program under different names. Upgrading in this situation may fail, or it may produce a duplicate installation, which can yield bizarre program-specific malfunctions. Red Hat has described a formal system for package naming to avoid such problems, but they still occasionally occur. It's therefore best to upgrade a package using a subsequent release provided by the same individual or organization that provided the original.

Verify that the package is installed with the **rpm -qi** command, which displays information such as when and on what computer the binary package was built. Listing 8.1 demonstrates this command. (rpm -qi also displays an extended plain-English summary of what the package is, which has been omitted from Listing 8.1.)

Managing Users
and Software

PART 2

Listing 8.1 RPM Query Output

```
$ rpm -qi samba
Name:      samba                        Relocations: (not relocatable)
Version:   2.0.7                        Vendor: Red Hat, Inc.
Release:   21ssl                        Build Date: Mon 14 Aug 2000
           ➥03:03:08 PM EDT
Install date: Wed 27 Sep 2000 08:04:12 PM EDT     Build Host:
           ➥porky.devel.redhat.com
Group      : System Environment/Daemons     Source RPM: samba-2.0.7-
           ➥21ssl.src.rpm
Size       : 7704190                         License: GNU GPL
           ➥Version 2
Packager   : Red Hat, Inc. <http://bugzilla.redhat.com/bugzilla>
Summary    : Samba SMB server.
```

Using GUI Tools

Many Linux distributions include GUI tools to help you install, remove, update, and query RPM packages. Red Hat and Mandrake, for instance, come with Gnome RPM (Figure 8.1). To add a package using Gnome RPM, follow these steps:

Figure 8.1 Gnome RPM is one of several GUI tools for manipulating packages installed on an RPM-based Linux computer.

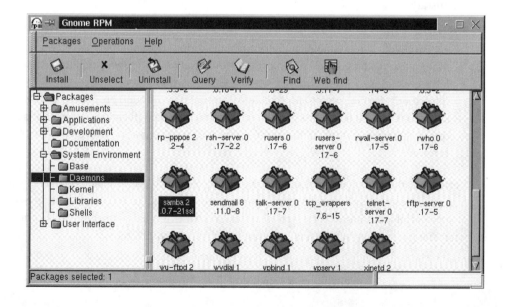

1. As root, start Gnome RPM by typing **gnorpm** in an xterm window.

2. In the main Gnome RPM window, click the Install button. Gnome RPM displays an Install dialog box in which you can select RPMs.

3. Click the Add button in the Install dialog box. In the file selection dialog box that appears, locate and select the RPM files you want to install, clicking Add after selecting each file. (Note that you can select multiple files, clicking Add after each file.) When you've selected and added all your files, click Cancel. You'll see the Install dialog box again, with your additions visible.

4. Make sure that there are check marks in the check boxes next to all the packages you want to install, and then click the Install button. Gnome RPM installs the packages.

You can use Gnome RPM in a similar manner to update, delete, or query RPM packages. GUI configuration utilities in other distributions, such as Caldera and SuSE, differ in details but have similar functionality.

Installing a Debian Package

Debian, Corel, and Storm Linux all use Debian packages rather than RPMs. Debian packages are incompatible with RPM packages, but the basic principles of operation are the same across both package types. Like RPMs, Debian packages include dependency information, and the Debian package utilities maintain a database of installed packages, files, and so on. You use the dpkg command to install a Debian package. This command's syntax is similar to that of rpm:

    dpkg [options][action] [package-files|package-name]

The action is the action to be taken; common actions are summarized in Table 8.3. The options (Table 8.4) modify the behavior of the action, much like the options to rpm.

Table 8.3   dpkg Primary Actions

dpkg Action	Description
-i or --install	Installs a package.
--configure	Reconfigures an installed package: runs the post-installation script to set site-specific options.
-r or -P or --remove or --purge	Removes a package.
-p or --print-avail	Displays information about a package.

Table 8.3 dpkg Primary Actions *(continued)*

dpkg Action	Description
-1 *pattern* or --list *pattern*	Lists all installed packages whose names match *pattern*.
-L or --listfiles	Lists the installed files associated with a package.
-C or --audit	Searches for partially installed packages and suggests what to do with them.

Table 8.4 Options to Fine-Tune dpkg Actions

dpkg Option	Used with Actions	Description
--root=*dir*	All	Modifies the Linux system using a root directory located at *dir*. Can be used to maintain one Linux installation discrete from another one, say during OS installation or emergency maintenance.
-B or --auto-deconfigure	-r	Disables packages that rely upon one being removed.
--force-*things*	Assorted	Forces specific actions to be taken. Consult the dpkg man page for details of *things* this option does.
--ignore-depends=*package*	-i, -r	Ignores dependency information for the specified package.
--no-act	-i, -r	Checks for dependencies, conflicts, and other problems without actually installing the package.
--recursive	-i	Installs all packages matching the package name wildcard in the specified directory and all subdirectories.

Table 8.4 Options to Fine-Tune dpkg Actions *(continued)*

dpkg Option	Used with Actions	Description
-G	-i	Doesn't install the package if a newer version of the same package is already installed.
-E or --skip-same-version	-i	Doesn't install the package if the same version of the package is already installed.

Debian-based systems often use a somewhat higher-level utility called dselect to handle package installation and removal. dselect provides a text-mode list of installed packages and packages available from a specified source (such as a CD-ROM drive or FTP site), and allows you to select which packages you want to install and remove. This interface can be very useful when you want to install several packages, but dpkg is often more convenient when manipulating just one or two packages.

Some Debian-based Linux distributions, such as Corel Linux, include GUI front-ends to dpkg; they're similar to the Gnome RPM program for RPM-based systems. If you're more comfortable with GUI tools than with command-line tools, you can use the GUI tools much as you'd use Gnome RPM to ease administration.

As an example, consider the following command, which installs the samba_2.0.6-cl-1.1_i386.deb package:

```
# dpkg -i samba_2.0.6-cl-1.1_i386.deb
```

If you're upgrading a package, you may need to remove an old package. To do this, use the -r option to dpkg, as in

```
# dpkg -r samba
```

> **NOTE** It's possible to use both RPM and Debian packages on a single computer, and in fact some distributions (such as Corel Linux) explicitly support this configuration. Using both package formats reduces the benefits of both, however, because the two may introduce conflicting packages and they cannot share their dependency information. It's therefore best to stick with whatever package format your distribution uses as its own native format.

Installing a Tarball

If you have Slackware Linux or another distribution that uses tarballs for distribution, you can install software by using the standard Linux tar utility. You can also use this method if you want to install a tarball on a Linux distribution that ordinarily uses a package management tool. We recommend using an RPM or Debian package if your distribution supports one of these file formats, however.

WARNING When installing a new version of a program over an older one on Slackware Linux, the new files will most likely overwrite the old ones. If you install a tarball on a system that normally uses packages, however, or if you install a tarball that was created using a different directory structure than what your current system uses, you may end up with duplicate files. This can cause substantial confusion, because you might end up continuing to use the old binaries even after installing the new ones. You should therefore remove the old package as well as you can, before installing a binary via a tarball. Check the directory structure contained within a tarball first, by using the tar command, as in **tar tvfz samba.tgz**. This command displays all the files in the tarball, including their complete paths.

Tarball installation is a fairly straightforward matter. As the root user, you issue commands similar to the following. These commands install the files from the samba.tgz file located in the /root directory:

```
# cd /
# tar xvfz /root/samba.tgz
```

Note that the first command (**cd /**) is critically important; without it, you'll install the files under whatever directory you're currently in, not in the usual directory tree. (It is possible, however, that the tarball you obtain might have to be installed under some directory other than /, in which case you should follow the directions that come with the package to install it.)

NOTE Chapter 11 describes the tar utility in greater detail.

Compiling Source Code

It's frequently desirable or necessary to compile a program from source code. Situations when you might want to do this include the following:

- You can't find a binary package for the program in question. This is particularly likely when you run Linux on a non-*x*86 system, such as a Macintosh or Alpha-based computer.

- The binary packages you've found rely upon newer or older support libraries than what you have available. Recompiling against your support libraries often works around this problem, although sometimes the source code itself requires libraries other than what you have available.

- You want to enable compile-time options that are not used in the available binary packages. These options may optimize a package for your computer or add functionality.

- You want to modify the source code. If there's a bug that's been fixed since the last binary package was released, or if you want to add a feature or modify a program in some way, you have little choice but to compile from source code.

In the first two cases, you can often compile from a *source RPM,* which is an RPM file containing source code rather than binary files. It's also possible to create Debian packages from source code, given appropriate control files. In the latter two cases, it's easiest to obtain a source distribution as a tarball, make your modifications, and install directly from the compiled code. Creating a package from modified or optimized source code is seldom worthwhile for a one-computer installation. If you maintain several Linux computers, though, you might want to read the RPM HOWTO document or Ed Bailey's *Maximum RPM* to learn how to generate a binary RPM from an original source code tarball. You can then distribute the customized package to all your computers after compiling it on just one system.

Compiling from Packages

Source RPM files are identified by the presence of `.src.` in the filename, rather than `.i386.` or some other architecture identifier. For example, `samba-2.0.7-21ssl.src.rpm` is the source RPM for the Samba 2.0.7 package that comes with Red Hat 7.0; `samba-2.0.7-21ssl.i386.rpm` is the matching compiled binary for *x*86 computers. If you wanted to compile the source RPM on LinuxPPC (Linux for Macintosh and other PPC-based systems), the result would be a file called `samba-2.0.7-21ssl.ppc.rpm`.

NOTE Some non-source RPM files are architecture independent. These can contain documentation, fonts, architecture-independent scripts, and so on. They're identified by a `.noarch.` filename component. These RPMs can be installed without modification on systems using any CPU.

To compile a source RPM package, you use the `--rebuild` operation to the `rpm` command, thus:

```
# rpm --rebuild samba-2.0.7-21ssl.src.rpm
```

If all goes well, you'll see a series of compilation commands run as a result. These may take anywhere from a few seconds to several hours to run, depending on the package and your computer's speed. On a typical 500MHz Intel-architecture computer, most packages compile in a few minutes.

Building a package requires that you have necessary support libraries installed—not just the libraries required by the final binary package, but also the matching development libraries. These libraries aren't always included in source RPM dependency information, so it's not unusual to see a compile operation fail because of a missing library. Your best bet when this happens is to examine the error message and then check the list of requirements on the program's home page. With luck, the failure message will bear some resemblance to a requirement listed on the package's home page. You can then locate an appropriate development RPM (which usually contains `devel` in its name), install it, and try again.

TIP You can often use the command **rpm -qpi** *packagefile* to locate the program's home page. The package maintainer often has a home page, as well.

Once a package has successfully compiled, you'll find one or more matching binary RPM files somewhere in the `/usr/src` directory tree. Most distributions name a directory in this tree after themselves, such as `/usr/src/redhat` on Red Hat systems. This directory contains an RPMS directory, which in turn has one or more subdirectories, one for each

architecture name, such as i386 or ppc. (Most packages built on Intel-architecture computers place binaries in the i386 subdirectory, but some use i586 or some other name, so
you may need to check multiple directories.) The RPM files you find in this subdirectory
are binary packages that you can install just like any other binary RPM. Source RPMs
usually create just one binary RPM file when built, but some generate multiple binary
RPM files.

Administrator's Logbook: RPM Source File Installation

System: E12345678

Action: Compiled Samba 2.0.7 from source RPM & installed resulting binary RPM.

It's possible to compile a Debian package from source code, but the process is somewhat
different for these. Instead of a binary Debian package, you must locate and use a control
file, which you can use in conjunction with a regular source code tarball.

Compiling Tarballs

If you don't want to or can't create a package file, you can compile source code from an
original source tarball and install the compiled software directly. You then give up the
advantages of RPM or Debian packages, however, including protection from accidentally
overwriting files with other packages, the ability to verify the contents of a package, and
so on. Whenever possible, it's best to use a binary package or to create your own binary
package from a source package, rather than install directly from a source tarball.

NOTE   Some administrators prefer using original source tarballs because they
know the source code hasn't been modified by the package maintainer, as is quite
common with RPM (including source RPM) files. Such changes seldom cause
problems, but if you're intimately familiar with a program in its "pure" form, you
may want to consider compiling and installing it from source rather than relying
upon a package file.

You can unpack a source tarball using a command like **tar xvzf *sourcecode.tgz***. This
usually produces a subdirectory containing the source code distribution. You can unpack
this tarball in a convenient location in your home directory, in the /root directory, in the
/usr/src directory, or somewhere else—whatever's convenient for you. Some operations

involved in compiling and installing the code usually require root privileges, though, so you might not want to use your home directory.

Unfortunately, it's impossible to provide a single procedure that's both complete and accurate for installing all source code tarballs. This is because no two source code packages are exactly alike; each developer has his or her own style and preferences in terms of compilation and installation procedures. Some elements are quite commonly included, however:

Documentation   Most source tarballs have one or more documentation files. Sometimes these appear in a subdirectory called doc or documentation. Other times there's a README file or an INSTALL file, and occasionally OS-specific files (README.linux, for instance). Read the ones that are appropriate to your installation.

Configuration options   Most large programs are complex enough that they require precompilation configuration for your OS or architecture. Today, this is often handled through a script called configure; to configure the package, you type **./configure.** The script checks for the presence of critical libraries, the nature of your compiler, and so on, and creates a file called Makefile that will ultimately control compilation. A few programs accomplish the same goal through some other means, such as executing the typed command **make config.** Sometimes you must answer questions or pass additional parameters to a configuration script to get the results you desire.

Compilation   To compile a package, you must usually type **make.** For some packages, you must issue individual make commands for each of several subcomponents, as in **make main.** The compilation process can take anywhere from a few seconds to several hours, depending on the package and the speed of your computer.

Installation   Small packages sometimes rely on you to do the installation; you must copy the compiled binary files to /usr/local/bin or some other convenient location. You may also need to copy man page files, configuration files, and so on. The package's documentation will include the details you need. Other packages have a script called install or a make option (usually typing **make install**) to do the job.

Post-installation configuration   After installing the software, you may need to configure it for your system by editing configuration files. These may be located in users' home directories, in /etc, or elsewhere. The program's documentation should include details. This step is just like what you do when installing from a binary package file.

Linux administrators have traditionally placed packages they compile themselves in the /usr/local directory tree—/usr/local/bin for binaries, /usr/local/man for man pages, and so on. This placement ensures that installing a program from a source tarball won't interfere with RPM- or Debian-based packages, which typically go elsewhere in the /usr tree. Most source tarballs include default installation scripts that place their contents in /usr/local, but a few don't follow this convention. Check the program's documentation to find out where it installs, so you'll be aware of such deviations and, if necessary, can change them by adjusting the Makefile or installation script.

Administrator's Logbook: Source Code Package Installation

System: E12345678

Action: Compiled & installed Samba 2.0.7 with SSL extensions. Located in /usr/local/samba.

Kernel Compilation

The Linux kernel is a particularly critical and complex component on any Linux system. It therefore deserves special consideration in any discussion of software installation and maintenance. Although you can install a precompiled updated kernel much as you can other precompiled packages, doing your own kernel compilation offers certain advantages, as described shortly.

The kernel compilation and installation process, although not extraordinarily difficult, has its own quirks, so this section covers the process in some detail, starting at setting the compilation options and proceeding through to rebooting the computer to use the new kernel.

Why Compile Your Kernel?

With any luck, your computer booted and ran immediately after you installed Linux on it. This fact means that the Linux kernel provided with the distribution works. Why, then, should you go to the bother of compiling a new kernel? Here are the most important advantages to custom kernel compilation:

Architecture optimization   The kernel includes optimization options for each of several classes of CPU—80386, 80486, and so on. Most distributions, including Red Hat 7.0, ship with kernels that are optimized for 80386 CPUs. By compiling a kernel for your particular CPU model, you can squeeze a little extra speed out of your system.

Removing unnecessary drivers   The default kernel includes drivers for a wide variety of hardware components. In most cases, these drivers do no harm because they're compiled as *modules* (separate driver files), which aren't loaded unless necessary. A few are compiled into the kernel proper, however. These consume memory unnecessarily, thus degrading system performance slightly.

Adding drivers   You may need to add a new or experimental driver to your system. This may be necessary if you're using an unusually new component, or if there's a bug fix that's not yet been integrated into the main kernel tree. Such changes often require you to *patch* the kernel—to replace one or more kernel source code files. For details on how to do this, check with the site that provides the new driver.

Changing options   You may want to change options related to drivers, in order to optimize performance or improve reliability. As you examine the kernel configuration procedure, you'll see many examples of such options.

Upgrading the kernel   You may want to run the latest version of the kernel. Sometimes you can obtain an upgrade in precompiled form, but occasionally you'll have to compile a kernel from source code, particularly if it's a very recent or experimental release.

Of course, kernel compilation isn't without its drawbacks. It takes time to configure and compile a kernel. It's also possible that the kernel you compile won't work. Be sure to leave yourself a way to boot using the old kernel, or you'll have a hard time booting your system after an upgrade. (The discussion in this chapter describes how to boot the computer into either the old or the new kernel, so you shouldn't have a problem if you follow these instructions.)

On the whole, compiling your own kernel is something that every Linux system administrator should be able to do, even if it's not something you do on every system you maintain. Using a custom-compiled kernel helps you optimize your system and use cutting-edge drivers, which can give your system an advantage. In some cases, this is the only way you can get certain features to work (as with drivers for particularly new hardware).

Obtaining a Kernel

Before you can compile a kernel, you must obtain one. As for other software packages, you obtain a kernel either precompiled or in source code form; and in RPM, Debian package, or tarball form. We favor installing a kernel from source tarball form, because it allows you to be sure you're working from an original standard base. Kernel RPMs, in particular, are often modified in various ways. Although these modifications can sometimes be useful, they can also interfere with the smooth installation of patches should they be needed. (On the other hand, the kernels distributed as RPMs sometimes *include* the very patches you might want to install, thus simplifying matters.)

One of the best places to look for a kernel is `http://www.kernel.org`. This site includes links to "official" kernel source tarballs. You can also find kernel files on major Linux FTP sites, such as `ftp://sunsite.unc.edu` and `ftp://tsx-11.mit.edu`. If you want to use an RPM or Debian package, check for kernel source-code files from your distribution's maintainer. If you use an RPM or Debian kernel package, you may need to download two files: one with the kernel source code proper, and one with the kernel header files. Tarballs typically include both sets of files in a single tarball.

A complete 2.2.17 kernel tarball is 16MB in size; a 2.4.0-test8 kernel tarball is 21MB. (Kernels are also available in bzipped tar files, which are somewhat smaller than the traditional gzipped tar files. You use `bzip2` to uncompress these files rather than `gzip`.) Because of their large size, these kernel files may take quite some time to download, particularly if you're stuck using a PPP dialup link.

Once you've downloaded the kernel tarball, you can unpack it in the `/usr/src` directory. The tarball creates or installs to a directory called `linux`.

> **WARNING** If your `/usr/src` directory already has a directory called `linux`, you should rename it to something else and create a new `linux` directory for the new source package. This will prevent problems caused by unpacking a new source tree over an old one, which can create inconsistencies that cause compilation failures.

You can unpack a kernel tarball just as you would any other source code tarball, for instance:

```
# tar xvzf ~/linux-2.4.0-test8.tar.gz
```

If your source tarball uses `bzip2` compression, you can use a command similar to the following to extract it:

```
# tar xvf ~/linux-2.4.0-test8.tar.bz2 --use-compress-program bzip2
```

Kernel Configuration Options

Once you've extracted your kernel tarball, you can proceed to configure it. Use any of the following three commands to accomplish this task:

```
# make config
```

This command runs a text-based configuration tool that asks you specific questions about each and every configuration option. You can't skip around arbitrarily from one option to another, so this method is quite awkward.

make menuconfig

Like make config, this option presents a text-based configuration tool. However, the make menuconfig tool uses text-mode menus, so you can skip from one option to another. This is a good way to configure the kernel if you're using a text-based console login.

make xconfig

This command also uses menus for configuration, but the menus are X-based, so you can configure the kernel using mouse clicks in X.

The kernel configuration options are arranged in groups. If you use make menuconfig or make xconfig, you can select one group to see a list of items in that group, as shown in Figure 8.2. Particularly in the 2.4.*x* kernels, groups often have subgroups, so you may need to examine quite a few menus before you find a particular driver or option.

Figure 8.2 Kernel compilation options are arranged hierarchically, with each main-menu option generating its own menu, which displayed in a separate window when make xconfig is used.

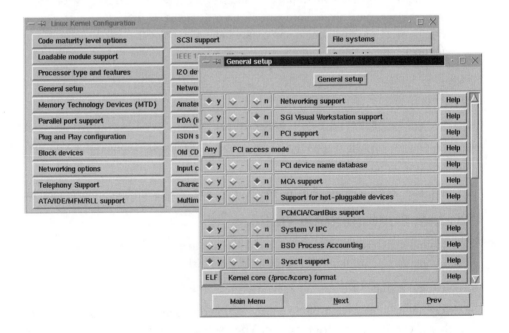

Describing every available kernel configuration option would be quite tedious, as well as inevitably incomplete, because options are constantly being added and changed. Therefore, Table 8.5 merely presents an overview of the main kernel headings in the 2.4.*x* kernel series. The 2.2.*x* kernel includes more main-heading items, but 2.4.*x* reorganizes many options into subheadings, thus reducing the clutter on the main kernel options menu.

Kernel Version Numbers

Each Linux kernel has a version number of the form *x.y.z.*

- The *x* number is the *major version number,* and in 2001 this number is 2.

- The *y* number denotes an important change to the kernel and has a special meaning. Even-numbered *y* values are considered *stable*—they're unlikely to contain major bugs, and they don't change much from one minor release to another. An odd *y* number denotes a *development* kernel, which contains features that are experimental. Development kernels may be unstable and may change substantially over time. Unless you're desperate to use a feature introduced in a development kernel, you shouldn't use one of these.

- The *z* number represents a minor change within a given stable or development kernel. In stable kernels, these represent minor bug fixes and occasionally the addition of important new (but well-tested) drivers. Within development kernels, incrementing *z* numbers represent major bug fixes, added features, changes, and (being realistic) bug introductions.

When Linus Torvalds believes that a development kernel is becoming stable and contains the features he wants in that kernel, he calls a *code freeze,* after which point new features aren't added, just bug fixes. When the kernel stabilizes enough, a *test release* in the next stable version is announced. This kernel has a number such as 2.4.0-test1. Once Linus is satisfied with the stability of the kernel, the *test* moniker is removed. At this writing, the current stable kernel version is 2.2.17, and the 2.4.0-test8 kernel is also available. Once 2.4.0 is released, a 2.5.*x* development series will begin, leading eventually to the release of a 2.6.0 or 3.0.0 kernel.

Table 8.5 Linux 2.4.*x* Kernel Configuration Options

Kernel Configuration Menu Item	Subsumed Options
Code Maturity Level Options	This menu provides options allowing you to select experimental drivers and features.
Loadable Module Support	Modern kernels typically include many features in loadable modules (separate driver files). This menu lets you enable support for these modules and set a couple of options related to it.
Processor Type and Features	You can configure the system to optimize the kernel for your particular CPU, as well as enable CPU-related options such as floating-point emulation (which is *not* required for modern CPUs).
General Setup	This menu contains an assortment of miscellaneous options that didn't fit anywhere else, such as types of binary program files supported by the kernel and power management features.
Memory Technology Devices (MTD)	This menu allows you to enable support for certain types of specialized memory storage devices, such as flash ROMs. Chances are you don't need this support on a workstation or server.
Parallel Port Support	Here you can add support for parallel-port hardware (typically used for printers and occasionally for scanners, removable disk drives, and other devices). Support for specific devices must be added in various other menus.
Plug and Play Configuration	The 2.4.*x* kernel includes support for ISA plug-and-play (PnP) cards. Prior kernels relied upon an external utility, isapnp, to configure these cards. You can use the kernel support or the old isapnp utility, whichever you prefer.

Table 8.5 Linux 2.4.*x* Kernel Configuration Options *(continued)*

Kernel Configuration Menu Item	Subsumed Options
Block Devices	Block devices are devices such as hard disks whose contents are read in blocks of multiple bytes. This menu controls floppy disks, parallel-port-based removable disks, and a few other block devices. Some other block devices, including most hard disks, are covered in other menus.
Networking Options	You can configure an array of TCP/IP networking options from this menu, as well as enable other networking stacks, such as DDP (used for AppleTalk networks) and IPX (used for Novell networks). Network hardware is configured in another menu.
Telephony Support	This menu lets you configure specialized hardware for using the Internet as a means of linking telephones.
ATA/IDE/MFM/RLL Support	Most *x*86 computers today use EIDE hard disks, and you enable drivers for these devices from this menu. Related older disk drivers are also enabled from this menu, as are drivers for EIDE CD-ROMs, tape drives, and so on.
SCSI Support	Here you enable support for SCSI host adapters and specific SCSI devices (disks, CD-ROM drives, and so on).
IEEE 1394 (FireWire) Support	This menu allows you to enable support for the new IEEE 1394 (aka FireWire) interface protocol, which is used for some video and disk devices.
I2O Device Support	This menu allows you to use I2O devices. Intelligent Input/Output (I2O) is a new scheme that allows device drivers to be broken into OS-specific and device-specific parts.
Network Device Support	This menu contains options for enabling support of specific network hardware devices. This includes PPP, which is used for dial-up Internet connections.

Managing Users and Software

PART 2

Table 8.5 Linux 2.4.*x* Kernel Configuration Options *(continued)*

Kernel Configuration Menu Item	Subsumed Options
Amateur Radio Support	You can connect multiple computers via special radio devices, some of which are supported by Linux through drivers in this menu.
IrDA (Infrared) Support	Linux supports some infrared communications protocols, which are often used by notebook and hand-held computers. You can enable these protocols and hardware in this menu.
ISDN Subsystem	Integrated Systems Digital Network (ISDN) is a method of communicating at up to 128Kbps over telephone lines. You can enable support for ISDN cards in this menu.
Old CD-ROM Drivers (not SCSI, not IDE)	Some old CD-ROM devices used proprietary interfaces. Linux supports these cards, but you must enable appropriate support with the settings in this menu. If you use a modern EIDE or SCSI CD-ROM, you do *not* need to enable any of these options.
Input Core Support	If you want to use a USB keyboard or mouse, enable support for these devices in this menu. You can also set a few other input device options here.
Character Devices	Character devices, in contrast to block devices, allow input/output one byte (character) at a time. Enable support for such devices (serial ports, mice, and joysticks, for instance) in this menu.
Multimedia Devices	If you have a video input or radio card in the computer, check this menu for drivers.
File Systems	This menu has options for supporting specific filesystems such as Linux's native ext2fs, or Windows's FAT.
Console Drivers	In this menu you can set options relating to how Linux handles its basic text-mode display.

Table 8.5   Linux 2.4.*x* Kernel Configuration Options *(continued)*

Kernel Configuration Menu Item	Subsumed Options
Sound	You can configure your sound card drivers in this menu.
USB Support	If your system uses any USB devices, you can enable support for USB—and for specific devices—in this menu. This menu includes options for much more than the USB keyboards and mice included on the Input Core Support menu. In fact, you need basic USB support from this menu even when using the Input Core Support keyboard or mouse drivers.
Kernel Hacking	This menu has a single option, which gives you some control over the system even if it crashes. It's useful primarily to kernel programmers.

You should take some time to examine the kernel configuration options. Each option has an associated Help item (see Figure 8.2). When you select it, you can see help text about the configuration option in question—at least, usually (sometimes the text is missing, particularly for new features).

Most kernel features have three compilation options: Y, M, and N. The Y and N stand for Yes and No, referring to compiling the option directly into the kernel or not compiling it at all. M stands for Module. When you select this option, the driver is compiled as a separate module driver file, which you can load and unload at will. (Linux can normally auto-load modules, so using modules is transparent.) Modules can help save memory, because these drivers need not be constantly loaded. Loading modules takes a small amount of time, however, and occasionally a module may not load correctly. It's generally best to compile features that you expect to use most or all of the time directly into the kernel, and load occasional-use features as modules. For instance, on a network server, you'd compile your network card's driver into the kernel, but you might leave the floppy disk driver as a module if that system's floppy disk is seldom used.

When you're done configuring the kernel, click Save and Exit in the main menu to save your configuration. The configuration program responds with a message telling you to type make dep to continue the compilation process; it then exits.

Compiling the Kernel

Once the kernel is compiled, you need to run several commands in succession:

```
# make dep
# make bzImage
# make modules
```

The first of these creates *dependency* information, so that the compiler knows each component's dependencies and can compile components as appropriate. This process typically takes a minute or two.

The second command, make bzImage, compiles the Linux kernel proper. Although variations of this command are possible, such as make zImage, these sometimes don't work well with large 2.4.*x* kernels. The result of running make bzImage is a kernel file located in /usr/src/linux/arch/i386/boot (i386 will be something else on non-*x*86 computers). This file is called bzImage. Running make bzImage typically takes several minutes. On very old hardware, it may take over an hour.

> **TIP** If you're using a computer with little RAM, try closing large memory-hungry programs, such as Netscape, before compiling the kernel. On particularly small systems, closing down X entirely can speed up kernel compilation.

The make modules command compiles the kernel module files. Depending on how many items you elected to compile as modules and the speed of your hardware, this process may take anywhere from a minute or two to over an hour.

> **NOTE** Red Hat Linux 7.0 requires a peculiar modification to the make bzImage and make modules commands. You must specify that the system use kgcc rather than the usual gcc for compilation. To do this, include CC=kgcc in the make command, as in *make CC=kgcc bzImage*.

If all these make commands execute without reporting any errors, you have a new kernel. It is not yet installed on the computer, however. That involves several additional steps.

Installing the Kernel and Modules

The kernel file proper, bzImage, must be placed somewhere suitable for booting. In principle, this can be anywhere on the hard disk. Most Linux computers use a tool known as the *Linux Loader (LILO)* to boot the kernel.

Versions of LILO prior to 21.3 suffered from the drawback that they could not boot a Linux kernel if that kernel resided above the so-called 1024-cylinder boundary. This boundary is a point on the disk corresponding to a numbering scheme used by the *x*86 BIOS to identify sectors on a hard disk. The standard BIOS calls can't read beyond the 1024th cylinder, and because LILO uses the BIOS, LILO can't read past that point, either. LILO 21.3 and later, however, can work around this problem on modern BIOSs (most of those issued since 1998) by using extended BIOS calls that can read past the 1024th cylinder.

If you use a pre-21.3 version of LILO or if your motherboard's BIOS was written before 1998, you may need to take steps to ensure that your kernel file falls below the 1024th cylinder—about 8GB on most systems. If you have a LILO later than version 21.3 *and* if your BIOS is more recent than 1998, you can place your kernel anywhere. You also need not be concerned about this if your Linux partitions all fall below the 1024-cylinder boundary.

If you need to restrict your kernel's position, one good way to do this is to create a small (5–20MB) partition below the 1024th cylinder and place the kernel in that partition. Typically, this partition is mounted as /boot. Even if you don't create such a partition, the Linux kernel often resides in the /boot directory.

To place the kernel file in /boot, you can issue a simple cp or mv command:

```
# cp /usr/src/linux/arch/i386/boot/bzImage /boot/bzImage-2.4.0-test8
```

This example copies the bzImage kernel file to a new name. It's a good way to make sure you can easily identify the kernel version, particularly if you experiment with different kernel versions or kernel options.

Installation of the kernel modules is handled by another make command in the kernel source directory: **make modules_install.** This command copies all the compiled kernel modules into a subdirectory of /lib/modules named after the kernel version—for instance, /lib/modules/2.4.0-test8. Once you've placed the kernel and its modules in reasonable locations, you must tell Linux to boot the new kernel. You can do this by editing /etc/lilo.conf, the LILO configuration file. This file should contain a group of lines resembling the following:

```
image=/boot/vmlinuz-2.2.16-22
        label=linux
        initrd=/boot/initrd-2.2.16-22.img
        read-only
        root=/dev/hda7
```

**Managing Users
and Software**

PART 2

This group of lines identifies the boot kernel (vmlinux-2.2.16-22 in this example), provides a label for the kernel (linux), and sets assorted other options. You should duplicate this set of lines and then edit *one* of the two sets. Change two things:

- Alter the image= line to point to the bzImage kernel file you've compiled and placed in the /boot directory.
- Modify the label= entry. You might call the new kernel linux-240t8, for example.

WARNING Do not simply change the existing boot description in lilo.conf. If you do so and if your new kernel is flawed in some important way—for instance, if it lacks support for your boot disk or filesystem—you won't be able to boot Linux. Duplicating the original entry and modifying one copy ensures that you'll be able to boot into the old kernel if necessary.

After you save the new lilo.conf file, type **lilo** to reinstall LILO with the new settings. The lilo program should respond by displaying a series of Added messages, one for each label provided in /etc/lilo.conf.

Testing Your New Kernel

At this point, you're ready to test your new kernel. To do so, shut down the computer and reboot. When the system reboots, one of two things will happen, depending on how LILO is configured:

- You'll see a prompt reading lilo:. If this happens, type the name for the new kernel image—this is what you entered on the label= line in /etc/lilo.conf.
- You'll see a list of kernel images and OSs. You should be able to select the new kernel image from this list by using the keyboard arrow keys and then pressing Enter.

Typically, older distributions use the lilo: prompt approach. Many newer distributions, including Red Hat 7.0 and Corel Linux, present a list of kernel images and OSs.

If all goes well, your new kernel will boot and your system will start up normally. You should then test all your system's hardware devices to be sure the kernel and its modules are working correctly. Try out your CD-ROM drive, floppy disk, modem, and so on. If you have problems with a device, recheck your kernel configuration options.

WARNING When upgrading from a 2.2.*x* kernel to a 2.4.*x* kernel, devices sometimes fail because the two kernels place the kernel modules in different locations within the /lib/modules/*version* directory tree. You can work around this problem by compiling drivers directly into the kernel or rearranging the module files to conform to 2.2.*x* kernel standards.

TIP Once you've tested your new kernel, you can save some disk space by going back into the /usr/src/linux directory and typing **make clean**. This command removes intermediary object files, thus clearing a substantial amount of disk space. It also causes subsequent kernel compilations to proceed more slowly than they otherwise would, however, because the system must recompile everything. If necessary, you can remove the entire /usr/src/linux directory tree— but some other programs rely on files in this directory in order to compile properly, so it's usually best to leave it alone.

Administrator's Logbook: Replacing a Kernel

System: E12345678

Action: Upgraded kernel from 2.2.16 to 2.4.0-test8.

Important options: Included Symbios 53c8xx SCSI and DEC Tulip drivers in kernel file proper; omitted unused EIDE drivers.

Boot options: Kernel file is /boot/bzImage-2.4.0-test8; booted from LILO as linux-240t8.

Checking for OS Updates

One particularly critical aspect of software installation is keeping your system up-to-date. As described in this section, OS updates are important for keeping your system secure and bug-free. Most distribution providers maintain Web pages or FTP sites from which you can download OS updates, and there are other sites you can check, as well, for updated software.

The Importance of OS Updates

In late 1999, a bug was discovered in named, the DNS server run on many Linux systems and included in the package called BIND. This bug allowed anybody with the requisite knowledge to break into a computer running named and acquire root privileges. The next several months saw countless systems compromised as *script kiddies* (delinquents with little knowledge, running prepackaged intrusion scripts) broke into computers running the standard BIND package on many versions of Linux. During most of this period, however, fixed versions of named were readily available on those distributions' Web pages. Had administrators spent five minutes locating, obtaining, and installing the updated server, they would have saved hours of frustration rebuilding compromised systems.

Of course, today's Linux distributions don't ship with that compromised version of named; their packages have been updated to fix the bug. The point of this story isn't that named versions from 1999 aren't to be trusted; it's that one must protect against the fact that important programs sometimes contain bugs that can open holes in a system's security. A security problem might be discovered tomorrow in a server you run today. If so, your system can be compromised. Indeed, if your system is always connected to the Internet, it's extremely likely that it *will* be compromised under those circumstances. (Many system administrators who ran appropriate monitoring software saw an abnormal number of probes of their DNS ports in early- and mid-2000, most of which were almost certainly attempts to break into those systems via the named bug.) Given the fact that security flaws are common, it's important that you keep your system's servers and other programs up-to-date.

Security problems aren't restricted to servers. Flaws are sometimes found in non-server programs that are run by local users. If your system has multiple users, these bugs can be exploited to gain root access. The fact that the compromise is local in origin doesn't make your task any easier: You must clean up the problem, most likely by wiping all data and restoring from a backup or reinstalling the OS.

In addition to security-related problems, bugs sometimes affect system stability or the reliability of specific programs. You can save yourself and your users a great deal of frustration by updating a buggy program to a more stable release. Fortunately, most core Linux programs are well tested and contain few glaring stability problems. Nonetheless, minor problems do occasionally crop up, so updating your system can be quite worthwhile.

On occasion, you may need to upgrade an entire system. You might be running Red Hat 6.1 and want to upgrade to Red Hat 7.0, for example. A major upgrade like this is usually done in response to new features rather than minor bug fixes. Red Hat 7.0, for instance, uses xinetd and XFree86 4.0 rather than inetd and XFree86 3.3. These changes are very important if you need features offered by xinetd and XFree86 4.0. Most Linux distributions offer ways to upgrade the OS as a whole, typically through the usual installation routines. These go through and replace every updated package, and then reboot into the updated OS.

> **WARNING** All package updates, and particularly whole-OS updates, have the potential to introduce problems. The most common glitches produced by updates relate to configuration files, because the updates often replace your carefully tuned configuration files with default files. You should therefore *always* back up a package's configuration files before updating the package. In the case of a whole-OS update, back up the entire /etc directory so that you can restore the originals if needed. Your administrative log files, too, can be critically important in making your system work again, particularly when the updated package requires a different format for its configuration file, as is true of the change from inetd to xinetd. Good notes on how you've configured one package can help you get its replacement in working order.

Locating Updates for Your Distribution

Most Linux distributors maintain Web pages or FTP sites with information on and links to updated packages. Table 8.6 summarizes the locations of these sites for many common distributions. The quality of these update sites varies substantially. Some are quite minimal, offering just a few updated packages and little or nothing in the way of explanation concerning the nature of the problems fixed. Others provide extensive information on the seriousness of problems, so you can better judge which packages are worth updating and which are not.

Table 8.6   URLs for Major Linux Distribution Updates

Distribution	Update URL
Caldera	`http://www.calderasystems.com/support/security/` and `ftp://ftp.caldera.com/pub/updates`
Corel	`http://linux.corel.com/support/updates.htm` (also see `http://www.debian.org/security/`)
Debian	`http://www.debian.org/security/`
Mandrake	`http://www.linux-mandrake.com/en/security/`
LinuxPPC	`http://www.linuxppc.com/support/`
Red Hat	`http://www.redhat.com/apps/support/updates.html`
Slackware	`http://www.slackware.com/getslack/`

Table 8.6   URLs for Major Linux Distribution Updates *(continued)*

Distribution	Update URL
Storm	`http://www.stormix.com/support/stormlinux/bugs/` (also see `http://www.debian.org/security/`)
SuSE	`http://www.suse.com/us/support/security/`
TurboLinux	`ftp://ftp.turbolinux.com/pub/turbolinux-updates/current/i386/`
Yellow Dog	`ftp://ftp.yellowdoglinux.com/pub/yellowdog/updates/`

Your distribution maintainer is usually the best source of updates for critical system components such as libc, XFree86, and major servers. By using an update provided by your distribution maintainer, you can be reasonably certain that the update won't conflict with or cause problems for other packages that come with the distribution. In cases such as the following, however, you may want or need to look elsewhere for updates.

Unavailable updates   If your distribution's maintainer is slow in producing updates, you may have little choice but to look elsewhere when you learn of a problem with an important package.

Prior self-updates   If you've previously updated a package using another source, you may want to stick with that source rather than return to the distribution maintainer's package. Presumably you've already worked through any compatibility issues, and it may be a nuisance to have to do this again if you revert to the original supplier.

Package substitutions   You might decide to replace a standard package with an altogether different program that provides similar functionality. For instance, if you use Postfix to replace sendmail on a Red Hat Linux 7.0 system, you won't find Postfix updates on Red Hat's Web site.

Package additions   Just as with substituted packages, you won't find updates for programs that don't ship with the original distribution. For example, you'll have to turn to Applix (`http://www.applix.com`) for ApplixWare updates.

Kernel updates   As described earlier in "Obtaining a Kernel," the Linux kernel can be updated via prepackaged files, but it's often beneficial to compile the kernel yourself from original source code.

Even if you don't intend to go to third parties or to official home pages for specific programs, you should consult sources other than your distribution's errata Web page for information on important security flaws and bug fixes. You will often learn of critical updates and security issues from such sources. Following are three of note.

Security newsgroups   The Usenet newsgroups `comp.security.unix`, `comp.os.linux.security`, and others devoted to specific products can alert you to important security issues. If you read these groups on a daily basis and take action based on important alerts you read there, you can greatly enhance your system's security.

Security Web pages   There are many Web sites devoted to security issues. Some helpful ones include `http://www.linuxsecurity.com`, `http://www.cert.org`, and `http://ciac.llnl.gov`.

Product Web pages   Check the Web pages for important individual packages to learn about updates. Although news about security-related updates should appear quickly on other forums, reports of feature changes and other updates may not travel so quickly. Nonetheless, some of these updates may be important for you. You'll need to decide for yourself which packages are important enough to monitor in this way, and how often.

Maintaining an up-to-date system can take a great deal of effort. In most cases, it's best to concentrate on security updates and updates to packages that are of most importance to your particular system. Occasionally updating the entire OS may also make sense, but this is a fairly major task and is frequently unnecessary. (Even in early 2001, Red Hat 5.2—a distribution that's roughly two years old—is still adequate for many purposes, although it needs many individual package updates to be secure.)

Administrator's Logbook: Updating Programs

System: E1234567

Action: Updated `samba-2.0.3` to `samba-2.0.7` to provide support for Windows 2000 clients.

In Sum

Installing, removing, and updating programs are very important actions for any Linux system administrator. Most Linux systems today use the RPM or Debian package formats, both of which allow for easy package handling by maintaining a database of packages and the individual files associated with these packages. When necessary, you can build a package file from source code, or install software without using an RPM or Debian package. This approach is particularly useful for the Linux kernel itself, which can benefit more than other programs from customizations unique to each computer. In all cases, ensuring that your programs are up-to-date requires some effort, because you must keep an eye on important security developments as well as watch for the addition of features you might want to make available on your system.

Part 3

System Optimization and Disk Management

Featuring:

- Benchmarks and the elements of performance
- Performance tuning and eliminating bottlenecks
- Linux support for filesystems
- Mounting and unmounting filesystems
- Updating and maintaining filesystems
- Backup strategies and media
- Linux and third-party backup and restoration tools
- Disaster recovery techniques

9

Performance Tuning

Performance tuning is truly an art form. Those who are particularly skilled at it can often take a system that seems barely sufficient for its intended task and make it fly. When a computer starts to react sluggishly, whether because of new software that is taxing its resources or some other factor, many people immediately conclude that a purchase order is the next step. Certainly the purchase of a new, high-end system could speed things up, but often there is a less expensive way.

This chapter provides some performance tuning tips that will allow you to maximize the performance of the computers in your system without the purchase of additional hardware. Use these tips to enhance the computers you administer, and you'll enjoy a boost in performance.

The Elements of Performance

Many elements are used to measure performance. Certainly it is valuable to compare the number of CPU cycles used to perform a task to the number of CPU cycles used by a different computer or the same computer after being configured differently. Memory usage, including swap memory usage, is another factor that can be used to gauge performance. Hardware performance is often measured in terms of number of failures and comparisons based on other factors like speed, and software is compared in a like manner.

Regardless of what element of performance you are testing, it is critical to ensure that the test isolates that element so that variations in other areas do not influence the final outcome. If you want to test CPU speed on two different systems, for example, you would not want one to have significantly more memory or any other feature that would make the playing field uneven from the beginning.

Hardware Performance

The hardware in a computer system is critical to its performance, so it's essential for system administrators, like yourself, to be able to determine when new hardware will actually provide a measurable benefit to the system in question. Making this determination requires measuring the performance of existing hardware and determining if it's creating a *bottleneck*, which is a component or process that limits the overall system performance. (Bottlenecks are covered in more detail shortly.) There are several different classes of hardware that are potential sources of bottlenecks.

CPU Cycles

The Central Processing Unit (CPU) of the computer carries most or all of the system's computational load. It's the CPU that performs spreadsheet calculations, compresses data for archiving, determines where to place a word when formatting a document, and so on. The CPU is therefore a major contributor to a system's performance—and a potential source of bottlenecks.

The importance of the CPU varies from one system to another, though; on a computer that's used for very CPU-intensive tasks, such as creating 3D animations or performing many types of scientific simulations, the CPU is extraordinarily important. Other tasks, such as serving files, are more affected by other subsystems, such as the disk or memory.

If your computer has an inadequate CPU, the most obvious fix is to upgrade the CPU. There may be other options, however. The trick is to get the computer to perform a task in fewer CPU cycles than it otherwise would. (Roughly speaking, a CPU cycle is a single "tick" of the CPU "clock"—most tasks require a fixed number of CPU cycles to perform.) You can sometimes reduce the number of CPU cycles required to run a program by recompiling the program with more efficient compiler options. Of most importance, most *x*86 Linux distributions use 386 optimizations, but if the computer uses a Pentium or faster CPU, 586 or even 686 optimizations may produce better performance.

TIP   The Mandrake and Stampede Linux distributions use 586 optimizations on their packages, and so can be marginally faster than other distributions. On the other hand, the 586 optimizations mean that these distributions don't run on 386 or 486 computers.

Memory

Many programs are *memory-intensive*—they consume a great deal of memory. Examples include high-resolution graphics packages, some databases, and some scientific simulations. If your system makes heavy use of such memory-intensive programs, it's important that you have both enough memory and fast memory.

Memory is measured in megabytes (MB). You can find how much your system has, and roughly how it's being used, with the `free` command, thus:

```
$ free
                 total     used     free   shared  buffers   cached
Mem:             95772    86748     9024    54480     5796    36164
-/+ buffers/cache:        44788    50984
Swap:           136512     7000   129512
```

The `total` column on the `Mem` line shows the total amount of RAM that Linux is using. The `used` column shows the amount of memory that's used, but the `Mem` line isn't the best to read in conjunction with this column, because it includes memory that Linux has dedicated to disk buffers. On most systems, the `used` column should show a value very close to the `total` column. Instead, check the `-/+ buffers/cache` line under the `used` column to see how much memory is in use. If your system has insufficient memory, it will use a lot of swap memory (indicated by a high value in the `used` column on the `Swap` line). This is disk space treated like memory. Because disk performance is slow compared to memory performance, it's best to minimize use of swap space.

Short of replacing or adding memory, there's not much you can do to improve the performance of the memory you've got; however, there are steps you can take to make Linux use its existing memory more efficiently. These techniques are covered later in this chapter.

Disk Performance

The disk subsystem—and particularly the hard disk—is a potentially important determinant of performance. Many processes, including file serving, databases, and software development, depend upon fast disk access. In addition, swap space resides on the hard disk, so if your computer has inadequate memory, disk performance becomes important in memory-intensive tasks, as well.

You can improve disk performance by replacing your hard disk or by supplementing it with another one. A less expensive option is to optimize your disk performance in any of several ways, described in more detail later in this chapter. Careful partition layout, Linux disk-tuning options, and so on can improve performance substantially.

Input/Output

Besides disk access, a variety of other I/O processes are also quite important, but less universally so. The video hardware is extremely important to some video-intensive tasks, such as displaying and moving windows in X, and in game playing. Network card I/O is important to servers and other network-intensive tasks. Even the lowly serial and parallel ports can be important to tasks such as printing.

For the most part, I/O speed is directly related to the quality of the relevant hardware. Sometimes the hardware quality interacts with the quality of drivers written for that hardware. For instance, historically, the fastest video hardware has first been supported in Linux using drivers that don't fully take advantage of the cards' features. The newest video cards therefore often perform poorly in Linux, at least until the XFree86 developers can produce improved drivers—a process that can take several months.

Occasionally, special driver parameters can improve the performance of an I/O device. Linux usually sets the best parameters at boot time, but you may want or need to adjust these settings in some circumstances. Chapter 12 covers adjusting the speed of serial ports, and this chapter includes tips for some other I/O devices.

Software Performance

Tools to measure software performance are typically expensive and are not often used. Typically software performance is measured in terms of speed and accuracy. Software speed is directly dependent on the skill of the programmer who wrote the software, but since you can't control that, you have only to look to the hardware and operating system when software performance appears to have degraded. Often a specific program that your users run frequently will be the clue to them that the system is running poorly.

Measuring Performance

There are so many ways to measure performance that it is difficult to make the measurement meaningful. One of the best benchmarks for Linux systems is the time it takes to compile a specific kernel from the command line without X running; this is certainly useful when comparing two identical computers or a single computer before and after a reconfiguration. Because kernel compilation under Linux exercises most functions that are exercised by normal benchmarks except floating-point performance, this comparison yields very useful data, which has the added benefit of being in an easily compared form. To make the comparison even better, you can shut down any external access, preventing user load from tainting the data. Of course, you need to use the same kernel source tree and the same `.config` file to ensure that you are comparing apples to apples. This is sufficient if your intent is to test the "guts" of the system.

For instance, you might compile a kernel and discover that the process requires 15:03 to complete. After setting several optimizations, you might find that the same process requires only 11:34—a substantial improvement. In performing such a comparison, though, you must ensure that nothing about the compilation itself has changed. You should compile the same source code from the same source tree. Also, be sure to do a **make clean** before each test compile. This command removes the intermediate object code files created from the source code files. If you don't do a **make clean**, the subsequent **make bzImage** (see Chapter 8) or similar command will simply relink the kernel against the previously compiled object files, resulting in a huge speed difference that doesn't reflect the results of your performance tuning.

To measure X performance, use the xbench tool. As described on its Web site (`http://charon.astro.nwu.edu/xbench`), this tool uses a measurement called xStones, which is a weighted average of several tests indexed to an old Sun station with a single-bit depth. xbench uses 13 low-level tests:

line	Draws vertical and diagonal lines of different lengths.
dline	Draws dashed lines.
wline	Draws wide lines.
rects	Draws rectangles.
fillrects	Draws solid filled rectangles.
tiledrects	Draws tiled rectangles.
stippledrects	Draws stippled rectangles.
invrects	Inverts rectangles on the screen.
arc	Draws arcs of varying angles between 5 and 360 degrees.
filledarc	Draws filled arcs of varying angles between 5 and 360 degrees.
filledpoly	Draws a filled polygon with five points.
bilblt	Test varies; see Web site for details.
imagestring	Draws a string.

The simple tests listed above really only test the graphics engine. Additionally, xbench uses one complex test to test the X server's overall performance. This test creates a window, clears an area, draws some text, scrolls the window, and destroys the window. This is a very old tool. If there was a newer a tool that measured the same type of activity, we'd use it. As it is, though, xbench is the usual benchmark for X performance.

Finding Bottlenecks

When you notice that one of your computers or an entire network is running slower than usual, it is time to assume the detective role and track down the problem. Where is the bottleneck that is preventing the data stream, whether on the network or on the backplane of an individual computer, from flowing at its previous rate? What is causing the sluggishness? Is it hardware, software, the network, or something in the operating system that is causing the problem? There are two tools we use to determine the problem: top and traceroute. These tools can find most of the bottlenecks in the average computer system that aren't related to hardware. If you don't find a bottleneck, chances are the problem is hardware that is beginning to fail or is wrongly configured. Such issues are discussed later in this chapter.

Using *top* or *gtop* to Find the Bottleneck

We use the top utility frequently to see how heavily loaded a particular computer is. The system information top displays includes uptime, the number of processes and the states of those processes, the percentages of CPU cycles and memory each process is using, the amount of time each process has taken, and a lot of other information. The information may be specific to the listed process or cumulatively computed from the process and its dead children. This information is invaluable in troubleshooting a system. The processes are listed in order from the most resource-intensive to the least intensive, and the display updates itself about every 5 seconds. Top reads global configuration information from /etc/toprc and user configuration information from a .toprc file in the user's home directory.

The normal top utility is text-mode, but graphical versions also exist. The graphical versions are available with the GNOME and KDE interfaces. The GNOME version is gtop, or the System Monitor, and the KDE version is ktop, or the Task Manager. As you've seen in previous chapters, we usually don't go for the GUI version of a tool unless it lends itself particularly well to a visual presentation. In the case of table of process information, you'll see that it does. Figure 9.1 shows the standard command-line top utility.

Looking at the sample output, you'll see that the system is running a process called vmware, which is taking up 27.7% of the CPU cycles. It also is using 46.1% of the memory. That's normal; this product is quite resource-intensive and slows down a system quite a bit. Sometimes, however, programs go haywire and start dominating the CPU or the memory and need to be shut down. The top utility will help you find such programs.

Figure 9.1 The top utility

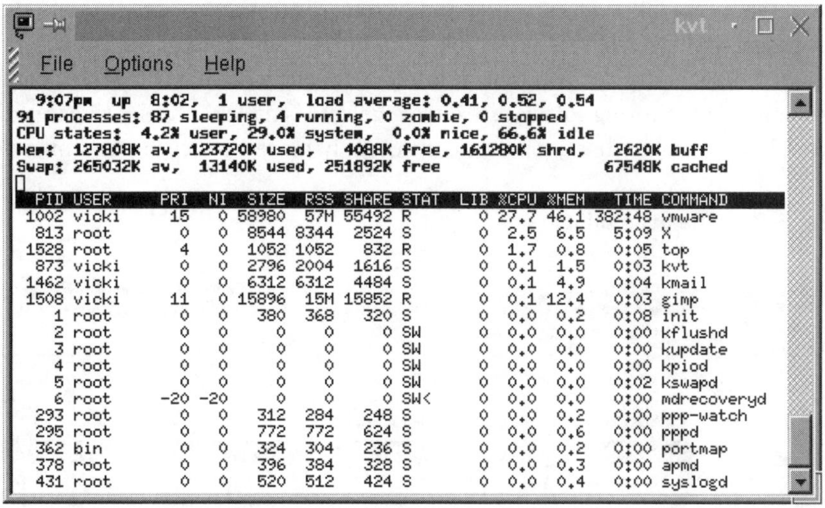

```
  9:07pm  up  8:02,  1 user,  load average: 0.41, 0.52, 0.54
91 processes: 87 sleeping, 4 running, 0 zombie, 0 stopped
CPU states:  4.2% user, 29.0% system,  0.0% nice, 66.6% idle
Mem:  127808K av, 123720K used,   4088K free, 161280K shrd,   2620K buff
Swap: 265032K av,  13140K used, 251892K free                 67548K cached

  PID USER     PRI  NI  SIZE  RSS SHARE STAT  LIB %CPU %MEM   TIME COMMAND
 1002 vicki     15   0 58980  57M 55492 R       0 27.7 46.1 382:48 vmware
  813 root       0   0  8544 8344  2524 S       0  2.5  6.5   5:09 X
 1528 root       4   0  1052 1052   832 R       0  1.7  0.8   0:05 top
  873 vicki      0   0  2796 2004  1616 S       0  0.1  1.5   0:03 kvt
 1462 vicki      0   0  6312 6312  4484 S       0  0.1  4.9   0:04 kmail
 1508 vicki     11   0 15896  15M 15852 R       0  0.1 12.4   0:03 gimp
    1 root       0   0   380  368   320 S       0  0.0  0.2   0:08 init
    2 root       0   0     0    0     0 SW      0  0.0  0.0   0:00 kflushd
    3 root       0   0     0    0     0 SW      0  0.0  0.0   0:00 kupdate
    4 root       0   0     0    0     0 SW      0  0.0  0.0   0:00 kpiod
    5 root       0   0     0    0     0 SW      0  0.0  0.0   0:02 kswapd
    6 root     -20 -20     0    0     0 SW<     0  0.0  0.0   0:00 mdrecoveryd
  293 root       0   0   312  284   248 S       0  0.0  0.2   0:00 ppp-watch
  295 root       0   0   772  772   624 S       0  0.0  0.6   0:00 pppd
  362 bin        0   0   324  304   236 S       0  0.0  0.2   0:00 portmap
  378 root       0   0   396  384   328 S       0  0.0  0.3   0:00 apmd
  431 root       0   0   520  512   424 S       0  0.0  0.4   0:00 syslogd
```

NOTE VMware is a tool for running multiple operating systems on a single computer. An alternative to dual-booting, it provides a virtual machine on an Intel-based computer. This virtual machine is a simulated computer in which an alternative operating system can be installed and run as if it were running on standard PC hardware while actually being isolated from the host's hardware and operating system. For more information, go to the VMware, Inc. site at `http://www.vmware.com`.

Other information provided by top includes the process ID (PID), which can be used to kill an errant program; the user who's running the program; the task priority (PRI) and nice value (NI), which determine how Linux allots CPU time to the task; various measures of memory usage (SIZE, RSS, and SHARE); the task's state (STAT)—R for running, S for sleeping, W for swapped out, and so on; and the total CPU time consumed (TIME).

The top utility also has an interactive mode, which allows you to perform tasks like killing a process, changing what information is displayed and how often it is updated, and renicing a process. (We'll talk about nicing and renicing a process in the "Tuning the System" section of this chapter.) The global /etc/toprc file can be used to restrict nonprivileged users to the secure mode of top, which disables this interactive mode.

Figure 9.2 illustrates GNOME's gtop version of the utility. Gtop is far more impressive in color, but you can get an idea of its value from the figure. The colored bars at the top clearly show the CPU usage by user and system, the memory usage (MEM), the swap memory usage (SW), which in this example is minimal, and the load average (LA), which is also minimal here. However, you must be able to discern what portion of the load is caused by running the monitoring software itself, or the data is useless. Comparing this display to Figure 9.1, you can see that gtop uses considerably more CPU cycles and memory than top.

Figure 9.2 The gtop utility

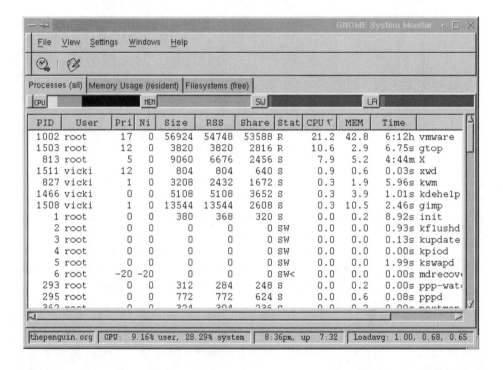

Figure 9.3 shows the KDE graphical alternative, Task Manager. Not only can you clearly see that almost all of the physical memory is being used (124,832 KB in use and 2,976 KB free), you also see that the amount of swap memory being used is 23,636KB out of 241,396KB total. The Task Manager also allows you to kill a task by highlighting it and clicking the Kill Task button or to pass a signal to a process by highlighting it and then selecting the signal to send from the Process menu. This is more comfortable to many administrators than the interactive mode of the nongraphical top. Again, in analyzing the results you have to realize that you're using additional resources by running the graphical version.

Figure 9.3   The KDE Task Manager

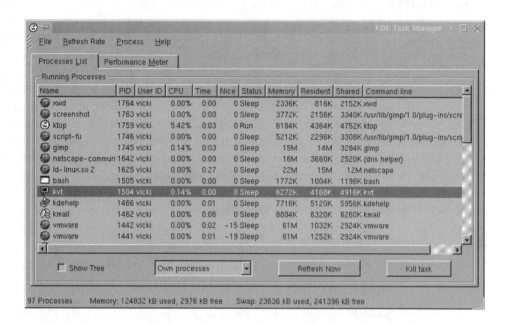

System
Optimization

PART 3

TIP   The amounts of physical memory used and free don't add up to the 128MB that the system has, because some memory is used to contain the kernel and shadow the BIOS.

Linux Memory Usage

Many new system administrators misunderstand the high usage of memory on a Linux system and, when they see statistics like thoes illustrated here, believe they need to add more physical memory. In reality, Linux makes very good use of the physical memory and will consistently use nearly all of it. Operating systems that don't do this simply waste the resource. To gauge your memory needs with top, look at how much swap memory is being used. If, as in this case, only a very small amount is being used, you don't need more memory. When the system does a lot of swapping and does so often, you need to consider adding either more swap space or more physical memory. If your swap is already around double the amount of your physical memory, add more physical memory. The free utility, described earlier, shows memory usage information only.

traceroute

The traceroute utility will help you track down problems in your network or determine that
a problem is actually outside your network. The traceroute utility prints the route that
packets take to a specific network host and three measurements of the time in milliseconds for
each hop. Listing 9.1 shows the traceroute command in action. Using this information, you
can determine whether there is a delay at one of the network stops that your data makes
between the sender and receiver, thereby providing useful information when you are troubleshooting a network problem. Listing 9.1 shows a slow increase in the times between the first
hop and the final one, but there's a jump at the final hop, suggesting that the destination is
overloaded or on a slow link. In this case, you can't do anything to improve network performance. If you'd seen a big jump *within* your network, though, it's possible that reconfiguring
your network or upgrading its hardware could improve performance.

Listing 9.1   Output of the traceroute Command

```
$ /usr/sbin/traceroute www.linux.org

traceroute to www.linux.org (198.182.196.56), 30 hops max, 40 byte
        ➥CApackets
  1  dsl-254-070.dsl-isp.net (216.254.70.1)  30.599 ms  46.390 ms
        ➥CA33.701 ms
  2  border9.fe4-0.speakeasy-6.nyc.pnap.net (209.191.175.196)
        ➥CA25.710 ms   37.445  ms   26.314 ms
  3  core2.fe0-0-fenet1.nyc.pnap.net (209.191.128.66)  26.032 ms
        ➥CA25.860 ms   25.5   97 ms
  4  POS3-3.GW12.NYC4.ALTER.NET (157.130.253.217)  26.243 ms
        ➥CA38.132 ms   25.969 ms
  5  505.ATM2-0.XR1.NYC4.ALTER.NET (152.63.22.66)  26.275 ms   25.030
        ➥CAms   26.302 ms
  6  189.at-1-0-0.TR1.NYC8.ALTER.NET (152.63.21.90)  27.014 ms
        ➥CA27.310 ms   26.042 ms
  7  124.at-6-0-0.TR1.DCA6.ALTER.NET (152.63.2.165)  35.369 ms
        ➥CA35.692 ms   34.126 ms
```

```
 8   187.at-6-0-0.XR1.TCO1.ALTER.NET (152.63.34.17)  31.948 ms
        ➥CA31.754 ms   34.152 ms
 9   193.ATM9-0-0.GW1.TCO1.ALTER.NET (146.188.160.41)  33.437 ms
        ➥CA35.940 ms   33.455 ms
10   uu-peer-oc12.core.ai.net (205.134.160.2)  47.416 ms   48.639 ms
        ➥CA44.509 ms
11   border-ai.invlogic.com (205.134.175.254)  42.543 ms   54.816 ms
        ➥CA63.588 ms
12   router.invlogic.com (198.182.196.1)  58.183 ms   58.595 ms
        ➥CA73.077 ms
13   www.linux.org (198.182.196.56)  117.648 ms   153.763 ms
        ➥CA111.498 ms
```

Tuning the System

Most of the default settings in a typical operating system—Linux as well as Windows NT—are set conservatively in an effort to serve the widest variety of installations. This section examines some of the aspects of a Linux computer system you can optimize beyond the default settings to give it better performance. Some of these will bring only minimal gains, but the overall effect will be positive. Of course, we cannot tell you generically which of these methods will bring the greatest benefit to your system, but we've been careful to warn you of any potential risks. You might want to use a less-critical system to test these optimizations, although they are all safe if performed as listed.

nice and *renice*

Introduced in Chapter 4, "Tools of the Trade," these two commands allow you to assign priorities to processes. The highest priority is –20, and the lowest priority is 19.

nice

The nice utility allows you to run a specified program with a modified scheduling priority. If you don't specify a new priority with the nice utility, the command's priority will be increased by 10, thereby making it give way to other processes; hence the name nice. Only privileged users can specify negative priorities, making a process more urgent.

> **TIP**   Some CPU-intensive programs are low priority. For instance, the SETI@home
> project (`http://setiathome.ssl.berkeley.edu`) distributes deep-space radio
> recordings to individual systems for processing in the search for extraterrestrial
> intelligence (SETI). A Linux version of the SETI@home software is available and can
> be run in the background. Chances are your own computer use is more important
> to you than the SETI@home software, so you can use `nice` to run the SETI@home
> software at low priority. Doing so ensures that SETI@home won't rob CPU time
> from more important processes, while still allowing you to participate in the project.
> You can use the same technique with any CPU-intensive but low-priority task.

renice

The `renice` utility is a little more versatile than `nice`. It may be used on users (the –u argument) to alter the scheduling priority of all of the processes owned by that user. When it's
used on a process group (`-g`), the scheduling priority of all processes in the process group
will be altered. When it's used on a process (`-p`), the priority of that process is altered. If
you combine more than one of these types in a single command, you must specify –p for
any individual processes that occur after a user or process group name in the `renice` command. For example, the following command would increase the scheduling priority of
process 247, 123, and all processes owned by root by a factor of 10.

```
# renice +10 247 -u root -p 123
```

Virtual Memory Tuning

You can use the files in /proc/sys/vm to tune the virtual memory system on your Linux
computers. Use the `cat` command to see the current settings and then the `echo` command
to set new values. The relevant `cat` command looks like this:

```
# cat /proc/sys/vm/freepages
```

```
64      96      128
```

These three numbers are the current settings for the variables: `min_free_pages`, `free_
pages_low` and `free_pages_high`. Free memory normally doesn't go below `min_free_
pages`. If the number of free pages falls to below the `free_pages_high` setting, back-
ground swapping is started. If it falls below the `free_pages_low` setting, intensive swapping is started. A "page" is 4KB. The boot default setting for `min_free_pages` on a system
with 8MB or more memory is $n \times 2$, where n is the number of megabytes of memory. The
`free_pages_low` setting for this machine would be $n \times 3$, and the `free_pages_high`
would be $n \times 4$. Machines with less than 8MB of memory use an n value of 8.

If "out of memory" errors occur or if the machine is primarily used for networking, it might be beneficial to increase min_free_pages to 64 or more. In this case, free_pages_ low should be set to double the min_free_pages setting.

On a server with 128MB of memory and a fairly low user load, settings of "256 512 768" tend to work well. If the system will be restricted to light server duty and fairly significant desktop usage, these settings are probably adequate. If the server load becomes heavier and the system seems to stall, you can experiment with increasing the settings using the guidelines noted above.

To adjust these settings, simply echo the desired values and redirect the output to /proc/ sys/vm/freepages as follows:

```
# echo "256 512 768" > /proc/sys/vm/freepages
```

Another tool is the /proc/sys/vm/overcommit-memory file, which you can use to allow overcommitting of resources. It contains only a flag setting (0 for off, 1 for on) to turn this feature off or on. Overcommitting allows you to do things with fewer resources than you would otherwise need. We don't recommend this, because if programs try to use the resources they've been told are available, the programs or system may crash. If you need more memory, add more physical memory.

The /proc/sys/vm/bdflush file determines the behavior of the bdflush kernel daemon. This daemon determines when existing "dirty" buffers should be written to disk. A "dirty" buffer is one that is awaiting a disk write. When memory is short, you can set the maximum number of dirty buffers that can exist in a buffer cache to a high value and/or the maximum number of dirty buffers that bdflush can write to the disk at once. This causes Linux to perform less frequent but longer-lasting disk writes. A low value makes disk writes more even in their frequency and duration. Other settings control the allocation of free buffers, and these can be adjusted to meet the system's needs as well. Read more about bdflush in /usr/src/linux/Documentation/vm.txt.

The /proc/sys/vm/kswapd file contains settings that control kernel swapping. You can control how many pages kswapd tries to free at one time and the number of pages kswapd writes in one turn (a *swap cluster*). You'll want to set the swap cluster setting reasonably large so that kswapd does its I/O in large chunks and the disk won't have to seek very often, but if you set it too high, the system will be bogged down with very lengthy swaps. The setting used by default for Red Hat will work for a server that is not heavily used, but you can experiment.

The file /proc/sys/vm/pagetable_cache contains two numbers, which represent the minimum and maximum cache size for each processor. On a low-memory, single-CPU system, particularly with less than 16MB of RAM, you should set these values to 0 so that

System Optimization

PART 3

you don't waste the memory. On SMP systems, these settings are used to allow the system to do fast page-table allocations without having to acquire the kernel memory lock. The default settings in Red Hat 7.0 are 25 and 50.

Serial Port Tuning

Serial ports in Linux default to pretty conservative values, so you can sometimes see great performance improvements in modem throughput (and any other metric that grades the performance of a serial device) by resetting these values with the `setserial` command. `setserial` is designed to set and/or report the specified serial port's configuration information, including its I/O port and IRQ setting. Chapter 12 discusses `setserial` in more detail.

If you set your serial port's speed appropriately and it still seems slow, you might try to tune your packet size as appropriate for your connection quality. If you have a particularly noisy phone line, choose a small packet size. If the line is high-quality and quiet, you might want to try a larger packet size. You can set these options with the `mru` and `mtu` parameters to the `pppd` utility, which is described in Chapter 12.

Filesystem Tuning

Filesystem settings are typically set quite conservatively to avoid putting the user's system at risk. Many settings can be tweaked to optimize that filesystem. Since Linux uses the ext2 filesystem, we'll be looking at ways to improve filesystem performance within an ext2 filesystem. Chapter 10 is devoted entirely to the discussion of Linux-supported filesystems. This section covers some utility programs you can use to improve a standard ext2 filesystem's performance.

Partition Issues

Before tuning the filesystem, it's important to understand how the *placement* of a partition influences its performance. Hard drives are made up of circular, thin platters that spin at very high speeds. As with all spinning objects, the outer edge must move faster than the inner edge. This means that tracks at the outer edges of a hard drive platter will be moving faster than those nearer the middle of the platter. Given the same linear data density, this means that data is read from and written to the drive faster from the outermost tracks. Hard drives write data to the disk from the outside in, so that the fastest areas are filled with data first. When partitioning your drive, the first partition will be faster than the last. The general consensus is that the swap and the /`tmp` partitions should be on the fastest parts of the drive, so put them near the beginning. Of course, if your drive has more than 1024 cylinders, the /`boot` partition will need to be within the first 1024 if you intend to use versions of LILO prior to 21.4.2. LILO prior to version 21.4.2 will not boot the system if the /`boot` partition falls outside of this boundary.

tune2fs

The tune2fs utility allows you to adjust some aspects of an ext2 filesystem. First, you can use the –c max-mount-counts parameter to adjust the maximum number of times the filesystem may be mounted before a filesystem check is automatically performed. The default is 20 on a Red Hat 7.0 system. To set it to 30, use tune2fs like this:

```
# /sbin/tune2fs -c 30 /dev/hdb3
```

A related parameter is -i interval-between-checks, which determines the maximum length of time between mandatory filesystem checks. The default on Red Hat 7.0 is 15,552,000 seconds (6 months). To set it to 9 months, use tune2fs like this:

```
# /sbin/tune2fs -i 23328000 /dev/hdb3
```

You might wish to increase these numbers on a filesystem that is seldom written to or is mounted read-only. This will prevent you from having to wait while the system performs an unnecessary filesystem check. We don't advise increasing them on a filesystem that is heavily written to, because you want to catch any filesystem problems as early as possible to avoid data loss.

The tune2fs utility can also be used to adjust the number of blocks on a filesystem that are reserved for root use only, as well as the percentage of the filesystem that will be reserved for root use only. The default under Red Hat 7.0 is 5 percent. To set the number of blocks, use the –r *reserved_blocks* option with a specific number of blocks:

```
# /sbin/tune2fs -r 50000
```

To set the reserved blocks using a percentage, use the –m *reserved_percentage* option:

```
# /sbin/tune2fs -m 10
```

Keeping blocks reserved for root use only is a lifesaver if a user fills up the filesystem; it allows root an opportunity to fix it. It also can be used to allow specific users and/or groups to use these specially reserved blocks, but for the reason just mentioned, you'll want to use this sparingly. Reserved blocks are most important on critical system filesystems, such as / and, if they're on separate partitions, /var and /etc. You may want to *decrease* the reserved block percentage on removable disks like Iomega Zip disks or floppy disks, and perhaps also on a separate /home partition.

WARNING Never use tune2fs to change parameters on a filesystem that is currently mounted read/write! Certain changes could destroy your data. Unmount the partition before making any changes.

---

hdparm

The hdparm utility retrieves and optionally sets hard drive parameters. It works reliably with kernel versions 1.2.13 and later. Some options are not supported in use with a kernel prior to 2.0.10.

> **TIP** The hdparm utility is designed to be used on IDE hard disks; there's no need to use it on SCSI hard disks. SCSI drives are handled by SCSI host adapters, the drivers for which automatically use optimum settings. You can still use hdparm to test your SCSI disk's performance, though, as described shortly.

On disks that experience a high I/O load, significant performance improvements have been reported by setting the IDE drivers to use *direct memory access (DMA)* and 32-bit transfers. The default kernel settings are quite conservative and have some room for tweaking.

The following command specifies 32-bit I/O over the PCI bus on the first IDE disk:

```
# /sbin/hdparm -c 1 /dev/hda
```

Some chipsets require a special sync sequence, which can be performed by replacing the –c 1 with –c 3. The value 3 works with almost all 32-bit IDE chipsets but costs slightly more in overhead. To disable 32-bit transfers, use –c 0.

To enable the use of DMA on device /dev/hda, use the following command:

```
# /sbin/hdparm -d 1 /dev/hda
```

DMA allows data to be transferred directly from the hard drive into memory, bypassing the CPU. In order to enable DMA, support for your motherboard chipset must be compiled into your kernel. To turn off DMA, use the –d 0 parameter instead. A few drives are known to have bad implementations of DMA and can cause filesystem corruption. If you see a recurring problem, try disabling DMA.

You can test the results of your changes by running hdparm in performance test mode:

```
# /sbin/hdparm -t /dev/hda
```

Your result will look something like the following:

```
/dev/hda:

Timing buffered disk reads:  64 MB in 5.81 seconds =  12.36 MB/sec
```

Make adjustments and rerun the `hdparm` test command until you've found the optimal settings. If you want to make these changes permanent, use the –k option with `hdparm` as shown:

```
# /sbin/hdparm -k 1 /dev/hda
```

Changing the number of sectors transferred on each interrupt by setting the –m option may buy you a minor performance gain, but we haven't seen a real change when we've used it.

mke2fs

The `mke2fs` command creates a second extended filesystem on a disk partition or other device. If your Linux machine typically works with very large files, you may be able to obtain a noticeable filesystem performance improvement by formatting your drives with larger block sizes. By default, the Linux filesystem uses 1024-byte blocks. If you're going to manipulate files that are bigger than a gigabyte in size, you might try setting the block size to 4K with the `mke2fs` command:

```
# mke2fs -b 4096 /dev/hda3
```

The `mke2fs` command creates a new filesystem on the partition specified. This operation destroys any data that had been on that partition, so don't use it except on an empty partition.

defrag

When you write a file to disk, it can't always be written in consecutive blocks. A file that is not stored in consecutive blocks is said to be *fragmented*. It takes longer to read a fragmented file because the disk's read-write head is required to move more. You want to avoid disk fragmentation, even though a good buffer cache with read-ahead ability makes it less of an issue. Luckily the ext2 filesystem is very careful in its block selection so as to minimize fragmentation.

The Debian distribution comes with a utility called `defrag`, which is released under the GNU GPL and is available for public consumption. You can download it from `ftp://metalab.unc.edu/pub/Linux/system/filesystems`.

chattr

Linux keeps track of the last time a file was modified and updates the timestamp appropriately. This process involves the use of the `find` and `fsck` commands, and it can be resource-intensive for systems that contain large amounts of constantly changing data, such as a newsfeed or mail server. In order to save the time and resources involved, you might choose to turn off the last-access-time modification as superuser with the `chattr` command:

```
# chattr +A filename
```

System
Optimization

PART 3

The chattr command may be used recursively. The command to skip the last-access-time modification on the /var/spool/mail directory would look like this:

```
# chattr -R +A /var/spool/mail
```

We don't generally use this technique, because we find that knowing when a file was last accessed is quite useful.

Bad Blocks

It's a good idea to check periodically for bad blocks on your hard drives. To locate and repair bad blocks on a filesystem, we use a sequence of three commands: dumpe2fs, badblocks, and e2fsck. First you must find out how many blocks are on the device you plan to check. To do this, you use the dumpe2fs command, which is in the e2fsprogs package in Red Hat Linux. The dumpe2fs command, as the name implies, dumps filesystem information from the superblock and block groups on the specified device. This information includes the basics like the OS type, inode count, block count, last mount time, mount count, last checked data, check interval, first inode, inode count, and more. The command to dump data on partition /dev/hda3 looks like this:

```
# /sbin/dumpe2fs /dev/hda3
```

Because we just want the number of blocks for use in locating bad blocks, however, we should pipe this command into a grep command, as follows:

```
# /sbin/dumpe2fs /dev/hda3 | grep "Block count"
dumpe2fs 1.19, 13-Jul-2000 for EXT2 FS 0.5b, 95/08/09
Block count:                533736
```

Knowing the total number of blocks on the partition you wish to check for bad blocks, you can then use the badblocks program. To check device /dev/hda3, which has a total of 533,736 blocks, starting at block 1 and outputting the results to a file called badblocks.rpt, use the following command:

```
# badblocks -o badblocks.rpt /dev/hda3 533736 1
```

WARNING Never use the –w option with a filesystem containing real data, since this option tells badblocks to perform write tests to every block on the device. This would, of course, write over any existing data on the partition. The –n option performs a nondestructive read/write test, which restores the original data after writing test data to each block.

Now that you've checked the disk itself for bad blocks, you should give the filesystem a chance to repair them. You do this using `/sbin/fsck.ext2` (or `/sbin/e2fsck`, which is the same program). When passed the flag -l followed by the `badblocks` output file, e2fsck will attempt to move any data contained in the questionable block to a healthy block. When run, e2fsck reports its five passes through the filesystem, including any problems it encounters, thus:

```
# e2fsck -f -l badblocks.rpt /dev/hda7

e2fsck 1.19, 13-Jul-2000 for EXT2 FS 0.5b, 95/08/09

Pass 1: Checking inodes, blocks, and sizes

Pass 2: Checking directory structure

Setting filetype for entry 'pump.sock' in /var/run (30156) to 6.

Setting filetype for entry 'fs7100' in /tmp/.font-unix (37489) to 6.

Pass 3: Checking directory connectivity

Pass 4: Checking reference counts

Pass 5: Checking group summary information


/: ***** FILE SYSTEM WAS MODIFIED *****

/: 96133/165792 files (0.6% non-contiguous), 300086/331332 blocks
```

In the above example, e2fsck found minor problems with two files, /var/run and /tmp/.font-unix. The utility corrected both problems automatically. On rare occasion, e2fsck may require your help in fixing problems. If this happens, your best bet is to accept the default option for each problem, unless you understand the ext2 filesystem intimately.

Eliminating Unnecessary Processes

Chapter 7 noted that unnecessary processes left running on a system pose a significant security risk. That reason alone is enough to merit altering the system so that these processes are not automatically started. If you need another reason, here it is: Any processes running on your machine use memory and CPU cycles. In other words, they waste resources that could be used by required processes.

So how do you determine which processes are unnecessary? You need to rely on a detailed familiarity with a system's hardware and software configuration and its application requirements. Some processes are obviously unnecessary. If you don't have a sound card, for example, kwmaudio would be a superfluous process and should be killed. If your system isn't a name server, named would be of no use. Use common sense, and eliminate processes you don't intend to use. You can find out what processes are running by using the ps -x command, thus:

```
# ps -x

PID TTY       STAT    TIME COMMAND
    1 ?         S      0:26 init
    2 ?         SW     0:04 [kflushd]
    3 ?         SW     0:16 [kupdate]
    4 ?         SW     0:00 [kpiod]
    5 ?         SW     0:07 [kswapd]
  448 ?         S      0:02 syslogd
  451 ?         S      0:00 klogd
  460 ?         S      0:46 named
  464 ?         S      0:00 rpc.portmap
  483 ?         SL     0:01 xntpd -p /var/run/xntpd.pid

< output truncated >
```

This output is likely to continue for some time, so you should pipe it through the more or less pager (as in **ps -x | less**), or redirect the output to a file so you can read it in a text editor. You can examine the list of processes to find what's unnecessary. If something isn't needed but seems to be started automatically at boot time, you'll have to locate the startup script and disable it, as discussed in Chapter 5.

Compiling for Efficiency

Most compiled programs can be compiled with specific settings that make them run more efficiently on your specific hardware/operating system combination. The kernel has a great many optimizations that can be used. Application software may have some optimization possibilities as well.

Optimizing the Kernel

Generally it is a bad idea to run any distribution's default kernel instead of recompiling a system-specific kernel. The stock kernel contains an abundance of drivers, to facilitate installation upon many different machines with different configurations. You probably won't need many of these drivers. For example, most installations don't need the support that's included for capabilities like Symmetric Multi-Processing (SMP) or Integrated Services Digital Network (ISDN). These "extras" use up memory, impairing system performance. As soon as possible after installation, you should recompile the kernel, leaving out drivers for hardware you don't have and eliminating functionality you won't use.

Another reason for recompiling is the fact that recent kernels allow for optimization based on the processor, but most distributions ship with kernels optimized for 386 systems. A kernel developed for a 386 machine will run slower on a more capable machine than will code compiled for that machine's processor. If the kernel must be portable among a variety of machines, you'll have to compile to the lowest machine's processor type, but other than that, you should select the appropriate processor type for the computer the kernel is to be run on.

The number of processor optimization options is growing. Back in kernel 2.2.5, there were five optimization schemes from which to choose. Table 9.1 lists the optimization schemes available in the 2.2.17 kernel, and Table 9.2 lists the 2.4.0-test9 kernel's optimization options. (It's possible to apply kernel patches to 2.2.x kernels to increase the number of optimizations they offer, but the effort isn't normally worthwhile.)

System Optimization

PART 3

Table 9.1   Optimization Schemes in the 2.2.17 Kernel

Optimization Scheme	Processors
386	AMD/Cyrix/Intel 386DX/DXL/SL/SLC/SX, Cyrix/TI 486DLC/DLC2 and UMC 486SX-S
486	AMD/Cyrix/IBM/Intel DX4 or 486DX/DX2/SL/SX/SX2, AMD/Cyrix 5x86, NexGen Nx586, and UMC U5D or U5S
586/K5/5x86/6x86	Generic Pentium-class CPUs, possibly lacking the TSC (time stamp counter) register
Pentium/K6/TSC	Intel Pentium/Pentium MMX, AMD K6 and K6-3D
Ppro	Intel Pentium II/Pentium Pro, Cyrix/IBM/National Semiconductor 6x86MX and MII

Table 9.2 Optimization Schemes in the 2.4.0-test9 Kernel

Optimization Scheme	Processors
386	All Intel, AMD, and Cyrix 386 CPUs, as well as the Cyrix 486DLC series and NexGen Nx586
486	All Intel, AMD, and Cyrix 486 CPUs, as well as the UMC U5D and U5S
586/K5/5x86/6x86/6x86MX	Generic Pentium-class CPUs, possibly lacking the TSC register
Pentium-Classic	Original Intel Pentium
Pentium-MMX	Intel Pentium MMX
Pentium-Pro/Celeron/Pentium-II	Intel Pentium Pro, Celeron, and Pentium-II
Pentium-III	Intel Pentium-III
K6/K6-II/K6-III	AMD K6, K6-2, and K6-III
Athlon/K7	AMD Athlon (K7), including the Duron
Crusoe	Transmeta Crusoe series
Winchip-C6	Original IDT Winchip
Winchip-2	IDT Winchip 2
Winchip-2A/Winchip-3	IDT Winchip with 3dNow capability

Additionally, the amount of memory is a factor when compiling a new kernel. If your system is blessed with more than a gigabyte of memory, you'll need to turn on Big Memory Support. You do this by selecting 2GB Maximum Physical Memory (instead of the default 1GB) when prompted.

There are many other kernel parameters that might give you a performance gain. Since these are CPU-specific, we'll leave it to you to evaluate their potential benefit to your systems. Chapter 8 covers other kernel compilation options and procedures.

Optimizing Applications

Just as the kernel code can be recompiled to optimize a computer system's performance, so also can the application code be optimized. If you download a tarball, read the documentation to see if there are system-specific optimizations that you might use. Most Linux software comes with an INSTALL file, which contains instructions for installation. Additionally, you'll likely find README files, which will tell you specific things to do for your operating system and/or hardware.

Tuning the X Window System

The X Window System, the subject of Chapter 16, is a critical part of a desktop system, since it provides the user a GUI environment in which to work. Users like graphical tools, and some Linux administrative functions are so complicated that the ability to perform them without graphical tools is all but forgotten. Network configuration, for example, is almost exclusively done via some graphical tool like netcfg or kppp. It's certainly possible to configure a network by editing the scripts, but fewer and fewer administrators do it that way anymore. As a result, most of the desktop systems you administer and probably many of the servers will be configured to run X. X is quite resource-intensive, though. Anything you can do to tune X is a good thing.

Window Managers and Integrated Desktop Environments

Window managers and integrated desktop environments (IDEs) can really chew up memory and CPU cycles. First, since it seems to be a source of confusion even for seasoned system administrators, you need to understand the difference between the two. A *window manager* is the interface between X and the user. It is the mechanism by which the user can move, resize, and otherwise manipulate the windows that X gives it. Some of these window managers have task bars, virtual desktops, file managers, and theme-association; others do not. An integrated desktop environment brings some inter-application consistency and additional tools to this environment. It provides things like a file browser and user desktop, along with assorted minor tools and utilities, and it influences the overall look and feel of the environment. An IDE comes with a specific window manager but may be used with a different window manager if that manager is IDE-aware. We'll talk more about the specifics in Chapter 16 when we discuss X in more depth, but the essential point is that an IDE runs atop a window manager. If you need to reduce overhead, you can get rid of the IDE, which will free up a lot of resources.

If you do that and are still not getting the performance you need (but still need the X environment), try changing window managers. If you're looking for performance instead of "pretty," try the Tab window manager (twm). This environment provides title bars, icon management, point-and-click, and other functions, but it does so with line-art instead of using the high-overhead 3D effects or shading. The switch to twm will buy you some performance improvement.

Removing Bad Modes from *XF86Config*

Another X performance issue involves the startup process, which although faster than Microsoft Windows, is much slower than it should be. What could make it go faster? If you watch the output of the startx command (press Shift+Alt+F1 to go back and look), you'll see many lines similar to this:

```
(--) SVGA:  NM2160: Removing mode (640x400) that won't display
    ➡properly on LCD
```

This line represents a video mode that was looked at and determined not to fall within the capabilities of your video card/monitor combination. Each time X is started, the system reevaluates these modes. One way to speed things up a bit is to remove any bad video modes from your XF86Config file. The mode line will look like this:

```
Modeline "640x400"  31.50  640  672  736  832  400  401  404  445
    ➡-hsync  -vsync
```

Simply comment it out by placing a # symbol in front of the word Modeline. The next time X is started, these modes won't be attempted, saving you a little time for each mode deleted. This will *not* improve performance once X is running, however.

Upgrading

"When should I upgrade my operating system?" is a question that plagues many system administrators. Do you upgrade simply because a newer version has come out? Do you upgrade individual packages whenever there is a bug fix? Do you reinstall from scratch or perform the distribution's upgrade?

It's usually best to back up the system, reinstall, and then dump configuration files and user files over the new system. This may cause you some trepidation at first, since you won't be sure that you remembered to put all the configuration data back; you may think you will overlook something. If you use the installation process's upgrade facility, you'll probably never have a problem with it. As you became more confident, however, you'll probably decide that you don't like having residue from the previous version mixed in with the new version, so you'll begin backing up the system, and doing a full install.

You should not blindly upgrade or reinstall a working, configured system just because a new version of the operating system has come out. The distribution's Web site will contain detailed information about what prompted the new version and what has been upgraded. Read those notes and do a cost-benefit analysis! Is the gain worth the time? Are there risks if you don't upgrade, and do these risks apply in your setting? Perform an upgrade if the new version offers several significant security fixes or a major change in overall kernel philosophy. If there are only a few security fixes, you can upgrade those packages only, and leave the rest alone. You'll get more comfortable with what requires an upgrade as you progress.

In Sum

A computer's performance can be influenced by many factors, both hardware and software. If your system isn't performing to your liking, you might try upgrading your hardware, but devoting some time to optimizing your computer may save you the cost of hardware upgrades. Indeed, some hardware upgrades won't do much good unless accompanied by appropriate software tuning. Enabling 32-bit DMA transfers on IDE hard disks is one such case. You can also tune your computer's use of the hard disk, of memory, and of the CPU by appropriate configuration options. Some optimizations (particularly for the CPU) require you to recompile software for your system, or at least to locate software compiled with better-than-386 optimizations.

One class of optimizations that's covered in this chapter relates to the placement of filesystems on the hard disk. Chapter 10 extends this topic and covers alternatives to the standard Linux ext2 filesystem, some of which may improve performance, particularly after a system crash or power outage.

System Optimization

PART 3

10

Filesystems and Disk Management

One of Linux's strengths as an operating system is its support for a wide variety of filesystems. Not only does Linux support its own native filesystem, the Second Extended Filesystem (*ext2fs* or *ext2*), but it also supports a wide array of filesystems used by other Unix-like OSs, Windows, MacOS, and others. This support makes Linux a particularly effective OS in a multi-boot environment, and it can also be quite useful for a Linux-only system. You can use Linux's extensive filesystem support to read removable media and even hard disks from other computers.

NOTE The word *filesystem* has two meanings. As used in this chapter, *filesystem* means a disk- or network-based data structure used for storing files. It also refers to the hierarchy of directories and files on a disk. In this second sense, the filesystem is a logical structure that you can view with a file manager or with Linux commands such as 1s. (Chapter 3 discusses filesystems in this second sense.) By contrast, the low-level data structures that constitute a filesystem in its first meaning are largely invisible to you as a user or system administrator—but their effects are important nonetheless, as illustrated throughout this chapter.

In order to access these filesystems, however, you must understand the tools that Linux uses to make this access possible. Most critically, you must recognize how Linux *mounts* and *unmounts* filesystems—that is, how the OS grafts a removable disk or hard disk partition onto its existing directory structure. In addition, you should be familiar with the tools available to help you prepare a filesystem for use and keep it working smoothly.

This chapter begins with an overview of Linux's filesystem capabilities, including the major filesystems it supports. The discussion then moves to practical issues of filesystem handling—how to mount and unmount both hard disk and removable-media filesystems. It concludes with a look at maintaining your filesystems and adding new ones.

Linux Filesystem Support

Linux filesystem support is excellent, but not perfect. Some filesystems don't work on a default installation of Red Hat Linux (or of other distributions, for that matter). These filesystems require that you locate the appropriate drivers and, in all probability, recompile your kernel. Other filesystems work, but their features are limited. Most importantly, many filesystem drivers are available in read-only forms—they can be used to read files from the foreign filesystem, but not write to the filesystem. Still others work in full read/write mode, but their feature sets don't mesh perfectly with Linux's assumptions and requirements. For all these reasons, you must understand the specific filesystems you're using in order to be aware of the limitations and work around them where possible.

Locating Filesystems

Most Linux filesystems come with the Linux kernel, and Red Hat Linux includes most of these filesystems in its default configuration. Many of these filesystems are available as kernel modules. You can find out which filesystem modules are available by typing the following command:

```
$ ls /lib/modules/x.y.z/fs
```

In this command, *x.y.z* is the kernel version number, such as 2.2.16. In response, you'll see a set of filesystem driver modules, such as hpfs.o. These modules are usually named after the filesystems they implement. Some of these driver files are support modules, however, and not independent filesystems. (This is particularly true of the nls_cp*.o modules, which implement language support used by FAT and Joliet filesystems.) Also, be aware that not all filesystems appear in this directory—some are built into the kernel file itself. Most importantly, the filesystem from which Linux boots (ext2fs in most cases) must be built into the kernel.

Preparing to Use a Standard Filesystem

If a filesystem you want isn't present on your computer, you can check the Linux kernel to see if it's present in the kernel source tree but not compiled for your system. To do so, you must check the filesystems available in the Linux kernel File Systems and Network Filesystems configuration menus (Figure 10.1 shows the kernel File Systems menu). Chapter 8 discusses the kernel configuration menus and kernel configuration options in greater detail.

> **NOTE**   In Linux kernels 2.2.*x*, network filesystems appear in their own kernel configuration menu. In the 2.3.*x* and 2.4.*x* kernels, network filesystems appear as a submenu off the main File Systems menu.

Figure 10.1   This 2.4.0-pre6 kernel has been patched to include ReiserFS support.

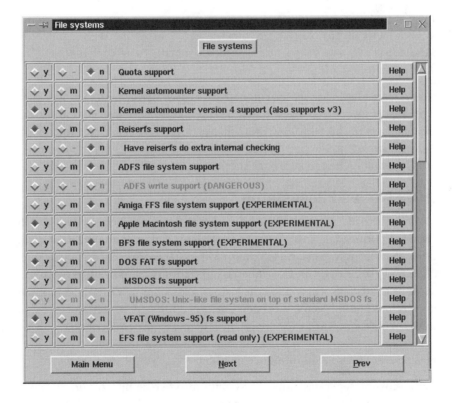

When you've opened the appropriate kernel configuration menu, you can scroll through the list of available filesystems to find the one you want. If you're unsure of what filesystem a given kernel option supports, click the Help button for that filesystem to see a brief description. Once you've selected your desired filesystems, you must recompile your kernel and kernel modules and then configure your system to use the new kernel, as described in Chapter 8.

Locating Unusual Filesystems

A few filesystems don't ship with the regular Linux kernel. Most of these are development filesystems—they're new enough that they have yet to be added to the kernel. The most interesting of these filesystems are the new journaling filesystems, which are described shortly, in "Journaling Filesystems." (That section includes pointers to these filesystems' homes on the Internet.) Journaling filesystems can greatly speed bootup times after a crash. If your Linux system operates in an environment in which speedy recovery from power outages or system crashes is important, or if you have hard disks larger than about 20GB, you may want to investigate these filesystems.

If you're looking for a specific filesystem and can't find it in the kernel, try doing a search on Deja News (http://www.deja.com/usenet/), or with a Web search engine such as Yahoo! (http://www.yahoo.com) or Google (http://www.google.com). There's a good chance you'll find a lead.

Most nonstandard filesystems require that you *patch* your Linux kernel—that is, add files to the kernel source tree. These patches usually come with instructions for accomplishing this task, so you should follow those instructions. You can then select the kernel driver as just described in "Preparing to Use a Standard Filesystem," and compile a kernel or kernel modules with the necessary support.

Linux Native Filesystems

A *native* filesystem is one that can be used as the primary filesystem for an OS. Linux can run using nothing but a single native filesystem; that is, it doesn't need a mix of two or more separate filesystems. An OS's native filesystems are often designed for a specific OS, although in some cases an OS "inherits" or "adopts" a native filesystem from a predecessor or related OS. Throughout its history, Linux has inherited and adopted filesystems and has had Linux-specific filesystems designed for it. (Chapter 3 details this history for Linux.) This is in contrast to *foreign* filesystems, which are designed for another OS. As a general rule, foreign filesystems don't mesh as well with Linux as do native filesystems. In some cases, these definitions become blurred, as you'll soon discover.

This discussion separates native filesystems into two camps: *traditional* and *journaling*. Other categorizations could also be made, but for our purposes this one is quite useful. "Traditional" does not mean insignificant or poorly performing. In early 2001, the most important filesystem for Linux, ext2fs, falls into the traditional category. These filesystems are, however, likely to fade away by mid-decade, if not earlier, in favor of one or more journaling filesystems.

Traditional Filesystems

Traditional filesystems are derived from filesystem technologies that go back to the 1970s, if not earlier. Some of these have admittedly been updated over the intervening years, and some even saw development in the 1980s and 1990s; but these filesystems share some important characteristics. Most notably, these filesystems all suffer from the need to perform an extensive filesystem check if they're not shut down properly.

In a traditional filesystem, when the computer writes data to disk, it necessarily does so in pieces. The computer may perform some disk reads to locate available disk space, then modify on-disk pointers to allocate space for a file, then write the data to the disk, and then update the on-disk pointers to complete the operation. The precise order of these operations varies from one filesystem and OS to another. Unfortunately, the filesystem as a whole may be in an inconsistent state at any given moment—one disk structure may indicate that space is allocated to a file, while another indicates that the same space is free.

Of course, once all operations are completed, the disk state is consistent. The problem comes when a disk is not properly unmounted. If the power fails or the computer crashes, the disk may wind up in an inconsistent state; and without the pending operations in memory, Linux cannot know *what* disk structures may be affected. Linux must therefore perform a lengthy check of the disk's contents to resolve inconsistencies. This is the reason for the long delay while Linux runs `fsck` on its disks when starting after a crash. (Linux also runs `fsck` after several normal startups, to ensure that no inconsistencies have crept onto the disk because of bugs or other problems.) Perhaps worse than the length of the disk check procedure is the fact that it sometimes uncovers serious corruption. In a worst-case scenario, you may lose all the data on a disk.

Traditional Linux-native filesystems include the following:

Minix   The Minix filesystem, which uses the type code `minix` at mount time, was Linux's first filesystem. This filesystem originated with the Minix OS, hence its name. By today's standards, the Minix filesystem is quite primitive; for instance, its maximum size is 64MB. Some people continue to use it on floppy disks, however.

Extended   The Extended Filesystem, more commonly known as *ext* or *extfs* and called `ext` in a `mount` command, was designed to overcome many of the Minix filesystem's limitations. It uses a different design that borrows heavily from other Unix filesystems. Extfs has been surpassed and was removed from the standard Linux kernel with the 2.2.*x* kernel series.

Second Extended   The Second Extended Filesystem, usually called *ext2* or *ext2fs*, uses a `mount` code of `ext2`. It's the standard filesystem for Linux systems using 2.0.*x* through 2.4.*x* kernels, although this is likely to change in 2001 or 2002. This filesystem is based on extfs but has substantially expanded capabilities. Ext2fs is the basis for development of one journaling filesystem, as described shortly.

Xia   The Xia Filesystem, called xiafs at mount time, was an extension to the Minix filesystem that competed with extfs and ext2fs. Released at about the same time as ext2fs, Xiafs was more stable, but ext2fs offered larger maximum partition and file sizes. Since then, ext2fs has become very stable, surpassing Xiafs in all important measures. In the end, ext2fs became the standard Linux filesystem. The Xiafs option was removed from the 2.2.*x* kernel.

ISO-9660   This filesystem is unusual in that its use is restricted to CD-ROM discs. In some sense, it's not really a native filesystem; but as CD-ROMs intended for use in Linux invariably use the ISO-9660 filesystem, it's included in this list. "Raw" ISO-9660 is very limited in filename length, and it lacks Linux's ownership and permissions. The Rock Ridge extensions to ISO-9660 correct this shortcoming, allowing CD-ROMs to contain these important features. Another filesystem, Joliet, is used in conjunction with at least a minimal ISO-9660 filesystem and provides long filenames for Windows systems. Linux can also read Joliet CD-ROMs, if appropriate support is compiled into the kernel. All three variants use the iso9660 filesystem type code.

In late 2000 and early 2001, the most important traditional Linux filesystem is clearly ext2fs. You'll only find extfs and Xiafs on museum pieces, and although the Minix filesystem continues to live in 2.2.*x* and 2.4.*x* kernels, its practical use is restricted to floppy disks. ISO-9660 and its extensions are important, but only for CD-ROMs.

Although ext2fs is a good filesystem by traditional filesystem standards, it has its limits. Most important at the moment is the disk check's duration problem; however, ext2fs is also limited to a maximum filesystem size of 16 terabytes (16,384GB) and a maximum file size of 4GB. Although 16TB disks are still not available for desktop computers at this writing, filesystems take sufficient development time that filesystem developers need to start planning for these disks well before their introduction. The 4GB file-size limit is an issue for some installations today, and it's likely to become more important to more people with the growth in popularity of applications such as video editing.

NOTE   Linux relies upon a *Virtual Filesystem* (VFS) layer to implement features used by all filesystems. In the 2.2.*x* kernels, the VFS imposes a partition-size limit of 4TB and a file-size limit of 2GB. The kernel developers have rewritten most of the code responsible for these limits in the 2.3.*x* kernel series, and any remaining stragglers will no doubt be dealt with by the time 4TB disks become available.

Journaling Filesystems

With small hard disks, the need to perform a disk check after a system crash or power outage is a nuisance, but a bearable one. Such a disk check typically takes no more than a few minutes, and because Linux seldom crashes, the check is not usually a major problem—unless it uncovers serious corruption on the disk, in which case files may be lost. On larger disks, however, the disk check takes a longer time. On big multigigabyte disks, which are extremely common today, a disk check can take several minutes—or even hours! Such a delay is more than a minor nuisance, particularly if it's imposed on a server that must be up at all times.

One solution to lengthy disk checks is to implement a *journal*, which is an on-disk list of pending operations. As the OS calls for on-disk changes such as file writes, the filesystem driver writes information on these changes to an on-disk file—the journal. When the OS makes *real* changes to the disk structures, it makes them in such a way that, when they're finished, the disk is in a consistent state; then the OS clears the journal. The result is that, should a power outage or system crash occur, the OS knows which files and disk structures may be affected by the problem, because all the pending changes are recorded in the journal. The OS can therefore undo or redo operations indicated by the journal, producing a consistent filesystem. This greatly reduces the post-crash startup time.

Some overhead is associated with maintaining a journal, but in practice, most journaling filesystems use more advanced designs than do non-journaling filesystems. This means journaling filesystems often (but not always) outperform traditional filesystems. These filesystems also typically support much larger maximum filesystem and file sizes than does ext2fs.

The main factor holding back journaling filesystems in Linux is the fact that none is yet part of the Linux kernel, at least not as of kernel version 2.4.0-test8. There are, however, several contenders for the next-generation Linux filesystem crown:

Third Extended   The Third Extended Filesystem (*ext3* or *ext3fs*) is an extension to ext2fs. The basic idea is to take ext2fs and add a journal. Because it's still a work in progress, it's unclear whether ext3fs will ultimately lift ext2fs's filesystem and file size limits. As you might expect, ext3fs's type code is `ext3`. You can obtain an early version of ext3fs from `ftp://ftp.uk.linux.org/pub/linux/sct/fs/jfs/`.

ReiserFS   This filesystem is a completely new design. The developers have been working on it for several years, but only in 2000 did it begin to be usable. Still, at the rollout of the 2.4.0 Linux kernel, ReiserFS isn't quite ready. This filesystem currently has a maximum size of 16TB and supports files of up to 4GB—the same limits as ext2fs. (It's possible these limits will change before ReiserFS is finalized, however, or in a future version.) Use the `reiserfs` type code to access ReiserFS partitions. The main ReiserFS Web site is at `http://devlinux.com/projects/reiserfs/`.

XFS   XFS is Silicon Graphics's (SGI's) journaling filesystem. It's been used on SGI Unix workstations and servers (which run the IRIX OS), and the company has ported it to Linux and released it under the GPL. This filesystem supports maximum filesystem sizes of up to 16,384 petabytes (PB; 1PB is 1024TB), and maximum file sizes of up to 8,192 PB. As such, XFS is the currently available filesystem that supports the largest media for Linux. This filesystem's type code is xfs. You can learn more at http://oss.sgi.com/projects/xfs/.

JFS   IBM's Journaled Filesystem (JFS) was originally developed for the AIX OS; however, IBM (like SGI) has released its advanced filesystem under the GPL and is actively supporting its porting to Linux. In addition to its journal, JFS supports a maximum filesystem size of 32 PB and a maximum file size of 4 PB. Use the jfs filesystem type code when mounting JFS partitions. More information is available at http://oss.software.ibm.com/developerworks/opensource/jfs/.

NOTE   Filesystems are sometimes classified according to the size of the pointers they use. Ext2fs, ext3fs, and ReiserFS are all 32-bit filesystems. This fact, in combination with other design features, is why these filesystems have the same maximum partition sizes. XFS and JFS, by contrast, are both 64-bit filesystems, which is why their maximum partition sizes are so large. (XFS and JFS differ in other details, hence the difference in their maximum sizes.)

All of these filesystems offer substantial improvement over ext2fs in that the journaling feature reduces startup time after a system crash or power outage. Increased partition and file sizes in XFS and JFS are also a great boon. XFS, JFS, and ReiserFS all support dynamic partition resizing, although the code to support it is not entirely stable and complete at this writing. You should check on the status of this feature if it's important to you.

In early 2001, all of these filesystems are usable, but none is yet completely reliable. ReiserFS is closest to this, but its lead may slip by the time you read this. If you have large hard disks and cannot cope with long disk checks at startup, you should study each of the filesystems discussed in this section to determine which is most stable. You may want to check recent Usenet News discussions by performing a search on http://www.deja.com/usenet/.

Although none of the journaling filesystems is yet a standard part of the kernel, some distributions already ship with support for ReiserFS. Specifically, Mandrake 7.1 and SuSE 6.4 include ReiserFS support. Future versions of these and other distributions may add support for ReiserFS as well as other journaling filesystems. You can also patch your kernel to support any of these filesystems. (Read the filesystem's documentation for detailed instructions.) With the exception of ext3fs, converting an existing system to use a journaling filesystem requires backing up, creating the new filesystem, and restoring your files.

Administrator's Logbook: Kernel Patching

System: E12345678

Action: Patched 2.4.0-test8 kernel with ReiserFS 3.5.26 support.

NOTE Prior to 2000, Linux's lack of a journaling filesystem has been one of the cited reasons for using mainstream commercial Unixes such as AIX or IRIX. As Linux's journaling filesystems mature, this argument will dissipate, helping to extend Linux's reach into the realm of larger servers.

Outside of reliability and speed, which may change by the time you read these words, ext3fs offers you the advantage of easily converting an existing ext2fs partition, by adding a journal file and changing the type you use in the mount command or /etc/fstab entry. You'll still be able to access the partition as an ext2fs partition if you like, but after conversion, you'll lose the ability to write to the partition using Linux's ex2fs drivers.

XFS and JFS are both available on other OSs and so may be desirable in some environments. (Neither SGI's IRIX nor IBM's AIX is available on *x*86 hardware, but the server version of IBM's OS/2 Warp 4.0—an *x*86 operating system—can use JFS. The capability to read these filesystems might also be useful if you need to move a hard disk from one system to another.)

Foreign Filesystems

In addition to its native filesystems, Linux supports a wide range of filesystems that are mostly used with other OSs. This filesystem support is important in dual-boot configurations, when exchanging removable media between OSs, and when using Linux to recover data from a hard disk that originally resided in another computer. In most cases, you do not want to use a foreign filesystem to store Linux's core files. These filesystems often lack features that are critical for Linux's use, such as ownership and permissions. In a few cases, the filesystems support these features, but Linux's implementation of the filesystem is weak in one way or another.

System Optimization

PART 3

Microsoft Filesystems

When used in a dual-boot environment, Linux must often coexist with one version or another of Windows. Also, removable media—floppy disks, Zip disks, LS-120 disks, and so on—are often created on Windows systems. It's therefore important that Linux support Microsoft's filesystems. Fortunately, Linux includes at least minimal support for all of the following filesystems in common use on Windows and on related operating systems:

FAT The *File Allocation Table (FAT)* is a data structure after which Windows *9x/* Me's filesystem is named. Originally used on DOS computers, FAT has been extended in two ways: the size of the FAT data structure, and the capacity to store long filenames. These extensions are described shortly.

HPFS Microsoft developed the *High-Performance Filesystem (HPFS)* for use with OS/2 1.2, when Microsoft and IBM were still partners. Subsequently, Microsoft included HPFS support in Windows NT through version 3.51, but dropped it with Windows NT 4.0. IBM continues to use HPFS in its OS/2 product line. Linux's HPFS support was read-only through the 2.2.*x* kernel series, but a read/write HPFS driver ships with 2.4.*x* kernels. This driver is unusual in that it stores Linux ownership, group, permissions, and other features using HPFS *extended attributes (EAs),* which OS/2 uses to store icons and other ancillary file data. The Linux filesystem type code for HPFS partitions is `hpfs`.

NTFS The *New Technology Filesystem (NTFS)* is the preferred filesystem for Windows NT and 2000 systems. NTFS is a fairly advanced journaling filesystem that supports a system of ownership similar to Linux usernames. Unfortunately, Linux's NTFS support is weak. Although read/write drivers have been available in the 2.2.*x* and later kernels, the write support is marked as being "dangerous" in the kernel compilation scripts. Also, these drivers don't support NTFS's security features. With the release of Windows 2000, Microsoft made changes to NTFS (often referred to as *NTFS 5.0*). Linux's NTFS drivers can cope with NTFS 5.0 partitions, but using the read/write support on these partitions is inadvisable, at least with the support available around the time of the 2.4.0 kernel's release. (In fact, the NTFS support in the 2.4.0 prerelease kernels detects NTFS 5.0 partitions and refuses to enable write support on them.) Linux's type code for NTFS partitions is `ntfs`. Red Hat 7.0 does *not* include a compiled NTFS driver in its default installation, so you must locate one or recompile your kernel if you want to access NTFS partitions from Red Hat 7.0.

NOTE Because Linux's NTFS write support is considered so dangerous, it must be enabled separately from the main NTFS support in the Linux kernel.

The most useful and stable Linux driver for Microsoft filesystems is the driver for FAT. This driver is extremely stable—in contrast to some foreign filesystems, it's quite safe to write to FAT partitions. FAT filesystems actually come in several varieties, differing along two dimensions:

- Bitness: The FAT data structure uses pointers that are 12, 16, and 32 bits in size. Increasing FAT size equates to increasing maximum partition size. The 12-bit FATs are used mostly on floppy disks; 16-bit FATs allow partitions of up to 2GB; and 32-bit FATs support partitions of up to 2TB. Linux's FAT drivers auto-detect the FAT size, which is often indicated as a suffix to the filesystem name, as in *FAT-16* and *FAT-32*.

- Filename length: The original FAT filesystem, as used by DOS, supported only eight-character filenames with an optional three-character extension (the so-called 8.3 filename limit). With Windows 95, Microsoft introduced an extension to FAT known as VFAT, which supported long filenames. Linux supports its own FAT extension, known as UMSDOS, which places Linux ownership and permissions information on FAT filesystems along with long filenames. VFAT and UMSDOS are incompatible extensions.

Because Linux auto-detects the FAT size, there's no need to use separate Linux filesystem types for different FAT sizes. Linux uses three type codes for each of the filename length options, however. If you mount a filesystem with the msdos type code, Linux restricts filenames to 8.3 limits. If you use the vfat type code, Linux uses VFAT long filenames. If you use umsdos, Linux uses UMSDOS long filenames. In most cases, vfat is the most appropriate type code with which to access FAT partitions, because it allows for exchange of files with long filenames between Linux and Windows systems.

> **NOTE** A common misconception is that FAT-32 and VFAT are somehow linked. They aren't. You can access a FAT-16 or even FAT-12 disk using VFAT long file names; and you can mount a FAT-32 partition with the Linux msdos driver to use only 8.3 filenames. (Windows 98 run in DOS mode also provides only 8.3-filename access to FAT-32 partitions, as well.)

UMSDOS is unusual because it allows Linux to treat a FAT partition like a native filesystem. You can run a Linux system entirely from a UMSDOS partition, and in fact some distributions support installing Linux directly on a UMSDOS partition. This configuration tends to be slow, however, because Linux's FAT support, although stable, isn't as fast as its support for ext2fs.

System
Optimization

PART 3

Apple Filesystems

If you run Linux on a Macintosh or need to exchange data with Macintosh users, you're likely to need support for a Macintosh filesystem. In early 2001, three such filesystems exist, although only two are in common use and only one sports Linux drivers:

MFS   The *Macintosh Filesystem (MFS)* was used by the earliest Macintoshes. It's almost never used on anything but 400KB floppy disks, which are extremely rare today. Linux does not include MFS support.

HFS   The *Hierarchical Filesystem (HFS)* was the replacement for MFS. Used on 800KB and larger floppy disks and all Macintosh hard disks until 1998, HFS is quite common in the Macintosh world. The Linux 2.2.*x* and later kernels include read/ write HFS support, using the filesystem type code hfs. The write support is considered experimental, however, and occasionally damages hard disks. It's therefore best to restrict use of this support to blank floppy disks. Macintosh CD-ROMs often use HFS rather than ISO-9660.

NOTE   Although 800KB Macintosh floppies use HFS, Linux cannot read these disks, even with an HFS-enabled kernel. These disks use an uncommon low-level disk-recording technique, and standard *x*86 hardware cannot cope with it. Apple switched to PC-style low-level recording technologies with its 1.44MB floppies, so Linux can read Macintosh 1.44MB floppies, as well as other removable media.

HFS+   The follow-on to HFS borrows many features from Unix-style filesystems, but it stops short of adding a journal. Currently, there is no Linux driver for HFS+. New Macintoshes invariably ship with their disks formatted for HFS+, but this filesystem is not used much on removable media. (The MacOS X installation CD-ROM is an exception; it uses HFS+.)

If you need to exchange removable media between Macintosh and Linux systems, you can do so. You must use HFS on these media, however; and if you use a floppy disk, it has to be a 1.44MB floppy or a rare 720KB HFS floppy. Alternatively, you can use FAT, because modern Macintoshes support FAT.

If you run Linux on a Macintosh, you may want to create an HFS partition to be used for data exchange between Linux and MacOS. Because Linux can't read HFS+ partitions, this data-exchange partition is a practical necessity when you want to share files across OSs.

Miscellaneous Filesystems

In addition to Microsoft and Apple filesystems, Linux supports a wide variety of other foreign filesystems. Most are of extremely limited utility and interest. Here are some highlights:

BFS BeOS uses its own journaling filesystem, known as BFS. A read-only Linux driver for this filesystem is available from http://hp.vector.co.jp/authors/VA008030/bfs/. The author claims to be working on read/write support, but it does not yet exist. Although BeOS is a single-user OS, BFS supports file ownership and permissions similar to those used in Linux. In theory, BFS could become a contender for a native journaling filesystem, but the others have a commanding lead in early 2001. BFS also lacks support for file access time-stamps, which may hinder its abilities as a native Linux filesystem. BFS's filesystem type code is befs.

NOTE The 2.4.x kernels include support for another filesystem known as BFS that is completely unrelated to the BeOS BFS. This BFS is used for storing critical system startup files on SCO's UnixWare OS.

FFS/UFS The *Fast Filesystem (FFS; aka Unix Filesystem or UFS)* was developed early in the history of Unix. It's still used by many Unix and derivative systems, including FreeBSD and Solaris. In principle, FFS/UFS could have been adopted as a native Linux filesystem, but Linux's write support for this filesystem is still considered dangerous, much as is Linux's support for writing to NTFS. FFS has been around long enough to spawn several minor variants, but one Linux driver handles them all. FFS's filesystem type code is ufs.

UDF The *Universal Disk Format (UDF)* is a filesystem designed for recordable CD, DVD, and recordable DVD media. Linux includes UDF support in the 2.4.x kernel series, but the write support is marked "dangerous" and is very limited in terms of supported hardware. This filesystem's type code is udf.

You can browse the Linux kernel configuration menus to learn about other filesystems supported by Linux. If you're looking for support of a specific filesystem and can't find it in the kernel menu, try a Web search.

Network Filesystems

Some filesystems are designed for use over a network, as opposed to on a hard disk. You can mount these filesystems in Linux much as you do disk-based filesystems, and then perform normal file-access operations on the filesystem. Network filesystems supported by Linux include the following:

NFS Sun's *Network Filesystem (NFS)* is the preferred method of file sharing for networks of Unix or Linux computers. The Linux kernel includes both NFS client support (so that Linux can mount another system's NFS exports) and core routines to help a Linux NFS server, which is separate from the kernel. NFS's filesystem type code is nfs.

System Optimization

PART 3

Coda   This is an advanced network filesystem that supports features omitted from NFS. These features include better security (including encryption) and improved caching. The Linux kernel includes Coda client support, and separate packages are needed to run a Coda server. The main Coda homepage is at http://www.coda.cs.cmu.edu/. Coda's filesystem type code is coda.

SMB/CIFS   The *Server Message Block (SMB)* protocol, which has been renamed the *Core Internet Filesystem (CIFS)*, is the usual means of network file sharing among Microsoft OSs. The Linux kernel includes SMB/CIFS client support, so you can mount SMB/CIFS shares. You can configure your Linux computer as an SMB/CIFS server using the Samba package (http://www.samba.org/). The filesystem type code for SMB/CIFS shares is smbfs.

NCP   The *NetWare Core Protocol (NCP)* is NetWare's file sharing protocol. As with SMB/CIFS, Linux includes basic NCP client support in the kernel, and you can add separate server packages to turn Linux into an NCP server. NCP's filesystem type code is ncpfs.

It's important to recognize that the network filesystem is completely independent of the filesystems used on both the server and client for disk access. Consider a Linux computer that's running Samba, sharing files for a Windows system. The server makes files available using the SMB/CIFS network filesystem. Locally, these files may be stored on *any* filesystem that Linux supports—ext2fs, ISO-9660, ReiserFS, FAT, or anything else. These filesystems all look identical to the client, except where the underlying filesystem has a limitation that obtrudes itself, such as 8.3 filename limits when Linux uses its msdos driver to access FAT, or the read-only nature of ISO-9660 or BFS. Likewise, if Linux uses NFS to mount a remote filesystem, it's unimportant whether the server is using ext2fs, FFS, HFS+, or anything else. This characteristic means that you can give a computer access to filesystems it cannot natively understand, as when Linux accesses HFS+ from a Macintosh running an NFS server, or when Windows Me accesses JFS through a Linux system using SMB/CIFS.

Chapter 15, "TCP/IP Linux Networking," covers network filesystem configuration in more detail.

Accessing Filesystems

The preceding discussion outlines the major filesystems available for the 2.2.*x* and 2.4.*x* Linux kernels. Actually *using* these filesystems requires practical knowledge of several Linux commands and configuration files. The most important of these in day-to-day operations are the commands used to mount and unmount filesystems. Some additional peculiarities arise when it comes to accessing removable media such as floppy disks, Zip disks, and CD-ROM discs.

Mounting and Unmounting Filesystems

Linux provides two methods for mounting hard disk filesystems: manual mounting via the mount command, and automatic mounting at boot time via entries in /etc/fstab. (It's also possible to auto-mount removable media, as described later in "Using Removable Media.") To stop using a filesystem, you must *unmount* it by using the umount command. (Yes, that's spelled correctly; umount is missing the first *n*.)

Using the *mount* Command

Linux uses the mount command to make a filesystem available. Here is the basic format of this command:

```
mount [-t fstype] [-o options] device dir
```

The *fstype* is the filesystem type, such as ext2, vfat, or jfs. You can often omit the -t parameter, and Linux will correctly detect the filesystem type. The preceding discussion of filesystems for Linux includes these type codes.

device is the Linux device file associated with the filesystem. For instance, /dev/sdb4 indicates the fourth partition on the second SCSI disk; /dev/fd0 indicates the first floppy disk.

dir is the mount point, which should be an empty directory. (You can use a nonempty directory, but then you lose access to the files stored in that directory for as long as the filesystem is mounted.)

The *options* are special codes that give Linux instructions on how to treat filesystem features. Some options apply to most or all filesystems, but others are filesystem-specific. Type **man mount** for a discussion of the filesystem options that apply to most of the standard Linux filesystems, and consult the filesystem's documentation for information on rarer filesystem options. Table 10.1 summarizes the most important filesystem options.

System
Optimization

PART 3

Table 10.1   Important Filesystem Options for mount Command

Option	Supported Filesystems	Description
defaults	All	Uses the default options for this file-system. It's used primarily in the /etc/fstab file (described shortly) to ensure that there's an options column in the file.
loop	All	Uses the loopback device for this mount. Allows you to mount a file as if it were a disk partition. For instance, entering **mount -t vfat -o loop image.img /mnt/image** mounts the file image.img as if it were a disk.
auto or noauto	All	Mounts or does not mount the file-system at boot time, or when root issues the mount -a command. Default is auto, but noauto is appropriate for removable media. Used in /etc/fstab.
user or nouser	All	Allows or disallows ordinary users to mount the filesystem. Default is nouser, but user is often appropriate for removable media. Used in /etc/fstab. When included in this file, user allows users to type **mount /*mountpoint***, where /*mountpoint* is the assigned mount point, to mount a disk.

Table 10.1   Important Filesystem Options for mount Command *(continued)*

Option	Supported Filesystems	Description
owner	All	Similar to user, except that the user must own the device file. Some distributions, including Red Hat, assign ownership of some device files (such as /dev/fd0, for the floppy disk) to the console user, so this can be a helpful option.
remount	All	Changes one or more mount options without explicitly unmounting a partition. To use this option, you issue a mount command on an already-mounted filesystem, but with remount along with any options you want to change. Can be used to enable or disable write access to a partition, for example.
ro	All	Specifies a read-only mount of the filesystem. This is the default for filesystems that include no write access, and for some with particularly unreliable write support.
rw	All read/write filesystems	Specifies a read/write mount of the filesystem. This is the default for most read/write filesystems.
uid=*value*	Most filesystems that don't support Unix-style permissions, such as vfat, hpfs, ntfs, and hfs	Sets the owner of all files. For instance, uid=500 sets the owner to whoever has Linux user ID 500. (Check Linux user IDs in the /etc/passwd file.)

System Optimization

PART 3

Table 10.1 Important Filesystem Options for mount Command *(continued)*

Option	Supported Filesystems	Description
gid=*value*	Most filesystems that don't support Unix-style permissions, such as vfat, hpfs, ntfs, and hfs	Works like uid=*value*, but sets the group of all files on the filesystem. You can find group IDs in the /etc/group file.
conv=*code*	Most filesystems used on Microsoft and Apple OSs: msdos, umsdos, vfat, hpfs, ntfs, hfs	If *code* is b or binary, Linux doesn't modify the files' contents. If *code* is t or text, Linux auto-converts files between Linux-style and DOS- or Macintosh-style end-of-line characters. If *code* is a or auto, Linux applies the conversion unless the file is a known binary file format. It's usually best to leave this at its default value of binary, because file conversions can cause serious problems for some applications and file types.
nonumtail	vfat	Normally, Linux creates short file names when using VFAT in the same way as Windows; for instance, longfilename.txt becomes LONGFI~1.TXT. Using this parameter blocks the creation of the numeric tail (~1) whenever possible, so the file becomes LONGFILE.TXT. This can improve legibility in DOS, but may cause problems if you use Linux to back up and restore a Windows system, because the short filenames may be changed after a complete restore.

Table 10.1   Important Filesystem Options for mount Command *(continued)*

Option	Supported Filesystems	Description
eas=*code*	Read/write hpfs	If *code* is no, Linux ignores OS/2's Extended Attributes (EAs). If *code* is ro, Linux reads EAs and tries to extract Linux ownership and permissions information from them, but doesn't create new EAs. If *code* is rw, Linux stores ownership and permissions information in EAs, overriding the settings provided by the uid, gid, and umask options.
case=*code*	hpfs, hfs	When *code* is lower, Linux converts filenames to all-lowercase; when *code* is asis, Linux leaves filenames as they are. The default for HFS and the read/write version of HPFS is asis; for the read-only HPFS in the 2.2.*x* kernels, it's lower.
fork=*code*	hfs	Sets the HFS driver handling of Macintosh resource forks. Options are cap, double, and netatalk. These correspond to the methods used by the Columbia AppleTalk Package (CAP), AppleDouble, and Netatalk networking systems for storing resource forks on Unix systems. If you use one of these networking packages and want to export Macintosh filesystems, you should use the appropriate code.

Table 10.1   Important Filesystem Options for mount Command *(continued)*

Option	Supported Filesystems	Description
afpd	hfs	Use this parameter if you want to export filesystems using Netatalk. Makes the filesystem fully read/write compatible with Netatalk, but causes problems with some Linux-native commands.
norock	iso9660	Disables Rock Ridge extensions for ISO-9660 CD-ROMs.
nojoliet	iso9660	Disables Joliet extensions for ISO-9660 CD-ROMs.

With these mount options at hand, you should be able to mount filesystems with the characteristics you desire. In most cases, Linux-native filesystems don't require any special filesystem options. Foreign filesystems, however, often benefit from one or more options. Filesystems that don't support Linux's permissions, in particular, usually benefit greatly from the uid, gid, and umask options. You might want to use a command similar to the following to mount a VFAT partition, for instance:

```
# mount -t vfat -o uid=500,gid=100,umask=002 /dev/hdc8 /dos/drive-e
```

This command gives ownership to all files on the VFAT partition to whoever has user ID 500 (usually the first user created on a Red Hat system); gives group ownership to group 100; and removes write access to the world but leaves write access for the owner and group. The result is that user 500 and anybody in group 100 can both read and write files on the partition, but users who aren't in group 100 can only read files on the partition.

Creating */etc/fstab* Entries

When Linux boots, it needs to know what filesystems to mount and at what locations in its directory tree in order to produce a usable system. If you've created separate partitions for /usr, /home, and /var, for instance, Linux must know to mount the appropriate partitions at these points—it will do you no good to have Linux mount your user files (which should go at /home) at /usr, where program files normally reside. Linux's solution to this problem is the /etc/fstab file, which contains default mount assignments.

This file comprises a series of lines, one per filesystem. Lines preceded by a pound sign (#) are ignored by Linux. Each line is a series of entries separated by whitespace, as illustrated in Listing 10.1.

Listing 10.1 A Sample /etc/fstab File

```
#device        mountpoint   fs      options      dump fsck
/dev/hda2      /            ext2    defaults      1 1
/dev/hdb7      /home        jfs     defaults      1 2
/dev/hda3      /dos         msdos   umask=0       0 0
server:/home   /server/home nfs     ro            0 0
/dev/cdrom     /mnt/cdrom   iso9660 noauto,user   0 0
/dev/fd0       /mnt/floppy  auto    noauto,user   0 0
```

The /etc/fstab file's columns contain the following information:

device   This column lists the device filename associated with the disk or partition. One of the devices in Listing 10.1, server:/home, is an NFS share. For this device, server is the name of the server, and /home is the directory it exports.

mountpoint   This column indicates the mount point for the filesystem. The first entry is usually /, the root filesystem. Linux normally reads the /etc/fstab file from the root filesystem, but once it gets this file, it remounts the root filesystem using the options specified in this file.

fs   You must specify the filesystem type code for most filesystems. If you use any nonstandard filesystems, such as jfs for the /home partition in Listing 10.1, you must ensure that you've compiled your kernel with that support. It's also critically important that the root partition's filesystem be compiled *into the kernel* (rather than as a module), or else Linux won't be able to read its startup files. The /mnt/floppy mount point in Listing 10.1 specifies a filesystem type code of auto. Linux can auto-detect many filesystem types, and this configuration is particularly convenient for removable-media devices such as floppy drives.

WARNING   Don't confuse the /etc/fstab filesystem type code of auto (which tells Linux to auto-detect the filesystem type) with the auto mount option (which tells Linux to mount the filesystem at boot time).

System Optimization

PART 3

options   You can specify options from Table 10.1, as well as any other options you discover, for any filesystem. The noauto,user combination used for the floppy disk and CD-ROM drive in Listing 10.1 is particularly useful for removable-media devices, because it allows ordinary users to mount and unmount these devices. Be sure not to put spaces between mount options, just commas.

dump   This column contains a 1 or 0, indicating that the dump utility should or should not back up the specified partition when it's run.

fsck   This column indicates the *file system check* order. When Linux boots, it checks filesystems with non-0 values in this column for corruption, in the order specified by this column's value. Normally, the root partition has a value of 1, while other Linux native filesystems have higher values.

When you install Linux, it creates an initial /etc/fstab file based on the information you gave the installation programs about your partitions. You can modify this configuration to add partitions not understood by the installation routines (such as BFS partitions, if you have BeOS installed); to fine-tune the configuration (such as adding extra parameters for FAT partitions); and to add variants, particularly for removable media. It's a good idea to test your mount options by issuing them directly with the mount command before adding them to /etc/fstab. (Of course, this doesn't make much sense for some options, such as noauto and user.) Once you've modified /etc/fstab, you can test its configuration by issuing the mount -a command. This causes Linux to reread /etc/fstab and mount any filesystems that are not mounted but that are listed without a noauto option in /etc/fstab.

You can also modify /etc/fstab using GUI configuration tools. Red Hat's Linuxconf, for example, includes this facility in its File Systems➤Access Local Drive area, as shown in Figure 10.2. You can add a new filesystem to the file by clicking Add, or edit an existing configuration by double-clicking the line in the list on the right side of the window. In either case, you can set base features (such as the device filename, filesystem type, and mount point) and filesystem options (such as read-only, user mountable, and so on). These options were discussed in preceding sections.

Using the *umount* Command

When you're done using a filesystem, you can issue the umount command to unmount it. The basic syntax for this command is as follows:

```
umount [-a][-f][-t fstype] mountpoint | device
```

The meanings of the options are as follows:

-a   If this option is specified, umount tries to unmount all the partitions specified in /etc/fstab. This is an option you should *not* issue in normal operation, although you might in emergency recovery systems after restoring a system to health.

Figure 10.2   GUI system configuration tools let you edit /etc/fstab via a point-and-click interface.

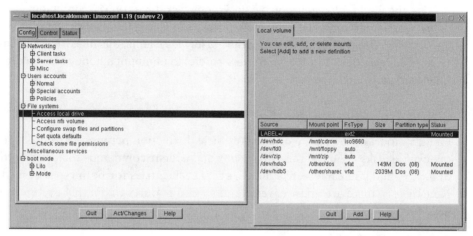

-f   When you specify -f, umount forces the unmount operation. This option can be useful if an ordinary umount command fails, which often occurs when an NFS server goes down.

-t *fstype*   If you use this parameter, umount unmounts filesystems of the specified type.

mountpoint   This is the mount point on which the device is mounted, such as /mnt/floppy or /home.

device   This is the device on which the filesystem resides, such as /dev/fd0 or /dev/hdb8.

Normally, you use umount without most options and specify only the mount point or the device, not both. For instance, you might type **umount /mnt/floppy** to unmount the floppy disk.

The umount command is most useful when applied to removable-media devices, because these devices are typically mounted and unmounted on a regular basis while Linux is running. Most installations leave hard disk partitions permanently mounted, so they need not be explicitly unmounted. Linux automatically unmounts these partitions when it shuts down, however; and you may need to temporarily unmount a normally mounted partition when performing certain types of system maintenance, such as moving the contents of a partition to a new hard disk.

System Optimization

PART 3

WARNING Linux locks most removable devices, such as CD-ROM and Zip drives, so that you can't eject the disk while it's mounted. When you unmount the disk, the Eject button will work again. Floppy disk drives on *x*86 computers, however, cannot be locked. It's therefore possible to eject a floppy disk while it's still mounted. Because Linux caches writes to its filesystems, this mistake can cause serious filesystem corruption. Be very careful to unmount a floppy disk before ejecting it.

Using Removable Media

Linux's model of the disk world makes little distinction between hard disks and removable disks. You use the same mount and umount commands to access both types of device, and you can create similar /etc/fstab entries for both types of media. Nonetheless, there are a few caveats and special features that apply to removable media devices only.

Accessing Floppy Disks

The most important caveat concerning floppy disks is about accidentally ejecting them, as noted in the preceding Warning. Beyond this, you can access floppy disks as if they were very small hard disk partitions. The usual device file for accessing floppies is /dev/fd0. If your system has two floppy drives, the second is accessible as /dev/fd1. There are also a number of specialized device access files, such as /dev/fd0H1440, which provide forced access to a disk of a specific capacity, such as 1440KB for /dev/fd0H1440. (In normal operation, /dev/fd0 can be used to access disks of any capacity.)

If you're presented with an unformatted floppy disk, you must format it. In DOS or Windows, this procedure is handled with a single command, FORMAT. In Linux, by contrast, you perform two actions. First, you do a low-level format using the fdformat command, as in **fdformat /dev/fd0**. (It's here that the capacity-specific device files can be most useful, because they can force a format at a specified capacity.) Second, you create a filesystem on the disk, as described in "Creating a Filesystem" later in this chapter.

Most filesystems that you use on hard disks can be used on floppy disks, with a few exceptions. Most notably, some journaled filesystems require journal files larger than floppies can hold. You can use Linux's ext2fs on floppy disks, but ext2fs has enough overhead that it's not the best choice. The Minix filesystem is popular on floppy disks because it includes support for Linux permissions and ownership, and it consumes less overhead than ext2fs. FAT filesystems, too, are popular on floppies, even for transfer between Linux systems. The drawback to FAT is that you lose Linux ownership and permissions unless you also archive files into a tar or similar carrier file.

Disk Access without a Filesystem

It's possible to access a floppy disk without using a filesystem *per se.* This is commonly done by writing a `tar` file directly to a floppy disk. Suppose you want to transfer a directory, `somedir`, between systems. You can do so by issuing the following `tar` command on the source system:

```
$ tar -cvev/fd0 somedir
```

This command copies the contents of `somedir` to a `tar` file on the floppy disk. You can reverse the process on the target system by issuing this command:

```
$ tar -xvf /dev/fd0
```

Of course, you can also transfer `tar` files in a similar way by mounting a disk with a filesystem and then using an appropriate `tar` file on the disk (such as `/mnt/floppy/somedir.tar`) rather than the device file (`/dev/fd0`). Why use direct access, then? It's most useful when transferring files between versions of Unix that don't share an appropriate common filesystem. You can be sure that a `tar` file written without a filesystem can be read by *any* Unix-like OS, because `tar` is so widely available. Support for any given filesystem is not so universal, although FAT filesystem support is extremely common on modern Unixes.

One unusual shortcut used for access to floppy disks is the Mtools package. It's a set of programs that allow access to FAT floppy disks (or, in principle, other removable media formatted with FAT) without explicitly mounting them. Mtools includes a series of commands named after DOS disk-access commands. These include `mdir` (to take a directory listing), `mcopy` (to copy a file), `mdel` (to delete a file), and `mformat` (to create a FAT filesystem on a floppy). These commands use a DOS-style drive letter in place of Linux's device identifier. For instance, to copy a file to a floppy, you would type `mcopy` `filename` `a:`. Mtools can be a very useful method for copying a few files to or from a FAT floppy, but if you want to give programs direct access to files on a floppy, you must mount it normally. Mtools comes with most Linux distributions. You can read more about it at `http://mtools.linux.lu/`.

A package similar to Mtools, called HFS Utilities, exists for accessing Macintosh floppies (`http://www.mars.org/home/rob/proj/hfs/`). These utilities use an `h` prefix to the DOS-style commands, as in `hdir` and `hformat`. The package also includes a GUI front-end.

System Optimization

PART 3

> **NOTE** As noted earlier, standard *x*86 PC hardware is incapable of reading the low-level data recording methods used by Apple for its 400KB and 800KB floppy disks. The HFS Utilities package doesn't provide a magical way around this limitation.

Accessing High-Capacity Removable Disks

High-capacity removable disks such as Iomega Zip disks, Imation LS-120 disks, and Castlewood Orb drives are becoming increasingly popular as typical file sizes increase. As a general rule, Linux has no problem with these devices, but there are a few caveats.

The most important of these is to ensure that the device's interface (ATAPI, SCSI, parallel-port, USB, or something else) is compatible with Linux. For the most part, EIDE/ATAPI and SCSI devices pose no problems. Most parallel-port drives can be made to work, but locating low-level Linux drivers for some of the rarer devices can be a challenge. USB drives are unsupported in the 2.2.*x* kernel series, but the 2.4.*x* kernels add support for some USB drives. Check with http://www.linux-usb.org for details on USB device support.

There are two ways to treat high-capacity removable devices: as big floppy disks or as removable hard disks. In the first case, you use the main device file to access the drive, as in /dev/hdb for an EIDE or ATAPI drive that's configured as the slave drive on the primary EIDE chain, or as in /dev/sda for a SCSI drive that's got the lowest SCSI ID number of all SCSI disks. Treating removable disks in this way is common for some media, such as magneto-optical drives. It has the advantage that you don't need to worry about partitioning the disks.

More frequently, removable disks are handled as if they were hard disks. In this arrangement, the disk is partitioned with fdisk (discussed shortly, in "Disk Partitioning") or a similar disk-partitioning tool. You then access the *partition* when creating and mounting filesystems. For instance, you might access /dev/hdb1 or /dev/sda4. One problem with this approach is that the partition number can vary from one disk to another. Iomega Zip disks commonly use the fourth partition, but some other disk types and tools use the first partition. You may therefore need to create multiple /etc/fstab entries to handle all the possibilities, particularly if you exchange disks with several people.

> **NOTE** Macintosh Zip disks are partitioned using the Mac's partition table, which is different from the partition table system used on *x*86 PCs. Linux's HFS driver, however, includes limited support for the Macintosh partition table, so you can mount Macintosh Zip disks as if they were big floppies (using /dev/hdb, /dev/sda, or similar "numberless" device files). Alternatively, you can compile Macintosh partition table support into your Linux kernel and mount the fourth partition on the removable disk.

You can use any filesystem on a large removable disk that you can use on a hard disk. In particular, ext2fs works well on removable disks. FAT and HFS are also popular choices, particularly when you want to exchange data with Windows or Macintosh users, respectively. The journal files used by journaling filesystems may consume a large percentage of a removable disk's capacity. For instance, ReiserFS creates a journal file that's 32MB in size—roughly a third the capacity of a 100MB Zip disk.

Reading CD-ROM Discs

CD-ROM discs are not terribly unusual in terms of how they're mounted and accessed. There are two differences to keep in mind:

- *Read-only access.* CD-ROM discs are by nature read-only. The rw option therefore has no effect, and you cannot write to CD-ROM discs.

- *Filesystem choices.* Although Linux can mount a CD-ROM created using just about any filesystem, ISO-9660 dominates the CD-ROM filesystem landscape. Many discs created for the Macintosh market, however, use HFS instead of or in addition to ISO-9660. Discs created with Linux or Unix in mind usually include Rock Ridge extensions, while Joliet is a common addition to discs created for the Windows market. It's possible to create a CD-ROM with ISO-9660, Rock Ridge, Joliet, and HFS, pointing to some combination of the same and different files.

> **NOTE** For purposes of mounting a disc for read access, CD-R and CD-RW discs and drives are just like CD-ROM discs and drives. It's not possible today to write directly to a CD-R or CD-RW disc or drive, however. To do this, you must use special software such as the mkisofs and cdrecord combination (discussed in Chapter 11), or a GUI front-end such as X-CD-Roast.

You can use the mount command's -t parameter, along with -o and the norock and nojoliet options, to specify how Linux will try to mount a CD-ROM. Table 10.2 summarizes the possibilities.

Table 10.2   Mount Options for CD-ROMs

Mount Options	Linux's Action
-t hfs	Mounts the CD-ROM using HFS, if possible.
-t iso9660	Mounts the CD-ROM using Rock Ridge, if present. If Rock Ridge is not present but Joliet is, and if Linux includes Joliet support, Linux uses Joliet; otherwise, it uses plain ISO-9660.

Table 10.2   Mount Options for CD-ROMs *(continued)*

Mount Options	Linux's Action
`-t iso9660 -o norock`	Mounts the filesystem using Joliet, if the CD-ROM includes a Joliet filesystem and the kernel includes Joliet support. Otherwise, plain ISO-9660 is used.
`-t iso9660 -o nojoliet`	Mounts the CD-ROM using Rock Ridge, if present. If Rock Ridge is not present, plain ISO-9660 is used.
`-t iso9660 -o nojoliet,norock`	Mounts the CD-ROM using plain ISO-9660.

Automating Removable-Media Access

Microsoft's OSs treat removable disks differently than does Linux. In a Microsoft OS, each removable disk has a *drive letter,* such as A: for the first floppy disk. There's no need to explicitly mount a removable disk; you can simply specify a file on a removable disk by inserting the drive letter in front of the file's name, as in A:\SOMEFILE.TXT. This approach is convenient for users but has the drawback of possibly making it unsafe to cache disk writes, so performance suffers. Some hardware notifies the OS when the user presses the Eject button, allowing the OS to finish any cached disk accesses before ejecting the disk. When using such a device, cached disk writes are possible.

This discussion is relevant to Linux because many new Linux users are accustomed to the Windows method of handling disks. These users expect to be able to read and write files on the disk without explicitly mounting the disk, much less relying on the superuser to do the job. Linux provides several workarounds for these users. Specifically:

- The user and owner mount options, which are normally used in /etc/fstab, allow users to mount and unmount removable disks. Although these options don't provide truly automatic access, they can be adequate for users with some Linux know-how. They're also a critical first step to some other possibilities.

- Window managers and file managers can often be customized to run specific commands when a user clicks on an icon or picks an item from a pop-up menu. Such a configuration can allow users who are uncomfortable with a text-based shell to issue mount and umount commands. Configuration details vary substantially from one program to another, so consult the appropriate package documentation for details.

- The default configurations for the KDE and GNOME desktop environments include automated access to CD-ROM and floppy disks similar to the access in Windows.

Double-click on the appropriate desktop icon, and the system mounts the disk and opens a browser window on the disk's contents. You can later select an *unmount* option from the appropriate icon's context menu to unmount the disk. These options rely on the presence of user or owner options in /etc/fstab.

- The *automounter* is a tool that monitors access attempts to specified directories and, when one is detected, mounts a specified device at that location. Once all opened files are closed, the automounter waits a specified time and then unmounts the device. This configuration can be convenient for mounting, but may pose problems for certain media types because of the delays when unmounting. Floppies can be particularly troublesome in this respect because you won't know when it's safe to eject a floppy, except by issuing a command such as df to see if the disk is still mounted.

Of these options, /etc/fstab configuration has already been described. GUI configurations (including those for window managers and desktop environments) vary a lot from one package to another, so you should check your package's documentation for details. The automounter requires the most elaborate configuration. To use this tool, follow these steps:

1. Check that your kernel configuration includes both the Kernel Automounter support in the Filesystems area and NFS Filesystem Support in the Network File Systems area. These options are included in the standard Red Hat 7.0 kernel. (Kernel compilation is discussed in Chapter 8.)

2. If it's not already installed, install the autofs package. The exact filename is autofs-3.1.5-5.i386.rpm in Red Hat 7.0, but it may be called something else in other distributions.

3. Edit the automounter's configuration file, /etc/auto.master. It normally contains a single line that lists the base automount point (/misc by default), the configuration file for that mount point (/etc/auto.misc by default), and a timeout value (60 by default). Change any of these parameters as needed. The remainder of this procedure assumes that you leave the defaults as is.

4. Edit the /etc/auto.misc configuration file. This file should list specific subdirectories within the base automount point (/misc), filesystem type codes, and device files for each device you want auto-mounted. For example:

```
floppy    -fstype=auto    :/dev/fd0
maczip    -fstype=hfs     :/dev/sda
```

This example sets the automounter to check /misc/floppy for floppy disk accesses using any filesystem (type auto) and /misc/maczip for HFS filesystems mounted on a SCSI Zip drive (/dev/sda).

System Optimization

PART 3

5. Start the automounter by typing **/etc/rc.d/init.d/autofs start**. It should start up automatically when you reboot the computer, as well. (If you're not using Red Hat, you may need to use another startup script, or start the automounter manually by typing automount **/misc file /etc/auto.misc**.

You *do not* create directories within the /misc directory for each mount point. Instead, the automounter detects attempts to access nonexistent directories and dynamically creates them when mounting the device. This fact can make the automounter ineffective if you use a file manager, since these programs typically only let you access existing directories. The automounter is useful, however, when you use command-line tools.

Using Swap Space

One type of disk access is critically important to Linux but has not yet been mentioned in this chapter: *swap space*. This is disk space that's set aside as auxiliary to system memory (RAM). Suppose your computer has 128MB of RAM, but you want to run 190MB worth of programs on the system. Swap space allows you to accomplish this, by treating disk space as if it were RAM. The result is that you can run all 190MB worth of programs— albeit more slowly on this 128MB computer than on a machine that has in excess of 190MB of RAM.

Linux typically assigns one or more disk partitions as swap space. These partitions use the type code 0x82 (*Linux swap*), as described in "Disk Partitioning." It's also possible to use an ordinary disk file as swap space. Normally, Linux sets up a swap partition during system installation, so this feature is handled automatically. You may want to adjust this default configuration, however.

You can find out how much swap space your system currently has by typing **free**, which produces output like the following:

```
                total     used     free   shared   buffers    cached
Mem:          127752    121416     6336    61108     26748     53316
-/+ buffers/cache:  41352     86400
Swap:         136512      4928   131584
```

Pay particular attention to the line labeled Swap. Under the Total column is the number of kilobytes of swap space available to the system. The Used and Free columns list how much of that space is in use and available, respectively. If the Used value begins to approach the Total value, you should consider adding more swap space.

TIP It's difficult to anticipate how much swap space a system will need, because it depends on how the computer is to be used. One oft-quoted rule of thumb is to create swap space equal to twice your system's physical RAM. This rule of thumb originates from the multiuser minicomputer and mainframe Unixes of the 1980s, however. It may not be appropriate to Linux workstations, or even to multiuser Linux systems with dozens or hundreds of megabytes of physical RAM.

To add more, follow these steps:

1. Set aside appropriate disk space. You can do this in either of two ways:

   - Create a new disk partition for the swap space. This approach can be difficult because it requires that you repartition your hard disk.

   - Create an empty file of the appropriate size on a Linux-native filesystem. For example, the command **dd if=/dev/zero of=/*swap* bs=1024 count=*n*** creates an appropriate file (called /*swap*) that's *n* kilobytes in size.

2. Issue the mkswap command on the new swap space you've created. For a partition, you'll type something like **mkswap /dev/sdc5**. For a file, the command will resemble **mkswap /*swap***. This command prepares the space to store swap information.

3. Use the swapon command to add the new swap space, as in **swapon /dev/sdc5** or **swapon /*swap***. Enter another free command, and you'll see that the available swap space has increased by the size of your new swap partition or file.

To make the use of swap space permanent, you should add an /etc/fstab file entry for the swap space. This entry uses the mount point and the filesystem type code entries of swap, but otherwise resembles other /etc/fstab entries. For instance, both of the following lines add swap space:

```
/dev/sdc5 swap      swap     defaults      0 0

/swap      swap     swap     defaults      0 0
```

Once you've added these entries, Linux uses the specified swap space after a reboot.

If you want to stop using a specific swap partition or file, you can use the swapoff command, which works much like the swapon command—for instance, **swapoff /dev/sdc5**.

Updating and Maintaining Filesystems

Before you can use a filesystem, you must prepare one. If you obtain a new disk, you must break it into partitions and create filesystems on those partitions. Only then will you be

System Optimization

PART 3

able to mount the filesystems. These steps are necessary when adding a disk and when replacing one, but the precise details of these operations differ. There's also the issue of filesystem maintenance. In some situations—particularly after a system crash or power failure—Linux must check its filesystems for integrity. You may need to supervise this process, so it's important to understand what goes on during such a check.

Disk Partitioning

If you've bought a new disk, your first task once you've connected it to your computer is to *partition* the disk. This procedure carves the disk into smaller chunks so that you can share the disk across multiple OSs, or subdivide the space used on a single OS to protect files on one partition should another develop problems. Chapter 2 briefly discusses these issues, and it describes partitioning a disk during a Red Hat Linux installation session. You can also use assorted partitioning tools after installation, to change your configuration or to add a new disk.

TIP   If you want to change an existing partition configuration, one of the best tools available is PartitionMagic, from PowerQuest (`http://www.powerquest.com`). This commercial package allows you to add, delete, move, resize, and copy FAT, HPFS, NTFS, ext2fs, and Linux swap partitions, without damaging their contents. PartitionMagic comes with a DOS version and a DOS boot floppy, so you can run it even on a Linux-only computer. If you regularly alter your partition setups, it's well worth having. Similar tools are available from others, but the only dynamic partition resizers that handle Linux ext2fs partitions are much more difficult to use than PartitionMagic.

Planning a Partition Layout

Before you begin working with partitioning software, it's important to design an appropriate partition layout. Unfortunately, it's hard to give simple and complete rules for doing this, because every system's needs are different. What's suitable for a high-level news server may be wholly inappropriate for a desktop workstation. Here are some rules of thumb to keep in mind:

- *Keep it simple.* The simpler the configuration, the better. Complex configurations can be difficult to maintain. Further, if a system has many partitions, it's more likely that one of them will run out of room while another has plenty of free space—an awkward situation.

- *Keep related data together.* Because the time required to access data varies with the distance from one point to another on a disk, it's best to keep related data in one area. One consequence of this rule is that in a multi-OS configuration, you should keep the partitions for each OS contiguous.

- *Put the most-used data in the center.* Heavily accessed partitions should go in the middle of a range of partitions. Swap partitions typically see a lot of use, so they should be positioned in between nonswap partitions.

- *Split OSs across disks.* If you have two or more operating systems, you may be tempted to put one OS entirely on one disk and another on a second disk. If you split both OSs across both disks, however, you'll achieve slightly better performance because two sets of disk heads are working in both OSs.

- *Isolate critical data.* Consider putting particularly important or much-used data on partitions separate from other files. This can reduce the risk of damage to those data should a disk error in another part of the disk occur. Similarly, if a heavily used partition runs out of disk space, the problems this causes can be isolated. Putting /home and, on some servers, /var and /tmp, on their own partitions are typical examples of this rule of thumb.

- *Put the Linux kernel under the disk's 1024-cylinder mark.* Until recently, the Linux Loader (LILO) couldn't boot the Linux kernel if it resided in an area past the 1024th cylinder. One easy way around this limitation is to create a small (5–20MB) partition under that point and mount it as /boot. You can then store the Linux kernel in this partition and put the rest of the system elsewhere, even past the 1024-cylinder point. The latest versions of LILO (including the version that ships with Red Hat 7.0) don't suffer from this problem, but as of early 2001, it's best to be safe in this respect.

NOTE The *1024-cylinder mark* is the point where the 1024th cylinder of the disk, as reported by an EIDE drive or SCSI host adapter, lies. On modern hard disks, this point works out to just under 8GB, but it can be much lower on some (mostly older) systems. This arrangement is important because the original *x*86 BIOS, and hence a wide range of software that relies upon the BIOS, couldn't read beyond 1024 cylinders. This limit has been lifted in modern BIOSes, but it's taken a while for the chain of utilities that use the BIOS (including LILO) to take advantage of the improved support for larger disks.

You shouldn't take any of these rules as being absolute. Indeed, they sometimes contradict one another. For instance, the data-isolation rule is at odds with the keep-it-simple rule. In the end, you'll need to decide which rules best reflect your own personal preferences and needs for the system, and create a partitioning scheme that reflects these factors. For new Linux administrators, we typically recommend a root (/) partition, a /home partition, a swap partition, possibly a /boot partition, and whatever partitions are necessary to support any other OSs that exist on the computer. Creating more partitions can be difficult because it's hard to judge how large to make them. Another administrator's experience is of limited use in making that judgment, because the systems may be used in radically different ways. Once you've gained some experience, or if you see a compelling reason to do so initially, you may want to separate out partitions for /var, /tmp, /usr, /usr/local, /opt, and other directories.

Linux Disk-Partitioning Software

Linux's main partitioning tool is called fdisk (for *fixed disk*). It's named after the DOS FDISK utility but works quite differently. To use fdisk, type its name followed by the device file you want to modify, such as /dev/sda or /dev/hdb, thus:

```
# fdisk /dev/hdb
```

WARNING Every *x*86 OS has its own disk-partitioning software. Linux's fdisk is unusually flexible, but can produce partitions that other OSs don't like. As a general rule of thumb, you should use each OS's partitioning tools to create its own partitions. Alternatively, you can use a more OS-agnostic tool, such as PartitionMagic, to do the job for all OSs.

On modern disks, you'll likely be told that the number of cylinders exceeds 1024. You can safely ignore this warning, except to know that it's best to place the Linux boot partition below the 1024-cylinder limit. Once fdisk is running, you see only a prompt that reads Command (m for help):. You type single-letter commands at this prompt in order to accomplish various tasks. You can type **m** or **?** to see what these commands are. Table 10.3 summarizes the most important ones.

Table 10.3   Important Linux fdisk Commands

fdisk Command	Meaning
d	Deletes a partition
l	Displays a list of known partition type codes
m or ?	Displays a summary of commands
n	Creates a new partition
p	Displays the disk's current partition table

Table 10.3   Important Linux `fdisk` Commands *(continued)*

fdisk Command	Meaning
q	Quits without saving changes
t	Changes a partition's type ID code
v	Verifies the partition table; checks that it's internally consistent and returns basic information
w	Saves (writes) changes and exits from the program

It's generally a good idea to start any `fdisk` session with a **p** command to let you see the current contents of the disk. This allows you to verify that you're modifying the correct disk, and gives you the partition numbers for partitions you might want to delete. You also need this information in planning where to put new partitions.

> **WARNING**   Don't make changes to any partitions that are currently mounted. Doing so can confuse Linux and possibly cause a system crash. You can unmount a partition and then delete it, if that's your intention. To change a partition's size, use a partition resizing tool such as PartitionMagic; or you can back the partition up, resize it, and restore the backup. Some early ext2fs partition resizers require that you separately resize a partition with `fdisk` and resize the filesystem with the partition resizer. Follow those tools' instructions, if you use them.

Once you've seen what (if anything) already exists on the disk, you can proceed to delete, add, and otherwise modify the partition table using `fdisk`'s commands. Consider the following `fdisk` exchange:

```
Command (m for help): p


Disk /dev/hdb: 255 heads, 63 sectors, 1216 cylinders
Units = cylinders of 16065 * 512 bytes


    Device Boot    Start      End    Blocks   Id  System
/dev/hdb1                257     1216   7711200    5  Extended
```

```
/dev/hdb2           1        192    1542208+   fb   Unknown

/dev/hdb3          193       256     514080    17   Hidden HPFS/NTFS

/dev/hdb5          257       516    2088418+    6   FAT16

/dev/hdb6          517       717    1614501     7   HPFS/NTFS


Command (m for help): n

Command action

   l    logical (5 or over)

   p    primary partition (1-4)

l

First cylinder (718-1216, default 718): 718

Last cylinder or +size or +sizeM or +sizeK (718-1216, default 1216):
+400M
```

In this situation, the initial configuration included five partitions, and the n command added a new one. fdisk gave the option of creating a *logical* or *primary* partition. The *x*86 partitioning scheme originally provided for only four partitions per disk, which soon became inadequate. The workaround was to use one of the original four *primary* partitions as a placeholder for a potentially large number of *logical* partitions. The "placeholder" primary partition is then referred to as an *extended* partition. In Linux, the primary partitions use numbers from 1 to 4; the logical partitions are numbered 5 and up. Linux doesn't care whether its partitions are primary or logical, so we recommend using mostly or exclusively logical partitions for Linux. This reserves primary partitions for OSs that do need them, such as DOS, Windows, and FreeBSD.

Linux's fdisk lets you specify partition sizes either in terms of an ending cylinder number or in bytes, kilobytes, or megabytes. The preceding example specified a 400MB partition starting at cylinder 718.

TIP   For the final partition on a disk, enter the size by specifying an ending cylinder number that corresponds to the maximum available. This practice minimizes the amount of unused disk space.

By default, fdisk creates partitions that use the type code 0x83 (*Linux native*). Such partitions are suitable for holding Linux's ext2fs or any of the journaling filesystems available for Linux. If you want to create a Linux swap partition or a partition to be used in another OS, however, you must change its type code. You do this with the t command, which prompts you for a hexadecimal code. If you don't know the code, type L at this point for a list. (You can enter a code that's not on the list if you like, but fdisk won't be able to identify the associated OS if you do so.) Linux's fdisk is one of the few partitioning tools that let you change the type code of an existing partition, using the t command. You can use this feature to convert a partition created with another tool for use by Linux.

> **NOTE** Linux doesn't actually use the partition type codes except during installation. Instead, Linux relies on the -t parameter to mount, or on Linux's autodetection algorithms, to determine the partition type. Many other OSs, however, rely upon the partition type codes to determine what partitions they use.

When you're done editing the partition table, look it over with the p command; then verify that everything's OK with the v command. Chances are that v will report your disk has some number of unallocated sectors. This is normal and reflects sectors lost to the standard PC method of accessing the disk. You should write down the partition numbers and your intended uses for them, so that you don't forget these details. Once you're satisfied with your new partitioning scheme, type **w** to commit the changes to disk and exit.

> **TIP** Linux's fdisk does *not* alter any on-disk structures until you enter the w command. If you create an unusable disk structure and want to start over again from scratch, you can type **q** to quit without saving the changes. When you start fdisk again, you'll see the same starting conditions you saw initially.

Creating a Filesystem

Filesystems aren't completely blank slates. To function, they rely upon the presence of certain key components, even when they contain no actual files. These initial data structures include pointers to the root directory and whatever data structures the filesystem uses to allocate space, boot sector code, and perhaps some files or directories required by the OS or filesystem (such as the lost+found directory that appears on every ext2fs partition). The process of writing these core data structures to disk is sometimes referred to as *formatting a disk*. This term is common in the Microsoft world, but it's ambiguous, because it can also refer to creating new magnetic marks the disk mechanism uses to locate individual sectors on the disk. To avoid ambiguity, it's common in the Linux world to refer to the process of writing sector marks as *low-level formatting*, and to laying out initial filesystem data structures as *high-level formatting* or *creating* (or *making*) *a filesystem*.

System
Optimization

PART 3

For floppy disks, the DOS and Windows FORMAT command performs both low-level and high-level formats, although it may skip the low-level format if that's already been done. In Linux, the fdformat program (described earlier in "Accessing Floppy Disks") performs a low-level format on floppy disks. Under any OS, special utilities are used to perform low-level formats on hard disks and high-capacity removable disks. These utilities are sometimes integrated into the BIOS, especially for SCSI disks. It's unlikely that you'll need to perform low-level formats on hard disks.

In Linux, each filesystem has its own utility to create a filesystem. These utilities are usually named mkfs.*fsname*, where *fsname* is a code for the filesystem; for instance, mkfs.ext2 to create an ext2 filesystem. Often these utilities go by other names, too, such as mke2fs. The mkfs utility is a front-end to all these specific filesystem-creation programs. Here is the syntax for this command:

```
mkfs [-t fsname] [options] device [size]
```

The options to this command are as follows:

-t *fsname*   Specify the filesystem type with this option. Then mkfs calls mkfs.fsname.

options   You can pass filesystem-specific options to the program that does the actual filesystem creation. Precisely what options are available varies from one filesystem to another; check the mkfs.*fsname* man page for details. Common options include the following:

-c   Checks the device for bad blocks.

-l   *filename*   Reads a list of known bad blocks from *filename*.

-v   Displays extra information during the filesystem creation process.

device   This is the only truly required parameter. Use it to tell the program on what device to make the filesystem, such as /dev/sdb1 or /dev/fd0.

size   You can tell the system to create a filesystem of a particular size, measured in blocks that are typically 1024 bytes in size. If you omit this parameter, the program creates a filesystem that fills the partition or device.

Red Hat Linux includes filesystem-creation utilities for ext2fs, the Minix filesystem, and FAT (the FAT tool is called mkfs.msdos; but as there are no differences at filesystem creation time between ordinary FAT and long filename-enabled VFAT, you can use this utility to create VFAT filesystems). In addition, the Mtools package includes another FAT filesystem creation program, and the HFS Utils package includes a program to create Macintosh HFS filesystems. The various journaling filesystem projects include their own mkfs.*fsname* utilities. Aside from FAT, Linux utilities to create most non-Linux filesystems are rare. In general, you should create filesystems such as HPFS, NTFS, or BFS in their own OSs. As an example, the following commands both create a FAT filesystem on a floppy disk:

```
# mkfs.msdos /dev/fd0
```

and

```
# mformat a:
```

TIP If you want to use ext2fs on floppy disks or other removable media, use the -m 0 parameter to mkfs.ext2. The -m parameter specifies the percentage of disk space that's reserved for use by root. This percentage can be safely set to 0 for removable disks, but it's best to leave it at its default value of 5 for most disk partitions, especially the root (/) partition.

Adding a Disk

As your system grows, it accumulates files. What's more, as time goes on, file sizes increase. Real-time video files, for instance, can easily consume literally gigabytes of disk space, compared to the kilobytes that were common for personal productivity applications of just a decade or so ago. To cope, you may want to add a new hard disk to an existing computer that's been in service for a while.

Most *x*86 computers sold today use EIDE disks. These disks are inexpensive and easy to find, but they have a disadvantage: A typical computer can support just four EIDE devices. Because common add-on devices, such as CD-ROM drives, tape backup drives, and high-capacity removable-media drives, also use the EIDE interface, you may be limited to just one or two EIDE hard disks. Beyond that, you'll have to either add another EIDE controller or add a SCSI adapter. SCSI adapters can host either 7 or 15 devices, depending upon the SCSI variant, and SCSI hard disks often outperform their EIDE cousins. Unfortunately, SCSI disks are generally more expensive than equivalent EIDE devices. Check your current inventory of disk devices before buying a new one to determine what type of device to buy.

When it comes to actually adding a disk, the procedures outlined earlier are the critical ones in terms of software configuration. Depending on the disk's intended role, you may want to transfer some files to the new disk, as well. Overall, the steps involved in adding a new disk are as follows:

1. Check your hardware and decide on a disk type and model.

2. Add the disk hardware, paying attention to characteristics such as EIDE master/slave status, and SCSI termination and ID.

3. Partition the disk in a way that's suitable for your system.

4. Create filesystems on the new disk's partitions.

5. Mount the new disk's partitions.

If you want to transfer data, you can do so in between steps 4 and 5. The usual procedure is to select a directory to move to the new disk. For instance, you might move /opt to a new disk. To do so, follow these steps:

1. Follow steps 1 through 4 just above.

2. Mount the new partition at a temporary location. This can be an existing mount point, such as /mnt/floppy; or one you create specifically for this purpose. The remaining steps assume that you're using /mnt/floppy as a temporary mount point.

3. Change to the base of the directory you want to move, as in **cd /opt**.

4. Type the following command to copy all files to the new filesystem:

```
# tar clpf - . | (cd /mnt/floppy; tar xpvf -)
```

> **NOTE** The -1 parameter keeps `tar` from moving into filesystems mounted on the source directory. If you want to transfer two current filesystems onto one new one, you'll need to omit this parameter. It's included in step 4 because omitting it can sometimes cause problems. In particular, be careful *not* to copy the /proc filesystem, which is a pseudo-filesystem that contains system information. Copying it is wasteful and potentially dangerous. Another potential pitfall lies in copying a filesystem on which the destination filesystem is mounted, which results in an endless loop unless the -1 `tar` parameter is specified. Both problems are most likely to occur if you attempt to move the root (/) filesystem.

5. Check, as best you can, that the new partition contains the files that it should.

6. Remove the files from their original location. For instance, type **rm -r /opt/***.

> **WARNING** Step 6 is potentially very dangerous. If there's been an error in copying the files, removing the originals will result in loss of data. You might want to skip this step for a while. If you do, you can mount the new partition over the contents of the original directory. You'll then access the new partition rather than the old directory. When you're satisfied that all is well, temporarily unmount the new partition and come back to perform step 6.

7. Unmount the new partition from its temporary location.

8. Mount the new partition at the (now empty) directory that held the original files.

9. Edit /etc/fstab to reflect the new filesystem mount point.

This procedure allows you to remove much of the load from one disk by spreading it across two. You may encounter complications, however. Specifically, if you want to move a directory that's normally in heavy use, such as /usr, you may have problems deleting the directory. In such cases, you may need to resort to an emergency boot disk to perform steps 6 and 9, skipping the intervening steps.

Replacing a Disk

Fundamentally, you can treat a disk transplant much as you do a disk addition; it's just that you're moving *everything* from one disk to another. Here are some special caveats to keep in mind:

- If you're replacing a disk because you can't add any more disks to your system, you'll need to temporarily disconnect a device, such as a Zip or CD-ROM drive, in order to perform the replacement. Alternatively, you can use a tape backup device as an intermediary storage device, but this is likely to be a slower procedure.

NOTE You can use a network storage device, such as a server system, as an intermediary storage device. If you do so, it's best to use tar to back up the files to the network server. Copying the files directly may result in the loss of important filesystem characteristics.

- Step 4 of the second procedure in "Adding a Disk" specifies use of the -1 parameter to tar. This parameter keeps the transfer restricted to one filesystem, which helps avoid problems with /proc or endless loops that result when copying the root filesystem. When moving an entire installation, it's best to do so one filesystem at a time.

- When you've finished copying all the files, edit /etc/fstab on the destination system to reflect the partition assignments as they will exist *after* you've removed the original disk. For instance, if the original disk is /dev/sda and the new one is /dev/sdb, removal of /dev/sda changes all the /dev/sdb partitions to equivalently numbered /dev/sda partitions. The new disk's /etc/fstab file should include references to itself as /dev/sda.

- Create a DOS boot floppy and put on it a copy of your Linux kernel and the LOADLIN.EXE program from the Linux installation CD. You'll use this floppy to boot your copied system for the first time. If you don't have a copy of DOS handy, FreeDOS (`http://www.freedos.org`) can serve this function quite well. Note the device identifier that the root filesystem will have when the original hard disk is removed.

- When you've copied everything and removed the old disk, boot with the DOS boot floppy. Type `LOADLIN` *`VMLINUZ`* `root=/`*`device`* `ro`, where *`VMLINUZ`* is your Linux kernel filename and /*`device`* is the device ID of the root partition. This procedure should boot Linux. You can then edit /etc/lilo.conf (if necessary) and type `lilo` to install LILO on the new disk. Thereafter, the new disk should boot without the aid of a floppy, just as did the original disk.

WARNING   Don't remove any partitions or overwrite any data on your old hard disk until you're sure all your important data exist on the new disk. If you miss a partition or make an error in copying the original disk's data, keeping the original around for a brief period can save you a lot of aggravation when you discover the problem.

Checking Filesystem Integrity

At every boot, Linux checks that its filesystems were shut down correctly. If they weren't, Linux initiates a filesystem check, which is performed by a utility called fsck.*fsname*, where *fsname* is the filesystem name. (Like mkfs.*fsname*, these utilities often go by other names, such as e2fsck for fsck.ext2. The fsck utility is a front-end that calls the appropriate filesystem-specific utility.) The filesystem check process is most important for ext2fs, because an unclean shutdown can leave ext2fs in an inconsistent state, resulting in lost or damaged files; a filesystem check prevents this. One of the prime advantages of journaling filesystems, as explained earlier, is that they require only very minimal filesystem checks after a system crash. Linux lacks programs for checking most foreign filesystems; you must normally use programs native to those OSs to perform such checks. (FAT is an exception to this rule; there is a Linux fsck.msdos program.)

The operations of a filesystem check vary from one filesystem to another. For ext2fs, it involves five separate passes through the filesystem, the first two of which take 90 percent or more of the program's running time. Each pass detects and corrects a different class of filesystem errors. If all goes well, this process completes automatically, without the need for human intervention; it just takes some time—a time that can be measured in tens of minutes or even hours on multigigabyte partitions.

Unfortunately, the filesystem check process sometimes *does* require human intervention. When this happens, you're likely to see a message that the operation failed and that you must run fsck manually. You must type the root password to gain limited access to the system, whereupon you should issue the fsck command on the partition that caused the problem, as in **fsck /dev/hda9**. The program is likely to ask you bewildering questions concerning whether it should duplicate specific *inodes* (directory structures associated with files) or store lost files in the lost+found directory. Unless you know a great deal about the design of the filesystem that's being checked, you should select the default for each of these questions. When this is over, issue the **shutdown now -r** command to reboot the computer and hope for the best.

Even when a filesystem has been cleanly unmounted, Linux sometimes issues an fsck on the filesystem at boot time. This is because ext2fs has a maximum mount count—a maximum number of times that Linux will mount the partition before it requires a check, in order to ensure that errors haven't crept onto the system. There's also a maximum *time* between checks, for similar reasons. You can determine these values for any given ext2fs partition by using the dumpe2fs program. (This program produces a lot of output, so you should pipe it through less, as in **dumpe2fs /dev/hda9 | less**.) Look for lines labeled Maximum mount count and Check interval. Typical values are 20 mounts and 6 months, respectively.

You can alter these values (and several others) using the tune2fs program. Include the -c parameter to adjust the maximum mount count, and the -i parameter to adjust the check interval. For instance, type **tune2fs /dev/hda9 -c 5 -i 1m** to reduce the limits to 5 mounts or 1 month. (You can also use d and w for units to the -i parameter, to indicate days and weeks, respectively.)

Naturally, filesystems other than ext2fs use different criteria for determining when to force a filesystem check. Most include flags that let them spot a filesystem that was not cleanly unmounted, but any given filesystem may or may not include equivalents to the forced checks by time or number of mounts included in ext2fs. Equivalents to the dumpe2fs and tune2fs programs may exist for specific filesystems, but not usually.

In Sum

Linux has unusually strong support for a wide variety of filesystems. In early 2001, Linux's weak point is its lack of a mature journaling filesystem, but work is underway on several contenders to fill this role. In terms of foreign filesystem support, Linux is unsurpassed; it can at least read, and often write, filesystems from all major *x*86 OSs, and from many non-*x*86 OSs.

Using filesystems under Linux entails issuing a mount command and accessing files using normal Linux programs and shell commands. You can add entries to /etc/fstab to have the computer automatically mount filesystems at boot time, or to allow non-root users to do so.

System
Optimization

PART 3

Filesystem creation and maintenance involves several tools, including the fdisk tool for partition creation, mkfs and its helper programs for filesystem creation, and fsck and its helper programs for filesystem integrity checking. Understanding how to use these tools is critically important for upgrading and maintaining your system.

11

Backing Up and Restoring

One of the most important system administration tasks is to reliably create and verify backups. Failure to do so might go unnoticed for several weeks or even months; unglamorous tasks like backups tend to slip through the cracks all too often. The first time a system on the backup list fails and there is no backup from which to restore it, however, you can count the seconds before someone gets a very serious reprimand—perhaps to the point of losing the job entirely. This might seem excessive, but if the data is valuable enough to make the backup list, you can bet that someone will miss it if it's gone.

If you work for a software company or any company that stores the working version of its "product" on the computers under your administrative control, backups are especially critical. Hundreds or thousands of employee-hours might be lost if the system failed without a recent backup. A system administrator is expected to prevent such loss and will probably not hold that title for long if unable to do so. Think of it as health insurance for your computers. You wouldn't go without health insurance, and neither should your computers.

Backup Strategies

Defining a backup strategy means deciding how much information you need to back up, and how often. At one extreme are *full backups* which, as you might guess, back up everything. If you do a full backup every night, you'll certainly be able to restore anything to the state it was in the previous night. But this is very time consuming and requires significantly higher media consumption than other methods, since you will be backing up everything every night. An alternative is the *incremental backup,* including only those files that have changed (or are likely to have changed) since the last backup. Most administrators try to develop backup strategies that combine these two methods, reducing the time expended backing up the system without sacrificing the ability to restore most of what was lost.

In addition to formal backups of a computer or network, you may want to archive specific data. For instance, you might want to store data from scientific experiments, the files associated with a project you've just completed, or the home directory of a user. Such archives are typically done on an as-needed basis, and may work best with different hardware than you use to back up an entire computer or network.

Combining Full and Incremental Backups

Including incremental backups in your strategy saves a great deal of time and effort. Much of the data on your system (whether a network or a single computer) is static. If data hasn't changed since the last reliable backup, any time spent backing it up is a waste. There are two ways to determine which files to include on an incremental backup. The first is to use commands that look for files newer than the date of the last full backup. The second method is to determine which data is most likely to be changed and to include this data, whether actually changed or not, on the incremental backup.

Most backup strategies combine full backups with incremental backups (often referred to as daily backups), to cover the more dynamic data. Typically each night, when the system's workload is at its lowest, a backup of one of these forms is performed.

One plan, illustrated in Table 11.1, is to rotate between four sets of tapes (or whichever medium you choose; we'll look at the backup media options shortly). Starting with set 1, do a full backup on Sunday when system usage is likely to be at its lowest and do an incremental backup every other day of that first week. Move to tape set 2 for the next week, doing the full backup on Sunday as before. Move on to tape sets 3 and 4 as appropriate. At the end of the fourth set, store the tape from Sunday of week 1 as the monthly backup and replace that tape with a new one. Other than the monthly tape, reuse the tapes from the previous month for the next sequence. Once a year, archive a monthly tape as the archive for that year.

Table 11.1   Backup Plan with Full and Incremental Backups

	Sun	Mon	Tue	Wed	Thu	Fri	Sat
week1	F	I	I	I	I	I	I
week2	F	I	I	I	I	I	I
week3	F	I	I	I	I	I	I
week4	F	D	D	D	D	D	D

This method has several advantages. Since it takes four weeks for the first tape to get recycled, restoring the system to the status from a specific day of the month requires only that you dump from the appropriate tape. Typically, the missing or errant file will be discovered within the month covered by the tape. If not, check the monthly tape. There are a few isolated scenarios that might not be covered; any file changed after the previous night's backup and deleted before the next night's would lose any of those changes, but this is a very solid plan overall.

Including Differential Backups

The term *differential backup* is sometimes used to refer to a backup consisting of all files that have changed since the previous backup at any level. This differs from an incremental backup, which includes everything that has changed since the last full backup, because the immediately previous backup might be a full backup, an incremental backup, or another differential backup. This type of backup is illustrated in Table 11.2. In view of the savings in time over the full/incremental plan shown above, it certainly merits consideration.

Table 11.2   Backup Plan with Full, Incremental, and Differential Backups

	Sun	Mon	Tue	Wed	Thu	Fri	Sat
week1	F	D	D	I	D	D	D
week2	F	D	D	I	D	D	D
week3	F	D	D	I	D	D	D
week4	F	D	D	I	D	D	D

System Optimization

PART 3

Comparing this method to that shown in Table 11.1, you can see that we have replaced the incremental backups with differential backups. The problem with doing this is that you now have to restore multiple backups if the system goes down on any other day than Sunday after the full backup, in order to get the system back to its previous state. For instance, if the system went down on a Friday night, you would have to load the previous Sunday's full backup and the differential backups for the following Monday through Friday. While the backup itself takes less time, restoring actually takes much longer. Table 11.3 illustrates an alternative strategy, combining all three backup methods.

Table 11.3   Backup Plan with Full, Incremental, and Differential Backups

	Sun	Mon	Tue	Wed	Thu	Fri	Sat
week1	F	D	D	I	D	D	D
week2	F	D	D	I	D	D	D
week3	F	D	D	I	D	D	D
week4	F	D	D	I	D	D	D

This version adds an incremental backup on Wednesdays. Since an incremental backup is available, if a problem occurred after Wednesday's backup, you could restore the previous full backup and the incremental backup from that day. Otherwise, you would have to restore the most recent full backup and then any incremental backups that are not followed by an incremental backup as well as the incremental backup. To clarify, if the system went down on Tuesday night after the backups ran, you'd have to restore three tapes: Sunday's full backup, Monday's differential backup, and Tuesday's differential backup. If the system went down on Friday night, you'd have to restore four tapes: Sunday's full backup, Wednesday's incremental backup, and Thursday's and Friday's differential backups.

Data-Specific Backups

There may also be a need for data-specific backups, which target data that has been added to the system and are performed on a routine basis like once or twice a month. This technique is often used for specific types of data for which long-term storage requirements might be different. For example, a company's payroll accounting data might be entered on the 15th and the last day of every month. If this data is simply included in an incremental backup, it will be written over within a month. The archived monthly backup would capture the previous month's end-of-month payroll but would not capture the mid-month payroll at all. The company might need to keep the data for the two payroll days, saving several months' or even years' worth of data. A separate backup of this data might be done on the 15th and the last day of the month, after the data is considered to be stable, and archived independently.

Basically, a backup strategy must be fitted to the computer system for which it is being designed. A little forethought will save a great deal of grief in the long run. Consider the types of data, whether the data is static or dynamic, and any known fluxes in the system, and create a backup plan that will ensure that all concerns are met.

Backup Media

What medium should you use for backups? Choose a media type based on how much data you'll be archiving, whether or not you intend to do unattended backups, how much money you have to spend on new hardware and media, and what hardware you already have available to you. The options are almost endless, and the costs are highly variable. In most cases that we've encountered, the hardware on hand was what we used. After some great technological leap, you might convince the boss that some new hardware is in order.

The options we'll discuss in the following sections include a variety of tape formats, CD-R backups, floptical disks, Bernoulli boxes and other removable drives, or even floppy disks. You should choose what makes the most sense for the system you're protecting given the resources at your disposal.

Tapes

Tapes are generally considered to be the best backup medium in terms of capacity and cost. Additionally, with the size of hard drives ever increasing, tape is the only real alternative for unassisted backup, since most other options require media switching. Tape drives may be internal or external. Often companies purchase internal drives for servers to facilitate automatic backups and external drives to be shared among several workstations. Instead of sharing an external drive, it's also possible to use one computer as a *backup server* for an entire network. Such a system can use NFS, Samba, or other tools to back up remote machines.

There are many different types of tape available. If you don't already have a tape drive and decide to use this backup approach, you'll want to consider which type of tape you'd like to use. Tape capacity is an important factor. Determine the space required for a full backup and increase it by at least 50 percent to determine what type of tape best meets your requirements. Keep in mind that there are autoloaders to allow unattended backups across multiple tapes. Another factor is what backup software package you intend to use; of course, the list of equipment supported by the package you choose will limit your choices. Here are some of the most common choices:

- 8mm helical scan
- 4mm helical scan (DAT)
- quarter-inch cartridge linear tape (QIC)
- Travan (a QIC derivative)

Helical Scan

Helical scan tapes use a rotating head/drum assembly to read and write, as illustrated in Figure 11.1. The head writes "swipes" on the diagonal instead of parallel to the tape's edge.

Figure 11.1   Helical scan

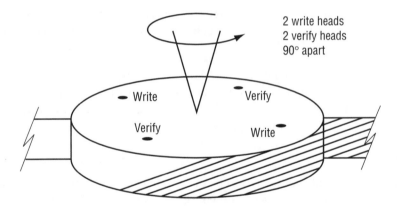

This is the same method used by VCR tapes. The 4mm helical scan tapes are very similar to digital audio tapes (DATs), but have slightly different magnetic tape properties, and so aren't reliably interchangeable. There is an 8mm version as well, which is similar to 8mm videotape. Most helical scan drives do internal data compression. Hardware data compression reduces the CPU load on the computer if you want to compress your backups, and it is more reliable than the compression used with some backup packages, such as tar. Any compression technique produces uneven *amounts* of compression, though; text tends to compress well, whereas binary formats don't compress as well, and some pre-compressed data (such as GIF images) may actually increase in size if "compressed" again.

> **WARNING** Many tape drive manufacturers, whether their products have hardware compression or not, quote estimated *compressed* capacities for their drives. If you don't use compression, or if your data aren't as compressible as the manufacturer assumes, you won't get the rated capacity from these drives.

Helical-scan drives typically start at about $500 and go up in price to well over $1,000. Low-capacity DAT tapes cost less than $10, but higher-capacity tapes cost $30 or more.

QIC and Travan Linear Tape

Quarter-inch cartridge linear tape (QIC) was developed in 1972 by the 3M Corporation (now called Imation). More recently, 3M released a QIC variant known as Travan, which dominates the low end of the tape marketplace in 2001. QIC and Travan tapes, like helical-scan tapes, look and work much like audio tape cassettes, with two reels inside, one taking up tape and the other holding it. The difference from helical-scan technology is that linear tape technologies write data in parallel bands that lie perpendicular to the length of the tape, rather than at an angle. This configuration simplifies the design of the tape head, thus reducing the cost of the tape drive. It's more difficult to achieve high data densities with this design, though.

The reels are driven by a belt that is built into the cartridge. A capstan, a metal rod that projects from the drive motor, presses the tape against a rubber drive wheel. As shown in Figure 11.2, the head contains a write head with a read head on either side. The write head writes data longitudinally, and one read head (depending on the direction the tape is running) attempts to verify the data that has just been written. If the data passes verification by the read head, the buffer is flushed and filled with new data from the system memory. If errors are found, the segment is rewritten on the next length of tape. (Very low-end QIC and Travan devices lack this *read-after-write* capability, and so are less reliable.) Capacity is added by adding more tracks. Capacities vary from a few megabytes for obsolete devices sold in the 1980s to over 10GB for modern devices.

Compared to helical-scan drives, QIC and Travan drives are noisy. Neither type has a clear advantage in capacity or reliability (although each type has its proponents who claim a reliability advantage). QIC and Travan drives cover a wider range of capacities and budgets, though, with low-end devices being less reliable and lower in capacity. As a general rule, QIC and Travan drives are less expensive to buy than are helical-scan drives, with prices starting at $200 or less. High-end units can cost over $1,000, though. The QIC and Travan tapes are more expensive, starting at $30 or so. This makes QIC and Travan a good choice if you expect to buy few tapes, but helical-scan drives may be better if you plan to buy many tapes.

Figure 11.2   Reading and writing linear tape

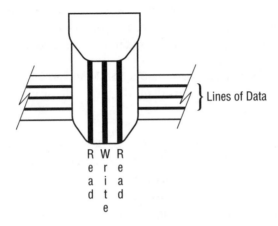

R W R
e r e
a i a
d t d
   e

} Lines of Data

Newer Options

Recent developments have provided new types of tape for higher-end systems. Among these are digital linear tape (DLT) in a single or multiple configuration, Mammoth (8mm) drives in a single or multiple configuration, and robotic storage management systems, which run without any human intervention. These systems are quite nice to have, but the cost is often prohibitive.

Digital Linear Tape   Digital Linear Tape drives vary in capacity and configuration from the low-end 10GB drives to the newer automated DLT tape libraries, which can store 1.5 Terabytes of data (compressed among up to 48 drives).

DLT drives use 0.5"-wide metal particle tapes; these are 60 percent wider than 8mm. Data is recorded in a serpentine pattern on parallel tracks grouped into pairs. As shown in Figure 11.3, the tape is passed through a head guide assembly (HGA), which consists of a boomerang-shaped aluminum plate with six large bearing-mounted guides arranged in an arc. The tape is gently guided by a leader strip and wound onto a take-up reel without the recorded side of the tape ever touching a roller. There are also mechanisms that continually clean the tape as it passes, to increase tape life.

A track is recorded using the entire length of the tape, and then heads are repositioned and another full-length path is laid down on the return trip. Some newer DLT tape drives record two channels simultaneously using two read/write elements in the head, effectively doubling the transfer rate possible at a given drive speed and recording density. DLT technology uses a file mark index located at the logical end of the tape to minimize search time.

Figure 11.3   The Digital Linear Tape (DLT) drive mechanism

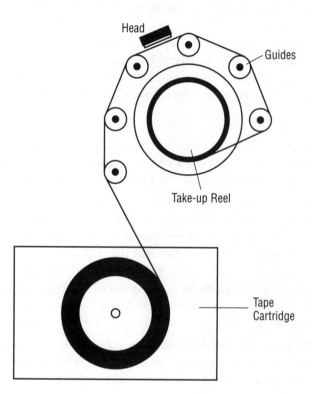

When we checked prices recently, a DLT library cost about $12,000—out of reach for most of us. Single-tape DLT drives are more in line with DAT prices, starting at a bit over $1,000. Still, if you have the need for high-capacity, reliable storage, there are few systems that can beat it. The cost per MB of data stored is actually quite reasonable.

Mammoth   Exabyte's Mammoth drive is another viable option for higher-capacity storage. The 5.25 " half-height Mammoth drives can read almost all of the earlier versions of Exabyte 8mm tapes in addition to the higher 20/40 GB tapes they were designed to use. The Mammoth drives are also available in library systems, which can store terabytes of data. The Mammoth tape drive cleans the read and write heads automatically at every load and unload. It has a good transfer rate, 180MB per minute, making it plenty fast for backups. The cost is still quite significant, ranging from around $1,000 for the 14/28 GB drives to around $11,000 or more for the 1.2/2.4 TB multidrive Mammoth2 models.

Robotic Systems   The emerging robotic systems vary widely in storage capacity and degree of automation. At the low end are auto-loading tape libraries that hold around six tapes and feed them into a single drive as guided by a scripted set of instructions. These are not uncommon and make backups a great deal easier when the backups don't fit on a single tape. Beyond these are several levels of complexity. At the top are completely robotic systems, which require no human intervention for day-to-day operations. There are so many different types that we'll leave their exploration to you.

Tape Interfaces

The technology underlying the tape mechanism is certainly important in evaluating tape technologies, but another issue is also quite important: how the tape interfaces with the computer. There are five interfaces that have been or are being used:

Floppy   The floppy interface was used on many inexpensive tape drives from the mid-1990s and earlier. Early versions of these drives were generally plagued by poor performance and weren't very dependable. When they did work, they were very slow, rewound the tapes so often that they tended to wear out quickly, and in the process ran quite hot. Linux supports floppy tape through the `ftape` utility. `ftape` supports drives that conform to the QIC-117 and one of the QIC-80, QIC-40, QIC-3010, and QIC-3020 standards. Few floppy-interfaced tape drives exceed 1.6GB in capacity, which is frustrating with modern hard-drive sizes.

Parallel-port   The parallel port was used by many early external tape drives. It's got many of the same drawbacks as the floppy interface, and has fallen into disfavor. Like floppy-interfaced drives, parallel-port drives are supported by the `ftape` package.

USB   The *Universal Serial Bus (USB)* is starting to be used by some low-end external tape drives. USB speed is limited, however, so high-speed drives typically don't use it. Linux's USB support is quite limited in the 2.2.*x* kernels, but is better in the 2.4.*x* kernels. USB tape drives in Linux are still very new, so you may encounter problems with such devices.

IDE/ATAPI   The IDE port is becoming popular for low-end internal tape drives. These devices are often referred to as *Advanced Technology Attachment Packet Interface (ATAPI)* drives. ATAPI units don't suffer from the speed problems of floppy, parallel-port, or USB devices.

SCSI   The *Small Computer System Interface (SCSI)* port has long been a favorite for mid-range and high-end tape drives. SCSI supports both internal and external devices, and many high-end tape drives are available *only* in SCSI form. Unfortunately, SCSI drives are often more expensive than their ATAPI counterparts.

As a general rule, the best interface type is SCSI, because it's fastest and supports the largest number of devices per interface (7 or 15, depending upon interface type, compared to 4 for IDE/ATAPI). IDE/ATAPI drives are acceptable for workstations or if you're working on a tight budget. In the future, USB drives might be acceptable if you need portability, but in early 2001, USB tape drives and Linux are an unproven combination. Floppy- and parallel-interfaced drives are old news. You might use one to back up a low-capacity system if you happen to have the drive available, but for most serious applications, something newer is more appropriate.

CD-R and CD-RW

A CD-ROM is a Write Once/Read Many (WORM) storage medium in which microscopic pits are inscribed on the aluminum layer of a plastic disc to represent data. Once inscribed, the tracks formed by the pits are read optically by a noncontact head, which scans in a roughly radial pattern as the disc spins just above it. The head moves at a constant linear velocity, thereby assuring a constant data rate. Since the head speed is constant, the disc must rotate at a decreasing rate as the data track is scanned from its beginning near the center of the disc to its end nearer the outer edge of the disc. (Many modern CD-ROM drives don't use a constant linear velocity, though, and so have variable data transfer rates from different parts of the disc.)

A CD writer (CD-R or CD-ROM Recordable) is simply a CD reader with a laser strong enough to burn optical equivalents of CD-ROM pits into a special CD-R disc that's coated with an optical dye. Some of these discs are intended to be multisession, meaning that you can write some portion of the disc and then fill the remaining space at a later time, while others are written to and cannot be supplemented later. On a CD-RW (CD-Rewritable), the laser can not only write data, it can erase the disc, leaving a clean surface as if the CD-RW hadn't been used. In any of the above forms, these discs are quite vulnerable to scratching and heat damage.

Writable CD-ROM's are becoming quite popular for backups as well. CD-RW discs only work in players equipped to recognize them. There is an increase in cost for the CD-RW discs over the CD-R discs. The price for a 50-pack of CD-R discs with jewel cases starts at around $19. The price for 50 CD-RW disks with jewel cases starts around $28 and goes up as the discs are certified at higher write speeds. CD-ROMs hold approximately 650MB of data, so you'll probably need several to do a full backup.

CD-R and CD-RW are relatively low-cost options for backup. Since each disc will only hold up to 650MB of data, and since hard-disk capacities are always going to exceed that, you are stuck changing discs when one gets full or buying a CD changer in addition to the writer and the media. This eliminates any real cost savings over tape. We prefer to use tape or some other high-capacity option.

Other Alternatives

Alternatives to tape and CD-R include floptical disks, Bernoulli boxes, and other removable drives. The perfect system would combine fast random access, dependability, and a high storage capacity.

Some Oldies

As hard drives continue to increase in capacity, innovation in backup systems is required to keep up. As a system administrator, you might find that you have older backup equipment that doesn't quite handle the job. You might also find that the word "free" overrides any arguments for a new backup system, requiring you to become familiar with the old one. These are a few of the legacy storage devices still in common use.

Floptical Drives   Floptical disk drives, intended to replace standard floppy disks, read and write data with lasers that are much more precise than the drive heads used on a standard floppy drive. They use a 3.5" Very High Density disk, which looks like a regular 3.5" floppy but has a capacity of up to 21MB. The floptical drives will also read the old 720KB and 1.44MB floppies, allowing you to replace your old 3.5" floppy drive instead of sacrificing an additional drive bay. Another selling point is that the 21MB disks don't require a proprietary format like most of the removable storage drives. Unfortunately, these drives didn't really catch on and didn't provide enough space-per-dollar to really take over the market.

Bernoulli Drives   The Bernoulli drive takes cartridges that are the dimensions of a 5.25" floppy disk but over 0.25" thick. They have a rigid case that makes them one of the most durable formats of removable storage available. Bernoulli cartridges hold 230MB of uncompressed data, which gave them an edge over the 120 megabyte QIC tapes that were common when this technology first hit the market. Largely due to increased capacity of modern tape drives, the Bernoulli drives are no longer being produced, so they probably should be avoided unless you already have one.

Removable Drives   Removable drives like the Iomega Jaz and Zip drives may be used for backup and were commonly used in this way until recent hard-drive capacities made them less practical. The first version of the Jaz drive had a 1GB capacity, and the newer version doubles that. Jaz 2 uses an UltraSCSI interface, which connects to a PCI bus, an ATAPI interface that connects to the IDE chain, a PCMCIA interface, or a parallel port. Being SCSI, these drives work with Mac computers too. The Zip drive uses either a 100MB disk or a 250MB disk. Although it is useful for transferring files that are too large to be held on a floppy between computers, it can hardly be considered a viable backup option.

Magneto-optical Drives   Another older technology is the magneto-optical drive. This type of rewritable drive uses a laser to heat the disk to a point where a magnet can change the location's polarity. A disk location that hasn't been "hit" represents a 0, and a location that has been hit represents a 1. This process requires two passes of the drive head, and the combination of laser and magnet makes the drive head very heavy. An improvement on this method, Light Intensity Moduled Direct OverWrite (LIMDOW), builds the magnet into the disk itself. While the capacity of the original magneto-optical disks topped out at about 2.6GB, the LIMDOW technology could more than quadruple this, making the technology potentially useful in creating backups. The largest capacity we have seen is 5.2GB, offered by some Hewlett Packard and Sony drives. These drives do have large price tags, however, starting at around $1000.

Media Storage

Media storage is important, too. Magnetic media are vulnerable to heat, moisture, and electrical or magnetic proximity and have a tendency to degrade over time (just as VCR tapes do). Magneto-optical drives, on the other hand, are a combination of both magnetic and optical technology. The fact that they store data magnetically altered with the help of a heating laser makes the medium more resistant to heat or electrical damage, so storage requirements are less restrictive. Purely optical technologies (CD-R and CD-RW) are the most likely to be of archival quality. CD-R storage lifetimes are estimated at 10–100 years, depending upon dye type and who's doing the estimating. Certainly locations that are characteristically damp, excessively dry, or very hot would pose a hazard to any storage media and should probably be avoided when planning media storage.

Hierarchical Storage Management

In many situations, the media are stored on-site. As unlikely as it sounds, if the building burned down, both the computers and the backups could be destroyed. Think of the World Trade Center bombing if you need an example. If it is possible, you should store at least some portion of the backups in a different location. One option would be to store the monthly and incremental backups on site but to store the annual backups off-site. This doesn't give you 100 percent recoverability, but it is a step in the right direction. Another option is to store weeks 1 and 2 on-site, weeks 3 and 4 off-site, and then to swap every second week. Look at the risks and the cost in employee hours to rebuild what would be lost, and make a smart decision about where to store the backups.

True hierarchical storage management is not limited to spreading the backups across multiple storage locations. It also provides some automated process by which files (on the hard drives) that are no longer used (static files) can be moved to tape or to some optical medium. This creates usable space on the hard drives in addition to meeting archiving needs.

For example, consider the fictitious WeAin'tThem Inc., a software company that creates and markets its own operating system. WeAin'tThem has a working (development) version of its software and a copy of the last released version for use in customer support. It does development work on a server system, which holds the developing software version (2.5), compilers and libraries that it requires, and the last released version (2.4). As the development of new modules continues, the disk fills up. When the developing software is released, version 2.4 is archived to tape, and a new development version (3.0) is begun. Now the system has versions 2.5 and 3.0 on it, and version 2.4 is safely tucked away in case a customer who had chosen not to upgrade due to hardware incompatibility needs customer support.

Backup Commands and Utilities

In the next section, we'll discuss various backup commands at your disposal. We'll look at utilities that facilitate the handling of the hardware itself, command-line backup commands, and GUI-based backup packages. Most of them are included with the main Linux distributions; the others can be downloaded from Internet sites.

Tape Utilities

Tape utilities are programs that help manage tape access and usage. These aren't backup programs, in fact they often do not write to the tape at all; instead, they perform functions necessary to the backup process like finding a specific position on the tape or allowing you to retension the tape.

mt   The mt utility performs a number of tape operations, such as moving to or finding a specified position on the tape, setting or checking the tape's tension, setting or checking the tape's compression, setting or checking the block size or density, and erasing the tape. The mt command is used when you need to rewind the tape prior to writing to it, to erase the tape, to reposition the head before a write, or to auto-eject the tape when the backup has been completed.

If you are using QIC tapes, you should always retension the tape before you write to it. For some reason, QIC tapes are much more sensitive to tension than are other tapes. The command to do this with a nonrewinding tape drive is:

```
# mt -f /dev/nftape reten
```

> **NOTE** This discussion uses /dev/nftape as the tape device. You may need to use another device file, as discussed shortly. In any event, mt is normally used with *nonrewinding* device files, which do not rewind the tape automatically after each access. *Rewinding* devices, by contrast, automatically rewind the tape after each access. The former are used when you want to store more than one backup per tape, and the latter are used when you want to write a single backup to a tape or access only the first backup that already exists on a tape.

The mt utility is also used to erase the tape. You'll usually need to do this before using ftape with a tape that was preformatted since ftape sometimes doesn't like the formatting that is on a new tape.

```
# mt -f /dev/nftape erase
```

The mt utility is useful when you want to move forward on the tape. The following sample command will move two files forward on the tape:

```
# mt -f /dev/nftape fsf 2
```

> **NOTE** In reference to a tape drive, a *file* is a single backup, which may contain many files from the disk. Think of it as a tarball stored on tape (which it may in fact be). You might store multiple backups on one tape, particularly when doing incremental or differential backups.

To put more than one backup on a single tape, you must use the mt utility with its eof keyword. The following command moves the tape just past the end of the written data, where the next backup can begin. Any attempt to read the tape after issuing this command will result in errors, but it's necessary if you want to write data to a tape without overwriting existing data.

```
# mt -f /dev/nftape eof
```

rmt The rmt utility is used by the remote dump and restore utilities to manipulate a tape drive located on a remote backup server in the same way that mt does with local tape drives. The rmt utility accepts requests specific to the manipulation of magnetic tapes, performs the requested manipulation, and then responds with a status indicator. rmt is not usually started separately but is rather used with an rexec or rcmd call, both of which are used to execute a command on a remote server.

Tape Device Names

Backup commands invariably require you to identify the tape device by name. The tape device name will vary depending upon the interface to which it is connected and the number of devices on that chain. There are IDE tape devices, SCSI tape devices, and `ftape` devices (both floppy-interfaced and parallel-interfaced). USB devices work like SCSI devices.

IDE/ATAPI Tape devices that use the IDE interface are accessed through the /dev/ht0 (rewinding) and /dev/nht0 (nonrewinding) device files. If you have more than one IDE/ATAPI drive, change the 0 to 1 or above to address the second and subsequent drives.

A modern computer motherboard usually will support two IDE chains, although they may not both be enabled in the system's BIOS. Each chain supports up to two devices (hard disks, tape drives, and so on). Historically, the motherboard did not provide the IDE connections itself but relied on the existence of an IDE controller card. Few systems use separate IDE controllers now. Although it is possible to accommodate additional IDE devices by adding an IDE controller card to a system that has two IDE chains on the motherboard, the requirement for each controller to have a unique interrupt makes this difficult to configure. For this reason, you're better off using SCSI if you need more than four devices.

SCSI The first SCSI tape drive is attached to /dev/st0 if it is rewinding or /dev/nst0 if it is nonrewinding. To refer to subsequent drives, increment the number as needed. Because SCSI host adapters support 7 or 15 devices, depending upon the adapter type, and each adapter uses a single interrupt, SCSI is well suited for systems with lots of disk and tape drives.

ftape An `ftape` device uses one of four methods of access depending upon the floppy tape drive itself. The /dev/rft0 (rewinding) and /dev/nrft0 (nonrewinding) devices provide access to the first device; incrementing the number provides access to additional `ftape`-driven drives. For compatibility, /dev/ftape and /dev/nftape are symbolic links to /dev/rft0 and /dev/nrft0, respectively. These device filenames work for both floppy-interfaced and parallel-port-interfaced drives driven via `ftape`.

Old 3.0*x* versions of `ftape` supported driver-level compression via the /dev/zqft0 and /dev/nzqft0 device files. This feature was removed from the 4.0 and later releases of the software, however, in order to provide improved error-recovery features.

CD-R and CD-RW Backup Tools

Archiving data to CD-R or CD-RW (subsequently referred to collectively as *CD-R* for brevity's sake) is an option if you have a small amount of data to store, but isn't really helpful when you're backing up an entire network. If you are doing incremental backups on a system that doesn't have many large files changing, CD-R might be an option. Sometimes, CD-R is useful for the archival backups mentioned earlier in this chapter. The long shelf life of CD-R media makes them a good choice for long-term archival storage, in fact. For larger backup jobs, though, tape is generally superior.

CD-R Commands

Writing to a CD-R is a two-step process:

- The data (whether data files or audio files) must be accumulated and assembled into an *image*, which also includes any required formatting information.
- The created files must be written to the CD-R, usually with the utility cdrecord.

NOTE You'll see later in this chapter that some GUI-based utilities perform these two functions without clearly identifying them as separate steps.

A certain amount of the free space on a CD-R must be reserved for storing the ISO-9660 filesystem (usually a few megabytes). This format, the standard file system for CD-ROMs, exists in three levels. Level 1 uses the 8+3 file naming convention and requires that the data be contiguous. Directory trees must not be nested more than eight levels deep under Level 1. The filenames on these discs can be viewed under both Linux and DOS. Level 2 allows longer filenames, and as a result, DOS may not be able to read all the files on a Level 2 disc. Level 3 does away with the requirement that the data be contiguous, keeping the less-restrictive file naming convention, and again DOS may not be able to read all its files. In order to make the ISO-9660 format more useful in the Unix world, Rock Ridge extensions were added. These extensions define a way to handle mixed-case filenames and symbolic links. If this disc is read on a system that doesn't have the Rock Ridge extensions, the filenames won't display in their long format. Microsoft developed a different way of storing long filenames on CD-ROM and CD-R discs, known as *Joliet*. You can create a Joliet CD-R from Linux, but for storing Linux files, Rock Ridge is superior, because Joliet doesn't support Linux file ownership or permissions. Creating a mixed Rock Ridge/Joliet CD-R is possible and useful in a mixed-OS environment.

mkisofs The mkisofs command creates the ISO-9660 filesystem image to be written to the CD by the cdrecord utility. This image includes the data files as well as the formatting information. The mkisofs utility does not, however, contain any CD-R driver code and therefore *does not* write the image to the CD-R. The developers chose this approach mainly to allow users to test an image from the hard drive before writing it to the CD-ROM. Historically, writing an image as it is being created was also potentially unreliable on slower computers.

System Optimization

PART 3

To create a CD-R image file, you must pass mkisofs the name of a directory to be turned into a CD-R, the name of an output file, and any of a large number of optional parameters. A fairly basic example is:

```
$ mkisofs -r -J -o output-file.iso /source/directory
```

This example creates an image file called output-file.iso from the contents of /source/directory. The -r parameter adds Rock Ridge extensions (with some changes to permissions and ownership to help make the disc portable), and the -J parameter adds a Joliet filesystem. The mkisofs man page includes extensive discussion of the many additional parameters available for this utility.

You may use the loopback capability of Linux to check whether the image created by mkisofs has a directory structure and permissions that match the original files. Loopback is the capability that allows you to mount a file as if it were a disk partition. To do this, use the following command, inserting the correct name for the created image and the correct path to the mount point you wish to mount the image on:

```
# mount -t iso9660 -o loop cd_image /mnt/tmp
```

TIP   We typically create a */mnt/tmp* file for mounting partitions or files that are not so permanently mounted as CD-ROM drives and floppy drives. You can use it to mount anything temporarily, regardless of device type.

Compare */mnt/tmp* to wherever your original files are located until you are convinced that the contents are the same. Then use the following command to unmount the CD-R image that you've created:

```
# umount /mnt/tmp
```

cdrecord   Once you've made and tested an image file, you'll use the cdrecord utility to actually write the CD-ROM image to the blank CD-R. cdrecord was designed for use with SCSI or ATAPI CD-recorders. It can write data, audio, mixed, and multisession discs and supports most CD recorders available. cdrecord is run from the command line and has a great many options. The man page is quite helpful, but the process is not simple. The simplest case, a pure data image copied to with an ISO-9660 filesystem on a sufficiently quick system using the device at SCSI target ID 6 as its target, allows you to run the command as follows:

```
# cdrecord -v speed=2 dev=0,6,0 cd_image
```

For better readability, the SCSI settings of the writer are stored in three environment variables: SCSI_BUS, SCSI_ID, and SCSI_LUN.

If you use cdrecord to overwrite a CD-RW, you must add the option blank=*blanktype* to erase the old content. The program can blank the CD-RW in several different ways, as summarized in Table 11.4.

Table 11.4   Options for Blanking a CD-RW Disc with cdrecord

blanktype **value**	**Description**
help	Displays a list of possible blanking types.
all	Completely erases the entire disc. This may take a long time.
fast	Erases key data structures on the disc; fast but incomplete.
track	Erases a single track.
unreserve	Unreserves a reserved track.
trtail	Erases the tail of a track.
unclose	Uncloses last session; allows writing additional information to a previously finished writing session.
session	Erases the last session.

On a sufficiently speedy machine, the output of mkisofs can be directed into cdrecord using a pipe. First you need to obtain the image size. To do this, use this form of the mkisofs command:

```
# mkisofs -R -q -print-size cd_image
```

Next, pipe the mkisofs command into the cdrecord command, passing the image size to cdrecord as shown:

```
# mkisofs  -R  cd_image  | cdrecord -v fs=6m speed=2 dev=0,6,0 -
```

X-CD-Roast   X-CD-Roast, illustrated in Figure 11.4, is an X-based front end for CD programs like mkisofs, cdparanoia, and cdrecord. It gives a nice interface from which to run these programs, which are usually command-line driven. This program is growing quite popular with Linux users and is available from http://www.erfurt.thur.de/ak/xcdroast.html.

Figure 11.4   The X-CD-Roast main screen

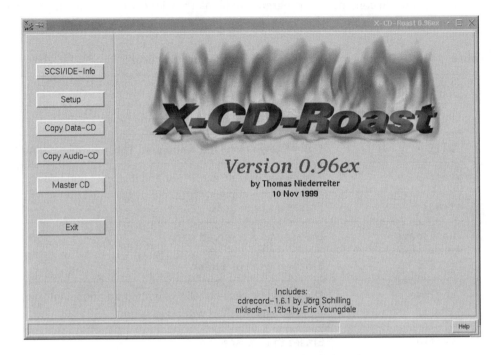

Device Access

You may have noticed in the example of `cdrecord` that the command didn't take a conventional device filename. Instead, this utility takes a SCSI device specification in the form

   bus,id,lun

where *bus* is the SCSI bus (0 on systems with just one SCSI host adapter), *id* is the SCSI ID number of the CD-R drive, and *lun* is the logical unit (LUN) of the drive (almost always 0). This identification ultimately leads the utility to use the *SCSI generic* devices (`/dev/sgx`, where *x* is a letter from a forward). Unlike SCSI devices for tape drives, hard disks, and so on, the SCSI generic devices are designed to allow access to any type of SCSI device, which is why `cdrecord` uses them—these devices allow the sort of low-level access that's required for writing to a CD-R drive. You must be sure that the SCSI generic support is compiled into your kernel (or available as a kernel module). This option is called SCSI Generic Support in the SCSI Support kernel configuration menu.

This all works well for SCSI devices, but what about IDE/ATAPI CD-R drives? For these, you must turn on a Linux kernel feature that allows an IDE device to masquerade as a SCSI device. The option is in the Block Devices kernel configuration menu and is called SCSI Emulation Support. Once this is compiled and active, your CD-R drive will turn up as a SCSI generic device.

NOTE Chapter 8 covers kernel compilation in more detail.

Most CD-R drives can be accessed as ordinary CD-ROM drives for read-only access. For SCSI devices, the appropriate device filenames are `/dev/scd0` (or higher numbers), and for IDE/ATAPI drives, the device filenames are `/dev/hda` through `/dev/hdd` or above, depending upon the chain to which the device is attached and its master/slave status. This read-only CD-ROM access does *not* help in making backups, but it can be useful in restoring data from a CD-R you've created.

Linux Backup and Restore Tools

Linux provides several command-line tools you can use to back up files: `dump` and `rdump`, `tar`, `cpio`, and `afio`. There are also several GUI third-party packages, which we'll look at shortly. Although some system administrators prefer to have a GUI where they can just click a few buttons to kick off the backup, many administrators are accustomed to working from the command line and find that method faster. Additionally, commands like `afio` allow you to Telnet to the computer controlling the backup, use the `ps` command to find out how long the backup process has been running, and use that information to determine how much longer it will take. Or you can incorporate these commands into a script and have that script page you when the process completes. We'll give you both options, and you can choose.

dump

The `dump` utility (which comes with most Linux distributions, including Red Hat) looks at the specified filesystem and determines what needs to be backed up as determined by a specified `dump` level. The `dump` format is inode-based, unlike that of `tar`, `cpio`, and `afio`. The `dump` format requires that all directories be written to the backup before other files in the backup. The directories are written in ascending inode order, and then the files are added in ascending inode order as well. The command must specify the incremental level for the dump and the subset of the filesystem to act upon.

NOTE   Because dump operates on a lower level of filesystem access than do most other backup utilities, any given dump program must have explicit support for any filesystem you use. The standard Linux dump utility handles ext2 filesystems, but not FAT filesystems or the experimental journaling filesystems described in Chapter 10. Trying to use dump on such filesystems won't cause problems, but neither will it work. Linux's dump may eventually be upgraded to handle more filesystems, though.

Basic *dump* Operation

The dump command's basic syntax is this:

   dump [-*level*] [-b *blocksize*] [-B *records*] [-f *file*] [-u] *directory*

The meanings of these parameters are as follows:

   -*level*   The incremental level.

   -b *blocksize*   The size (in bytes) of a dump block.

   -B *records*   The size of the tape in dump blocks. Combined, blocksize and records allow dump to handle tapes that are smaller than the data to be backed up; if dump must back up more than *blocksize* × *records* bytes, it pauses when it reaches this limit and prompts you to change tapes.

   -f *file*   The file to which the backup should be written—normally a tape device file, as described earlier.

   -u   This parameter causes dump to store data about its backup history in /etc/ dumpdates. Without this parameter, incremental backups won't work correctly.

   directory   The directory or filesystem device file to be backed up.

The incremental dump backs up a file if it has changed since the previously recorded backup. A standard dump incremental scheme begins at level 0 and extends to level 9, 0 being a full dump and 1–9 being incremental. Each incremental level backs up all files changed since the last backup of a lower incremental level. If you perform a series of dump operations (say, one per day) using the same non-0 dump level, the result is a series of incremental backups, as described earlier in this chapter. If you increase the dump level with each backup (say, 1 on Monday, 2 on Tuesday, and so on), the result is a series of differential backups, as described earlier in this chapter.

dump in Action

Suppose you want to implement an incremental backup strategy in which you do a full backup on Sundays and back up all files changed since Sunday every other day of the week. The dump commands for the Sunday would be something like this, assuming that you need to back up /, /usr, and /var to a SCSI tape unit at /dev/nst0:

```
# dump 0uf /dev/nst0 /
```

```
# dump 0uf /dev/nst0 /usr
```

```
# dump 0uf /dev/nst0 /var
```

The dump commands for each of the remaining days of the week would look like this:

```
# dump 5uf /dev/nst0 /
```

```
# dump 5uf /dev/nst0 /usr
```

```
# dump 5uf /dev/nst0 /var
```

You could also use any other non-0 dump level for the incremental backups. A level of 5 gives you the flexibility of performing an unscheduled differential backup by using a higher level, should there be some critical files you need to back up. You can also perform an incremental backup that resets the normal incremental file count should you make a lot of changes early in the week that you don't want to subsequently back up again. Of course, if you deviate from your usual backup schedule, you should carefully label your backup tapes to prevent confusion.

As an example, let's look at the output from a dump of /usr/local/bin, because a relatively small directory makes the output manageable. The command we'll use is:

```
# dump 0uf /dev/nst0 /usr/local/bin
```

The output looks like this:

```
DUMP: Date of this level 0 dump: Thu Sep 21 08:09:35 2000
DUMP: Date of last level 0 dump: the epoch
DUMP: Dumping /dev/hdb1 (/) to /dev/nst0
DUMP: mapping (Pass I) [regular files]
DUMP: mapping (Pass II) [directories]
DUMP: estimated 120147 tape blocks.
DUMP: Volume 1 started at: Thu Sep 21 08:09:41 2000
DUMP: dumping (Pass III) [directories]
DUMP: dumping (Pass IV) [regular files]
DUMP: DUMP: 230552 tape blocks on 1 volumes(s)
DUMP: finished in 148 seconds, throughput 1557 KBytes/sec
```

System Optimization

PART 3

```
DUMP: Volume 1 completed at: Thu Sep 21 08:12:09 2000
DUMP: Volume 1 took 0:02:28
DUMP: Volume 1 transfer rate: 1557 KB/s
DUMP: level 0 dump on Thu Sep 21 08:09:35 2000
DUMP: DUMP: Date of this level 0 dump: Thu Sep 21 08:09:35 2000
DUMP: DUMP: Date this dump completed:  Thu Sep 21 08:12:09 2000
DUMP: DUMP: Average transfer rate: 1557 KB/s
DUMP: Closing /dev/nst0
DUMP: DUMP IS DONE
```

This output is pretty self-explanatory. The dump wrote 230,552 blocks onto one tape in 148 seconds.

Dumping Remotely

It's possible to specify a remote backup server with dump by modifying the form of the dump device filename. Instead of a simple device file, you must specify the backup server's name, a colon, and the device filename on that server, thus:

   # **dump 0uf buserver:/dev/nst0 /usr**

On some networks, though, this can result in a slow backup. A better option may be to pipe the backup through rsh:

   # **dump 0uf - /usr | rsh buserver dd of=/dev/rmt0**

One problem with a remote backup like this is that the backup server must be running rshd (or in.rshd), the remote shell daemon. This utility has great potential as a security hole, particularly on any system that's connected to the Internet. What's worse, you must normally run rshd with its -h parameter to allow root access, which increases the potential for security problems. On the whole, it's best to use this access method only when the backup server is well-protected behind a firewall. Ideally, the backup server should have no other network duties, should have no users aside from those necessary to maintain it, and should be devoid of any software that a cracker might find useful in penetrating your network, should the worst occur.

Historically, remote use of dump has been through a separate rdump utility. On most Linux systems today, rdump is a symbolic link to the ordinary dump utility, which has acquired rdump's network functionality.

restore

Use the `restore` utility to extract a backup that was made with `dump`. `restore` has two modes: interactive and noninteractive. The interactive mode allows you to select one or more files to restore, while the noninteractive mode restores the entire backup. You must use a nonrewinding tape device if you have multiple archives.

Restoring Interactively

Let's assume that you need to restore `/usr/local/bin` from the backup we made earlier with `dump`. Load the appropriate backup tape and run the following command:

```
# restore -i -f /dev/nst0
```

The –i flag tells `restore` to start an interactive session. When this command executes, you will get a `restore>` prompt. Use the `ls` command to see what is on the tape. Here it indicates that the `local` directory structure is on the tape. It doesn't list what's under `local`, simply the directory itself.

```
restore> ls

.:

local/
```

Since we know that the `bin` directory, which contains what we want to restore, is under `local`, we can type `add bin` at the `restore` prompt to add the `bin` directory to the list of items to be restored and then type `extract`:

```
restore> add bin

restore> extract
```

If there had been multiple archives on a single tape, you'd use the –s option to specify which you wanted to restore. For example, the command to restore from the second archive on the tape is:

```
# restore -i -s 2 -f /dev/nrst0
```

Noninteractive Restore

To restore files as a batch, first change directory to the location where you'd like to restore; the paths used are relative. If the tape contains multiple archives, you may use the `mt` command described earlier in this chapter to find the correct tape position, or you can use the –s option to restore as we did in the interactive example.

You can get a listing of files on the tape by using the –t option. To look for a specific file, use:

```
# restore -t -f /dev/nst0 local/bin/ntpd
```

System Optimization

PART 3

The response should look like this:

```
Dump    date: Thu Sep 21 11:38:21 2000
Dumped from: the epoch
Level 0 dump of /usr on opus:/dev/hdb6 (dir /local/bin)
Label: none
    375916     ./local/bin/ntpd
```

If you want a listing of all the files on the tape, omit the last argument as follows:

```
# restore -t -f /dev/nst0
```

Here is an excerpt of the results:

```
Dump    date: Thu Sep 21 11:38:21 2000
Dumped from: the epoch
Level 0 dump of /usr on opus:/dev/hdb6 (dir /local/bin)
Label: none
        2     .
    358337     ./local
    374625     ./local/bin
    375916     ./local/bin/ntpd
    376041     ./local/bin/sudo
    375917     ./local/bin/ntpdate
    375918     ./local/bin/ntptimeset
    375919     ./local/bin/ntpdc
```

You may list specific files to restore using the –x option as follows:

```
# restore -x /usr/local/bin -f /dev/nst0
You have not read any tapes yet.
Unless you know which volume your file(s) are on you should
start with the last volume and work towards the first.
Specify next volume #: 1
set owner/mode for '.'? [yn] y
```

Remote Restore

As with dump, restore can be used to restore files from a tape device in a remote backup server computer. The backup must have been done with an inode-based backup utility like dump or rdump. The specification of the device must be preceded by a colon, as shown below:

```
# restore rf buserver:/dev/nst0
```

Historically, remote restores have been done through a separate rrestore command. On modern Linux systems, this command is a symbolic link to the ordinary restore command, which has acquired network functionality.

tar

tar is one of the older tape archiving tools, but it is probably the most portable. Solaris tar, as ported to Linux, backs up to tape or a file on a file-by-file basis, excluding special files such as device files. GNU tar (included in all Linux distributions) is better in that it does back up device files. One of the primary problems with tar, especially problematic with compressed tar archives, is error recovery. Corrupted tar backups typically lose hundreds of kilobytes of data before being able to "resynchronize" and begin restoring data again. If the backup becomes corrupted, compressed tar archives cannot be recovered at all since the archive is made up of one big compressed image of the archived files. While this provides for greater compression than if each were compressed separately, any corruption of the file makes the entire archive unusable.

Basic *tar* Features

tar does not have any compression functionality built into it but instead uses the external gzip or compress utilities to provide this feature. In addition to the data recovery problems, another disadvantage to a gzipped tar archive is that you cannot add a file to an existing archive, and in order to extract an individual file from an existing archive, you must uncompress and search the entire archive. A less critical drawback to the tar program is its lack of any form of buffering. While buffering is not absolutely necessary to the creation of system backups, it significantly increases throughput and speeds up the process tremendously.

As you'll see if you check the man pages, tar is an enormous package, with many options. This book could easily devote a chapter to explaining how to use the tar package. Most of what you'll do, however, can be covered with a few common commands. Table 11.5 lists the primary tar commands, and Table 11.6 lists the qualifiers for these commands. Whenever you run tar, you use exactly one command and you usually use at least one qualifier.

Table 11.5 tar Commands

Command	Abbreviation	Purpose
--create	c	Creates an archive.
--concatenate	A	Appends tar files to an archive.
--append	r	Appends files to an archive.
--update	u	Appends files that are newer than those in an archive.
--diff or --compare	d	Compares an archive to files on disk.
--list	t	Lists archive contents.
--extract or --get	x	Extracts files from an archive.

Table 11.6 tar Qualifiers

Qualifier	Abbreviation	Purpose
--directory *dir*	C	Changes to directory *dir* before performing operations.
--file [*host*:]*file*	f	Uses file called *file* on computer called *host* as the archive file.
--listed-incremental *file*	g	Performs incremental backup or restore, using *file* as a list of previously archived files.
--one-file-system	l	Backs up or restores only one filesystem (partition).
--multi-volume	M	Creates or extracts a multi-tape archive.
--tape-length *N*	L	Changes tapes after *N* kilobytes.
--same-permissions	p	Preserves all protection information.

Table 11.6   tar Qualifiers *(continued)*

Qualifier	Abbreviation	Purpose
--absolute-paths	P	Retains the leading / on file-names.
--verbose	v	Lists all files read or extracted.
--verify	W	Verifies the archive after writing it.
--exclude *file*	(none)	Excludes *file* from the archive.
--exclude-from *file*	X	Excludes files listed in *file* from the archive.
--gzip or --ungzip	z	Processes the archive through gzip or gunzip.

Of the commands listed in Table 11.5, the most commonly used are --create, --extract, and --list. The most useful qualifiers from Table 11.6 are --file, --listed-incremental, --one-file-system, --same-permissions, --gzip, and --verbose.

WARNING   The tar --one-file-system option is critically important to backups. Ordinarily, tar backs up everything under the directory it's been given as input. Although this works fine if you feed tar the name of a directory that has nothing mounted on it, it can cause problems for certain types of mounts. For example, if you tell tar to back up the root directory (that is, /), the program backs up everything mounted on that directory or any subdirectory, including NFS or Samba shares served by other machines. Worse, tar also backs up the Linux /proc filesystem, which is a virtual filesystem that represents the computer's status, including all its memory. At restoration time, tar tries to overwrite the /proc filesystem's contents, which is likely to cause serious problems, possibly even including a system crash. For this reason, it's best to always use --one-file-system and feed tar the names of each partition you want to back up.

The tar command backs up files to or from *files*. Because Linux treats hardware devices as if they were files, you can tell tar to back up to or from an appropriate hardware device file, in order to use that device directly. (This approach works best for tape devices; for CD-R and CD-RW drives, it's necessary to pipe tar's output through CD-R control software like cdrecord, and for disk devices, it's best to store the archive as a regular file on a filesystem, although you *can* store the archive "raw" to the device.)

A Sample *tar* Operation

A typical tar command to back up a computer looks like this:

```
# tar --create --verbose --gzip --one-file-system --same-permissions
      ➡ --file /dev/st0 / /home /usr/local
```

This command can be expressed somewhat more succinctly using command abbreviations:

```
# tar cvzlpf /dev/st0 / /home /usr/local
```

In either form, this tar command backs up the root (/), /home, and /usr/local filesystems to /dev/st0 (the first SCSI tape device). The assumption here is that the computer has three Linux partitions, corresponding to the three specified directories. A system with different partitions would need to specify the appropriate local partitions.

For an incremental or differential backup, you could add the --listed-incremental parameter, as in this example:

```
# tar cvzlpf /dev/st0 --listed-incremental /root/increments / /home
      ➡ /usr/local
```

This command stores information on the incremental backup in the /root/increments file, and uses the contents of that file to designate which files are to be backed up. To perform a series of incremental backups, you would issue the command as above. Before running another backup, you would make a copy of the increments file. After making the backup, overwrite the new increments file with the backup. This way, tar will back up the same files the next time you use this option, plus any additional ones that have changed. To perform a differential backup, you would leave the increments file alone and refer to it each time you do a backup. tar will then modify the increments file, and will back up only files changed since the last incremental backup.

If you want to create multiple archives on a single tape, you must use the mt command, described earlier in this chapter, in conjunction with a nonrewinding tape device. You can then step past existing archives to read or write second, third, and subsequent archives.

Archiving to a Local Directory

You can use tar to create compact archives of files that you can then move around, store on floppy disks or the like, and transfer over a network. The command

```
# tar cvzf archive.tgz /usr/local/bin
```

creates a compressed archive of the `/usr/local/bin` directory and names that archive `archive.tgz`. The archive is created in the directory from which the command was issued. The output looks something like this:

```
tar: Removing leading '/' from archive names
usr/local/bin/
usr/local/bin/gpg-check
usr/local/bin/gpg-encrypt
usr/local/bin/gpg-sign
usr/local/bin/gpg-sign+encrypt
```

The command `tar xvzf archive.tgz` uncompresses the archive and sends the output to a directory under the current directory; `tar` uses relative pathnames by default. If the `usr/local/bin` directory doesn't exist in the present working directory, it will be created there.

The command to read a listing of an archive's contents with `tar`, following the same format, is `tar tvzf archive.tgz`. The output will include the file paths and the equivalent of an `ls -l`.

If you wish to use full paths—to write to `/usr/local/bin` without regard to the directory from which the command was run—you can use the P qualifier. The resulting commands would be

```
# tar cvzPf archive.tgz /usr/local/bin
```

and

```
# tar xvzPf archive.tgz
```

The output would list the full paths instead of the relative paths listed earlier and would be identical for the archive and extract commands:

```
/usr/local/bin/
/usr/local/bin/gpg-check
/usr/local/bin/gpg-encrypt
/usr/local/bin/gpg-sign
/usr/local/bin/gpg-sign+encrypt
```

Unpacking this archive with the command we used before would put the files into `/usr/local/bin` instead of */current/directory*`/usr/local/bin`.

System
Optimization

PART 3

On occasion, you may want to move files from one location on a disk to another. You can use cp to do this, but cp tends to drop ownership and other information. Rather than remember the cp parameters to work around these problems, you may want to use tar. You can use a Linux pipe to do the job, tarring files to a process that untars them in another location, thus:

```
# cd /source-dir
# tar cpf - . | (cd /destination-dir; tar xpvf -)
```

The result of the preceding two commands is a duplication of the contents of /source-dir in /destination-dir, including ownership, permissions, symbolic links, and so on. This command can be very useful if you want to back up to a backup hard disk. If your system goes down, you can swap in the backup hard disk, boot with an emergency boot floppy, and be running the backup system in a matter of minutes.

Archiving to Another Computer Remotely

To write the archive to a file on another computer, you simply precede the archive name with the name of the computer followed by a colon. This option, like the remote dump access described earlier, uses the rshd or in.rshd daemon on the destination system, so you can access a remote tape drive directly. Thus the archival commands would be something like:

```
# tar cvzf remote:/dev/st0 /usr/local/bin
# tar xvzf remote:/dev/st0
```

Archiving to a Floppy Disk

Yes, Virginia, it is possible to back up your system to floppy disks, but it will be painful. Each floppy disk will hold 1.4MB of data. This technique is most useful for copying large files from one system to another using floppies, or copying files between Linux and other Unix systems that don't share common filesystems. By writing a tarball directly to floppy, you bypass the need for a filesystem. Assume that you have a file /tmp/biggraphic.gif, with a size of 1.88MB. Obviously this won't fit on a standard 3.5" floppy. You can use the tar command with the –M option as follows:

```
# tar -cvMf /dev/fd0 /tmp/biggraphic.gif
```

When the backup image reaches the floppy's capacity, you will be prompted for a new floppy:

```
Prepare volume #2 for /dev/fd0 and hit return:
```

Put the second floppy in the drive and press the Enter key, and tar will continue the backup process. Each time the floppy capacity is exceeded, you will get this same prompt with an appropriate volume number.

To extract the file from the floppies, put the first volume in the drive and use the following command:

```
# tar -xvMf /dev/fd0
```

You will be prompted to put in the subsequent floppies, as you were when the archive was written. Unfortunately, the tar command won't allow you to compress a multi-volume backup. If you attempt to do so, you will get the following error:

```
tar: Cannot use multi-volume compressed archives

tar: Error is not recoverable:  exiting now
```

Although tar will write to standard output with the -0 argument, it will not read a file list from standard input, unlike many other archiving utilities. Many consider this to be a major disadvantage. The next two archiving utilities, cpio and afio, have this capability.

cpio

The cpio utility, named for the cp command and input/output or I/O, was designed to have the advantages of both dump and tar, including the ability to backup and restore special files and to provide for the extraction of single files or directories from a cpio archive. Its primary use is to transfer files from one computer to another rather than archiving. However, because cpio reads from standard input and writes to standard output, it is a great candidate for scripted backups. Because the output may be redirected to either a file or a raw device, this command is quite versatile and is frequently used in place of tar. The use of cpio has dropped off somewhat with the advent of the afio tool.

Archiving to a Local Directory

Since cpio expects the list of files to archive to come from standard input, it is typically used with the find command. Input and output follow standard redirection rules. cpio uses the o argument to create an archive. Just as with tar, the i argument is used to unpack the archive and the t argument is used to list the contents of the archive.

Let's start with a simple example. To archive the files in the current directory into a file named archive.cpio, use the following command:

```
# find . | cpio -o  > archive.cpio
```

The output will look something like this:

```
cpio:  .: truncating inode number

cpio:  usr/local/bin: truncating inode number

cpio:  usr/local/bin/gpg-check: truncating inode number

cpio:  usr/local/bin/gpg-encrypt: truncating inode number
```

```
cpio:  usr/local/bin/gpg-sign: truncating inode number
cpio:  usr/local/bin/gpg-sign+encrypt: truncating inode number
```

To dump the archive to the current directory, use the i argument:

```
# cpio -i  < archive.cpio
```

The output of this command will be a count of the blocks written.

To obtain a listing of the files contained in the archive, use the t option as follows:

```
# cpio -t < archive.cpio
```

This command will output the list of the files that would be written out if the archive were dumped. The output would look like this:

```
cpio:  .
cpio:  usr/local/bin
cpio:  usr/local/bin/gpg-check
cpio:  usr/local/bin/gpg-encrypt
cpio:  usr/local/bin/gpg-sign
cpio:  usr/local/bin/gpg-sign+encrypt
```

Archiving to Tape

As with tar, this is the archiving operation you'll use for regular backups. To archive to tape instead of to a file on the same disk drive or network, replace the archive name with the device name of the tape drive. If the tape drive were the first device on the SCSI chain, the device name would be /dev/st0. The commands to write, retrieve, and list the files contained in the present working directory to that tape drive would be:

```
# find . > /dev/st0
# cpio -i < /dev/st0
# cpio -t < /dev/st0
```

The output will look pretty much the same as the example earlier.

Archiving to Another Computer Remotely

To make cpio write to another computer, you can use the -F parameter to specify a remote server name and filename on that server. This process uses the rshd or in.rshd daemon on the backup server. You can specify a tape device filename on the backup server to send data to that device. Thus the command would be something like:

```
# find . | cpio -o  -F buserver:/dev/st0
```

Archiving to a Floppy Disk

Because of the severely limited storage capacity, archiving to a floppy disk makes sense only for copying a few files, not for backing up a system. To write to a floppy, simply replace the tape device name with the device for the floppy, usually /dev/fd0. The resulting command would look like this:

```
# find . | cpio -o > /dev/fd0
```

To extract the file from the floppy, use the following command:

```
# cpio -i < /dev/fd0
```

To list the files on the floppy, use –t instead of –i.

afio

The afio utility ships with some, but not all, Linux distributions. It doesn't come with Red Hat 7.0, but is part of the Red Hat Power Tools package, and is readily available from Linux archive sites, including RPM Find (http://rpmfind.net/linux/RPM/AByName.html). Some administrators consider afio the most useful backup program, thanks to its compression algorithm. Instead of compressing the entire archive as one like tar, afio compresses the data file by file, so that if corruption occurs, no more than one or two files will be lost. The rest of the archive is recoverable even though compressed. When you've experienced the frustration of trying to restore a tarred archive and discovering after 30 minutes that the archive is corrupted, you'll really come to appreciate afio.

Another feature of afio that you'll come to appreciate is its double-buffering capability. afio uses a memory buffer to store data until a separate write process writes the data in the buffer out to the tape or other medium. This allows afio to continue working even if the tape drive can't keep up with the data stream. Tape drive wear caused by stops and starts is greatly reduced since the tape drive nearly always has data waiting to be written.

Archiving to a Local Directory

Since afio expects the list of files to archive to come from standard input, it is typically used with the find command. afio uses the -o argument to initiate a backup. Just as with tar, the -i argument is used to unpack the archive and the -t argument is used to list the contents of the archive.

Let's start with a simple example. To archive the files in the current directory to an archive named archive.afio, use the following command:

```
# find . | afio -o /root/archive.afio
```

> **_WARNING_** If you create an afio archive in the same directory you're backing up, the archive will contain an early copy of itself, increasing its size. It's therefore best to create the archive in some other directory.

To dump the archive to the current directory, use the -i argument:

```
# afio -i /root/archive.afio
```

To obtain a listing of the files contained in the archive, use the t option as follows:

```
# afio -t /root/archive.afio
```

To add compression to the mix, add the -Z option to the afio command line. To create a compressed archive, for instance, use the following command:

```
# find . | afio -oZ /root/archive.afio.gz
```

Archiving to Tape

In order to archive to tape instead of just to a file on the same disk drive, the archive name should be replaced by the device name of the tape drive. If the tape drive were the first device on the SCSI chain, the device name would be /dev/st0. The resulting commands would be:

```
# find /usr/local/bin | afio -o /dev/st0
```

```
# afio -t /dev/st0
```

```
# cd /; afio -i /dev/st0
```

Archiving to Another Computer Remotely

To write the archive to a file on another computer or to read an archive stored on another computer, you simply precede the archive name with the name of the computer followed by a colon. This function, as with similar functions of dump, tar, and cpio, relies upon the rshd or in.rshd daemon on the backup server computer. Thus the archival commands would be something like:

```
# find /usr/local/bin | afio -o buserver:/dev/st0
```

```
# afio -t buserver:/dev/st0
```

```
# cd /; afio -i buserver:/dev/st0
```

Archiving to a Floppy

Again, this operation is primarily for backing up a few files, not whole systems. If you remember from the tar example, each floppy disk will hold roughly 1.44MB of data. Assume that you have that same file, /tmp/biggraphic.gif, which is 1.88MB. The afio command will automatically make multiple volumes if it senses that the current floppy's capacity has been reached. No special arguments must be passed, although this example uses the -v parameter to increase the verbosity of messages from the program:

```
# ls /tmp/biggraphic.gif | afio -ov /dev/fd0
```

When the backup image reaches the floppy's capacity, you will be prompted to put in a new floppy as shown:

```
"/dev/fd0" [offset 1m+421k+0]: No space left on device

afio: Ready for volume 2 on /dev/fd0

afio: "quit" to abort, anything else to proceed. >
```

Put the next floppy in the drive and press the Enter key, and afio will continue the backup process. You'll see something like this to tell you it's continuing:

```
afio: "/dev/fd0" [offset 1m+421k+0]: Continuing
```

Each time the floppy capacity is exceeded, you will get the same "Ready for volume…" prompt with an appropriate volume number. When the archive has been completely written, you'll see this:

```
tmp/biggraphic.gif -- okay
```

To extract the file from the floppies, put the first volume in the drive and use the following command:

```
# afio -iv  /dev/fd0
```

You will be prompted to put in the subsequent floppies with the same command as was used when the archive was written.

Third-Party Tools

Several backup tools have been developed, by vendors and individuals alike. Many of these tools are free, and a few even include the source code. Most of these backup packages are GUI-based, since tar, cpio, and afio work quite well from the command line. Some of these packages are included with established distributions, and some are not.

AMANDA

The Advanced Maryland Automatic Network Disk Archiver, AMANDA, is a client-server backup utility developed at the University of Maryland. It allows the administrator of a local area network to back up drives from any of the networked hosts to a single backup server. Later versions can use Samba to back up Windows hosts as well. The AMANDA front-end can use the dump utility or GNU tar to perform the backup/restore functions. It is available on a number of platforms, and there are no restrictions on the platforms the clients and server must use. However, if even one system in the LAN uses a pre-2.4.0 version of AMANDA, all must use pre-2.4.0 versions. AMANDA 2.4.0 and subsequent versions are not compatible with preceding versions.

AMANDA is available for download at ftp://ftp.amanda.org/pub/amanda/ as well as from many other network sites.

Taper

Taper is a simple but reasonably complete archiving utility, shown in Figure 11.5. It will archive to some parallel port tape devices, SCSI tape drives as supported by the kernel, IDE tape drives as supported by the kernel, or floppy tape drives.

Figure 11.5 The Taper main screen

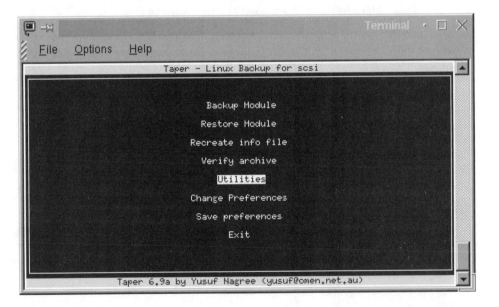

Taper allows you to search the archive for a particular file and has a recovery module for corrupt archives. It allows for unassisted backups.

Taper is available in the Red Hat distribution and from the Taper Web site at http://www.e-survey.net.au/taper/ or from ftp://ftp.clark.net/pub/dickey/ncurses/. You will need at least ncurses 4.1 to compile Taper. The forms library is also required.

BRU

Enhanced Software Technologies (EST) began developing their backup product in 1985 for Unix. The first Linux-specific version was marketed in 1994. Red Hat partnered with EST and started offering a trial version of BRU backup and restore on the Linux Applications CD included with the boxed set of Red Hat version 6.1. EST is also partnered with SuSE Linux and Caldera OpenLinux.

BRU is a very polished product, with tremendous visual appeal. The introductory screen is shown in Figure 11.6 and is even nicer in color.

Figure 11.6 The BRU main screen

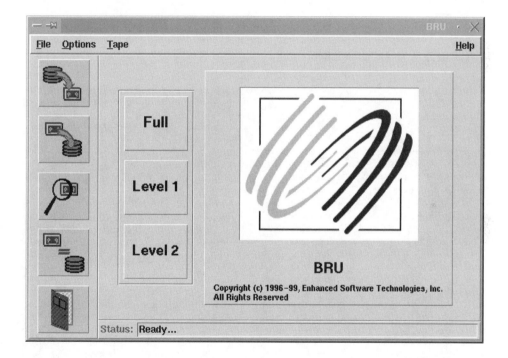

The BRU backup and restore utility has received a great deal of public recognition and was voted the "Best of Show" in its category at the 2000 LinuxWorld Conference. It is a highly scalable package, which performs well when backing up single workstations as well as a networked client/server backup strategy.

BRU will make a full backup, a Level 1 backup (equivalent to an incremental backup), and a Level 2 backup, which backs up all files modified since the last Level 1 backup.

KDat

KDat is KDE's tar-based tape backup utility. Although KDat is simple, it performs all of the functions you need in an archive utility and comes in the KDE kdadmin package. Although the name suggests it works only with DAT drives, this isn't so; it works with any tape device supported by Linux. KDat allows you to create backup profiles for frequently used backup criteria so that you don't have to redefine the backup every time. It has some nice features, like management of multiple archives on a single tape, support for GNU incremental backups, and a quick-search algorithm that allows you to seek a specific file in an existing archive without having to read the entire archive. KDat relies on the Qt and KDE libraries, so you must have these on your system if you plan to use it. (It can be used from environments other than KDE, though.) Figure 11.7 shows KDat in action.

Figure 11.7 The KDat archiving utility

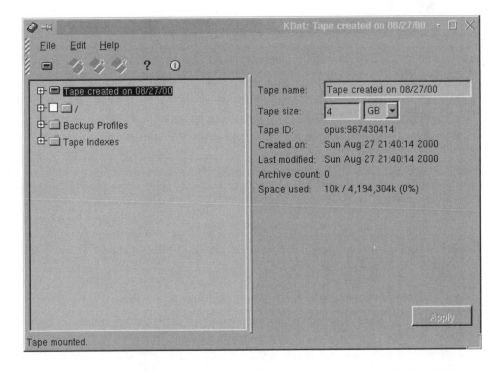

Tips while Restoring

Although restoring files from a backup is a rather simple procedure if the backups were done properly, there are definitely some things to remember here to avoid mishaps.

- Be sure you understand whether the paths specified by the backup software are relative or absolute so that you restore to the intended location. If you are restoring over the top of an existing system, you must be sure that you are in the correct directory so that you don't write over files unintentionally. If a backup was made using relative paths, writing to the wrong place is unlikely to cause any harm, because it will simply place everything under the present working directory. If you have created a backup with absolute paths, however, the files will overwrite the files already there. That is, an absolute-path backup of /usr will write over the existing /usr tree. It is certainly OK to write over this tree intentionally, but many have done so inadvertently to their dismay.

- Read the tape label just before putting it in the drive. It's unfortunately easy to grab a tape, put it down in a stack of tapes, and then pick up the wrong one. You may not discover that you are extracting the wrong archive until the process finishes, leaving you to extract the correct backup in your "free" time.

- Buy reasonably good quality media. You don't have to buy the best, but definitely buy a tape that is going to stand up to the recurring use. Name-brand tapes are more likely to survive repeated uses than are generic or minor-brand tapes. This applies to CD-Rs as well. For archival CD-R storage, gold/gold media (which appear gold on both sides) and silver/blue (silver on top, blue on bottom) are likely to last longer than are gold/green media. The storage media that work best for you may depend on your tape or CD-R drive; for some drives certain types of tapes last the longest, or certain CD-R brands produce the fewest duds. Pay attention to trends and save your company some money by buying the type the drive likes.

- Never pull tapes out while they are active; let the tape finish and rewind. If you've used a nonrewinding device file, let it finish the current process and then rewind the tape with mt. Most tape drives automatically rewind a tape when you insert it in the drive, if it's not already rewound, so removing a non-rewound tape won't save you any time in the long run. Pulling an active tape out of the drive is a good way to damage the tape.

- If you get errors when trying to read or write to a tape, try cleaning the drive heads with the appropriate cleaner tape. Often dirty heads cause a tape drive to report write or read errors incorrectly.

- If you get errors when you write a CD-ROM, try a slower write speed or a better quality of media.

- Before using a tape drive for real backups, perform a test backup of a lot of static data (such as the contents of the /usr directory tree) and use your tape software's comparison feature (such as tar's --diff or --compare commands). If the software reports changes to files that should not have changed, you should track down the source of the problem. One of us once discovered a bizarre incompatibility between a tape drive and an Iomega Zip drive when used on one SCSI host adapter. The problem caused errors when reading data from the tape drive. The incompatibility vanished when both drives were connected to another host adapter. You want to discover such difficulties *before* you need to use the drive for actual data recovery.

Backing Up the Operating System

Preceding sections of this chapter have discussed backup tools and commands, but in practice it's necessary to know *what* to back up. There are two philosophies concerning backups: minimal and complete. A minimal backup backs up only those files that are unique to your system, such as configuration files and user data. A complete backup backs up the entire computer. Each approach has its pluses and minuses.

Minimal Backups

The idea behind a minimal backup is that, in the event of a disaster such as a hard disk crash, you can obtain new hardware (if necessary), reinstall Linux from scratch, and restore a small backup from tape, CD-R, or some other medium to recover a working system that's identical or nearly identical to the system you'd been using. Linux is reasonably well suited to such an approach, because configuration files, user files, and most other system-specific files are confined to specific directories, such as /etc, /home, /usr/local, and /var.

Suppose that you want to back up these four directories, leaving the bulk of the Linux system in /usr (aside from /usr/local) "backed up" in the form of the original Linux installation CD-ROM. You might use a command like the following to perform this task using tar and a SCSI tape drive:

```
# tar cvplf /dev/st0 /etc /home /usr/local /var
```

Minimal backups have certain advantages, including speed, a reduced need for tapes, and the capability to recover the system without creating an elaborate disaster recovery plan (you'll reinstall a complete system and then use it to restore your system-specific data). On the down side, you can easily miss something important (including software upgrades installed after the initial system installation), and to work properly, you'll need to take careful notes on what you installed during system installation and afterward, in order to create an initial post-restore configuration that matches your system's state at backup time. On the whole, it's usually better to perform a complete backup, unless you don't have the tape capacity to conveniently back up your entire system. Some systems can benefit from a mixed approach: Use a complete backup on occasion, and minimal backups more frequently. This approach resembles an incremental backup, but is more hit-or-miss.

Complete Backups

A complete backup backs up *everything* on the computer, with the possible exception of selected files you know you won't be wanting after a restore—for instance, you might explicitly exclude the /tmp directory's contents. In principle, you can perform a complete backup by backing up the / directory and all its subdirectories, but as described earlier, you want to avoid backing up the /proc filesystem, because it's not a disk-based filesystem at all. This filesystem stores information on the computer's state, so backing it up is a waste of tape at best, and restoring it can cause serious problems, potentially even including a system crash.

A complete backup takes more time and tape than a minimal backup, and restoring such a backup after a disaster requires some preparation, as described shortly. On the plus side, once you've recovered such a backup, you won't need to fine-tune your configuration or worry about missed files or program upgrades—if done properly and completely, your recovered system will be a virtual clone of its state before being backed up.

Depending upon your software, you may be able to perform a complete backup by backing up / and specifying files or directories to exclude, or by backing up each filesystem independently. For instance, to back up / and exclude /proc using tar, you might issue the following command:

```
# tar cvpf /dev/st0 / --exclude=proc
```

This particular command omits the leading / from /proc, because tar stores files in its archive in a relative manner by default. If you include the / in /proc, tar will *not* exclude /proc. The potential for confusion may make it easier to get the correct results by using the -l parameter to tar and specifying each filesystem you want to back up, thus:

```
# tar cvplf /dev/st0 /home / /usr/local /boot
```

This command backs up four filesystems (/home, /, /usr/local, and /boot), but of course you should adjust the filesystems for your computer. You can list the filesystems in any order, but keep in mind that it will be quicker to restore files from the filesystems you list first. This example lists /home first, on the theory that users may accidentally delete files from their home directories and want them restored.

System Optimization

PART 3

Disaster Recovery Techniques

Backing up your system regularly and methodically goes a long way toward protecting it, but there are still situations that call for something different. If you forgot to run LILO or can't boot the kernel you just made, you don't need to reinstall, but you do need some sort of disaster recovery. Disaster recovery methods allow you to log onto your system, so that you can fix it or retrieve important files before damaged equipment takes the system down permanently. There are several methods to choose from, depending on the problem and what you need to do to repair it. Among these are booting in single-user mode, from an emergency boot disk, and in rescue mode.

Single-User Mode

Single-user mode boots your computer to run level 1. The local filesystems are mounted as usual, and the system's initialization scripts are run, but there is no network access. You are placed in a system maintenance shell where `root` may use the console but no one else is allowed to log in at all. If your system boots but does not allow you to log in when it has completed booting, try rebooting and entering `linux single` at the LILO boot prompt:

```
LILO boot: linux single
```

Since this method uses the ailing system's own initialization scripts, any error in these scripts may still be a problem; no daemons run in this mode, however, so problems caused by a daemon's failure to start will likely be fixable in this mode. Single-user mode also uses the system's own kernel, so if the kernel is causing a panic, this won't help either. If a filesystem has problems, single-user mode will attempt to mount it as usual and will probably fail at that point.

Single-user mode is great for getting on a system when you've forgotten the `root` password, allowing you to run LILO when you have forgotten to do so after creating a new kernel image, and to fix some other problems that don't prevent the system from reaching single-user mode. You can take advantage of the fact that no one else can log in to perform functions like installing software, making backups (if the system can stay in single-user mode for a long time without disruption), and doing other standard maintenance functions that benefit from `root` solitude.

Using a Boot Floppy

Chapter 2's discussion of installing Linux, as demonstrated on a Red Hat system, noted that creating a boot floppy is a useful installation option. In the early days of Linux, the packaged distributions came with at least one boot and one root floppy. These floppies were required for installation. The boot floppy contained all the files needed for a LILO-initiated bootup of a particular system. The root filesystem was contained on the root floppy. Using this method, you could boot the installed system using the boot floppy and specifying the location of the installed root partition, or you could boot the image on the root floppy.

Install Boot Disk

There are two flavors of boot disks these days. The first is used to boot into the installation and is typically referred to as an *install disk*. These days, most CD-ROM distributions provide a bootable CD-ROM, removing the need for a boot disk. Still, if your computer BIOS does not allow booting from a CD-ROM or if your CD-ROM is not functioning, you'll need to create the boot disk by copying the correct boot image to a floppy. If your distribution does not come with a ready-made boot disk, you must create one using one of the boot disk images from your installation CD-ROM. Some bootable CD-ROMs can be used directly in much the same way as an emergency floppy.

There are three images that can be used for this disk because different install methods require that different capabilities be built into the kernel. If your distribution came with a premade boot disk, it probably is equivalent to one made from `boot.img`, since it is the most commonly used boot image. There is also a `bootnet.img` image to be used for installing from a non-PCMCIA network device. A `pcmcia.img` image is available for installation via a PCMCIA device like some CD-ROM drives, Ethernet adapters, or hard drives.

Since the install disks allow you to boot your system and use a virtual terminal, they can sometimes be used to repair flaws, but some of the same restrictions apply as with single-user mode. The boot disk contains only a kernel image, so all the initialization is performed using the system's own files.

There are several ways to create an install floppy. If you have a working Windows system, you may create the disk by using `RAWRITE.EXE`. This binary is located in the `dosutils` directory on a Red Hat CD-ROM. To use it, execute the command and tell it which of the images in the `images` directory you wish to write to floppy and which device to write to.

If you are lucky enough to have a Linux or other Unix machine available, you can create the disk using `dd` with a variation on the following command:

```
# dd if=/mnt/cdrom/images/boot.img of=/dev/fd0
```

On some systems you'll need to specify the block size. See the man page for the `dd` command for more details. You may also use the `cat` command as follows:

```
# cat /mnt/cdrom/images/boot.img >/dev/fd0
```

You must not use the `cp` command, because the idea is to transfer the raw image without any formatting, and the `cp` command requires a formatted disk.

Emergency Boot Floppy

The second type of boot floppy is a standalone boot image created specifically for your system after an install or by running the command /sbin/mkbootdisk. This disk is typically referred to as an emergency boot floppy. It contains a root filesystem along with customized boot data for the system it was built from rather than the generic data provided with the distribution boot floppy. The standalone boot floppy can be used to boot your system if you cannot or do not wish to run LILO or some other boot manager.

It is important to remember that a boot floppy uses files on the existing system when it boots. It needs to find the second-stage boot loader, which is typically /boot/boot.b, the initialization files, and a kernel image on the computer you are booting. If the problem you are trying to fix is in one of these files, you won't be able to boot using a boot floppy. You'll need to use Red Hat's rescue mode.

Rescue Mode

A Linux distribution's *rescue mode* boots a small but complete Linux system completely independent of the installed Linux system. From this mode, you can mount the computer's devices, edit configuration files, run a filesystem check, or do a number of other repair functions depending upon the problem. Since both single-user mode and boot disks depend upon files from the installed system itself and certain types of problems cannot be fixed these ways, rescue mode is the only way to fix some problems that you'll encounter.

Many distributions' CD-ROMs include the ability to boot into a rescue mode of one sort or another. This section focuses upon Red Hat's rescue mode, but the principles are the same for other distributions.

If LILO has been overwritten by another operating system, you cannot boot from the kernel and initialization files on your hard drive, because there is no way to access them; so you need to use rescue mode. If hardware problems make it impossible to boot using your own initialization scripts, use rescue mode and mount that drive to retrieve whatever you can before it dies. If you've made a mistake in /etc/fstab and incorrectly given the mount point for the / partition, you can use rescue mode to edit the file and reboot. You can even use rescue mode to recover a complete tape backup to a new hard disk after an old one has died.

To boot into rescue mode, you need to boot from a Red Hat boot disk or by booting a floppy containing either the PCMCIA boot image or the bootnet image. When you reach the boot prompt, simply type **linux rescue**. When the system boots, you will be in rescue mode and will have a Bash # prompt. You will be able to run any of the following commands:

anaconda	gzip	mkfs.ext2	ps
badblocks	head	mknod	python
bash	hwclock	mkraid	python1.5
cat	ifconfig	mkswap	raidstart
chatter	init	mlabel	raidstop
chmod	insmod	mmd	rcp
chroot	less	mmount	rlogin
clock	ln	mmove	rm
collage	loader	modprobe	rmmod
cp	ls	mount	route
cpio	lsattr	mpartition	rpm
dd	lsmod	mrd	rsh
ddcprobe	mattrib	mread	sed
depmode	mbadblocks	mren	sh
df	mcd	mshowfat	sync
e2fsck	mcopy	mt	tac
fdisk	mdel	mtools	tail
fsck	mdeltree	mtype	tar
fsck.ext2	mdir	mv	touch
ftp	mdu	mzip	traceroute
genhdlist	mformat	open	umount
gnome-pty-helper	minfo	pico	uncpio
grep	mkdir	ping	uniq
gunzip	mke2fs	probe	zcat

If your root filesystem is undamaged, you can mount it and use the chroot command to run commands as if the original root filesystem were your root directory. You can mount all the partitions on this root filesystem and essentially run your own system. Under Red Hat 6.2 and beyond, you are required to create your own devices, so before you can mount /dev/hda1, you'll need to use the mknod command to create /dev/hda, /dev/hda1, and /dev/hda2.

```
# mknod /dev/hda b 3 0
# mknod /dev/hda1 b 3 1
```

```
# mknod /dev/hda2 b 3 2
# mkdir /mnt/olddisk
# mount -t ext2 /dev/hda1 /mnt/olddisk
# mount -t ext2 /dev/hda2 /mnt/olddisk/usr
# chroot /mnt/olddisk
```

This example reflects a system that exists as two separate partitions: / and /usr. If you don't know the partitioning scheme of the system you're attempting to fix, you can use fdisk to determine it (after you've created the device file for your hard disk, that is). The fdisk utility will allow you to determine partition types and sizes; this is usually enough information to make a good guess as to the scheme being used. If you are wrong, don't worry; attempting to mount the wrong partition will not harm the system.

Third-Party Recovery Software

Recently, several third party-vendors have begun marketing recovery packages. In the past, backups were considered by many to be sufficient. Because recovery utilities are common in Windows, users converting from that environment often want to see these tools in Linux.

BRU

Enhanced Software Technologies (EST) uses the technology behind its BRU backup-and-restore package discussed earlier as the backbone to a line of data recovery products.

QuickStart Data Rescue   The QuickStart Data Rescue package provides the ability to perform disaster recovery using a single boot disk. Once booted with the QuickStart Data Rescue disk, your system will be able to detect most tape drives. After the tape drive is detected, you will be able to use the graphical interface to reinstall your system with the configuration as it was captured in the original use. Normally, if a system crashes, you need to reinstall the operating system and perform some configuration tasks (to make the system see your tape drive, for instance) before you can even begin to dump the needed elements from tape. With QuickStart Data Rescue, you just boot from the disk and start putting your data back.

QuickStart System Replicator   QuickStart System Replicator provides a simple method for replicating systems when there is a need to efficiently produce multiple, similarly configured systems. Build the first system, and use the replicator to produce as many duplicates as you need. Make the necessary changes to IP addresses, user accounts, etc., and you're all set.

Undeleting Files

It's easy to accidentally delete a file. Part of the purpose of backups is to allow recovery of such files, but if the file hadn't been backed up before its accidental deletion, the backup does no good. Therefore, there are undelete utilities available, and certain window managers use a trash can icon by default, which doesn't immediately delete files, instead storing them in a temporary limbo before deleting them. The rm command does not actually erase the deleted file from the disk but instead removes the file's inode or index pointer, leaving the data in place until that same inode is reused. Because the data still exists, it is often possible to retrieve it. We'll mention only one data recovery utility here, although there are several more available or under development now.

GtkRecover   GtkRecover (see `http://www.linuxave.net/~recover/gtkrecover.html`) is a nice little program that finds all the residue from deleted files on your drive and dumps those matching your criteria to a directory that you specify. Figure 11.8 shows GtkRecover prompting for information about a deleted file.

Figure 11.8   GtkRecover prompts for information to help locate deleted files.

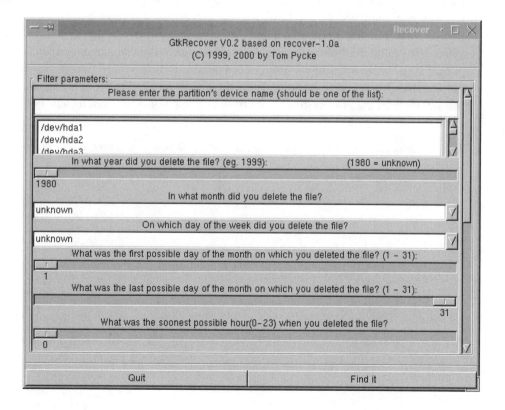

GtkRecover searches your drive for any deleted inodes that have yet to be reassigned and filters them based on your answers to a specific list of questions. The inodes dumped to the directory have no association with their previous filename or other file characteristics, so there is some detective work left, but this tool is quite useful if you need to recover deleted files.

Undeletion Mini-HOWTO To learn more about undeleting files, see the very good Undeletion mini-HOWTO at `http://www.linuxrx.com/HOWTO/sunsitesources/mini/Ext2fs-Undeletion.html`.

In Sum

Backup is an important topic, and one that covers a lot of territory. Effective backups rely upon an appropriate choice of hardware, selection of a reasonable backup schedule, and use of good backup software. Linux works with most modern backup hardware and provides many choices of backup software. Your backup schedule, of course, is yours to set.

Backing up your data is not enough. You must have a good recovery plan in case of disaster. At a minimum, you should be able to boot an emergency recovery disk of some sort in order to restore data from a backup. This same or another recovery disk should allow you to edit your main system's files, in case you accidentally damage some critical file like `/etc/fstab`. There are also assorted tools available to help you recover data, even without a conventional system backup. All of these tools and techniques play an important role in safeguarding your system's data from accidental loss, or even from sabotage by a cracker.

Take a break and obtain your beverage of choice. When you return you'll learn about serial communications.

Part 4

Communicating with Devices and Scripting

Featuring:

- Understanding serial devices
- Configuring terminals and modems
- Configuring serial printers
- The printing process in Linux and the lpd print spooler
- Creating printers in Red Hat Linux
- Kernel support for printing
- Remote printing
- Bash shell scripting
- Administrative scripting in other languages

12

Serial Communications, Terminals, and Modems

Throughout much of the history of computing, the RS-232 serial port has been an important piece of hardware. The serial port allows us to connect two computers together or to connect a computer to another device, such as a printer or mouse. The general-purpose nature of the serial port has allowed it to be used for a wide variety of tasks. The down side to serial ports is that they're slow. The RS-232 serial port on x86 computers is usually capable of a maximum transfer rate of 115,200 bits per second (bps). This compares to 100Mbps (100,000,000 bps) for modern Ethernet devices. For this reason, and because of the development of a variety of specialized interfaces (such as the PS/2 mouse port), the serial port is not as important today as it once was. Nonetheless, there are many jobs for which the serial port is still well suited. This chapter covers those jobs, which include linking "dumb" text terminals to a Linux system, using modems to connect to other systems over telephone lines, and using printers connected via serial ports. (Although mice are often connected via the serial port, their configuration and use is comparatively simple; it is covered in Chapter 16, "The X Window System." Most printers are connected via parallel ports; and their configuration is covered in Chapter 13, "Printers and the Spooling Subsystem.")

> **NOTE** Although this chapter emphasizes the traditional RS-232 interface, a new type of serial port has gained in popularity since 1999: the *Universal Serial Bus (USB)*. USB is much faster than RS-232 and so lacks many of RS-232's downsides. This chapter points out where RS-232 and USB differ.

Understanding Serial Devices

Before digging into the details of how to use serial ports to accomplish specific goals, it's helpful to understand precisely what a serial port is and how Linux treats the low-level serial port hardware. These details dictate what can and cannot be done with a serial port under Linux, and how you communicate with the serial hardware.

Standard Serial Devices

Most *x*86 computers come with two built-in RS-232 serial ports. These devices typically use 9-pin male connectors on the computer, as shown in Figure 12.1, but some serial ports (particularly on older computers and non-computer devices) use 25-pin connectors. The connectors on modems, printers, and other serial devices are usually female.

Figure 12.1 Modern *x*86 motherboards include a wide variety of connectors in standardized locations.

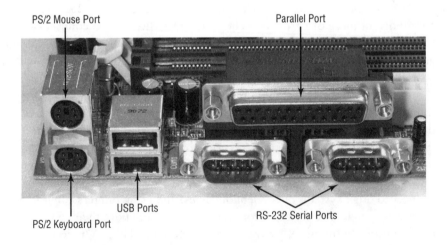

USB connectors are physically quite different from RS-232 connectors, as you can see in Figure 12.1. Some of the advantages of USB ports over standard RS-232 serial ports are:

Higher speed   USB supports speeds of up to 12Mbps, roughly 100 times as fast as standard RS-232.

Multi-device support   RS-232 ports support just one device per port. USB, by contrast, allows you to connect multiple devices to a single USB connector, although you must use a *hub* to do this job. A hub simply links several USB devices to a single USB port.

Hot swappable devices   You can attach and detach USB devices while the computer is running. This is risky with RS-232, since a short could conceivably damage the device or the computer.

As a general rule, RS-232 serial devices are well supported in Linux. USB devices, by contrast, are poorly supported in the 2.2.*x* kernel series, but USB support in the 2.4.*x* kernels is much better. Therefore, if you plan to use USB devices, you should upgrade to a 2.4.*x* kernel, or patch your 2.2.*x* kernel to include USB support. A few Linux distributions ship with 2.2.*x* kernels patched with USB support.

Enabling Serial Support in the Kernel

Whether you use RS-232 or USB, it's necessary that you understand the kernel configuration options needed to use the devices. You may not need to deal with these options explicitly, because most distributions ship with appropriate kernel support enabled, at least for common devices and uses. (USB support, being so new, is often omitted, at least in many distributions released in mid-to-late 2000.) You can read more about kernel configuration in Chapter 8, "Software Administration."

For RS-232 devices, kernel configuration options lie in the Character Devices kernel configuration menu (Figure 12.2). Specifically, to use the standard two serial ports, you should select Y or M to the Standard/Generic (Dumb) Serial Support option. You don't need to select kernel options for specific RS-232 serial devices, such as modems or printers. Details of communicating with specific devices are handled by appropriate user-level programs, such as pppd or lpd.

Configuring Linux's USB support is somewhat more complex, because you need to select several options in the USB Support kernel configuration menu (Figure 12.3). Remember that this support is only available in 2.4.*x* kernels, or in 2.2.*x* kernels patched with the appropriate USB driver. Specifically, you need to select one or more options in each of three option classes:

Support for USB   This top-level option is required if you want to use any USB device.

Figure 12.2 The Linux Character Devices kernel configuration menu includes the main RS-232 serial devices option.

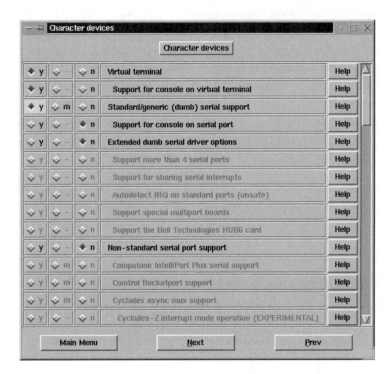

USB controller support There are two classes of low-level USB controllers: Universal Host Controller Interface (UHCI) and Open Host Controller Interface (OHCI). Select whichever one your motherboard or plug-in USB card supports. If you don't know which your system uses, select both. For UHCI, you have a choice of the main driver or an alternate driver. In most cases, the main driver works well, but if you have problems with it, try the alternate driver.

Specific device support You must select drivers for specific classes of USB devices, and in some cases even for specific models. The bulk of the USB Support kernel configuration menu is composed of USB device classes, so scan through it to locate your devices. In some cases, you may also need to select options in other kernel configuration menus; for example, some USB cameras require you to enable Video for Linux support in the Character Devices menu.

Using Serial Device Files

Traditional RS-232 devices use device filenames of the form /dev/ttyS*n*, where *n* is a number from 0 up. To communicate with a serial device, you (or a program you use) send

Figure 12.3 USB support requires selecting drivers for specific USB devices.

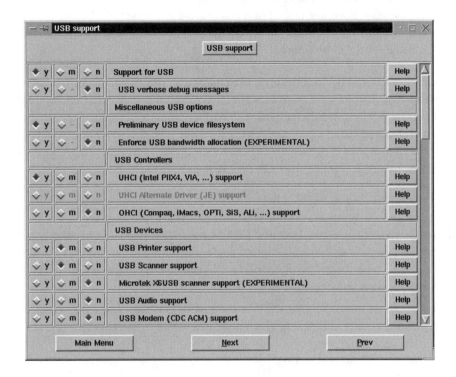

Administrator's Logbook: Enabling USB Support

System: E12345678

Action: Patched 2.2.17 kernel with USB support and recompiled, enabling support for USB mice and modems. Installed in LILO as 2217-usb.

---

characters to this device file. For instance, the following command sends the string ATDT555-4321 to a modem attached to /dev/ttyS0, causing the modem to dial 555-4321.

```
$ echo "ATDT555-4321" > /dev/ttyS0
```

> **NOTE**   In the past, the /dev/cua*n* devices were used as a variant method of accessing serial ports. Use of /dev/cua*n* is discouraged today, however, and support for these devices may disappear in the future, although it's still present up to at least the 2.4.0-test6 kernel.

Because the serial device interprets the characters, there is no need for cross-device standardization of commands sent over the RS-232 serial port; modems accept different commands than do printers, which use different commands than mice, and so on. There are, however, some Linux commands that can affect how the serial interface works. Of particular importance is the setserial command, which sets the RS-232 port's parameters, such as its speed. This command's syntax is as follows:

```
setserial [-ab] device [parameters] ...
```

The -a and -b options cause the program to display information on the hardware's settings, such as the interrupt request (IRQ) used by the port. -a results in a multiline display, and -b produces a less complete single-line output. You can pass a wide assortment of parameters to the program in order to change how it configures the port. These are the most important parameters:

port *portnum*   Sets the I/O port number to *portnum*. The I/O port is a hexadecimal number, such as 0x03f8, which indicates where in memory the input to and output from the serial port occur. Unless you're using very unusual hardware, you shouldn't need to adjust this setting.

irq *irqnum*   You can tell Linux to use an unusual IRQ number with this parameter. As with the port parameter, chances are you won't need to use this option.

uart *uarttype*   RS-232 serial ports are controlled by *universal asynchronous receiver/transmitters (UARTs)*, which come in several varieties. Linux usually detects the UART type correctly at bootup, but if it gets this detail wrong, you can correct the matter by using the uart parameter. (An incorrect port type is likely to produce unreliable serial port operation.) Most modern motherboards use 16550A UARTs, so *uarttype* would be 16550A for these boards. Very old hardware may use earlier UARTs, such as the 16450; and some devices use more recent ones, like the 16650.

baud_base *speed*   This parameter sets the speed of the serial port. The usual value for *speed* is 115200, which is the fastest speed in bps that most serial ports support.

These options and parameters just scratch the surface of setserial's capabilities. Read its man page for more information on esoteric features you can control with the program. This utility is most useful when you use simple programs and daemons with the serial port. More sophisticated programs and daemons can set the serial port's speed and other features themselves.

Unlike the RS-232 serial port, there isn't a single device file for each USB port on your computer. Instead, Linux maps each device to its own device file. The reason for this arrangement is simple: Using a hub, it's possible to connect more than one USB device to each USB port. Suppose a USB port hosts a printer, a mouse, and a modem. Each of those devices acquires its own entry in /dev or /dev/usb, so you can address each device appropriately. Precisely how you handle these devices varies from one device and program to another. For instance, you would normally reference a USB mouse in your XFree86 configuration file, as described in Chapter 16, whereas you'd reference a printer's file in /etc/printcap, as described in Chapter 13. Table 12.1 summarizes some of the more common USB device files, including their *major* and *minor* numbers, which define the interface between the device file and the kernel's drivers. It's important to realize that the device filenames are largely arbitrary; you can access a device under any filename you like, so long as that filename identifies a device file created via mknod with the appropriate type, major number, and minor number, as described shortly. Some USB devices, such as disk devices and speakers, are treated as if they were non-USB devices, such as SCSI disks and ordinary sound cards, respectively. Others use new major and minor numbers, and usually new device filenames.

Table 12.1   Methods of Accessing USB Devices in the 2.4.0 Kernel

Device	Device Filename	Type	Major Number	Minor Number
Disk devices	/dev/sd*n*	Block	8	0–240
Modem	/dev/ttyACM*n*	Character	166	0 up
Mouse	/dev/mouse*n* or /dev/mice	Character	13	32 and up or 63, respectively
Printer	/dev/usblp*n*	Character	180	0 and up
Scanner	/dev/usbscanner*n*	Character	180	48–63
Speakers	Normal audio devices, such as /dev/audio and /dev/mixer	Character	Varies	Varies

Table 12.1   Methods of Accessing USB Devices in the 2.4.0 Kernel *(continued)*

Device	Device Filename	Type	Major Number	Minor Number
USB-to-parallel adapter	/dev/usblp*n*	Character	180	0 and up
USB-to-RS-232 adapter	/dev/ttyUSB*n*	Character	188	0 and up

If you need to create a device file to access a USB device, you may do so with the mknod command. The syntax of this command is:

    mknod *filename type major minor*

In this command, *filename* is the device filename, *type* is either b for block devices or c for character devices, and *major* and *minor* are the major and minor numbers listed in Table 12.1. Be aware that many USB devices' major and minor numbers have changed during the development of Linux's USB code and may change again in the future. These are sometimes documented in files in the /usr/src/linux/Documentation/usb directory, but documentation on this point is still spotty in late 2000.

Unusual Serial Devices

Some serial devices are rare and nonstandard implementations of RS-232 ports. The problem with the standard implementation of RS-232 serial devices is that it's difficult to add ports beyond the two included on most motherboards. Adding third and fourth ports presents only minor difficulties—most add-on ports come configured to "share" interrupts with the first two ports, but it's necessary to reconfigure these boards to use unique IRQs because Linux doesn't normally work well with this arrangement.

> **NOTE**   Internal modems normally include serial port hardware along with modem hardware. Adding such a modem works just like adding a serial port. It's sometimes helpful to disable an unused motherboard serial port before adding an internal modem, so that the internal modem can take over the identity of one of the first two regular ports. This can normally be done in the computer's BIOS setup screens. Some internal modems don't have serial port hardware. These devices are often called *WinModems*, *controllerless modems*, or *software modems* (although the first term technically applies only to 3Com products). There are Linux drivers for a few such devices—check http://www.linmodems.org for details. Many don't work under Linux, however, and so should be avoided.

The problem with using a unique IRQ for each serial port is that the $x86$ architecture allows for only 15 interrupts, and some are required for other devices, so it's not possible to assign unique IRQs to more than a handful of serial ports. To overcome this problem, some companies have developed *multiport serial cards*, which place several RS-232 ports on one card and one IRQ. Because these devices use nonstandard hardware, they require their own unique drivers. If you have need of such a device, check the Linux kernel configuration area for character devices (Figure 12.2). Depending upon the type of device, you may need to select the Extended Dumb Serial Driver Options item or Nonstandard Serial Port Support. In either case, you must select appropriate options for your specific board. You should study these options before buying the hardware, so you're sure you get something supported in Linux.

Configuring Terminals

One of the most common uses for a serial port on a multiuser system is as a port for a *terminal*. A terminal is a device or computer that's used as a means of controlling another computer. Because most $x86$ computers have two RS-232 ports plus their normal keyboard and monitor, it's possible for three people to simultaneously use a single computer if two people access the computer via terminals. (Of course, you can add more serial ports or use networking connections to further increase that number, if you like.) Although most Linux distributions don't come preconfigured to use terminals, it's not difficult to add this capability to a system.

> **NOTE** Terminal access is almost always performed through RS-232 ports. You can use an RS-232-to-USB adapter, however, to connect RS-232 terminals to a Linux computer via the computer's USB ports.

Understanding Terminals

To understand terminals, it's helpful to think back to the days when Unix systems came in boxes the size of a dishwasher, if not larger. In those days, dozens or hundreds of users accessed a Unix system through dumb terminals—devices that roughly resembled today's iMac computers, at least to the naked eye. Inside these dumb terminals, though, was extremely simple circuitry, no hard disk, and only enough memory to handle the local display and a few extra lines of text. With virtually no processing capability, they were input/output devices, not computers. These devices could take what a user typed at the keyboard and echo it out a serial port, and they could display what was received from the serial port on the screen. These capabilities were very useful when a "real" computer cost millions of dollars and had to be used by many people. Such terminals were the primary means of accessing Unix systems through the 1980s. They were common in corporate and educational settings and are still in use today. (Your local library may use dumb terminals to provide patrons with access to its online book catalog, for example.)

NOTE Dumb terminals are text-only devices; they cannot be used to run X-based programs such as StarOffice or the GIMP. There is, however, another variety of terminal that can be used with X programs: an *X terminal*. X terminals usually interface through a network port, not a serial port. The NCD X Terminal mini-HOWTO document (`http://www.linuxdoc.org/HOWTO/mini/NCD-X-Terminal.html`) provides information on these devices.

Because of Linux's Unix heritage, Linux includes the software necessary to support dumb terminals; using it is a matter of changing a few default configurations. Once this is done, you can plug in a dumb terminal and use it. Why would you want to do this? For the same reasons large organizations used (and still use) dumb terminals, such as stretching resources and providing access to a computer to more people than would otherwise be possible. If you don't need to run X programs, a dumb terminal can provide perfectly adequate access to a Linux computer.

Instead of a dumb terminal, you can use an outmoded computer. If you have an old 8088-based PC gathering dust in a closet, for instance, you can wipe it off, set it up, link it to a Linux computer, and use a simple DOS *terminal program* to make it work like a dumb terminal. Similarly, specialized devices like palmtop computers often come with terminal programs, so you can access a Linux computer from such devices.

TIP On rare occasion, X can lock up, leaving Linux unresponsive. Technically, Linux hasn't crashed, and it's usually possible to recover from such problems—*if* you have some way in other than the system's keyboard. Such a way in is often remote access through Telnet, but this isn't always an option. Using dumb terminal access, even from a palmtop computer, can let you kill or reconfigure X, thus recovering control of the system without using the Reset switch.

When you use another computer as a terminal, you must normally link the two computers through a *null modem* cable. These cables link one computer to another, and they're wired differently than the cables that link a computer to a modem. Most computer stores sell null modem cables.

If you want to use one Linux computer as a terminal for another, you can do so, although it's more common to use Ethernet hardware and the Telnet or SSH program to log in to one computer from another. Linking two Linux computers via serial ports requires you to use a Linux terminal program on one computer, as described later in this chapter, in "Calling a Remote Text-Mode System."

> **NOTE** Linux uses *virtual terminals* to provide text-mode access to a Linux system from its main keyboard and monitor (which are collectively referred to as *the console*). To configure Linux to use "real" terminals, you extend this configuration to support serial devices as well as the console, as described shortly.

Configuring a *getty* Program

In most cases, the goal when using a terminal (either dumb terminal hardware or a terminal emulator) is to have the terminal display a Linux login: prompt when the user starts the terminal. Linux normally presents these prompts using a program called getty, or some variant of that, such as mingetty, mgetty, or agetty.

> **NOTE** The original getty program goes by that name. Various replacements use similar names and do similar things. The word getty can therefore refer to either the original getty program or the class of similar programs that fill basically the same role. For the most part, the word is used in the latter sense in this chapter.

Linux runs getty programs from the /etc/inittab file. In Red Hat 7.0, the default /etc/inittab file contains the following lines:

```
# Run gettys in standard runlevels
1:2345:respawn:/sbin/mingetty tty1
2:2345:respawn:/sbin/mingetty tty2
3:2345:respawn:/sbin/mingetty tty3
4:2345:respawn:/sbin/mingetty tty4
5:2345:respawn:/sbin/mingetty tty5
6:2345:respawn:/sbin/mingetty tty6
```

Each line in the /etc/inittab file contains colon-delimited entries that tell the system about certain specific types of services to be run. The preceding entries tell Linux to run the /sbin/mingetty program for each of the first six virtual consoles in run levels 2 through 5. The result of these entries is that you can type Alt+1 through Alt+6 (in combination with Ctrl, if you're currently running X) to shift to any of six virtual consoles. You can log in to any of these to run programs, even under different usernames.

To expand the default configuration to support terminals run over a serial port, it's necessary to add some further entries to /etc/inittab. To do so, follow these steps:

1. Install the mgetty package. On a Red Hat 7.0 system, the package name is mgetty-1.1.22-1.i386.rpm, and is on the second CD-ROM.

NOTE Different distributions use different getty programs by default. Red Hat's mingetty can't handle serial port traffic, but some default getty programs can handle the serial port, so this step may not be necessary with all getty programs. If you use something other than mgetty, however, some of the following details may differ; consult your getty program's documentation for details.

---

2. To add support for a terminal attached to /dev/ttyS0, add the following line to /etc/inittab just after the existing mingetty lines:

   ```
   S0:2345:respawn:/sbin/mgetty -s 57600 -r /dev/ttyS0
   ```

3. Type **telinit Q** to tell Linux to reexamine the /etc/inittab file and make appropriate changes—namely, to run mgetty.

You may need to make adjustments to step 2 for your particular needs. Specifically, step 2 specifies that the terminal run at 57,600 bps (the -s 57600 parameter) and that it use /dev/ttyS0. The -r parameter indicates that the connection is direct—that is, not via a modem. Modem logins, as described shortly, require a few changes to this configuration.

Once logged on using a terminal, the user can run Linux text-mode programs, including administrative tools like Linuxconf (assuming the user has sufficient privileges, of course). Some programs, however, rely on text-positioning protocols. These protocols were originally used with particular models of dumb terminals, and so are frequently named after those terminals. Examples include VT-100 and VT-220. In many cases, mgetty can determine the type of terminal that's connected. In other cases, you may need to do this manually by setting the TERM environment variable. For instance, if you're using a VT-100 terminal, you could type the following after logging in:

```
$ export TERM=vt100
```

If you find that your display does strange things, type **env | grep TERM** to see what the system thinks the terminal type is, and adjust it as appropriate. Some dumb terminals emulate others, and most terminal programs emulate one or more popular dumb terminals.

Administrator's Logbook: Enabling Serial Port Logins

System: E12345678

Action: Added support for logins from /dev/ttyS0 via mgetty. Used 57,600 bps port speed and mgetty package.

File modified: /etc/inittab

Using a Serial-Port Console

Terminals can be very convenient for accessing a Linux system in certain circumstances, but they do have a major limitation: they're useful only after the system has completely booted. There are situations in which you may want to run a computer without a monitor, as when you place a server in some out-of-the-way location. If you do this, you won't be able to see the computer's boot-time messages or interact with the system when console maintenance is required (as when fsck encounters a problem when rebooting after a crash). Moving a monitor to such an isolated computer and squatting in front of it to perform maintenance can be a pain (sometimes literally!), so Linux provides a solution: a *serial-port console*. In this arrangement, Linux uses the serial port for all console operations. You can then run a null-modem cable to some other computer and use a terminal program on that computer whenever you need to perform console operations on the isolated system.

In order to use a serial-port console, you must do three things:

1. Select the Support for Console on Serial Port option in the Character Devices Linux kernel configuration menu (see Figure 12.2).

NOTE   To select this option, you must compile Linux's standard serial support into the kernel by selecting Y to Standard/Generic (Dumb) Serial Support. If you compile the standard serial support as a module, you will not be able to add serial-port console support.

---

2. Recompile the Linux kernel with this new option enabled.

3. Start Linux while passing it the parameter console=ttyS0 (making an appropriate substitution for the serial port you use). The usual way to do this is to add a line to your /etc/lilo.conf entry for a kernel and type **lilo** to reinstall LILO. The line reads:

```
append="console=ttyS0"
```

Communicating with Devices

PART 4

Assuming the new kernel and /etc/lilo.conf entries are the default, Linux uses the specified serial port as its console. You can therefore put the system into single-user mode or recover after a system crash or power outage from a dumb terminal or another computer running a terminal program—even another Linux system. This access does *not*, however, extend as far as letting you select the OS to boot using LILO or modifying your computer's CMOS BIOS settings; these settings rely upon the BIOS, not Linux, for input, and so cannot be redirected by Linux.

> **WARNING**   Some Linux distributions, including Red Hat, use specially formatted text to display startup messages in color. Some terminal programs may misinterpret these codes in various unhelpful ways, as in a request to begin a file transfer. For this reason, you're best off using a very minimal terminal program, or disabling terminal program features like server-requested file transfers.

Configuring Modems

One of the most common RS-232 serial devices is the telephone *modem*. This word is an acronym for *modulator-demodulator*, because a modem functions as a way to convert analog data to digital form (that is, *modulate* it) and reverse the process (*demodulate* the data).

Most telephone modems are RS-232 devices, but there are two major exceptions to this rule:

- *Internal software modems*—These devices, mentioned earlier, have no serial port circuitry. A few have Linux drivers available (check http://www.linmodems.org for details), but many don't. It's usually best to avoid software modems for use in Linux.

- *USB modems*—Modems that interface through the USB port are becoming popular. If a USB modem uses the *Communication Device Class Abstract Control Model* (CDC-ACM) protocol, it should work with the USB support in the 2.4.*x* Linux kernels.

> **NOTE**   Internet access provided by *Digital Subscriber Line (DSL)* and cable TV systems is also often referred to as modem-based. Although these devices do modulate and demodulate data, their use is very different from what's described in this section. Cable and DSL modems are more akin to Ethernet routers and bridges, so Chapter 15, "TCP/IP Linux Networking," is relevant to configuring these devices.

Some internal modems—particularly older models—use a serial port in conjunction with conventional modem circuitry. These devices function just like ordinary external modems, which plug into an RS-232 port. No matter what interface the device uses, you can configure a modem in many ways. The configuration details differ depending upon who initiates a connection, your computer or a remote computer. When one of your users initiates a connection, you must configure the system to perform *dial-out* access. In order to support remote users calling your system, you must configure your system to accept *dial-in* access of one form or another.

Dial-out Modem Uses

Small Linux systems, such as desktop workstations, often require dial-out access. The user of such a system may need to contact another via a modem to check e-mail or perform other simple text-based tasks. Moving up in complexity, the modem can be used to initiate a *Point-to-Point Protocol* (*PPP*) connection in order to allow Web browsing, FTP transfers, and so on. Finally, it's possible to send faxes from a Linux computer using a modem. These features are generally most desirable for single-user workstations, but sometimes they're helpful even on multiuser systems. This is particularly true of sending faxes; you can configure a shared printer queue (see Chapters 13 and 15) to use a fax modem rather than a printer, thus providing outgoing fax services to an entire network of computers.

Calling a Remote Text-Mode System

One of the simplest types of outgoing modem connection is a text-based link to another computer. The idea behind such a link is similar to that of using a serial port along with a dumb terminal or a computer running a terminal program. The difference is that a pair of modems and the telephone network sit between the two computers. In such a setup, the dial-out computer ordinarily functions as the terminal; the dial-in system runs a `getty` program and receives the call, as described shortly, in "Accepting Text-Mode Logins."

Using modems in text mode is now much less common than it was before the rise of the Internet and PPP connections. It can still be a good way to handle simple access needs, however. Further, some companies still operate *bulletin-board systems* (*BBSes*), which provide product information, file downloads, and discussion forums for those without Internet access.

To call a remote text-based system, you must use a terminal program. Two popular terminal programs on Linux are the text-based `minicom` and the X-based Seyon (shown in Figure 12.4). Details of how to use these programs differ, but the basic principles are the same:

- Before you run a program, you may need to create a symbolic link so that /dev/ modem points to the device file onwhich your modem resides (such as /dev/ttyS0).

Figure 12.4 The Seyon terminal emulator lets you use Linux as if it were a dumb terminal.

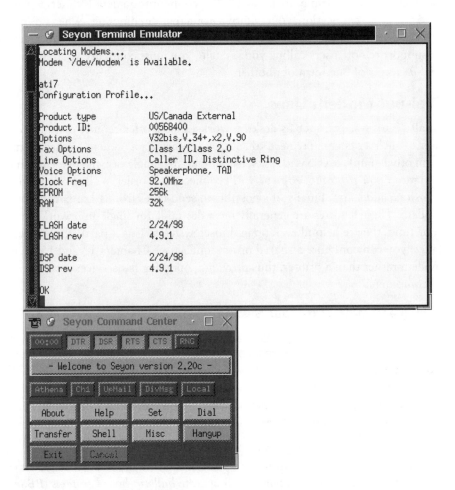

Alternatively, you can configure the program to use the desired device file directly—for instance, by clicking Set in the Seyon Command Center window, clicking Port, and entering the desired device filename.

> **NOTE** The user who makes a connection *must* have permission to both read and write the modem's device file. Red Hat Linux's startup scripts change the ownership of the /dev/ttySn device files whenever anyone logs onto the console, so the console user always has access to the modem, if it's an RS-232 serial device. Other distributions use a special group for these files, along with 664 or 660 permissions, so all members of that group can access the modem. You can add any users who should have modem access to the group. Use the ls -l command on the modem device for your system to find out how it's configured, and make any necessary changes to the device's permissions or your group configuration.

- When you run the program, you may need to adjust the serial port's parameters—most importantly, the port speed. In Seyon, you can do this by clicking Set, then Baud, and then the button corresponding to your desired speed. When using a modern 56Kbps modem, a port speed of 115Kbps is appropriate.

- To dial a number, type **ATDT** followed by the number, such as **ATDT555-1234** to dial 555-1234. AT is the standard modem code for *attention*, and signals the modem that you're about to give a command. D stands for *dial*, and T refers to touch-tone dialing. (If your phone system doesn't support touch-tone dialing, use **ATDP** to dial using rotary pulses.)

- If you dial a number on a regular basis, you can add it to a dialing directory. In Seyon, you can see preconfigured numbers by clicking the Dial button. You can edit these entries by clicking Edit in the Dialing Directory window, which produces a simple text editor showing the configuration file. You can dial a number by selecting it in the Dialing Directory window and clicking Go. This action sends the appropriate AT commands to dial the number.

- When you're done using the program, hang up the modem by logging out of the remote system, turning off the modem, or picking an appropriate option in the program, such as the Hangup button in Seyon's Command Center window.

Seyon stores configuration information in the ~/.seyon directory, so every user may have customized settings. minicom requires that root run it with the -s parameter to create a configuration file called /etc/minirc.dfl, after which a user can create a custom configuration called ~/.minirc.dfl by changing defaults established by root.

Once you've connected to a remote system using a terminal program, you can use that system according to whatever rules it uses. These rules vary substantially from one system to another. For instance, if you connect to a Linux computer, you can typically use Linux

Communicating with Devices

PART 4

text-mode commands and utilities; but BBSes often use custom menu-based environments in which you type letters or digits to move around the system.

Making a PPP Connection

Today, establishing a PPP link is perhaps the most common use for a dial-out modem. PPP allows you to tie a system to the Internet using full TCP/IP networking features. A PPP-linked system can therefore browse the Web, transfer files via FTP, send and receive e-mail, and so on. Because PPP links are usually transitory and modem links are slow by modern Internet standards, it's uncommon to find servers running on PPP-connected computers. Some Internet Service Providers (ISPs) do offer accounts that can be used constantly; however, it's usually less expensive to acquire faster service through a cable modem or DSL for always-on connections.

Testing Basic Connectivity   The first step in linking a computer to the Internet via PPP is to acquire an account from an ISP. (If you want to link two computers that you control, such as an Internet-connected server at work and a home system, check "Accepting PPP Connections" later in this chapter for information on setting up a system to function as a PPP server.) Fortunately, ISPs are extremely common. You can find listings for them in your local telephone directory, probably under "Internet Services" or some variant of that.

Before you go further in configuring PPP access, you should check that your modem and device files work correctly by checking the instructions in "Calling a Remote Text-Mode System," earlier. You can call your ISP's dial-in number with Seyon or `minicom` to check basic modem functionality. Depending upon how your ISP's system is configured, you may see a `login:` prompt or gibberish when you connect. The main test is that you can get your own modem to dial; if this works, then you can be sure you have no problems relating to your own modem or modem device file permissions.

Connecting via PPP Scripts   Most ISPs today use the PAP or CHAP authentication protocols. These protocols allow you to identify yourself to the ISP in an automated fashion. In Linux, you must configure a file, called `/etc/ppp/pap-secrets` or `/etc/ppp/chap-secrets`, to support these authentication methods. Both files use the same format. Each line contains information for one account and takes this form:

```
client    server    secret    IP_address
```

> **TIP** If you're not sure which system your ISP uses, you can create one file and use a hard or symbolic link to make it accessible under both names. For instance, create /etc/ppp/pap-secrets and then type **ln -s /etc/ppp/pap-secrets /etc/ppp/chap-secrets**.

The meanings of each element are:

client   The username on the ISP's system.

server   The name of the ISP's server. This value is normally *, which means Linux accepts any server (because the ISP may change its server's name without notice).

secret   The password to the ISP's system.

IP_address   The numeric IP address or addresses that Linux will accept. This value is normally blank, meaning that the system accepts any IP address.

As an example, the following file can be used to log on to an ISP using the username agb and the password comehere:

```
agb   *   comehere
```

WARNING   The PPP secrets file, no matter what its name, is extremely sensitive, because it contains your ISP username in an unencrypted form. You should ensure that it's readable *only* by root (that is, that it's owned by root and has 0600 permissions). You should also use a different password on your ISP than you use on any other system, so that if this file is compromised, it can't be used to gain illicit access to other systems.

To initiate a PPP connection using command-line tools, you must have appropriate PPP scripts. Sample scripts are available with the PPP package for most distributions. In Red Hat 7.0, these scripts are in the /usr/share/doc/ppp-2.3.11/scripts directory. Their names are ppp-up, ppp-up-dialer, and ppp-down. The first two are responsible for initiating a PPP connection, and the third breaks a PPP link. You should copy all three scripts to /etc/ppp or to a location on your path, such as /usr/local/bin. You must then modify the ppp-up and ppp-up-dialer scripts to suit your configuration. In particular:

- In ppp-on, locate the lines that begin TELEPHONE=, ACCOUNT=, and PASSWORD=, and modify them so that they're appropriate for your ISP and account. (The ACCOUNT and PASSWORD variables may not be required if you use PAP or CHAP, but they should contain dummy variables in that case.)

- Check that the DIALER_SCRIPT variable in ppp-on points to the correct location of ppp-on-dialer. The default location is /etc/ppp.

- Check the call to pppd in the last lines of ppp-on. (pppd is the tool that handles the PPP negotiations; the scripts merely provide it with the information it needs to do its job.) Most of the parameters to this call are quite cryptic, but you should at least be able to confirm that it's using the correct modem device filename and speed (115200 is appropriate in most cases, but the default is 38400).

Communicating with Devices

PART 4

- Check the ppp-on-dialer script. This script includes a "chat" sequence—a series of strings the program expects to see from the modem or remote system in one column, and a series of responses in another column. You may need to log on using Seyon or minicom and capture to disk the prompts your ISP uses to ask for your username and password, and modify the last two lines of the script in order to make it work. Alternatively, you may need to comment out the last two lines by preceding them with pound signs (#) and remove the backslash (\) from the CONNECT line if your ISP uses PAP or CHAP.

NOTE   The chat program expects a single line; its input is only formatted in columns in ppp-on-dialer for the convenience of humans. The backslashes ending most lines signify line continuations, so that chat interprets multiple input lines as a single line. Only the final line should lack a backslash.

When you're done making these changes, type **ppp-on** (preceding it with a complete path, if necessary) as root to test the connection. If all goes well, your system should dial the modem, link up, and give you Internet access. If this fails to occur, check the last few lines of /var/log/messages with a command such as **tail -n 20 /var/log/messages**. There should be some sort of error messages, which may help you to diagnose the problem.

WARNING   Debugging text-mode PPP connections sometimes bears an uncanny resemblance to voodoo. The problem is that there are many minor variant implementations of PPP, both on the ISP side and on the Linux side. Some combinations are incompatible or require unusual pppd parameters. You can read the pppd man pages and try pppd parameters in the ppp-on script if you have problems. You may also be able to find help on your ISP's Web site, if you have some alternate means of accessing it.

Many ISPs send *domain name system (DNS)* server information to clients during PPP authentication. If yours doesn't, you'll need to enter this information into your /etc/resolv.conf file. This file should contain one to three lines listing DNS server addresses, as provided by your ISP. For instance:

```
nameserver 192.168.1.1
```

If your PPP configuration doesn't set this information automatically and you don't set it manually, you'll be able to access sites on the Internet by numeric IP address (such as 216.224.70.176), but not by names (such as www.sybex.com). You only need to configure DNS information once, not once per connection.

Administrator's Logbook: PPP Dialout Scripts

System: E12345678

Action: Added PPP dialout functionality to Bob & Sally's Family ISP.

Files Added/Modified: ppp-on, ppp-on-dialer, ppp-off, and pap-secrets, all in /etc/ppp.

Connecting Using a GUI Utility   Because of the difficulties associated with establishing a PPP connection using scripts, many users prefer to use a GUI front-end. These tools use the same underlying pppd program as do conventional scripts, but their point-and-click interface makes it easier to enter information on your ISP and account. It's generally possible to dispense with chat scripts when using GUI utilities, which further lessens the possibility of error.

All systems that use KDE, including Red Hat Linux, come with a GUI utility called KPPP (shown in Figure 12.5). You can use KPPP even if you don't use KDE. Alternatively, you can use a GUI dialer that's not associated with a specific environment, such as X-ISP

Figure 12.5   KPPP allows you to enter PPP account information and connect to an ISP using a GUI interface.

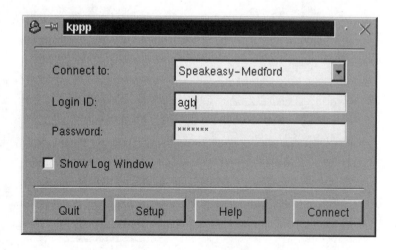

(http://users.hol.gr/~dbouras/). Most GUI dialers function in basically the same way, although some details differ. To use KPPP, follow these steps:

1. Launch KPPP by typing kppp in a terminal window or by launching it from KDE's K menu (usually K ≻ Internet ≻ Kppp). The first time you launch the program, it will have no ISP entries in the Connect To field (Figure 12.5 shows KPPP configured to use an ISP).

2. Click Setup to enter an ISP's information. The result is the KPPP Configuration dialog box shown in Figure 12.6, but with no accounts defined.

3. Click New to create a new account. KPPP displays the New Account dialog box shown in Figure 12.7.

Figure 12.6   You can adjust KPPP's settings from the Configuration dialog box.

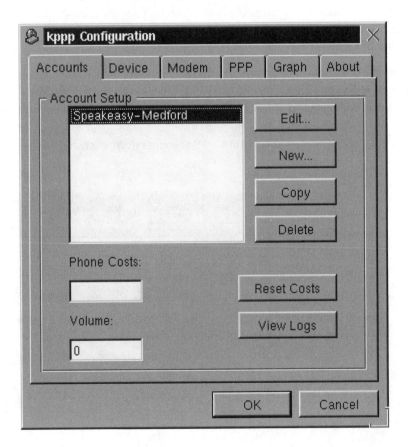

Figure 12.7 The New Account dialog box allows you to enter critical information provided by your ISP.

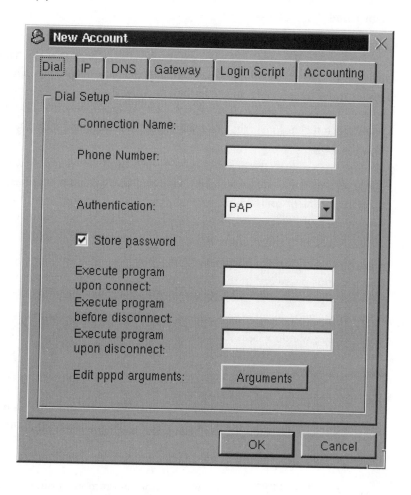

4. Enter a name and telephone number in the Connection Name and Phone Number fields, respectively. You can use any name you like; this entry is used to help you identify an account if you have several. The phone number should be one provided by your ISP.

5. Select the authentication method your ISP uses. In most cases, you can leave this set to its default of PAP.

6. Click through the remaining tabs on the New Account dialog box and enter any information provided by your ISP. The information that's most likely to need setting is the DNS server information. Enter an IP address in the DNS IP Address field and

click Add. Repeat this process if your ISP provides two DNS server addresses. In some cases, you may need to create a login script, similar to the one described for script-based PPP dialups.

7. Click OK in the New Account dialog box.

8. In the Configuration window, click the Device tab. Check that the Modem Device is set appropriately, and set the Connection Speed to 115,200. (You may want to use a lower speed if your modem is particularly slow. In general, you should use a connect speed of at least twice the modem's official speed, because modems support compression technologies that increase their effective speed when handling uncompressed data.)

9. Check the remaining tabs in the Configuration window. You may want to adjust a setting such as the modem's volume. Many additional settings are useful if you encounter problems making a connection or if you're familiar with the program, your modem, or PPP connections generally and want to enable an advanced option.

10. Click OK in the Configuration dialog box.

11. In the main KPPP window (Figure 12.5), enter your ISP username in the Login ID field and your password in the Password field. Note that these are your username and password *on the ISP*, not on the local system.

12. The first time you connect or if you encounter problems, it's often helpful to check the Show Log Window item. This results in a window that displays what KPPP sends to the modem and receives back in response; it can be very helpful in diagnosing connection problems.

13. Click Connect to initiate a connection. If all goes well, KPPP displays a Connecting To window that shows the connection status. When a connection is made, another window appears showing the time the system's been connected. You can click the Details button to see assorted statistics on the connection or the Disconnect button to end a connection.

Just as with script-based PPP connections, it's not uncommon to run into problems with a GUI-based PPP tool. A particular ISP may require an unusual set of PPP options, or it may use an odd PPP implementation that cannot be made to work well with Linux. (One of us once signed up for service through an ISP but couldn't get it working from Linux. Others reported the same problems with this ISP on Usenet newsgroups.) If you encounter problems, your best bet is to use the KPPP menus to experiment with alternate settings. You should also try using a terminal program to log on to the ISP, in order to see if the ISP uses any peculiar login prompts, which might best be handled through KPPP's scripting features (step 6).

Sending Faxes

All modern modems can be used as fax machines. Sending a fax from a computer results in an exceptionally clear fax at the receiving end because the output was generated digitally, rather than scanned from an original (unless of course you use a scanner to create a digital image to be faxed). There are several fax packages available for Linux, including mgetty+sendfax (http://alpha.greenie.net/mgetty/) and HylaFAX (http://www.hylafax.org/). The mgetty+sendfax package is a variant of mgetty, described earlier. This program comes with most Linux distributions. On Red Hat 7.0, the appropriate RPM package is called mgetty-sendfax-1.1.22-1.i386.rpm. You should install it and the regular mgetty package, upon which mgetty+sendfax depends.

In order to use mgetty+sendfax, you must configure it as follows:

1. *Install the package.* Locate and install mgetty+sendfax. It's usually called mgetty+sendfax, mgetty-sendfax, or mgetty, depending on your distribution. (On Red Hat 7.0, it's on the second CD-ROM.)

2. *Configure mgetty+sendfax.* Most distributions place mgetty+sendfax's configuration files in /etc/mgetty+sendfax. You should adjust at least four files:

   fax.allow   This file contains a list of users who are allowed to send faxes. Place one username per line in this file.

   faxheader   This file contains the header information for outgoing faxes. You should adjust it to list your fax number.

   sendfax.config   This file contains miscellaneous fax configuration information. Most of the items in this file are well commented. Change the fax-id item to your fax number. The fax-devices item is also critically important. It should list your fax device filename (without the leading /dev/), as in ttyS1 or modem.

   faxrunq.config   This file contains additional, miscellaneous fax configuration information. At a minimum, you should set the fax-devices item to point to your fax device filename, the same as you did on the same line in sendfax.config.

3. *Launch faxrunqd.* This is a daemon that watches for faxes to appear in the fax queue directory. Installing the mgetty+sendfax package normally creates this directory, usually at /var/spool/fax. To use your system to send faxes on a regular basis, you should configure it to run faxrunqd at system start-up, say by adding it to /etc/rc.d/rc.local or a similar startup file. When you do, be sure to include an ampersand (&) on the startup line, because faxrunqd does not normally start up in the background.

When you've finished configuring mgetty+sendfax, you can send a fax with the faxspool command. The syntax of this command is:

```
faxspool [options] phone-number file [file...]
```

Communicating with Devices

PART 4

Options include -n (to set normal resolution, as opposed to the default of fine), -C *program* (to call the specified program to generate a cover page), and -t *hh:mm* (to send the fax at the specified hour and minute). The phone number is the number to which the fax is to be sent. faxspool recognizes several file types, including .ps (PostScript), .t (ASCII text), .dvi (TeX DVI output), and .g3 (preformatted fax G3 files). The program uses the filename extension to identify the file type, so it's imperative that the filename extension match what faxspool expects for the file type.

It's possible, but somewhat tricky, to implement a print queue that sends output via a fax modem. One package that can help in this respect is GFax (http://www.gmsys.com/gnome-gfax.html). This program sets up a print queue that, when used, displays an X-based dialog box in which you can enter the destination fax number. One utility that allows Windows computers to send faxes via a Linux server that runs Samba is Respond (http://www.boerde.de/~horstf/). This program works much like GFax, but on Windows clients. Both programs rely upon an underlying fax-sending mechanism, such as mgetty+sendfax.

Dial-in Modem Uses

In a dial-in configuration, you set up your modem to accept incoming calls. Typically, the modem either reports to the computer that it's detected a ring, and the computer then commands the modem to answer the call; or the modem answers the call automatically and then reports to the computer that it's received a call. In either case, you must configure Linux to accept the call, and perhaps to process the incoming data in different ways depending upon what *type* of call it is.

Accepting Text-Mode Logins

One of the simplest cases is that of a text-mode login. Suppose you want to set up a system so that employees can call the computer from home to check their e-mail using text-mode programs like pine or mutt. The configuration for such a system can be very similar to that for a terminal, described earlier. In that configuration, it was necessary to add a line to /etc/inittab to link a serial port to a getty program, so that the getty program could process input from a dumb terminal. The only conceptual difference between that situation and a dial-in modem is that the modem (a pair of them, actually, but the Linux system deals directly with only one) sits between the terminal and the Linux computer. You should follow the steps outlined in "Configuring a getty Program" to set up a modem for dial-in text-mode access. The only difference is in step 2 of that procedure, which requires a slightly different modification to /etc/inittab:

```
S0:2345:respawn:/sbin/mgetty -s 57600 /dev/ttyS0
```

This line differs from the one presented earlier only in the absence of the -r parameter. The mgetty program was designed for use with modems (hence the m in mgetty), so the -r parameter *disables* some normal mgetty functionality. Specifically, mgetty normally sends command codes to the modem to prepare it to receive calls, and mgetty responds to a modem's connect messages by passing it the Linux login: prompt. Removing the -r parameter from the /etc/inittab line re-enables these features.

Administrator's Logbook: Accepting Remote Logins

System: E12345678

Action: Configured system to accept remote logins via /dev/ttyS1, using 57,600 bps port speed and mgetty.

File modified: /etc/inittab

Accepting PPP Connections

It's sometimes desirable to configure a Linux system to accept PPP logins. So configured, an Internet-enabled Linux computer can function as a gateway between a remote computer running any of several operating systems and the Internet. This setup can be convenient if you have a system at work with always-on Internet access and a modem, and you want to provide yourself or your employees with Internet access at home or when you or they are on the road. Many ISPs use Linux systems running PPP servers to handle dozens, hundreds, or more users.

NOTE 56Kbps modems operate with a speed asymmetry—upload speeds are slower than are download speeds. This state of affairs exists because the high upload speeds require that one system (the ISP's computer in a normal configuration) have a special connection to the telephone network. Unless you acquire such a connection, your dial-in PPP system will be limited to 33.6Kbps speeds, even if you have a 56Kbps modem.

There are many ways to accept PPP connections. The method described here is comparatively simple to set up, but it requires that the calling system use a connection script or manually enter authentication information. No matter how you do it, there are several configuration features you must set. In essence, a PPP link requires that the Linux computer function as a router between the dial-in systems and the rest of the network. Therefore, these systems require router support in the Linux kernel (which is standard in most Linux distributions, including Red Hat 7.0). You must also be able to assign an IP address

Communicating with Devices

PART 4

to the dial-in systems. Normally, this is done on a static basis according to the serial port, as you'll shortly see.

To configure a Linux system as a PPP server, follow these steps:

1. Configure the computer to accept a remote login via a `getty` program, as described in the previous section.

2. Modify the `/etc/ppp/options` file so that it contains the following entries (you may need to modify the netmask to conform to your network; this value should be the same as the netmask of the PPP server):

   ```
   asyncmap 0

   netmask 255.255.255.0

   proxyarp

   lock

   crtscts

   modem

   login
   ```

3. Create a file called `/etc/ppp/options.port`, where *port* is the port file, such as `ttyS0` for the first serial port. This file contains the IP address or hostname of the PPP server followed by a colon (`:`) and the IP address or hostname of the PPP client. You should be sure that the PPP client hostname is available for use on the network. For instance:

   ```
   192.168.1.3:192.168.1.200
   ```

4. Create an `/etc/ppp/pap-secrets` file entry for any users who should be able to use the PPP link. This entry is similar to the one for dial-*out* PPP access, but it lists a *local* username and password. For instance, the following allows the user `abell` to connect to a PPP server using the password `watson`:

   ```
   abell   *   watson
   ```

5. Check the permissions on the `pppd` file. You should set it uid `root` by typing **chmod u+s /usr/sbin/pppd**, if necessary. When you've done this, typing **ls -l /usr/ sbin/pppd** should reveal the following permissions:

   ```
   -rwsr-xr-x   1 root   root   140656 Mar   7 10:25 /usr/sbin/pppd
   ```

6. To run `pppd`, users dialing in must normally type a slightly cumbersome command—it's not very complex by Linux system administration standards, but it's a bit of an annoyance. You can reduce the annoyance factor by setting up a global alias to run

this command. Once set up, a user need only type **ppp** to launch pppd on Linux. You can set this up by entering the following line in /etc/bashrc (assuming your user's account is configured to use Bash as the default shell):

```
alias ppp="exec /usr/sbin/pppd -detach"
```

With these steps followed, a user should be able to use PPP to connect to the computer and any network to which it's attached. The PPP server requires manual login via a standard Linux login: prompt, after which the client must send the ppp command to start pppd on the Linux system. This can all be handled in a login script or by a manual procedure from some PPP dialers, such as the one that comes with Microsoft Windows.

Receiving Faxes

If you've configured your system to accept dialup text-mode logins using mgetty, as described in "Accepting Text-Mode Logins," your system is automatically configured to receive faxes. When a call comes in on the line to which the modem is attached, the modem determines whether the call is a data call or a fax call. If it's a data call, mgetty passes control of the serial line over to appropriate programs to handle data transmission. If the modem detects an incoming fax, mgetty initiates fax reception and places incoming faxes in the /var/spool/fax/incoming directory.

Incoming fax files use the standard G3 fax file format. You can view these files with several programs, such as KDE's KFax (shown in Figure 12.8). Such programs are typically quite simple; they allow you to view or print the file, but not much else.

TIP   mgetty includes options to send configuration strings to the modem so that it functions as *only* a data modem or as *only* a fax modem. These options are -D and -F, respectively. They can be added to the appropriate lines in /etc/inittab.

Communicating with Devices

PART 4

Configuring Serial Printers

Most printers connected to Linux computers use the parallel interface, as discussed in Chapter 13. The parallel interface offers one great advantage over the traditional RS-232 interface: speed. Modern parallel ports are theoretically capable of transferring 2MB/s, compared to the 0.014MB/s of an RS-232 serial port. This hundred-fold speed difference

Figure 12.8 KFax includes options to zoom in and out, change to a new page in a fax, or print a fax.

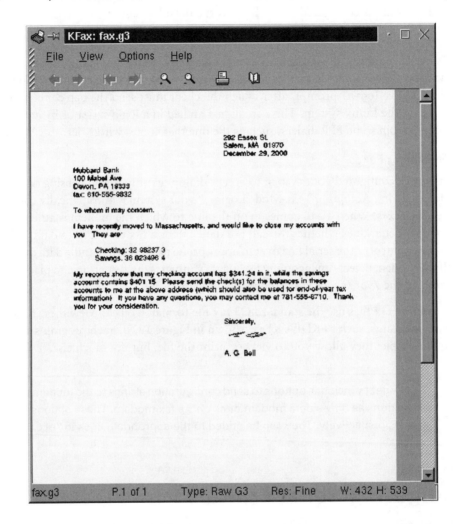

is important for printers—especially modern color printers, which often take massive bitmaps as input.

Despite the advantages of parallel ports, some printers use RS-232 serial ports. This interface is least problematic when the printer understands PostScript, because most Linux programs that can print can create PostScript output, which is more compact than the bitmap output that Ghostscript creates. (See Chapter 13 for a discussion of Ghostscript and how to use it in a Linux printer queue.)

Since 1999, USB printers have started to become popular. The USB interface is capable of 1.5MB/s speeds—roughly comparable to a parallel port. If you want to use a USB printer in Linux, you'll need a 2.4.*x* kernel, or at least a back-port of the USB drivers to a 2.2.*x* kernel.

Special Considerations for Serial Printers

For an RS-232 serial printer, the configuration details that differ from a parallel-port configuration are in the /etc/printcap file. Specifically:

- You must specify an appropriate serial port, such as /dev/ttyS1, on the lp= line.
- You must set the speed of the port using the br# line. (The pound symbol is used in place of an equal sign with this option.) For best results, you should set the speed as high as your serial port and printer allow—ideally 115,200 bps (br#115200).

To use a USB printer, you must specify the appropriate USB printer device file on the lp= line—probably /dev/usblp0 or something similar, as described in Table 12.1. You do *not* set the port speed for USB printers as you do for RS-232 serial printers.

In the case of both RS-232 and USB printers, you must have appropriate support in the Linux kernel for the port in question. All major Linux distributions include RS-232 support, but you may need to add this support for USB printers, as just described.

When to Use a Serial Printer

If you have a choice, use a parallel printer in Linux, or one that uses an Ethernet interface if you have a network. These interfaces provide the best speed, particularly when printing graphics—and Ghostscript converts text into graphics when printing to non-PostScript printers, so unless the printer supports PostScript, most Linux printing is graphics printing.

The USB interface is almost as fast as the parallel interface and so can be a good choice in this respect. The fact that USB printer support is still so new in Linux, however, makes this interface a second choice, particularly if you're using a distribution, such as Red Hat 6.2, that includes no USB support by default. (Red Hat 7.0 and some other recent distributions add USB support to their 2.2.*x* kernels.) Because USB printer support is so new, you should check http://www.linux-usb.org for compatibility information on specific models.

The RS-232 interface is decidedly sluggish, so it should not be used for a printer if you can avoid it. Modern printers that include RS-232 support also invariably support parallel or

Communicating with Devices

PART 4

USB interfaces, so there should be no trouble using these printers via more capable interfaces, at least from the printer's side of things. There are two situations in which you might be forced to use an RS-232 port:

Port depletion on the computer   Most x86 computers have just one parallel port. If you're using it for one printer, you may need to use an RS-232 port for a second printer. You can buy add-on parallel-port cards for such situations, however, so unless you want to connect many printers to one computer or cannot add a card for some reason, you can usually work around a lack of parallel ports.

Old serial-only printers   A few printers don't include parallel, USB, or Ethernet ports. Fortunately, such printers are usually PostScript models, so they're not as badly impacted by RS-232's speed problems as are non-PostScript models.

In Sum

The RS-232 serial port is a low-speed but very flexible means of interfacing computing equipment. It can be used to link two computers together (directly or through a modem), to connect dumb terminals to a computer, or to interface a printer to a computer. Linux's support for these functions is quite good, but it relies on a large number of additional software packages, such as pppd for PPP links, getty for login access, and the printing system for printers. Understanding these tools is vital for using RS-232 serial ports under Linux.

USB is a recent serial port standard that surpasses the old RS-232 standard in many ways, including speed and flexibility. Many devices are available in USB interfaces, ranging from mice to scanners to disk drives. Linux's support for USB is still new, but with the 2.4.x kernels it is good enough to allow you to use many of these devices. If you're using a Linux distribution that doesn't include either the 2.4.x kernel or a version of the 2.2.x kernel that's been patched with USB support, however, you'll need to upgrade the kernel to use USB devices.

13

Printers and the Spooling Subsystem

Printers are critical tools for most businesses, and that makes the ability to set up and administer printing a very important system administration task. You will find that many of the emergency calls you receive are from users who cannot print a document they need for an upcoming meeting. Even when something small goes wrong with a printer, it seems like a crisis to anyone who needs that printer at that specific time. A successful system administrator must understand the printing process and be able to successfully troubleshoot basic printing problems.

Printing under Linux works somewhat differently than does printing under most non-Unix OSs. If all works well, these differences are transparent to your users, but you must understand many of Linux's printing details and peculiarities in order to set up and troubleshoot a Linux printing queue. You must also understand how these queues interact with clients if the computer functions as a print server for other computers. This chapter outlines the types of printers commonly used today, the tools Linux provides for controlling printer operation, and basic installation and configuration.

Printer Basics

Printers are classified both by the way they print and the way they connect to the computer. There are three main types of printers and four types of printer interfaces you may encounter. Familiarity with these printer basics makes you a more capable system administrator and helps your users to trust that you know what you're doing. A brief introduction to types of printers and the ways they interface the computer will be helpful. If you already know these basics, you can skip ahead to "The Printing Process in Linux."

Types of Printers

Printers differ radically in the way they create images on paper. Impact printers mechanically strike characters against inked ribbons to transfer an image to paper. These have limited and specialized uses in today's business world; more common are nonimpact printers, which transfer images by other means. Impact printers include line printers, daisy-wheel printers, and dot-matrix printers. Nonimpact printers include laser printers and ink-jet printers. Some of the earliest common printers for mainframe computers were line printers—big, fast, and noisy. Daisy-wheel printers were introduced in 1970, offering the same print quality as typewriters. Soon after, the dot-matrix printer effectively replaced the daisy-wheel. Laser printers hit the scene in 1975 but the cost was prohibitive, so most businesses continued to use dot-matrix printers. In 1976 when the first ink-jet came out, it too was cost-prohibitive. In 1988, Hewlett-Packard released the DeskJet ink-jet printer, which was priced at $1000. Although many users kept their dot-matrix printers instead of paying for the better capability, this series of printers opened the door to widespread use of ink-jets by home users. Laser printers were still far too expensive and didn't do color like the ink-jets. In 1992, Hewlett-Packard introduced the LaserJet 4, which supported resolutions up to 600×600. Color laser printers were introduced in 1994. The market now is pretty much shared between ink-jet and laser printers. There are, however, a few printer types that are important in niche markets, such as dye sublimation and thermal wax transfer printers, which are popular in graphic arts departments.

Dot-Matrix Printers

Dot-matrix impact printers have a number of pins (usually between 9 and 24) arranged in a vertical line. The printer shoots some of them into an inked printer ribbon, leaving a number of dots on the paper, which produces a fuzzy, low-quality representation of the intended letter. The fuzziness is due to the mechanical nature of the pins; they simply cannot be made small enough to hide the fact that the letters are made up of dots. To its advantage, however, this type of printer first introduced the possibility of printing graphics since it was not restricted to letters like the daisy-wheel printers that preceded dot-matrix models in the marketplace.

Today, dot-matrix printers are rare because they're slow, noisy, and produce lower-quality print than competing ink-jet and laser printers. Nonetheless, they cling to life in certain applications. The primary advantage of these printers is that, because they rely upon impact technology, they can print multi-part forms. You'll therefore see dot-matrix printers in use in some retail establishments for printing receipts and invoices.

Linux support for dot-matrix printers is quite good. A handful of printer languages, led by Epson's ESC/P, have long dominated the dot-matrix market, and Linux's Ghostscript utility supports these common dot-matrix printer languages. Therefore, if you find yourself needing to support a dot-matrix printer, chances are you can get it working from Linux.

Ink-Jet Printers

Whereas dot-matrix printers rely on impact through an inked ribbon to create images on the paper, ink-jet printers shoot small drops of ink through nozzles onto the page. Like the pins of a dot-matrix print head, ink-jet nozzles can be arranged to form characters or other images but create smaller dots that are less easily discerned as such. The printing mechanism moves horizontally as the paper is slowly drawn through the printer. Early models produced dots large enough that the print quality was on a par with that of dot-matrix printers, but the technology quickly improved to the point where the images rival laser printers in image quality.

Generally cheaper to buy than laser printers, ink-jet printers are more expensive to maintain. The system contains 1–6 ink cartridges, which have to be replaced or refilled when empty. (Each cartridge produces 1–3 colors; all modern ink-jets are color printers, although the earliest models printed only black.) These cartridges can be quite expensive and may print only a few pages before requiring replacement, leading to high per-page costs. Ink-jet printers work best with specially coated paper that prevents the ink from spreading as it dries. Care should be taken when removing a printed sheet from an ink-jet printer, since the ink will smear unless it is allowed sufficient time to dry. Regular printer paper may be used, but the image is often slightly blurred by the way the drops of ink soak into it.

> **NOTE** You can buy ink refill kits for most popular ink-jet printer models. These kits can greatly reduce the cost of printing, but refilling can be a messy process and doesn't always work correctly. Printer manufacturers discourage this process, and they may refuse warranty service if they discover you've been refilling, although refill manufacturers claim any such action is illegal. To the best of our knowledge, this claim has never been tested in court.

Laser Printers

Laser printers offer the best print quality. Introduced commercially by Hewlett-Packard in 1984, they have come to dominate the office market as their price has fallen compared to other printer types. A laser printer transfers a full-page image to paper electrostatically, much like a photocopier. But while a photocopier begins by copying the image from its source photographically, a laser printer begins with computer data, which the printer's onboard processing converts into instructions that drive a laser beam, tracing the image onto a cylindrical drum. Figure 13.1 illustrates the process. The fineness of the laser beam enables laser printers to achieve very high resolution for both text and graphics, in the range of hundreds of dots per inch (dpi).

Figure 13.1   Laser printing

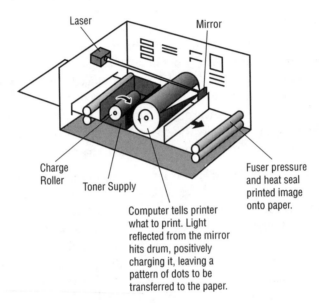

Modern laser printers are several times faster than the average ink-jet and are good for use where large volumes of printing need to be produced quickly and at high quality. Laser printers are less sensitive to paper characteristics than are ink-jets, so you can get by with less expensive paper. The toner used in place of ink in laser printers is also less expensive than ink-jet ink, at least on a per-page basis. (Toner cartridges usually cost more than ink-jet cartridges, but the toner cartridges print many more pages.) Most laser printers in 2001 print only black, but color models are slowly growing in popularity.

Obsolete and Rare Printer Types

The history of computer printing is littered with technologies that have seen their heyday and have now faded into obscurity. There are also printer types that are produced and used in certain niche markets. These technologies include:

Daisy-wheel printers   Daisy-wheel printers are named after the appearance of their print heads, which resemble the petals of a flower. At the tip of each "petal" is a raised image of a character. These petals are struck against an inked ribbon, much as in a dot-matrix printer. These devices were a common means of producing high-quality text at one time, but they've been made obsolete by laser printers, which produce better text faster and less noisily.

Line printers   Line printers use impact technology, much like daisy-wheel and dot-matrix printers. These printers use a series of wheels with letters on them. Each wheel spins independently, so an entire line of text can be composed and printed at once, hence the name. The Linux *line printer daemon* (`lpd`) program takes its name from this type of printer but works with other printer types. These printers are still in use with large mainframe computers.

Dye-sublimation printers   These printers use dyes rather than inks to create their images. The printer heats the dyes until they turn gaseous, and the gas then hits the paper, producing a colored dot much like that produced by an ink-jet printer. These printers produce excellent color output, but they're expensive and slow.

Thermal wax transfer   This technology uses colored waxes rather than the colored inks of ink-jet technology. These printers fall between dye-sublimation and ink-jet printers in both print quality and cost.

Plotters   A plotter uses pens, dragged across the paper by a robotic arm, to produce output. These devices are often used to produce large pages of line art, as in architectural drawings.

You're unlikely to encounter any of these printer types, but you might, particularly if you're administering a Linux print server used in a graphics art department or some other environment where a specialized printer type is desirable. The main thing to be concerned about with these printers is compatibility with Linux's Ghostscript utility. As described shortly, printers used with Linux must either understand the PostScript printer language natively or must be supported by Ghostscript. Unusual printers may satisfy neither requirement. If the printer is supported, however, you can treat it just like any other printer.

Printer Interfaces

Printers can be made accessible to a computer in several ways. In the simplest case, a printer can be connected directly to a standalone workstation via the parallel, RS-232 serial, or Universal Serial Bus (USB) port. In the business world, however, the connection will more likely be to a networked workstation or to a dedicated print server. A print server is a computer or dedicated network device that has one or more printer interfaces and a network interface. The print server accepts print jobs from other computers on the network, and directs those jobs to the printer. A Linux computer can function as a print server, either in a dedicated fashion or in addition to performing other tasks. In Linux, a file named `printcap` contains the basic configuration for each printer. Some printers have network interface cards built directly into them and can also be accessed by setting up the appropriate entry in the `printcap` file. We'll talk more about this file in a little while.

Parallel Port

Most printers connect to computers via the parallel port. These can be anything from dot-matrix printers to modern laser printers. Parallel printers use an interface by which data is transferred on more than one wire simultaneously. A parallel port carries one bit on each wire, thus multiplying the transfer rate obtainable over a single cable by the number of wires. Along with data, control signals are sent on the port as well to say when data is ready to be sent or received.

There are now enhanced high-speed parallel ports, conforming to the IEEE 1284 standard, which provide communication with external devices, including printers. These advanced ports support bidirectional transfers to 2MBps. Keep in mind, however, that high-speed parallel ports are intended to run devices within 20 feet of the computer; short, high-quality cables are essential to high throughput. Signals sent on cables longer than 20 feet will degrade in proportion to the length of the cable.

Most of this chapter's discussion of Linux printing support and configuration applies to printers connected to a parallel port. Typically, though, only a few configuration details need to be changed if you're using an RS-232 or USB printer.

RS-232 Serial Port

RS-232 serial ports were initially developed for use by modems, but they now support a number of other devices like serial mice and serial printers. RS-232 serial ports are slower than parallel ports, so they aren't used very often for printers, which usually require high-speed interfaces, particularly when printing graphics. Some printers can be used as either parallel or RS-232 serial depending on the way you connect them to the computer.

 RS-232 serial ports can handle situations where there is more distance between the printer and the computer. A serial printer can run 50 feet at around 38.4Kbps (4.8KBps, roughly 500 times slower than the 2MBps of a parallel port). The cable length can be extended via an electrical interface like EIA-530 (aka RS-422).

Chapter 12, "Serial Communications, Terminals, and Modems," shows how to configure serial printer connections.

USB Ports

The latest type of printer interface is the USB port. This is an updated type of serial port that supports much higher speeds than the older RS-232 serial port—up to 1.5MBps, or very close to parallel-port speeds. USB also allows you to connect up to 127 devices to a single port, whereas both parallel and RS-232 serial ports allow only one device per port. These facts have made USB devices increasingly popular, and not just for printers—keyboards, mice, scanners, tape backup devices, modems, digital cameras, and more are available in USB form. Among printers, USB is most common in low-end and mid-range ink-jet printers, and particularly those marketed for Macintosh users. (Current Macintoshes lack both parallel and RS-232 serial ports.)

From a Linux perspective, the main drawback to USB is that USB is still new enough that Linux's support for USB is immature. In fact, USB support in the 2.2.*x* Linux kernel series is essentially nonexistent. The 2.4.*x* kernels do include USB support, but distributions at the start of 2001 (including Red Hat 7.0) don't use 2.4.*x* kernels by default. Many distributions *do*, however, include a back-port of the 2.4.*x* USB support to their 2.2.*x* kernels. This is true of Red Hat 7.0. The end result is that you *can* use a USB printer, but you may need to update your kernel or choose an appropriate distribution. Because USB printers are comparatively untested under Linux, you may also encounter problems because of the immature drivers.

Networked Printers

The term *networked printer* refers to a printer attached to a computer accessible via the network or to a printer that has a built-in network card and is assigned its own IP address. The latter is sometimes called an Ethernet printer. (Note that a parallel, RS-232 serial, or USB printer may become a networked printer simply by attaching it to a print server.) A networked printer is set up via the same printcap file and requires less configuration than other connection types, since Linux can print to any networked printer that supports the LPD protocol (and most do). You must set up a printcap entry on any other computers on the network that need access to a networked printer.

The Linux Printing Process

Printing under Linux begins with a process called *print spooling*. A print spooler is a program that accepts print jobs (requests for a certain document to be printed) from a program or network interface, stores them in a spool queue, and then sends them to a printer one at a time. Print spooling is critical on a system where a second or subsequent print job might be sent before the first job has been completed. The print spooler holds these jobs and allows an administrator to manage them. Typically, this management includes deleting jobs, reordering jobs, or restarting the printer or its queue. The most common print spooling software package for Linux has historically been the line printer daemon or lpd package, which was borrowed from BSD's Net 2 package. Other print spoolers include LPRng and CUPS. Red Hat and Caldera are two distributions that use LPRng by default. Debian gives a choice of lpd or LPRng. Many others use lpd. Both systems are quite similar in practice, and this chapter emphasizes their way of doing things.

Tools of the Printing Trade

No matter what specific printing system you use, there are certain common utilities and configuration files of which you should be aware. These include the /etc/printcap file (or its equivalent), Ghostscript, and the printer queue's filter set. The details of these packages and their configuration determines what printers you can use, and precisely how programs print on the computer.

The *printcap* File

The lpd and LPRng print spoolers use a configuration file called /etc/printcap. This name is short for *printer capabilities*, and that's what the file describes. It contains entries providing configuration data for all the printers connected to the computer, either locally or via network. Each printer's entry contains information such as the printer's name, its spooling directory, the maximum file size it can accept, and so on. The spooler reads this file each time it starts and each time it is called.

The printcap file has a complicated format and is usually created with some sort of configuration tool. These tools make the job of creating a printcap file much easier. Red Hat Linux uses the Printtool utility, discussed later in the chapter.

You'll see an example of a printcap file on a Red Hat system when we look at the lpd spooler.

CUPS and some other printing systems don't use a printcap file; instead, they use other files, located in the /etc/cups directory in the case of CUPS, such as /etc/cups/printers.conf. The format of these files is different from the format of a printcap file, but they accomplish the same tasks.

Ghostscript

Traditionally, Unix programs have been written under the assumption that a printer is one of two things: a line printer that understands little or no formatting, or a PostScript printer. PostScript printers can accept downloadable fonts, bitmapped graphics, vector graphics, and many other features. In fact, PostScript is a full-blown programming language, comparable in many ways to C, Perl, and the like. PostScript, however, is designed for creating printed output, so it's heavy on graphics manipulation features.

Because Linux has inherited so many Unix programs, Linux has also inherited the PostScript-centric nature of its printer system. Unfortunately, PostScript printers have traditionally been more expensive than otherwise similar non-PostScript printers, and many Linux developers have been unable to afford PostScript printers. In order to create more than primitive monospaced text-only output, therefore, Linux requires a helper application. This application is *Ghostscript* (http://www.cs.wisc.edu/~ghost/), which converts PostScript into a wide variety of other formats, including formats that can be understood natively by many non-PostScript printers.

When using a non-PostScript printer, then, the printing process proceeds as follows: An application (WordPerfect, xfig, Netscape, or whatever) produces a PostScript file. This file is fed into a Linux printer queue, which sends the file through Ghostscript. The queue then passes Ghostscript's output on to the printer. The result is that you can configure the application as for a PostScript printer, even when the printer is really a low-end ink-jet that could never understand PostScript.

All major Linux distributions ship with Ghostscript, but not with the latest version of the program. Ghostscript is unusual in its licensing. The latest versions are free for *noncommercial* distribution, but any distribution for money requires negotiation of license terms with the copyright holder, Aladdin. Older versions of Ghostscript, however, are available under the GNU General Public License (GPL), and so can be distributed on commercial Linux CD-ROMs without dealing with onerous licensing issues. In most cases, the older GNU Ghostscript is quite adequate. If you want the latest Ghostscript features, check the Ghostscript Web site; you can download the latest version and use it, so long as you don't include it in any product you distribute for money.

TIP Unless your printer understands PostScript natively, most or all of your Linux printing will rely upon Ghostscript to handle the printer. Therefore, it's critically important that your printer either be a PostScript printer itself or be supported by Ghostscript. The Linux Printing Support Database (http://www.linuxprinting.org/printer_list.cgi) is a cross-reference database of printer models and their Ghostscript drivers, including comments on how well these drivers work. Consult it before buying a printer or if you're having trouble getting a printer to work in Linux.

Ghostscript itself typically requires very little in the way of configuration. It includes drivers for many different printers, and the program that calls it (such as the print queue or magic filter) specifies what driver to use. In some cases, though, you may want to add fonts to Ghostscript or even recompile it with unusual drivers. If you need to add fonts to Ghostscript, it can be done by editing the /usr/share/ghostscript/*version*/Fontmap file, where *version* is the Ghostscript version number (5.50 in Red Hat 7.0). Most programs that print with unusual fonts embed them in their output PostScript files, so there's no need to add fonts to Ghostscript explicitly.

Magic Filters

One critical piece of information that the print spooler software finds in the printcap file is the magic filter, or print filter, to be used with a given printer. A *magic filter* is software that receives a file from standard input, performs an action based on the file's type, and then outputs the result on standard output.

When a print spooler such as LPRng is called with a filename or stream as an argument, it examines the printcap entry for the specified printer. If the appropriate stanza specifies a print filter, lpd sends the document or stream through that filter, thereby producing output in the proper format. The printer will not print properly if sent a file it does not understand. There are numerous file formats used for printing: straight text, PostScript, image files of various types, and so on. The print filter decides what to do with each file type—whether to send it directly to the printer, process it through Ghostscript, or process it through some other program.

With a plain text file, for example, the magic filter has nothing to do. If it receives a PostScript file, however, the magic filter for a non-PostScript printer would call Ghostscript to translate the file for printing. Three packages that provide these filters are rhs-printfilters (used by Red Hat), APSFilter (used by most distributions and discussed later in this chapter), and magicfilter. You must ensure that any program called by your filter, like Ghostscript, is on the system as well. If you stick with the default printer tools used by your distribution, this should be adequate. If you adjust your print filter configuration, though, you'll need to carefully review its documentation to learn what other tools it requires.

The LPRng Print Spooler

LPRng is a modern re-implementation of the old lpd printing system. LPRng includes equivalents to most of the lpd tools and utilities, although some of the details differ. Most of the information presented here about LPRng also applies to the older lpd system.

Both LPRng and the original lpd system are built around the line printer daemon, lpd. This is the program that monitors print requests and kicks off the appropriate subprogram to accomplish the desired task. The Line Printer Daemon Protocol is defined in Request For Comment (RFC) 1179. The term lpd is used to refer both to the daemon itself and more broadly to the set of programs used to perform the various functions associated with a print spool. These include the lpd, lpr, lpq, lpc, and lprm programs. The most important is the daemon itself, lpd, which provides the spooling functionality.

NOTE It's important to distinguish between the original lpd package and the lpd program. The former indicates a specific set of programs with a particular history. The latter indicates a program of a particular name, versions of which come with both the original lpd package and the newer LPRng. Much of the following discussion of lpd refers to the program, not the specific package; this discussion applies to both the original lpd package and the new LPRng package.

Basic *lpd* Functionality

A master line printer daemon runs constantly to keep track of any print spooling needs on the system. The master lpd is started at boot time in the same way as other daemons we discussed when we talked about system initialization. Red Hat Linux has an lpd script in /etc/rc.d/init.d, which is run at boot time. You can start or stop LPRng at other times by issuing a command consisting of the full path to the lpd script, a space, and one of the following: start, stop, status, or restart. When the line printer daemon is started, it reads the /etc/printcap file, discussed earlier. Listing 13.1 shows an example of a printcap file.

Listing 13.1   An Example printcap File

```
lp|lp0|lexmark:\
        :sd=/var/spool/lpd/lexmark:\
        :mx#0:\
        :sh:\
        :lp=/dev/lp0:\
        :if=/var/spool/lpd/lexmark/filter:
lp1|hp4000:\
        :sd=/var/spool/lpd/hp4000:\
        :mx#0:\
        :sh:\
        :rm=tennessee:\
        :rp=hp4000:\
        :if=/var/spool/lpd/hp4000/filter:
lp2|epson:\
        :sd=/var/spool/lpd/epson:\
        :mx#0:\
        :sh:\
        :if=/var/spool/lpd/epson/filter:\
        :af=/var/spool/lpd/epson/acct:\
        :lp=/dev/null:
```

Communicating with Devices

PART 4

This `printcap` file example contains the configuration for a directly connected Lexmark Optra 40, a remote HP LaserJet 4000, and a remote SMB/Windows Epson Stylus Color 800. The first line assigns the local printer's name, in this case `lp|lp0|lexmark`. This is actually a specification for *three* names, each separated from the others by vertical bars (`|`). In this case, users can refer to the printer as `lp`, `lp0`, or `lexmark`, with identical results. `lp` is the default for the first printer on most systems. The next uncommented line sets the spooling directory for the printer to `/var/spool/lpd/lexmark`. The line beginning with `:mx` sets the maximum file size in kilobytes; the 0 in our example sets it to unlimited. The next line sets up the printer to suppress the page header, which when present provides information on who ran the print job, to make sorting print jobs easier in a busy printing environment. The next line sets the printer device name to `/dev/lp0`. This device name is the printer's hardware device file—the file to which LPRng ultimately sends its output. This name may or may not bear any resemblance to the print spool name defined earlier. The line beginning with `:if` provides the path to the file that contains the filter information for any print types defined for that printer. These options and more are documented in the `printcap` man page.

The sample `printcap` file contains stanzas (sections) for two more printers. The `lp1|hp4000` entry is for a printer located on a machine with a hostname of `tennessee`, located on the same network as the local machine. The difference in this stanza is that instead of an `lp` line, it contains an `rm` line, which specifies the machine to which the printer is connected; and an `rp` line specifying the queue name on that machine. This second queue also has its own spool directory.

The `lp2|epson` entry is for an SMB/Windows 95/NT printer. The standard Red Hat print queue format doesn't place information on SMB print servers in the `printcap` file; instead, that information is located in the `.config` file in the spool directory. For an SMB printer, you must include a username and password for the host machine. For security reasons, the username and password on the Windows machine should *not* be the same as that user's account on the Linux machine. We'll discuss printing to a networked Windows printer later in the chapter.

After reading through the `printcap` file and printing anything left in the queue, the line printer daemon goes into a passive mode, waiting for requests to print files, reorder print jobs in the queue, or display the waiting print jobs. It uses the system calls `listen` and `accept` to determine whether any such requests are made.

As mentioned above, the line printer daemon package includes other programs necessary to the printing functionality. These binaries perform specific functions, which we'll look at next.

lpr

The lpr program is the spooling command that makes requests of lpd. lpr makes contact with the line printer daemon when it needs to put a new print job into the spool. The format is basic:

```
lpr path-to-file [arguments]
```

When you print from an application under Linux, the program runs lpr, specifying a stream from which to read. This data may take any of several forms, including PostScript, raw text, JPEG graphic, and so on. lpr passes the data to lpd, which checks the printcap file for specifics about the printer. If the printcap entry includes a filter line, lpd sends the data (document) through that filter as discussed earlier. Once the document is filtered, lpd sends it to the queue specified in the printcap entry for that printer.

Commonly used arguments to lpr include:

-Pqueuename	Forces output to a particular printer instead of the default printer or the printer specified by the PRINTER environment variable. *Do not* include a space between -P and *queuename*.
-h	Suppresses the printing of a header page.
-m mail_addr	Sends mail to *mail_addr* upon completion of the print.
-#num	Prints *num* copies of each file.
-T title	Title to print on cover page.

lpq

The lpq command controls the queue examination program, which lists the print jobs currently waiting in the queue. The lpq command returns the user's name, the job's current place in the queue, the files that make up the print job, a numeric identifier for the job, and the total size of the job in bytes. To check the queue for a specific printer, use the -P option, as with the lpr command. To check the queue for jobs owned by a specific user, enter a username as an argument. In action, lpq looks like this:

```
$ lpq -Php4000
Printer: lp is lp@localhost
Printer: lp@speaker  'raw'
 Queue: 3 printable jobs
 Server: pid 12180 active
 Unspooler: pid 12181 active
```

```
Status: printing 'user@speaker+179', file 1 'yacl-egcs.txt', size
    ➥4172, format 'l' at 18:06:54
```

Rank	Owner/ID	Class	Job	Files	Size	Time
active	user@speaker+179	A	179	yacl-egcs.txt	4172	18:06:54
2	user@speaker+182	A	182	tweener.txt	4879	18:07:05
3	user@speaker+186	A	186	kms94.ps	125700	18:07:16

NOTE The output format of LPRng, as shown above, differs from the format of the original lpd's lpq. LPRng's listing is more complete, but lpd's provides much of the same critical information, including a job ID number and the name of the file being printed.

---

lpc

The LPRng System Control program, or lpc, provides the capability to disable or enable a print queue, to reorder the print jobs in a queue, and to obtain status information about a printer, a queue, or a job. These commands are applicable to any printer in the /etc/printcap file as specified by the associated name or to all printers.

If issued without an argument, the lpc session will be interactive and a lpc> prompt will be returned. You can also include the lpc command in a script, using the following format:

> lpc [*subcommand*]

The available subcommands are as follows:

> abort   Terminates any printing in progress and then disables further printing to the specified printer(s). The queue is left intact so that the waiting print jobs will be printed when the start command is next issued. Sometimes, if a printer has stopped printing for no apparent reason, issuing the abort command followed by the start command will get things going again.

> disable   Turns the queue off so that it won't accept any more jobs, although the superuser can still queue print jobs. Printing is not halted, so anything in the queue already or added by the superuser will print. When a printer is to be deactivated, you should issue the disable command followed by the stop command.

> down   Turns the specified print queue off, disables printing to that queue, and logs a message to the printer status file. Subsequent attempts to run the lpq command will indicate that it is down and output the status message.

> enable   Enables spooling on the specified printer's queue so that it will accept new jobs.

> exit   Terminates the interactive lpc session.

reread   Tells the `lpd` daemon to reread its configuration file.

start   Enables printing and starts a spooling daemon for the specified printer(s).

stop   Stops `lpd` after the current job has been completed and disables printing.

topq [*printer*] [*jobs*]   Places the jobs in order at the top of the queue (after the currently printing job) for the specified printer(s). Unless `topq` has been used to reorder them, the jobs will be in FIFO order (first in first out).

up   Enables the queue for the specified printer and starts a new printer daemon for that queue.

As an example, suppose you want to reorder the jobs in the `lexmark` print queue so that job 186 from the earlier `lpq` example prints before job 182. (Ordinarily, job numbers are assigned in ascending order according to print order.) You might use the following command to accomplish this goal:

```
# lpc topq lexmark 186 182
```

lprm

The `lprm` command allows you to remove a job or jobs from the spool queue of the default printer. You may pass a `-P` option with a printer name to specify a different printer. Entering the `lprm` command with the number of a job in the queue removes that job. You can also use `lpq` to see the job numbers in a queue, as described earlier.

Issuing `lprm` with an argument of – removes all jobs the initiator owns, clearing the queue entirely if issued by the superuser. If the superuser issues the `lprm` command followed by a username, all jobs for that user will be removed. Thus, if you wish to remove job 11 and you are the owner or the superuser, you may issue the following command:

```
$ lprm  11
```

If you're the superuser and you want to remove all the jobs owned by `someuser`, you could enter the following command:

```
# lprm  someuser
```

Alternative Printing Utilities

Red Hat 7.0 ships with LPRng and the `rhs-printfilters` package as the basic printing system and print filter set, respectively. These are not the only options available, however. In fact, some distributions ship with alternative systems, such as the older `lpd`, the newer CUPS, or alternative magic filters. It's almost always easiest to use whichever package comes with your distribution, but you may want to consider replacing a package under some circumstances.

Communicating with Devices

PART 4

Alternatives to LPRng

There are several spooling packages on the market. Traditionally, lpd has been the most popular, but Linux distributions are beginning to abandon it, for various reasons. One disadvantage is that the original lpd package's lpr, lpc, lpq, and lprm are each GUID commands, and all except lpc are also SUID. This means that anyone running these binaries temporarily assumes the privileges of the owner of the binary (SUID) or the group of the binary (GUID). This allows restricted access to resources that are not meant to be manipulated by the basic user. This is a potential security problem since any user who finds a way to break out of the program or to exploit some weakness in the program may use these privileges—especially if the user or group is root—to wreak havoc system-wide.

There are also a great many things that a spooling program could do that lpd doesn't do. Among these are load balancing between different print queues and tighter authorization constraints. Nonetheless, you may still find yourself using lpd with some distributions. If you do, the preceding discussion of LPRng is applicable, aside from a few minor details like the exact format of lpq's output. LPRng is a more secure and streamlined package, and so is generally preferable to lpd.

LPRng is an enhanced version of the lpd package. It provides the lpr, lpc, and lprm programs in an implementation that requires much less overhead and doesn't require SUID root. It supports dynamic redirection of print queues, load balancing, automatic job holding, very clear diagnostics, security checks, load balancing among multiple printers, and improved handling of permission and authorization issues. For secure printing, LPRng supports Kerberos 5, MIT Kerberos 4 extensions to LPR, PGP, and simple MD5-based authentication. LPRng ships with Caldera OpenLinux 2.4, Red Hat 7.0, and Debian 2.2. You can learn more about LPRng at http://www.astart.com/lprng/LPRng.html.

The Common Unix Printing System (CUPS) is another package that aims to overcome lpd's limitations. It takes a more radical approach than does LPRng, though, entirely abandoning the printcap file and adding new network printing protocols. CUPS does incorporate common lpd-style printing programs, such as lpr, to ease the transition from one system to another. Most importantly, CUPS provides a means for applications to query the printing system about a printer's capabilities, which CUPS extracts from PostScript Printer Description (PPD) files you install. With the standard lpd system, either the applications must make assumptions about a printer's capabilities (such as paper size), or you must configure every application individually. If CUPS catches on, programs will be able to obtain this information automatically, easing administrative effort. Currently, though, few applications take advantage of CUPS's unusual features. This spooler is an optional component of Mandrake 7.2. You can learn more at `http://www.cups.org`.

If you want to experiment with an alternative printing system, do so on a test system, at least initially. Some packages may not get along well with these new systems, because their `lpd` compatibility is not perfect. Once you've determined that your major applications work with the new system, you can consider installing it on your main systems, possibly including any print servers you maintain.

Alternative Filter Packages

The `rhs-printfilters` package is quite adequate for most uses. It can distinguish raw ASCII text, PostScript, various graphics file formats, and a handful of others. If you use these filters as part of your `printcap` file, as described earlier, then the filter will automatically handle the printing of any of these file types. These print filters are also integral to using a standard Red Hat print queue to print to a printer that's hosted on a Windows print server. This filter package is not the only print filter available for Linux, however. Alternatives include:

APSFilter   This package aims to be a platform-neutral filter package. It handles more file formats than does the standard Red Hat `rhs-printfilters` package. You can learn more at `http://www.apsfilter.org`.

Magicfilter   Like APSFilter, Magicfilter is a full-featured filter package, which can handle more file formats than can the standard Red Hat filters. The package is available from `ftp://sunsite.unc.edu/pub/Linux/system/printing/`.

Many distributions ship with either APSFilter or Magicfilter, so you may already be using one of these without knowing it. In most cases, switching from one filter package to another provides few benefits and many hassles, because printing systems are built from a rather long chain of programs. If one link changes something that a subsequent link relies upon, the system stops working. Unless you've investigated your alternative package and find that it does something the one you're currently using doesn't do, therefore, it's generally best to stick with whatever comes with your distribution.

Configuring Printers under Red Hat

Each Linux distribution includes a preferred tool to add an entry to the `printcap` file and create the printer's spool directory under `/var/spool/lpd`. Red Hat uses a program called Printtool. This GUI tool, shown in Figure 13.2, creates entries for the `/etc/printcap` file and provides links to the corresponding magic filters as well. You start this tool by typing `printtool` in an `xterm` window.

Communicating with Devices

PART 4

Figure 13.2   Red Hat's Printtool facility

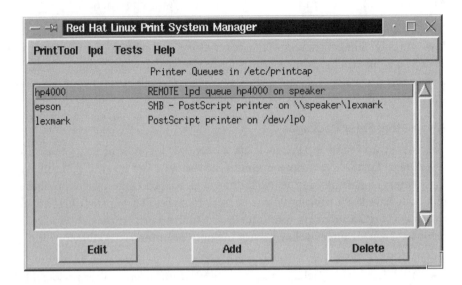

To add a printer using Printtool, follow these steps:

1. Start the Printtool utility. You'll see its main screen, as shown in Figure 13.2, although you may not see any defined printers.

2. Click Add. Printtool responds by displaying the Add a Printer Entry dialog box, in which you can select from among five different printer types (see Figure 13.3).

Figure 13.3   You can elect to define a local printer, three different types of network printer, or a "direct to port" printer that bypasses the usual queue setup.

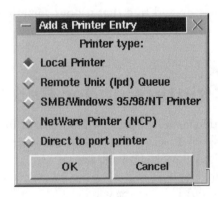

3. Click the printer type you want to define. The remaining instructions assume you opt for a local printer. The network printer definitions are similar, but ask for information on the print server name rather than a local printer port.

4. Click OK in the Add a Printer Entry dialog box. Printtool displays information about the printer ports it has detected. (If you opt for a network printer, it may display tips or warnings concerning your type of network connection instead.) This port detection doesn't always detect all your ports, particularly if you're using an RS-232 serial or USB printer. You can safely ignore these omissions.

5. Click OK in the information screen. Printtool displays the Edit Local Printer Entry dialog box shown in Figure 13.4. (The network printer dialog boxes are similar but have fields for identifying the print server and printer rather than the Printer Device field shown in Figure 13.4.)

6. Enter the identifying information for your printer—the name or names you want to use for it, the spool directory, and the printer device file (or network identifying information). *Do not* click OK yet.

7. Click Select next to the Input Filter field. Printtool displays the Configure Printer dialog box shown in Figure 13.5. Here you should set several characteristics of your printer and how you want it to be handled:

   A. Select your printer type in the Printer Type list. This list is *not* a complete list of printers; instead, it lists broad classes of printers. Many laser printers, for instance, emulate certain HP LaserJet models, so you would select the appropriate LaserJet model from the list. Also, there's just one entry for all PostScript models on this list. Your selection here will determine what other options are available.

Figure 13.4   The Edit Local Printer Entry dialog box lets you configure basic features of your printer queue.

Communicating
with Devices

PART 4

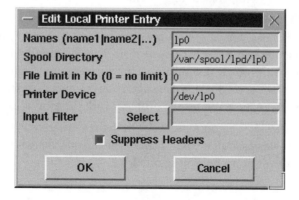

Figure 13.5 The Configure Filter dialog box is used for configuring Ghostscript and a few miscellaneous print queue options.

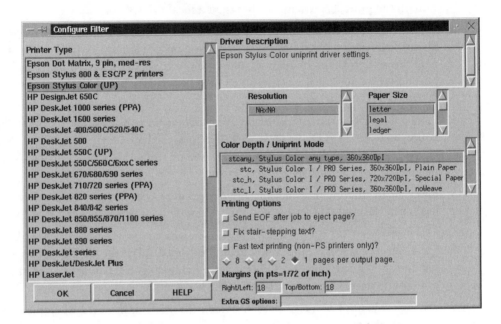

B. Select your printer's resolution in the Resolution field, if it's available. You won't be able to adjust your printer's resolution on a job-by-job basis, unless it understands PostScript natively and you use a program that accomplishes the task.

C. Select the paper size in the Paper Size field.

D. Select any other options in the Color Depth / Uniprint Mode field. This field is used for setting miscellaneous Ghostscript options that apply to specific printer types.

E. Set any miscellaneous printing options you like in the Printing Options area. It's generally best to leave these at their defaults initially. If your last page doesn't print or if you get text printouts in which each line begins horizontally after the end of the preceding line (so-called "stair-stepped" text), then you can return to this dialog box and fix the problem with these options.

8. When you've set your options, click OK in the Configure Filter dialog box. You'll see the Input Filter field in the Edit Local Printer Entry dialog box (Figure 13.4) change to show the printer type you selected.

9. Click OK in the Edit Local Printer Entry dialog box. The queue should appear in the main Printtool window (Figure 13.2).

10. Select LPD ➤ Restart LPD in the Printtool window's menu to restart the line printer daemon.

At this point, the printer should be defined. You can click its name in the Printtool window and select the tests under the Tests menu item to test the configuration. The Print ASCII Test Page item prints plain ASCII text, and the Print Postscript Test Page item prints a PostScript file. These printouts include tips on fixing minor problems, should they appear on the printouts. If the printout doesn't appear at all, and if you're using a local printer, try the Tests ➤ Print ASCII Directly to Port option. If the printout doesn't appear from this item, then you've may have selected the wrong printer device file in step 6 or the drivers may not be loading. (The problem could also be more prosaic, as in a failure to turn on the printer.)

To filter PostScript files for non-PostScript printers, most Linux distributions use GNU Ghostscript instead of Aladdin Ghostscript, which supports more printers than the GNU version. If you find that Printtool does not support your printer, you may wish to install Aladdin Ghostscript. The magic filters used by Printtool are taken from the `rhs-printfilters` package, which supports PostScript and other common input types.

Printing with Other Distributions

Other Linux distributions, such as Debian, SuSE, and Slackware, use essentially the same printing process as we've described for Red Hat, but they may use different spooler software and/or configuration tools. Mandrake users can use the same Printtool utility just described.

Debian

Debian offers a choice between the standard `lpd` package and LPRng, discussed earlier. There are several options for configuration tools. APSFilter version 5 is a good choice, since it adds support for LPRng.

Another very usable option is the Magicfilter package. Magicfilter will ask you a few questions about your printer and then configure it for you. It is a good option if you're not getting the results you want with the APSFilter package.

Many Debian users simply edit the `printcap` file by hand. The man page for `printcap` clearly lists the options and what they represent. As long as the format is followed, the entry should work.

Communicating with Devices

PART 4

SuSE

The printing system on SuSE Linux is based on APSFilter but has some SuSE-specific enhancements. SuSE's APSFilter will recognize all common file formats (including HTML, if html2ps is installed). There are three ways to set up printers on SuSE systems:

- An interactive tool called YaST will let you configure PostScript, DeskJet, and other printers as supported by Ghostscript drivers. YaST will create /etc/printcap entries for several types of printers (raw, ASCII, auto, and color) in local, network, Samba, or Novell Netware configurations. YaST will also create the appropriate spool directories. YaST will add apsfilterrc files, which allows you to fine-tune things like paper size, paper orientation, resolution, printer escape sequences, and some Ghostscript settings. Launch YaST by typing **yast** at a command prompt.

- SuSE's APSFilter package contains a setup script that is a modified version of the original APSFilter's setup script. To invoke it, run the command **lprsetup**. The lprsetup program contains online help and default answers to questions about adding, deleting, or setting up a line printer on your system. It prompts for data, showing the default answer in brackets [ ]. Pressing the Enter key accepts the default. After you have answered all of the questions, lprsetup creates the spooling directory, links the output filter, and creates an /etc/printcap entry for the printer.

- You can configure the print queues manually, by editing /etc/printcap in your favorite editor. If you want to use APSFilter in this way, you'll need to configure the package manually. Consult the APSFilter documentation for details. This procedure is most likely to be useful if you don't want to use a magic filter for some reason—say, if you only print PostScript files and have a PostScript printer.

Slackware

Slackware uses APSFilter to set up printing. You must have the following packages installed:

```
a1/lpr.tgz
ap1/apsfilt.tgz
ap1/ghostscr.tgz
ap1/gsfonts.tgz
```

Run the following command as root to begin printer setup:

```
# /usr/lib/apsfilter/SETUP
```

Setup is actually quite easy with APSFilter's setup utility. Still, most Slackware users like the "rawness" of Slackware and prefer not to use GUI-based tools at all. They, like the Debian users mentioned earlier, prefer to hand-edit the printcap file.

Kernel Support

Printer port support is built largely into the kernel source files. Parallel ports require that several modules be included. RS-232 serial printing is accomplished with much less fuss and requires no real printer-specific adaptation when the kernel is configured. USB printing requires the use of a 2.4.*x* or USB-patched 2.2.*x* kernel compiled with support for both USB and USB printers, as described in Chapter 12. Remote printing requires no printer-specific kernel options.

Parallel Port Printers

If you are unsure whether your kernel has parallel port printer support built in, look at /var/log/dmesg to see if a line containing lp0, lp1, or lp2 appears. A 2.2.16 kernel with an HP DeskJet 690C printer attached might produce the following dmesg lines:

```
parport0: PC-style at 0x378 [SPP]

parport_probe: succeeded

parport0: Printer, HEWLETT-PACKARD DESKJET 690C

lp0: using parport0 (polling).
```

A kernel earlier than 2.1.33 will not say parport, since this method was not introduced until later, but you should still see something like lp0 or lp1 in your output. Depending upon the exact kernel options, the exact printer in use, and whether or not the printer is powered on when the system boots, you may or may not see any reference to the specific printer model attached to the parallel port. Another way to check is to cat the /proc/devices file and grep the output for lp. If lp is contained within this file, printing is enabled in the running kernel. Use this command:

```
$ cat /proc/devices |grep lp
6 lp
```

If your kernel has compiled printer support as a module, these tests may not work, because the printer device won't turn up until you try to print. Therefore, don't be too concerned if you don't see any evidence of a printer device. Try printing. If it doesn't work, try checking /proc/devices, as just described. If there's no evidence of a printer device, it's possible that your kernel printer modules aren't loading for some reason.

The *lp* Device Driver

Under kernels earlier than 2.1.33, the printing device was /dev/lp0, /dev/lp1, or /dev/lp2, depending on which parallel port your printer was connected to. This is a static attachment, so any of these may be correct on your system. If one doesn't work, try the next. When the lp driver is built into the kernel, the kernel will accept through LILO an lp= option to set interrupts and I/O addresses.

Syntax:

```
lp=port0[,irq0[,port1[,irq1[,port2[,irq2]]]]]
```

Example:

```
lp=0x3bc,10,0x278,5,0x378,7
```

This example would set up three PC-style ports, one at 0x3bc with an IRQ of 10, one at 0x278 with an IRQ of 5, and one at 0x378 using IRQ 7. Some systems will have only one parallel port set up in this way.

The *parport* Device

The parport device was added to kernels 2.1.33 and newer to correct several of the problems that existed in the old lp device driver. The parport device can share the ports between multiple device drivers and dynamically assign available parallel ports to device numbers rather than simply equating an I/O address with a specific port number: a printer on the first parallel port might not be assigned /dev/lp0 using parport. The development of the parport device brought about the capability to run many new devices via the parallel port, including Zip drives, Backpack CD-ROMs, and external hard disks. It is possible to share a single parallel port among several devices, and all the corresponding drivers may safely be compiled into the kernel.

You must have CONFIG_PARPORT and CONFIG_PARPORT_PC set to YES in your kernel configuration if your parallel port is PC compatible (all IBM-compatibles and some Alpha machines have PC-style parallel ports). If your printer is not serial, you must have CONFIG_PRINTER set to YES in your kernel configuration. Use the same tests as listed above to check for printing support.

RS-232 Serial Devices

A printer attached to a standard RS-232 serial port requires only that the serial port be enabled and that the printcap entry be set up correctly. Serial support is almost always built into the kernel by default to accommodate modems and other serial devices, and these ports support printing capability as well. Chapter 12 discusses Linux support for RS-232 serial connections.

USB Devices

USB printers require special attention in Linux, because of the need for USB-patched 2.2.*x* or 2.4.*x* kernels. In particular, you need both basic USB support (including support for either the UHCI or OHCI USB controller, whichever your USB port uses) and support for USB printers. Once this support is compiled and the appropriate device files are installed, USB printers may be accessed using the /dev/usblp*n* device, where *n* is a number from 0 up. (This file may appear in a subdirectory of /dev, such as /dev/usb.) Chapter 12 covers USB devices in more detail.

Remote Printing

On a network, a workstation may be configured to print to a printer attached to a different host machine on the network or to a standalone printer with an internal network interface card (NIC). In the first case, the host machine might be a Linux or Unix box or a machine running some version of Microsoft Windows. In the second case, the printer runs its own server software that's functionally identical to a Linux/Unix or Windows print server.

Linux to Linux

In the case of Linux-to-Linux printing, you'll need to configure printing on both the server (the machine to which the printer is attached) and the client (the machine that submits a print job). There are two steps to this overall configuration, beyond basic network setup:

1. Configure the server to print to the printer it controls. You should test local printing functions as described earlier in this chapter. You can perform this configuration manually or via a GUI utility such as Printtool.

2. Configure the client to print to the network printer hosted by the server, as described earlier in this chapter. You can perform this configuration manually or via a GUI utility such as Printtool.

Both of these steps have been covered in the preceding discussion. Once you configure the print server to print locally, it's automatically configured to accept remote print jobs, at least if you're using LPRng as delivered with Red Hat 7.0. This makes printer setup very easy, but it's also a potentially big risk, because it means that any miscreant who wants to can send huge print jobs to your printer. The older lpd printing system is a bit less promiscuous by default. To accept remote print jobs with the old lpd, you must enter the names or IP addresses of the computers from which lpd will accept the jobs in the /etc/hosts.lpd file (or in /etc/hosts.equiv, but this file grants permission to use a range of additional services, so it's best not to use it in most cases).

To block random Internet systems from using your LPRng print server, you should edit the /etc/lpd.perms file. This file includes a lengthy set of comments describing the details of its configuration. To simply block all but local machines, you can use entries that take one of two forms:

```
ACCEPT SERVICE=X REMOTEIP=127.0.0.1/255.0.0.0
REJECT SERVICE=X NOT REMOTEIP=192.168.98.0/255.255.255.0
```

or

```
ACCEPT SERVICE=X REMOTEHOST=localhost
REJECT SERVICE=X NOT REMOTEHOST=*.threeroomco.com
```

These examples block connections that do *not* originate from the 192.168.98.0 IP block or from the threeroomco.com domain, respectively, while still allowing connections from the server itself. You can do much more with the lpd.perms file than you can with the old-style lpd's hosts.lpd file. For instance, you can allow or deny access based on the remote user, and you can allow or deny users or machines access to specific LPRng features. The default lpd.perms file contains many examples, so it's well worth examining if you want to fine-tune your configuration.

> **NOTE** Although LPRng leaves your print server open to outsiders' printing on it by default, its more sophisticated security features make it a more secure printing package *if* you configure it properly.

When Windows Is Involved

Things get a bit more complicated when either the local or the destination machine is running some version of Microsoft Windows. Windows printers use a protocol called the Server Message Block (SMB), renamed the Common Internet File System (CIFS), to provide shared printing. Trying to get Windows and Linux computers to share printers using their native tools is like trying to get two people who don't understand the same language to have a conversation. Fortunately, Linux includes a package that teaches Linux to "speak" the Windows file and printer sharing language of SMB/CIFS: Samba.

Samba is such an important tool for mixed networks that it is the subject of a companion volume in the Craig Hunt Linux Library, Roderick W. Smith's *Linux Samba Server Administration* (Sybex, 2001). There's a brief introduction to Samba in Chapter 15 of this book. Briefly, Samba is an open source software suite that provides SMB/CIFS file and print services to clients that might be running any version of Windows, OS/2, or other OSs. Samba runs on Linux, other versions of Unix, VMS, and other OSs. Other sources of information about Samba include an excellent SMB-HOWTO and several Samba mailing lists. The main Samba Web page is http://www.samba.org.

Since we're dealing with printing in this chapter, the next two sections show how to configure Samba to print from a Windows machine to a printer attached to a Linux box and from a Linux machine to a printer attached to a Windows machine.

Printing from Windows to a Linux Printer   Assuming that you have configured a Linux computer to print to a local printer, you have only to set up a Samba share to allow the Windows computers on the LAN to print to it. You'll do this in the smb.conf file that is created when you install Samba. (This file is located in /etc/samba in Red Hat 7.0, but may be in /etc, /etc/samba.d, or elsewhere on other distributions.) Add printing configuration to your smb.conf as shown in Listing 13.2:

Listing 13.2   A Sample smb.conf File Allowing Networked Windows Computers to Print to a Linux Printer

```
[global]
        workgroup = ARBORETUM
        printing = bsd
        encrypt passwords = Yes


        load printers = Yes
        log file = /var/log/samba-log.%m
        lock directory = /var/lock/samba


[printers]
        comment = All Printers
        security = Server
        path = /var/spool/samba
        browseable = No
        printable = Yes
        public = Yes
        create mode = 0700
```

Samba configuration involves setting up global options that apply to all shares (in the [global] section of the smb.conf file) and options for specific shares or share types. Listing 13.2 shows only one share—the [printers] share. This share is special because it creates a separate printer share for *each* printer that's defined in /etc/printcap. This option relies upon the load printers = Yes parameter in the [global] section. (Alternatively, you can share just some printers by creating share definitions for each one individually.)

Also of critical importance is the `workgroup = ARBORETUM` global parameter. This sets the Samba server's *NetBIOS workgroup name*, which is similar to a domain name. If this option is set incorrectly, you won't be able to see the Samba server in the Windows computers' Network Neighborhood browsers. In the case of Listing 13.2, the server is a member of the `ARBORETUM` workgroup.

One other critical Samba configuration issue relates to authentication. Unlike Linux-to-Linux printing, SMB/CIFS printing sends a password between machines to authorize printing. By default, Samba accepts *cleartext* (unencrypted) passwords and checks them against the normal Linux login passwords. Since Windows 95 OSR2 and Windows NT service pack 3, however, Microsoft has programmed Windows computers to send encrypted passwords by default. Because SMB/CIFS uses a different password encoding method than does Linux, Samba can't rely on the normal Linux password database when using encrypted passwords. Therefore, you must create a new password database using Samba's `smbpasswd` utility, which allows you to set Samba's encrypted passwords much as the Linux `passwd` utility lets you set Linux's login passwords. To use this utility to add a user, pass it the `-a` parameter and the username you wish to add (this username must correspond to an existing Linux user):

```
# smbpasswd -a someuser
New SMB password:
Retype new SMB password:
```

The passwords don't echo when you type them. If you've not used the utility before, it will complain that it can't open the `smbpasswd` file, but will create a new one despite this error. To use the encrypted passwords, you must add an `encrypt passwords = Yes` parameter to the `[global]` section of `smb.conf`, as shown in Listing 13.2.

> **WARNING** Windows 9x and Me systems store passwords locally that you send to servers. This can be a potentially major security problem, particularly if users' Samba and Linux login passwords are identical. There are many ways to reduce the risk posed by Windows' storing passwords locally. The least difficult of these is to ensure that the Samba encrypted passwords don't correspond to normal Linux login passwords. You might also separate the Samba server from other Linux servers and workstations or use a separate printing-only account on the Linux server for printing (users would have to enter this password, not their normal Linux login password, to print from Windows).

Printing from Linux to a Windows Printer To print from Linux workstations on a network to a printer attached to a Windows machine, each Linux machine needs a `printcap` entry for that printer. This is fairly easy to create using Red Hat's Printtool, which has an option for setting up an SMB/Windows 95/NT Printer (see Figure 13.3). Other spooling packages have similar setup options. Next you must ensure that you have the script `/usr/bin/smbprint`, which comes with most Samba packages, including the one that ships with Red Hat 7.0. The `smbprint` script intercepts a normal printer queue's process to send the print file through a utility called `smbclient`, which can be used to communicate with SMB/CIFS servers. Thus, if `smbprint` is called from a print queue's filter, it bypasses part of the normal printing mechanism and initiates an SMB/CIFS print request. Most smart filter packages know how to handle this task.

In Sum

Much of the complexity of printing derives from the fact that there are so many options available—there are many different types of printers, as well as differences from one model to another; Linux provides an assortment of printing utilities; and network printing presents an assortment of additional options and challenges. Understanding each of these areas and their interactions can help you create a workable Linux printing system. There's no point in buying an unsupported printer for use in Linux, for instance. Fortunately, each piece of the Linux printing puzzle, from physically connecting a printer to configuring a Linux computer as a print server, is understandable. If you approach the task one step at a time, you can get your Linux system working, and even serve printers to other computers in the process.

14

Making Your Job Easier with Scripts

A well-written script can be a system administrator's best friend at times when there is much to be done and not enough hands to do it. Large, repetitive tasks are especially easy to script—and especially tedious to perform if you don't. As you get accustomed to scripting, you'll discover many more uses for it. You'll find yourself writing scripts even to perform the smaller tasks.

This chapter begins with and focuses most strongly upon the Bash shell scripting language, but there are several other types of scripts, including Perl language scripts, Python language scripts, awk scripts, and sed scripts. Even more variations are in use, but these seem to be the most popular among Linux system administrators today. This chapter touches upon each of these script types, and also covers system initialization scripts and scheduling scripts to run at times of your choosing.

Determining which type of script to use is a tricky process. Since the role of a script is to perform some lengthy task quickly and efficiently, system administrators often simply use what they know best. Bash shell scripts are quite common. Perl and Python are used frequently, as well, and are the favorites for CGI programming in support of Web site development. These two are really not well suited to anything that requires real-time response or multithreading, however. Of the two, Python scales better and is easier to read and understand. For more information, look at `http://www.perl.com` and `http://www.python.org`. Although still used and maintained, scripts written in the `awk` text processing tool and the `sed` stream editor have very specialized uses and seem to be falling out of favor as new scripting tools are developed. (Java and Tcl/Tk scripts are not included in this discussion because neither seems to see significant use as a system administration tool.)

> **NOTE**   Shell scripts are actually computer programs. They differ from most programs, however, in that they're written in *interpreted* languages—that is, languages that are interpreted directly from human-readable form rather than first being converted into machine code by a compiler. This makes shell scripts slower to execute than their compiled brethren, but the same fundamental principles apply to all programming languages. Because of the complexity of any programming language, this chapter cannot provide a complete description of even a single scripting language, but it will provide a quick introduction to get you on your way to writing your own scripts or modifying existing ones.

Common Scripting Language Features

No matter what the scripting language, there are certain common features you should understand. Most of these features are common not just to scripting languages, but to compiled languages as well. These features do take slightly different forms in different languages, however. For instance, each language has its own rules for identifying variables, and equivalent commands can be represented by different words in different languages, much as words with the same meaning are different in different human languages. It's important before proceeding further that you understand some of these fundamental features of programming languages.

Identifying a Script

One common feature of all executable files in Linux is that they must be identifiable as such. In part, this is handled through the execute bit on the program file. Beyond this, though, the Linux kernel must know *how* to execute the file. It would do no good to try to execute a Bash shell script as a binary program file, for instance. Linux solves this small problem by looking at the first two characters of the file, which constitute a code for the file's program type. Shell scripts are identified by the code sequence #!, followed by a path to the program that's able to execute the script. For instance, a Bash shell script begins with the following sequence:

```
#!/bin/bash
```

Because the # symbol identifies a *comment* (a line or part of a line that's ignored by the interpreter, thus allowing you as a programmer to describe the intent of the code), this line is ignored by the Bash interpreter itself. The Linux kernel, however, can use this information to launch /bin/bash and pass it the shell script.

> **NOTE** Other implementations of Unix use the same method of identifying shell scripts, which is one reason that most shell scripting languages work on a wide variety of Unix-like platforms.

Sometimes you'll see references to *shell scripts* without reference to a specific language. These scripts are written in a very general way and can be executed by Bash or other command-shell scripting languages. These scripts frequently begin with #!/bin/sh. On most Linux systems, /bin/sh is a symbolic link to /bin/bash, so the two have the same effect. It's possible to change that symbolic link, though, so it's best to explicitly identify a Bash script *as* a Bash script. Perl scripts, Python scripts, and so on should also be identified by referring to the appropriate binary file.

If you omit the line identifying the script type, Linux will usually try to process it as a Bash script. It's best to include this line, however, for your own documentation purposes and to eliminate the possibility that whatever goes on the first line may be misinterpreted by Linux, resulting in an inability to run the script.

Variables

Programming languages are built on the idea of manipulating data. Scripts that you write as an administrator are likely to process the contents of data files, filenames, and so on. In order to manipulate such data, programming languages support *variables*—symbolic representations of the data you wish to manipulate. In most computer languages, variables are collections of one or more letters, such as x, balancedue, or filename. The rules for naming variables differ substantially from one language to another—some have limits on filename length, others allow or disallow certain nonalphabetic characters, some require certain characters, and so on.

Shell scripts frequently manipulate filenames and similar alphabetical data in variables. For instance, a variable called filename might contain (not surprisingly) a filename. Some operation might then load a *new* filename into that variable. The code in the script can then pass these filenames to subroutines or other programs, and you as a programmer need not know what the filenames are. Many scripting languages contain specialized methods of assigning values to filenames. Bash, for instance, lets you assign filenames to a variable and loop through all the filenames in a directory to perform some operation on all of those files.

Control Statements

Because scripts (and programs generally) usually do repetitive work, it's necessary that languages include some means of directing the flow of a program. For instance, if you write a script to search every file in a directory for certain characteristics, you need some way to tell the program to repeat the search over some set of files. Similarly, you may need to tell the program to jump to another part of itself—say, to skip some instructions that aren't relevant to a particular file, because it doesn't meet certain criteria. These tasks are handled by what are collectively known as *control statements*. These statements control the flow of the program.

There are several types of control statements, although some are more important than others, and some languages discourage the use of some statements. The major types are:

Conditionals   A conditional expression tells the program to do one thing if a particular condition is met, and to do another if that condition is not met. (There are also conditionals that support more than two options.) For instance, you might use a conditional if you want to copy all files whose names begin with a to another directory. Your conditional statement would execute one set of operations if the filename begins with a and another if it doesn't.

Loops   A loop allows the program to perform the same task repeatedly, although usually on different data. For instance, you might use a loop to examine all the files in a directory. The loop would execute once for each file, and then terminate.

Subroutines   A subroutine isn't a control statement *per se*, but it is an important aspect of many programming languages. A subroutine isolates a segment of code to perform a specific task. The main program can then execute the subroutine, often as if it were a simpler command. For instance, you might write a subroutine to calculate a circle's circumference given its diameter, and then call it when you need this computation.

Jumps   A jump sends execution of the program to another point. Jumps can be used to implement loops and subroutines, but they're generally frowned upon by today's programmers because they can produce a tangled mess of program code, in which it's difficult to determine the sequence of execution (often referred to as *spaghetti code*).

It's possible—and often necessary—to combine two or more of these types of control statements to perform a task. For instance, a loop might contain one or more conditionals, in order to take different actions depending upon the type of data stored in the variables the loop examines. Most loops actually incorporate conditional-style logic to control termination. That is, the loop executes until some condition is met, such as reaching the end of a set of inputs.

Commands

Commands perform concrete actions. Commands can perform numeric computations, open files, move files, run programs, and so on. Languages vary substantially in how many commands they support. Some support very minimal command sets; to do anything interesting, you must call prepackaged subroutines or other programs. Others include massive command sets that can do just about anything you might want. Sometimes it's difficult to tell the difference between a command and a prepackaged subroutine or outside program.

Shell scripting languages focus their command sets on file manipulations. Other scripting languages have other priorities. Perl, for instance, specializes in manipulating *strings* (collections of alphanumeric characters).

The Bash Shell Scripting Language

Most Linux distributions make the Bash shell the default for all users. This shell provides the command-line prompt that's familiar to most Linux users. The Bash shell also provides a scripting language that allows users and administrators to automate repetitive tasks or even develop programs. This scripting language is well suited to automating repetitive tasks that you might ordinarily do at a command prompt. It can call other programs and utilities, so you can easily use common Linux utilities, such as `grep` and `find`, within a Bash script.

Variables

Most variables in Bash scripts are strings—they hold alphanumeric sequences such as words or filenames. These variables are assigned via the equal sign, as in the following example:

```
IPCHAINS="/sbin/ipchains"
```

In this example, the string /sbin/ipchains is assigned to the variable $IPCHAINS. This variable can then be used to call the /sbin/ipchains program, to pass its name to other programs, or be manipulated in various ways. Assigning a variable in this way is very useful if you intend to change the variable's value. It's also sometimes used to make it easy to modify a script. For instance, if you move the `ipchains` program to /usr/sbin, you can change the variable assignment rather than many calls that use the $IPCHAINS variable.

To use a variable, you precede its name with a dollar sign ($). Thus, to call /sbin/ipchains, you could place the string $IPCHAINS on a line by itself (or followed by appropriate parameters for this utility). The only time you *don't* use the $ is when assigning a value to a variable. You can combine two or more variables by assigning them to a third, thus:

```
IPCHAINS="/sbin/ipchains"
OPTIONS="-A input -d 255.255.255.255 -j ACCEPT"
COMMAND="$IPCHAINS $OPTIONS"
```

The result of these three lines is a variable, COMMAND, that contains a complete ipchains command, including several options. You can use this ability to combine variables to provide greater flexibility. By combining variables in different ways based on the script's input (using conditionals and loops to guide the process), you can greatly expand the flexibility of a script.

Bash scripts can inherit certain variables from the user's work environment. These variables are therefore referred to as *environment variables*. These variables may be set by Bash scripts that are run automatically when a user logs in, and they typically contain information such as a list of directories to be searched for executable programs (PATH), the user's home directory (HOME), and many others, most of them used by specific programs. You can find out what environment variables are available to you by typing **env** at a Bash command prompt—but be aware that these variables can change from one user to another.

Another type of variable is that passed to a script from the calling program or command typed by the user. These are identified by numbers—1, 2, 3, and so on. The fact that variables are preceded by $ symbols distinguishes these variables from literal numbers. These variables are known as *parameters*, and they allow the user to pass information to the script. As a very simple example, Listing 14.1 is a script that echoes the first and third words typed after the script name.

Listing 14.1   A Simple Script Demonstrating Parameter Variables

```
#!/bin/bash
echo "$1 $3"
```

If you type this script into a file called echo-part, type **chmod a+x echo-part**, and run it, the result might look like this:

```
$ ./echo-part the cow jumped over the moon
the jumped
```

The other words typed on the command line are assigned parameter variables, but because the echo line only specifies echoing the first and third, those are the only ones that produce output. When you run the script, you can tie together two or more words so that they appear in one variable by enclosing those words in quotation marks. For instance, using the same program, you might do this:

```
$ ./echo-part "the cow" jumped "over the moon"
the cow over the moon
```

Conditional Expressions

Bash and other shells include functionality that allows evaluating a variable and using the results to determine how to proceed. For instance, you might want to check the $USER variable, which holds the current user's login name, to see if it is equal to vicki before starting the script vicki_script. If the values are the same, the script starts; otherwise, it echoes an error message to the screen.

These tests and checks are accomplished with statements containing *conditional expressions*. These conditional expressions may be used in conditional statements or loops.

Quite often a script will check whether a given file or variable exists before attempting to make use of it. This checking is done with one of the conditional expressions listed in Table 14.1.

Table 14.1   Conditional Expressions and Their Meanings

Conditional Expression	Meaning
-a *file*	True if *file* exists.
-b *file*	True if *file* exists and is a block file.
-c *file*	True if *file* exists and is a character file.
-d *file*	True if *file* exists and is a directory.
-e *file*	True if *file* exists.
-f *file*	True if *file* exists and is a regular file.
-g *file*	True if *file* exists and is set-group-id.
-h *file*	True if *file* exists and is a symbolic link.
-k *file*	True if *file* exists and its "sticky" bit is set.

Table 14.1 Conditional Expressions and Their Meanings *(continued)*

Conditional Expression	Meaning
-p *file*	True if *file* exists and is a named pipe (FIFO).
-r *file*	True if *file* exists and is readable.
-s *file*	True if *file* exists and has a size greater than zero.
-t *fd*	True if file descriptor *fd* is open and refers to a terminal.
-u *file*	True if *file* exists and its set-user-id bit is set.
-w *file*	True if *file* exists and is writable.
-x *file*	True if *file* exists and is executable.
-O *file*	True if *file* exists and is owned by the effective user ID.
-G *file*	True if *file* exists and is owned by the effective group ID.
-L *file*	True if *file* exists and is a symbolic link.
-S *file*	True if *file* exists and is a socket.
-N *file*	True if *file* exists and has been modified since it was last read.
file1 -nt *file2*	True if *file1* is newer by modification date than *file2*.
file1 -ot *file2*	True if *file1* is older by modification date than *file2*.
file1 -ef *file2*	True if *file1* and *file2* have the same device and inode numbers.
-o *optname*	True if shell option *optname* is enabled.
-z *string*	True if the length of *string* is zero.
-n *string*	True if the length of *string* is not zero.
string1 = *string2*	True if the strings are equal.
string1 != *string2*	True if the strings are not equal.

Table 14.1   Conditional Expressions and Their Meanings *(continued)*

Conditional Expression	Meaning
string1 < *string2*	True if *string1* sorts before *string2* lexicographically.
string1 > *string2*	True if *string1* sorts after *string2* lexicographically.
arg1 -eq *arg2*	True if *arg1* is equal to *arg2*. Both must be integers.
arg1 -ne *arg2*	True if *arg1* is not equal to *arg2*.
arg1 -lt *arg2*	True if *arg1* is less than *arg2*.
arg1 -le *arg2*	True if *arg1* is less than or equal to *arg2*.
arg1 -gt *arg2*	True if *arg1* is greater than *arg2*.
arg1 -ge *arg2*	True if *arg1* is greater than or equal to *arg2*.

Conditional expressions are typically used in the formation of an if, for, or while loop. For example, consider the -a option, which simply tests whether a file exists. If you want to determine whether the user who is logged in has a .bash_profile and execute that profile if it exists, you can use the following if statement:

```
if [ -a /home/$USER/.bash_profile ]

    then

    . /home/$USER/.bash_profile

fi
```

Loops

Perhaps you want to execute a program once for each of a certain number of files. For instance, you need a simple script that will play all the .wav files existing in a given directory. The script would use a for loop as in Listing 14.2.

Listing 14.2   A Simple Script to Play Audio Files

```
#!/bin/bash
for d in `ls *.wav`; do play $d; done
```

Communicating
with Devices

PART 4

> **WARNING**   The characters preceding ls and following *.wav in the preceding example are back-quotes, also called back-ticks, which are usually located on the key above Tab on the keyboard, along with the tilde (˜) symbol. If you use regular single-quote characters (located next to the Enter key), the above script will not function correctly.

The preceding example uses several features to accomplish its goal:

- The ls *.wav command works just as it would when typed at a command prompt—it lists all the files that end in .wav. These are effectively expanded as input for the script.

- The for d in part of the script uses the expansion of the ls *.wav to initiate a loop that executes once per file. This loop structure is extremely important to many file-manipulation tasks. The variable $d receives the name of each file in turn, then the rest of the loop executes with that variable set. On the next go-through, the second filename is assigned to d, and so on until all the files are exhausted.

> **WARNING**   This loop syntax uses spaces to delineate files, so if a filename includes a space, your script won't be able to parse the files correctly. For instance, if you have a file called Londo Cats.wav, the script in Listing 14.2 will try to play the files Londo and Cats.wav, but chances are neither exists, so the file won't be played. This is one of the reasons experienced Linux users don't create files with spaces in their names.

- The semicolons (;) separate individual commands on one line. Each for statement affects multiple commands.

- The do play $d command calls the Linux play utility and passes the name of a .wav file (stored in the $d variable) to the play utility. This results in the desired effect, one file at a time.

- The done command signals the end of the for loop.

> **NOTE**   The play command is a front-end to the Linux Sound Exchange (sox) package and plays any sound file to the default sound device.

On the business end, let's say that anyone who works on the Help desk taking customer calls is required to write a document each time, detailing the conversation and any work that was done in support of that call. This policy has been in place for a year now and the directory containing these files is fairly large. Because a lot of text is contained in these documents, you reason that they will probably compress quite well. You want to add the extension .2001 to show the year in which the files were created. You might create something like Listing 14.3 to perform these tasks.

Listing 14.3   A Script to Rename and Compress All the Files in a Directory

```
#!/bin/bash
for d in `ls /usr/local/calldocs/*` ;
    do mv $d $d.2001 ;
gzip $d.2001 ;
done
```

Sometimes you need to run through a file line by line, executing some command on each line that matches a certain set of criteria. This is most easily done with a `while` loop. Suppose you're providing mandatory network training for five users, weekly until all users have been trained. To determine who is up for training, you maintain the `/etc/training_list` data file. A person's training is categorized in segments from A through D, with D signifying a fully trained user. Network training is C training (training for users at level C). Assume that `/etc/training_list` is as shown in Listing 14.4.

Listing 14.4   A Sample `/etc/training_list` Data File

```
sam|501|34|A
tom|502|23|B
terry|503|43|B
john|504|12|C
mike|505|67|D
sarah|506|45|C
leonard|507|78|B
meg|508|15|D
tom1|509|33|B
```

```
larry|510|67|C
jeffrey|511|45|D
mark|512|23|C
chris|513|34|D
anne|514|24|A
ellen|515|16|B
jake|516|27|C
pat|517|45|C
```

You might create a script like Listing 14.5 to determine which employees remain to be trained. (This script uses the cut command, discussed later in this chapter.)

Listing 14.5   A Script for Updating the Training File

```
#!/bin/bash
#remove the old tobetrained file if one exists
if [ -e /home/$USER/tobetrained ]; then
    rm /home/$USER/tobetrained
fi


cat /etc/training_list |
while read line
do
        training=`echo $line|cut -d"|" -f4`
        if [ $training = C ];
        then
          name=`echo $line|cut -d"|" -f1`
          echo $name >> /home/$USER/tobetrained
        fi
done
```

The training script in Listing 14.5 first declares its command interpreter to be the shell /bin/bash. Next, the script removes the tobetrained file in the user's directory if one exists. This is necessary since we are appending to the file rather than writing over it. Next, we read the /etc/training_list file line by line looking at the fourth field. We compare the letter in the fourth field to determine if it's a C, indicating whether the user is in the C training group. If the letter is a C, we get the name from that line and write it out to the tobetrained file.

Other Types of Scripts

Although Bash shell scripts are quite common and can accomplish a lot, there are other types of scripting languages available for Linux. Each of these has its own advantages and disadvantages. This section covers Perl, Python, awk, and sed scripts, although only enough to give you an idea of what these tools can accomplish.

Perl Scripts

Teaching you the Perl scripting language is not, of course, our intent for this chapter. Rather, we want to prepare you for working with Perl scripts you'll likely run across while performing your Linux system administration duties. To this end, we'll take a brief look at Perl fundamentals to give you the basic familiarity you'll need.

Perl doesn't have a lot of structural requirements. Comments must begin with a pound sign (#), and all lines of code must end in a semicolon. White space is irrelevant, meaning that the entire program could be written as one line if you wanted it that way. Obviously, reading and maintaining such a program would not be easy, so it's a good idea to use indentation for indicating the script's logical flow.

Perl variables are defined using a statement in this form:

```
$variable = value;
```

To check a variable's value, you use two consecutive equal signs: ==. This is most often done in an if statement, a for loop, or a while loop. Perl uses if, for, and while statements much the same as Bash shell scripts do:

- An if statement compares the value to the variable once and then moves on. A simple if statement looks like this:

```
if ($variable == 3){

    print ("The value is 3");

}
```

- A for loop cycles through a number of values comparing them to a variable or a constant. When the list has been exhausted, the loop ends. A simple for loop looks like this:

```
#set the maximum length to 0
$maxlength= 0 ;
#cycle through each length and compare it to the maxlength
foreach (keys %in) {
    $maxlength= length if length > $maxlength ;
}
#increment the maxlength variable
$maxlength++ ;
```

- A while loop continues to cycle through performing whatever function is contained therein until the while statement is no longer true. A simple while loop looks like this:

```
while ($variable <= 3){
    change_variable;
}
```

There are several ways to initiate a Perl script. First, you may call the Perl interpreter with the script name as an argument, like so:

$/usr/bin/perl scriptname

You may also cat the script into the Perl interpreter, like this:

$cat scriptname | perl

Unfortunately, both of these initiation methods require that you know that this particular command is a Perl script and not a Python script, Bash shell script, or compiled executable. It is far easier, given the number of commands available on a Linux system, to execute the Perl script by using the script name as a program executable. Your shell facilitates this if you have set the permissions string to make the script executable and have included an interpreter line in the following format as the first line of the script:

#!/usr/bin/perl [*optional arguments*]

This causes the shell to execute the script as if you had typed the complete Perl line at the prompt, as follows:

$/usr/bin/perl *[optional arguments] scriptname*

Following is a very basic Perl script written to provide a text-based menu. Using this script, you can prompt the user for input, read the input, and perform some task based on that input. This script was written by a programmer who was first learning Perl; it illustrates some of the basic concepts of the language.

Listing 14.6   An Example Perl Script to Create a Menu

```perl
#!/usr/local/bin/perl


while ($function != 3) {
    print ("Please select the function you'd like to perform:\n");
    print ("Enter 1 for a directory listing.\n");
    print ("Enter 2 for the convert program.\n");
    print ("Enter 3 to exit.\n");
    $function = <STDIN>;
    if ($function == 1) {
        system (ls);
    } elsif ($function == 2) {
        system ("convert 6");
    } else {
        $function = 3;
    }
}
```

NOTE   This script's function #2 calls the convert program, but it doesn't do anything useful.

Python Scripts

Python is a fairly intuitive scripting language that uses a more natural format than does Perl or shell scripting. Lines don't have to end in semicolons, and there are fewer braces and parentheses.

- An if statement in Python looks like this:

```
if variable = 3:
    print "variable = 3."
```

- A for loop in Python looks like this:

```
for i in [1,2,3,4,5]:
    print "This is number", i
```

- A while loop in Python looks like this:

```
variable = 0
while variable <= 3:
        print "variable = ",variable
        variable = variable+1
```

To help you decide which language you prefer (Python or Perl), the Python script in Listing 14.7 performs the same function as the Perl script in Listing 14.6.

Listing 14.7 An Example Python Script to Create a Menu

```
#!/usr/bin/python
import os
function = 0
while function != 3:
    print "Enter 1 for a directory listing."
    print "Enter 2 for the convert program."
    print "Enter 3 to exit."
    function = input ("Please select the function you'd like to
        ➥perform: ")


    if function == 1:
```

```
    os.system ("ls .")
elif function == 2:
    os.system ("convert 6")
```

awk and *sed* Scripts

Although awk and sed scripts are not used as frequently as they were a few years back, they certainly still have value. So many new scripting tools have hit the market that the awkward language of awk and sed scripts has been left behind. When your intent is to make changes to a file line by line, Python is often the better choice. On the other hand, you're more likely to find awk or sed than Perl or Python on non-Linux Unix platforms. This isn't to say that Perl and Python are rare, but they're not as common as are sed and awk.

awk

awk is a text-processing tool you can use to easily make recurring changes or replacements in a document. (The program was written by Alfred Aho, Peter Weinberger, and Brian Kernighan; and the name awk is derived from the first initial of each surname.)

This tool uses C-like language to manipulate structured data one line at a time. awk command files are scripts composed of one or many functional blocks enclosed in curly brackets. Each individual block within the file may be associated with a conditional expression that is used to determine whether that block should be executed upon the current line. As you might guess, when there is no conditional expression, the block is executed on every line in the file.

The very straightforward example awk script shown in Listing 14.8 takes a file and numbers its lines by a specified increment. Although simple, this operation is useful when you are debugging a script or some C source code, because syntax-error messages usually include the line number. After the BEGIN keyword, the variables are given values. The next block actually prints the number and the line represented by $0. The next line increments the line counter by the specified increment. If there were code that needed to be executed just before the file is closed, a block labeled END could be added to the end of the script.

Listing 14.8   A Sample awk Script

```
/#/bin/awk
BEGIN {
    line = 1;
```

```
    increment  = 1;
}


{
# Prints the number and echoes the line.
printf("%5d %s\n", line, $0);
line += increment;
}
```

To execute this from a file, save the code to a file with the extension .awk and issue the following command. (The .awk extension is not required, but including it clarifies which type of script you are calling.)

$awk -f file.awk file > newfile

Each line matching the conditional expression is prefixed with a line number. If there are no lines matching the conditional expression, each line of the file is echoed to the new file, and no line numbers are added.

Here is another example, with the actual actions added to the command instead of in a file:

$awk '{print $1, $2, $3}' file > newfile

Since $0 represents the command, and $1 represents the first word in each line, the result in this case will be a file called newfile containing the first three words of each line in file. This is often the quickest way to output a report in a different format.

Several books are available that illustrate the use of awk. A popular one is *Sed & Awk (Nutshell Handbook)*, by Dale Dougherty and Arnold Robbins (O'Reilly, 1997). The awk utility, or the GNU version called GAWK, is included with most Linux distributions and available for most flavors of Unix.

sed

As its name suggests, sed is a stream editor. It allows for the search and replacement of regular expressions and more—a valuable capability when the task at hand involves updating a file. You can use sed to automate the update of a text file by searching for a string and changing it as required. It is also quite useful when you need to change the output of a command before piping it into another command. If you have ever issued a command such as :s/phrase/newphrase/ to replace one phrase with another within an editor, then you know how to use sed commands. When using sed, however, this change is automatically applied globally because sed works on each line in the file.

sed can be executed with the actions as a command-line argument. It is sometimes beneficial to do this if, for example, the output of a very long file needs slight alteration so that it can be printed to a new file in the format requested by the boss. Here is a fairly simple example:

```
$cat /tmp/calendar |sed -e 's/Jan/&uary/' | sed -e 's/Feb/&ruary/' |
  ➥sed -e 's/Mar/&ch/' | sed -e 's/Apr/&il' | sed -e 's/Jun/
  ➥&e/'| sed -e 's/Jul/&y/' > newfile
```

In this example, a calendar file containing dates within the first seven months of the year needs to be altered so that the abbreviated month name is replaced by the full name of that month. The edited calendar is to be written out to newfile. First we cat the file into our sequence of sed commands. The -e tells sed that the next thing is a sed command to be executed. This command's placement within single tick marks distinguishes it from the rest of the line. The s means that we wish to substitute the second phrase for the first. Thus this command line meets our file-alteration needs, its length well justified when it saves many keystrokes in a file with say, 1000 lines.

Like awk, the sed command is included with most Linux distributions and available for most flavors of Unix.

System Initialization Scripts

Often when you are using some recently developed utility, you need to start the utility at boot time and aren't able to depend on an existing script to do this. For these situations, you need to write your own initialization script and add it to the initialization scripts that we discussed in Chapter 5. This is actually quite easy to do if you follow the example of an existing script. These scripts are all Bash shell scripts and share a common format.

Adapting Bash Shell Scripts

Many of the scripts that you'll work with are Bash shell scripts. These scripts are generally good enough as is. You won't have to change very many of them. Nevertheless, it is important to know how to do so, because there are special circumstances that will require you to write a script or edit an existing script.

Writing an Initialization Script

Let's say that you have downloaded a tarball of mynewutility from an Internet site. Obviously, there is no mynewutility script in the /etc/rc.d hierarchy, since the utility isn't part of the standard distribution. When you have finished installing the utility and configuring it, you'll probably want to make it start at boot time like the other daemons in the /etc/rc.d hierarchy. To accomplish this, you'll need to write an *initialization script* to manage the new utility.

Let's look at the existing script for the printer daemon and adapt it for use to manage mynewutility. Red Hat 7.0's printer startup script is /etc/rc.d/init.d/lpd, shown in Listing 14.9.

Listing 14.9 A Sample Initialization Script for lpd

```
#!/bin/sh
#
# lpd          This shell script takes care of starting and stopping

#              lpd (printer daemon).
#
# chkconfig: 2345 60 60
# description: lpd is the print daemon required for lpr to work \
#              properly. It is basically a server that arbitrates \
#              print jobs to printer(s).
# processname: /usr/sbin/lpd
# config: /etc/printcap

# Source function library.
. /etc/init.d/functions

# Source networking configuration and check that networking is up.
if [ -f /etc/sysconfig/network ] ; then
        . /etc/sysconfig/network
        [ ${NETWORKING} = "no" ] && exit 0
fi


[ -x /usr/sbin/lpd ] || exit 0
```

```
[ -e /etc/printcap ] || exit 0

RETVAL=0

fixup () {
    # Fixup the printcap file in case it has continuation characters
    # at the end of each entry, like old versions of printtool did.
    if [ -w /etc/printcap ] ; then
    TMP1=`mktemp /etc/printcap.XXXXXX`
    gawk '
        BEGIN { first = 1; cont = 0; last = "" }
        /^[:space:]*#/  { if(cont) sub("\\\\$", "", last)}
        { if(first == 0) print last }
        { first = 0 }
        { last = $0 }
        { cont = 0 }
        /\\$/ { cont = 1 }
        END {sub("\\\\$", "", last); print last}
    ' /etc/printcap > ${TMP1} && cat ${TMP1} > /etc/printcap
        ➥&& rm -f ${TMP1}
    fi
}

start () {
    echo -n "Starting lpd: "
# run checkpc to fix whatever lpd would complain about
    /usr/sbin/checkpc -f
    # start daemon
    daemon /usr/sbin/lpd
    RETVAL=$?
```

```
        echo
        [ $RETVAL = 0 ] && touch /var/lock/subsys/lpd
        return $RETVAL
}

stop () {
        # stop daemon
        echo -n "Stopping lpd: "
        killproc /usr/sbin/lpd
        RETVAL=$?
        echo
        [ $RETVAL = 0 ] && rm -f /var/lock/subsys/lpd
        return $RETVAL
}

restart () {
        stop
        start
RETVAL=$?
        return $RETVAL
}

# See how we were called.
case "$1" in
    start)
        start
        ;;
    stop)
        stop
        ;;
```

```
status)
    status /usr/sbin/lpd
    RETVAL=$?
    ;;
restart)
    restart
    ;;
condrestart)
    # only restart if it is already running
    [ -f /var/lock/subsys/lpd ] && restart || :
    ;;
reload)
    echo -n "Reloading lpd: "
    killproc /usr/sbin/lpd -HUP
    RETVAL=$?
    echo
    ;;
fixup)
    fixup
    ;;
*)
    echo "Usage: lpd {start|stop|restart|condrestart|reload|
        ↪status|fixup}"
    RETVAL=1
esac


exit $RETVAL
```

The format of initialization scripts is fairly uniform. The standard SysV initialization scripts have some features that we really like. At the beginning of the script is a comment detailing what the script is intended to do.

> **NOTE**   It's also helpful to add comments that identify any specific system char-
> acteristics the script requires to run successfully, although this is not done in
> most of the existing scripts. This might be a comment such as "In order for the
> lpd script to run successfully, the printers must have been configured, and a
> properly formatted /etc/printcap must exist." This setup is not critical to the
> functioning of the script, but it simplifies things for a new system administrator
> trying to gain a deeper awareness of the computer system.

After the comments, the /etc/init.d/functions library script is run. This script sets up functions that are used within initialization scripts. The library script contains functions that are useful to multiple initialization scripts and otherwise have to be duplicated in each script.

Next, the script checks certain conditions that are required for the printer daemon to function properly. First, the script checks whether the network is up. If it isn't, the script attempts to start it. If the network variable in the network script is set to no, the lpd script exits, because lpr and lpd communicate using the network facilities. Next, the script verifies that lpd exists and is an executable file. It also verifies that an /etc/printcap file exists.

The next section of the lpd script contains functions required for the line printer daemon. These include a fixup function, which changes an /etc/printcap file in the old format to the new format. Also required are a start function, which starts the line printer daemon; a stop function, which kills the line printer daemon and removes its lock file; and a restart function, which stops the old line printer daemon and starts a new one.

The next part of the script contains the menu functionality that allows you to specify which one of the script functions you'd like to perform. This is a case statement like those in C and other languages, setting the following alternatives:

- If the script was called with the start argument, then call the start function.
- If the script was called with the stop argument, then call the stop function.
- If the script was called with the status argument, then use the status function from the /etc/rc.d/init.d/functions library to determine whether the line printer daemon is running.
- If lpd was called with the restart argument, then run the restart function.
- Starting lpd with the condrestart argument causes the system to restart lpd only if it is currently running.
- Running the lpd script with the reload argument tells the script to send a HUP signal to the line printer daemon.
- Lastly, running /etc/rc.d/init.d/lpd fixup runs the fixup function in this file.

The last line in the lpd script is the return of the $RETVAL variable, which has been generated by the function that the script performed.

Now that you understand this existing script, creating your own initialization script for mynewutility will be relatively easy. Let's assume that mynewutility requires networking to be active and that the executable is located at /usr/sbin/mynewutilityd. We only need start, restart, stop, and status functionality in this case. The new script will look something like Listing 14.10.

Listing 14.10 An Initialization Script for mynewutility

```
#!/bin/sh
#
# mynewutilityd  This shell script takes care of starting
#                and stopping mynewutilityd.
#
# chkconfig: 2345 60 60
# description: mynewutilityd is a fictitious daemon used
#              to illustrate startup script functions.
# processname: /usr/sbin/mynewutilityd


# Source function library.
. /etc/init.d/functions


# Source networking configuration and check that networking is up.
if [ -f /etc/sysconfig/network ] ; then
        . /etc/sysconfig/network
        [ ${NETWORKING} = "no" ] && exit 0
fi


[ -x /usr/sbin/mynewutilityd ] || exit 0


RETVAL=0
```

```
start () {
    echo -n "Starting mynewutilityd: "
# start daemon
    daemon /usr/sbin/mynewutilityd
    RETVAL=$?
    echo
    [ $RETVAL = 0 ] && touch /var/lock/subsys/mynewutilityd
    return $RETVAL
}


stop () {
    # stop daemon
    echo -n "Stopping mynewutilityd: "
    killproc /usr/sbin/mynewutilityd
    RETVAL=$?
    echo
    [ $RETVAL = 0 ] && rm -f /var/lock/subsys/mynewutilityd
    return $RETVAL
}


restart () {
    stop
    start
RETVAL=$?
    return $RETVAL
}


# See how we were called.
case "$1" in
    start)
```

```
        start
        ;;
    stop)
        stop
        ;;
    status)
        status /usr/sbin/mynewutilityd
        RETVAL=$?
        ;;
    restart)
        restart
        ;;
*)
        echo "Usage: mynewutilityd {start|stop|restart|condrestart
            ➥|reload|status }"
        RETVAL=1
esac


    exit $RETVAL
```

Of course, this script will not run unless you use the chkconfig or ntsysv utility to add it to the scripts for your preferred run level, thus:

```
#chkconfig –level 2345 mynewutilityd on
```

Tailoring the *rc.local* Script

The rc.local script is likely to need your editing, because it is the script where you place so-called *local changes*—those that are specific to one computer and don't represent daemons that are added as part of a package. In fact, it's common to start unusual daemons (like the fictitious mynewutility discussed above) by adding them to rc.local.

Let's take a look at the default version of rc.local for Red Hat 7.0 (Listing 14.11).

Listing 14.11 The rc.local Script for Red Hat 7.0

```
#!/bin/sh
#
# This script will be executed *after* all the other init
# scripts.
# You can put your own initialization stuff in here if you
# don't want to do the full Sys V style init stuff.

if [ -f /etc/redhat-release ]; then
    R=$(cat /etc/redhat-release)

    arch=$(uname -m)
    a="a"
    case "_$arch" in
            _a*) a="an";;
            _i*) a="an";;
    esac

    NUMPROC=`egrep -c "^cpu[0-9]+" /proc/stat`
    if [ "$NUMPROC" -gt "1" ]; then
        SMP="$NUMPROC-processor "
        if [ "$NUMPROC" = "8" -o "$NUMPROC" = "11" ]; then
            a="an"
        else
            a="a"
    fi
fi

# This will overwrite /etc/issue at every boot.  So,
```

```
# make any changes you want to make to /etc/issue here
# or you will lose them when you reboot.
echo "" > /etc/issue
echo "$R" >> /etc/issue
echo "Kernel $(uname -r) on $a $SMP$(uname -m)" >> /etc/issue

cp -f /etc/issue /etc/issue.net
echo >> /etc/issue
fi
```

The default rc.local file is simple. It only contains code to create the /etc/issue and /etc/issue.net files. The /etc/issue file is used to write the text introduction to the login prompt. The result on an *x*86 computer using Red Hat 7.0 looks like this:

```
Red Hat Linux release 7.0 (Guinness)
Kernel 2.2.16-22 on an i586
```

The rc.local file first declares its interpreter, just like all the other scripts that we've looked at in this chapter. Next, rc.local checks whether the file /etc/redhat-release exists and is a regular file. If the file is both, the variable R is set to the content of the file.

The case statement that follows the redhat-release check exists to determine whether the correct word in the upcoming string should grammatically be a or an; if the value of $arch has an initial vowel, the script uses an; otherwise, it uses a.

Next, an if statement is used to determine whether there is more than one processor; and second, if there is more than one processor, whether the word for the number of processors begins with a vowel, as in 8 (eight) and 11 (eleven). This determination is only important if the system is using multiple processors, in which case the /etc/issue will look something like this:

```
Red Hat Linux release 7.0 (Guinness)
Kernel 2.2.16-22 on a 2-processor i586
```

The last few lines of the script simply write out the data to the /etc/issue file and copy it to /etc/issue.net.

If you have not created the mynewutilityd script, you can start the mynewutility daemon in the rc.local file by adding the following line at the end of the file:

```
daemon mynewutilityd
```

Communicating with Devices

PART 4

Administrator's Logbook: Changes to Red Hat 7.0 default /etc/rc.d/ rc.local script

Added a line to start the daemon mynewutilityd, which is part of the mynewutility package downloaded from www.mynewutility.org, to add basic newutility functionality to our network.   VS 16 Jul 00

Cautions about Changing Existing Scripts

Many system administrators advise that it is not a good idea to revise and adapt existing scripts. Actually changing an existing script on your system is sometimes necessary, although certainly you should exercise caution when you change one. Should you decide to tailor an existing script to your specific usage, it is a good practice to start by making a copy of the script with an extension like .orig to identify it as the original version. You also need to add comments noting within the tailored script what specifically was changed and why.

Generally, anything that makes your system different from the default arrangement should also be included in an administrative log entry. When you are troubleshooting a problem, this helps to clarify differences between a machine that is working properly and one that isn't. Sometimes it is the change that caused the malfunction, and other times it might be the lack of this change which is problematic.

Consider the example discussed in this chapter, where you have added a check to the mynewutility script. This check determines whether a process called necessary is running, and the script only continues if the process is running. A log entry to accompany this might look like the one in the Administrator's Logbook example on this page, for "Changes to Red Hat 7.0 default /etc/rc.d/init.d/mynewutilityd script."

Administrator's Logbook: Changes to Red Hat 7.0 default /etc/rc.d/ init.d/mynewutilityd script

Edited /etc/rc.d/init.d/mynewutilityd adding a check to determine whether the necessary process was currently running. If necessary is not running, the script attempts to run it. If it runs successfully, proceed with the initialization of the mynewutility daemon.   VS 14 Aug 00

Administrator's Logbook: Changes to Red Hat 7.0 default `/etc/rc.d/`
`init.d/mynewutilityd` **script** *(continued)*

```
#check for necessary process

if ! pgrep necessary

 then

    /usr/bin/necessary

    if ! pgrep necessary

       then

          exit

    fi

fi
```

Using the *cron* Facility

The `cron` daemon makes it very easy to set up a recurring event based on the need to run it at a given time, day, or date. `cron` searches `/var/spool/cron` for `crontab` files, which are named after existing user accounts; any `crontabs` that are found are loaded into memory. The daemon also searches for `/etc/crontab` and the files in the `/etc/cron.d/` directory.

In this system, `/etc/crontab` contains entries that run files in `/etc/cron.hourly` on an hourly basis, files in `/etc/cron.daily` on a daily basis, files in `/etc/cron.weekly` once a week, and files in `/etc/cron.monthly` once a month. Listing 14.12 shows the default `/etc/crontab` file for Red Hat Linux 7.0.

Listing 14.12   The Default Red Hat 7.0 `/etc/crontab`

```
SHELL=/bin/bash
PATH=/sbin:/bin:/usr/sbin:/usr/bin
MAILTO=root
HOME=/
```

Communicating with Devices

PART 4

```
# run-parts
01 * * * * root run-parts /etc/cron.hourly
02 4 * * * root run-parts /etc/cron.daily
22 4 * * 0 root run-parts /etc/cron.weekly
42 4 1 * * root run-parts /etc/cron.monthly
# sysstat
0 * * * 0,6 root /usr/lib/sa/sa1 600 6 &
5 19 * * * root /usr/lib/sa/sa2 -A &
```

In the first line, the shell is established as the Bash shell, and a path is set up. The MAILTO line sets up who is to receive the output from these commands, including error messages and simple notifications that the files were run. The home directory is set to /.

The first five fields of the run-parts lines establish the run times for the files contained in the listed directory. The five fields used in /etc/crontab are as follows:

minute	0–59
hour	0–23 (24-hour format)
day of the month	1–31
month	1–12
day of week	0–7 (where both 0 and 7 are Sunday)

Asterisks represent any value. In the /etc/cron.hourly line, then, the string

```
01 * * * *
```

indicates that the files contained in the /etc/cron.hourly directory should be run at one minute after each hour. The /etc/cron.daily line uses

```
02 4 * * *
```

which indicates that the files contained therein should be run at two minutes after the fourth hour of each day. The /etc/cron.weekly line,

```
22 4 * * 0
```

identifies that the files it contains are to be run at 4:22 on Sunday. The /etc/cron.monthly directory contains files that are to be run at 4:42 on the first day of the month, based on the string:

```
42 4 1 * *
```

Values can be lists, ranges, or steps. *Lists* are comma-separated values as follows:

```
1,3,5,7,9
```

Ranges look like this:

```
1-5
```

You can combine the two like this:

```
1-5,7,9
```

Steps are ranges in which a certain set of numbers are skipped. The form is N/m, where N is typically a range and m represents the numbers to skip. Thus the following in the hour field indicates that the line should be run every other hour:

```
0-23/2
```

To indicate every other possible value for the field, you can use

```
*/2
```

The sixth field of the run-parts lines identifies the user in whose name the command should be run; in this case, root. The seventh field is the command itself. You can simply create an executable script and place it in the appropriate directory.

If the cron job only applies to one user, it should be added to that user's personal crontab file via the crontab command. This command installs, uninstalls, or lists the user's crontab file, /var/spool/cron/$USER, depending on the argument you use. The two forms for the crontab command are as follows:

```
crontab [-u username] file
crontab [-u username] [-1] [-r] [-e]
```

The first crontab syntax is used to replace the user's crontab file with another, so a file-name with which to replace the specified user's existing crontab must be given on the command line. If no user is specified, the name of the user executing the command is used.

The second crontab syntax is the more common format. The –1 option causes the crontab to be displayed. The –r option removes the existing crontab, and the –e begins a session to edit the crontab. The default editor (as specified by the VISUAL or EDITOR environment variable) is used.

The format for the user's `crontab` file excludes the username, since that file is intended to be used only to start programs as the user who invoked the `crontab` command. The `cron` daemon wakes up every minute and checks for changes in `/etc/crontab`, so there is no need to restart the daemon if you change the default files.

Running a Script at a Specific Time

The at command is used to run a command once, at a given time.

> **NOTE** The cron utility can do almost everything that the at command can do, so you may choose to use cron exclusively. There is only one exception: You can set an at job during a cron run, but you can't use cron to modify cron jobs. This feature isn't often required, though.

The at command allows a variety of time formats. It accepts times of the form *HH*:*MM* to run the job at that specific hour and minute of the day. If the time is past, it assumes the next day. You can add a suffix of AM or PM. To specify a specific day to run the job, give a date in the form month-name day with an optional year, or by giving a date of the form *MMDDYY*, *MM*/*DD*/*YY*, or *DD*.*MM*.*YY*. The at command will also accept times such as now +*time-units*, where the *time-units* can be expressed as minutes, hours, days, or weeks. Once the time is accepted, an at> prompt will appear where you are to type the command to be run at the given time.

Here are several different at commands. The first one runs on the 23rd of October:

```
$ at 102300
at> who -u >who.log.102300
```

This one runs at noon today, or tomorrow if it's already past noon:

```
$ at 12:00
at> backup_script &
```

This one runs one hour from now:

```
$ at now + 1 hour
at> clean_up_script &
```

Commands Often Used in Shell Scripts

There are several fundamental commands that appear often in shell scripts. They include cat, cut, echo, sort, and xargs. We'll discuss them with some depth here, giving you examples that illustrate their usefulness in script writing.

cat

```
cat filename
```

Although the cat command has optional arguments, they are not typically used in scripts, so we won't discuss them here. In scripts, cat is typically used to output a file's contents, most often for use in a pipe sequence.

For example, the command *cat /etc/issue* produces the following output:

```
Red Hat Linux release 7.0 (Guinness)
Kernel 2.2.16-22 on an i586
```

cut

```
cut [options] filename(s)
```

The cut command is often used in scripts or in a piped command, to cut specific fields or characters from a file in a delimited format. The default delimiter is a tab, but you can change this with the -d option, so that the fields in a comma or pipe-delimited file may be cut out, too.

Consider a file in this format:

```
12   34   54   23   12   34
32   67   85   18   62   10
```

The command to output fields 1 and 5 from each line of a tab-delimited file looks like this:

```
cut -f1,5 filename
12   12
32   62
```

Now let's assume a pipe-delimited file in the following format, perhaps listing the names of system administrators responsible for backing up the system on each of the seven days of the week.

```
john|mary|terri|leonard|jacob|geoffrey|eric
tom|jeff|mike|larry|moe|curly|harpo
```

To cut out the name of the person responsible for the fourth day of weeks 1 and 2, you'd use this command:

```
cut -d"|" -f4 filename
leonard
larry
```

The cut command has several options to provide for actions besides cutting by whole fields. You can cut specific bytes, characters, or fields. You've seen that fields are specified by the -f parameter. To designate the retrieval of bytes, use –b; and for characters, use –c. To indicate the inclusion of all data between the *n*th byte, field, or character and the end of the line, add a hyphen character (-) after the number, as shown in the following examples:

```
cut -d"|" -f4- filename
leonard|jacob|geoffrey|eric
larry|moe|curly|harpo
```

To indicate the inclusion of all data between the *n*th byte, field, or character and the *m*th byte, field, or character, use N-M as shown here:

```
cut -d"|" -f4-6 filename
leonard|jacob|geoffrey
larry|moe|curly
```

Finally, to indicate all the data on a line up to and including the *n*th byte, field, or character, precede the number with a hyphen (-) as shown here:

```
cut -d"|" -f-4 filename
john|mary|terri|leonard
tom|jeff|mike|larry|moe
```

Now that you have a basic idea of how to use the cut command, let's look at an example that's particularly suited to Linux system administration. Say, for example, that you need to set a variable to your IP address for use in a script. You could cut the value from the output of /sbin/ifconfig like this:

```
ip_address = /sbin/ifconfig ppp0 | grep inet |cut -d":" -f2 |cut
  ➥-d " " -f1
```

echo

```
echo [options] string
```

The echo command is equally useful in scripts and on the command line. Its purpose is to display the string given as its argument. This is quite handy for showing the value of an environment variable or sending output into a piped command sequence. Let's say that you need to find out the value of the HISTSIZE variable. You can echo out its value like so:

```
echo $HISTSIZE
1000
```

The echo command was used to echo a blank separator line into a data file in the rc.local script that we discussed earlier in this chapter, as follows:

```
echo >> /etc/issue
```

echo can also be used to echo a message to the user of the script, as shown here:

```
if [ ! -e /bin/executable ];
then
echo "The file /bin/executable does not exist."
fi
```

sort

```
sort [options] [file(s)]
```

The sort command applies the sort, as defined by the specified options, to each of the files listed and concatenates them all to standard output (stdout). The options for sort include –b, which says to ignore initial blanks in the sorted lines; -c, which checks to see if the file has already been sorted; -d, which considers alpha and numeric characters; -f, which ignores case by evaluating everything as if it were uppercase; -n, which sorts numerically; -o, which allows you to specify an alternate output file; and -r, which reverses the sort.

Assume the following numbers must be sorted:

```
66, 567, 3, 38, 64, and 543
```

A standard sort will sort the numbers incorrectly:

```
3
38
```

```
543
567
64
66
```

A numeric sort (sort −n) will sort them correctly:

```
3
38
64
66
543
567
```

Now let's try sorting these names: Fred, Tom, Abe Lincoln, and Constable Bob. A standard sort will return the following:

```
Abe Lincoln
Constable Bob
Fred
Tom
```

xargs

```
xargs [options]
```

The xargs command reads space-delimited arguments one line at a time from stdin and assembles as many of them as will fit into one command line.

As an example, consider that a command using find to generate the input sometimes passes so many arguments that Bash cannot handle the complete command and generates an error like this:

```
$ cat `/usr/bin/find .`
bash: /bin/cat: Argument list too long
```

Here, the find command has generated output that causes the expanded command to exceed the maximum length. To get around this, use xargs to pass only the number of arguments allowed. Instead of accepting the arguments on the command line, `xargs` accepts them through a pipe as follows:

```
$ /usr/bin/find . | xargs cat
```

The second command will apply the `cat` command to every filename output from the `find` command, giving the intended results.

Using Pipes

The `sort`, `echo`, and `cut` commands described in the preceding sections are especially useful in scripts where you need to set a variable equal to some portion of the output of a command, or where you need to change the order of data before passing it on to the next function that will use it. Linux *pipes* can be useful in this respect because they allow you to send the output of one program or command into another program or command. Pipes are often used on the command line, but they can also be used in many scripting languages.

The script for updating the training file that we looked at earlier (Listing 14.5) uses both the `echo` command and the `cut` command in the piped sequence:

```
name=`echo $line|cut -d"|" -f1`
```

And the following `cat` statement produces a sorted version of the `/etc/training_list` file.

```
$cat /etc/training_list | sort -d > sorted_list
```

In Sum

Linux's ability to handle many scripting languages can prove quite useful to your system administration duties. One of the most-used scripting languages is Bash, which is tightly integrated into the Bash shell you probably use to enter text-mode commands. This shell scripting language lets you combine Bash commands, Linux programs, and variables using basic programming concepts like loops and conditional statements, in order to automate what would otherwise be tedious tasks. Other scripting languages include Perl, Python, `sed`, and `awk`.

You can use any scripting language in conjunction with Linux's mechanisms for running programs at specific times, `cron` and `at`. These utilities can be very useful for scheduling tasks such as backups that you want to perform at specific times, particularly when you might not be around to launch the jobs manually.

Linux's startup scripts are written in Bash, so understanding the details of this scripting language can help when you need to modify the standard start-up scripts or create new ones.

Communicating with Devices

PART 4

Part 5

Networking and Troubleshooting

Featuring:

- Understanding and configuring TCP/IP networking
- File sharing
- Internet servers and super servers
- Configuring the X Window System
- Building a user interface atop X
- Setting up a mail server
- Protecting against spam
- General troubleshooting techniques
- Troubleshooting specific problems

15

TCP/IP Linux Networking

Perhaps more than any other computer technology, networking has changed our lives. Today it's possible to shop, read newspapers, obtain music and software, do research, correspond with colleagues, and even earn a living entirely online. Although there are costs associated with this new use for computers, society as a whole is rapidly embracing the Internet.

Today's networking protocols began life on Unix systems. At the core of the Internet (and of most local networks) lies a protocol known as the *Transmission Control Protocol/ Internet Protocol (TCP/IP)*. TCP/IP was first developed on what are by today's standards primitive versions of Unix. As a clone of Unix, Linux has a tightly knit set of TCP/IP networking tools. Indeed, many of Linux's networking tools are the same as those used on "traditional" Unix systems.

This chapter introduces TCP/IP networking in Linux. It begins with an overview of the design of TCP/IP and then launches into the details of TCP/IP configuration in Linux. One very common use of TCP/IP networking is to provide file and printer sharing on a small network, so that users of one system can directly use files and printers on another. This chapter therefore describes this use, although only in broad strokes. TCP/IP is also used for providing many Internet services, such as Web and FTP servers, so these topics are touched upon. Two other chapters in this book (16 and 17) cover additional TCP/IP topics: The X Window System and mail servers.

Understanding TCP/IP Networking

Chances are, you're familiar with how network tools function, at least from the user's point of view. As with so many aspects of our world, however, there's considerable complexity hidden beneath the surface of common network tools like e-mail and remote printing. Understanding the basic design of TCP/IP networking can be invaluable when you're configuring a system to use these features—and particularly when troubleshooting TCP/IP problems. This section therefore presents an overview of critical design features of TCP/IP and of computer networking in general. If you are already familiar with these concepts, feel free to begin with the "TCP/IP Configuration" section instead.

Network Stacks

The basic goal of networking, from the point of view of high-level software, is to transfer information from a specific program running on one computer to a specific program running on another computer. For instance, when you run a Web browser such as Netscape, the goal is to transmit a request for specific documents from Netscape Navigator to a Web *server* program (such as Apache) on a remote computer. Apache responds by returning one or more documents to Navigator. This process of exchanges may repeat many times.

> **NOTE**   The term *server* has two meanings. First, it can refer to a *program* that runs on a computer. Apache is a Web server, for example. Second, it can mean the *computer* that runs a server program. Likewise, *client* can refer to either a program that requests information of a server program or a computer that requests information of a server computer. When these terms are applied to entire computers, confusion can quickly result in some environments because a single computer can function as both client and server simultaneously.

One of the problems encountered in achieving the goal of data exchange between programs is in controlling access to the network. If programs like Netscape were allowed to control the network hardware directly, chaos would soon ensue, as programs would interfere with one another. At the core of the solution to this problem lies the concept of a *network stack*. This is a set of small software modules, functioning in series, each of which interfaces with two others (or with one other and the network hardware or a human). Network applications—both clients and servers—lie at the top of the network stack. These applications communicate with the layer below them, and so on until the bottom layer is reached, at which point the data leave the computer and traverse the network to the destination system. At that point, the process is reversed, and data travel up the stack to the destination application. This application can then send a reply via the same method. Figure 15.1 illustrates this process.

Figure 15.1 Information travels "down" and "up" network stacks, being checked and packed at each step of the way.

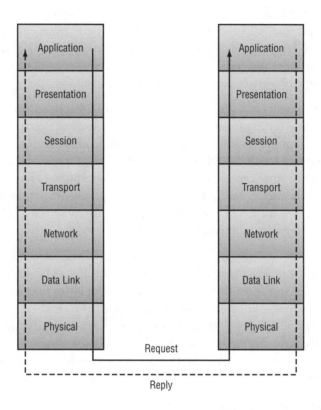

At each stage in their journey down a network stack, data are checked or encapsulated in additional information. These "wrappings" function much like an envelope around a letter sent via the Post Office; they help the data reach their ultimate destination. Unlike a physical letter, though, data sent via TCP/IP may be split up into multiple packets. Rather than send a 2MB file in one chunk, TCP/IP breaks it down into many packets of about 1.5KB each. Part of the encapsulation process ensures that the recipient computer is able to reassemble the original file from its many individual packets. TCP/IP was designed to be fault-tolerant, so it's possible for the receiving system to request that a specific packet be re-sent if it doesn't arrive. Individual packets may travel different routes from source to destination and the system still functions.

In principle, each layer of a network stack may be swapped out and replaced with an equivalent component without affecting higher or lower layers. For example, Figure 15.1's Physical layer corresponds to network hardware, such as Ethernet cards. The Data

Link layer consists of drivers for the network hardware. In principle (and sometimes in practice), you can swap out one network card for another, or change one driver for another, without having to adjust any other components of the network stack. In practice, however, you may need to adjust the driver if you change the network card. At the Application layer, you can change applications without adjusting the network hardware or any of the "invisible" software that lies between the two—you can use Lynx rather than Netscape Navigator for Web browsing, for instance.

Figure 15.1 presents an idealized view of a network stack, known as the *Open Systems Interconnection (OSI) model*. In practice, TCP/IP is often described in terms of its own model, which contains fewer layers. TCP/IP's model considers hardware separately, so it doesn't extend to the Physical layer; and TCP/IP merges the Session and Transport layers into one and the Application and Presentation layers into one. These differences are unimportant for our discussion, however; the critical points are that data are packed and unpacked as they traverse the network stack, and that the stack helps control network access, including data addressing.

TCP/IP is not the only network stack in existence. Others, such as AppleTalk and NetBEUI, can also be used. These alternate network stacks can be described by the same OSI model depicted in Figure 15.1, but each has its own idiosyncrasies, so it's not normally possible to swap a layer from one stack for a layer from another stack. (The Physical and to some extent Data Link and Application layers are shared between stacks, however.) TCP/IP is the basis for the Internet, and so is the most common network stack. Linux also includes support for several less-common network stacks, such as AppleTalk and Novell's IPX.

Network Addresses

One critically important component of any network protocol is *addressing*. If you're at one computer and want to use resources located on a server, you must have some method of telling your computer how to reach the server. To a human, the network address most frequently takes the form of a *hostname, computer name*, or *fully qualified domain name (FQDN)*, such as www.sybex.com. This hostname is sometimes preceded by a code indicating what type of server you want to use on the remote system, such as http:// for a Web server (Web servers use the *Hypertext Transfer Protocol*, or *HTTP*). When so used, the hostname is referred to as a *Uniform Resource Locator (URL)*.

Hostnames are hierarchical in nature, with each portion of the hierarchy separated by a period (.). The leftmost component of the hostname (such as www in www.sybex.com) is sometimes called the *machine name*. This component identifies a single specific computer. The remainder of the hostname (such as sybex.com) is the *domain name*. It refers to a collection of computers. Domain names are themselves hierarchically arranged. *Top-level domains (TLDs)*, such as `.com`, `.org`, and `.us`, contain *domains* such as `sybex.com` and `linux.org`, which can be broken down into their own subdomains or have computers assigned directly to them. Thus, the number of levels in the hierarchy is variable. One domain might have many levels (such as `a.very.deep.domain.structure.in.the.uk`), whereas another can be quite shallow (such as `oneroomco.com`, which could conceivably point directly to a single computer).

Unfortunately, although hostnames of this form are reasonably easy for people to understand, computers work better with numbers. Therefore, although the Internet includes provisions for using hostnames, at its core it relies upon a different addressing scheme: *IP addresses*. IP addresses are 32-bit numbers that are generally expressed as four decimal numbers separated by dots (`.`), as in 192.168.204.98. IP addresses are broken into two components: a *network address* and a *machine address*. This division simplifies the job of *routers*, which are devices that send traffic between networks, because it means the router can be programmed in terms of networks rather than individual computers. A *network mask* (*netmask* for short) marks the network address portion of an IP address with binary 1's. For instance, 255.255.255.0 places a binary 1 in each bit of the first three bytes of an address, indicating that those first three bytes are the network address, and that the final byte is the machine address. An IP or network address can be combined with a network mask using a shorthand form in which the number of leading binary 1's in the netmask follows the IP address, as in 192.168.204.0/24. This is the same as the 192.168.204.0 network with a netmask of 255.255.255.0 (twenty-four 1's, expressed in binary).

> **NOTE** In a hostname, the most significant portion (the machine name) is in the *leftmost* position of the address. In an IP address, the most significant portion (the machine address) is in the *rightmost* position of the address.

Traditionally, the available range of IP addresses is broken up into networks of various *classes*, as indicated in Table 15.1. As indicated by the classes' netmasks, these classes differ in size—each Class A network can contain over 16 million computers; Class B networks can host 65,534 computers, and Class C networks can each have only 254 computers. More recently, however, networks have been merged or split up in nontraditional ways in order to make more efficient use of the dwindling supply of IP addresses. Each of the three major classes of IP addresses supports a range of *private* IP addresses (shown in Table 15.1), which routers do not route. These IP addresses can be used internally for private networks without acquiring "official" IP addresses. There are also Class D and E networks, which have special meaning and are reserved for future use.

Table 15.1   IP Address Classes and Private Address Ranges

Class Name	Range	Netmask	Private Addresses
Class A	1.0.0.0– 127.255.255.255	255.0.0.0	10.0.0.0– 10.255.255.255
Class B	128.0.0.0– 191.255.255.255	255.255.0.0	172.16.0.0– 172.31.255.255
Class C	192.0.0.0– 223.255.255.255	255.255.255.0	192.168.0.0– 192.168.255.255

> **NOTE**   The Internet is fast running out of IP addresses. Although a 32-bit address provides a theoretical limit of about 4 billion addresses, the actual limits are somewhat lower, and the number of Internet-connected computers is growing at a staggering rate. For this and other reasons, work is underway on *IPv6*, a new means of addressing for TCP/IP networks. IPv6 uses a 128-bit address, which permits roughly 3.4×10^{38} addresses—that's 2.2×10^{18} addresses per square millimeter of land surface on the Earth, which ought to last us a while.

As a practical matter, it's necessary to link IP addresses to hostnames and vice-versa. This task is accomplished through the *Domain Name System (DNS)*, which uses a highly distributed system of DNS servers. Each DNS server is responsible for its own domain or subdomain. These servers are arranged in a hierarchical manner mirroring the domain name structure. At the top of this hierarchy are the *root servers*, which know the addresses of the servers that handle the TLDs. Each TLD server knows the addresses of servers that handle each of its domains, and so on. Eventually, a server in this hierarchy is *authoritative* for a domain, meaning that it can say with authority whether a given hostname exists, and if it does, what its IP address is. A similar hierarchy allows *reverse DNS* lookups, so that a name can be found, given an IP address.

Typically, an organization's DNS server performs two tasks:

- It fields name queries from computers inside its domain. It queries an appropriate root server and follows the chain of referrals from that server to locate an authoritative server for the requested domain. It then passes the result of this query (typically an IP address or a code saying that the name is invalid) back to the requesting client.

- It accepts queries from outside sources regarding the names and IP addresses of systems within its domain.

When you configure a Linux system for networking, chances are you need only know the IP addresses of from one to three DNS servers. You can then point your Linux system at those DNS servers to let them do the dirty work of traversing the tree of servers to resolve domain names into IP addresses. Linux can function as a DNS server, but configuring Linux in this way is well beyond the scope of this book. For that information, consult a book such as Craig Hunt's *Linux DNS Server Administration* (Sybex, 2000).

A final address type is the network card's *hardware address*. The card uses this to tell when packets are addressed to it. Part of the job of the network stack is to find a hardware address matched to any given IP address. The stack does this by broadcasting a query to all the computers on the local network. (For more distant systems, the computer need only send the packet to a local *router*, which can then forward the data appropriately.) In most cases, you need not concern yourself with the hardware address, although one exception is noted later in this chapter.

Ports

Once a packet has been routed to a destination system, the target computer needs to know what to do with it. This information is conveyed, in part, through the use of multiple *ports*. Each TCP/IP packet is addressed to one of 65,536 ports, which you can think of as being similar to extensions on a business telephone system. By convention, specific server packages listen for traffic on specific ports. For instance, Web servers listen on port 80 and mail servers listen on port 25. The file /etc/services lists the port assignments used by common servers. As a user, you don't normally need to be concerned with port use, because client programs know which ports to call. As a system administrator, you must occasionally deal with port assignments. For instance, you may need to add an entry to /etc/services if an appropriate entry isn't present.

> **NOTE** TCP/IP ports are distinct from hardware ports, which are used to link devices like printers and modems to the computer. An Ethernet card usually has one Ethernet port, but that one Ethernet port supports thousands of TCP/IP ports.

Client programs also use ports to call *out* of a system. Linux assigns outgoing ports to programs on an as-needed basis, so you don't need to be concerned with this detail. When a server replies to a client, it does so using the port that the client used, so Linux knows to which program it should deliver the return packet. Both client and server programs keep track of the IP addresses with which they're exchanging data, so they can keep packets from different sessions separate.

Networking and
Troubleshooting

PART 5

TCP/IP Configuration

With the theory of TCP/IP out of the way, it's time to move on to practical Linux TCP/IP configuration. Most distributions, including Red Hat 7.0, allow you to configure TCP/IP at system installation; but this isn't always practical, because you may need to install hardware or locate new drivers before you can proceed. Even if you use installation-time configuration options or a separate GUI interface, it's helpful to understand the underlying text-mode tools. This chapter therefore emphasizes text-based TCP/IP configuration tools and utilities.

Configuring Network Hardware

The first step in TCP/IP configuration is to set up the hardware. A working network includes a wide variety of network hardware, such as hubs or switches, routers, servers, and so on. The possibilities are so broad, in fact, that it's impossible to cover them all here. Therefore, this chapter focuses upon configuring a single Linux system in a network. In this context, hardware configuration consists of locating and installing an appropriate network interface card (NIC) and ensuring that your system contains appropriate drivers for that card.

> **NOTE** Many isolated Linux systems use the *Point-to-Point Protocol (PPP)* to link the system to the Internet via a telephone modem. Chapter 12 describes PPP; this chapter is more concerned with networking via dedicated networking hardware.

Linux supports a wide variety of networking hardware. The most common type of networking hardware today is Ethernet, which comes in several varieties, including 10Base2 (also known as *thin coax*), 10Base5 (a.k.a. *thick coax*), 10BaseT, and 100BaseT. Most of these varieties operate at speeds of up to 10Mbps, but 100BaseT supports 100Mbps speeds. Even faster varieties operate at up to 1000Mbps (1Gbps). The Linux kernel supports most modern Ethernet adapters. To discover what devices your Linux distribution supports, check the kernel configuration options under Ethernet (10 or 100Mbps) in the 2.2.*x* kernels or Network Device Support ➢ Ethernet (10 or 100Mbit) in the 2.4.*x* kernels. You can also check with a device's manufacturer to see which Linux drivers to use. Some manufacturers provide Linux drivers for their boards, but these are usually just the drivers from the Linux kernel.

Some networks don't use Ethernet, but instead use other types of networking hardware, such as Token Ring. Although Linux's support for these more exotic types of hardware isn't as complete as for Ethernet, you can usually find drivers for at least some NICs for most network types. As with Ethernet, you should consult the kernel's configuration options and boards' manufacturers to discover what's supported.

If you compile a driver directly into your kernel, it will automatically load and detect your network card. If your driver is compiled as a module (which is typical of freshly installed Linux systems), however, you may need to add an entry or two to the `/etc/modules.conf` file (called `/etc/conf. modules` on some distributions). Specifically, you may need to set up an alias between `eth0` and the name of your NIC's driver. If you have multiple NICs, you may need to add multiple lines to make these associations, as in:

```
alias eth0 tulip
alias eth1 via-rhine
```

These lines tell Linux to use the `tulip` driver for `eth0` (the first Ethernet device) and the `via-rhine` driver for `eth1` (the second Ethernet device). Of course, to set up these lines, you will need to have located the appropriate driver for your board, as described earlier. You can see what drivers are present on your system by typing **`ls /lib/modules/`*`x.y.z`*`/net`**, where *`x.y.z`* is your kernel version.

TIP One of the best reasons to configure networking when you install Linux, especially if you're less than intimately familiar with your networking hardware, is that most Linux installation routines include tools that detect the type of network hardware you have installed, so you don't need to figure out this detail.

Once you've configured the hardware and rebooted, Linux should auto-detect the hardware at boot time. When it does, it displays a brief message to this effect, such as the following:

```
eth0: Macronix 98715 PMAC rev 32 at 0xda00, 00:80:C6:F9:3B:BA, IRQ 9.
eth1: VIA VT3043 Rhine at 0xdc00, 00:80:c8:fa:3b:0a, IRQ 10.
eth1: MII PHY found at address 8, status 0x782d advertising 05e1 Link
    ➥0000.
```

These lines indicate that Linux has detected two Ethernet cards: `eth0` uses a Macronix 98715 (a chip that uses the `tulip` driver), and `eth1` uses a VIA VT3043 Rhine chip (which uses the `via-rhine` driver). These messages also include the Ethernet devices' hardware addresses—the six-byte hexadecimal values, such as `00:80:C6:F9:3B:BA`. These values can be important on some networks, as described later in this chapter. If you don't see such lines at boot time, you should re-examine your configuration to be sure you haven't mistyped a device driver name, and that you've correctly identified the NIC's hardware.

TIP Boot messages scroll by so quickly that you're likely to miss them. After you've booted, you can type **dmesg** to see these messages replayed. Further, you can pipe the results through grep, as in **`dmesg | grep eth`**, to isolate just the Ethernet-related messages.

One peculiarity of network hardware under Linux is that these devices don't have the usual device file entries in the /dev directory. Nonetheless, networking devices are named (as in eth0 or eth1). Networking tools communicate these names to the Linux kernel directly, not by accessing device files.

Using DHCP for Configuration

The easiest way to configure most computers for networking is to use the *Dynamic Host Configuration Protocol (DHCP)*. This is a networking protocol that allows one system (the *DHCP server*) to maintain information about a network's important characteristics and to feed this information to other systems (the *DHCP clients*). A network administrator maintains the information on the DHCP server, and all other systems need only be told to use a DHCP client program. The client program, when started, sends out a *broadcast* asking for help from a DHCP server, which then responds with all the important network information.

NOTE   Some DHCP servers respond only to registered clients. The server uses the NIC's hardware address to identify clients. You may need to provide this information to your network administrator or ISP. For Ethernet devices, the code in question is a six-byte hexadecimal value. Linux Ethernet drivers display this value on the screen at boot time, as described earlier.

There are three DHCP clients in common use on Linux systems: dhclient, dhcpcd, and pump. (Red Hat 7.0 uses pump.) In most cases, you need only install the appropriate package on the system. When the computer starts, it uses an appropriate startup script to call the DHCP client. In Red Hat 7.0, the /etc/sysconfig/network-scripts/ifup script contains the call to pump; but many other distributions place DHCP client scripts somewhere in the /etc/rc.d directory. If you install a DHCP client and don't want to reboot before using your network, you can call the client program directly; for instance, by typing /sbin/pump on a Red Hat 7.0 system.

Some Linux distributions that rely upon GUI configuration tools may require you to set an option in this tool to call the DHCP client automatically at boot time. You can usually bypass this requirement by placing a call in a boot script such as /etc/rc.d/rc.local, but it may be simpler to check the appropriate configuration option. In Red Hat's Linux-conf, it can be found in the Config ➢ Networking ➢ Client Tasks ➢ Basic Host Information module, shown in Figure 15.2. Click the tab for your NIC and select the Dhcp option.

Figure 15.2   In many distributions you can set many networking options from a single GUI configuration tool.

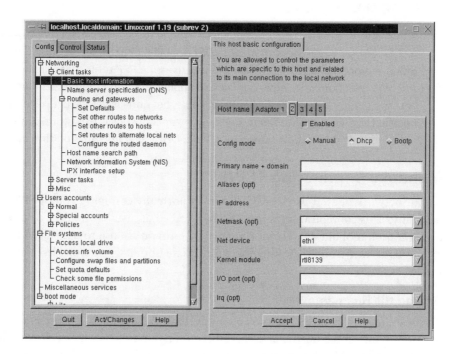

Unfortunately, although DHCP is supposed to simplify network configuration, it doesn't always work quite the way it should. One particular class of problems relates to servers that use multiple network interfaces, particularly when only one of these should be configured via DHCP. Most DHCP clients allow you to specify an interface to configure. For instance, you could use **pump -i eth1** to tell pump to configure your eth1 interface. You may be able to modify your startup scripts to force your DHCP client to work on only the desired interfaces.

Sometimes problems with a DHCP client can be quite intractable. Fortunately, the fact that there are three DHCP clients for Linux provides you with a way out: You can try another client. Before you remove the original client, though, you should locate and back up its configuration file. You may need to restore and modify this file to start a new client, particularly if you use a DHCP client from another distribution, because different distributions use slightly different startup script formats.

DHCP is capable of setting most aspects of a Linux system's network configuration. DHCP cannot, however, install the network drivers. Some DHCP configurations also omit some information—most commonly the hostname—so you may need to do a few manual adjustments even if your system uses DHCP. (The next section describes manual TCP/IP configuration.)

> **NOTE** Some *Digital Subscriber Line (DSL)* installations use an automatic configuration protocol called PPPoE. This protocol uses the PPP tools that are normally used over telephone modems, but instead applies them to Ethernet connections. There are several Linux PPPoE clients available, but none is yet the Linux standard. Check http://www.rodsbooks.com/network/network-dsl.html for pointers to several. If your DSL installation uses PPPoE, DHCP will *not* work on that system.

Manually Configuring TCP/IP

If your network doesn't use DHCP, you must normally configure your TCP/IP settings manually. This configuration is most easily handled at installation time or using a GUI configuration tool like Linuxconf (Figure 15.2). If you choose to use such a tool, you should have little trouble locating the appropriate options, given the descriptions that follow.

Setting the Hostname

The hostname is most important to computers that want to contact yours as a server. You can't normally set the hostname that's stored on a remote DNS server, however, so you must rely upon the DNS administrator to accomplish this task. You can, however, set the name that your computer believes itself to be. This can be important because some protocols, such as mail, embed the sender's address in outgoing messages. If your hostname is set incorrectly locally, recipient systems may become quite confused or even refuse connections.

You can set your system's hostname using the hostname command. Entered without any parameters, this command reports the system's current name. You can pass a name to the command, however, to set the hostname. For instance, the following command sets the hostname to gingko.oneroomco.com:

```
# hostname gingko.oneroomco.com
```

> **NOTE** The commands described here for manual TCP/IP configuration can be added to a startup script, such as /etc/rc.d/rc.local, if you want to automate the process. It's usually better to use the distribution's standard network startup scripts for this purpose, though.

Unfortunately, setting the hostname one time with this command does not set it permanently; after you reboot, Linux sets its hostname using values stored in configuration files. Details vary from one distribution to another, but you should pay particular attention to the /etc/HOSTNAME, /etc/hostname, /etc/sysconfig/network, and /etc/hosts files. The first three are common locations for Linux to store the name that it sets using the hostname command when it boots. The /etc/hosts file is a bit different, because it lists mappings of hostnames to IP addresses—it can be used in place of DNS on a small network, and it can augment DNS even on a large network. If you see your IP address in /etc/hosts, be sure it's mapped to your correct hostname.

> **TIP** If you can't find your system's hostname reference, try typing **grep -r hostname /etc/***. This command should return a list of files in the /etc directory tree that contain the word hostname. One of these is almost certainly the file that sets your hostname. Sometimes this file uses a definition from another file to set the hostname, so you can modify the source file or bypass the definition in another file by modifying the name-setting file directly.

Activating an Interface

To use a network, you must activate an interface. To do this, use the ifconfig command, which tells Linux to begin using a device and to associate it with a specific IP address. The basic syntax for this command is:

```
ifconfig interface [options] [address]
```

The meaning of each parameter is:

interface	This is the network interface, such as eth0.
options	You can specify several different options to ifconfig. The most important are up and down, which force the system to activate or deactivate an interface, respectively. (up is the default, so you can omit it when activating an interface.) You can also use the netmask *mask* option to set the netmask—by default, ifconfig uses a netmask based on the class of network to which the address belongs, as shown in Table 15.1. You can read about more options in the ifconfig man pages.
address	This is the IP address to which the computer will respond on this interface, such as 192.168.203.7. If you omit the address, ifconfig reports on the status of an interface, rather than configuring the interface to use an address.

Networking and Troubleshooting

PART 5

In its simplest form, an `ifconfig` command can be quite short:

```
# ifconfig eth0 192.168.203.7
```

You may need to add more options. In particular, if your IP address uses a nonstandard netmask, you may need to specify one, as in:

```
# ifconfig eth0 netmask 255.255.255.128 eth0 192.168.203.7
```

It's a good idea to check on a configuration after setting it up. You can also use `ifconfig` to gather useful debugging information even long after an interface has been activated. For example:

```
# ifconfig eth0
eth0      Link encap:Ethernet  HWaddr 00:A0:CC:24:BA:02
          inet addr:192.168.203.7  Bcast:192.168.203.255
          ➥Mask:255.255.255.0
          UP BROADCAST RUNNING  MTU:1500  Metric:1
          RX packets:7173469 errors:6 dropped:0 overruns:0 frame:6
          TX packets:6294646 errors:0 dropped:0 overruns:0 carrier:0
          collisions:66163
```

This output shows that eth0 is up and running, using the hardware address 00:A0:CC:24:BA:02 and the TCP/IP address 192.168.203.7. Further statistics include the *Maximum Transfer Unit (MTU)* size of 1500, received (RX) and transmitted (TX) packets (including errors), and collisions. This information can be invaluable when debugging a connection. A huge number of errors or collisions can signal that your network is overburdened or that your hardware is faulty, for example.

NOTE *Some* errors and collisions are normal. The preceding example shows a total of 66,163 collisions and 13,468,115 packets sent or received, for a collision rate of about 0.5%. The error rate (6 of 7,173,469 received packets and no transmit errors) is also quite low. It's difficult to specify a threshold above which errors or collisions indicate problems, because these values can vary from one network to another. Collisions occur inevitably on Ethernet networks when two systems try to transmit at the same time. Collision rates therefore go up with total network traffic.

Configuring the Routing Table

It's important that a computer know to which network interface it should send data. When there is just one NIC, this may seem a trivial task, but it's not quite so trivial in Linux, because all Linux systems support a *loopback* (or *localhost*) *interface*, which directs the network traffic back to the Linux system. This interface is very useful in troubleshooting and for some basic Linux features, such as X. It's normally assigned an address of 127.0.0.1 and is configured automatically by default startup scripts. You therefore need not concern yourself about the loopback interface, but you must tell your system how to route all other network data.

This task is accomplished with the route command, which has the following syntax:

```
route [add | del] [target] [gw gateway]
```

Each parameter has a specific meaning:

add | del	Specify add if you want to add an entry to the routing table, or del if you want to remove one. When starting up an interface, you use the add parameter.
target	The *target* is the IP address or network address to which the route applies. A network address looks just like an IP address, but it uses trailing 0's in the machine portion of the IP address, as in 192.168.203.0. One special target is the default route, which is 0.0.0.0. You can use the keyword default in place of 0.0.0.0, if you like. The default route is the route taken by all traffic that's not matched by more specific rules. You normally specify a gateway system with the default route; traffic to most sites that aren't on your local network then travels through the gateway system.
gw *gateway*	A gateway is a system that knows how to send packets to another network. The terms *gateway* and *router* carry very similar meanings, and are often used interchangeably. Your ISP or network administrator can provide you with the IP address of an appropriate gateway.

NOTE There's normally no need to specify explicitly the NIC or even the IP address with which a route is associated, because the route command can discern this information based on the target or gateway address. If your network is unusually complex, you can force the route to be associated with a device by using the dev *device* parameter.

Networking and Troubleshooting

PART 5

Typically, you specify two routes for traffic passing out of a Linux computer: one for traffic destined for the local network and one for a default route, which passes through a gateway. You can accomplish this task by issuing two commands, such as:

```
# route add 192.168.203.0
# route add 0.0.0.0 gw 192.168.203.1
```

The first of these commands adds a route for local traffic—anything addressed to the 192.168.203.0 network goes out over the appropriate NIC. The low-level TCP/IP protocols include routines that allow a computer to locate any other computer that's connected to its local network segment. The second command takes over when packets are destined for an address other than the 192.168.203.0 network (or any other network defined by an explicit route). In this case, the system directs the packets to 192.168.203.1, which should be a router capable of passing the packets on to the appropriate destination. (In fact, it may pass them on to another router, and so on for quite a few *hops* on the network.)

NOTE If you're configuring systems on a local network that will not be connected to the Internet, there's no need to specify a gateway route.

You can examine your routing table by issuing the route command without any options (or with the -n option, if you want to see IP addresses rather than machine names). For instance:

```
# route -n
```

```
Kernel IP routing table
```

Destination	Gateway	Genmask	Flags	Metric	Ref	Use	Iface
192.168.203.0	0.0.0.0	255.255.255.0	U	0	0	0	eth0
127.0.0.0	0.0.0.0	255.0.0.0	U	0	0	0	lo
0.0.0.0	192.168.203.1	0.0.0.0	UG	0	0	0	eth0

This output reveals three routes: one for the 192.168.203.0 network, one for the localhost interface (which is actually configured as an entire network), and one for the default route. Most desktop and even server systems will have routing tables that resemble this one. If a computer has multiple NICs, or if its network is unusually complex in any of several ways, the routing table may have additional entries.

Most Linux systems include calls to route in startup scripts. In Red Hat 7.0, /etc/rc.d/init.d/network is responsible for starting networking, including setting the route, but it calls several others to do the work. Ultimately, `/etc/sysconfig/static-routes` holds the information on routes that are added automatically. You can therefore modify this file, use Linuxconf to do the job, or add calls to route to some other startup script, such as `/etc/rc.d/rc.local`.

Specifying DNS Servers

In order to resolve hostnames into IP addresses for arbitrary systems on the Internet, Linux must know the IP address of at least one DNS server. Linux stores this information in the `/etc/resolv.conf` file, along with information on its own default domain name. A typical `/etc/resolv.conf` file looks like this:

```
domain room1.threeroomco.com

search room2.threeroomco.com room3.threeroomco.com

nameserver 192.168.203.1

nameserver 192.168.203.20
```

There are three important keywords used in this file:

domain	This specifies the domain to which the system belongs. Linux tries to resolve names using the specified domain first. For example, if you use the machine name gingko and the above /etc/resolv.conf file, Linux first searches for a computer called gingko.room1.threeroomco.com. This feature allows you to omit the domain name portion of a machine name when a target computer is in the same domain as the source machine.
search	The search option works much like the domain option, but you can specify several domains to be searched using this parameter, separated by spaces or tabs.
nameserver	Each nameserver line specifies the IP address of a single DNS server. This must be an IP address, not a machine name—after all, it's name resolution that the DNS server is supposed to do. You can specify as many DNS servers as you like, one per line, but Linux only uses the first three. Normally, only the first is used; but if the first DNS server becomes inaccessible, Linux goes on to the next.

WARNING Configuring a system to search too many domains or subdomains can increase the time it takes to resolve a domain name. It could also cause you to contact one machine when you meant another, if they bear the same machine names but exist in different domains.

You don't need to do anything special after entering information in /etc/resolv.conf in order to use these DNS servers. Also, Linux remembers these settings (unlike some other network configuration options) when you reboot, so you don't need to adjust any startup scripts.

Administrator's Logbook: Basic TCP/IP Configuration

System: E12345678

Actions: Configured computer to use DHCP for network assignment on eth0, and to set eth1 to use a fixed configuration.

eth1 configuration:

    IP address: 192.168.203.7

    Netmask: 255.255.255.0 (default)

    Gateway: none (use DHCP-assigned gateway on eth0)

    DNS: none (use DHCP-assigned DNS servers)

Testing the Setup

With any luck, you now have a working network configuration. You should perform some tests to be sure it's working. If you're impatient, skip ahead to test 6; but if you have problems, try the following tests in order:

1. Check the basic Linux TCP/IP stack by pinging the localhost address. Type **ping 127.0.0.1**. You should see a series of output lines similar to the following, indicating that the localhost address is responding:

   ```
   64 bytes from 127.0.0.1: icmp_seq=1 ttl=255 time=0.3 ms
   ```

   Press Ctrl+C to stop this sequence. If this test doesn't work, your configuration is very badly damaged. Every Linux system should pass this test, even immediately after installation.

2. Ping your NIC's external address (as in **ping 192.168.203.7**). This tests the association of the address to a NIC via `ifconfig`, as well as basic network driver functions.

3. Ping a machine on your local network by IP address. A good system to ping is usually your router/gateway. If this test works, you can be sure that your network hardware and drivers are functioning. If it fails, double-check your `ifconfig` setup and investigate the possibility of using a more up-to-date driver for your network card.

NOTE It's possible to configure a computer to ignore pings. Computers can also be offline, or the route to a remote computer can be broken in various ways. It's therefore possible that a ping test will fail despite a flawless configuration of your own system. If this happens, try another system before declaring the test failed.

---

4. Ping a machine beyond your local network by IP address, as in **ping 198.182.196.56** (this pings www.linux.org, but this address may change in the future; it's best to locate an address using `nslookup`). If this test works, your gateway configuration is correct. If previous tests succeeded but this one fails, check your routing table, paying particular attention to the gateway.

5. Ping local and remote machines by machine name rather than IP address, as in **ping www.linux.org**. If this test works, your DNS configuration is correct.

6. Use more sophisticated network tools, such as a Web browser or Telnet client. It's extremely unlikely that these will fail when pings work, but it's best to be complete.

If the preceding tests all pass, then your network settings are at least minimally correct. Of course, it's possible you'll run into more subtle problems, such as slow network performance or an inability to reach specific systems. Some such problems can be caused by local configuration problems, such as an incorrect routing table. Network debugging can be a complex task. If you have peculiar problems, you may want to post a message to the `comp.os.linux.networking` newsgroup.

File Sharing

One of the most common uses for networking on small networks is to implement *file sharing*. The idea behind this technology is to allow the users of one computer (the client) to access the files on another computer (the server) as if the server's files were stored on a disk local to the client. The benefits of this arrangement include:

- Saving on total disk space by storing files needed by many clients on just one system.

- Enabling individuals to work from any computer while accessing the same files.
- Making collaboration simpler than it would otherwise be, because there's no need to move files around on floppy disks.

Like many networking applications, file sharing requires the use of both client and server software. There are several file-sharing packages available on many OSs. This chapter restricts discussion to just two: the *Network File System (NFS)*, which is used by Linux and Unix systems; and *Samba*, which is the Linux implementation of the *Server Message Block (SMB*; a.k.a. *Common Internet Filesystem*, or *CIFS)* protocol used by DOS, Windows, and OS/2.

NOTE   Both NFS and SMB/CIFS are built at the top level of the OSI network model. Some file sharing protocols, including SMB/CIFS, can optionally use a variety of protocol stacks, but in Linux both of these use TCP/IP.

Sharing with Unix or Linux: NFS

NFS is tightly woven into Linux and Unix systems, and it supports the filesystem features (such as ownership and file permissions) upon which Linux and Unix systems depend. It's therefore the file sharing solution of choice on networks dominated by Linux or Unix computers.

NOTE   For a complete guide to NFS administration in Linux, see the forthcoming *Linux NFS and Automounter Administration*, by Erez Zadok (Sybex, 2001).

Configuring an NFS Server

To configure a Linux system as an NFS server, follow these steps:

1. Install an NFS server package. In Red Hat Linux 7.0, this package is called `nfs-utils-0.1.9.1-7`.

2. Edit the `/etc/exports` file to share specific directories, as described shortly.

3. Start the NFS server. On Red Hat systems, you can do this by typing **`/etc/rc.d/init.d/nfs start`**. (If the NFS daemon is already running, you should use `restart` rather than `start` in this command. You can discover if this server is running by typing **`ps ax | grep nfsd`**. If it's running, you'll see one or more entries for processes called `nfsd`.)

To ensure that the NFS server starts at boot time, check the `/etc/rc.d/rc3.d` and `/etc/rc.d/rc5.d` directories for a file called `S??nfs`, where `??` is a number. These files, if present, should be links to `/etc/rc.d/init.d/nfs` (or an NFS startup script in some other directory on some distributions). If these files don't exist, you must create them. The following command should accomplish this goal on Red Hat systems, but you may need to adjust the linked-to file on some distributions:

```
# ln -s /etc/rc.d/init.d/nfs /etc/rc[35].d/S60nfs
```

The most critical configuration file for an NFS server is /etc/exports. This file determines which computers may mount an exported directory, as well as various limitations placed on these mounts. Each line in /etc/exports defines one *export*, or directory that's shared. The line begins with the path to the directory and continues with a list of systems that are authorized to use the export, including any client-specific options enclosed in parentheses. Listing 15.1 shows a sample /etc/exports file.

Listing 15.1   An /etc/exports File Showing Some Common Options

```
/home larch(rw) birch(rw,map_static=/etc/birch.map)
     ➥gingko.threeroomco.com(ro)
/home/fred 192.168.34.23(noaccess)
/mnt *.threeroomco.com(rw)
/opt 192.168.34.0/24(ro)
```

You can list hostnames in several different ways in /etc/exports, as illustrated by Listing 15.1. These methods include:

Individual hostnames   You can list the hostnames individually, as in all the systems on the /home export in Listing 15.1. If the clients are part of the same domain as the server, you can omit the domain name, as was done with larch and birch in the example. Alternatively, you can keep the entire hostname.

Individual IP addresses   Instead of using a hostname, you can export a share to a system by specifying its IP address. Using an IP address enhances security slightly. This is the approach used by the /home/fred export in the example.

Domains   You can specify a domain by using a wildcard character, as in *.threeroomco.com, which exports the directory to any computer in the threeroomco.com domain. This approach can be convenient, but it also increases the potential for abuse should a DNS server be compromised.

IP address blocks   You can export a directory to a block of IP addresses by specifying a network address and netmask in abbreviated format, as in 192.168.34.0/24.

> **WARNING** You can export a share to any computer by omitting the hostname entirely. This may be convenient on a small private network, but it is also quite dangerous, particularly if your computer is accessible to the Internet as a whole.

You should specify one or more options for most exports and clients. You'll do this by specifying the options in parentheses after the client name. Listing 15.1 makes heavy use of the rw and ro options, which provide read/write and read-only access to a share, respectively. (Some NFS servers default to read-only access, while others default to read/write access, so it's best to be explicit on this matter to avoid confusion.) The noaccess option blocks all access to a directory. Listing 15.1 uses this option to prevent the computer at 192.168.34.23 from accessing the /home/fred directory, even if the /home directory is exported to that computer.

One particularly important option is map_static, which is used to specify a file that describes a mapping of client and server user and group IDs. Every Linux or Unix system assigns a user a username, but the username is just a convenient label. Underlying the username is a numeric *user ID*. The same user may have different user IDs on two different systems, even if the usernames are identical on both systems. NFS relies on user IDs, so if map_static is not used, a user might be able to access the *wrong* user's files on a server. The contents of the mapping file consist of three columns, separated by spaces: uid or gid (to indicate whether the code to be changed is a user or group ID, respectively), the ID on the client, and the ID on the server. Listing 15.2 presents a sample mapping file. In this file, user ID 501 on the client is mapped to user 504 on the server, and group 103 on the client becomes group 100 on the server.

Listing 15.2 A Sample NFS Mapping File

```
uid   501   504
uid   503   503
gid   103   100
```

> **WARNING** If you use a mapping file at all, it's important that it include *all* the users' mappings, even if the user has the same ID on both systems. If you omit a server user ID, then the associated user ID on the client is likely to be gibberish. This may be fine if the user doesn't exist on the client, but it's not OK if the user does exist on the client.

Various other options exist on some or all NFS servers and may be of interest to advanced administrators. Type man exports to learn more about this file and its options.

One thing to keep in mind about NFS is that it operates on a *trusted host* security model. That is, if you list a computer in /etc/exports, you turn over some of your security to that system. NFS exports Linux's username and permission information to the client, but if the remote system's security has been compromised in any way, it's possible that a user of the client might be able to damage files on the server. For this reason, it's generally unwise to export sensitive directories, such as /etc, especially with read/write permissions.

Over the years, there have been several Linux NFS servers. The latest version on most distributions uses special features in the Linux kernel to accelerate the server. You must therefore include NFS server support in your Linux kernel if you recompile your kernel. (All major distributions include this feature in their default kernels.) Unfortunately, this means that an NFS server may break if you upgrade your kernel, particularly from 2.2.*x* to 2.4.*x* kernels. You may therefore need to look for an updated NFS server (or an older one that doesn't use the kernel acceleration) if you upgrade your kernel.

Administrator's Logbook: Exporting Directories via NFS

System: E12345678

Action: Configured NFS exports: /home and /opt to local network computers (see /etc/exports for details).

Mounting Remote NFS Exports

Linux includes NFS client support in its kernel, and all major distributions compile this support in their standard kernels or as modules. You should therefore have little trouble mounting NFS exports, as long as the server recognizes your system as a valid client. Linux uses its regular mount command for mounting NFS exports. The syntax is as follows:

```
mount [-t nfs] server:/path /mountpoint
```

In most cases, the -t nfs parameter isn't required; Linux can figure out that it's an NFS export you're specifying. *server* is, of course, the name of the server, and */path* is the path to the exported directory on that server. */mountpoint* is the local mount point. For instance, the following command mounts the /home share from birch on the client, at /shared/homes:

    # **mount birch:/home /shared/homes**

You must normally be root to issue the mount command in this way, but you can add an entry to /etc/fstab to automate this process or allow other users to mount NFS exports. The entries to do this look just like those to mount a local filesystem, as described in Chapter 10, except that they include the NFS-style *server:/path* specification rather than a local device file. They also must specify a filesystem type of nfs.

However it's done, once an NFS export is mounted you can use it much as you do a local filesystem. Assuming your users have appropriate permissions on the remote system, they may read from and write to remote files. Of course, a network filesystem is not likely to be as fast as a purely local one.

Sharing with Windows: Samba

Ordinarily, NFS is the best choice to share files with other Linux or Unix systems. Windows and related operating systems, however, don't include NFS client packages by default, although they are available as add-ons. Instead, these OSs use SMB/CIFS networking protocols to achieve the same goals. Although NFS and SMB/CIFS serve the same purpose, they differ in many important details. SMB/CIFS was designed with DOS and Windows in mind, so it is the best protocol for file sharing with these systems. Fortunately, all modern Linux distributions include a server for SMB/CIFS: Samba.

Samba is a very complex package—it contains many more options and features than do any of Linux's NFS packages. This is largely because Samba must make a Linux computer look like a Windows system, which complicates the file-sharing task. Windows treats filenames and file attributes differently than does Linux, so it's necessary to include workarounds in Samba. Windows networks also include a variety of features that partly replicate functions of normal TCP/IP networking, such as an alternative naming system. These topics go far beyond the scope of a single chapter, so if you need to set up more than a minimal Samba file server, you should consult a book devoted to the topic, such as Roderick W. Smith's *Linux Samba Server Administration* (Sybex, 2001).

In Red Hat 7.0, Samba comes as three packages: samba-common-2.0.7-21ssl, samba-2.0.7-21ssl, and samba-client-2.0.7-21ssl. The first of these includes core Samba files, the second contains Samba server files, and the third contains Samba client files.

NOTE If any of your systems run Windows 2000 or Windows ME, you may want to be sure you're running Samba 2.0.7 or later. Although Samba 2.0.5a and 2.0.6 sometimes work with these clients, they can produce subtle problems. This is particularly true when using Samba as a client to Window servers. Versions of Samba prior to 2.0.5a don't work at all with the latest versions of Windows. You can find updated packages at http://www.samba.org.

Samba Configuration Options

The most common use of Samba is as a server. Samba's server functions are controlled through a single configuration file: smb.conf. This file contains several sections, each beginning with an identifying name in square brackets, such as [global] or [some-share]. Most of these sections identify *shares*—directories that Samba makes available, similar to NFS exports. The [global] definition, however, assigns default values and important global features. Within each definition, you can control Samba's features by assigning a *value* to a *parameter*, thus:

```
parameter = value
```

Samba is unconcerned with the case of parameters and most values (although a few values, such as Linux pathnames, are case-sensitive). Samba treats any characters that follow a semicolon (;) or pound sign (#) as a comment; these characters are ignored.

On most Linux systems, the smb.conf file resides in the /etc, /etc/samba, or /etc/samba.d directory. (Red Hat 7.0 uses /etc/samba.) If you compile Samba yourself, you can specify where the smb.conf file will go; the default value is /usr/local/samba/lib.

In addition to or instead of configuring Samba by editing its configuration file directly, you can use any of several GUI tools. Linuxconf, for example, includes Samba configuration options, as shown in Figure 15.3. (These options are not present in Red Hat 7.0's version of Linuxconf, but they do exist in earlier versions of Red Hat and in other distributions that use Linuxconf.) Samba also includes a utility called the *Samba Web Administration Tool*, which is a daemon that can be accessed from a Web browser. To use it, enter http://servername:901 as the URL, where servername is the server's name or IP address. (You must first launch SWAT, however, which is usually done by adding an entry to /etc/inetd.conf or /etc/xinetd.conf, both of which are briefly described later in this chapter.)

Networking and Troubleshooting

PART 5

Figure 15.3 GUI configuration tools let you manage Samba using a point-and-click interface.

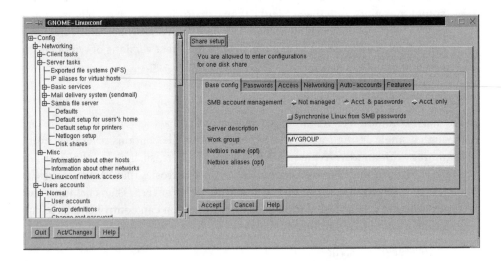

Samba is usually run from startup scripts in the /etc/rc.d directory tree. If they're not already present, you should create appropriate links in the /etc/rc.d/rc3.d and /etc/rc.d/rc5.d directories. On a Red Hat system, the following command should work, but you may need to adjust these pathnames and filenames on other distributions:

ln -s /etc/rc.d/init.d/smb /etc/rc.d/rc[35].d/S35smb

You'll need to start Samba manually if you've just set it up this way, or restart it after you make changes to its configuration. You can do this by typing **/etc/rc.d/init.d/smb start** or **/etc/rc.d/init.d/smb restart**, respectively.

Setting Global Options

Samba includes many global options (those that appear in the [global] section of smb.conf). Some of the most important of these are shown here:

```
[global]
        workgroup = ARBORETUM
        netbios name = GINGKO
        server string = Big Server
        encrypt passwords = Yes
        os level = 1
```

```
preferred master = No
domain master = No
hosts allow = 192.168.34. elm
```

These options mean the following:

workgroup	Windows networks are organized into *workgroups*, which are collections of computers sharing the same workgroup name. This name is specified by the workgroup parameter. If you don't set this parameter to match your network's workgroup, you may not be able to access the Samba server. (Many Windows networks use domains rather than workgroups. Domains also have names that you set using the workgroup parameter.)
netbios name	A computer's NetBIOS name is the name by which other computers know it, and the netbios name parameter sets this feature. If this parameter is not set, Samba takes the default value from the computer's machine name; for instance, gingko.threeroomco.com becomes GINGKO.
server string	This parameter sets a comment that's visible when you browse a workgroup using the Windows Network Neighborhood tool. It's purely a cosmetic feature of Windows networking.
encrypt passwords	This parameter is critically important, and it causes a great deal of trouble to new Samba administrators. By default, Samba accepts only cleartext passwords, which are transmitted without encryption. This characteristic can be a security risk, however; it's better to transmit passwords in an encrypted form, which makes it difficult or impossible to decipher an intercepted password. Using encrypted passwords on Samba, however, requires maintaining a separate Samba-only password list. (Samba checks cleartext passwords against Linux's normal password database.) Early versions of Windows 95 and Windows NT 4.0 used cleartext passwords, but Windows 95 OSR 2, Windows NT 4.0 SP 3, and all later versions of Windows use encrypted passwords. The section "Setting Password Options" describes Samba's encrypted password handling in more detail.

Networking and
Troubleshooting

PART 5

os level | The os level parameter controls how Samba announces itself for master browser elections. These elections determine which computer maintains a list of local computers for the convenience of other systems. You should set this value low (say, to 1) unless you're an experienced Samba administrator and understand the consequences of taking on master browser duties.

preferred master, domain master | These two parameters also affect whether Samba takes on master browser duties. If set to Yes, preferred master causes Samba to attempt to take on this role, which can be quite detrimental if the server isn't configured to win elections. Therefore, we recommend setting this value to No unless you understand the election process. Likewise, domain master determines whether Samba tries to become the domain master browser (as opposed to the local master browser, which is slightly different).

hosts allow | This parameter is an important security feature. If used, it blocks Samba access to all but the specified computers. You can list computers by hostname (not the NetBIOS name, if they differ) or by IP address. If a hostname begins with a period, or if an IP address with fewer than four elements ends with a period, that signifies an entire network of computers. In the preceding example, for instance, all computers on the 192.168.34.0/24 network are allowed access. Although this parameter isn't necessary, it's a good idea to use it, particularly if the server is connected to the Internet at large.

The most critical of these parameters are workgroup and encrypt passwords. When you first install Samba, it's not likely to be configured to function on your workgroup, so chances are you *must* set the workgroup parameter to use the server. Likewise, unless you're using fairly old clients, you must normally either configure Samba to use encrypted passwords or reconfigure your clients to use cleartext passwords.

Setting Password Options

If you set encrypt passwords = Yes, you must set up an encrypted password file on Linux. To do this, you can use the smbpasswd program, which adds a username and password to the encrypted password file (/etc/samba/smbpasswd on Red Hat 7.0 systems) or edits that information. For each user on your system, you should issue the command:

```
# smbpasswd -a username
```

The program will ask you to enter the password twice. The first time you run this program, it may notify you that it can't find the smbpasswd file, and so is creating it.

If you prefer to use cleartext passwords and the normal Linux password database, you can do so by changing any recent Windows clients to send cleartext passwords. On Red Hat systems, the directory 7.0/usr/share/doc/samba-2.07/docs contains several .reg files that can be used to make the appropriate changes to Windows systems. Copy the file named after the version of the OS you're running (such as Win98_PlainPassword.reg for Windows 98) to a floppy disk, move that disk to the target Windows system, and double-click the file to adjust the client's configuration. You'll need to reboot before the changes will take effect.

Configuring File Shares

File shares comprise the bulk of most smb.conf files, particularly on servers that have many shares. This share demonstrates the most common file-sharing options:

```
[bigshare]
        comment = Shared Program Directory
        path = /home/samba/bigshare
        read only = No
        browseable = Yes
        create mask = 0666
        directory mask = 0777
```

The meanings of this share's parameters are as follows:

comment	The comment parameter works much like the server string parameter, except that comment sets a comment that's associated with a specific share.
path	The path parameter sets the directory that's to be shared. This can be any directory on the computer, although of course it's unwise to share some directories, such as /etc, for security reasons.
read only	By default, Samba doesn't grant write access to directories it shares. You can allow users to write to Samba shares by including the read only = No parameter. writeable and writable are antonyms of read only, so writeable = Yes is synonymous with read only = No.

`browseable`	This parameter, if set to Yes, causes a share to appear in Network Neighborhood browse lists under Windows. It's generally best to set this parameter to Yes.
`create mask and directory mask`	These parameters set the maximum permissions on files and directories that users create via Samba. In the example, these are set at high values, so that all users can read and write each other's files. Of course, you may want to restrict permissions rather than expand them. The default values are 0744 and 0755, respectively.

There is a special share name that deserves explicit mention: [homes]. If you use this share, you should omit the path parameter, and Samba provides a share that corresponds to the user's home directory. For instance, if jennie logs onto the server, the share appears on the client as JENNIE and shows the user's home directory files. This share is extremely useful and popular on servers used for storing individual users' files (as opposed to shared program files).

In addition to file sharing, Samba supports printer sharing, as discussed in Chapter 13. The easiest way to enable printer sharing is to create a [printers] share, which should have the print ok = Yes parameter set. This causes Samba to share each of the printer queues defined in /etc/printcap. Because these Linux printer queues are normally defined as PostScript printers, you should treat them as PostScript printers from the Windows clients.

TIP Apple LaserWriter drivers tend to work well with printers that use Ghost-script on Linux for printing.

Using Samba as a Client

Samba includes two client programs: smbclient and smbmount. The first of these is a program that allows you to perform file transfers in a manner similar to a text-mode FTP client program. By contrast, smbmount allows you to mount a share on the Linux directory tree, much as you can mount an NFS share using the Linux mount command. (In fact, since Samba 2.0.6, you can use mount instead of smbmount.) There are also assorted GUI front-ends to these packages, so that you can browse an SMB/CIFS network from Linux much as you can from Windows.

All of the Samba client programs rely upon settings in the [global] section of smb.conf to control aspects of their operation, such as the claimed NetBIOS and workgroup names of the computer. You should therefore be sure these features are set correctly before using Samba as a client.

To use smbclient, you start it and pass the name of the server and the share you want to access, thus:

```
$ smbclient //server/share
```

After you type this command, smbclient prompts you for a password, which should match the password associated with your username on the server. (If your username on the server is not the same as on the client, you can use the -U *username* parameter to specify your username on the server.) The commands available in smbclient are similar to those in the text-mode ftp program, or from a Linux shell—ls to see the available files; put and get to transfer files to and from the share, respectively; cd to move to a new directory; and so on. You can type **?** or **help** to see a summary of commands.

Although smbclient can be a good way to transfer a few files quickly, smbmount is more flexible if you want to be able to directly modify files on the server. You might use this tool to use a Linux program to edit a file that's stored on a server, for instance. To use smbmount, issue the command in the following form:

```
$ smbmount //server/share /mountpoint
```

> **NOTE** If you don't issue the smbmount command as root, two programs must be set user ID (suid) root for this to work: smbmnt (a helper program to smbmount) and smbumount (used to unmount SMB/CIFS shares). You can issue the command **chmod a+s /usr/bin/smbmnt /usr/bin/smbumount** to accomplish this task.

Like smbclient, smbmount asks you for a password before it mounts the share. Once a share is mounted, you can access the files on it as if they were on a local disk, with certain caveats. Some filesystems may be shared read-only, so you may not be able to write files to these shares. SMB/CIFS doesn't support Linux-style ownership and permissions, so by default, all files are owned by the individual who issues the smbmount command. When you're done with a share, you can unmount it with the smbumount command; enter it as

```
$ smbumount /mountpoint
```

As mentioned earlier, you can use mount instead of smbmount with Samba 2.0.6 and later. To do so, you call mount with a filesystem type of smbfs, thus:

```
# mount -t smbfs //server/share /mountpoint
```

This procedure works best when the caller is root, unless you create an /etc/fstab entry that allows ordinary users to issue the mount command, as described in Chapter 10. When this is the case, you should omit the filesystem type, server, and share names when issuing the mount command (as in **mount /mountpoint**).

Networking and Troubleshooting

PART 5

Several GUI front-ends to smbmount are available. Details of operation differ from one program to another, but as a general rule, these utilities present a GUI view of the local network, as demonstrated by LinNeighborhood (http://www.bnro.de/~schmidjo/), shown in Figure 15.4. When you double-click a share to open it, a dialog box asks for your username and password, and the program then opens a window on the share using the file manager you specify when you configure the program. GUI front-ends don't really add fundamentally new functionality to Linux's SMB/CIFS capabilities, but they do make these networks more accessible to those who aren't familiar with Samba's text-mode tools. You may therefore want to install LinNeighborhood, or a similar package, such as Kruiser (http://devel-home.kde.org/~kruiser/) or xSMBrowser (http://www.public.iastate.edu/~chadspen/).

Internet Servers

If you want to be able to use a computer when you're away from it, you must install some variety of server on that computer. Likewise, if you want others to be able to use a computer, a server is necessary. The appropriate server depends on your precise needs, however. There are some commonalities to configuring servers, but every one involves at least some unique aspects, so you should consult the appropriate documentation.

Available Servers

Linux supports a wide variety of Internet server packages. Although these can be used on a local network alone, they're more often used to provide services to a wide variety of computers on the Internet at large. A few of these servers are discussed to a greater or lesser extent elsewhere in this book. Many are complex enough that entire books are written about them. You can usually find more information in documentation files that come with the servers, or on Web pages devoted to the servers. A complete listing of servers available for Linux would be too long to reproduce here; but some of the most important server types include:

FTP servers   The *File Transfer Protocol (FTP)* is one of the Internet's most important protocols, although it's one of the least flashy. FTP allows individuals to transfer files to or from an FTP server. Links on Web pages to program files are often FTP links. Several FTP servers are available for Linux, such as *Washington University FTP (WU-FTP*; http://www.wu-ftpd.org/) and *ProFTP* (http://www.proftpd.net). Red Hat Linux ships with WU-FTP, but you can install any other FTP server for Linux, if you prefer.

Mail servers   If you want your computer to receive mail addressed directly to it, you must run a *mail server*—a.k.a. a *Mail Transport Agent (MTA)*. (If your ISP collects

Figure 15.4   LinNeighborhood and other GUI SMB/CIFS browsers provide a user interface similar to that of Network Neighborhood in Windows.

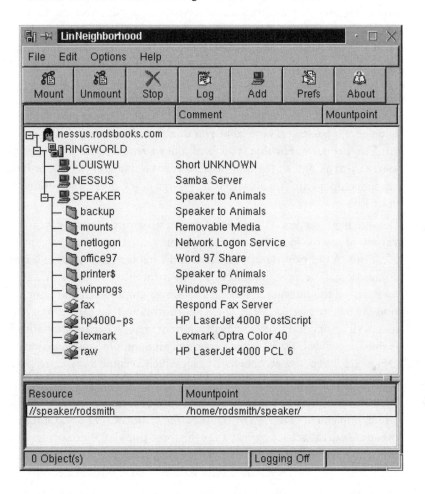

and holds mail for you, you may not need an MTA; instead, you can use a mail program that retrieves mail using a protocol such as the *Post Office Protocol [POP].*) All major Linux distributions come with an MTA, which is usually configured by default in a reasonable way for a standalone workstation. Red Hat Linux ships with sendmail (`http://www.sendmail.org`), but various alternatives are available and are used by some other distributions. Chapter 17 covers sendmail, but if your system is to be used exclusively as a mail server, you should consider purchasing a book devoted to the topic, such as Craig Hunt's *Linux Sendmail Administration* (Sybex, 2000).

News servers   The *Network News Transport Protocol (NNTP)* controls the transfer of *Usenet news*—a global discussion forum in which users post queries, solutions, and other discussions of topics as diverse as vegetarian cooking, Linux, and the International Space Station. News servers typically exist at ISPs and large organizations, such as universities. They exchange articles with each other, resulting in the global span of Usenet news. You can run a news server yourself, either if you're in charge of the news server for a large organization or if you want to run a small news server for internal use or to maintain local copies of the newsgroups in which you're interested. Red Hat Linux comes with *Internet News (INN)*, one of the more popular news server packages. Note that you don't need a news server if you just want to *read* Usenet news. For that, you need a news *reader*, such as tin (http://www.tin.org), Knews (http://www.matematik.su.se/~kjj/), or Netscape's news reader component. You also need access to a news server, such as one maintained by your ISP.

Remote login servers   If you want to run programs remotely, you must run some variety of *remote login server*. This is a program that accepts logins from remote locations. A getty program (discussed in Chapter 12) is a login server for dial-up connections. The most familiar login server for most people is Telnet, which accepts logins from the Internet at large. (This server comes with all major Linux distributions.) Unfortunately, Telnet sends all information, including passwords, in cleartext, so it's not good from a security point of view. A better alternative in this respect is the *Secure Shell (SSH)*, which encrypts all data. One implementation of SSH is OpenSSH (http://www.openssh.com), which became a standard part of Red Hat Linux with version 7.0 of the distribution.

Web servers   One of the most visible types of Internet server is the Web server, which implements the *Hypertext Transfer Protocol (HTTP)*. On Linux, Apache (http://www.apache.org) is by far the most popular Web server. Apache is complex enough that to do more than basic configuration, you should read a book on the topic, such as Charles Aulds' *Linux Apache Server Administration* (Sybex, 2001).

X servers   An *X server* is a program that displays the windows created by X-based programs. On an isolated workstation installation of Linux, the X server (typically XFree86) runs on the same computer as the X programs that are being run. You can, however, connect to a remote computer (using a login protocol like Telnet or SSH) and run X programs from that remote system using your local X server. Note that, unlike most servers, the X server runs on the computer that's nearest you; the remote system runs the client programs. This makes sense when you think of it from the program's point of view; to the program, the server—and you—are at the distant location, and the server provides remote services (a display and input devices). Chapter

16 covers XFree86 (`http://www.xfree86.org`), the X server that ships with all major Linux distributions.

WARNING   All servers are security risks. Bugs in servers, misconfigured servers, and flaws in local security (such as poor password selections by your users) make it possible for undesirables to break into your computer. In addition, some servers provide other possibilities for abuse. For instance, it's easy to misconfigure a mail server so that it can be used to *relay* mail from anywhere to anywhere. Those who send unsolicited bulk e-mail ("spam") frequently look for open relays to obscure their true locations. Because of the great potential for abuse, you should run as few servers as possible on your Linux computer. Many Linux distributions install many servers by default, so you should check through your `inetd.conf` or `xinetd.conf` file (described shortly) and disable anything you're not using.

Using a Super Server

One problem with servers is that when they're running, they consume system resources—primarily memory, but also some CPU time. These resources might be better used by other processes, particularly when the servers are used only occasionally. Systems that host many seldom-used servers therefore turn to a *super server* to control the servers. A super server is a program that looks for incoming packets addressed to several other servers. When the super server detects such packets, it launches the appropriate server program. When the individual servers aren't needed, they don't run. This approach can save a great deal of memory when you want to run several servers, most of which aren't in use at any given moment.

Another benefit to using a super server is that it's usually possible to implement additional security features with such a server. One approach to this is to use an intermediary package, such as TCP Wrappers (introduced in Chapter 7), to filter connection requests. TCP Wrappers can examine the IP address of the calling system and allow or deny access based on this address. This can be extremely useful if some servers, such as a Telnet or SSH server, should only be accessible from certain computers.

Using *inetd*

The most common super server in most Linux distributions is `inetd`. This server was a standard part of Red Hat through version 6.2. With version 7.0, however, Red Hat switched to `xinetd`, which is described shortly. The `inetd` server is controlled through the `/etc/inetd.conf` file. Each line in this file corresponds to a single server. An example that uses TCP Wrappers follows.

```
ftp stream tcp nowait root /usr/sbin/tcpd in.ftpd -l -a
```

The meaning of each element of this entry is as follows:

ftp	This is the code for the service, as found in the /etc/ services file. inetd "listens" on a particular port for connection requests, and this code—or more precisely, the port number associated with this code in /etc/services—determines to what port number inetd listens.
stream	This is the socket type, which determines some aspects of how the server interacts with the TCP/IP stack. Common options are stream and dgram.
tcp	This is the type of TCP/IP connection—tcp or udp. Most network servers use TCP, which establishes a lasting two-way connection; but some use UDP, which is less robust but requires less overhead because it doesn't establish a full two-way connection.
nowait	Datagram-based services (those that specify dgram rather than stream) either remain connected to the caller and specify wait here, or they are multithreaded and split off a separate thread to handle the connection. This latter type specifies nowait. This entry isn't meaningful for streaming connections, but by convention they specify nowait.
root	inetd launches every server using a particular username. Many servers must be launched as root, but some may be launched under some other username to increase security.
/usr/sbin/tcpd	This entry is the name of the server that's to handle the connection. In the case of this example, the server is tcpd—the name of the TCP Wrappers program. If you want to bypass TCP Wrappers, you would specify the server program directly.

`in.ftpd -l -a`	The final entry is any parameters that are to be passed to the server. When the "server" is TCP Wrappers, you pass the name of the real server, along with any parameters that server requires. TCP Wrappers then checks that the incoming request is allowed and calls the real server (`in.ftpd` in this example), along with whatever parameters you specify (such as `-l` and `-a`).

In the default `inetd.conf` file, you'll find entries for most common servers. Most of these entries are commented out with pound signs (#), however. You can therefore uncomment the appropriate entries when you add a server of a particular type. Conversely, if you remove a server or want to disable it, you can comment out the appropriate line if it's active.

TIP   One easy first step to securing a Linux server is to comment out all unnecessary lines from `inetd.conf`. In fact, none of the servers listed in this file is necessary for Linux to boot. Some servers may *sound* like they're critically important, but they aren't. The `login` server, for example, is a very low-security remote login server, as described earlier; it is *not* required for ordinary text-mode logins or even for remote logins via Telnet or SSH. You can go through `inetd.conf` and comment out all the servers except those you're sure that you need.

After you've made changes to `/etc/inetd.conf`, you must send the server a SIGHUP signal to tell it to reload its configuration file. You can do this as follows:

```
# ps ax | grep inetd
  468 ?          S        0:00 inetd
# kill -SIGHUP 468
```

The process ID number (468 in the preceding example) may be different on your system. If possible, you should immediately test that your changes took effect. If you added or removed a server, make this test by trying to connect to the server.

Using *xinetd*

Although `inetd` is the most common super server, it's not the only one. One moderately popular `inetd` replacement is `xinetd` (pronounced "zi-net-dee"), which can be obtained from `http://www.synack.net/xinetd/`. Red Hat 7.0 ships with `xinetd` rather than inetd. This program's greatest advantage is that it combines many of the features of TCP Wrappers in the super server proper. It's particularly useful on systems that have multiple network cards, because it can block access to particular servers based on the network card.

The xinetd configuration file is /etc/xinetd.conf. Its format is different from that of inetd.conf, but it contains much of the same information. Rather than placing information on a single line, xinetd.conf creates multiple-line entries. Listing 15.3 shows the xinetd.conf equivalent of the sample inetd.conf entry shown earlier. This listing also shows the use of the interface option, which tells xinetd to listen *only* on the interface associated with the specified IP address. In this example, if the computer has two network interfaces, only one will respond to incoming FTP traffic.

Listing 15.3   A Sample xinetd.conf Service Entry

```
service ftp
{
        socket_type     = stream
        protocol        = tcp
        wait            = no
        user            = root
        server          = /usr/sbin/in.ftpd
        server_args     = -l -a
        interface       = 192.168.203.7
}
```

Most of the entries in the xinetd.conf service definition correspond to entries in the similar inetd.conf service definition. One exception is the interface entry, which has no inetd.conf equivalent. Another difference is that there's no call to tcpd in the xinetd.conf definition. This is because xinetd incorporates functionality similar to that of TCP Wrappers. In particular, you can use only_from to specify a list of IP addresses, networks, or computer names that are allowed to use a service; or you can use no_access to "blacklist" computers or networks, blocking them from using a service. You can also block access based on time of day, limit the total number of connections to a service, and so on. These options and many more are detailed in the xinetd.conf man page.

The default Red Hat 7.0 xinetd.conf file is quite short. Instead of listing entries for all services in a single file, Red Hat 7.0 uses a xinetd.conf file that sets only global default options. Files for specific servers appear in the `/etc/xinetd.d` directory. This configuration makes it easy for server packages to set themselves to run when they're installed. If you're using `xinetd` on another distribution, you may prefer to maintain a single monolithic `xinetd.conf` file with entries for all your servers. Both approaches are perfectly valid.

After making changes to your `xinetd` configuration, you must restart the server. You do this much as you restart `inetd`, as described earlier.

General Super Server Considerations

Because a super server doesn't keep the real servers loaded at all times, you do *not* normally need to restart the super server if you update the underlying server. You can upgrade your Telnet server, for instance, and the super server will immediately begin using the new version. The exception to this rule is if the updated server needs to be called in a new way—if its name or location has changed, for instance.

The drawback to using a super server is that it necessarily takes some time to launch its "child" servers. The result is that the server computer won't respond immediately to requests; it may take anywhere from a fraction of a second to several seconds for the system to respond to a request. This can be a major drawback for some servers, such as Web servers. You'll have to judge for yourself whether the delay is worth the improvement in memory use and (perhaps) security of using a super server.

Some servers don't work very well, if at all, from a super server. Most installations don't run Samba or sendmail through `inetd` or `xinetd`, for instance; although it's possible to run these servers through a super server, the performance penalty is too great. You should therefore not think that you've shut down all unnecessary servers once you've cleared out superfluous servers from `/etc/inetd.conf`, `/etc/xinetd.conf`, or `/etc/xinetd.d`. You may need to clean more from the `/etc/init.d` directory tree or from other system startup files.

In Sum

TCP/IP networking is the most popular type of networking today. It's the protocol that's used on the Internet, and many local networking tasks use TCP/IP as well. Configuring Linux for TCP/IP networking involves using a handful of different tools to activate a network interface, tell Linux how to route packets, and so on. Most distributions allow you to configure these options when you install the OS, or you can do it after-the-fact through either a GUI configuration utility or by editing configuration files in a text editor.

File sharing is one of the most popular networking tasks on small networks. This task builds on basic TCP/IP networking features, allowing you to store files on a single computer for use by many systems. This can be a great boon in many work environments, boosting productivity by allowing individuals to work at any computer and to exchange files among themselves easily.

Linux supports a wide variety of TCP/IP-based Internet servers, which can provide private and public services to remote systems. Many of these servers are the topics of entire books. Chapters 16 and 17 introduce two of these services, the X Window System and mail servers.

16

The X Window System

G_raphical user interfaces (GUIs)_ are practical necessities for many computer uses today. Although it's possible to accomplish a lot with text-mode tools, many users are more comfortable in a GUI environment than with text-mode programs. GUIs are also extremely useful for certain classes of programs, such as graphics editors. Some OSs, such as MacOS, integrate their GUIs extremely tightly into the OS as a whole. Linux uses a looser arrangement, however. In Linux, the GUI is entirely separate from the core of the OS. In fact, several different GUIs are available for Linux, but the most common by far is known as the _X Window System_, or _X_ for short.

Most modern Linux distributions, including Red Hat, make every effort to configure X properly at installation, and to set up defaults that make for an appealing and easy-to-use GUI environment. Such configurations may lead a new Linux user to believe that Linux is more like Windows or MacOS than it is. In fact, X is very different from these operating systems in many ways, leading to distinct advantages and disadvantages to X as compared to the GUIs in other OSs.

This chapter begins with a look at basic X concepts, such as X as a network protocol. The chapter then proceeds to an overview of X configuration—although, with any luck, this will be handled automatically at system installation time. Then, a discussion is provided of each of three important components of a working X environment: the window manager, widget sets, and the desktop environment. This chapter concludes with a look at some of the issues involved in running X-based applications on a Linux system.

X Concepts

You're probably already familiar with GUI environments, be it from using Windows, MacOS, or some other OS; or from using X on Linux or Unix as a user (as opposed to as a system administrator). Much of your knowledge from these experiences can be useful in using and administering X. You should be aware of several unique aspects of X, however. Many of these characteristics make X much more flexible than are most other GUIs, but some can be limiting or create confusion on the part of new X users.

X as a Network Protocol

Compared to most other GUI environments, X's most unusual characteristic is that it's a very network-oriented tool. The basic idea behind X is this: When an X-based program is launched on a Linux computer, the program attempts to connect to an *X server*. The X server provides a screen on which the program can display its output, and a keyboard and mouse to provide for input.

When you set up a Linux computer as a workstation, it defaults to using a *local* X server for these functions. This X server uses the computer's standard keyboard, mouse, and monitor. Therefore, no actual network accesses are involved. A Linux program can easily direct its X requests to an X server running on another computer, however. When this happens, the result is that you can use one computer (on which an X server is running) to run software that's located on another computer (the client). Typically, you use a remote login client (such as Telnet; see Chapter 15) and an X server on the local system, with a login server and X client (the program) on a remote system. After logging in to the remote system, you issue appropriate commands to make its X programs use your local display, and launch an X server locally. The remote system need not even have a display or X server. This arrangement is illustrated in Figure 16.1.

Figure 16.1   The X server runs on the computer at which a user sits; the X client may be located miles away from the user.

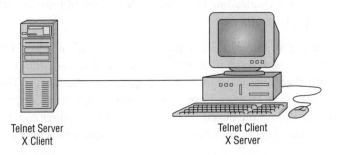

Telnet Server
X Client

Telnet Client
X Server

The terminology of the client/server relationship is confusing to most Linux newcomers, because most people think of servers as running on powerful computers that are located remotely. In most cases, it's the client that runs on the computer at which the user sits. This relationship is reversed in the case of X. To understand and remember this, it's helpful to think about it from the application's point of view. To the X program, the X server provides network services, just like a file server or Web server. The fact that there's a human seated in front of the X server is irrelevant to the program.

> **NOTE** One network product, the *Virtual Network Computing (VNC)* server (http://www.uk.research.att.com/vnc/), can be used to remotely access a Linux computer much as can be done through an X server. In VNC's network model, however, the server runs on the same computer as do the X programs; the user runs a small client program that communicates with the VNC X server. Effectively, VNC adds an extra layer to the line of communications, in the process reversing the usual X client/server relationship so that it's more intuitively reasonable to most users.

Even if you use X only locally, on a single computer, the network-centric design of X has important consequences. These include:

- X can be configured to use a *font server* (described shortly) to handle font rendering. Some distributions, including Red Hat 7.0, use a font server by default. You can, however, use a single font server for all the computers on your network, which can simplify font administration.

- Like all network servers, X uses assorted security measures. On some distributions (but not Red Hat), you may find that you can't run X-based programs if you use su to acquire root privileges. If your X security is lax, users of other computers may be able to snoop on your display or display their own programs on your screen.

- X programs rely upon certain environment variables to tell them what display to use. These variables are normally set correctly in default Linux installations, but these settings may become damaged. You must also change them if you want to use a remote display.

- X is typically slower than other GUI environments. The need to process display data through network protocols, even when the display is local, causes some slowdown. This effect is likely to be quite modest on modern hardware, but you might notice it with some applications or on older hardware.

On the whole, X's network-centric nature makes for a great deal of flexibility in a network environment. You can run the same programs *from* many computers, while running these programs *on* just one computer. The complexity and speed hit of X can be a drawback on an isolated workstation, however.

Networking and Troubleshooting

PART 5

X Security

If you're using X only locally, chances are your distribution has configured X in a reasonable way. On some distributions, however, you may need to loosen security a bit if you want to use X programs after you've used su to acquire root privileges. If you want to run X programs remotely, too, you'll need to make a couple of adjustments.

To use an X server, the client computer has to know *which* X server to use. This is done through the DISPLAY environment variable, which you can set using the following command (assuming you're using the bash shell):

```
$ export DISPLAY=hostname:displaynum
```

In this command, *hostname* is the name of the computer on which the server runs (that is, the computer at which you're sitting), and *displaynum* is the number of the display. *displaynum* is normally 0 or 0.0 for the primary X display, but it may be a higher number if the computer runs multiple X servers, as described shortly in "X Virtual Consoles." It's important to realize that you issue this command on the computer that hosts the X programs you intend to run, not on your local computer.

Most X servers are configured by default to refuse connections except from the local system. Some distributions also refuse connections except from the user who's logged on locally. When this happens, you won't be able to use X programs after you use su to acquire root privileges. There are various ways to tell X to be more lenient in the connections it accepts. The simplest is to use the xhost command, which uses the following syntax:

```
xhost [+|-][hostname]
```

To add a client to the list of allowed hosts, use *+hostname*; to remove a client, use *-hostname*. If you omit the hostname, the X server accepts or refuses *all* connections, no matter what the client. This can be a potentially major security problem when adding permissions. Unlike the DISPLAY environment variable, this command must be issued on the X *server* computer—the one at which you sit.

TIP   If you regularly run programs on a variety of computers from a single Linux computer, you can add appropriate xhost commands to your .xsession or other startup file (described later in this chapter) to allow these connections by default. You can use localhost as the *hostname* to ensure that all local users (including root) can use your display, so you can use su and then run X programs as the alternative user.

As an example, consider the following: You're sitting at the computer dino.pangaea.edu, and you want to run a program that's located at larch.threeroomco.com. Assuming both computers are Linux or Unix boxes, you would follow these steps:

1. Log in to dino.pangaea.edu.

2. If dino isn't already running X, start it by typing **startx**.

3. Issue the command **xhost +larch.threeroomco.com**.

4. Use Telnet or Secure Shell (SSH) to log in to larch.threeroomco.com from dino.pangaea.edu.

5. Type **export DISPLAY=dino.pangaea.edu:0** on your larch login.

6. Run whatever programs you want to run using your larch login.

7. When you're done, type **xhost -larch.threeroomco.com** on dino to remove larch from dino's accepted host list.

X servers are available for a wide variety of computers, not just Linux and Unix boxes (see the sidebar "Alternatives to XFree86" later in this chapter). You can therefore follow a similar procedure if dino runs some other OS. Most X servers for Windows and other OSs, however, are fairly lax on security, so you don't need to use the xhost commands; these X servers accept connections from just about anywhere to begin with.

If your computer (dino) sits behind a firewall, especially one that uses IP masquerading, you may not be able to follow these steps, because the outside client won't be able to breach the firewall to connect to your X server. There are two common workarounds to this problem:

Use VNC   VNC, mentioned earlier, reverses the client/server configuration, so the server falls outside the firewall. Assuming your firewall doesn't block outgoing VNC connections, you can use a local VNC client and run the VNC X server on the remote system. Consult the VNC documentation for details of its use.

Use SSH   SSH can be configured to *tunnel* X connections through its own connection. When this happens, the SSH server looks for X connection attempts from local programs and passes them back to the system on which the SSH client (and X server) runs. When properly configured, this works automatically, so you can skip steps 3, 5, and 7 from the above procedure. If this doesn't work initially, check the file /etc/ssh/ssh_config on the client; its ForwardX11 line should read yes. The server's /etc/ssh/sshd_config file should include a line that reads X11Forwarding yes.

X Virtual Consoles

Chapter 10 described the use of *virtual consoles* for text-mode logins. If you use a text-mode login, you can hit Alt+F1 through Alt+F6 to switch between different screens, each of which can display a different login session. You can therefore use one to log in with your normal username, another to log in as root, and so on; or log in multiple times as one user and switch easily between different programs. If you're running X, you can switch to a virtual text-mode console by pressing Ctrl+Alt+F*n*, where *n* is the console number.

Virtual consoles are not restricted to text-mode logins, however. When X runs, by default, it takes over an unused virtual console (typically console 7). You can therefore switch back to X from a text-mode console by pressing Alt+F7 (if X is running). Of potentially greater interest, it's possible to run multiple X sessions, each in its own virtual console. You can then switch between them by pressing Ctrl+Alt+F*n*, where *n* is a number from 7 up. To launch a second X session, follow these steps:

1. If you're already running in X, press Ctrl+Alt+F1 to get to a text-mode login: prompt. Log in.

2. Type **startx -- :1 vt8** to start X on virtual terminal 8. You should see X start up.

3. Press Ctrl+Alt+F7 to switch back to your original X session or Ctrl+Alt+F8 to switch to the new one.

Why would you want to start a new X session? After all, most window managers support multiple workspaces, so you can easily keep lots of windows open on different screens. You can even use su within an xterm to launch programs as different users. Using multiple X sessions does have certain advantages, however:

- You can run different window managers in different sessions. This isn't ordinarily a compelling reason to run multiple sessions, but it can be useful if you want to evaluate a window manager or if you need to use one for some programs but prefer another for other programs.

- You can start X in different resolutions. Your normal startup might be in 1280×1024 resolution, but if you need to test software at 800×600, you can run a separate 800×600 session. You can use the -bpp (for XFree86 3.*x*) or -depth (for XFree86 4.0) parameter to startx, along with an appropriate XF86Config setting (as described shortly), to force X to start at a given resolution when you start at a given bit depth. For example, the following command starts XFree86 4.0 at 32-bit color depth, which you can associate with a specific resolution:

```
$ startx -- :1 -depth 32 vt8
```

- You can start multiple X sessions as different users, complete with a different desktop environment and assorted X customizations. This can be useful when testing different environments or when debugging a particular user's configuration.

Configuring an X Server

Configuring X entails making adjustments to one primary file: XF86Config. This file resides in the /etc/X11 directory on Red Hat systems, but some distributions place the file in /etc. You can configure X by directly editing its XF86Config file or by using an X configuration tool. In most cases, X is configured reasonably during system installation, but sometimes the installation routines bungle the job. You might also need to adjust the configuration to change configuration details or if you change your video hardware.

Most Linux distributions released in the latter half of 2000, including Red Hat 7.0, ship with two versions of XFree86: 3.3.6 and 4.0 or 4.0.1. XFree86 3.3.6 is stable and supports a large number of video cards. XFree86 4.0 is less well tested and supports fewer video cards, but it includes additional features, such as the ability to bind two video cards' displays into a single desktop. For the average user, it's best to leave the X configuration as whatever your distribution selected. In some cases, though, you may want to upgrade to XFree86 4.0 (or downgrade to 3.3.6). Consult the main XFree86 Web site (http://www.xfree86.org) to learn more about the differences between these two versions of XFree86.

> **NOTE** Some distributions, such as Red Hat 7.0, install components of both versions of XFree86. Typically, the font and support files from version 4.0 are installed, along with a server file for version 3.3.6. This setup may seem strange, but it works. Use the 3.x configuration instructions when adjusting such a system.

XFree86 3.x

XFree86 3.x (including the latest, and perhaps last, in that line, 3.3.6) has long been the standard X server in Linux. You can configure XFree86 3.x through its XF86Config file or by using any of several X configuration tools. This section describes this configuration, so that you can adjust your system's X settings should the need arise.

To determine whether your system is running XFree86 3.x, check for a link to an X server in the /etc or /etc/X11 directory. In Red Hat 7.0, this link is called /etc/X11/X. If this link points to a file called XFree86, the system is configured to use XFree86 4.0. If the link points to a file named XF86_*Server*, where *Server* is a server name such as SVGA or Mach64, the system is configured to use XFree86 3.x.

The *XF86Config* File

The XF86Config file contains settings that are grouped into several different sections (you may want to load this file into a text editor to review your settings while reading the following items):

Files   The Files section includes paths to directories that contain important files. Most important of these are the FontPath lines, which point X to its font files and font servers, as described shortly.

ServerFlags   You can set a few miscellaneous controls in this section. Chances are you won't need to make any adjustments here.

Keyboard   This section defines the keyboard. Aside from the keyboard repeat rate, which you may want to adjust via the AutoRepeat line, these settings are mostly things that you won't need to adjust.

Pointer   Your mouse's settings are set in this section. The Protocol line specifies the type of mouse you're using—PS/2 for most modern PS/2-interfaced mice, Microsoft for Microsoft serial mice, and so on. (The XF86Config man page includes information on the allowable values for this option.) You specify the device file to which the mouse is attached using the Device line. Mistakes on these two lines are common sources of X difficulties. If set incorrectly, X won't start, will start without any pointer showing, or will start, but you won't be able to move the mouse pointer.

Monitor   This section defines the characteristics of your monitor. Of most interest are the HorizSync and VertRefresh lines, which define the horizontal and vertical refresh rates of which your monitor is capable. You should find this information in your monitor's manual. This section also contains many Modeline parameters, which you should not adjust unless you understand how video hardware works.

Device   The XF86Config file contains one or more Device sections, which provide information on your video card. With most modern video cards, this section is quite short. You should not adjust these settings unless you add RAM to your video card or replace the board entirely (in which case, you may want to run an X configuration utility to do the dirty work).

Screen   There are usually several Screen sections, which reference the Monitor and Device sections by name. You may want to adjust the Screen section for your monitor/video card combination to configure it for your preferred screen resolution and bit depth. There are two important options in the Screen section:

DefaultColorDepth   This option sets the color depth that X uses when it starts. The default is 8, which results in a mere 256-color display. The value 16 is usually a better choice on modern hardware. Values 24 and 32 work well on some systems, but occasionally produce problems.

Subsection "Display"   Each Screen section has one or more Display subsections, which define the characteristics of a given color depth. The Depth line identifies the color depth for which the subsection is written, and the Modes line identifies the resolutions at which X will work in this color depth. You can use this feature to define different resolutions to be associated with different color depths. Your video card may be incapable of producing 32-bit color at your highest resolution, so you can specify a lower maximum resolution for the 32-bit display. You can then start multiple X servers, as described earlier, using the color depth as a cue to use a different resolution.

As a general rule, it's easiest to create an XF86Config file using an X configuration tool, as described shortly. Hand-editing XF86Config may be useful, however, when you change hardware. You can edit the horizontal and vertical refresh rates if you replace a monitor, for instance, and X will automatically use the new settings to locate the optimal refresh rate. Hand editing can also be useful when fine-tuning your configuration; for example, you can add a DefaultColorDepth line to the Screen section.

Using an X Configuration Tool

All major Linux distributions include X configuration tools that run during system installation. These tools are usually available after installation, as well. Examples include:

xf86config   This is the crudest of the common X configuration tools. It runs entirely in text mode, and asks you a series of questions about your hardware and desired configuration. There's no possibility to go back and correct an error, so you must kill the program and start again if you make a mistake. Because of its crude user interface, xf86config can be used before X is running or if X is seriously misconfigured.

Xconfigurator   This program is another text-mode X configuration tool. Unlike xf86config, though, Xconfigurator uses color text and text-mode dialogs rather than simple streams of text. This makes Xconfigurator easier to use.

XF86Setup   This utility, shown in Figure 16.2, works only once X is running. You can therefore use this utility to reconfigure an X server that's working nonoptimally, but you can't use it to get X working at the outset. (Most distributions, including Red Hat, use GUI X configuration tools similar to XF86Setup to configure the system initially. These work because the setup routines run using the lowest-common-denominator VGA X server, which works on all but the most ancient video displays.)

Figure 16.2 GUI X configuration tools let you select options using list boxes, buttons, and so on.

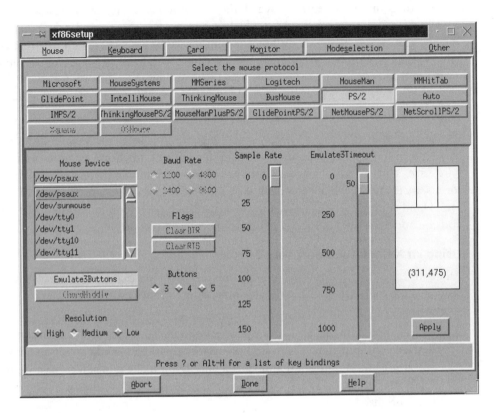

You should have several pieces of information handy before you begin configuring your X server. Although some configuration utilities can probe for some of this information, you'll need to know some of it yourself. These critical features are as follows:

Mouse type Most modern computers use a PS/2 mouse, but there are several other options (displayed near the top of the window in Figure 16.2).

Mouse device Most distributions create a link so that you can access a mouse as /dev/mouse. You may need to do the same, or specify the mouse device directly. /dev/psaux is the usual device file for PS/2 mice. Serial mice can usually be addressed as /dev/ttyS0 or /dev/ttyS1.

Video card information Some X configuration utilities let you select a card from a long list of model names. Others require you to know the chipset used on the card.

For very old cards, you may need to know what RAMDAC and clock chips the boards use. In all cases, you should know how much RAM the card boasts.

Monitor capabilities You must know the maximum horizontal and vertical refresh rates of your monitor. You can obtain this information from the monitor's manual.

Desired resolutions You'll be asked to specify what resolutions you want to use, as well as what color depths.

TIP Laptop computers can be particularly tricky to configure for X, because laptop displays are unusually finicky about acceptable resolutions and display refresh rates. Check `http://www.cs.utexas.edu/users/kharker/linux-laptop/` for a collection of links to Linux users' experiences with various laptops. Most of these include ready-made `XF86Config` files you can use instead of building one yourself.

XFree86 4.0

XFree86 4.0 is a major upgrade over version 3.3.6. This upgrade adds many new features and entails substantial changes to XFree86 configuration. With luck, you won't have to concern yourself with these changes, because they'll be handled automatically at system installation. If you want to upgrade from 3.3.6 to 4.0, or if you need to modify your installation, you'll have to deal with these changes.

Changes from XFree86 3.*x*

XFree86 4.0 offers several improvements over XFree86 3.3.6, including:

Multihead displays You can install multiple video cards in a single computer, attach them to monitors that you place next to each other, and have X create a single virtual desktop that spans both displays.

New driver architecture In XFree86 3.*x*, each X server contained one or more drivers for specific video cards. To use an S3 board, you'd use an X server called XF86_S3; to use an ATI Mach64 board, you'd use XF86_Mach64. XFree86 4.0, by contrast, uses a single X server, XFree86, which loads a driver module (located in /usr/X11R6/lib/modules/drivers) for your specific video hardware. This design is less awkward and easier to extend, although you as a user and administrator are unlikely to notice much difference.

DDC support The *Data Display Channel (DDC)* is a protocol that's been standard in most video hardware since the mid-1990s. It allows monitors to communicate their maximum refresh rates to video cards and video display software. XFree86 3.*x* doesn't support DDC, so you must enter this information manually. XFree86 4.0 adds support for DDC.

TrueType font support XFree86 4.0 adds support for TrueType fonts (the standard font type in Microsoft Windows). In practice, TrueType fonts have been available in Linux for some time through separate font servers, as described shortly in "Configuring a Font Server." Built-in TrueType support is an added convenience.

DRI support The *Direct Rendering Interface (DRI)* is a hardware acceleration standard that allows Linux programs to take advantage of video boards with 3-D hardware acceleration features. As of XFree86 4.0.1, only the 3dfx chipsets are supported, but this support is likely to expand in 2001 and beyond.

New configuration file format The new XFree86 options mandate a new configuration file format. The configuration file may still be called XF86Config, or it may be called XF86Config-4 on some systems (including Red Hat 7.0).

You can check to see whether you're running XFree86 4.0 by looking for a link called X in /etc or /etc/X11. If this link points to /usr/X11R6/bin/XFree86, your system is configured to use XFree86 4.0. If the link points to some other file, your system uses version 3.*x* or possibly a third-party X server (see the sidebar "Alternatives to XFree86").

Configuring XFree86 4.0

For an administrator, the XFree86 4.0 change that's most important is the change to the configuration file format. The general organization of the new XF86Config file is similar to that of 3.*x*'s XF86Config, so you should read "The XF86Config File" earlier, for details. In addition, the new file adds a few extra sections:

ServerLayout This section defines some overarching features of the server. Specifically, this section binds specific input and output devices. Chances are you won't need to adjust this section from its default.

Module This section specifies server modules you want loaded. Modules can provide functionality such as TrueType support and DRI support. You probably won't have to adjust this section of the file.

DRI If you're lucky enough to have a video card with 3-D acceleration features supported by XFree86, you can define who may access these features in this section. A simple line allows all users to access DRI functions:

```
Mode 0666
```

In Red Hat 7.0, there's only one standalone X configuration utility: xf86cfg. This is an X-based configuration tool (see Figure 16.3). To configure X with this utility, you can right-click the icon for a component in the main section of the window and select Configure from the resulting pop-up menu.

Figure 16.3   xf86cfg lets you configure XFree86 4.0 in a point-and-click fashion.

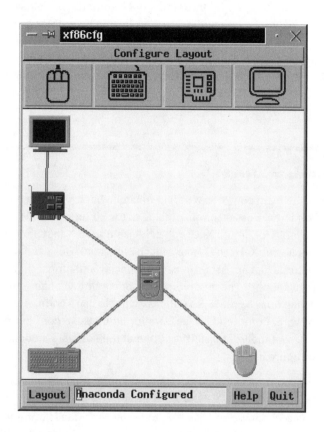

WARNING xf86cfg assumes it works on /etc/X11/XF86Config, not the
/etc/X11/XF86Config-4 file used by Red Hat 7.0. You must therefore temporarily rename the file, or create a link, to use this utility in Red Hat 7.0.

In addition to using xf86cfg, you can configure XFree86 4.0 by issuing the command
XFree86 -configure. This command creates a file called /root/XF86Config.new, which
should be at least minimally functional. You can then modify it via xf86cfg or manual
editing, should you need to tweak it.

**Networking and
Troubleshooting**

PART 5

TIP   XFree86 4.0 uses DDC by default, but it sometimes yields less-than-optimal results. For example, one author uses an Iiyama VisionMaster Pro 450 monitor, which is able to display 1280×1024 at 100Hz, but DDC produces only an 85Hz display at this resolution. This problem can be overcome by copying the appropriate Modeline lines for a 100Hz 1280×1024 display from a 3.3.6 XF86Config file to the 4.0 XF86Config file. (These lines are clearly marked in the default 3.3.6 XF86Config file.)

Alternatives to XFree86

XFree86 is the most common X server in Linux, but it's not the only one available for Linux, nor is it the most common outside of the Linux world. Two commercial X servers are available for Linux: Xi Graphics' Accelerated X (http://www.xig.com) and MetroLink's Metro-X (http://www.metrolink.com). Both servers offer an assortment of features that are useful in certain specific situations, such as multiscreen and touch-screen support. These servers also sport somewhat different lists of supported hardware than does XFree86, so you may want to use a commercial server with some video hardware. Commercial X servers for Linux use a configuration file similar to XF86Config, but their details differ. Consult the software's documentation to learn how to configure it.

Non-Linux systems frequently use X servers other than XFree86. Commercial Unixes often ship with their own X servers. X servers are also available for non-Unix systems, such as Windows and MacOS. Examples include Hummingbird's eXceed (http://www.hcl.com/products/nc/exceed/), Starnet's X-Win32 (http://www.starnet.com), MicroImage's MI/X (http://www.microimages.com/freestuf/mix/), Tenon's Xtools (http://www.tenon.com/products/xtools/), and PowerLAN's eXodus (http://www.powerlan-usa.com/exodus.html). These programs typically use GUI configuration utilities. Those that run inside the host OS's GUI (such as all the Windows and Macintosh products) typically don't require special mouse or video configuration. They usually do require font configuration, however, and often offer features that are meaningless in Linux, such as the ability to run an X session within a single host OS window.

Alternatives to XFree86 *(continued)*

If you run a network and want to provide X-based access to multiple users, an *X terminal* is another X option you may want to investigate. An X terminal is a computer that's specialized to run X. Such a computer has little memory, no hard disk, and an anemic CPU. X servers typically include large color displays. The "NCD X-Terminal Mini-HOWTO" document covers many details of X terminal configuration.

Starting X Automatically

When you installed Linux, you may have been asked whether you wanted to start the OS in text mode or graphics mode. If you selected the former option, you see a text-based login prompt and can launch X only after logging in. If you selected the latter option, and if the system's X configuration is correct, you should be greeted by an X-based login program whenever you start the system. On older versions of Linux, this X-based login was handled by a program known as the *X Display Manager (XDM)*. More recent versions of Linux typically use similar utilities that are associated with the KDE or GNOME projects (described shortly). These updated packages are known as the *KDE Display Manager (KDM)* or the *GNOME Display Manager (GDM)*. All three programs serve a similar function, however: They let you log on to the computer. For simplicity's sake, the rest of this chapter refers to all these programs as *XDM*.

Whether the computer boots into text or graphics mode is handled by the /etc/inittab startup script. Near the start of this script, you should find a line that resembles the following:

```
id:5:initdefault:
```

The critical component of this line is the digit—5 in this example. This digit indicates the default *run level* for the computer, as described in Chapter 5. Run level 1 is a single-user mode that's often used for emergency maintenance; run level 6 forces the computer to reboot; and the intervening run levels are defined by the distribution. On most distributions, including Red Hat 7.0, run level 3 is used for text-mode startup, and 5 indicates full GUI startup via XDM. (These numbers are arbitrary; for instance, SuSE Linux uses 2 and 3 instead of 3 and 5.)

Although Linux starts at a run level specified in /etc/inittab, you can change the run level of a running system using the telinit command, as in telinit 3 to change to run level 3.

Networking and Troubleshooting

PART 5

> **TIP**   If you plan to change your X configuration, it's best to switch out of full GUI login mode first. Use `telinit 3` to switch to a text-mode login. You can then change your X configuration and type **startx** to launch X. If there's a problem with the configuration, you'll be dropped back to a working text-mode session. You can then correct the problem and, when X is working, use `telinit 5` to return to a full GUI configuration. If you change your X configuration without testing it in this way, you run the risk of creating a system that can't start X, but that keeps trying to do so, thus blocking your use of the console.

Configuring a Font Server

A *font server* is a network server that delivers font bitmaps to computers that request them. The font server may work from font bitmaps or fonts in scalable outline formats, such as PostScript Type 1 or TrueType fonts. When the server uses the latter, it *rasterizes* the font—that is, the server converts the font into a bitmap of the size the client requests. The principle benefit to using a font server is that you can configure a font server on a single computer with all the fonts you want, and you need not install those fonts on other computers on the network. Instead, you tell those computers to access the font server that's been configured in the way you desire. Some distributions use font servers because XFree86 3.*x* does not by default understand TrueType fonts (although XFree86 4.0 does). It's easier to add TrueType support to a separate font server program than to the XFree86 3.*x* font handler, so using a local font server is a good way to provide TrueType font support in Linux.

> **WARNING**   Check the license terms of any font before adding it to a font server. In the United States, outline fonts are considered computer programs, and therefore may be copyrighted and subject to terms of use similar to those of other programs. These terms may forbid the use of a font on a font server or require a per-client payment.

Adding Fonts to a Font Server

Some Linux distributions don't use font servers by default, although they're perfectly capable of doing so. Other distributions, including Red Hat, use font servers as a matter of course, although they're usually configured to be accessible only to the local computer. You can check your system's configuration by examining the XF86Config or

XF86Config-4 file (located in /etc/X11 in Red Hat, but in /etc on some other distributions). Early in this file, there should be one or more lines that begin with FontPath:

```
FontPath    "/usr/X11R6/lib/X11/fonts/Type1"

FontPath    "unix/:-1"

FontPath    "tcp/dino:7101"
```

Each of these lines specifies a location where fonts may be found. The first line indicates a directory on the X server computer's hard disk, but the next two specify font servers. The unix/:-1 server is the default Red Hat 6.2 server, which is private to the local computer. (Red Hat 7.0 changes this to unix/:7100.) The tcp/dino:7101 server is a network-accessible font server running on port 7101 of the computer called dino. (See Chapter 14 for a discussion of ports and hostnames.) This line has been added to the default configuration; it is *not* a standard part of any distribution's configuration.

The default Red Hat 7.0 font server is controlled from the file /etc/X11/fs/config. This file includes several settings, the most important of which are the following:

catalogue   This setting is a comma-delimited list of directories that contain fonts. The list may span multiple lines and ends when a directory is not followed by a comma.

default-point-size   You can set the default size of fonts, in 10ths of a *point* (a common measure of font size), for when a program doesn't specify a font size. Red Hat sets this value to 120, which corresponds to 12 points.

default-resolutions   Point sizes relate to physical size, but computer displays vary in the number of pixels displayed on any given size of screen. Because computer graphics (including font displays) work on pixels, point size can vary depending upon the size of your monitor and the resolution at which you run it. Most displays use a resolution of between 72 and 100 dots per inch (dpi). The resolution may vary both horizontally and vertically. Your screen might be 75×80 dpi, for instance. You can set the default resolution using the default-resolutions setting, which lists both horizontal and vertical resolutions, separated by commas. You can specify a second default resolution after the first, separated from the first by commas.

If you want to add fonts to your system, you must specify the path to those fonts, either directly in XF86Config or by including the path in /etc/X11/fs/config. You must also create an appropriate configuration file *within* the font directory to tell the system about the fonts you've added. It's best to separate fonts of different types in different directories; for instance, TrueType fonts in one directory and Type 1 fonts in another. To create X font information files for a directory, follow these steps:

1. Use a text-mode login or open an xterm window.

2. Change to the target font directory.

3. If the directory contains TrueType fonts, issue the command **ttmkfdir .
   >fonts.scale**. This action creates the `fonts.scale` file, which contains font names
   associated with each font file and other critical information.

NOTE   Older versions of xfs and XFree86 don't support TrueType fonts. Most
modern Linux distributions ship with this support, however.

4. If the directory contains PostScript Type 1 fonts, do the following:

   A. Obtain and install the `typelinst` package. (It may be obtained from http://
   rpmfind.net/linux/RPM/TByName.html, among other places.)

   B. Type **typelinst** to create a `fonts.scale` file for the Type 1 fonts in a directory.

5. Issue the command **mkfontdir -e /usr/X11R6/lib/X11/fonts/encodings**. This
   creates a `fonts.dir` file from the `fonts.scale` file or from font information in bitmapped fonts in the directory.

6. Check the `fonts.dir` file. It should begin with a number (indicating the number of
   fonts defined in the file). Each subsequent line should then begin with a font filename
   and conclude with an X font specification, which includes the font name and
   assorted other information.

At this point, your configuration files point to the new font directory, which should contain a `fonts.dir` file that correctly identifies the new fonts. You can either shut down X
and restart it or issue the following commands to begin using the newly defined fonts:

```
# killall -USR1 xfs
# xset fp rehash
```

WARNING   If there's an error in your new font configuration, X may behave
very strangely or fail to start. This can be particularly troublesome if your system
is configured to boot directly into X, because Linux may lock itself into a cycle of
trying to start X, failing, and trying again, making the system inaccessible from
the console. You should therefore ensure that you have access to the system
through some other means, such as a dumb terminal (Chapter 10) or a Telnet
login. Alternatively, if you encounter problems, you can modify the configuration
from an emergency boot floppy.

To check that your changes have taken effect, you can use the `xfontsel` program, shown
in Figure 16.4. This program allows you to display all the fonts that are available on the
X server from which it's run.

Figure 16.4   Choose the font by clicking fmly, and set point size and other characteristics, if you like.

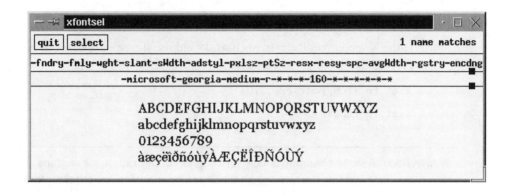

NOTE Like most X programs, xfontsel takes its fonts from the *X server*, not the computer on which the program runs. Therefore, the same program run from the same computer might have different fonts available to it when run via X servers on different computers.

Configuring a New Font Server

If you want to use the networking capabilities of a font server, you can set up one system to serve fonts to others on your network, thus simplifying your administrative tasks. To do this, follow these steps:

1. Create a new font server configuration file. You can base it on the /etc/X11/fs/config file, but should place it somewhere else, such as /etc/xfsconfig.

2. Create font directories that contain the font files you want to share, as well as the fonts.scale and fonts.dir configuration files, as described earlier.

3. Modify your new font server configuration file so that it serves fonts from the directories you created in step 2 or from existing font directories.

4. Add a line to a convenient startup script (such as /etc/rc.d/rc.local) to launch xfs using this new configuration file, serving fonts using port 7101 (which is more or less standard for this purpose). This line should resemble the following:

   /usr/X11R6/bin/xfs -port 7101 -config /etc/xfsconfig &

5. Type the command you entered in the startup script in step 4 to launch the font server.

6. Configure each X server that should use the font server. This can be done by editing the X server's XF86Config file, as described earlier. The entry should resemble the following:

```
FontPath    "tcp/fontserv:7101"
```

7. Restart the X servers on the systems that should use the new font server. Alternatively, type the following commands:

```
# xset fp +tcp/fontserv:7101

# xset fp rehash
```

WARNING As with changing a local font server configuration, these steps can cause serious problems, including an inability to start X. You should therefore use caution, especially on the first system you reconfigure. Also, this configuration can cause X servers to fail if the font server crashes or if network problems make the font server inaccessible.

The best use of a network font server is on a network that contains several X servers and on which you want to use fonts that don't come standard with the X servers. Many X servers for Windows, MacOS, and other OSs use standard X fonts or X font servers rather than the underlying OS's font mechanisms. Font servers can therefore provide a consistent set of fonts to these X servers, as well as to Linux or Unix systems. Consult the X server's documentation to learn how to point the X server to a network font server.

Unusual Font Servers

A few applications use their own font servers or include features that resemble those of font servers. This practice is particularly common on word processors, because X's font handling doesn't include some features that are required for good printed output. There are two common approaches to this problem:

- Include a unique font server in the program package. This server often runs on port 7102 and provides the features of an ordinary X font server plus the features required for word processors. ApplixWare and WordPerfect Office 2000 both take this approach, and in fact both use the FontTastic font server from Bitstream. It's possible to use this font server from other applications, but you must modify your Linux startup scripts to start the server automatically when the system boots. (Ordinarily, the application starts the font server when a user launches the application.)

- Implement font-rendering code in the application proper. This approach is used by WordPerfect 8 and earlier; TeX; and most viewers of *Portable Document Format*

(PDF) files, such as Acrobat Reader. This method is simpler in some respects than adding a new font server, but it's less useful to other programs, which typically can't intercept the first program's font handling.

The nonstandard font handling used by these programs can be a source of frustration to both users and administrators, because you may find it necessary to install the same fonts several times to use them in key programs. You may also discover that the same font looks very different in different programs because of different font-rendering capabilities. Unfortunately, there is no easy fix to these problems. For details on specific programs, check the "Font HOWTO" document, which comes with most distributions or can be found at `http://www.linuxdoc.org`.

Building a User Interface atop X

X comprises several different layers. At the lowest level, there is the X server itself, which is mainly a video driver and set of programming interfaces for that driver. These interfaces allow the programmer to display windows, but the windows are incomplete. Additional layers of X provide certain critical features. Specifically, the *window manager* provides borders, resizing functions, and usually additional features; *widget sets* provide programmers with features that are useful inside windows, such as scroll bars and menus; and *desktop environments* combine many programs together into a coherent set. The following sections describe each of these X components in turn.

Window Managers

The window manager determines much of the overall look and feel of an X environment. The window manager is responsible for handling the decorations that surround windows, the window placement, and the launching of some types of programs. It's usually not too difficult to switch to a new window manager, but different distributions use different methods to determine which window manager to use.

The Role of Window Managers

Functions that may be provided by the window manager include:

Window borders   Window *borders* serve a decorative purpose and make it clear where the window ends. On many window managers, they also provide window-sizing features.

Drag bar   The *drag bar* is the component at the top of most windows that you can click to drag the window about. Some window managers allow you to double-click the drag bar to expand the size of the window.

Window widgets   Window *widgets* are the small icons visible on most windows' drag bars or elsewhere. These icons allow you to close a window, maximize it, minimize it, or perform other tasks.

Window placement and sizing features   The window manager determines where on the screen a window appears. (Programs can request particular placements, but the window manager determines a default placement strategy.) The window manager also allows you to move windows around, usually by dragging a drag bar. You can also adjust the sizes of windows by using widgets or borders.

Window-fronting actions   Certain actions bring windows to the front of a stack or allow you to use a window. Most window managers today use a click anywhere in the window to perform either action; but some use other actions, such as a click only in the drag bar. Some allow you to type text into a window without it being at the front of a stack. Most provide several options to handle window-fronting actions.

Desktop background   Most window managers include a provision to modify the desktop's background color or use a bitmap as a background image.

Program launch facilities   Window managers invariably provide some means of running programs. Typically, a window manager can be configured by editing a text file. This file contains a list of programs that the window manager can launch. You can then select the programs by clicking the desktop background or by selecting the program from a menu provided at the top or bottom of the screen.

Virtual desktops   Most window managers include some means of controlling multiple *virtual desktops*. Typically, you can click small icons to select one of several desktops, each of which has its own set of windows. You can therefore devote one desktop to one set of related applications and another to another set, reducing the clutter on your screen.

Some of these window manager features—particularly the last few—may be duplicated or supplanted by desktop environments. If you don't want to use a full desktop environment, though, the availability of these features in window managers can be very helpful.

Most window managers provide similar functionality, but details differ. Some, such as Enlightenment (`http://www.enlightenment.org`), are designed to provide maximal "eye candy"—they include extensive features to alter the appearance of windows. Others, such as wm2 (`http://www.all-day-breakfast.com/wm2/`), are visually and even functionally Spartan. Figures 16.5 and 16.6 illustrate how radically different two window managers can appear. Figure 16.5 shows a text editor window running in kwm, the window manager that comes with KDE. (Most of the illustrations in this book show kwm windows.) Figure 16.6 shows the same text editor running in wm2.

Figure 16.5   Most modern window managers, such as kwm, roughly mimic the default look
of windows in Microsoft Windows.

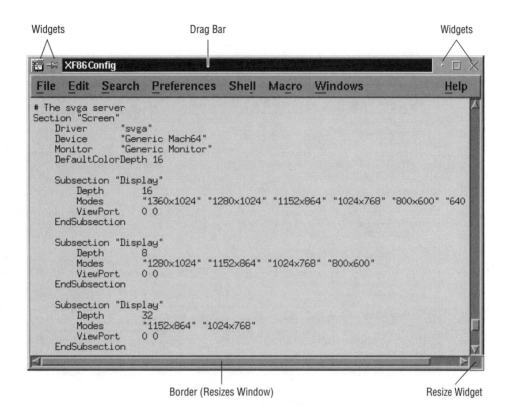

Setting the Window Manager

Window manager preference is a very personal matter. If you want to experiment, you
can try several different window managers to see which you prefer. Linux distributions
use a configuration script in the user's home directory to run programs the user wants to
run at login time. If this file is absent, the system uses a default script. The name of this
script varies with your login preferences, but it's usually located in the /etc/X11 directory
tree, often in /etc/X11/xinit. On Red Hat 7.0, the user-customizable configuration
script is called .xsession, and it must have execute permissions. Other distributions may
call this script other things, such as .Xlogin. When launching X from a text-mode login
via startx, yet another script is commonly used: .xinitrc. To replace the default set of
login actions with something else, follow these steps:

1. Load the .xsession file from your home directory into a text editor (on a fresh
   account, this file won't exist, so you may need to tell your editor to create it).

Figure 16.6   Some window managers have their own unique looks and provide unusual feature sets.

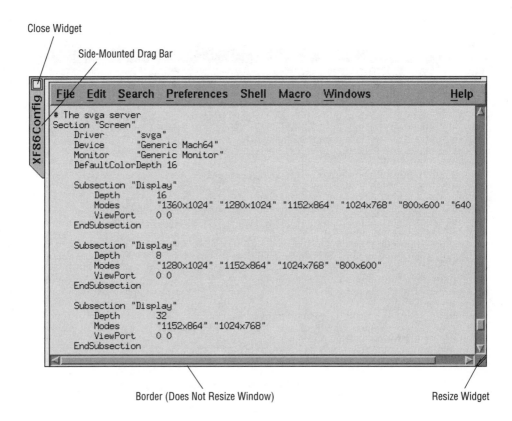

2. Type the names of any programs you want to run automatically when you log in, including your window manager. If you want a program to run and stay running while other programs run, be sure to follow its startup line with an ampersand (&), or the script will stop running until you've closed that program. In most cases, the final program launched from .xinitrc should be your window manager, and it should *not* include an ampersand. This way, when you exit from the window manager, you'll log off the account. As an example, the following file launches an xterm window and the wm2 window manager:

    ```
    xterm &
    wm2
    ```

3. Save the .xsession file and exit from the text editor.

4. Type **chmod 755 ~/.xsession** to give the file execute permissions. (You can use more restrictive permissions, such as 0700, if you don't want others to see which programs you run automatically.)

Thereafter, when you log on, Linux will launch whichever programs (including the window manager) you set in the .xsession file when you log on again in X. You may, however, have to select a particular login option in your XDM program. If you use KDM, for example, you should choose Default from the drop-down list of Session Types. If you don't know where to begin in your exploration of window managers, an excellent starting point is the window managers Web site at http://www.plig.org/xwinman/. This site features descriptions of the most common window managers and desktop environments for Linux, including links to the projects' Web sites.

Widget Sets

The widget set provides tools to programmers to produce menus, buttons, dialog boxes, and other components that fit *inside* a window or that use windows to perform a simple task. (Look back at Figures 16.5 and 16.6, which show the same program run in different window managers. Note that the scroll bars and menus look exactly the same, although the drag bars and window manager widgets are quite different.) You as a user have little control over which widget sets you use. This is because the widget set is chosen by the programmer, not by the user. (Of course, you can choose a program because of the widget set it uses.) There are roughly half a dozen widget sets in common use today, including the *GNOME Toolkit (GTK)*, *Qt*, *Motif*, and *Athena*. Many other widget sets are available, but few are used on more than a handful of programs.

The wide array of widget sets available is part of the reason for the inconsistent user interfaces found on Linux programs. Each widget set has its own unique look, so programs built with different widget sets have menus, dialog boxes, and so on that vary widely. Since 1998 or so, however, new programs have increasingly been built upon GTK or Qt. As widget sets go, these two are fairly similar in appearance, so Linux programs today are less variable than they were in the mid-1990s.

Desktop Environments

A desktop environment is a collection of programs and tools designed to provide a user-friendly experience to a Linux user. A desktop environment uses the same widget set in all its component applications and may include additional features to help integrate its tools, such as an address book shared across multiple applications.

Networking and Troubleshooting

PART 5

NOTE Newcomers to Linux often confuse the window manager with the desktop environment. Although a window manager is one component of a desktop environment, the latter is a much more comprehensive package. Comparing the two is like comparing a slice of bread to a four-course meal.

The Role of Desktop Environments

Why should you run a desktop environment? In some cases, you shouldn't. Desktop environments consume a great deal of memory and disk space. If you're running a server or low-memory system, you're better off using a standalone window manager and, perhaps, a few small utilities. (You can run individual components of desktop environments even when you don't run the whole thing, as described shortly in "Mixing Desktop Environment Components.") In fact, if the system is a server, you might prefer to not run X at all, to save memory for the server processes.

If you intend to use a computer as a desktop workstation, however, a desktop environment can provide many useful features. Most importantly, the desktop environment gives you a set of consistent tools to interface with many of Linux's system settings. You can adjust features such as your mouse's tracking rate, default fonts used by a variety of applications, and the appearance of your window manager, all using a single control program. This can be a great boon to Linux users, and especially to those who are unfamiliar with Linux's many configuration files.

NOTE Although there's some overlap between a desktop environment's settings and those adjusted through GUI configuration tools such as Linuxconf, for the most part the two are independent. The desktop environment sets features that individual users may want to customize, whereas Linuxconf and similar utilities adjust systemwide features that affect all users.

In addition to providing an interface for setting system features, a desktop environment includes a selection of mini-applications—programs such as calculators, image viewers, audio CD players, and addictive card games. Perhaps most importantly, a desktop environment provides a *file manager,* which displays files in a window, allowing you to open, copy, move, and delete files using a mouse. KDE and GNOME are both embarked upon producing office suites similar to Microsoft Office, but these projects are still in their infancies.

Available Desktop Environments

The two most common desktop environments available on Linux are the *GNU Network Object Model Environment (GNOME)* and the *K Desktop Environment (KDE)*. There are also several less-used desktop environments available. Brief descriptions of these environments follow:

GNOME   GNOME is built atop the GTK widget set, which was originally developed for the *GNU Image Manipulation Program (GIMP)* graphics utility. In its 1.0.*x* versions, GNOME uses Enlightenment as the default window manager, but this is changing to Sawfish with the 1.2.*x* versions (included in Red Hat 7.0). In any version, you can easily reconfigure GNOME to work with other window managers, although some integrate better with GNOME than do others. GNOME features an ever-increasing number of mini-applications and configuration modules. It's currently the favored desktop environment on Red Hat and Debian systems. You can learn more at `http://www.gnome.org`.

KDE   KDE uses the Qt widget set, which at one time was a controversial choice. When KDE was originally developed, Qt used a license that didn't meet with full approval among all open source developers, which was one of the reasons for the development of GNOME, using the open source GTK widget set. Today, however, Qt's license has changed, and it meets with the approval of most open source developers. Unlike GNOME, KDE is tightly tied to its own window manager, kwm. KDE is somewhat more advanced than is GNOME. Red Hat 7.0 ships with KDE 1.1.2, but version 2.0 was released in October of 2000. KDE includes a large number of mini-applications and configuration utilities. Most Linux distributions today favor KDE as their default desktop environments. The KDE project's home page is at `http://www.kde.org`.

XFce   XFce is a lightweight desktop environment compared to GNOME or KDE. Like GNOME, it's built around GTK. Like KDE, it uses its own window manager (XFwm). XFce includes a modest selection of mini-applications and configuration utilities. You can learn more at `http://www.xfce.org`.

CDE   The *Common Desktop Environment (CDE)* is the only commercial desktop environment available for Linux. Although popular on many commercial versions of Unix, CDE is fairly uncommon on Linux. CDE uses the Motif widget set, which has historically been the widget set of choice for commercial Unix and Linux applications. CDE for Linux can be obtained from Xi Graphics (`http://www.xig.com`), under the name *DeXtop*.

Roll-your-own   It's possible to assemble your own desktop environment. To do this, start with the window manager of your choice and add configuration utilities, mini-applications, a file manager, and so on. Typically, you configure the window manager to launch important utilities from its built-in menus, and configure your system to start the window manager, file manager, and any other tools you want open at all times when you log in. The result is typically a much less integrated environment than what you get with a conventional desktop environment, but it may be more to your liking. Chances are this approach will consume less memory than will a conventional desktop environment, too.

Even if you use a distribution that favors one desktop environment, you can use another. With most distributions, doing so is merely a matter of installing the environment from the distribution's CD-ROM and selecting it from a menu on the XDM login screen. In the event that the XDM doesn't provide this feature (as the original XDM doesn't), you can start the environment by placing an appropriate command in the ~/.xsession or equivalent file. For instance, to start KDE, the command is startkde; for GNOME, it's gnome-session. It's possible for one user of a system to use one desktop environment and for somebody else to use another.

Mixing Desktop Environment Components

Although most desktop environments come with a wide array of utilities that integrate with one another to a greater or lesser extent, it's usually not necessary to run these tools within their parent environments. You can run KDE's kscd CD-ROM player from within GNOME, for instance—or when you're not running any desktop environment at all. You can use this fact to your advantage, picking the best parts of each environment. The drawback is that mixing components in this way reduces their interoperability. Programs from two environments might not share a common address-book file, for example, whereas two matched programs could share this file.

One further drawback to mixing components in this way, or to keeping two or more environments installed for the convenience of your users, is that the disk-space requirements can be substantial. Each environment is likely to consume hundreds of megabytes of disk space, although you might be able to get by with less for a very minimal installation. If you want to use just a handful of components, you may be able to install them in just a few megabytes.

X Applications

X applications use X to display information and to accept input from the user. They rely on the window manager that the user selects and the widget set that the programmer selects. In some cases, applications share settings or can interact with desktop environments. Usually, though, X applications don't rely on desktop environments.

NOTE   Occasionally, you'll see a program referred to as "a KDE program" or "a GNOME program." With the exception of a few utilities that are integral to these environments, this does *not* mean that the program relies upon the specified desktop environment to run. It does most likely mean that the program uses the underlying widget set of the desktop environment, and it may mean that the program can use settings from and interact with other programs in the desktop environment. If you see an appealing "KDE program" but run GNOME, go ahead and try the program. Chances are it will work, although you may need to install libraries or desktop environment components to use the program.

On rare occasions, you may find that an X application doesn't function well with a particular window manager or with some other component you have installed, such as a specific X server. If an application's windows don't move around or stack in the way you expect, you might want to try another window manager, at least for diagnostic purposes. If the problem goes away, you may consider switching window managers permanently; or you can look for an update to the program or window manager; or you can contact the authors of the program and window manager to report a bug.

A few programs (particularly those based on the Motif widget set) can't display graphics properly at 24-bit color depth with some video boards. A handful of these programs also have problems at 32-bit color depth. If you have such problems, you may be able to correct them by dropping down to 16-bit color depth. An upgrade to your X server may also help; Accelerated-X and XFree86 4.0 both correct these problems.

In Sum

X is the GUI environment that's most often used in Linux. Unlike the GUIs in Windows or MacOS, X is built up of multiple components, which can be swapped in and out as the user (or programmer) desires. X is also a network-oriented GUI, allowing users to run programs on one computer but use another computer as the screen, keyboard, and mouse. You can add a networked font server to simplify your font configuration tasks on a network of systems that employ X servers. These facts make X an extremely flexible GUI environment, but they also produce drawbacks: X is slower than most other GUI environments, and the extent of choice offered by X makes for less consistency across applications and systems.

Networking and Troubleshooting

PART 5

17

Setting Up Your Mail Server

For many organizations, the most important network service is e-mail. Although Web servers and file servers transfer a huge quantity of data, e-mail is critically important for outside communications. Your users may correspond with colleagues, clients, and vendors through e-mail, and even exchange important data files as attachments to e-mail messages. It's therefore important that your organization host at least one reliable e-mail server. Fortunately, Linux is well-suited to this task, and in fact a wide variety of mail server packages is available for Linux.

This chapter begins with a discussion of the core e-mail protocols, including the difference between push and pull protocols. Next, there is a discussion of how to configure send-mail, the most popular push mail program on the Internet. If your users read mail from systems other than the mail server, you'll need to configure a pull mail protocol such as POP or IMAP, which are discussed next. The chapter concludes with a discussion of the bane of all e-mail administrators, unsolicited bulk e-mail (*spam*).

NOTE Configuring a large mail server is a major undertaking. This chapter can help get you started and is adequate for learning how to configure a mail server for a workstation or small network. If your needs are larger, though, you would do well to consult additional documentation, such as Craig Hunt's *Linux Sendmail Administration* (Sybex, 2001).

Understanding E-Mail Protocols

To configure a system as a mail server, it's necessary to understand something about how e-mail is delivered. The most important thing to understand is the difference between push and pull e-mail protocols. It's also important to know something about the capabilities of each of today's three most common e-mail protocols: SMTP, POP, and IMAP.

NOTE This section presents an overview of the e-mail protocols themselves. Configuring the servers for these protocols is covered in subsequent sections of this chapter.

Push and Pull Protocols

Broadly speaking, e-mail can be delivered in one of two ways:

- The sender can initiate a transfer, usually as soon as the e-mail is ready to be sent. This method uses a *push* protocol. It requires that the recipient run a mail server at all times. The sender can use a client program to communicate with the server, or one server can communicate with another. (In the latter case, one server takes on the role of the client, but it may work as a client while simultaneously functioning as a server for other connections.)

- The recipient can initiate a transfer, usually when the user wants to read e-mail. This model is known as a *pull* protocol. The mail server in this case holds mail it has received (typically via a push protocol). The recipient's system does not need to be available at all times, but the sending system must be constantly available—or at least, available at predictable times.

The most common push protocol on the Internet today is the *Simple Mail Transfer Protocol (SMTP)*. This protocol is quite old by Internet standards, but it has served well and is likely to remain in common use into the indefinite future. A server that implements SMTP is often referred to as a *Mail Transfer Agent (MTA)*.

Two pull protocols are in common use: the *Post Office Protocol (POP)* and the *Internet Message Access Protocol (IMAP)*. POP is much simpler and is somewhat more common in 2000, but IMAP offers several additional features (described shortly) and is gaining slowly in popularity. All these protocols are available in various versions.

Individuals use e-mail client packages known as *Mail User Agents (MUAs)*. These programs can typically initiate SMTP sessions, and usually POP or IMAP sessions as well. Those programs that run on Linux can usually read mail directly from a local Linux mail queue maintained by the MTA.

The simplest e-mail exchange between computers involves just two computers and a single protocol (probably SMTP). In this scenario, one user composes an e-mail message and issues a command that causes the e-mail software to connect to the destination system and transmit the message. The recipient computer then holds the message in a local mail queue, and the addressee reads the message using a mail program on the recipient computer.

Most mail transfers on the Internet today are more complex, however. They typically involve several transfers, which are illustrated in Figure 17.1. These steps are as follows:

1. The sender composes a message using an MUA on one computer (let's call it `franklin.example.com`). Depending upon the MUA, the mail may be sent immediately or queued locally. A recipient address (let's say `susan@express.gov`) is included in the message.

2. At some point, `franklin` connects to a mail server for its domain (let's call it `osgood.example.com`) and sends the e-mail. In this transfer, `franklin` uses SMTP and functions as a client to `osgood`'s server.

3. Unless the mail's recipient is local, `osgood` uses the *Domain Name System (DNS)* to look up the computer that functions as the mail server for the recipient domain (`express.gov`). This may be a computer that goes by the same name, or it may be a different computer (such as `pony.express.gov`).

4. Once `osgood` has the address of the recipient system, `osgood` connects to that system using SMTP and transfers the e-mail. In this transfer, unlike in step 2, `osgood` is the client; `pony.express.gov` is the server.

5. `pony` may queue the mail for local delivery, or it may pass the mail to another system, depending upon its configuration and the recipient's name (`susan`). For the purposes of this discussion, let's say that `pony` is a temporary way station, and it passes mail to `railroad.express.gov`. This transfer is also likely to use SMTP, with `pony` as the client and `railroad` as the server.

6. The message goes into a queue on `railroad`, associated with the recipient (`susan`). Sooner or later, `susan` uses yet another computer (say, `air.express.gov`) to connect to `railroad` and retrieve mail. This transfer is likely to use POP or IMAP. Here, `railroad` is the server, while `air` is the client.

7. `susan` reads her e-mail on `air`, using an MUA. If she wants to reply, she can do so, initiating a series of actions similar to those outlined here. The e-mail might or might not pass through the same computers, though; an organization can configure different systems to function as incoming and outgoing mail servers.

The details of an e-mail transfer may range from a simple two-computer situation up to the full set of steps described above, or potentially even more. Precisely what operations

Figure 17.1   E-mail frequently passes through several computers from its source to its
destination.

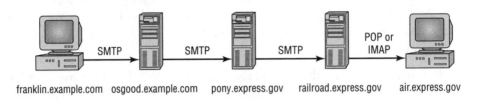

franklin.example.com   osgood.example.com   pony.express.gov   railroad.express.gov   air.express.gov

are involved varies substantially from one transfer to another. One critically important
point, however, is that most of the MTAs first receive the mail as a server and then
retransmit the mail as a client. This operation is known as *relaying* mail, and the server
that performs this task is a *mail relay*. As described later in this chapter, configuring a
mail server to relay only authorized mail is a critically important aspect of MTA
configuration.

The next-to-last computer in the delivery chain (`railroad.express.gov` in the preceding
example) often functions as a server for both SMTP and POP or IMAP. This does not
need to be the case, however; if `susan` logs on to `railroad` and reads her mail with a local
MUA, there will be no pull transfer involved.

In configuring an individual computer to function as a mail server, you don't need to be
concerned with all the possible variations on mail delivery. What's important is the role
that your computer plays with respect to those computers that communicate directly with
it. If you were configuring `railroad.express.gov`, for example, you would need to configure both SMTP and POP or IMAP servers, but no special configuration of the SMTP
server would be required to allow it to accept mail that's already been relayed from other
systems.

SMTP

SMTP is the most prevalent push protocol for e-mail today. An SMTP server usually listens on port 25 (see Chapter 15 for a discussion of port numbers). The transfer of an e-
mail message actually involves a series of text-mode commands. In fact, you can redirect
`telnet` to use port 25 and send e-mail without involving an MTA or MUA on the sending
side, as illustrated in Listing 17.1.

Listing 17.1   An Example SMTP Exchange Using `telnet`

> `$ telnet nessus.rodsbooks.com 25`
>
> `Trying 192.168.1.3...`
>
> `Connected to nessus.rodsbooks.com.`
>
> `Escape character is '^]'.`
>
> `220 nessus.rodsbooks.com ESMTP Sendmail 8.9.3/8.9.3; Mon,`
>
> ↳`18 Sep 2000 20:33:22 -0400`
>
> **`MAIL FROM:<rodsmith@speaker.rodsbooks.com>`**
>
> `250 <rodsmith@speaker.rodsbooks.com>... Sender ok`
>
> **`RCPT TO:<rodsmith@nessus.rodsbooks.com>`**
>
> `250 <rodsmith@nessus.rodsbooks.com>... Recipient ok`
>
> **`DATA`**
>
> `354 Enter mail, end with "." on a line by itself`
>
> **`This is a demonstration message. It contains no useful`**
>
> **`information.`**
>
> `.`
>
> `250 UAA09955 Message accepted for delivery`
>
> **`QUIT`**
>
> `221 nessus.rodsbooks.com closing connection`
>
> `Connection closed by foreign host.`

This exchange used only four SMTP commands: `MAIL FROM`, `RCPT TO`, `DATA`, and `QUIT`. There are additional SMTP commands, some of which may be necessary when communicating with certain hosts—for instance, many hosts require that the client identify itself using the `HELO` command. Listing 17.1, though, illustrates the simplicity of the core SMTP protocol.

Networking and Troubleshooting

PART 5

> **NOTE**   The details of the replies from the SMTP server vary. The key information resides in the numbers that begin lines, such as 250 and 354. The English text that follows many of these lines is intended for human consumption and varies from one MTA to another. Therefore, if you try a test similar to that shown in Listing 17.1, you may see somewhat different replies if your system doesn't use sendmail as the MTA. All SMTP MTAs respond to the same commands, however, and return the same numeric replies.

In Listing 17.1, the message is addressed to a user on the MTA's system. Therefore, the message is ultimately queued for local delivery—the MTA does not need to forward it to another system. In the procedure outlined in "Push and Pull Protocols," however, the ultimate recipient of the message does not have an account on most of the MTAs through which the message passes. In these cases, the MTA accepts the message for relay. Once the MTA receives the message, it turns around and transmits the message to another system. Although this may seem inefficient, it can be quite beneficial, because it allows a reliable system to hold mail for dial-up users in case of a network disruption, and it allows an organization to assign one computer to relay mail to several distributed mail servers, in order to off-load the work of storing the mail and functioning as pull servers.

MUAs typically function as SMTP clients, so the MUAs can send mail through an SMTP server. Linux MUAs have a choice in the SMTP server they use: They can use the server that runs on the local computer or they can connect to an outside SMTP server. The first option is how Unix systems, and hence Linux computers, have traditionally been configured. Small Linux workstations, however, may do at least as well if the MUA is configured to connect to an outside SMTP server. This can eliminate the need to configure the MTA to deliver outgoing mail.

POP

POP is the simpler of the two common pull e-mail protocols. In fact, there are two variants of POP: POP-2 uses port 109, and POP-3 uses port 110. Most POP mail servers support both protocols, but it's possible to configure a computer to respond to just one or the other, as described later, in "Configuring POP and IMAP."

As with SMTP, it's possible to initiate a call to a POP server using `telnet` (redirecting the call to port 109 or 110). Listing 17.2 illustrates such an exchange.

Listing 17.2   A POP E-Mail Retrieval Session

```
$ telnet nessus.rodsbooks.com 110
Trying 192.168.1.3...
Connected to nessus.rodsbooks.com.
Escape character is '^]'.
+OK POP3 nessus.rodsbooks.com v7.64 server ready
USER rodsmith
+OK User name accepted, password please
PASS password
+OK Mailbox open, 1 messages
RETR 1
+OK 619 octets
Return-Path: <rodsmith@speaker.rodsbooks.com>
Received: from speaker.rodsbooks.com (rodsmith@speaker.rodsbooks.com
        ➥[192.168.1.1])
        by nessus.rodsbooks.com (8.9.3/8.9.3) with SMTP id UAA09955
        for <rodsmith@nessus>; Mon, 18 Sep 2000 20:33:36 -0400
Date: Mon, 18 Sep 2000 20:33:36 -0400
From: rodsmith@speaker.rodsbooks.com
Message-Id: <200009190033.UAA09955@nessus.rodsbooks.com>
X-Authentication-Warning: nessus.rodsbooks.com:
        ➥rodsmith@speaker.rodsbooks.com [192.168.1.1]
        ➥didn't use HELO protocol
Content-Length: 68
Lines: 2
Status: RO

This is a demonstration message. It contains no useful
information.

.
```

```
DELE 1
+OK Message deleted
QUIT
+OK Sayonara
Connection closed by foreign host.
```

The POP protocol uses about a dozen commands, five of which are shown in Listing 17.2: USER, PASS, RETR, DELE, and QUIT. SMTP doesn't require the use of a username or password, because it's designed to deliver information to a user. POP, by contrast, does require authentication, because it can be used to retrieve and delete potentially sensitive e-mail messages. A POP session therefore begins with the USER and PASS commands, which convey this information.

> **WARNING** POP transmits passwords in *cleartext,* meaning that they're not encrypted. If the networks used aren't secure, a troublemaker could intercept the password and use it to retrieve or delete your e-mail. If you use the same password on other computers, the troublemaker could do worse. You should therefore use your POP password *only* on the system that contains your POP account and change the password frequently.

The RETR command retrieves a numbered message; this command is the opposite of the SMTP DATA command. The retrieved message includes message *headers,* however, which show the path the message has taken to reach its destination. A POP client may optionally issue the DELE command to delete a message. If this command isn't issued, the message remains behind on the server.

POP offers little in the way of message management tools; the intention is that the user maintain a local collection of e-mail messages, organized into folders by the user's local MUA. POP simply provides a single e-mail queue for each user. (In fact, it's the MTA that maintains the mail queue; the POP server merely accesses this queue, much as an MUA running on the mail server does.)

IMAP

At first glance, IMAP serves the same function as does POP: It allows for remote pull retrieval of e-mail from a mail server. IMAP is a more sophisticated protocol than is POP, however. Rather than POP's dozen commands, IMAP sports two dozen. These commands include mail manipulation tools, so that the user can arrange mail into folders on the mail server, rather than maintaining them on the client. This has two principal advantages:

- It's easier to examine and manipulate mail *without* reading it. This fact may be critically important if you're using a mail server over a slow dial-up PPP link and you receive an e-mail with a huge attachment. You can delete the e-mail, leave it, or move it into a folder without tying up your slow PPP connection handling the mail. Later, when you have more time or are using a faster connection, you can read the mail and its attachment.

- You can use any number of clients to seamlessly access the same mail messages. This can be extraordinarily useful if you use multiple computers or OSs, because it eliminates the need to archive messages outside of your mail programs or arrange to retrieve the same message multiple times, once into each mail program.

Like POP, IMAP is available in several variants, the most common of which is IMAP-4, which uses port 143. IMAP's command set is much more complex than is POP's. Although it's possible to use IMAP from a Telnet connection to port 143, the operation details tend to be tedious, as shown by Listing 17.3. The client must precede each command with an identifying code beginning with the letter A, as in A2 or A0014. Because IMAP stores mail in local mailboxes, it's necessary to pick one with the SELECT command before performing other operations. IMAP allows the client to read messages with the FETCH command, but that command takes various parameters to fetch different *parts* of a message, such as the text or specific classes of header. The client can also copy messages into specific folders (as in the A4 COPY 1 demos command, which copies message 1 into the demos folder), as well as create, delete, and otherwise modify the folders themselves.

Listing 17.3   IMAP Uses More Commands, and More Complex Commands, Than POP.

```
$ telnet nessus 143
Trying 192.168.1.3...
Connected to nessus.rodsbooks.com.
Escape character is '^]'.
* OK nessus.rodsbooks.com IMAP4rev1 v12.264 server ready
A1 LOGIN rodsmith password
A1 OK LOGIN completed
A2 SELECT mbox
* 1 EXISTS
* NO Trying to get mailbox lock from process 1557
```

```
* 0 RECENT
* OK [UIDVALIDITY 969392188] UID validity status
* OK [UIDNEXT 4] Predicted next UID
* FLAGS (\Answered \Flagged \Deleted \Draft \Seen)
* OK [PERMANENTFLAGS (\* \Answered \Flagged \Deleted \Draft
         ➡\Seen)] Permanent flags
A2 OK [READ-WRITE] SELECT completed
A3 FETCH 1 body[text]
* 1 FETCH (BODY[TEXT] {89}
This is a demonstration message. It contains no useful
information.
)
A3 OK FETCH completed
A4 COPY 1 demos
A4 OK COPY completed
A5 LOGOUT
* BYE nessus.rodsbooks.com IMAP4rev1 server terminating connection
A5 OK LOGOUT completed
Connection closed by foreign host.
```

Fortunately, users do not need to be very concerned with the details of IMAP's operation, because IMAP client programs—which include most modern MUAs—handle the details. Users can use an MUA's feature set to interface to the IMAP server, hiding the details.

In the end, the principal advantage—and disadvantage—of IMAP is that it allows users to store e-mail messages on the mail server. This is very useful when users need to access mail from several different computers, but it increases the need for disk space on the mail server.

Configuring Sendmail

MTA configuration is critically important to most mail servers, because the MTA is usually the most important part of the server. The most common MTA today is *sendmail*. This MTA ships with Red Hat Linux and many other Linux distributions. Fortunately, most Linux distributions use reasonable sendmail configurations by default, so if you're lucky, you may not need to touch your system's sendmail configuration. Unfortunately, sendmail can be a tricky package to configure, so if you do need to change your system's configuration, you may need to spend some time learning about sendmail.

Alternatives to Sendmail

Sendmail is the most popular MTA in use today, but it's far from the only one available. Indeed, some Linux distributions don't even ship with sendmail; they use other MTAs. Linux Mandrake ships with Postfix (http://www.postfix.org), and Debian and its derivatives ship with Exim (http://www.exim.org). Another popular MTA is qmail (http://www.qmail.org), although it's not the default choice of any distribution in early 2001.

When should you consider using an MTA other than sendmail? One good reason to use an alternative MTA is if your distribution ships with one. Replacing Postfix or Exim with sendmail is possible, but it takes some effort and may cause problems for MUAs or other utilities that make assumptions about the mail configuration on a computer. Another reason to use an alternative MTA is if you dislike sendmail's configuration options. As described shortly, sendmail configuration is a bit tedious, and some people simply dislike it. Finally, sendmail is a fairly old program, loaded with inefficiencies. Alternative mail servers may be able to run more quickly or handle a heavier load than can sendmail—but handling e-mail doesn't tax most servers, even when running sendmail.

If you want to try another MTA, which should you use? If your distribution of choice comes with a specific MTA, that one's a good candidate. Postfix and qmail are both designed in a modular manner, which improves speed and (in theory) reduces the potential for security problems. Of these two, Postfix is more compatible with sendmail's command options, and so is typically an easier replacement MTA for a system that ships with sendmail by default.

If you choose to use an alternative MTA, you'll need to locate documentation other than the "Configuring Sendmail" section of this chapter, because other MTAs use different configuration files and procedures. Your best bet is to read the documentation for your MTA of choice on its Web page.

Networking and Troubleshooting

PART 5

Configuring Domains

Every computer on the Internet has a name, such as the fictitious pony.express.gov. If a computer runs an MTA, it's possible to address mail to users of that system, such as susan@pony.express.gov. Frequently, however, a business or other organization prefers to use a shorter e-mail address. Rather than using pony.express.gov, the desire is to use express.gov. This shortened address is easier for individuals to remember, and it doesn't tie the mail down to a specific mail server. The trouble is that there probably is no machine associated with the express.gov name; that's a domain name to which machine names are attached. To overcome this problem, the Domain Name System (DNS) offers a feature known as the *mail exchanger (MX) record.*

An MX record is associated with a domain and points to a specific computer within the domain (or in some other domain). MTAs attempt to deliver mail to the computer associated with an address's MX record, if one exists. If there is no MX record for an address, the MTA tries to find a regular computer associated with the address. For instance, consider the express.gov domain. This domain contains, among others, the mail server pony. The DNS configuration for express.gov includes an MX record that points to pony. Therefore, when an individual addresses mail to susan@express.gov, the sending MTA looks up the MX record for express.gov and contacts pony.express.gov's MTA to transmit the mail. If the mail's sender had specified the address as susan@pony.express.gov, the sending MTA would find no MX record, but would find a regular address record for pony.express.gov and so would contact that computer. Either way, the mail is delivered to susan.

Unless your mail server computer doubles as your domain's DNS server, you can't configure an MX record from the mail server. If you're setting up a mail server for a domain, you should coordinate that aspect of configuration with the individual who handles the DNS server for the domain. If you need to do this yourself, the task can be handled by adding a line to the master record for the domain, which is controlled from a file somewhere on your DNS server, probably in the /var/named directory (the exact name of this file is highly system-specific, but is probably named after the domain). The relevant line looks something like this:

```
@       IN  MX   5     pony.express.gov.
```

The leading ampersand (@) is a code that means the record applies to the default domain name. IN stands for *Internet;* it's present on all records for most domains. MX is the mail exchange record indicator, naturally. The 5 is a preference code; remote MTAs attempt delivery first to the mail server with the lowest priority code. (A domain may have multiple mail servers, so that if one crashes, mail can still be delivered.) The final component of this line is the name of the mail exchanger computer itself. It's important that this name end in a period (.), or else DNS will try to add the domain name to it, resulting in a doubling of the domain name portion of the name and a broken MX record.

For more information on DNS configuration, consult a book on the subject, such as Craig Hunt's *Linux DNS Server Administration* (Sybex, 2000).

> **NOTE** If you want to configure a system to accept mail but don't want the system to accept mail for the entire domain, you can omit DNS configuration. You might do this if you want a system to accept mail addressed directly to it, bypassing the normal organizational mail server.

Sendmail Configuration Files and Procedures

Sendmail is controlled through the sendmail.cf configuration file, which normally resides in the /etc directory. On a default Red Hat 7.0 installation, this file is 1471 lines long (including comment lines). Some of these lines are reasonably understandable to a novice, but others are quite obscure. Although you can adjust this file directly if you're an expert, most users are far better off editing an m4 *source file* instead, and using the m4 utility to convert this into a sendmail.cf file.

On Red Hat Linux, the m4 source file from which sendmail.cf was generated is called /etc/sendmail.mc, and it's a mere 46 lines long, including comments. Most of its options are far more intelligible than the sendmail.cf options it produces. Other distributions place their m4 source files elsewhere; for instance, in SuSE Linux, the file is called /etc/mail/linux.mc, and it's 178 lines long—but most of its lines are comments.

The following sections describe some of the most commonly changed sendmail configuration options. After you make a change to the m4 source file, you can compile it into a sendmail.cf file. To do this, you must first install the sendmail-cf-8.11.0-8 package (on Red Hat 7.0; on other distributions, it may be called something else, or it may be integrated into the main sendmail package). Once you've installed this package, you can issue a command like the following:

```
# m4 /etc/sendmail.mc > /etc/sendmail.cf
```

> **WARNING** Before you issue this command, back up the existing sendmail.cf file by copying or renaming it. Backing up sendmail.mc is also a good idea. This will ensure that you have something that's at least partly functional in case you make changes that render the file useless.

Networking and
Troubleshooting

PART 5

Once you've created a new `sendmail.cf` file, you should restart sendmail using the following command (which you may need to adjust on distributions other than Red Hat):

```
# /etc/rc.d/init.d/sendmail restart
```

You should then check that your changes have had the desired effect by attempting to send or receive mail, as appropriate. If the changes don't have the desired effect, restore the original `sendmail.cf` and `sendmail.mc` files, and try again.

Address Masquerading

One of the most common changes to an e-mail configuration is configuring *address masquerading*. In this configuration, a mail server claims to have a name other than the computer's true hostname. This is most commonly done for one of two reasons:

- To give outgoing e-mail the MX record's address rather than the mail server's true hostname. For instance, you might want `pony.express.gov` to masquerade as `express.gov`. This practice can help ensure that replies to outgoing messages are addressed to *user@express.gov*, which may be desirable if your domain has multiple mail servers or if the domain's active mail server occasionally changes.

- To make the mail appear to come from a valid host rather than from a dial-up account or a computer that's hidden behind an IP masquerading router. Consider a workstation that connects to the Internet through a PPP dial-up link. Chances are this computer doesn't have a valid hostname configured; or if it does, the computer is not always accessible. Therefore, you want to give outgoing mail a legitimate address, such as that of your ISP's mail server.

NOTE   When using a dial-up ISP, it's generally best to configure sendmail to use the ISP's mail server as a relay. This configuration is covered in the next section, "Configuring Relays."

Address masquerading may appear to be a bit dishonest, and in some sense it is. Indeed, those who send spam frequently use this technique in an effort to hide their true identities. If used appropriately, though, address masquerading is a legitimate practice. If you're in doubt, consult your network's or ISP's mail administrator.

To perform address masquerading, add or change the following two lines in the `sendmail.mc` file:

```
MASQUERADE_AS(desired-address.com)
FEATURE(masquerade_envelope)
```

You should change *desired-address.com* to the address you want to use as the return address, of course. The first line causes the From: header to change. This header is the one that most MUAs use to determine the sender and the address to which replies are sent. The FEATURE(masquerade_envelope) line causes sendmail to make additional header substitutions, which can be useful if an MUA uses a nonstandard header to determine the sender's address. These options *do not* change the Received: headers, which are the most diagnostic for tracing mail back to its true source.

> **NOTE** Some MUAs can change the From: header. Changing your sendmail configuration may therefore be overkill. If you set a From: address using an MUA, that setting overrides anything set using sendmail's masquerading features.

Configuring Relays

As described earlier, in "Push and Pull Protocols," it's common for an e-mail message to be relayed several times between its source and its destination. There's a good chance you must cope with this situation in one way or another. In some cases, you may want or need to use an *outgoing relay,* in which your computer passes its mail to another system, which delivers the mail to its destination. In other cases, you may need to configure a computer so that it *functions as* an outgoing relay; other computers (such as mail clients on your own domain) connect to your Linux box to send their mail. Each configuration requires its own options.

Using an Outgoing Relay

All other things being equal, sendmail is capable of delivering mail to any other MTA to which the sendmail program can connect. In most cases, this means that sendmail can deliver mail to any system on the Internet that runs its own SMTP server. It's often desirable to configure a Linux computer to deliver mail directly, because this makes efficient use of network resources and bypasses a potentially unreliable mail relay. The Linux computer might *be* the official mail server, as well. There are, however, possible problems and limitations associated with sending mail directly. These include:

Unreachable destinations If the destination mail server is unavailable because it's crashed or because of network problems, sendmail must hold the mail locally until the problem clears up. It must also periodically reattempt delivery. These actions consume CPU time, disk space, and network resources, although in all probability, very little of each. Of potentially greater importance, if the system that's sending the mail has an intermittent Internet connection (such as a PPP link), subsequent send attempts may fail because that connection is down, thus resulting in a failure to deliver the mail at all, rather than a short delay.

Networking and
Troubleshooting

PART 5

The DUL   The *Dial-up User List (DUL)* is a list of IP addresses associated with dial-up (typically PPP) connections. (See http://www.mail-abuse.org/dul/ for more information on the DUL.) Many mail servers use the DUL to block mail from these connections, because spammers sometimes abuse dial-up lines to send spam. If your ISP has placed your dial-up number on the DUL, some recipients will reject your direct mail on this basis. Relaying your mail through the ISP's official server will work around this problem; the DUL affects *only* e-mail that's sent directly from a listed address.

ISP blocks of port 25   Also in an effort to fight spam, some ISPs block outgoing connections from their dial-up addresses when directed at port 25 (the SMTP port) on remote systems. If your ISP does this, you won't be able to send mail directly at all; you *must* relay mail through your ISP's mail server.

Remote antispam measures   Some mail servers take fairly extreme antispam measures, some of which may block your access attempts even if you're not hit by a DUL entry or an ISP that blocks your port-25 access attempts. For instance, a remote site might block your e-mail if your claimed hostname doesn't match the hostname associated with your IP address, as would most likely be the case when you use a PPP account.

For all these reasons, it's generally a good idea to configure a dial-up Linux computer to relay mail through your ISP's mail server. On the other hand, some ISP's mail servers are themselves notoriously unreliable, so you may prefer to brave the risks of sending mail directly. By contrast, if your computer is connected to the Internet in a more permanent fashion, relaying mail offers fewer advantages—but then, it also typically offers few or no *dis*advantages if your ISP or organization provides a mail server for this purpose. You may want to consult with your ISP or network administrator to learn more about the advantages and disadvantages on your particular network. Of course, you can also add your own personal experiences—if you know that your organization's mail server is unreliable, then sending mail directly can be quite desirable.

The default Red Hat configuration (and the default configurations for other distributions) sends mail directly. To change this configuration detail, you must add the following line to your sendmail.mc or equivalent m4 configuration file:

```
FEATURE(`nullclient', `mail.example.net')
```

> **NOTE** Options passed through the FEATURE command in sendmail.mc are often enclosed in single quotes. Unlike most configuration tools, though, m4 requires different opening and closing quotes. The opening quote is the back-quote character, which is usually available on the key to the left of the 1 key on a keyboard. The closing quote is the usual single quote character, which is on the key to the right of the semicolon (;) key on most keyboards.

You should, of course, change *mail.example.net* to your organization's or ISP's mail relay system. When you've rebuilt sendmail.cf and restarted sendmail, the result should be that all mail sent through your local copy of sendmail is relayed through the mail relay system you specify.

> **TIP** One objection that's frequently voiced to using an ISP's mail relay comes from users who use multiple ISPs. Because most ISPs reject mail relay attempts from outside their domains, a configuration like this will work from only one ISP. One way around this problem is to create *two* sendmail.cf files, one for each ISP. Name each one something appropriate, such as sendmail.cf.isp1 and sendmail.cf.isp2. You can then modify your PPP dial-up scripts (described in Chapter 12) to copy the customized files over the regular sendmail.cf and restart sendmail. The result is that sendmail will relay through whichever ISP's mail server is appropriate.

Configuring Sendmail to Relay for a Domain

Configuring sendmail to use another mail server as a relay is often convenient on small Linux systems that function as workstations. Linux is often used as the mail server that relays for others, however. This configuration works best when the Linux server has a dedicated connection to the Internet that is always up. By default, Red Hat Linux 7.0 is configured so that it doesn't relay mail from other systems. This is an antispam measure, but it gets in the way of the use of a Linux server as a relay for your own computers. The trick is to *loosen*, but *not remove*, the antirelay restrictions.

> **NOTE** To have sendmail function as a relay, it must also be configured to receive mail. This usually works correctly at installation, but if you're having problems, check the section entitled "Receiving Mail."

To allow sendmail to relay mail from certain classes of computers, you must add a FEATURE line to `sendmail.mc` or its equivalent file. This FEATURE line includes one of the following options:

`promiscuous_relay` This *extremely dangerous* option tells sendmail to relay any mail that comes its way. Don't use this option, because it virtually guarantees that spammers will, sooner or later, abuse your system.

`relay_based_on_MX` This option configures sendmail to accept relays from other computers, so long as those computers' domains are configured to show your system as the MX. This option is fairly lax on security, because it essentially lets somebody else (whoever controls the DNS server for the remote system) determine whether your system will function as a relay.

`relay_entire_domain` If you set this option, sendmail accepts mail from any host within the domain to which it belongs. This can be a convenient way to quickly configure a Linux system as a limited mail relay.

`relay_local_from` This option tells sendmail to accept relays if the sender uses the server's address as its own. This can be convenient in some cases, but it's also easily abused.

`relay_hosts_only` This option works with an access database (described shortly) to allow you to list individual hosts as acceptable or unacceptable for relaying.

`access_db` This feature allows you to use an access database (described shortly) to list domains for which sendmail will relay.

As an example, the default `sendmail.mc` file for Red Hat Linux includes the following line:

```
FEATURE(`access_db')
```

You can modify this line to use some other relay option, if one is appropriate for your network. Alternatively, you can adjust the access database file. This file is called /etc/mail/access on Red Hat 7.0, but it may appear elsewhere on some distributions. The file consists of lines, each containing a single domain name, machine name, or IP address followed by a tag that indicates how sendmail will treat messages received from the sender. (Lines beginning with pound signs [#] are comments and are ignored.) The default Red Hat 7.0 configuration looks like this:

```
# by default we allow relaying from localhost...
localhost.localdomain           RELAY
localhost                       RELAY
127.0.0.1                       RELAY
```

Valid tags are as follows:

OK   Forces sendmail to accept the mail, even if other rules would reject it.

RELAY   Accepts for relay mail that comes from or goes to the specified domain. The default configuration accepts local mail for relay; technically, when a local program sends mail through sendmail, it's functioning as a mail relay, so this configuration is required if you want to send mail.

REJECT   Refuses mail that comes from or goes to the specified domain. Sendmail generates a *bounce* message to let the sender know the attempt failed.

DISCARD   Works just like REJECT, except that sendmail does *not* generate a bounce message.

nnn text   Works like REJECT, but returns an error code *nnn* to the sender, along with *text* as a message.

You can specify domains either by domain name (as in badspammer.net) or by a partial IP address (as in 192.168.98, which matches all computers with IP addresses in the 192.168.98.0/24 network). The safest way to configure sendmail to relay is to specify a network by IP address, because this is harder to forge than is a domain name.

Suppose you want to configure sendmail to relay mail from the 192.168.98.0/24 network. You could add the following entry to /etc/mail/access:

    192.168.98   RELAY

Before you can use this entry, however, you must convert the text-mode /etc/mail/ access file into a binary format that's stored in /etc/mail/access.db. You do this by entering the following command:

    # **makemap hash /etc/mail/access.db < /etc/mail/access**

TIP   On Red Hat Linux, you don't need to issue the makemap command, because the sendmail start-up scripts do this automatically.

Once you've entered the command, you can restart sendmail, and it will be configured to relay mail from the 192.168.98.0/24 network. It's best to test your setup by configuring an MUA on another computer to use the system you've adjusted as the outgoing mail server. You should also check that you've not made the system too lax by doing the same from a computer that should *not* be able to use the system as a mail relay.

Networking and Troubleshooting

PART 5

Receiving Mail

Linux can receive mail sent via SMTP, as well as send it. To do so, sendmail must be run in *daemon mode*—that is, it must always be running, watching for connections on port 25. To run sendmail in daemon mode, it must be started with the -bd switch, as in **sendmail -bd**. This is the default configuration for sendmail in Red Hat Linux 7.0. You can check to see whether sendmail is running this way by using the ps command:

```
$ ps ax | grep sendmail
 2536 ?        S       0:00 sendmail: accepting connections
```

The statement that sendmail is "accepting connections" indicates that sendmail is indeed running in daemon mode. What if it's not, though? In that case, you must either start sendmail manually or modify your start-up scripts. In Red Hat 7.0, the relevant script is /etc/rc.d/init.d/sendmail, but the appropriate script may be called something else on other distributions. You should locate the call to sendmail in the start-up script and ensure that it includes the -bd parameter. In the case of Red Hat 7.0, the start-up script sets this parameter based on the contents of the DAEMON variable set in the /etc/sysconfig/sendmail file, which is loaded early in the sendmail start-up script.

Another requirement for sendmail to receive mail is that the program be configured to accept mail for the machine names by which it's known. For instance, consider the fictitious mail server pony.express.gov. If the DNS records for express.gov include an MX record pointing to pony.express.gov, that machine must accept mail addressed to express.gov as local, despite the fact that the machine name is not express.gov. Fortunately, this task is easily accomplished: You need only add the computer's aliases to /etc/mail/local-host-names and restart sendmail (this file is called /etc/sendmail.cw on some distributions). For instance, the following /etc/mail/local-host-names file tells the system to accept mail addressed to express.gov and postit.gov, in addition to whatever name the computer uses as its hostname:

```
express.gov

postit.gov
```

One question you should ask yourself is whether you *want* your system to receive SMTP mail. The average workstation doesn't need this capability, because another computer functions as a mail server for the workstation's users; the workstation uses a pull mail protocol to retrieve mail from the server. If you change the /etc/sysconfig/sendmail or /etc/rc.d/init.d/sendmail start-up script so that DAEMON=no rather than yes, you'll still be able to send mail from local programs, but you'll need to use a pull mail protocol to receive mail. If a system doesn't need to receive SMTP mail, it's a good idea to configure it in this way. Doing so eliminates the possibility that a miscreant might gain entry to the system through a bug in sendmail, and it also eliminates the possibility of a spammer abusing a misconfigured system to relay spam.

Configuring POP and IMAP

Fortunately, setting up the POP and IMAP protocols is not very difficult. Compared to sendmail, the POP and IMAP servers require very little in the way of configuration. If you're building a departmental mail server, though, you may need to configure user accounts, and this may require some thought. It's also possible to use a Linux system as a POP or IMAP client. In many cases, you do this via MUAs; however, there's a special program that lets you grab POP or IMAP mail and serve it through a regular Linux mail queue.

Running POP and IMAP Daemons

The first step to running POP or IMAP is to install the appropriate server package. In Red Hat 7.0, it's called `imap-4.7c2-12`, and it includes servers for both POP and IMAP. Other distributions ship with similar packages.

> **NOTE** Just as sendmail isn't the only SMTP server, the POP and IMAP servers included in the `imap-4.7c2-12` package aren't the only POP and IMAP servers. You'll most likely need to look for an alternative package if you use qmail as your MTA, because qmail stores e-mail in different locations than do most other MTAs, which confuses most POP and IMAP servers. The qmail Web site includes links to alternative POP and IMAP servers that work with qmail. Exim and Postfix are compatible with the standard `imap` package, however.

The POP and IMAP daemons are normally run from a *super server,* as described in Chapter 15. Red Hat 7.0 and Mandrake 7.2 use the `xinetd` super server, but most other distributions in early 2001, as well as earlier versions of Red Hat and Mandrake, use `inetd`. The configuration of these programs differs.

If your distribution uses `inetd`, the `/etc/inetd.conf` file probably contains the following lines relating to POP and IMAP servers:

```
pop-2   stream  tcp  nowait  root  /usr/sbin/tcpd  ipop2d

pop-3   stream  tcp  nowait  root  /usr/sbin/tcpd  ipop3d

imap    stream  tcp  nowait  root  /usr/sbin/tcpd  imapd
```

Networking and Troubleshooting

PART 5

Chapter 15 includes a discussion of the /etc/inetd.conf file format. For the moment, though, it's sufficient to know that these three lines indicate servers for POP-2, POP-3, and IMAP protocols. Whenever a connection is attempted to the appropriate port, inetd launches the ipop2d, ipop3d, or imapd programs to handle the task.

By default, these three lines are commented out—that is, they're preceded by pound signs (#) to deactivate the servers. Once you've installed a POP or IMAP server, you must do two things to activate it if you're using inetd:

1. Uncomment the appropriate server lines in /etc/inetd.conf. For example, if you want to use IMAP but not POP, uncomment only the imap line.

2. Restart inetd by typing **/etc/rc.d/init.d/inet restart**.

If your distribution uses xinetd rather than inetd, the procedure is somewhat different. Both Red Hat and Mandrake ship with imap packages that install xinetd start-up scripts in the /etc/rc.d/xinetd.d directory. These scripts are called imap, imaps, ipop2, ipop3, and pop3s. The script names that end in s are for secure versions of the protocols, which use encryption to protect the password from sniffing. By default, all of these protocols are disabled when installed. To enable one or more protocols, follow these steps:

1. Open the script corresponding to the protocol you want to enable in a text editor and edit the line reading disable = yes so that it reads disable = no. Save the file.

2. Repeat step 1 for any additional protocols you wish to enable.

3. Restart xinetd by typing **/etc/rc.d/init.d/xinet restart**.

Once you've done this, your system should be configured as a server for whichever pull mail protocols you've selected. You can test the server by using an appropriate MUA on another computer or by using a Telnet program to test the server manually, as shown in Listings 17.2 and 17.3.

Setting Up Mail-Only Accounts

Ordinarily, Linux accepts mail only for recipients who have an account on the server. For example, if mail is addressed to nemo@pony.express.com, and if pony.express.com has no user called nemo, the server bounces the mail—the sender receives back a message that includes an error message stating that nemo isn't a valid recipient. Therefore, you must normally create user accounts for all e-mail recipients, even if the computer is used *only* as a mail server.

NOTE There are exceptions to this rule. For instance, it's possible to configure mail *aliases,* where one e-mail address corresponds to a different username. Most systems come preconfigured with certain aliases for critical accounts such as postmaster, which is the user responsible for mail server configuration.

If a computer is to function as a mail server from which users access their mail *only* using a pull mail protocol, and if you don't want to grant users access to the system using normal command shells, you should adjust users' /etc/passwd entries so that the shells point to something useless. A normal user's /etc/passwd entry looks something like this:

```
george:x:502:100:George W.:/home/george:/bin/bash
```

The final component of this line—/bin/bash in this example—tells Linux what program to run when the user logs on through Telnet or SSH, or at the console. You can change this entry to something that won't grant any useful access, such as /dev/null or /bin/false. The account then becomes useless for shell access, but it can still be used for pull mail retrieval.

TIP Instead of specifying a completely useless program as a shell, you may want to specify the passwd program. Doing so allows users to change their passwords by using a Telnet or SSH program to log on to the server. Once the password has changed, the user is immediately logged off.

If you use a utility such as useradd to create accounts, you can create them using such "dummy" shells to begin with. With useradd, you use the -s parameter to specify the shell, so you can add -s /dev/null to create an account that uses /dev/null for its shell from the start. If you prefer to use GUI configuration tools, you may be able to accomplish the same goal. In fact, Red Hat's Linuxconf includes an option to create mail-only accounts, as shown in Figure 17.2. When you create an account in this way, Linuxconf uses /bin/false as the shell and assigns the user to the group popusers.

Using fetchmail to Acquire Mail from an ISP

Imagine this scenario: You're configuring a mail server for a small company. This company uses a low-end digital subscriber line (DSL) connection for Internet access, and the ISP doesn't allow the company to run its own mail server. Instead, the company contracts with another ISP to provide e-mail accounts under its desired domain name (let's call it oneroomco.com). E-mail from this ISP can be retrieved via IMAP, and the DSL ISP's e-mail is accessible via POP. Outgoing e-mail is sent directly via SMTP. Your task is to provide a single unified e-mail structure, so that internal e-mail remains local, without

Figure 17.2 Linuxconf includes a special option to create user accounts designed explicitly for mail-only use.

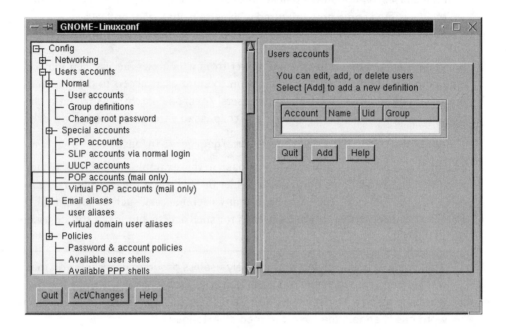

cluttering the DSL connection, and so that e-mail to either the DSL ISP's POP account or the mail ISP's IMAP account is pushed into a local mail queue. This arrangement is illustrated in Figure 17.3.

This chapter has already described many features required of the `mail.oneroomco.com` server in Figure 17.3. Mail relaying and the local POP server, for instance, were covered in previous chapters. (Figure 17.3 shows outgoing mail being sent directly, but it could as easily be relayed through either ISP's server.) The main missing piece is the retrieval of mail via POP and IMAP from the ISPs.

A tool that's extremely helpful in configuring remote mail retrieval via POP or IMAP is fetchmail. This tool is a dedicated pull mail *client* program. It connects to a remote POP or IMAP server, retrieves the mail from that server, and injects the mail into the local system's mail queue. When fetchmail is used in conjunction with a conventional SMTP server, the result can be a mail system that works almost as if it were connected directly to the Internet. The main difference users might notice is that, because fetchmail must initiate mail connections, incoming mail may be delayed by some period of time—a few

Figure 17.3   Small businesses frequently want to provide internal mail services, but must use pull mail protocols to retrieve their own e-mail.

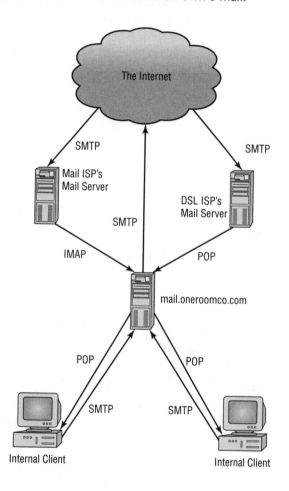

minutes or hours, typically, depending upon the frequency with which you configure fetchmail to check for new mail.

> **NOTE**   You can use fetchmail on even smaller systems than a small business's mail server. Many individuals use fetchmail to grab their mail, which can then be read using any Linux MUA. This can greatly simplify your life if you use multiple mail ISPs or if you want to use an advanced mail-filtering tool to sort your mail or weed out the spam.

Networking and
Troubleshooting

PART 5

Configuring fetchmail

The fetchmail program supports a large number of configuration options, so this chapter can cover only its basics. Consult the fetchmail man pages or Web site (`http://www.tuxedo.org/~esr/fetchmail/`) for more details. At its core, fetchmail is controlled by a configuration file called `.fetchmailrc`, located in the calling user's home directory. A typical `.fetchmailrc` file looks like this:

```
set postmaster "george"

set bouncemail

set properties ""

set daemon 1800

poll mail.a-dsl-isp.net with proto POP3
        ↪user "oneroomco" there with password "password"
        ↪is sally here options fetchall forcecr

poll mail.mailisp.com with proto IMAP
        ↪user "georgew" there with password "password"
        ↪is george here user "sallys" there with
        ↪password "sallyp" is sally here
```

The configuration file format is designed to be reasonably easy to interpret, but some features deserve comment:

`set postmaster`   This option lets you specify a local user who is to receive mail that appears to be misaddressed, as well as error messages.

`set bouncemail`   This option directs fetchmail to generate bounce messages and mail them to the sender in case of an error.

`set properties`   fetchmail itself doesn't use this configuration line, but it passes whatever appears inside the quotes to any scripts that it calls.

`set daemon`   You can configure fetchmail to run in the background and retrieve mail every specified number of seconds. The instruction `set daemon 1800` tells fetchmail to check for new mail every half hour. Alternatively, you can omit this line and call fetchmail from a cron job.

`poll`   Each `poll` entry tells fetchmail about a single remote mail server. You must specify the server name, the protocol to be used, the remote username, the remote password, the local user to receive the mail, and any additional options you want to specify. You can include multiple user accounts on one `poll` entry.

TIP   Rather than directly editing the .fetchmailrc file, you may want to try using fetchmailconf. This utility, which is installed separately from fetchmail in Red Hat 7.0, is a GUI configuration tool for fetchmail. Using this tool can help ensure that you generate a usable .fetchmailrc file.

WARNING   Because the .fetchmailrc file contains passwords, it's critically important that this file be protected from unauthorized access. In fact, fetchmail refuses to run if .fetchmailrc can be read by anybody but the owner.

Using fetchmail

Once you've configured fetchmail, you should test it. You can do so with the following command:

```
$ fetchmail -d0 -k
```

The -d0 option ensures that fetchmail does *not* enter daemon mode; this invocation will be a one-time call, even if .fetchmailrc specifies daemon mode. Likewise, -k tells fetchmail to leave any retrieved messages on the mail server. This ensures that you won't lose your mail if there's a problem that causes the mail to be lost between retrieval and injection into your local mail queue.

Once you've tested your fetchmail configuration and worked out any kinks, you can set it up for regular use. There are several possible ways to do this:

- You can use fetchmail's daemon mode to have it stay active and check for mail at regular intervals. If you want fetchmail to start automatically when the computer boots, you'll need to add an appropriate entry to a start-up file, such as /etc/rc.d/rc.local. Unfortunately, some people find that fetchmail occasionally crashes, so this mode may not be the best choice if you need the best reliability.

- You can run fetchmail from a cron job. For instance, to have fetchmail retrieve mail every hour, you can create a simple script (see Chapter 14) to do this and place that script in /etc/cron.hourly. If you use this approach, be sure *not* to specify daemon mode in your .fetchmailrc file.

- You can run fetchmail as part of a network start-up script. This approach is particularly useful for those who use PPP dial-up accounts, because you can configure the system to start fetchmail when the Internet connection initializes and to shut it down when the connection ends.

- You can run fetchmail manually, by typing **fetchmail** whenever you want to check for new mail.

Most of the automated methods run fetchmail as `root` by default, so the `.fetchmailrc` file must be placed in the `/root` directory. You can create a cron job that runs as an ordinary user, but this requires somewhat more effort to configure than dropping a script in a subdirectory of `/etc`. Consult the cron man pages for more information on this topic. Normally, it doesn't matter whether fetchmail runs as `root` or as an ordinary user; either way, the program calls sendmail to deliver the mail locally. Depending upon who should know the passwords contained in `.fetchmailrc`, though, you might want to be cautious about the user under whose name fetchmail runs.

Antispam Measures

In computer circles, *spam* refers to junk e-mail—ads for dubious hair-loss remedies, illegal pyramid schemes, mysterious messages in languages you don't understand, and so on. Sadly, spam is a major problem for e-mail administrators. There are two aspects to this problem: preventing your system from being used as a source of spam, and blocking incoming spam that might annoy your users and consume system resources. A few steps can help prevent your system from becoming a source of spam. Blocking incoming spam is a tougher problem, but there are still some actions you can take to at least reduce the volume of spam your site sees.

The Problem of Spam

To individual users, spam is typically an annoyance. A user who receives half a dozen or a dozen spams a day must typically spend a few seconds determining that a message is spam and deleting it. (This can easily work out to several hours a year wasted just deleting spam!) On occasion, a spam may be offensive, as when it advertises an X-rated Web site or contains racist slurs. If the user has a slow network link, the spam may take some time to transmit—we've seen spams 150KB in size, and this is certainly not the world record for spam size.

To a mail administrator, spam is a more serious problem. In addition to being an annoyance to users, spam consumes disk space and network bandwidth. These may not be major factors to a small site, but large ISPs may need to increase hard-disk sizes or buy more network bandwidth to cope with spam. What's worse, spam generates complaints. This is particularly true if your own server becomes a source of spam. If somebody uses your system to send out thousands of ads for an aphrodisiac floor wax, chances are you'll get complaints in return—perhaps enough to seriously disrupt your life for a day or more. It's therefore critically important that your mail server not become a spam source.

> **WARNING**   Even if all your users are well-behaved and would never dream of sending spam, your mail server may become a source of spam if it's configured as a relay or if the mail server is broken into.

To learn more about spam prevention than can be covered in this space, check the *Mail Abuse Prevention System (MAPS)* Web site, http://www.mail-abuse.org. Schwartz and Garfinkel's *Stopping Spam* (O'Reilly, 1998) also provides a good overview of the topic.

Preventing Outgoing Spam

Your first spam concern should be to ensure that your server doesn't become a spam source. There are two ways your system can send spam: One of your users can decide to send spam, or somebody who's *not* a legitimate user of your system can hijack it to send spam. Each potential problem requires different solutions, although there are some commonalities.

Policing Your Own Users

If you operate a small mail server for a limited number of people, you can probably control outgoing spam by speaking to the users of your system. In an office of half a dozen people, for instance, you can simply tell everybody not to spam. Perhaps the most difficult aspect of doing this is conveying to your users precisely what spam is. Spam has many features. Most importantly, it is the following:

Unsolicited   E-mail readers don't ask for spam. Typically, spammers collect e-mail addresses from postings to Usenet newsgroups or by setting address-collecting "robots" loose on the Web. Some spam comes when users willingly leave their e-mail addresses on spammers' Web sites. Some companies seem to think that such an action makes it OK to send ads to individuals, but unless careful precautions are observed, this isn't so. If you want to set up an advertising list, be sure your recipients *want* to be on that list. The MAPS Web site includes many pointers to help you avoid inadvertently spamming. This said, not all unsolicited e-mail is spam. A journalist may legitimately e-mail somebody to ask for an interview, for instance. If e-mail is unsolicited, though, it deserves careful scrutiny to determine whether it's legitimate or spam.

Bulk   Spam is invariably sent in large quantities—to hundreds or thousands of recipients. There are legitimate uses for bulk e-mail (such as mailing lists to which readers subscribe), but if you send e-mail in bulk, you should ensure that the recipients *want* to be on the mailing list. Some spammers have taken to trying to hide the bulk nature of their spams by creating individualized message subjects or otherwise tweaking the messages. These changes don't alter the fact that the message, as a whole, is sent to quite a few recipients.

Often commercial   Spam is usually commercial in nature. This isn't a requirement of spam, however. An unsolicited bulk e-mail warning of a new computer virus may not be commercial, but it is nonetheless spam. (In practice, such messages are often hoaxes, too.) Commercial e-mail does not need to be spam, but if your message is commercial in nature, you should be sure your recipients want to receive it.

On a small site, once you've informed your users about what spam is and why they shouldn't send it, the biggest risk is that somebody might mistakenly believe that the rules don't apply to a particular message, such as a warning about a new virus or a plea to find a lost child. Although such messages may seem important or even heart-wrenching, sending them in bulk is still spamming. These messages are often hoaxes. Even when they're not, there are appropriate means of disseminating such information.

If you're dealing with a larger domain, you may have a larger problem. The worst such situation for you as an administrator is if you're in charge of an ISP's mail server. ISPs are frequently abused by spammers. The spammer opens a throwaway account, sends tens or hundreds of thousands of messages, and vanishes. The ISP is left with the task of fielding the complaints and generally cleaning up the mess.

If you're in charge of a large domain's e-mail server, this chapter cannot provide enough information for you—either for spam control or even for basic mail configuration. You should read one or more books on e-mail, all the documentation for your mail server, and then some. Depending upon the size of your domain, you may need to hire an administrator just to handle the e-mail.

Blocking Unwanted Relays

Even a small site can fall victim to a relay job. Spammers routinely scan the Internet for open relays—SMTP mail servers configured to relay mail from outside domains. Spammers use relays for several reasons:

Offloading the work   In an SMTP session (see Listing 17.1), it's possible to send the text of a message just once, listing multiple recipients. The SMTP server then contacts each of the recipient MTAs to deliver the message. A spammer can therefore use a slow dial-up link to send one copy of a message to many recipients, thus reducing the spammer's own online time.

Obscuring the origin   Using a mail relay obscures the origin of the spam. Each server through which a message passes adds a header that identifies the server and the system from which the server received the message. If a spammer uses a relay, the ultimate recipient may believe that the relay sent the message, thus deflecting blame.

This strategy can be particularly effective if the spammer adds fake headers that indicate a bogus point of origin.

Avoiding detection by the ISP   The spammer's own ISP may have the means to detect spam as it moves through its own system. Using another computer as a relay, thus bypassing the ISP's legitimate relay, can help the spammer avoid detection—probably not for long, but for long enough to make the minimal effort worthwhile.

It's safest to configure a Linux system to not relay mail at all. Sendmail can be configured to work in precisely this way, as it is by default in Red Hat 7.0. "Configuring Sendmail to Relay for a Domain," earlier in this chapter, described several means of allowing sendmail to relay legitimate e-mail. Some of these methods are extremely dangerous and should not be used. `promiscuous_relay` is the worst of these, followed by `relay_local_from` and `relay_based_on_MX`. The best way to configure sendmail as a safe relay is to specify IP addresses in the `/etc/mail/access` file, as described in "Configuring Sendmail to Relay for a Domain." If this is impractical for some reason, `relay_entire_domain` is probably not too unsafe.

If you make any extensive changes to your sendmail configuration, it's best to test your system to be sure it's not an open relay. To do this, initiate a Telnet connection to `mail-abuse.org` *from the system you want to test:*

```
$ telnet mail-abuse.org
```

You should see in response the output of the MAPS system's attempts to use your system as a relay. The response should be a series of "relaying denied" messages, followed by a statement that the system blocked all relay attempts. If not, review your configuration to be sure you've not included any unwanted relaying options. You may also want to check for an updated version of sendmail from your distribution's provider, particularly if you're using an old version of sendmail—prior to version 8.9.0, sendmail's default configuration was to relay all mail by default.

Stopping Incoming Spam

Blocking relays and outgoing spam is part of what it takes to be a good Internet citizen. Taking these steps will not, however, stop your users from being flooded with spam. To alleviate this problem, you must take additional steps. Two broad classes of spam filters are available: *blackhole lists,* which block spam based on a list of IP addresses you may want to refuse for one reason or another, and filters based on header contents, such as message subject lines.

> ***WARNING*** No system of spam detection is perfect; all spam filters produce occasional errors. These errors fall into two categories: *false alarms,* in which nonspam messages are mistakenly blocked, and *misses,* in which spam gets past the filter. Reducing the number of misses usually raises the number of false alarms and vice versa. You must decide how many legitimate e-mails you want to sacrifice when blocking spam and set your spam filters appropriately.

Blackhole Lists

Blackhole lists are implemented using DNS servers, but the DNS servers are configured in a peculiar way: They return legitimate lookups for IP addresses that the service maintainer has decided are known or potential spam sources. In the simplest configuration, you can tell sendmail to refuse to take delivery of any message from such a site. The most common blackhole lists are described below.

MAPS RBL   The MAPS *Realtime Blackhole List (RBL)* is perhaps the most conservative service. To be listed in the RBL, a site must have engaged in any number of spamming or spam-supporting activities, and shown little or no evidence of ceasing such activities. This means that the RBL produces few false alarms, but also lets quite a bit of spam through. List server address:

```
rbl.maps.vix.com
```

List Web page:

```
http://www.mail-abuse.org/rbl/
```

MAPS RSS   The MAPS *Relay Spam Stopper (RSS)* lists sites that are known to be open relays that have been used at least once by spammers. Open relays that have not been used by spammers are not on the RSS list. Unfortunately, a large number of legitimate sites are poorly configured, and some of these find themselves on the RSS. Fortunately, most such sites quickly clean up their servers and are removed from the RSS. The RSS therefore produces occasional false alarms. List server address:

```
relays.mail-abuse.org
```

List Web page:

```
http://www.mail-abuse.org/rss/
```

MAPS DUL   The MAPS *Dial-up User List (DUL)* is a list of IP addresses associated with dial-up accounts—mostly IP blocks submitted by ISPs themselves, associated with their PPP lines. Unlike the RBL and RSS, the DUL isn't a list of sites that have done anything wrong. Spammers, however, frequently use direct connections from throwaway dial-up accounts to send spam directly (without using a relay), so block-ing these addresses impedes one potential avenue for spam. Unfortunately, it also blocks at least some legitimate e-mail, from users who use these ISPs and prefer not to use the ISP's own mail servers. The DUL therefore produces a rather high false alarm rate, although it also catches a lot of spam. List server address:

```
dul.maps.vix.com
```

List Web page:

```
http://www.mail-abuse.org/dul/
```

ORBS   The *Open Relay Behavior-modification System (ORBS)* is similar in prin-ciple to the MAPS RSS, but takes a more proactive approach: A site does not need to have actually been used as a spam relay to find itself on the ORBS list; it needs only to *be* an open relay. This means that ORBS blocks more spam than does RSS, but it also creates more false alarms. List server address:

```
relays.orbs.org
```

List Web page:

```
http://www.orbs.org
```

Sendmail 8.9.3, which ships with Red Hat 6.2, has the ability to use the MAPS RBL with minimal fuss. To do so, add the following line to your `sendmail.mc` file and recompile `sendmail.cf`:

```
FEATURE(rbl)
```

To use any of the other lists, you must patch some of the standard sendmail m4 scripts. It's probably easier in this case to upgrade to sendmail 8.10 or later, which includes support for using arbitrary blackhole lists. If you use sendmail 8.10 or later, the `sendmail.mc` line to use the MAPS RBL looks like this:

```
FEATURE(dnsbl, `rbl.maps.vix.com', `Rejected - see
    ➥http://www.mail-abuse.org/rbl/')
```

Red Hat 7.0 ships with sendmail 8.11.0, so it can use any blackhole list in this manner. In addition to using the `dnsbl` code, which identifies this as a call to use a blackhole list, this command includes the name of the site that hosts the list and an error code that's to be returned with each bounce. The first is critically important for basic functionality of the antispam measure. You can find the blackhole server addresses listed above. The latter isn't required for basic operation, but you should include some descriptive text and a Web site address so that somebody whose e-mail bounces in error can take steps to correct the problem. The descriptions above also include the main Web site address for each blackhole list, so you can include the address in the error message for bounced e-mail.

Mail Header Tests

A second broad class of spam rejection technique is that of using the contents of the e-mail's headers to reject spam. You can have your mail server reject mail with specific subject lines ("Get rich quick!"), from specific senders (ads@badspammer.net), or by any other criterion you choose. Some of these tests at least potentially overlap what blackhole lists do—ideally, one or more blackhole lists should block "spam haven" sites, so sender tests should not, in theory, be necessary. You may find it's helpful to add your own header-based sender blocks, however. These tests can be more specific than blackhole tests, because header-based sender blocks can include the *username* of the sender. Rather than block all senders of a large site, therefore, you can block the spammers—*if* you can find some way to identify them. (Spammers tend to change accounts frequently, so this task is remarkably akin to the torture of Sisyphus, who forever toils to roll a boulder uphill, only to have it roll back down again.) You might also choose to use your own tests to add a few sites without subscribing to a blackhole list that produces a lot of false alarms to eliminate those sites.

One way to implement a mail header test is to add the test to the /etc/mail/access file, as described earlier in this chapter, in "Configuring Sendmail to Relay for a Domain." Instead of using the RELAY key to enable relaying, though, you would use the REJECT or *nnn text* keys to reject mail. For example, you might use the following file to block a few problem sites:

```
localhost.localdomain        RELAY
localhost                    RELAY
127.0.0.1                    RELAY
badspammer.net               550 Spam not accepted
spamguy@somebigisp.net       REJECT
```

The 550 Spam not accepted line causes sendmail to reject mail from badspammer.net with a 550 error code and the error message "Spam not accepted." All other things being equal, you should try to include an informative rejection message for these entries. The REJECT code causes sendmail to reject all mail that originates from spamguy@somebigisp.net (but not from other users of somebigisp.net).

Mail header tests based on the e-mail's subject, the program used to send the mail, and other features can also be performed, but they're usually done by add-on programs. Specifically, procmail is a mail-filtering tool that can be used as an antispam tool, as well as for other tasks, such as sorting your mail so that mailing list e-mail is separated from personal e-mail. One particularly popular antispam tool that's built on procmail is Spam

Bouncer (`http://www.spambouncer.org`). You can install `procmail` from your Linux CD-ROM (if it's not already installed) and then install Spam Bouncer from its Web site, which contains complete instructions for doing this. Once this is done, suspected spam will be shunted into separate mail folders or, if you so choose, deleted outright.

> **WARNING** In our experience, Spam Bouncer has a particularly high false alarm rate. We *strongly* suggest that, if you try this tool, you first configure it to retain suspected spam for your review, so that you can see what types of messages it mistakenly categorizes as spam.

In Sum

E-mail is an extremely important feature of modern networking. Linux can function quite well as a small or even a large e-mail server, providing both push and pull e-mail protocols. By default, Red Hat Linux provides an e-mail configuration that will work with many networks, but you may need to adjust the default settings to handle limited relaying, multiple domain names, or domain name masquerading. If you want to provide pull e-mail servers, you'll need to install them, but configuration is straightforward compared to sendmail configuration. If you run any push e-mail server, you should be concerned about spam and ensure that your server isn't configured in such a way that a spammer can take advantage of it. Rejecting incoming junk e-mail may seem more critical in the short term, but it's more difficult to configure correctly than it is to block outgoing spam.

18

Troubleshooting Your Linux System

Troubleshooting is an art, requiring both a natural analytical ability and an extensive knowledge of the Linux system. It is also one of the most high-profile aspects of the Linux system administrator's job. If something isn't working, you can bet there will be "shoulder surfers" around to watch while you fix the problem. The more familiar you are with the Linux filesystem covered in Chapter 3, the booting and initialization processes covered in Chapter 5, and the login process detailed in Chapter 6, the more smoothly your troubleshooting experience is likely to go. Most of the troubleshooting that we've run into has involved an inability to boot the system, an inability to log into the system, or the inability to initialize some service.

There are a number of sources for information about commonly encountered difficulties in Linux and their solutions. These sources give you a place to start when you aren't sure what the problem is or how to track it down. You can run searches on `http://www.deja.com/usenet` to see if you can find a post where someone else has had a similar problem. Often, if these don't give you the complete answer, they at least get you pointed in the right direction. If you have an error message, enter the entire thing (or at least the part that would be common to other systems) within parentheses and then the word `Linux`. Often this brings up the answer to the problem; simply follow that example to fix it, and you're done.

Also look on your distribution's Web site to see if a fix has already been posted. If the fix is a software package, read the description to make sure that it is intended to fix your problem. (If is a security fix, you should download and apply it anyway.)

General Troubleshooting Techniques

Our basic philosophy about troubleshooting is to dive in and swim around. While it is far better to pare down the solution space to a problem if you can, new system administrators are sometimes too timid about trying to fix a problem. If you don't know where to start, check the last few lines of the /var/log/messages file to see if the problem is generating error messages. If not, run through the boot process to see if the problem could logically be there. If you don't find something that seems relevant, move on to the initialization process. Certainly it is better if you see something that points you in what seems to be a logical direction, but for some people the most difficult part is getting started. Once you're in under the hood, you will likely see something that just doesn't look right, and you're off and running. From that point, approach the problem methodically.

Remember to contemplate what you expected as well as what you saw. What run level was the system supposed to boot into? Could this be an X problem? Sometimes a problem with X will leave you at a run level 3 login prompt, making the problem even more confusing. If you were supposed to boot into run level 5 but the system stops at run level 3, see if you can log in at run level 3. If you can, then try to start up the X server. If it doesn't start, there will most likely be error messages to help you find the problem.

Here are some basic troubleshooting precepts:

- *Read, read, read!* Always read the README or INSTALL text files included with packages that you are installing from scratch. Always read the HOWTO (if one is available) for any packages you are configuring. Look on the Linux Documentation Project site to see if there is information about what you're doing. LDP is available at http://www.linuxdoc.org.

- Always look to the /var/log/messages file to determine whether a problem that you are attempting to correct is sending any error messages there. This is one of the easiest ways to find the problem, but new system administrators often go digging into configuration files without even looking at the error log.

- Someone, somewhere has almost certainly had the same problem before. Look to sites like http://www.deja.com/usenet, which archive Linux distribution mailing lists, to see if you can find a reference to it.

- Be patient and methodical. You're unlikely to find solutions in the last few hours of a 12-hour troubleshooting session. You can probably no longer look at the problem methodically after so long. Rest your brain and your eyes, and then try again. Don't forget to eat and sleep!

- If something worked yesterday but suddenly doesn't work today, it is probably not a configuration problem. Again, look at `/var/log/messages` to see if there is a message that will point to the problem. Check anything that has changed since the last time it worked to determine whether something that was changed has caused the error. If you still don't find it (and you know that no one has changed the configuration from the working one), don't spend a lot of time reworking configuration files; consider hardware.

- Remember that many services have a debugging switch that allows you to pass in certain parameters and/or increases the number of messages that the service logs to `/var/log/messages`. Also use the `verbose` switch wherever it exists to ensure that you receive the most information possible about what the service is doing. Also, some services have syntax checkers (for example, `tcpdchk` for networking) to determine whether the configuration files have errors. `tcpd` also has a great utility called `tcpdmatch`, which allows you to see whether your system would accept connections from a hostname that you pass as a parameter.

- Remember that many services depend on the ability to look up an IP address from a hostname with `nslookup` or even to look up a hostname in reverse with `nslookup` and the IP address (reverse lookup).

- Login problems are often due to an error in the related PAM file:

`login`	`/etc/pam.d/login`
`rlogin`	`/etc/pam.d/rlogin`
KDM	`/etc/pam.d/kdm`
GDM	`/etc/pam.d/gdm`
XDM	`/etc/pam.d/xdm`
SSH	`/etc/pam.d/sshd`

- When specifying a library path, ensure that you've spelled everything correctly and that the case is correct.

- The compiler never lies, although it can obfuscate. If you have an error message that you don't understand, there is a problem in the code. The compiler may interpret the true source of the problem as being OK, though, and report an error some lines later, when the compiler's interpretation finally breaks down. Compiler messages are also sometimes just plain cryptic. Look to determine what the error means. To confuse the issue a bit, bad hardware does sometimes cause the compiler to give you an error that might send you down the wrong path.

Networking and Troubleshooting

PART 5

- Simply rebooting is not a good fix. If you don't know what caused the problem and rebooting fixes it, you still won't know what caused it when it happens the next time. Find the problem and fix it. You might need to restart a service or a daemon, but at least if that fixes it, it guides you into the problem space, allowing you to find the solution.

- Join a Linux user group if there is one in your area. If there isn't one, start one. The exposure that you get to different problems will help you avoid those problems on your systems.

- Remember to sync after you make changes in rescue mode before you exit. This writes any residual information in the buffers to the hard drive. Not doing this may cause your "fix" to be lost after a reboot.

- Don't be afraid of the system. Very few things that you do are going to break the computer (except getting mad and throwing it on the floor). Experiment a bit. Log each step so that you can undo what you did. Make sure you have a boot disk or a rescue disk or CD-ROM. Of course, you don't want to delete files with reckless abandon, but it is OK to copy something to another partition and then remove the suspect file to see if it fixes the problem. If you mess up badly, boot into rescue mode and copy the files back to where they go and reboot.

The rest of the chapter looks at common problems and their solutions. We focus on questions that are asked frequently in the various Linux lists and newsgroups and that are pretty much distribution-independent. There are many Frequently Asked Questions (FAQ) documents available that provide information about specific areas. Look for a FAQ whenever you are preparing to configure something for the first time. If there is not a FAQ, rely instead on a HOWTO, if that is available.

Boot Problems

The problems we discuss in this section prevent the system from booting up fully. Boot problems are among the most frustrating, but they are also among the easiest to troubleshoot since the problem space is relatively restricted. If you know the boot process inside and out, the symptoms of the problem tend to point to the one or two possible solutions that produce exactly those symptoms. At that point, troubleshooting the problem becomes easy. Find some indicator of which of the possible problems you are dealing with, and fix it.

LILO Messages and Their Meanings

Chapter 5 briefly discussed the fact that on startup, LILO prints one letter of the LILO prompt for each of the tasks it has to do. Therefore, if only one or two letters print out, the process aborted at whatever task it was trying to accomplish. To begin troubleshooting, you only have to discern which task that was. Let's take a closer look at the diagnostic meaning of LILO's startup display.

Display	Diagnosis
(nothing)	LILO hasn't been loaded. It may not be installed, or some pre-LILO process has failed. For instance, the Linux partition might not be active or might not have been selected by an earlier boot loader.
L *error-code*	The main part of LILO has loaded, but it's unable to locate the second-stage boot loader, /boot/boot.b. The two-digit *error-code* can help to further diagnose the problem, as detailed in the LILO documentation.
LI	The main part of LILO has loaded, and it can locate the second-stage boot loader, /boot/boot.b; but this second-stage loader won't run. This problem is most frequently caused by a mismatch between the BIOS's disk geometry settings and those used by Linux. (See below for a description of disk geometry settings.)
LI1010, etc.	When LILO returns a string of LI101010 . . . at bootup, the problem is that LILO can't locate your kernel image. This is usually caused by recompiling the kernel and copying the new one over the old without running LILO again. Since LILO only reads /etc/lilo.conf and writes a new boot sector onto your hard drive when you run lilo, not when the system boots, it must be rerun to update that boot sector whenever /etc/lilo.conf changes. If you forget to do this, the system will not boot. To fix this, you can boot with the install/rescue floppy, mount the root directory on /mnt and rerun LILO using the command lilo -r /mnt. An alternative is to boot from an install/rescue floppy, mount the root directory on /mnt, run the command chroot /mnt to make the system treat /mnt as the root directory, and then run LILO normally.
LIL	The second-stage boot loader runs but can't function properly. This frequently indicates a geometry mismatch or a problem with the hard disk.
LIL?	LILO has loaded the second-stage boot loader into the wrong address. This is usually caused by moving /boot/boot.b without re-running lilo.
LIL-	LILO has detected a damaged descriptor table, /boot/map. This can be caused by disk geometry mismatch or by moving the descriptor file without re-running lilo.
LILO	The program has loaded and run correctly. Subsequent problems are likely related to the kernel or other Linux startup files.

Networking and Troubleshooting

PART 5

> **NOTE**   Hard disks are composed of one or more *platters,* each of which has associated with it one or two *heads.* These heads move across several different *tracks,* forming virtual *cylinders* across the stacked platters. Each cylinder is broken up into multiple *sectors,* each of which holds 512 bytes on most hard disks. Early hard disks could be defined by the number of cylinders, heads, and sectors they used; hence the term *CHS geometry* or *disk geometry.* The x86 BIOS and the standard x86 partitioning table use this method of describing a disk. The trouble is that all modern hard disks lie about their CHS geometries. Furthermore, the lies told by the disks sometimes cause problems, so BIOSes and OSs frequently change these lies to other lies. With so much fabrication occurring, the situation sometimes collapses in chaos when two different software components believe different things about the disk's geometry. This can be the source of some LILO problems, if LILO uses one CHS geometry setting and another tool uses another setting.

Making the System Boot a New Kernel

To change the default boot kernel from `linux` to `linux_new`, edit the `/etc/lilo.conf` file to change the `default=linux` line to `default=linux_new`. If you don't see a `default` line, simply add one. Not long ago, `lilo` simply took the first listed kernel image as the default image, so older `lilo.conf` files won't have the `default` parameter. Don't forget to rerun `/sbin/lilo` after you make any changes to the `/etc/lilo.conf` file.

Here is a sample `/etc/lilo.conf` file:

```
boot=/dev/hda
map=/boot/map
root=/dev/hda1
install=/boot/boot.b
prompt
timeout=50
message=/boot/message
linear
default=linux
image=/boot/vmlinuz-2.2.16-22
        label=linux
        read-only
```

```
image=/boot/vmlinuz-2.2.16-22-new
        label=linux_new
        read-only
```

Hardware Not Detected at Boot

If hardware in your system isn't recognized at bootup, it may be possible to get Linux to see it using an append line in /etc/lilo.conf. Say you have more than one network interface card (NIC) in your computer but Linux doesn't detect this on boot. Assuming that the problem is not that you are running a modularized kernel and the correct module doesn't exist, you can try appending the hardware data about the card. The append statement will look something like the following, except that the parameters will be replaced by values reflecting your hardware:

```
append="aha152x=0x140,12,7,0,0 sb=240,5,1,5,300"
```

Making a New Boot Floppy to Replace a Lost One

There are two ways to replace a lost or destroyed boot floppy with a new one:

- Insert an unused floppy into the first floppy drive and run (as root) **lilo -b /dev/fd0**. This will make an exact copy of your hard drive boot sector on that floppy so that the next time something kills your boot record, just insert that floppy and boot from it. When you get a login prompt again, log in as root and type **lilo** to re-create a valid master boot record on the hard drive.

- If you're on a Red Hat-based Linux system, you can run a utility called mkbootdisk. Typing **mkbootdisk** *kernel_version* will create a boot disk for the specified kernel. For example, **mkbootdisk 2.2.16** will create a boot disk for a 2.2.16 system. This utility defaults to the floppy drive, but it can be redirected to any device with the -device parameter.

Dual-booting with Another OS Like Windows

It is very easy to set up a system to dual-boot Linux and another operating system on a second disk. Because Windows likes to be on the first disk, you should switch the disks around, making the Windows disk /dev/hda and the Linux disk /dev/hdb. Remember to have a rescue disk or CD-ROM around when you're doing this, since LILO won't know where things are anymore. Boot into rescue mode and mount the Linux disk. Edit the /etc/lilo.conf file to include the Windows partition. Assuming that Windows is on the first disk (/dev/hda), Linux is on the second disk (/dev/hdb), and the partition containing /boot is correctly included below the 1024-cylinder mark of the disk it is on, your lilo.conf file should look like the following.

```
boot = /dev/hda
map = /boot/map
install = /boot/boot.b
prompt
timeout = 50
default = linux

image = /boot/vmlinuz-2.2.16
    label = linux
    read-only
    root=/dev/hdb1
other = /dev/hda1
    label = msdos
```

Run lilo to write out LILO's new configuration, sync the disks since you are in rescue mode, and reboot.

Can't Remove LILO from the Master Boot Record

It's possible that you'll install Linux on a computer and then discover that you need to recycle the computer for use with Windows, DOS, or some other OS. Many new Linux administrators have problems with this, though, because after they've removed Linux, LILO hangs on like an albatross around the computer's neck. Fortunately, there are ways to deal with this problem. If your system still has Linux installed and you want to remove LILO from the MBR, you log in as root and use the LILO uninstall command as follows:

```
# lilo -u
```

If for some reason you have deleted Linux from your system and installed some version of Microsoft Windows, you can use the Windows FDISK command to rewrite the Master Boot Record and then reboot:

```
C:> FDISK /MBR
```

Kernel Won't Load or Loads Only Partially

There are two possibilities here. Either the kernel image has become corrupted in some way or LILO is being passed an incorrect parameter. You see this if someone adds an incorrect append line in /etc/lilo.conf.

Often this is an incorrect mem line. The mem option isn't usually needed but occasionally you'll run across a system for which LILO doesn't recognize the correct amount of memory. If you need to help LILO recognize a large amount of memory, such as 256MB, add the line mem=256M to the /etc/lilo.conf file and then run lilo. If you incorrectly add mem=2256M or some other too-large number, your kernel will not fully load. If you incorrectly add mem=256m using the lowercase m, that will also inhibit the kernel's ability to fully load.

When LILO is run, it catches some of the errors in the /etc/lilo.conf file. If you specify a kernel image that doesn't exist, the lilo program will generate an error message. If you've specified a boot device that doesn't exist, you will see a message like this:

```
Fatal: open  /dev/hdb: Device not configured
```

Login Problems

Because gaining access to your systems is so important, you must be able to diagnose and repair login problems. Knowing the login process step by step is the key to this ability. Once you've been doing Linux system administration for a while, these problems will be easy for you to fix.

Lost Password

One of the most frustrating problems occurs when you have a system and no one seems to remember the root password. With luck this won't happen often. Sometimes, though, the root password is needed and not known and needs to be reset.

The Rescue Mode Method

If you've lost the root password to your system and need to gain root access, you can boot to single-user mode and change root's password. First issue the following command at the boot prompt, assuming that you want to boot a kernel with the label linux:

```
boot: linux single
```

If you don't know the name of the kernel image you want to boot, press the Tab key when you see the boot prompt, and all of the kernel images LILO recognizes will be listed. When the system finishes booting, you'll be in single-user mode. To change root's password, use the passwd command:

```
# passwd root
```

Sync the disk to make sure all of your changes are written out to the disk.

```
# sync;sync;sync
```

Networking and Troubleshooting

PART 5

Exiting will automatically reboot the system.

```
# exit
```

The *init* Method

Another way to change root's password is to pass a different init parameter to LILO when the system boots. You want to tell the system to mount the root filesystem in read-write mode so that you can write your changes when you run the passwd command and also to prevent the initialization scripts from running. At the boot prompt, enter the following (again assuming that you want to boot a kernel with the label linux):

```
boot: linux init=/bin/sh rw
```

When the system finishes booting, use the passwd command and sync the disks just like before. Now instead of rebooting, use the init command to change to run level 6, which is a reboot level:

```
# exec /sbin/init 6
```

Login Incorrect after Entering Username

If you enter the username at the login prompt and are not prompted for a password but instead are given a "Login incorrect" error and returned to the login prompt, you have an error in the /etc/pam.d/login file, probably in the auth line that calls /lib/security/pam_unix.so.

System Flashes Quick Message and Drops Back to *login* Prompt

If you try to log in to your system and see a message quickly flash before you are returned to the login prompt, you probably have an error in /etc/pam.d/system-auth in one of the required session lines. The message that is flashing is "Module is unknown"; it means there is a typing error in the path or name of the PAM library to be accessed, so that the library cannot be found. If the message looks more like "Login incorrect," the error is probably in the pam_unix.so line of the auth section of /etc/pam.d/system-auth. If you see no message at all, look to the second line of the auth section. We recommend logging in and making changes to /etc/pam.d/login to determine what changes result. Remember to leave one virtual terminal logged in so you don't have to go into rescue mode to fix the file you have tampered with.

Login incorrect Message

If you get this message when attempting to log in remotely as root to a Linux machine, the system is functioning normally; the problem is what you're trying to do. You really don't want to be able to log in remotely as root. That is a major security hazard. The more secure way is to log in as another user and, once logged in, use the su command to assume superuser privileges. If you're still convinced that you want to log in as root, you can enable your system to allow this. The /etc/securetty lists the virtual consoles and ttys from which root is permitted to log in. Since logging in remotely brings you in on a pseudoterminal, you need to add some pts/*n* lines to the /etc/securetty file. How many pseudoterminals you need to add depends on the number of remote connections. It's important to remember that doing this is a *bad idea*. Don't do this unless you absolutely have to. If you have to do this to test something, add the pts lines, do the test, and remove the pts lines immediately.

Network Problems

Troubleshooting an apparent network problem should be done in stages. Find out whether a local machine can ping the remote host and whether the remote machine can ping it back. If the local ping is successful but the remote machine's ping fails, look for problems in the configuration of the remote machine. If you can't find the source of the problem, look for a remote machine that can ping the local machine and compare the configuration of both remote machines. Most Ethernet cards have link lights that indicate whether the card is able to send data packets. The best way to learn to troubleshoot a network is to do it.

Following are a few networking problems related to Linux or software configuration. We cannot address the much wider problem space presented by networking hardware, simply because there are too many possible combinations and configurations to cover here.

Unknown Host Message

If you get this error when trying to Telnet or use various other networking tools, the hostname cannot be resolved into an IP address. This could be the result of a name server problem, a network problem, or a typing error. Try to ping the IP address instead of the hostname. If you can ping the host by numeric IP, the problem is with the name server setup. Otherwise, verify that the name you typed in is the correct one. If it is, try to ping another machine on the same network as the one causing you problems. If you can, the problem is almost definitely with the setup of the problematic host or possibly the cable that runs to it from the network.

Another possibility, especially on small local networks that don't use DNS internally, is a problem with the /etc/hosts file. This file can be used as a substitute for DNS on local networks; it contains the mapping of hostnames to IP addresses. An example resembles the following.

```
127.0.0.1 localhost
192.168.1.1 speaker.rodsbooks.com speaker
192.168.1.2 teela.rodsbooks.com teela luckyone
```

Each line begins with a single IP address and is followed by one or more hostnames. (Typically, a full hostname is first, followed by one or more hostnames that lack the domain name, or synonyms.) If your network uses /etc/hosts, be sure that the file is present and that its contents are reasonable.

You may also want to check the /etc/host.conf file. This file tells Linux in what order to try various hostname resolution methods, among other things. It normally contains a line like the following:

```
order hosts,bind
```

This line specifies that Linux will use /etc/hosts followed by DNS (which sometimes goes by the moniker *BIND*, for *Berkeley Internet Name Daemon*). This line may contain additional entries, or entries in alternative orders. If it's missing either entry shown here, name resolution may be impaired on your local network or on the Internet as a whole, respectively.

Network Unreachable Message

This message means that the local machine doesn't have a network route to the remote system. Verify the address you used. Use the netstat -r command to determine whether there is a route to the remote host's network.

Kernel Compilation

Compiling a kernel is not difficult if you know the process. Nevertheless, there are some common errors that appear on mailing lists with some frequency.

make menuconfig Generates an Error about *ncurses.h*

You may type **make menuconfig** and get the following error:

```
make[1]: *** [lxdialog.o] Error 1
make[1]: Leaving directory `/usr/src/linux-2.2.16/scripts/lxdialog'
make: *** [menuconfig] Error 2
```

The problem is that you do not have the package installed that contains ncurses.h. This can be a little confusing because you may have the ncurses RPM installed and still get this error. On systems using the Red Hat Package Manager (RPM), you need to install the ncurses-devel RPM in order to use make menuconfig.

Signal 11 Error

Sometimes when a user or a system administrator compiles a new kernel, gcc returns the following error:

```
gcc: internal compiler error 11
```

Signal 11 is a segmentation violation, which generally means that the program is trying to write into memory it doesn't own. The problem is usually caused by bad memory in your computer. If you immediately try to run the make command again and it goes a bit further, the problem is almost surely hardware. There is a great site that details signal 11 errors at http://www.bitwizard.nl/sig11.

Do I Need to Reconfigure the Kernel with Every Upgrade?

It's possible to copy your kernel configuration settings from a kernel you've previously compiled yourself to a new one. The commands to accomplish this task are:

```
# cd /usr/src/linux
# cp /usr/src/old-kernel/.config ./
# make oldconfig
```

When you configure your kernel, the system stores your configuration choices in a file called .config. The preceding command sequence copies the .config file from your old kernel's source directory to the new kernel's directory, then tells the system to use the old kernel's configuration file. The make oldconfig command, in particular, forces the compilation scripts to go through the old configuration file and update any entries that may need updating. You'll be prompted to decide whether to compile any new drivers, for instance. The end result is that you'll have a fresh kernel configuration *much* more quickly than you would have if you'd gone through the usual make xconfig or make menuconfig procedure, as described in Chapter 8.

WARNING It's probably best to avoid using this procedure if you're upgrading from a 2.2.x to a 2.4.x kernel, or a similar major upgrade. These kernel upgrades include so many changes that chances are good the make oldconfig procedure will fail.

Networking and
Troubleshooting

PART 5

Id: Unrecognized Option *-qmagic*

This message means that you should get a newer linker. The linker is in the `binutils`
RPM or is available as a tarball from `http://sources.redhat.com/binutils`.

Filesystem Problems or Questions

The filesystem is covered in great detail in Chapter 10. As a Linux system administrator,
the more you know about the ext2 filesystem the better. You should get familiar with the
inode concept and the filesystem layout especially, including the intended uses of the
directories off /. Here are a few of the most common filesystem-related questions.

Creating a Linux Filesystem on a Floppy Disk

To create a filesystem on a 3.5-inch, high-density floppy, issue the following command:

```
# /sbin/mke2fs /dev/fd0
```

The system will reply:

```
mke2fs 1.18, 11-Nov-1999 for EXT2 FS 0.5b, 95/08/09
Filesystem label=
OS type: Linux
Block size=1024 (log=0)
Fragment size=1024 (log=0)
184 inodes, 1440 blocks
72 blocks (5.00%) reserved for the super user
First data block=1
1 block group
8192 blocks per group, 8192 fragments per group
184 inodes per group


Writing inode tables: done
Writing superblocks and filesystem accounting information: done
```

Creating a Windows Filesystem on a Floppy Disk

To format a 3.5-inch, high-density floppy, you can use this command:

```
# /sbin/mkdosfs /dev/fd0
```

You get a lot less information from your system in this case. The output looks like this:

```
/sbin/dosfs 2.2 (06 Jul 1999)
```

An alternative utility included on many systems is mformat, which you can use as follows:

```
# mformat a:
```

This program doesn't return any output at all, unless it encounters a problem running the command.

/proc/kcore

Many new Linux system administrators see the size of the /proc/kcore file and want to delete it to free up the space. The /proc filesystem, however, is a virtual replica of your system, designed to give you information. It doesn't take up any hard disk space. /proc/kcore is a method of accessing your system's RAM. You can read from this file to access memory—*any* memory. For this reason, the file is owned by root and has r-------- (0400) permissions, to keep unauthorized individuals from accessing it. Any attempt to delete or change the permissions of this file is pointless. Like all files in the /proc filesystem, it takes up no real disk space. The fact that its size is the same as the amount of memory on your system is irrelevant since it is not taking up disk space.

Which Interrupts Are Available?

The /proc/interrupts file contains a list of interrupts and what they correspond to. When you are adding hardware and need to set an interrupt for it, you can use this list to determine which interrupts are available. For instance, here's a sample output from this file:

```
$ cat /proc/interrupts
          CPU0
   0:  387900164      XT-PIC  timer
   1:        232      XT-PIC  keyboard
   2:          0      XT-PIC  cascade
   7:      42467      XT-PIC  MAD16 WSS
   9:  124577099      XT-PIC  eth0
  10:    1438087      XT-PIC  eth1
  11:   24242763      XT-PIC  i91u
```

Networking and
Troubleshooting

PART 5

```
     13:              1              XT-PIC  fpu
   NMI:              0
```

This shows that interrupts 0, 1, 2, 7, 9, 10, 11, and 13 are all in use. Many of these are used by devices that you can't disable or change, such as the keyboard and the cascade device. (Interrupt 2 really just ties into interrupts 8–15; the *x*86 uses two interrupt controllers, each of which can handle eight interrupts. They're linked together by having the second send an interrupt to the first whenever the second receives an interrupt.) Other interrupts, such as 7, 9, and 10, may be configurable, because they correspond to devices (a sound card and two Ethernet cards, respectively) that can use any of several interrupts.

One caveat concerning /proc/interrupts is that this file turns up devices only *after* their drivers have loaded. If you have some device for which the driver is a kernel module, but that module hasn't been loaded, you'll see no entry in /proc/interrupts. For instance, the preceding listing doesn't include interrupt 6, which is normally used by a floppy disk. If /proc/interrupts were examined after mounting a floppy disk, the appropriate entry would appear.

If you suspect your system is suffering from an interrupt conflict between two or more devices, try using them separately, and check the /proc/interrupts entries. If both devices turn out to be using the same interrupt, this could be the trouble. On the other hand, some PCI devices are designed to share interrupts, so this could also be normal. ISA cards should never share interrupts, though.

X Window System Problems

Problems with X can be tricky to diagnose. Sometimes a full /home or /tmp filesystem will prevent X from starting. Errors in the /etc/X11/XF86Config file can also prevent X from starting. If you suspect an X problem, create a backup copy of XF86Config and run Xconfigurator or some other X configuration tool. Chapter 16 details the X Window System.

Booting into X, Login Prompt Disappears when Anything Is Entered

If you are attempting to boot to run level 5 and X won't start, you may get to a run level 3 login screen, but typing anything will just cause that screen to go blank and then restart with an empty log in again. This can be a problem with the font path specified in the XF86Config file, or a problem with the X Window System font server, xfs. Usually this is fixed by running Xconfigurator again.

Cannot Allocate Colormap Entry

If you see the following message when you attempt to start an application, you probably do not have enough video memory for all of the colors that you are trying to use:

```
Warning: Cannot allocate colormap entry for color_code
```

You basically have two choices: get a card with more video RAM, or stop using so many colors. Netscape is most often the application that is using too many colors from the colormap. Netscape, and some other applications, can be forced to use its own colormap. To do this, start Netscape with the following command:

```
$ netscape -install
```

Bypassing X

Sometimes an administrator will set up the system to boot directly into X (run level 5). If there is a problem with the video card configuration, the system will hang at startup. (In actuality, the system keeps trying to start X, but repeatedly fails, leading to an inability to use the console.) To bypass X and boot into text mode so you can fix the X configuration, add a 3 after the label you type at the boot prompt, thus:

```
boot: linux 3
```

This will cause the system to boot into run level 3. You can then run Xconfigurator again to fix the video card configuration.

Another way around this problem is to log onto the system using Telnet, SSH, or a serial port. You can then fix the X configuration problem and the XDM login screen will appear. Alternatively, you can set the run level to 3 by editing /etc/inittab, as discussed in Chapter 16.

The System Runs Very Slowly When Running X or Making a Kernel

You probably have too little memory in the system. If you have less RAM than all the programs you're running at once, Linux will swap to your hard disk, and swapping is slow. The solution is either to run fewer programs at once or to buy more memory. You may be able to reclaim some memory by recompiling your kernel and including fewer options.

Odds and Ends

Some solutions, tips, and techniques don't fit into any of the previous categories but are too valuable not to include.

Networking and Troubleshooting

PART 5

You've Deleted the Red Hat Package Manager and Can't Reinstall It

If you've deleted the RPM binary, you can't reinstall it without a package manager. You'll need to copy one onto a floppy from another system, mount the floppy, and copy it back. It doesn't even have to be the current version of RPM. After you have a working `rpm` binary, reinstall the correct version from an `.rpm` file.

Shutting Down a System on the Network Remotely

Sometimes you may want a "quick and dirty" method of shutting down a computer from a network login. You can do this as follows:

1. Create a user called `shutdown`.

2. Change the default shell from Bash to `/sbin/shutdown` for that user.

3. Make sure the account's password is set unless you want anyone to be able to shut down the machine.

When you use a remote login utility like Telnet or Secure Shell (SSH) to "log on" as the `shutdown` user, the computer will respond by shutting down.

NOTE   Many distributions ship with the `shutdown` account predefined. The account is typically disabled by using an asterisk (*) as the password field in `/etc/shadow`, however. You can enable the account by typing **passwd shutdown** as root and entering an appropriate password.

Permission Denied when Attempting NFS Mount

If you configure NFS according to the NFS HOWTO or Chapter 12 but see a "Permission Denied" message when you try to connect, you might have forgotten to enable NFS on the machine you're attempting access from. To test this, use `chkconfig` as follows:

```
$ chkconfig --list nfs
nfs    0:off   1:off   2:off   3:off   4:off   5:off   6:off
```

Run levels 3 and 5 should be on. If not, use the `chkconfig` command to turn NFS on in those run levels.

```
# chkconfig --level 35 nfs on
```

After issuing this command, recheck using `chkconfig`:

```
$ chkconfig --list nfs
nfs    0:off   1:off   2:off   3:on    4:off   5:on    6:off
```

Some people automatically turn services on in run levels 2, 4, and 5, so if your output indicates that these levels are on, this is fine. These changes only start the daemon on reboot, so if you want to test whether turning on the NFS daemon solves your problem, run the NFS initialization script like this:

```
# /etc/rc.d/init.d/nfs start
```

If you still get the "Permission Denied" error, check the /etc/hosts.allow file on the mounting machine. The three lines below should be included. Change the IP as appropriate. These lines let any machine on the 192.168.1.0 subnet mount the export.

```
portmap: 192.168.1.0/255.255.255.0

rpc.mountd: 192.168.1.0/255.255.255.0

rpc.nfsd: 192.168.1.0/255.255.255.0
```

The *free* Command Reports Less Memory Than the Machine Has

There are two common problems of interpretation of the output of the free command. To understand these, let's consider some sample output, created on a machine with 96MB of physical memory:

```
$ free
              total     used     free   shared  buffers  cached
Mem:          95772    87968     7804    51148     5572   28008
-/+ buffers/cache:     54388    41384
Swap:        136512    12308   124204
```

The total column lists both RAM (on the Mem line) and swap space (on the Swap line). As you can see, 95,772KB is less than 96MB (98,304KB). Most of this discrepancy is caused by the Linux kernel itself, which typically consumes about 2–4MB of RAM. (The kernel image stored in /boot is usually compressed, and parts of it are discarded soon after being loaded, so its size isn't a good gauge of how large the in-memory kernel is.) You also lose some RAM to shadowed ROMs, I/O space, and other artifacts of your computer's architecture.

The second problem many people have is that the amount of memory used is very high (or, alternatively, the amount free is very low), as reported by the used (or free) column's entry on the Mem line. This is largely an illusion, however, because Linux dynamically assigns memory to disk cache duty. This speeds up disk access by temporarily storing information from disk in RAM. If the RAM becomes needed for other purposes, Linux ditches some of the disk cache. The -/+ buffers/cache line reports a truer estimate of the amount of memory used. As you can see, it shows a much less extreme memory load than does the Mem line. You might also want to check the Swap line, because if a great deal of swap space is in use, the system's performance will be degraded as a result.

If you're still convinced that Linux isn't seeing all of your system's memory, the most likely explanation is that the system has a BIOS that's not working well with Linux's memory probes. Typically, such systems report just 64MB, or sometimes only 16MB, of RAM. The fix is to use a mem= append line in /etc/lilo.conf, as described earlier in this chapter, under "Kernel Won't Load or Loads Only Partially." As discussed there, however, the danger of getting this setting wrong is that the system won't boot at all. It's therefore wise to create a *duplicate* of a normal /etc/lilo.conf entry and include the mem= setting in only one. You'll then have a fallback position should your modification prevent a normal system boot.

Determining Which Packages Are on the System

Using the Red Hat Package Manager, use the Query All option:

```
# rpm -qa
```

Using the Debian Package Manager, use the -l option:

```
# dpkg -l
```

You can also pipe the output into a grep command to find a particular package:

```
# rpm -qa |grep binutils
# dpkg -l |grep binutils
```

modprobe Can't Locate Module *module-name*

The problem is that modprobe, insmod, or rmmod is unable to find the specified module. To stop the message, add the following to the /etc/modules.conf file. This often happens when you try to rebuild your kernel, defining something as a module that wasn't a module before, but don't also remake the modules. Enter this command to fix the problem:

```
alias module-name off
```

Be sure to use the name of the module exactly as listed in the error message.

The "You don't exist. Go away" Error Message

This is our favorite error message! It means that you are using some program that attempts to verify the user by checking the UID/login in /etc/passwd. If /etc/passwd gets corrupted, you'll see this message. You'll have to dump the passwd file from a backup or re-create it. Of course, you'll need to do this from some form of emergency boot, as discussed earlier or in Chapter 11. Another possibility is that utmp didn't properly register your session when you logged in. Log out and log back in again.

The Screen is Full of Gibberish

You probably sent a binary file to the console. Linux has a reset command that will reset your screen:

```
$ reset
```

In Sum

Linux problems come in many forms, ranging from an inability to boot the computer to strange behavior when you try to run programs or perform everyday tasks. The best way to learn how to solve these problems is to encounter them and work through them yourself. The hands-on experience doing that is more valuable than any listing of problems you can obtain from a book. Nonetheless, this chapter provides tips to point you in the right direction in solving several different types of problems. You should also take to heart the general problem-solving strategies outlined at the start of the chapter, because these will serve you well even with exotic problems we can't anticipate.

Index

Note to the Reader: Throughout this index **boldfaced** page numbers indicate primary discussions of a topic. *Italicized* page numbers indicate illustrations.

Index

Index

Code Listings *(continued)*